Reconstructing the criminal
Culture, law, and policy in England, 1830–1914

Reconstructing the criminal

Culture, law, and policy in England, 1830–1914

MARTIN J. WIENER

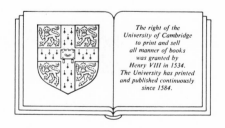

The right of the
University of Cambridge
to print and sell
all manner of books
was granted by
Henry VIII in 1534.
The University has printed
and published continuously
since 1584.

CAMBRIDGE UNIVERSITY PRESS

Cambridge

New York   Port Chester   Melbourne   Sydney

Published by the Press Syndicate of the University of Cambridge
The Pitt Building, Trumpington Street, Cambridge CB2 1RP
40 West 20th Street, New York, NY 10011, USA
10 Stamford Road, Oakleigh, Melbourne 3166, Australia

Cambridge University Press 1990

First published 1990

Printed in the United States of America

Library of Congress Cataloging-in-Publication Data
Wiener, Martin J.
Reconstructing the criminal: culture, law, and policy in England,
1830–1914 / by Martin J. Wiener.
p.   cm.
ISBN 0-521-35045-X
1. Criminology – England – History – 19th century.   2. Criminal
justice, Administration of – England – History – 19th century.
I. Title.
HV6022.G7W54   1990
364.942'09'034 – dc20   90-1593
                                          CIP

British Library Cataloguing in Publication Data
Wiener, Martin J. (Martin Joel), 1941–
Reconstructing the criminal: culture, law, and policy in
England, 1830–1914.
1. Great Britain. Crime & punishment, history
I. Title
364.941

ISBN 0-521-35045-X hardback

For Meredith Skura

Contents

Acknowledgments

While writing this book I have received generous support from the American Council of Learned Societies and the National Endowment for the Humanities. I am also indebted to Rice University, and in particular to Dean of Humanities Allen Matusow, for encouragement and support, including a leave that enabled me to bring the work to completion. Indeed, Rice has provided an ideal environment for thinking and writing. Many of the ideas here originated in discussions with colleagues, especially Tom Haskell and Bob Patten, and with graduate and undergraduate students. The manuscript also profited greatly from the detailed reading and criticism of Roger Chadwick, Randall McGowen, and Stanley Palmer and from the guidance through the thickets of English law provided by Steve Hedley and David Sugarman; none of them have agreed with all of my interpretations, and their disagreements have forced me to clarify my own thinking. Vic Bailey, George Behlmer, and David Smith provided further valuable suggestions and criticisms.

For permission to consult and to use material from papers in their possession I would like to thank the Bodleian Library, Oxford, the British Library, the Hon. Mrs. Crispin Gascoigne, the Essex Record Office, the Home Office, and the Modern Records Centre at the University of Warwick; for permission to use copyright material I would like to thank Sir William Gladstone, Bt., and the Howard League for Penal Reform. I am especially grateful to M. M. White and John Allen of the Home Office for assistance beyond the call of duty. The interlibrary loan staff of the Fondren Library rendered indispensable aid. I also owe much to the research assistance of Jim Peterson (whose life was tragically cut short) and Joanne Klein. Sandy Perez's secretarial efforts were unflagging. At Cambridge University Press, Frank Smith was ever encouraging, and Phil Alkana's copyediting was well-nigh flawless. All these debts, however, dim in comparison to that owed to Meredith Skura, a life partner in every sense of the term.

Introduction: criminal policy as cultural history

Interpreting criminal policy

Over the past generation, serious crime rates and public fear of crime have dramatically risen throughout the Western world. Explaining and dealing with crime has become a major preoccupation of academicians, politicians, and public administrators. Criminal and penal policy, which for some decades seemed to be reasonably successful, has not only become riven by practical difficulties but, more important, by philosophical debates and ideological conflicts. Diane Johnson, who has explored contemporary anxieties in fiction and in a biography of Dashiell Hammett, observed: "[I]f our responses to crime are arbitrary and inadequate, it is because we are not really agreed on the nature of culpability, have lost confidence that we can really decide what is 'right.'"[1] This crisis of both practice and belief has been most obvious in the two leading English-speaking countries, the United States and Great Britain. The British experience is particularly striking. Long the model of a law-abiding and closely knit society, Britain has come to face continued increases in reported crime, prison overcrowding, and riots, a decline of public confidence in the institutions of criminal justice, and a general uncertainty about the principles or practice of punishment.

This contemporary crisis of criminal policy has helped to stimulate a reorientation of thinking about the *history* of crime and punishment. With crime apparently an inescapable problem, with the entire state apparatus for dealing with it looking less competent and less trustworthy than hitherto, and with confidence in our ability to either explain or solve it at a discount, the historical record of crime and criminal policy has become both more interesting and more problematic. For many years, the history of criminal policy in Britain had been almost universally constructed as a story of reform: a gradual advance out of a medieval world of disorder and cruelty to the twentieth century,

---

[1] "Worst Wishes," *New York Review of Books*, Feb. 16, 1984, 40.

in which serious crime had been largely conquered at the same time that the
rights and needs of the criminal had been ever more fully respected.[2]

This comforting interpretation was established over the fortunate period
from the early nineteenth century to the mid-twentieth century, when English
institutions weathered domestic and international storms more ably than those
of perhaps any other people.[3] Even as both the nation's world power and
economic dynamism obviously began to falter, the criminal law remained an
area of unquestioned success. The English way of reconciling respect for individual liberty with a very high degree of public order and cooperation was the
envy of the world. Rare was the foreign visitor who failed to remark upon the
uncoerced yet pacific and law-abiding character of everyday life. However, in
a new era of sharply rising crime and political polarization, such self-
satisfaction has no longer been tenable. As in economic and imperial history,
contemporary failures have opened doors to a more probing examination of
the past. Thus, the last two decades have witnessed a virtual explosion of historical scholarship on crime and criminal justice, in which assumptions of a
steady march of progress have been sceptically scrutinized.

While historians staked out this new field, the character of historical inquiry
itself has been changing. Historical scholarship is being reinvigorated by a
dissolution of sharp distinctions that had become intellectually constricting. The distinctions between the "external" and "internal," the "social" and
"intellectual," and the "practical" and "symbolic" aspects of past experience
have been yielding to a deepening sense of how thoroughly such categories in
fact interpenetrate each other in the unitary process of human living.[4] We
have begun to appreciate how, as Keith Michael Baker has put it, "all social
activity has an intellective dimension that gives it meaning, just as all intellectual activity has a social dimension that gives it point."[5] If it is necessary to
locate ideas in a social context, historians must also locate social activity in an

---

[2] See, for example, Sir Leon Radzinowicz, *History of English Criminal Law and Its
Administration, I: The Movement for Reform, 1750–1833* (London: Stevens, 1948); Lionel
Fox, *The English Prison and Borstal Systems* (London: Routledge, 1952); Gordon Rose,
The Struggle for Penal Reform (London: Stevens and Sons, 1961).

[3] Since Scotland has possessed its own legal system and, to a significant degree, its own
administration of criminal justice, this work will be primarily concerned with England and
Wales.

[4] See, for example, W. J. Bouwsma, "Intellectual History in the 1980s: From History of
Ideas to History of Meaning," *Journal of Interdisciplinary History 12* (Autumn, 1981),
279–91; Peter Stearns, "Toward a Wider Vision: Trends in Social History," in *The Past
Before Us: Contemporary Historical Writing in the United States*, ed. Michael Kammen,
(Ithaca: Cornell University Press, 1980), pp. 205–30.

[5] "On the Problem of the Ideological Origins of the French Revolution," in *Modern
European Intellectual History: Reappraisals and New Perspectives*, ed. D. LaCapra and
S. L. Kaplan (Ithaca, Cornell University Press, 1982), p. 199.

intellectual or cultural context. As John Toews stated: "The plowing of a field, the abuse of a child, or the storming of a fortress [are] as much contextually situated, meaningful social actions as the construction of a philosophical argument, the choice of a metaphor, the publication of a journal, or the performance of an opera."[6] The idea of human experience in a "pure" form, free of interpretation, is a chimera.[7]

The confluence of these developments in practical policy and in the discourse of history and the human sciences in general has opened up new possibilities for understanding the history of criminal discourse and policy. Crime and punishment are eminently dual entities, at once social facts and mental constructs. Just as it has been asked what sorts of social dimensions have given point to the mental activity of thinking about crime, we also need to inquire what sorts of intellective dimensions have given meaning to the social activity of dealing with crime.

In attempting this inquiry, *Reconstructing the Criminal* seeks to bring two types of historical works closer together. I hope to persuade historians of crime and criminal justice that their field will be enriched by the use of more literary approaches than they have been accustomed to draw upon. At the same time, I hope to bring the growing body of work on criminal justice to the attention of historians of Victorian and Edwardian ideas and sensibility and to demonstrate its value for their cultural concerns. As one anthropologist has

[6] John Toews, "Intellectual History after the Linguistic Turn: The Autonomy of Meaning and the Irreducibility of Experience," *American Historical Review 92* (Oct., 1987), 882–3.

[7] Important statements of this insight as it relates to the work of historians are the essays by Roger Chartier and Dominick LaCapra in LaCapra and Kaplan, *op. cit.*, and the several works of Hayden White. Not surprisingly, literary critics have taken the lead in developing this argument; a well-put representative statement of it is made by John Bender, *Imagining the Penitentiary: Fiction and the Architecture of Mind in Eighteenth Century England* (Chicago: University of Chicago Press, 1987), Introduction and Ch.1. There is of course a danger, as Toews argues, that this view can be carried to the point of arbitrarily imposing the modern historian-critic's meanings upon the past. This result has indeed marred the recent work of many literary scholars (including Bender's), giving these arguments a bad reputation among many historians. Such runaway interpretationism is not, however, a necessary result of this understanding. As Gertrude Himmelfarb has observed about nineteenth-century social surveys, "ideas are implicit in the facts themselves, 'facts' that are, in effect, intellectual constructs. In this sense a social document may be read as a literary text to elicit meanings that are not overt – on the condition, however, that it is read in its contemporary context, that the words are given their contemporary connotation, and that the ideas deduced from them reflect the sensibility and consciousness of contemporaries rather than of the historian." *The Idea of Poverty: England in the Early Industrial Age* (New York: Knopf, 1984), p. 10. Of course, it is not possible to determine definitively just what that proper "contemporary connotation" might be. One can, however, keep that aim steadily in view, resisting the temptation to too much critical "creativity."

observed, law is not simply a corpus of practical rules, but a part of the ongoing "discourse about good and bad states of society."[8] Harriet Martineau's early Victorian observation that "the treatment of the Guilty is all important as an index to the moral notions of a society" is even more broadly true than she realized.[9] The making and administering of criminal policy has much light to throw on the more general history of moral discourse; moreover, when placed in that somewhat unfamiliar context, criminal policy itself takes on some fresh contours.

This account may also offer a useful perspective on present-day criminological and penal dilemmas. It closes with the triumph of the welfarist-therapeutic penal ethos, which has fallen in recent years into such disarray. By understanding the ethos that occupied the cultural high ground before it and how it came to replace that ethos, we gain a deeper appreciation of its strengths and weaknesses and perhaps of the strengths and weaknesses of the attitudes and views that seek to fill the gap left by its retreat.

In brief, this work aims to show how practical policy enacts and reshapes cultural premises while also suggesting new perspectives on a present problem. I have combined original analysis of source documents with fresh use of the findings of many other scholars in a variety of fields of study concerned with modern English history to delineate a cultural interpretation of Victorian and Edwardian criminal policy.

In the history of English criminal law and its administration, two longstanding historiographical orientations have resisted efforts to relate criminal policy to broader developments in society and culture. For the sake of simplicity, we might call these *internalism* and *pragmatism*. Adherents of the first, who are traditionally based in law schools, see criminal law, like law generally, as a highly autonomous field of thought and action that develops with its own internal logic (or at least dynamic). Their work carefully respects its formal statements and professional definitions. Like John Langbein attacking Douglas Hay's influential essay on the social-political uses of eighteenth-century criminal justice, they insist that "legal institutions lead a complex life of their own."[10] Langbein and his colleagues assuredly have a point. Nonlawyers should proceed carefully on the subtle terrain of legal history and appreciate the special characteristics of the world of the law. Legal internalism

---

[8] Sally Humphries, "Law as Discourse," *History and Anthropology 1* (1985), 251.

[9] Harriet Martineau, *How to Observe Morals and Manners* (London; C. Knight, 1838), p. 124.

[10] "Albion's Fatal Flaws," *Past and Present 98* (February, 1983), 96–120; see also A. W. B. Simpson, "The Horwitz Thesis and the History of Contracts," *University of Chicago Law Review 46* (1979), 533–601.

is always a necessary, but not sufficient, part of the story of criminal justice. Just as similar assumptions of autonomous (and generally rational) development have been found wanting in recent years by those writing the history of medicine,[11] so upon critical scrutiny – as many legal scholars themselves (both those influenced by the older movement of Legal Realism and those associated with the newer one of Critical Legal Studies, or CLS) have pointed out – the supposed self-contained rationality of the law tends to evaporate, merging into the mesh of interests, values, and sensibilities that make up the fabric of the common life.[12] In Mark Kelman's useful phrase, "we are nonrationally reconstructing the legal world over and over again."[13]

While legal internalists have eyed with suspicion forays into their field by nonspecialists insensitive to the delicate fabric of legal life, other historians have criticized efforts at discovering underlying logic or structure in the development of criminal justice policy as overly abstract.[14] Such pragmatists see the history of British criminal justice, like the history of other institutions and practices, proceeding through ad hoc expedients, taken by practical men dealing on a day-to-day basis with largely unforeseen situations, responding to ever-shifting circumstances. The classic statement of this view of policymaking was set forth by G. K. Kitson Clark, who described Victorian policymakers as driven by "the need to find a practical solution to the immediate problem which necessity, or their sense of humanity, presented to them."[15] Scholars in this tradition have stressed, in Victor Bailey's phrases, "the tentativeness, variability and complexity" and "the makeshift nature" of devel-

---

[11] Among others, see Charles Rosenberg, *No Other Gods: On Science and American Social Thought* (Baltimore: Johns Hopkins University Press, 1976); Paul Starr, *The Social Transformation of American Medicine* (New York: Basic Books, 1982); *Madhouses, Maddoctors, and Madmen: The Social History of Psychiatry in the Victorian Era*, ed. Andrew Scull, (Philadelphia: University of Pennsylvania Press, 1981); *The Anatomy of Madness: Essays in the History of Psychiatry*, ed. William Bynum, Roy Porter, and Michael Shepherd (London: Tavistock Publications, 1985); *Medical Fringe and Medical Orthodoxy, 1750–1850*, eds. William Bynum and Roy Porter (London: Croom Helm, 1987). As Bynum and Porter note, "Scholars of all stripes agree nowadays that ... the frontiers between orthodox and unorthodox medicine have been flexible; indeed, the very distinction between the two is one that has been socially constructed" [*Medical Fringe*, 1].

[12] As one CLS scholar has put it, "legal reasoning comprises a species of practical reasoning inseparably intertwined with moral values and social policies." [Hugh Collins, *The Law of Contract* (London: Weidenfeld & Nicolson, 1986), p. x].

[13] Mark Kelman, "Interpretive Construction in the Substantive Criminal Law," *Stanford Law Review 33* (1980–81), 672.

[14] Of course, these two groups are not mutually exclusive; they share many common interests and assumptions and in practice often overlap.

[15] *An Expanding Society: Britain 1830–1900* (Cambridge: Cambridge University Press, 1967), p. 147.

opments in the procedures and institutions of nineteenth-century criminal justice.[16]

Such pragmatic or empiricist views have much truth, perhaps especially so for English history. As an Archbishop of Canterbury once observed in writing about punishment, "the English tend rather to deal with the situation confronting them, and afterwards to discover on what principles they have done so."[17] Yet if principles were often only retroactively discovered, this did not at all mean they were merely later rationalizations of muddlings through. A prejudice against abstract theorizing or overt ideologizing has been an enduring part of the English self-image, but this has often served simply to obscure the sources and contexts of policy concerning criminals and others. More generally, it is obvious that even the most practical men do not act in a conceptual or moral vacuum. Determining what constitutes practicality and common sense requires prior interpretations of experience; and thus we are brought back to wider social and cultural questions.

Moreover, both internalists and pragmatists have tended to take for granted the sort of naive positivism that has become increasingly implausible. Thus, crime has traditionally been assumed to be an objective fact that constitutes a problem, and criminal policy as a more or less straightforward response to that problem.[18] Instead, it may be more fruitful to approach crime, as many social scientists and historians have begun to do, as a socially constructed category

[16] "Introduction," *Policing and Punishment in Nineteenth Century Britain*, ed. Victor Bailey (New Brunswick, N.J., Rutgers University Press, 1981), p. 18. Important examples of such pragmatism are to be found in this book, and in Sean McConville, *A History of English Prison Administration Volume One 1750–1877* (London: Routledge, 1981). The best full length work in this tradition is Margaret DeLacy, *Prison Reform in Lancashire, 1700–1850: A Study in Local Administration* (Stanford, Calif.: Stanford University Press, 1986); DeLacy, however, does go beyond the atomizing tendencies of this approach to venture a number of important generalizations.

[17] William Temple, *The Ethics of Penal Action* (1934), quoted in Fox, *The English Prison and Borstal System*, p. 3.

[18] Thus, even the immensely knowledgeable and thorough work by Sir Leon Radzinowicz and Roger Hood, *History of English Criminal Law and Its Administration Volume 5: The Emergence of Penal Policy* (London: Stevens, 1986), which is exhaustive in its exploration of official papers to trace policy arguments and administrative reform, remains in its perspective rather old-fashioned. Radzinowicz and Hood approach the making of policy in a social, political, and cultural vacuum, taking the arguments they carefully trace at face value, as those of objective and reasonable men not significantly different from policymakers today except in being less informed and probably more prejudiced. They also see the issues as presented to their policymakers from without, as objective problems of social behavior for which they had to find solutions. The authors do not ask how these problems were constructed, and what they may tell us of the social, political and cultural forces of the time. [For a fuller statement of this criticism, see Martin J. Wiener, "The March of Penal Progress?," *Journal of British Studies 26* (1987), 83–96.]

and its treatment as shaped by particular and contingent interpretations of reality. Even official criminal statistics are best seen as "condensed interpretations of the world ... compressing numerous decisions, preoccupations, and practices."[19] As the French historian, Michelle Perrot, put it, "there are no 'facts of crime' as such, only a judgmental process that institutes crimes by designating as criminal both certain acts and their perpetrators. In other words, there is a discourse of crime that reveals the obsessions of a society."[20] Criminal law and policy, from this standpoint, have an inescapably subjective or sociocultural dimension.

If this is so, then Victorian and Edwardian concerns with crime and its treatment need to be located in the wider culture more thoroughly than has been done. In what ways ought this to be done? The leading paradigm for such location in recent years has been political, in which not only the old Whig historiography of progress, but also both internalist and pragmatist stances, have been challenged as modes that mystified the underlying and determinative power relations. Michael Ignatieff and David Garland have argued that penal policy has always been determined by unacknowledged deep structures of power.[21] The point of criminal policy, they and others have insisted, has always been to reproduce existing social power relations. Therefore, criminal policy should be understood as the record of varying, and on the whole increasingly successful, strategies of social domination. The fundamental quest of penal reform since the eighteenth century, in Michel Foucault's phrase, was always "not to punish less, but to punish better; to punish with an attenuated severity perhaps, but in order to punish with more universality and necessity; to insert the power to punish more deeply into the social body."[22]

---

[19] David Downes and Paul Rock, *Understanding Deviance* (Oxford: Clarendon Press, 1982), p. 177. See also R. S. Sindall, "Criminal Statistics of Nineteenth Century Cities," *Urban History Yearbook*, 1986. Thus, as Joanna Innes and John Styles have concluded, "there can be no history of criminality separate from the history of law enforcement." ["The Crime Wave: Recent Writing on Crime and Criminal Justice in Eighteenth Century England," *Journal of British Studies* 25 (1986), 402.]

[20] "Delinquency and the Penitentiary System in 19th Century France" [1975], in *Deviants and the Abandoned in French Society*, eds. Robert Forster and Orest Ranum (Baltimore: Johns Hopkins University Press, 1978), p. 219.

[21] In this they have been much influenced by the work of Michel Foucault – particularly *Discipline and Punish: The Birth of the Prison* [1975] (New York; Pantheon, 1978). Michael Ignatieff, *A Just Measure of Pain: The Penitentiary in the Industrial Revolution 1750–1850* (New York: Pantheon, 1978); David Garland, *Punishment and Welfare: A History of Penal Strategies* (Alddershot: Gower, 1985).

[22] *Discipline and Punish*, p. 82. A similar argument is made in regard to the treatment of the mentally ill in the nineteenth century by Andrew Scull, *Museums of Madness: The Social Organization of Insanity in Nineteenth Century England* (New York: St. Martin's Press, 1979). For a general form of this argument, see Michael Katz, "Origins of the Institutional State," *Marxist Perspectives* (Winter, 1978), 6–22.

In a less subtle way that is still part of the same interpretative tradition, V. A. C. Gatrell recently identified the central theme of criminal policy in Britain over the past two centuries as the rise of the "policeman state."[23]

This paradigm has proved powerful and useful, but also constricting in a number of ways. If earlier generations were too complacent about the upward directionality of British history, revisionists have surely succumbed to the opposite vice; their picture of an onward march of surveillance and control embodies an unconvincingly gloomy photographic negative image of Whiggism. To replace humanitarian reform by social control is to offer one simplism in place of another. Human motives and even interests are more complex and more problematic, and the institutions of criminal justice have responded to a greater variety of motives and served a wider array of interests than that of "social control."[24]

More fundamentally, if internalist and pragmatist historians have failed to perceive how discourse and practice cannot proceed untouched by power relations, the recent analysts of power have tended to see nothing else, filling all historiographical cavities with political interpretations. A literary theorist in this school, Fredric Jameson, has declared that "everything is 'in the last analysis' political."[25] But, like economic man, dominative man is a useful

---

[23] "Crime, Authority and the Policeman-State 1750–1950," in *The Cambridge Social History of Britain 1750–1950*, ed. F. M. L. Thompson (Cambridge: Cambridge University Press, forthcoming).

[24] These points have been made as part of a larger debate about the concept of social control. See Martin J. Wiener, "Social Control in Nineteenth Century Britain," *Journal of Social History* 12 (1978–79), 314–21; Wiener (ed.), *Humanitarianism or Control: Nineteenth Century Reform Reappraised, Rice University Studies* 67, no. 1 (Winter, 1980); F. M. L. Thompson, "Social Control in Nineteenth Century Britain," *Economic History Review*, 2nd series, *34* (1981), 189–208. Gertrude Himmelfarb has noted the elastic nature of this concept: "The difficulty with the theory of 'social control' is that it can be neither proved nor disproved, since it can account for anything and everything: the restriction of poor relief or its expansion, the provision of education for the poor, or the failure to provide such education, the passage of a Ten Hours Bill or the defeat of that bill, a religious movement that catered to the poor or one that ignored the poor." *The Idea of Poverty*, p. 41n. Several leading revisionists have in fact changed their original positions to allow space for other motives, interests, and functions. See Michael Ignatieff, "State, Civil Society, and Total Institutions: A Critique of Recent Social Histories of Punishment," *Crime and Justice 3* (1981); David Garland, "Foucault's *Discipline and Punish*: An Exposition and Critique," *American Bar Foundation Research Journal* 1986: 847–80. "There are elements of the penal system," Garland now argues, "which malfunction and so are not effective as forms of control or else are simply not designed to function as control measures in the first place." [*ibid.*, p. 873]

[25] *The Political Unconscious* (Ithaca, N.Y.: Cornell University Press, 1981), p. 20. Or, as Michel Foucault put it some years earlier, "The individual is an effect of power." [Michel Foucault, *Power/Knowledge: Selected Interviews and Other Writings 1972–1977*, ed. Colin Gordon (New York: Pantheon, 1980), p. 98.]

fiction as long as we do not mistake him for man himself. It is difficult to see why one mode of explanation – the political – should occupy a privileged position in cultural and social analysis. Indeed, one would expect our recent insights into the creative role of culture to widen, not narrow, our field of vision. Now that we appreciate the degree to which cultural entities are more than simply products or reflections of deeper realities, but are themselves active agents in constituting human realities, why should we seek to understand their activity in solely, or even predominantly, political terms? By what warrant are we to adopt an exclusionary political master narrative?

If social discourse and action are always to some degree structured by political relations, these relations are no first cause, but are themselves historical products that have been shaped by the very forms of thought and action through which they are expressed. At any given moment, there are many possible ways to define interests and exert power. The important question is why certain possibilities rather than others are developed, and this question cannot be answered without also looking beyond politics – even the politics of discourse.[26] How the power to judge and punish is exercised depends always upon particular readings of human nature and society, and these develop out of imperatives that are not solely political ones. Indeed, criminal policy can be usefully seen not only as an inevitably political art or science, but conversely as an equally inevitably esthetic or philosophic form of politics. Just as sociopolitical historians of science have valuably argued that solutions to problems of knowledge are also solutions to problems of social order, the reverse is also true. Solutions to the problem of social order as embodied in policies for crime and other forms of deviance are also solutions to the problem of knowing

---

[26] The movement in legal scholarship known as Critical Legal Studies has much to contribute to general historians. Despite its association with a political understanding of law, the implications of CLS are broader and in some ways subversive of simplistically political interpretations. Against the Legal Realist description of law as straightforward reflection of interests, Robert Gordon, speaking for CLS generally, has stressed that "the formation of 'interests' themselves is saturated in some of the basic categories and assumptions of law." "An Exchange on Critical Legal Studies between Robert W. Gordon and William Nelson," *Law and History Review* 6 (Spring, 1988), 146. More explicitly, James Boyd White has suggested that law is "best regarded not as a machine for social control, but as ... a system of constitutive rhetoric: a set of resources for claiming, resisting and declaring significance. It is a way of asking and responding to questions; of defining roles and positions from which, and voices with which, to speak; of creating and maintaining relations; of justifying and explaining action and inaction. It is one of the forms in which a culture lives and changes, drawing connections in special ways between past and present, near and far. The law, of which legal punishment is a part, is a system of meaning; it is a language and should be evaluated as such." *Heracles' Bow: Essays on the Rhetoric and Poetics of the Law* (Madison, Wisc.: University of Wisconsin Press, 1985), p. 205. As with conventional languages, the influences shaping criminal law are many and various.

human beings and, indeed, the cosmos. In this sense, the perspective of politics can be balanced and enriched by those of philosophy and poetics.

Structures of action are also structures of thought; to describe them fully is also, as Clifford Geertz has put it, "to describe a constellation of enshrined ideas" or, in Raymond Williams's valuable term, to expose "structures of feeling."[27] In this work, the transformation of English thought and policy about crime during the nineteenth and early twentieth centuries is located within such changing mental constellations and affective structures related to (though not determined by) specific social developments. No complete history of English criminal policy is provided here. Rather than replacing internalist, pragmatist, Whig, or revisionist perspectives, this work places the stories they offer in a new frame.

Indeed, in the present state of our knowledge, it is not possible to write even a complete *cultural* history of a century's criminal policy. The scope of this work is therefore deliberately limited in two further ways. First, it is by and large confined to the milieu of the central government's policymaking classes – those who made or administered the penal laws. Popular views of crime and punishment do not figure much in our story. Eventually, when we know much more about these other levels and milieus, historians will be able to integrate central and local, and elite and popular, dimensions into a truly complete account of the meanings of crime and punishment in modern English history – an account toward which this present work is meant to contribute.

Second, this work focuses on a consensus within officialdom, rather than on conflict, on images and values that were widely held at a given moment within that social stratum, rather than those that were in intense dispute. This choice reflects both my desire to provide the reader with a clear and coherent account, and my conviction that in recent years the shared elements of middle- and upper-class culture have received short shrift in favor of those that were contested. Here too, this work can only stand as a contribution from one particular point of view toward more complete histories of crime and punishment, and Establishment culture, in modern English history.

From willfulness to wreckage

This work will explore two broad patterns of assumption and concern among the policymaking classes – patterns that were rooted in changes in (but not

---

[27] Clifford Geertz, *Negara* (Princeton: Princeton University Press, 1980), p. 135; Raymond Williams, *Marxism and Literature* (Oxford: Oxford University Press, 1977), pp. 132–5. By this Williams meant "not feeling against thought, but thought as felt and feeling as thought" [p. 132].

reducible to mere expressions of) social structures and relations. They have been noticed by scholars working in a variety of specialized areas, but their general significance has not been appreciated. Here it will be argued that these patterns gave form to central government's criminal policy over a century and more.

The decades after 1820 saw a heightened concern with unregulated human power, both personal and collective. The advancing individualism of the age had a dark, anarchic side that few failed to sense. Many traditional limitations upon individual freedom of action were being dismantled, while traditional structures of authority were being challenged. Virtually all the developments of the age were working to multiply the effective force of human desires and will. As a consequence, the question of control came to the fore. Social historians have noted this question in terms of class relations, but it extended beyond that to gender and generational relations, for example, and to the construction of personal identity. In social policy, this question underlay efforts to moralize the uprooted, rapidly growing, and youthful populace. In personal life, it promoted among the middle classes concern with regulating one's passions and planning one's life.

Victorian criminal policy was molded in the midst of these developments. Images of the criminal reflected rising anxieties about impulses and will out of control; crime was a central metaphor of disorder and loss of control in all spheres of life. Criminal and penal policy articulated the effort to counter this perception by fostering disciplined behavior and a broad ethos of respectability. As the brutality of the law was lessened, its reach was extended to cover more persons and more forms of behavior. Vagrants, drunkards, and other "immoral" and "disorderly" persons, on the one hand, and white-collar offenders, on the other, were brought more fully under the purview of criminal policy. At the same time, judicial interpretations of criminal liability tied the law more closely to the task of inculcating moral character by narrowing the grounds of excuse. In tandem with these changes, punishment was reconstructed so that its discretionary, public, and violent character yielded to forms more calculated to promote the development of inner behavioral controls. In convicted criminals, this reorientation was accomplished through the uniform and impersonal disciplinary regime of the new prisons, and in potential criminals, through the clarity and certainty of its penalties. At all levels prosecution was made easier, punishment more certain, and penalties more predictable, impersonal, and uniform. The guiding vision of this reconstructed system of criminal justice was that of the responsible individual. Members of the public were to be considered more rational and responsible than they had been hitherto. It was believed that treating men (and sometimes women) thus was the best way of making them more so in fact, an aim that was crucial to Victorian fears and hopes. Underlying early Victorian reform of criminal policy was the supposition that the most urgent need, and possibility, of the age was to make people self-governing and that the way to do this was to hold them, sternly and unblinkingly, responsible for the consequences of their actions.

During the last quarter of the nineteenth century, however, the cultural substructure of criminal policy began to shift again as a very different pattern of concern began to take shape among the policymaking elite. Although fears of both social and personal disorder were steadily allayed by the success of Victorian efforts at control, this very success, taking place while both scientific and social thinking were profoundly altering, nurtured the new anxiety. As technology and economic advances kept extending the scale and complexity of life, and as the natural sciences put forth new deterministic models of understanding the human world, the Victorian image of the individual weakened. Reflective persons were coming to feel dwarfed by their natural and social environment. At the same time, upper-middle-class discontent was growing as a result of the life-constricting repressiveness of triumphant respectability. Consequently, fears of a dam-bursting anarchy began to be replaced by opposite fears of a disabled society of ineffectual, devitalized, and overcontrolled individuals molded by environmental and biological forces beyond their control. By the Edwardian era, members of the social strata from which policymakers were drawn became sensitive to the limitations of a program of control and were concerned instead with finding new ways to re-enable, even revivify, both the populace and themselves.

Again, criminal policy reflected and participated in this deep cultural shift. At the same time that upper-middle-class individuals began to feel less autonomous and less vital, they began to preceive criminal offenders as less threatening and less responsible for their behavior and instead saw them as social wreckage and stepchildren of nature, rather than willful enemies of society. As self-realization began to replace self-discipline as the organizing theme of middle-class lives, the prison and its impersonal disciplinary regime appeared ever less a satisfactory answer to crime. Criminals appeared now to require direct therapeutic intervention rather than deterrence or discipline. Consequently, the link between liability to criminal sanctions and moral blame was loosened, while these sanctions were made less punitive and more welfarist. Fines and probation were substituted for imprisonment, prison regimes in general became less severe, reformative modes of incarceration were created for youths and inebriates, new efforts were instituted to detect mental weakness, and facilities for aid and supervision after release were developed. By the aftermath of the First World War, as a new generation took the reins at the Home Office and the Prison Commission, images of man and of criminal policy in Britain had altered dramatically and roughly in tandem. In a society whose culture as well as politics was post-Victorian, a new interpretation of criminality and a new approach to the treatment of criminals had become established. As the explosive image of the criminal had reflected Victorian concerns, twentieth-century anxieties found an expression in an image of a debilitated offender.

1

The origins of Victorianism: impulse and moralization

The rise of the problem of criminality

Victorian observers looking back on the previous century, V. A. C. Gatrell has noted, "would have been struck by their forefathers' relative indifference to crime as a 'problem', and by their relative satisfaction with the apparently arbitrary and capricious mechanisms which contained it."[1] Early Victorians, in contrast, saw a "constant and uninterrupted increase of crime"[2] everywhere they looked. The criminal statistics that began to be published annually from 1805 painted a disturbing, if not frightening, picture. Between 1805 and 1842, the numbers of persons committed to trial for indictable offenses (nontrivial crimes, roughly corresponding to the older category of felonies) had risen nearly sevenfold, far outracing the growth of population.[3]

We now know how little this superficially impressive fact tells us about "real" crime, reflecting as it does both improving record keeping and greatly expanding enforcement.[4] Modern historians have found contemporaries' excited accounts of this supposed "crime wave" to be highly misleading. Most offenses during the period of greatest concern, David Philips has concluded, were "prosaic and undramatic, involving smalll amounts being stolen, squalid robberies, burglaries and assaults, in which roughness was common, but not fatal violence, and in which the items taken were usually small amounts of coal, metal, clothing, food, money or personal possessions."[5] However, the apparent factuality of the statistics of ever-rising commitments played a crucial

---

[1] "Crime, Authority and the Policeman-State, 1750–1950," in *The Cambridge Social History of Britain, 1750–1950*, ed. F. M. L. Thompson (Cambridge: Cambridge University Press, forthcoming).

[2] "The Increase of Crime," *Blackwood's Edinburgh Magazine LV* (Jan.–June 1844), 533.

[3] See V. A. C. Gatrell and T. B. Hadden, "Criminal Statistics and Their Interpretation," in *Nineteenth Century Society*, ed. E. A. Wrigley (Cambridge: Cambridge University Press, 1972), pp. 372–4.

[4] See Gatrell and Hadden, *ibid.*

[5] David Philips, *Crime and Authority in Victorian England: The Black Country* (London: Croom Helm, 1977), p. 287.

role in underpinning contemporary concerns. The annual statistical returns, along with particular heinous or threatening crimes, were widely noted in the press, and much social meaning was read into them. "It is too evident," observed the Scottish social-reforming minister, Alexander Thomson, in 1852, "that our criminals are steadily increasing, not only in absolute numbers, but in relative proportion to the rest of the population."[6] Others, drawing on a wide variety of data of varying reliability, came up with sometimes startling figures of multiplying numbers of criminals.[7]

Not only were contemporaries almost unanimous in perceiving an ever-rising amount of criminality of all kinds, and particularly offenses committed by juveniles, but their fears of violent crime became more intense. The reformist *Law Magazine*, in drawing the line in 1850 at abolishing the death penalty, cited "the immense increase which has notoriously taken place in the whole catalogue of personal injuries, from common assaults up to attempts to shoot, stab, and poison."[8] The worrisome social changes of the day seemed to be generating not only more drunkards and prostitutes, not only more boy thieves, but more "cutthroats" and "ruffians." As the drunkard and the prostitute were being constituted as deviant types for social and psychological study, similarly the criminal, usually of violent inclinations, was becoming more clearly than ever a distinct category of social perception and analysis.

On the most straightforward level, it is clear that public interest in criminality – both popular and serious – was growing; crime and the criminal became during the first half of the century subjects of innumerable works of fiction and fact. Popular crime literature and theatre, particularly detailing real and imagined murders, proliferated.[9] "Crime," Louis James has observed, "was the best seller.... A 'stunning good murder' provided all the known highest-circulation broadsheets."[10] From 1848 to 1849, two broadsheets (whose readership was primarily working class) recounting the gory details of a dual murder were said to have sold $2\frac{1}{2}$ million copies.[11] "Fires are our best friends, next to murders," Henry Mayhew was told by sellers, "if they are *good* fires."[12] Although newpapers, confined by their price to a largely

---

[6] Alexander Thomson, *Social Evils: Their Causes and Their Cure* (London: Nisbet, 1852), p. 1.

[7] See Geoffrey Pearson, *Hooligan: A History of Respectable Fears* (London: Macmillan, 1983), p. 164.

[8] *Law Magazine 44* (Aug.–Nov. 1850), 122.

[9] See Richard Altick, *Victorian Studies in Scarlet* (New York: Norton, 1970).

[10] Louis James, ed., *English Popular Literature 1819–1851* (New York: Columbia University Press, 1976), pp. 39–40.

[11] *ibid.*

[12] Henry Mayhew, *London Labour and the London Poor* (4 vols.; New York: A. M. Kelley, 1967) Vol. 1, p. 238.

middle-class readership, were more restrained in their coverage, the two class
cultures were not as far apart as one might expect. Middle-class newspapers
also carried large amounts of crime news, here also weighted toward the violent. Moreover, this middle-class literature was also steeped in violence and
crime, as moral reformers and *The Times* complained.[13] The highly respectable *Morning Post*, for example, regularly provided "horrifying . . . details" of
"barbarous murder[s]",[14] often using them as starting points for reflections on
the savagery existing within civilization and ratifying its readers' apparent
sense of the danger surrounding them. On one day in 1845, four separate
murders occurring over the previous weeks were discussed in side-by-side
accounts, several giving gory details.[15]

What meaning did contemporaries give to the "crime wave"? Liberals as
well as Conservatives tended to see in it a message of moral decay. Crimes, as
the Liberal barrister and school inspector Jelinger Symons put it in 1849, were
"the offshoots of an extent of moral disease which they by no means accurately
measure, but of which they attest the magnitude."[16] Indeed Symons, a member of official commissions that investigated the plight of handloom weavers
and of miners, nonetheless contended that the central problem of the age was
not material deprivation, but the relaxation of "moral restraint."[17] In part,
this concern for "moral restraint" served as a focus for middle- and upper-
class fears of working-class insubordination. Yet spreading moral disorder was
also felt by both elite and nonelite men in regard to other social relations,
those patterned by gender and generation as well as by class.

Perhaps in response to tendencies toward a widening freedom of action for
women, concern among the educated and governing classes with bastardy and
with prostitution strikingly mounted. As aspects of the menace of unregulated
female sexuality, both these forms of deviance threatened early and mid-
Victorian paternal authority in all classes,[18] and the early Victorian period
promoted both to the status of major social problems. Both problems,
along with those of promiscuity and indecency in general, were often linked to
the growth of women's waged labor, particularly the intermixing of the sexes

[13] See Gertrude Himmelfarb, *The Idea of Poverty* (New York: Knopf, 1984), pp. 414,
416.
[14] Jan. 8, 1845.
[15] Feb. 1, 1845.
[16] J. Symons, *Tactics for the Times as Regards the Condition and Treatment of the Dangerous Classes* (London: John Ollivier, 1849), p. 15.
[17] *ibid.*, p. 58.
[18] See John Gillis, *For Better, For Worse: British Marriages 1600 to the Present* (New
York: Oxford University Press, 1985), Ch. 4, and Judith Walkowitz, *Prostitution and
Victorian Society* (Cambridge: Cambridge University Press, 1980), pp. 33–5.

at work.[19] Women's independence threatened to incite not only unregulated sexuality, but crime. Most female criminality was seen as rooted in prostitution, the most common form of independent economic activity by women.[20] Moreover, maternal desertion of domestic duty was perhaps the leading explanation for the rising scourge of juvenile delinquency. The temperance activist Thomas Beggs, in the same year as Symons' warnings, bemoaned the dangerous consequences of married women's employment: "Young children are left at home under very inadequate conduct and almost without restraint, left to play at will and expand into every lawless form."[21]

The young were increasingly perceived as posing a new problem. The late eighteenth century acceleration of population growth had produced a falling average age. By 1821, almost half the population was under 20 years of age.[22] Children aged five to fourteen, who had made up a little over one-sixth of the population in the late seventeenth century, made up about one-quarter by the 1820s.[23] At the same time, the continual expansion of the market economy and the growth of industry seemed to undermine the long-standing controls of apprenticeship and other forms of prolonged youth dependence.[24] As Symons observed after his service on official inquiries, "the tendency of manufacturing

[19] See Jane Humphries, "'. . . The Most Free From Objection . . .' The Sexual Division of Labor and Women's Work in Nineteenth Century England," *Journal of Economic History 47* (1987), 929–48. Humphries describes Symons and some other members of the 1840 Commission on Children's Employment in Mines as "obsessed" with sexual dangers.

[20] In his study of transportation, Michael Sturma has noted that "contemporaries who showed an interest in female convicts concerned themselves less with the crimes of women than with their moral condition. Women did not receive sentences of transportation for prostitution. Nevertheless, it was the sexual behavior of the women which was the principal, at times the only, criterion used in evaluating their conduct. Sexual license was both a reflection and index of criminality, and so one finds that 'the hardened offender' and 'the abandoned prostitute' often became synonymous." ["Eye of the Beholder: The Stereotype of Women Convicts, 1788–1852," *Labour History 34* (Canberra) (1978), 4.]

[21] Thomas Beggs, *An Inquiry into the Extent and Causes of Juvenile Depravity* (London: Gilpin, 1849), p. 72.

[22] John Springhall, *Coming of Age: Adolescence in Britain 1860–1960* (Dublin: Gill and Macmillan, 1986), p. 65.

[23] E. A. Wrigley and R. Schofield, *The Population History of England 1541–1871* (Cambridge: Cambridge University Press, 1981), pp. 528–9.

[24] After his better-known early social optimism of the "hidden hand," worked out before the pressures of demographic and economic change began to tell, even the father of market philosophy, Adam Smith, came to worry about the moral basis of a commercial society. In his 1790 revision of the *Theory of Moral Sentiments* Smith reverted toward a more theological position, placing greater stress on the need to reinforce weakening moral influences. Here Lawrence Dickey has seen "the perception that for a commercial society to function properly – in a 'civilized' way – it would have to maintain a high degree of collec-

machinery has been to throw the social importance of industry, in great measure, into the hands of children, investing them with consequence and independence before their minds are schooled in self-government. Hence the precocity of the passions and the growth of juvenile vice in manufacturing places."[25]

Symons was here simply summing up widely held views. Anxieties about what industrialism was doing to accepted generational and gender roles were rife. The Bradford Tory factory reformer, Parson Bull, had exhorted in 1833,

> Parents of Bradford how say you? Do you consent that your little girls and boys when a day older than 13 shall be held in the eyes of the law as independent of you? Is it for your comfort? Is it for their good? Will it mend their morals? Will it strengthen the bonds which hold society together? Oh worse than madness thus to strike at the very root of all social order and to spread the seed of anarchy and confusion all around![26]

Not only capitalism and factories, but also according to most contemporaries the rapid growth of towns seemed to be promoting moral dissolution.

tive vigilance and 'propriety' with regard to its morality. The problem, of course, was that the *actual* interplay between commercial and moral values in society was tilting the balance between the two toward the pursuit of the former *at the expense* of the latter. In the face of that development, Smith realized that the virtuousness of prudent and frugal men could no longer be taken for granted." From "Historicizing the 'Adam Smith Problem': Conceptual, Historiographical, and Textual Issues," *Journal of Modern History 58* (1986), 608. After Smith, this problem of what Fred Hirsch has called the "depleting moral legacy" of commercial society moved, indeed, to center stage. [From F. Hirsch, *Social Limits to Growth* (Cambridge, Mass: Harvard University Press, 1976), pt. 3].

[25] *Tactics for the Times*, p. 49.

[26] Quoted in Theodore Koditschek, *Class Formation and Urban-Industrial Society* (New York: Cambridge University Press, 1990). Such contemporary perceptions of a shift in the balance of power between generations seem to have had a basis in everyday life. Olive Anderson has noted that "it is now very clear that in [early Victorian] Lancashire textile towns life was exceptionally good for the young, but exceptionally bad for middle-aged and elderly men, although often not for middle-aged and elderly women." The young were better off partly because a wider range of jobs was open to them, but chiefly because the earning power of textile operatives reached its peak in their late teens and twenties. As their dexterity, strength, and endurance declined, middle-aged men had to move into lower-paying jobs, and ended their work careers hawking, street-sweeping, and rag-gathering. Older women, on the other hand, were often valued as child-minders and housekeepers, since many younger married women worked in the factories. Thus, older men lost relatively in relation to both younger men and to women. All this, Anderson observed, was "in considerable contrast to the state of affairs not only in rural areas, but also in nonindustrial towns, where widespread parental ownership of the means of production, a restricted labour market, and the predominance in the male labour force of craftsmen, retailers and professional men usually favoured the middle-aged and elderly." ["Suicide and Industrialization," *Past and Present. 86* (Feb., 1980), 165.]

One frequently cited reason was their anonymity. The Tory *Blackwood's Magazine* warned in 1844 that "the restraints of character, relationship and vicinity are . . . lost in the crowd. . . . Multitudes remove responsibility without weakening passion."[27] Indeed, towns, with their crowding, fast pace, and younger population, could dangerously *stimulate* the passions. Symons, speaking for many, observed that

> in all large and crowded communities crime is sure to abound, unless vigorously met by counteracting influences . . . the depraving character of these crowded communities, both physically and morally [is undeniable]. . . . Everything is of slower development in the country than in towns, where the communication of thought, and the contagion of habit and example, are more rife and rapid; the passions vegetate and develop themselves with more vigour. . . .[28]

The public health reformer, Edwin Chadwick, warned not just of physical but moral danger from these unhealthy and unregulated young. He wrote that

> the noxious physical agencies depress the health and bodily condition of the population, and act as obstacles to education and to moral culture; that in abridging the duration of the adult life of the working classes they check the growth of productive skill, and abridge the amount of social experience and steady moral habits in the community: that they substitute for a population that accumulates and preserves instruction and is steadily progressive, a population that is young, inexperienced, ignorant, credulous, irritable, passionate, and dangerous. . . .[29]

Intertwined, for Chadwick, with bad sanitary arrangements' direct effects on mortality was their threat to general moral health and social stability by the way they undermined generational authority: "The diappearance by premature death," he noted, "of the heads of families and the older workmen . . . must to some extent involve the necessity of supplying the lapse of staid influence amidst a young population by one description or another of precautionary force." The mobs of Bethnal Green, Bristol, and Manchester were always youthful: "the great havoc . . . was committed by mere boys."[30]

Thus, it was close to an early Victorian cliché to note, as did the Reverend Sydney Turner, the first Inspector or (Juvenile) Reformatories, in 1857, that "crime has its roots in unlicensed appetites, in bold, rebellious will, in

[27] "Causes of the Increase of Crime," *Blackwood's Edinburgh Magazine 56* (July–Dec., 1844), 7–8.

[28] *Tactics*, pp. 48, 49.

[29] *Report on the Sanitary Conditions of the Labouring Population* [1842], ed. M. W. Flinn, (Edinburgh: Edinburgh University Press, 1965), p. 268.

[30] *ibid.*, pp. 266–7.

vicious and enthralling habits."[31] Such fears of unbridled self-will were often
not only social, but – as the growth of Evangelicalism in the first half of
the century testified – also had a personal dimension. What was feared were
not only the unleashed impulses of others, but one's own; not only the young
around one, but the child in oneself. It has been noted that psychological
discourse often served as a projective screen for social conflicts, but it is
sometimes forgotten that social discourse served the same function for psychological conflicts. The specter of mingled chaos and tyranny did not require
prior contemplation of society, but could arise from within. The cruelty and
lack of restraint of so many slaveholders in the United States, the Evangelical
Earl of Carlisle noted in 1853, were all too "natural":

> take ... human nature, such as we observe it in the world immediately
> around ourselves, such as we feel it within our own bosoms – put it in
> contact with the recognized codes and published laws of slave-holding
> states, impregnate it with the habits and maxims of the surrounding so-
> ciety, transfer it, apart from check or observation, to the remote plan-
> tation or obscure barracoon, and ... work out for yourself the inevitable
> result.[32]

Popular fiction of the 1830s and 1840s, including Dickens's *Oliver Twist*,
highlighted and seemed to ratify important aspects of the ongoing factual discussion on crime.[33] One aspect was the perception that crime constituted a
world of its own, one that invertedly mirrored the respectable world as a
nightmare mirrors the day world. A second facet was the youthfulness of the
criminal world.[34] Thirdly, many of these works were suffused by fascination
with and an intense horror of violence.[35] The climax of *Oliver Twist* is Sikes's

---

[31] Sydney Turner, "Responsibility in Aims and Means," *Transactions of the National Association for the Promotion of Social Science [hereafter NAPSS] 1857*, p. 5. Turner was delivering the opening sermon to the first meeting of this influential mid-Victorian society; on its influence, see Chapter 3.

[32] Introduction to Harriet Beecher Stowe, *Uncle Tom's Cabin* (London: George Routledge, 1853), p. vi.

[33] See, among others, Altick, *Scarlet*, and Keith Hollingsworth, *The Newgate Novel 1830–1847* (Detroit: Wayne State University Press, 1963). The most penetrating work on images of crime in this era deals solely with the United States but is highly suggestive for understanding British culture as well: David Brion Davis's *Homicide in American Fiction 1798–1860: A Study in Social Values* (Ithaca: Cornell University Press, 1957).

[34] The most popular criminal subject for fictionalized treatment in these years, Jack Sheppard, was hanged at age 22; the Sheppard penny theatre craze of the 1830s was followed, it was complained, by boys of nine turning to crime.

[35] On Dickens's fascination with violence, see John Bayley, "*Oliver Twist*: 'Things as They Really Are,' " in *Dickens and the Twentieth Century*, ed. John Gross (Toronto: University of Toronto Press, 1962), pp. 47–64 and John Carey, *The Violent Effigy* (London: Faber and Faber, 1973), pp. 11–53.

murder of Nancy, a moment from which the whole tenor of the novel changes, the language heightens, and the rest of the work follows at a feverish intensity; the whole world seems to draw back in horror. As he usually did, Dickens was tapping a seam that ran through early nineteenth-century culture in both the outpouring of broadsheets detailing lurid crimes and their punishment and in the products of "high" culture like De Quincey's "Murder as a Fine Art," of fascination with extreme impulses and the fragility of controls against their expression. For all his indignant objection to being classed with the melodramatists, Dickens was deeply marked by the genre.

Accounts of criminality in the 1830s and 1840s – like those of prostitution – usually took the form of melodrama. As literary critics have pointed out, melodrama confronts basic anxieties – "the sense of an enemy, the loss of control, the apparent triumph of anarchy."[36] Not surprisingly, therefore, it became a natural stylistic mode for the early and mid-Victorian period.[37] Moreover, at the heart of melodrama lies the fear of the unleashing of aggressive impulses and forces, the sense of the fragility of the barriers civilization has erected. During these years not only theatrical, but also literary and even nonfictional representations of crime tended to follow the lines of melodrama, drawing sharp lines between good and evil characters, placing the good into harrowing dangers while in the end bringing the evil to punishment and banishing chaos. Moral issues were starkly clear, and criminality was dramatically at war with virtue.[38] Crime fiction, on stage or in print, rarely involved intellectual puzzles of detection; the criminal was usually known from early on, and interest focused on portraying his perverted psychology and actions. The focus of attention was on impulses breaking bounds, on the nature and actions of the villain.[39]

Stark moralism was joined to an equally stark emotionalism in a genre well suited to express anxieties about weakening controls. In its melodramatic

[36] Winifred Hughes, *The Maniac in the Cellar: Sensation Novels of the 1860s* (Princeton: Princeton University Press, 1980), p. 175.

[37] Louis James observed its "dynamic of emotional conflict and change" that made it highly appropriate for the era. *English Popular Literature 1819–1851*, p. 87.

[38] As the Reverend William Tuckniss declared in his introduction to the fourth volume of Henry Mayhew's *London Labour*, contemporary London was "the great arena of conflict between the powers of darkness and the ministry of heaven." [*London Labour and the London Poor*, Vol. IV (1862), p. xv.] This struggle between good and evil was externalized, particular characters being dominated by one or the other; "when the villain began to develop a conscience, in later domestic melodrama," Winifred Hughes has observed, "it spelled the end of his primitive vitality and foreshadowed the eventual decline of the melodramatic form itself." [*Maniac*, p. 10.] See also Frank Rahill, *The World of Melodrama* (University Park, Penn: Penn State Univeristy Press, 1967).

[39] These points are emphasized in Davis, *Homicide*, especially pp. 120–5, 142–3.

constructions, the world of early nineteenth-century criminality exhibited the lineaments of a nightmare of respectability.[40] The popular stage echoed the street literature, which was based on actual crimes, where extreme, violent passions were graphically displayed and then violently punished. The typical best-selling crime was the murder of a lover, particularly of a young woman by her male lover. In typical fictional plot, men killed their mistresses when they got pregnant or insisted on marriage, thereby interfering with plans for social rising through more suitable marriages. Sometimes in these dramas women would kill lovers who refused to marry them.[41] The primitive excess of the killings – bludgeonings, burnings, dismemberments – Beth Kalikoff has observed, "finds stylistic and thematic analogues in Victorian pornography . . . . The frantic, chaotic murders and ritualized executions of street literature reflect a resounding determination to punish criminals with the violence that characterizes their attack on legal, sexual, and moral authority."[42]

The genre of the Newgate novel that flourished during this period exhibited a fascination with unchained impulses and willfulness, suggesting anxiety about the very values of individual self-shaping and assertion of will against circumstance that were constantly upheld by contemporary moralists. This fiction was dominated by its energetic, passionate, and willful villains. The sociological explanation of crime as a product of poverty or social neglect, associated with Bulwer Lytton or Dickens, has probably been overstressed by later writers seeking origins of modern views. Complaints of the immorality of these stories focused less on such explaining away of criminality and more on their intense portrayal of a life filled with unchecked emotions and immediate gratification. W. M. Thackeray was characteristic in objecting to Newgate novels not because they justified or excused crime, but because they glamorized it, habituating their readers to a profitable world of dissoluteness and impulsive violence: "We have our penny libraries for debauchery as for other useful knowledge; and colleges like palaces for study – gin-palaces, where each starving Sardanapalus [king of Nineveh who was the symbol of luxurious effeteness] may revel until he dies."[43] As Gertude Himmelfarb has noted,

> No one suggested that Ainsworth's characters were degraded because of poverty or society. On the contrary, the criticism was that young boys

[40] Martin Meisel has described the excited stagings of *Jack Sheppard*, filled with mobs and passions. [*Realizations: Narrative, Pictoral, and Theatrical Arts in Nineteenth Century England* (Princeton, N.J.: Princeton University Press, 1983), p. 297.]

[41] See Beth Kalikoff, *Murder and Moral Decay in Victorian Popular Literature* (Ann Arbor, Mich.: University of Michigan Press, 1986), p. 17.

[42] *ibid.*, pp. 18–19.

[43] Gertrude Himmelfarb, *The Idea of Poverty* (New York: Knopf, 1984), p. 409.

would be *enticed* into a life of crime by the example of Jack Sheppard and the promise of an adventurous, romantic, carefree life, not because it was the only livelihood available to them.[44]

Himmelfarb has valuably drawn attention to the neglected writing of G. W. M. Reynolds, particularly his enormously popular *Mysteries of London*, which together with its sequel, *Mysteries of the Court of London*, were "probably the longest, best selling fiction of the time."[45] Reynolds, a political radical, portrayed in these works no virtuous struggling workers or unjust capitalists, but a world of decadent, self-indulgent aristocrats and brutal, drunken criminals, both types ruled by their impulses: "A pornography of violence – deliberate, brutal, gratuitous violence – characterizes the scenes of low life, just as a pornography of sexuality pervades those of high life."[46] Himmelfarb noted how his injections of social criticism sit awkwardly with his narratives. "'In England,' he interrupts his story to protest, 'men and women die of sta vation in the streets. In England women murder their children to save them from a lingering death by famine.' But his characters do not die of starvation in the streets; they live comfortably off the proceeds of their crimes, dying of alcoholism and debauchery, of violence at each other's hands, or on the gallows. And the women do not murder their children to save them from starvation; they murder or plot to murder them for their own selfish and wicked reasons."[47]

If more sober than Reynolds's representations, the portrayal of criminality by his less successful (though better known to posterity) journalistic contemporary, Henry Mayhew, also took on melodramatic hues. In his greatest work, *London Labour and the London Poor*, to distinguish the main body of the working class from deviants and criminals, Mayhew lumped the latter together and painted them in extreme hues: "I am anxious that the public should no longer confound the honest, independent working men, with the vagrant beggars and pilferers of the country; and that they should see that the one class is as respectable and worthy, as the other is degraded and vicious." These vagrants

---

[44] *ibid.*, p. 431.

[45] Himmelfarb, p. 435. In an obituary notice of Reynolds, who died in 1879, the *Bookseller* called him "the most popular writer of his time."

[46] *ibid.*, p. 441. "Reynolds's early serials in particular," Julian Symons observed in his history of crime fiction, "are much concerned with torture and violence." *Bloody Murder* (Harmondsworth: Penguin Books, 1985), p. 43.

[47] *ibid.*, p. 448. Whereas Himmelfarb sees the tension in *The Mysteries of London* between social realism and melodrama as a flaw, Anne Humphreys has pointed out its resolving power: "The conventional melodramatic frame of this novel turns out to be the true enduring principle that controls the chaos of the modern city." "[The Geometry of the Modern City: G. W. M. Reynolds and *The Mysteries of London*," *Browning Institute Studies 11* (1983), 79.]

and pilferers, only 5 percent of whom were "deserving," he labeled a "moral pestilence . . . a stream of vice and disease . . . a vast heap of social refuse."[48]

The world of Mayhew's unrespectable poor blended imperceptibly into the antisociety of criminality: "That the costermongers belong essentially to the dangerous classes none can doubt; and those who know a coster's hatred of a 'crusher', will not hesitate to believe that they are, as they themselves confess, one and all ready, upon the least disturbance, to seize and disable their policemen."[49] Although Mayhew faulted the local authorities for leaving these street folk few alternatives in denying them the right of carrying on their trade, he did not see a change in official attitudes as getting to the root of the problem. While hard hearts and closed minds among the respectable had helped the social cancer grow, sympathy and tolerance alone would not remove it. In *The Criminal Prisons of London* (coauthored with John Binny), his next work after *London Labour*, Mayhew defined "our criminal tribes" as "that portion of our society who have not yet conformed to civilized habits."[50] These "tribes" were likened to Bedouins nad gypsies, preferring to indulge their appetites when they can and, when in need, resorting to plunder rather than submitting to the discipline of steady work. Why, Mayhew then asked (betraying the fear that self-discipline and work were not necessarily inevitably gaining) do they continue thus, in the heart of modern civilization?

> Still the question becomes – why do these folk not settle down to industrial pursuits like the rest of the community? . . . It is a strange ethnological fact that, though many have passed from the steady and regular habits of civilized life, few of those who have once adopted the savage and nomadic form of existence abandon it, notwithstanding its privations, its dangers, and its hardships. This appears to be due mainly to that love of liberty, and that impatience under control, that is more or less common to all minds. Some are more self-willed than others, and, therefore, more irritable under restraint; and these generally rebel at the least opposition to their desires. It is curiously illustrative of the truth of this point, that the greater number of criminals are found between the ages of 15 and 25; that is to say, at that time of life when the will is newly developed, and has not yet come to be guided and controlled by the dictates of reason. The period, indeed, when human beings begin to assert themselves is the most trying time for every form of government – whether it be parental, political, or social; and those indominable natures who cannot or will not brook

[48] *London Labour* Vol. III, pp. 371, 377, 397, 429.

[49] *ibid.* Vol. I, p. 101.

[50] Henry Mayhew and John Binny, *The Criminal Prisons of London and Scenes of Prison Life* (London: Griffin, Bohn, and Company, 1862), p. 384. Most of this work was written by 1856.

ruling, then become heedless of all authority, and respect no law but their own.[51]

Mayhew and Binny defined habitual criminals as "those persons who feel labour to be more irksome than others, owing to their being not only less capable of continued application to one subject or object, but more fond of immediate pleasure, and, consequently, less willing to devote themselves to those pursuits which yield only prospective ones." They found this explanation to fit with the criminal character, for they noted that such persons were distinguished by an inordinate love of amusement and an indomitable repugnance to regular labor:

> Crime, then, it may be safely asserted, is *not* due, as some say, to an inordinate density of the population, nor to a love of intoxicating liquors, nor to an inability to read and write, nor to unwholesome dwellings, nor to a non-observance of the Sabbath; but simply to that innate love of a life of ease, and aversion to hard work, which is common to *all* natures, and which, accompanied with a lawlessness of disposition as well as a disregard for the rights of our fellow-creatures, and a want of self-dignity, can but end either in begging or stealing the earnings and possessions of others.[52]

While among men this "innate love of a life of ease" led chiefly to theft, among women it led to the even easier alternative of prostitution:

> females, among the poorer classes of society, who are born to labour for their bread, but who find work inordinately irksome to their natures, and pleasure inordinately agreeable to them, have no necessity to resort to the more daring career of theft to supply their want, but have only to trade upon their personal charms in order to secure the apparent luxury of an idle life.[53]

Thus, across political and religious persuasions, a wide variety of observers held a similar vision of a work-evading population of the "unrespectable," in which deviance blended imperceptibly into criminality. The boundaries of this underclass were drawn differently, depending in part on one's politics; however, the fear was widespread that this condition would not be easily soluble, but rather was deeply rooted in human nature, in the "natural man" (and woman) who lay underneath the thin crust of civilization. As the Reverend Richard Parkinson pointed out in 1839, in soliciting support for the

---

[51] *ibid.*, p. 384.
[52] *ibid.*, pp. 385–6.
[53] *ibid.*, p. 455.

Manchester Night Asylum, "There is but a thin gauze veil between virtue and crime [in each individual], which once broken through ... can never be wholly repaired."[54]

The specter of savagery

The anxieties over moral disorder that shaped images of criminality extended more broadly through early Victorian social and psychological discourse. There we repeatedly find a polarity between restraint, frequently identified with "civilization" itself, and instincts or impulses, identified with "barbarism" or "savagery." The specter of instinctualism seems to have been simultaneously projected onto several objects – the lower classes at home, primitive peoples abroad, and the deeper layers of the psyche within even the "respectable" classes.

The psychological imagination

Where eighteenth-century physicians had seen sexuality as a powerful but natural part of the human constitution whose suppression produced many more disorders than its overindulgence, in the early nineteenth century the passions and their proper management became an increasing question of medical concern.[55] With interest focusing upon the emotions, the will, rather than the mind, was coming to be seen as the most problematic aspect of human nature. The shift in psychiatric concern from intellectual defect to malfunctions in impulse control was signified by the new concept of "moral insanity."[56] J. C. Prichard, a physician and ethnologist, coined the term in 1833, comparing the morally insane to savage tribes. In both "the passions were under no restraint," and the will was surrendered impetuously to the emotions.[57]

[54] Quoted in Thomas Laqueur, "Bodies, Death and Pauper Funerals," *Representations no.1* (Feb. 1983), 131.
[55] See Roy Porter, "Love, Sex and Madness in Eighteenth Century England," *Social Research 53* (Summer, 1986), 211–42. John Pickstone has also remarked on the heightened dualism of early nineteenth-century physiology and "the presumption that the body and its passions are to be kept in check by the rational mind." "Ferrier's Fever to Kay's Cholera: Disease and Social Structure in Cottonopolis," *History of Science 22* (1984), 413.
[56] See Vieda Skultans, *English Madness: Ideas on Insanity 1580–1890* (London: Routledge, 1979); Andrew Scull, *Museums of Madness: The Social Organization of Insanity in Nineteenth Century England* (New York: St. Martin's Press, 1979).
[57] J. C. Prichard, *A Treatise on Insanity* (London: Sherwood, Gilbert and Piper, 1853), p. 175. Phrenologists had helped shift attention from the intellect to the emotions; as A. Hayward has noted ["Murder and Madness: A Social History of the Insanity Defence in

The passions, of course, were natural to all men and women. There was an instinct-driven "natural man" lying in wait within even ostensibly civilized persons.[58] With this possibility, insanity tended to be interpreted as an eruption of the inner savage. The leading midcentury manual of psychiatric medicine observed that "there is a latent devil in the heart of the best of men; and when the restraints of religious feeling, of prudence and self-esteem, are weakened or removed by the operation of mental disease, the fiend breaks loose, and the whole character of the man seems to undergo a sudden and complete transformation."

This danger existed in all; even in "the most modest . . . woman":

> Every medical man has observed the extraordinary amount of obscenity, in thought and language, which breaks forth from the most modest and well-nurtured woman under the influence of puerperal mania; and although it may be courteous and politic to join in the wonder of those around, that such impurities could ever enter such a mind, and while he repudiates Pope's slander, that 'every woman is at heart a rake,' he will nevertheless acknowledge, that religious and moral principles alone give strength to the female mind; and that, when these are weakened or removed by disease, the subterranean fires become active, and the crater gives forth smoke and flame.[59]

If interpretations of mental illness evoked "subterranean fires," it is hardly surprising that sexuality was bulking larger in writings on the etiology of insanity. More and more disorders were being traced to an excess or a failure of management of sexual passions.[60] Masturbation – a powerful symbol of private loss of control over impulse, particularly among young males – made its appearance in medical texts as a major problem.[61] Like other passions, sexual

Mid-Victorian England," unpublished M. Litt. thesis, Oxford University 1982, p. 55]: "One of the main reasons moral insanity gained credence among the medical profession resulted from the manner in which phrenologists had established the idea that the non-rational aspects of the mind were as important in the causation of madness as derangement of the intellectual faculties."

[58] As Vieda Skultans has observed of the early Victorians: "Like the forces of anarchy and disorder, insanity was thought to be a universal presence ready to break loose." "Moral Order and Mental Derangement," in *Symbols and Sentiments*, ed. Ioan Lewis (London: Academic Press, 1977), p. 225.

[59] J. C. Bucknill and D. H. Tuke, *A Manual of Psychiatric Medicine* (Philadelphia: Blanchard & Lea, 1858), p. 273.

[60] See Elaine Showalter, *The Female Malady: Women, Madness and Culture in England, 1830–1980* (New York: Pantheon, 1985), pp. 131–2.

[61] Roy Porter has noted that eighteenth-century physicians very rarely linked masturbation with insanity; those who warned of the dangers of aberrant sex focused on possible physical damage. Nor was there much medical (as opposed to moral) fear expressed in the

impulses appeared less self-limiting by nature and instead required deliberate control (and denial). As Nina Auerbach noted in regard to the reluctance to recognize female sexuality, "[T]he repressiveness of Victorian culture is a measure of its faith in the special powers of woman, in her association with mobility and unprecedented change, with a new and strange dispensation, with an unofficial but widely promulgated and frightening mythology."[62] Even more (though less noticed by recent historians), one could say that sexual repressiveness in general, and the dogma of child innocence, was also a measure of the fear of youth, with which, of course, sexuality was particularly associated.

The social imagination

A preoccupation with instinct had entered social discourse with Thomas Malthus, who placed "the passion between the sexes" in a new role of material, as well as moral, nemesis. As is well known, Malthus frontally attacked the general eighteenth-century approval of population growth. But he also challenged the leading strand of Enlightenment thinking that more generally inclined toward a benign view of human instincts. Instead, he argued that the ineradicable instinct of sexuality virtually ensured that population would rise to absorb any increase in food supply, preventing any lasting improvement in the condition of society. Malthus's powerful impact on the imagination of his age must be seen as due to more than his arguments, which were hardly irrefutable, and indeed were to be disproved by events. Rather, he seems to have touched a raw nerve with his picture of human nature commanded by peremptory instinct that resists accommodation, which can either, in unusual cases, be denied at the cost of "inextricable unhappiness" or more commonly be surrendered to, thus carrying with it for the mass of the population inevitable immiseration. This dilemma might explain why, as Gertrude Himmelfarb has reminded us, his later, more hopeful modifications were by

eighteenth century of female sexuality; eighteenth-century writers in general showed little interest in the psychopathology of the individual whore, concentrating instead on prostitution as a social issue, as the product of "luxury," contrasting with what Porter has called the "deep fascination which the psychology of prostitution – that strange dialogue of power, submission, and irresponsibility – held for nineteenth-century thinkers." ["Love, Sex and Madness," 233–4.] "Psychological typing of sexual deviants," he concluded, "was a development almost wholly reserved for the nineteenth century. . . . The Georgian age knew only acts" [234].

[62] Nina Auerbach, *Woman and the Demon* (Cambridge, Mass: Harvard University Press, 1982), p. 188.

and large ignored and abuse was heaped on him in terms that to a modern ear seem clearly excessive. Southey's characterization of Malthus to a civil servant friend as a "voider of menstrual pollution" elicited the reply that if the "cursed book" were true, its truth was so dangerous that "a man ought to be rather indicted for it than for a publication of the Grossest Obscenity." Long after Malthus had softened his doctrine by introducing the "remedy" of moral restraint, William Hazlitt accused him of regarding mankind, and the poor especially, as "so many animals *in season*."[63] Indeed, Malthus's implications went even further; his writing reversed not only the eighteenth-century association of personal fecundity with the health of society, but the related association of personal with social vitality. As Catherine Gallagher has pointed out, for Malthus "the social body is growing 'old' [and weak] precisely insofar as the actual demographic proportions of the society are increasingly weighted toward youth...."[64] For since in his model a declining average age of the population betokened a society in strain, Malthusianism not only pointed explicitly to the evil consequences of population growth, but also implicitly to the social dangers of bodily vigor and thus of youthful energies.

Malthusian images of unhealthy, self-destructive vitality pervaded early Victorian social description, both fictional and factual. A hallmark of modern scholarship has been criticism of the "confusions" and "paranoia" of early and mid-Victorian writers on the world of the poor, of the way they mixed descriptions of the "decent" majority and "indecent" minority poor and overstressed the latter, of their unfortunate preference for the picturesque or melodrama over realism as a mode of presentation. Thus, it has been frequently argued, the realist professions of both social novelists and social scientists were turned into moralizing and sensationalist practices, defeating not only their own realism, but also their reformism, as these repelling portraits of the "lower depths" erected insuperable barriers to empathy.[65] But this sort of easy criticism of the early Victorians for failing to have twentieth-century notions of realism does not take us very far. Such distinctions between realism and moralism, or between realism and sensationalism, presume that the early Victorians had access to a reality free from moral or sensational characteristics. For most social observers of the time, however, social reality, being human, *was* moral, *was* sensational in its nature. If, as Gertrude Himmelfarb perceptively put it, "the Malthusian image of pauperization was so dramatic it unwit-

---

[63] Quoted in Himmelfarb, pp. 124–5.

[64] "The Body Versus the Social Body in Malthus and Mayhew," *Representations 14* (Spring, 1986), 86.

[65] An especially sharp, and thorough, argument along these lines is Sheila M. Smith, *The Other Nation: The Poor in English Novels of the 1840s and 1850s* (Oxford: Clarendon Press, 1980).

tingly spilled over to the image of poverty itself,"[66] it is time to explore just what gave this and related images of deviance their dramatic power.

Even professedly radical writers like Dickens were obsessed with popular deviance and disorder; his early works overflow with chaotic crowd scenes, turbulence and confusion. In her thorough study of early Victorian literary treatment of the poor, Sheila Smith chided Dickens for "offer[ing] for enjoyment [from his first work, *Sketches by Boz*] ... social horrors at a safe distance." Paricularly in his descriptions of the slum district, St. Giles's, she complained, "[H]e reduces the people to wild objects producing a frisson of delight in the beholders." Smith recalled Forster's account of the young Dickens's delight in St. Giles's because it afforded him "wild visions of prodigies of wickedness, want, and beggary." "He uses the place and its inhabitants," Smith observed, "to conjure up his 'wild visions'; this is not so much the romance of reality as romance imposed upon reality."[67] Dickens's descriptions of St. Giles's exerted a great influence on contemporaries, helping to create, as Harriet Beecher Stowe put it, a literary "fashion."[68]

Dickens's artistic greatness could overcome such misrepresentation. But, Smith noted, when a lesser writer like Kingsley imitated Dickens's account of the slum, "the distorted sensationalism is very obvious; it's there in the relentless accumulation of horrible details ... and also in the extravagance of the language – 'those narrow, brawling torrents of filth, and poverty, and sin, – the houses with their teeming load of life were piled up into the dingy, choking night'." In such accounts, the world of the poor seemed overflowing with "frantic, hectic activity."[69]

The new factory life was similarly given a particular twist by imaginative writers, as they assimilated it to the quite different life of the London slums. The romantic Tory Disraeli did this most obviously in his *Sybil*, painting a Wodgate that seemed barbaric and primitive indeed. He shaped the facts he drew from factory inspectors' reports to create an impression of unrelieved squalor and anarchic lack of civilization. Disraeli may have been extreme, but he was by no means untypical. Dickens's *Hard Times* conjures up a like picture of industrial life. It introduces Coketown with a simile to savagery: "It was a town of red brick, or of brick that would have been red if the smoke and ashes had allowed it; but as matters stood it was a town of unnatural red and

---

[66] Himmelfarb, p. 175. Himmelfarb is less blamable here than are most previous writers, empathizing as she does with the general early Victorian efforts at moralization, if not with the particular case of Mayhew; there, an apparent desire to dismantle a "progressive" reputation seems to have thrust empathy to the rear.

[67] *The Other Nation*, p. 58.

[68] Quoted *ibid.*, p. 58.

[69] *ibid.*, pp. 59–60.

black like the painted face of a savage."[70] "Savagery" had negative associations indeed for Dickens; in an essay written while starting on *Hard Times*, he had fiercely denounced the myth of the "noble savage" as, in fact, the reality of "a wild animal."[71] Even the judicious Elizabeth Gaskell could describe the Manchester populace as "a Frankenstein, that monster of many human qualities ungifted with a soul, a knowledge of the difference between good and evil."[72] In general, most early Victorian social novelists, regardless of their benevolent, reformist intent, nonetheless conceived of the poor, as Smith unhappily concluded, as "a nation of savages, a constant reproach to the apparent civilization of the rest of society."[73]

While realist fiction sensationalized the world of the poor, nonfictional writing was doing much the same. Mayhew's *London Labour* began with the claim that society consisted of two races, "the wanderers and the settlers." Among the former were numbered

> the pickpockets – the beggars – the prostitutes – the street-sellers – the street-performers – the cabmen – the coachmen – the watermen – the sailors and such like. In each of these classes – according as they partake more or less of the purely vagabond, doing nothing whatsoever for their living, but moving from place to place preying upon the earnings of the more industrious portions of the community, so will the attributes of the nomad tribes be more or less marked in them. Whether it is that in the mere act of wandering, there is a greater determination of blood to the surface of the body, and consequently a less quantity sent to the brain, the muscles being thus nourished at the expense of the mind, I leave physiologists to say. But certainly be the physical cause what it may, we must all allow that in each of the classes above mentioned, there is a greater development of the animal than of the intellectual or moral nature of man, and that they are all more or less distinguished for their high cheek-bones and protruding jaws – for their use of a slang language – for their lax ideas of property – for their general improvidence – their repugnance to continuous labour – their disregard of female honour – their love of cruelty – their pugnacity – and their utter want of religion.[74]

In such ways, imaginative writing's imagery of popular savagery also permeated supposedly factual social reportage. Although in his early writings Mayhew asserted an explicit antimoralistic sociological perspective on poverty, and stressed the tragic power of circumstances to shape lives, his environmen-

[70] Book 1, Ch. 5.
[71] "The Noble Savage," *Household Words VII, no. 168* (June 11, 1853), 337.
[72] *Mary Barton* (1847), Ch. 15.
[73] *The Other Nation*, p. 69.
[74] Vol. 1, pp. 2–3.

talism increasingly faded before vivid descriptions of his subjects' seemingly unbuttoned way of life. This fascination with "immorality" shaped a subtext that, as both Himmelfarb and Karel Willams have argued, subverted his antimoralistic and socially critical declarations.[75] Like the early Dickens, Mayhew's social criticism merged with a fascination with immorality and impulsiveness, with results that offended twentieth-century observers were either to explain away or to use as a point of attack.

A central problem of both Mayhew's *London Labour* and his subsequent *Criminal Prisons of London* (1862), is the "degraded" life of the poor and its implications for society. About this life, Mayhew, like Dickens, sought to rouse the consciences of respectable readers. After describing scenes of immorality and crime, he insisted that "we are the culpable parties in these matters. That the poor things should do as they do is but human nature."[76] The degradation of these "wandering tribes" of the poor was, Mayhew suggested, the natural result of privation and insecurity. To suppose that a precarious occupation would beget provident habits was "against the nature of things." The most precarious calling naturally engendered the greatest degree of improvidence and intemperance: "It is not the well-fed man but the starving one that is in danger of surfeiting himself."[77]

Yet these efforts at social explanation were followed by renewed and overheated descriptions of just how sensual and violent the poor were.[78] "If we knew but the whole of the facts concerning them and their sufferings and feelings," Mayhew observed, "our very fears alone for the safety of the state would be sufficient to make us do something in their behalf. I am quite satisfied, from all I have seen, that there are thousands in this great metropolis ready to rush forth, on the least evidence of a rising of the people, to commit the most savage and revolting excesses."[79]

Mayhew's reformism, like that of the novelists, often took the form of vividly describing with great repugnance the savagery that civilization tolerated, indeed maintained, in its midst:

> The consciences of the London costermongers, generally speaking, are as little developed as their intellects; indeed, the moral and religious state of

[75] See Himmelfarb, Ch. 14; Karel Williams, *From Pauperism to Poverty* (London: Routledge, 1981), Ch. 5.

[76] Vol. 1, p. 43.

[77] Vol. l, p. 6.

[78] After debunking overheated moralists by insisting on costers' sexual monogamy despite their rarely becoming legally married, Mayhew proceeded to give lengthy descriptions of the indecency and sexual promiscuity whose typicality he had just denied, citing children who had "their tastes trained to libidinism long before puberty at the penny concert, and their passions inflamed with the unrestrained intercourse of the two-penny hops." [1, p. 101.]

[79] Vol. II, p. 5.

these men is a foul disgrace to us, laughing to scorn our zeal for the 'propagation of the gospel in foreign parts,' and making our many societies for the civilization of savages on the other side of the globe appear like a 'delusion, a mockery, and a snare,' when we have so many people sunk in the lowest depths of barbarism round about our very homes.

That they are ignorant and vicious as they are, surely is not their fault. . . . Is it possible, then, that men who are as much creatures of the present as the beasts of the field – instinctless animals – should have the least faculty of prevision? or rather is it not natural that, following the most variable climate of any – they should fail to make the affluence of the fine days mitigate the starvation of the rainy ones? or that their appetites made doubly eager by the privations suffered in their adversity, should be indulged in all kinds of excess in their prosperity – their lives being thus, as it were, a series of alternations between starvation and sur-feit?[80]

As with the social novelists, the effect of Mayhew's intercessions on behalf of the streetfolk was, as Himmelfarb put it, "to make them seem even more 'brutish,' a 'race' apart. The more passionate he was in their defense, the more indignant at the society that tolerated such vice and degradation, the more vicious and degraded they appeared."[81] Yet if Mayhew worked against his own manifest intentions, it was in the service of another "program," less explicit, but understood by his readers – to chart the extent of domestic "savagery," and thus the limits of progress, and the task still before the civilizing enterprise.[82] As long as civilization remained precarious – a percep-tion that Mayhew's work, like Dickens's, underlined – tolerance was an unaffordable luxury and empathy an inadequate, even counterproductive, social stance.

The ethnological imagination

Intensified images of domestic savagery were paralleled by diminished toler-ance for the ways of savages abroad. Here Dickens's and Carlyle's repugnance for "primitives" echoed, in extremis, the movement of more professional opinion. Dickens's 1853 denunciation of the idea of the "noble savage" made hysterical use of current ethnological descriptions:

I consider him a prodigious nuisance, and an enormous superstition. . . .
I call a savage a something highly desirable to be civilised off the face of

[80] Vol. 1, p. 101.
[81] *Idea of Poverty*, p. 327.
[82] From this standpoint, Reverend Tuckniss's moralistic introduction to the final volume of *London Labour* was not as disconnected to the text as modern scholars have assumed.

the earth. I think a mere gent (which I take to be the lowest form of civilisation) better than a howling, whistling, clucking, stamping, jumping,
tearing savage . . . cruel, false, thievish, murderous; addicted more or less
to grease, entrails, and beastly customs; a wild animal with the questionable gift of boasting; a conceited, tiresome, bloodthirsty, montonous
humbug.[83]

In ethnological discourse, though such violent language was eschewed,
civilization had indeed been coming to appear ever more antagonistic to
nature, as the Enlightenment myth of the Noble Savage had fallen out
of favor. Early Victorian Englishmen of the middle and upper classes, concerned about population explosion at home and political extremism across the
Channel, striving to transform the work habits of this rapidly growing domestic labor force as well as an even more rapidly growing number of colonial
subjects, were ill disposed to find anything benign, let alone admirable, in
the uncivilized. Ethnology in Britain thus came to stress, against much
eighteenth-century tradition, the critical distinction between savagery and
civilization. The anthropologist George Stocking has described this shift:

> Not yet, or no longer, able to subject themselves to the discipline of labor
> and delayed gratification, indulgent of their instinctive passions, savages
> were at the mercy of the forces of nature. By contrast, civilization,
> whether one viewed it as a natural outgrowth of human capacity or as a
> divinely assisted process, tended to be seen as a triumph over rather than
> an expression of the primal nature of man, just as it was a triumph over
> external nature.[84]

In contrast to the previous century, ethnological images of savagery highlighted the lack of effective controls upon the passions. In line with this expectation, as Stocking points out, "the major sociocultural evolutionists" of
midcentury all "took for granted some early condition of primitive promiscuity." This was a condition they saw among contemporary "primitives" as
well, whatever the state of the evidence. John McLennan's highly influential
Primitive Marriage (1865) not only described many instances among savages of
male sexual violence and female sexual "depravity," but explicitly connected
its picture of primitive mankind with continuing problems of "civilized" savagery. "Savages," McLennan declared, "are unrestrained by any sense of deli-
cacy from a copartnery in sexual enjoyments; and indeed, in the civilized state,
the sin of great cities shows that there are no natural restraints sufficient to
hold men back from grosser copartneries."[85]

---

[83] "The Noble Savage," 337.

[84] George Stocking, *Victorian Anthropology* (New York: The Free Press, 1987), p. 36.

[85] Quoted *ibid*., p. 202. This connection was almost a mid-Victorian convention, though
more often made in the other direction, as when Mayhew and Binny described criminal
women as "living almost the same barbarous life as they would, had they been born in the
interior of Africa." [*Criminal Prisons*, p. 466.]

The linkages could at times come even closer. For example, the young Francis Galton, exploring in Africa in the 1850s, had joined a Hottentot punitive raid upon members of another tribe who had stolen some cattle; he reported that he not only appreciated what such excitement might mean to "savage minds," but he even had a glimpse of "what fearful passions exist in our own minds [once] they are thoroughly aroused."[86] Though usually (with Galton as with others) such insights were suppressed by the reassurance of the fortunate distance between savagery and civilization, they remained a continuing source of unease beneath the surface of Victorian self-satisfaction.

The political imagination

In such ways, contemplation of domestic and foreign savages focused rising concerns about both sexual appetite and aggression. For the early Victorians, aggressiveness took on many of the problematic characteristics of sexuality and for much the same reasons. As sexual tolerance waned, so too did tolerance of collective or personal violence. The French Revolution and the Gordon Riots became powerful symbols in early Victorian cultural life for the consequences of what the Evangelical banker Henry Thornton had called "a general deliverance from restraint."[87] In the 1830s and 1840s, men of the middle and upper classes lived with the specter of the currents of impulse breaking through their collapsing banks and bringing flood where once there had been fruitful irrigation.[88] Often images of the unleashing of sexuality merged with those of aggression – not only with conservatives, but even, and perhaps especially, with those who were counted friends to "progress." For all his scorn of the Establishment, Dickens hated mobs and their violence.[89] In *Barnaby Rudge* (1841), the Gordon rioters "howled like wolves," "thirsted like wild animals"

---

[86] Quoted in *ibid.*, p. 93.

[87] Unpublished recollections, quoted in Standish Meacham, *Henry Thornton of Clapham* (Cambridge, Mass.: Harvard University Press, 1964), p. 65.

[88] This concern wrought a profound alteration in English political thinking and historiography. Frank Turner, examining Victorian images of the classical world, has noted such a sea change in the historiography of Rome: Thomas Arnold's *History of Rome* (1823–42), the most extensive British work on the subject to appear in the first half of the century, sharply downgraded the high standing the republic had held in eighteenth-century eyes, seeing its turmoils as the result of sin. Arnold's work, as Turner pointed out, was "indicative of the immense intellectual distance that lay between the political thought of the eighteenth and the first quarter of the nineteenth centuries. Concern with order had replaced prescriptive admiration for ancient liberty and balanced polity, and that concern would inform virtually all later Victorian interpretations of the Roman Republic." [Frank M. Turner, "British Politics and the Demise of the Roman Republic: 1700–1939," *Historical Journal 29* (1986), 589.]

[89] See Philip Collins, *Dickens and Crime* (Bloomington, Ind.: Indiana University Press, 1968), p. 47.

for blood, their "savage faces" glaring upon their victims.[90] As George Lillie Craik, a utilitarian writer whose account of these riots Dickens read, had observed, "passions more dangerous to society than those which instigated these furious and reckless rioters cannot be named or imagined. They were such as could not be allowed to rage uncontrolled without all society being quickly torn in pieces."[91] Like Craik, Dickens complained not of the harshness or indiscriminateness of the state's response, in which hundreds were killed, but only – and bitterly – of its tardiness and weakness.[92]

Why should a man who became known as a biting, and to some an irresponsible, critic of authority find it so necessary to mobilize his great vituperative resources against every popular upsurge? Bourgeois hypocrisy hardly seems a sufficient explanation. In Dickens, as in many of his contemporaries, social disturbance, besides stirring direct social anxieties, seemed to have crystallized intense personal fears of the release of aggressive passions from within as well as from without. As with Reynolds, these fears found imaginative foci in all social strata. *Barnaby Rudge* has not only the mob, but its leader, the aristocratic Lord George Gordon, in whose incoherent speech is revealed "struggling through his Puritan's demeanour . . . something wild and ungovernable which broke through all restraint."[93] In *Oliver Twist*, three years earlier, Mr. Fang, a police magistrate who drinks to excess, uses his position to bully all who appear before him. A year later, in *Nicholas Nickleby*, violence and the threat of violence (sexual at least as much as any other) pervades middle- and upper-class life. Lecherous, violent, and sadistic figures from the "respectable" classes crowd the book's pages; the flogging schoolmaster, Wackford Squeers, is only the most memorable of them. In the book that immediately followed *Barnaby Rudge*, Dickens (like the Earl of Carlisle) described

---

[90] Chapter 64.

[91] *Sketches of Popular Tumults; Illustrative of the Evils of Social Ignorance* (London: C. Knight & Co., 1837), p. 66.

[92] Mobs continued to simultaneously fascinate and repel Dickens, a man uniquely in touch with the early and mid-Victorian reading public. When he turned at last to deal directly with the French Revolution in *A Tale of Two Cities*, his denunciation of the callous aristocracy softened not at all his repugnance for the consequent popular rising. As John Gross noted, "He doesn't record a single incident in which it might be shown as beneficent, constructive or even tragic. Instead, it is described time and again in terms of pestilence and madness." [*Dickens and the Twentieth Century*, p. 192.] With such a specter of a potential plague of insanity perhaps lying in the back of his mind, Dickens was always prone to be provoked by actual mobs into fierce diatribes in which his everyday scorn of blind and callous government was forgotten. Instructive here are his violent responses to the Indian Mutiny of 1857 and the Jamaican insurrection of 1864.

[93] Ch. 35.

slaveholders in the United States as a veritable nation of Squeerses – men not in any way "accustomed to restrain their passions," men whose "brutal, sanguinary, and violent" habits were those of a "brutal savage."[94] And of course, the French aristocracy is similarly portrayed a few years later, in *A Tale of Two Cities*, most vividly in the image of the murderous carriage heedlessly crushing a child. Savagery – rooted in human nature, not class – could break out at any social level.

The imagery of passion and riot found its way into the more sober and factual writing of the time. In his percipient work on Victorian historians, J. W. Burrow paused at Macaulay's uncharacteristically intense description of the chaos England had narrowly escaped at the conservative overthrow of James II:

> Never, [Macaulay noted] within the memory of man, had there been so near an approach to entire concord among all intelligent Englishmen as at this conjuncture; and never had concord been more needed. All those evil passions which it is the office of government to restrain, and which the best governments restrain but imperfectly, were on a sudden emancipated from control; avarice, licentiousness, revenge, the hatred of sect to sect, the hatred of nation to nation. On such occasions it will ever be found that the human vermin which, neglected by ministers of religion, barbarous in the midst of civilisation, heathen in the midst of Christianity, burrows among all physical and all moral pollution, in the cellars and garrets of great cities, will at once rise into a terrible importance.[95]

Burrow observed that "the [Glorious] Revolution is respectability clamped down on universal riot and licence, a return of chaos and old night." Underneath the celebration of the progress of rational liberty is a drama in which, in Burrow's words, "blind instincts and dangerous classes meet in a frightening subterranean moral equation whose outward symptoms and symbols are the slums of great cities: Macaulay's Whitefriars, Carlyle's Faubourg Saint Antoine, and the murky, teeming landscape of Dickensian courts and alleys. Fears for one's own rational identity and apprehensions of social revolution seem often bound together by the same moral and imaginative geography, and it was one which made the prospect of a world turned upside down, even in retrospect, difficult to contemplate calmly."[96]

---

[94] Charles Dickens, *American Notes for General Circulation* (London: Chapman and Hall, 1842), Ch. 17.

[95] *History of England*, quoted in J. Burrow, *A Liberal Descent: Victorian Historians and the English Past* (Cambridge: Cambridge University Press, 1981), p. 84.

[96] *ibid.*, p. 84.

Domesticating the passions: the discourse of character

"Nearly every respectable attribute of humanity is the result not of instinct, but of victory over instinct."

J. S. Mill, *Nature*[97]

Early Victorian social policy, in one of its guises, was a series of efforts to contain and master popular impulsiveness. The social discourse of the state and of voluntary societies and philanthropic individuals, as well as the discourse of personal relations, came to center around ways to develop character – "moral order implanted within the individual," as Samuel Smiles was later to define it. Character signified not so much certain fixed and externally validated standards of behavior, like aristocratic honor or the plebeian standard of neighborliness, but rather a psychological state in which the passions were habitually mastered by reflection, the pressures of the present controlled by the perspective of the future.

The habitual deferral of imperious present desires for calm future benefit became the central trope of middle–class moral discourse, whether of a utilitarian or an Evangelical nature. Evangelicals stressed deferral until the next life, seeking to teach men to ground all action in a profound awareness of eternity. True Christians, William Wilberforce affirmed, "are walking by faith and not by sight."

> By this description is meant, not merely that they so firmly believe in the doctrine of future rewards and punishments, as to be influenced by that persuasion to adhere in the main to the path of duty, though tempted to forsake it by present interest, and present gratification; but farther, that the great truths revealed in Scripture concerning the unseen world, are the thoughts for the most part uppermost in their minds. This state of mind contributes, if the expression may be allowed, to rectify the illusions of vision, to bring forward into nearer view those eternal things which from their remoteness are apt to be either wholly overlooked, or to appear but faintly in the utmost bounds of the horizon and to remove backward, and reduce to their true comparative dimensions, the objects of the present life, which are apt to fill the human eye, assuming a false magnitude from their vicinity.[98]

The utilitarian counterpart of Evangelical farsightedness was consequentialism, which was not simply a pragmatic standard (as it later became), but a

---

[97] This essay was written in the early 1850s but first published posthumously in *Three Essays on Religion* (1874).

[98] *A Practical View of the Prevailing Religious System of Professed Christians* (Boston: Manning & Loring, 1799), pp. 118–19.

moral ideal. Despite the thrust inherent in its eighteenth-century origins toward the ratification of existing appetites and desires, nineteenth-century utilitarians rarely took that path. Instead, they almost always felt a moral imperative to assist persons to perceive their long-term interests in the welter of immediate preoccupations. As even Bentham himself put the problem:

> The good which constitutes the ground of the prohibitory measure, the reason that operates in favor of it, is comparatively prominent; the evil not equally so; its place is comparatively in the background. Hence it is [that], as in too many other instances, a good, however small, is by its vicinity to the eye enabled to eclipse and conceal the evil, however large.[99]

The rationality utilitarians sought to promote was defined operationally as the process of accurate calculation. Calculation meant gauging consequences or looking to the future. The Benthamite calculator was a man whose attention was habitually focused upon distant consequences. Utilitarianism thus sought to habituate men to consequential thinking, which did not come naturally or easily, that required and promoted impulse control. The principle of utility, James Mill wrote, "marshalls the duties in their proper order, and will not permit mankind to be deluded, as so long they have been, sottishly to prefer the lower to the higher good, and to hug the greater evil, from fear of the less." An individual who automatically focused his mind on the long-run consequences of his acts would come to defer gratification. By this means, as Mill argued, he would gain mastery over his "animal nature" that impelled him, to his ultimate harm, toward immediate, usually sensual gratification.[100] Or, as the economist Nassau Senior put it in 1836, "to abstain from the enjoy-

[99] *Jeremy Bentham's Economic Writings*, ed. W. Stark (London: Published for the Royal Economic Society by Allen & Unwin, 1952–54), Volume III, p. 411.
[100] *Fragment on Mackintosh*, quoted in William Thomas, *The Philosophic Radicals* (Oxford: Clarendon Press, 1979), pp. 103–4. In his three-volume *History of British India*, Thomas observed, "Mill's method characteristically combines puritanism and utility" [p. 105]. But such a method was not as sharp a revision of his master's philosophy as it might seem; James Steintrager has reminded us that Bentham himself juggled description and prescription: "hedonic calculation, on occasion, might be a description of the way men behave but it ought always to be the norm." [*Bentham* (Ithaca, N.Y.: Cornell University Press, 1977), p. 17.] That is to say, men *ought* to calculate their long-term advantage (and be aided and pushed into doing so) whether they were presently disposed to or not. Contrary to his twentieth-century interpreters, Bentham had no faith that men would arrive at this norm on their own: "I would no more," he cautioned, "use the word liberty in my conversation when I could get another that would answer the purpose, than I would brandy in my diet, if any physician did not order me: both cloud the understanding and inflame the passions." [Quoted in Douglas G. Long, *Bentham on Liberty* (Buffalo, N.Y.: University of Toronto Press, 1977), p. 173.]

ment which is in our power, or to seek distant rather than immediate results, are among the most painful [and necessary] exertions of the human will."[101]

Even as it had formed a vehicle for the rising anxieties over license, Malthusianism was increasingly reshaped by these programs to dispel that specter. Malthusian population theory was most widely disseminated in the moralistic and even Evangelical form developed particularly by the Reverend Thomas Chalmers. Chalmers's Christian individualism stressed how God's laws of nature formed a probationary system that required and rewarded self-mastery and self-help, and Malthus himself moved through successive editions in that direction. His fourth (1807) and fifth (1817) editions contained explicit references to "probation," and to "the necessity of practising the virtue of moral restraint in a state allowed to be a state of discipline and trial." The practical application of Malthus's population theory to poor relief by Chalmers in Glasgow brought approval from the master, and by 1831 Malthus could repudiate "the gloomy aspect" given by many to his theory and look forward to a "fundamental change in the habits and manners of the great mass of our people" – that is, the entrenchment of moral restraint in popular character.[102]

The discourse of character had a complex and ambiguous relation to the discourse of humanity, also waxing in the early nineteenth century, a relation that can only be suggested here. Character formation both limited and reinforced humanitarianism. On the one hand, as in child rearing, the demand for severity with oneself could counteract the softer feelings and legitimize the infliction of pain. On the other hand, less obviously but in the long run more decisively, the zeal to rein in the expression of impulses, in particular those not only of sexuality but also of aggression, nurtured an intolerance of open displays of aggression and open infliction of physical pain. Thus, in seeming contradiction to their dour philosophies, devout Evangelicals and committed utilitarians took the lead in many humanitarian movements. Macaulay's scornful remark that the Puritans put down bear-baiting out of hatred more of the pleasure of the baiters than of the pain of the bear had closer application to his father's, and even his own, generation; the two forms of repugnance were not as distinct as he may have assumed.[103] A social ideal of character build-

---

[101] *Political Economy* (1836), quoted in Walter Houghton, *The Victorian Frame of Mind 1830–1870* (New Haven: Yale University Press, 1957), p. 249.

[102] Quoted in Boyd Hilton, *The Age of Atonement: The Influence of Evangelicalism on Social and Economic Thought* (Oxford: Clarendon Press, 1988), pp. 90–1. Peter Mandler has shown such "christian individualism" to have been influential well beyond the ranks of Evangelicals. ["Tories and Paupers: Christian Political Economy and the Making of the New Poor Law," *Historical Journal* (forthcoming).]

[103] The character-building theme was woven through early Victorian humanitarianism. The Bishop of St. David's reminded the annual meeting of the Royal Society for the Prevention of Cruelty to Animals in 1846 that their mission was not simply to help animals

ing declared war upon the direct indulgence of appetites both sensual and aggressive.

Despite a powerful strain of social conservatism running through it, the discourse of character, whether Evangelical or utilitarian, entailed a far-reaching reconstruction of the moral order. It stood poised against not only the rising specter of popular license but also the hierarchical moral order inherited from the Hanoverian world. Character stood against the fecklessness of both rioting plebeians and gambling and dueling aristocrats.[104] Noel Annan's description of Evangelicalism, though not the whole story, identifies a central strand and could be applied equally well to Benthamism:

> [Evangelicalism] challenged at every point the way of life of the upper classes. Aristocracies live by a code. They ask whether a man is brave, generous, well-bred, and fanatically loyal to his kin and kind; and they detest sneaking opportunists, cagey trimmers, toadies and those who reason why. The way to ensure that one's actions are never squalid is to act instinctively by the light of honour – and if that means to act recklessly without thought for the consequences of one's actions, well, that is better than acting with calculation according to the rules of the counting-house. The Evangelicals never tired of putting this code in the pillory. . . . Recklessness led to gambling, gambling to the duel, the duel to murder. They particularly abhorred the sin of pride, 'the passion which strikes the deepest root in the breast of a Nobleman' . . . self-denial, humility, moral as distinct from physical courage, and self-control were the virtues which afforded the best evidence of salvation.[105]

but, more fundamentally, to improve humanity (particularly members of the lower classes): the uneducated individual "is after all but a child in the maturity of his physical powers . . . a savage in the midst of all the refinement of our civilization"; the curbing of animal cruelty was an essential step in the civilizing of the English savage. Quoted in Brian Harrison, *Peaceable Kingdom* (Oxford: Clarendon Press, 1982), p. 116.

[104] At the heart of upper-class gambling, as with other characteristic aristocratic pastimes, was an indulgence of the impulse of the moment. In J. C. D. Clark's sympathetic view, eighteenth-century gambling expressed the "exaltation of recklessness and careless sacrifice echoing the virtues of the battlefield." [*English Society 1688–1832* (Cambridge: Cambridge University Press, 1985), p. 107.] And gambling indeed led frequently to one kind of armed encounter, the duel. Established in the sixteenth century to replace the casual violence of assassination and vendetta, by the eighteenth century it had become a legitimating institution that perpetuated such contained but nonetheless often deadly violence into a supposedly more law-abiding and humane era. "Each duel," Clark observed, "was . . . a gesture of contempt towards the prudent, rational, calculating values which plebeians might be thought necessarily to hold. It seemed to express the atavistic insight that 'without shedding of blood is no remission'." [*ibid.*, p. 109.]

[105] Noel Annan, *Leslie Stephen: The Godless Victorian* (London: Weidenfeld and Nicolson, 1984), pp. 149–50. See also Donna T. Andrew, "The Code of Honour and Its Critics: The Opposition to Dueling in England 1700–1850," *Social History* 5 (1980), 409–34, and V. G. Kiernan, *The Duel in European History: Honour and the Reign of Aristocracy* (Oxford: Clarendon Press, 1988).

Tropes of consequentialism permeated the various discourses of improvement of the period, even the medical. As both lay and professional constructions of health were highlighting fear of the passions, so they also contained signposts for character building. Conceptions of treatment of illness and the maintenance of health left much space for personal responsibility and individual exertion of will. *Man's Power over Himself to Prevent or Control Insanity* was the apt title of an 1843 handbook on the treatment of mental illness.[106] "Hortatory rhetoric – an appeal to conscience as much as to reason," Bruce Haley has pointed out, "is typical of the Victorian literature of health."[107]

Victorian physiologists developed models of human functioning and particularly of mental process that, although increasingly materialist and determinist, left an important, even decisive, role for self-mastery and self-creation. W. B. Carpenter, described as "possibly the most representative orthodox mid-nineteenth century British physiologist,"[108] placed at the summit of his basically materialist model of brain process the will operating as an agency of consciousness rising above and controlling automatic brain function. As John Stuart Mill had argued in a well-known passage in his *Autobiography* (quoted by Carpenter in the preface to his *Mental Physiology*), "though our own character is formed by circumstances, our own desires can do much to shape these circumstances ... our will, by influencing some of our circumstances,

---

[106] Cited in Skultans, "Moral Order," p. 230.

[107] Bruce Haley, *The Healthy Body and Victorian Culture* (Cambridge, Mass: Harvard University Press, 1978), p. 17. Many movements to promote control over one's bodily habits flourished in the nineteenth century, from temperance, vegetarianism, and sexual purity to the "practical science" of phrenology. All were preoccupied with helping individuals aid their future well-being by developing control over their impulses and appetites. [See Brian Harrison, *Drink and the Victorians* (London: Faber, 1971); David de Giustino, *Conquest of Mind: Phrenology and Victorian Social Thought* (London: Croom Helm, 1975); Roger Cooter, *The Cultural Meaning of Popular Science* (Cambridge: Cambridge University Press, 1984); Angus McLaren, *Birth Control in Nineteenth Century England* (London: Croom Helm, 1978). For transatlantic parallels, see Ian Tyrrell, *Sobering Up: From Temperance to Prohibition in Antebellum America, 1800–1860* (Westport, Conn.: Greenwood Press, 1979); Stephen Nissenbaum, *Sex, Diet and Debility in Jacksonian America: Sylvester Graham and Health Reform* (Westport, Conn.: Greenwood Press, 1980).] The fervent concern of health reformers was shared in more moderate form by most physicians. For them as well, health was hardly separable from character, bodily order from moral order. Their medical advice usually stressed health as a personal achievement and its maintenance as a personal responsibility. [See Gerald Grob, *Mental Institutions in America: Social Policy to 1875* (New York: Free Press, 1973), pp. 153–4.] Bruce Haley has summed up the message of this medical literature: "To be truly healthy, a person must always be reaching out morally and intellectually.... All life ... involves work." [*Healthy Body*, p. 257.]

[108] Anita Clair Fellman and Michael Fellman, *Making Sense of Self: Medical Advice Literature in Late Nineteenth Century America* (Philadelphia: University of Pennsylvania Press, 1981), p. 115.

can modify our future habits or capabilities of willing."[109] The exercise of will could, over time, be rendered virtually automatic by being transformed into habit. Even the most thoroughly materialist physiologist, Henry Maudsley, who was to write persuasively of the "tyranny of [physiological] organization," stressed as late as 1883 how habit was the instrument of the will:

> The conscious energy of past functioning becomes the unconscious energy of present functioning, which thereupon is able to work without attention and almost without exertion. Will loses its character, so to speak, in attaining to its unconscious perfection; and meanwhile the free, unattached, path-seeking consciousness, and will ... the pioneers and perfecters of progress, are available to initiate new and to perfect old functions.[110]

The concept of habit as congealed will was to serve as a bridge between the voluntarism of the first half of the century and the increasing determinism of later Victorian naturalism. Despite their internecine struggles, nonprofessional health reformers and physicians agreed in urging their patients and the public to realize that the expression they gave to their will would be implanted by habit in their whole constitution, with long-range consequences for all aspects of their lives. Although everyday behavior was increasingly being described as mechanical, in the sense of following from structural patterns laid down in the body (particularly in the brain), people nonetheless were ascribed indirect responsibility for it because such patterns were developed gradually through experience.[111] The lesson to be drawn was the need to develop right habits, because with time habits became ever more automatic. Maudsley summed up this mode of thought when he declared that each individual had "a solemn responsibility under which he is to determine rationally in himself, by help of circumstances, that which may thereby be determined in his future conduct, and in some measure in his prosperity."[112] Such opportunities

---

[109] *Autobiography* [1872] (New York: Oxford University Press, 1944), p. 119.

[110] *Body and Will* (London: K. Paul, Trench, & Co., 1883), p. 93.

[111] As the case of phrenology demonstrates, even a rather extreme physicalism was quite compatible in practice with a vigorous moralism.

[112] Quoted in Haley, *Healthy Body*, p. 45. This responsibility was further heightened by the growing belief that not only one's own future, but the very nature of one's descendants was at stake. Rather than undermining the character-building project, hereditarian thinking could actually reinforce its "future orientation." The mechanism of inheritance, whose importance was stressed more and more as the century went on, was understood until the turn of the twentieth century chiefly in Lamarckian terms of the inheritability of acquired characteristics. The existing state of human nature was seen as the outcome of all the decisions and actions of all the (reproducing) members of previous generations, the product of a long chain of willed circumstances. Thus, as Charles Rosenberg has argued, "Nineteenth century social hereditarianism provided a framework within which behavior was explicable in terms of will and consequent action. One could change, one could *will* to

depended, however, upon strict self-discipline. "Self-conquest," insisted one typical health reformer, "is the preparatory step."[113]

Even more than physical medicine, psychiatry was directed toward strengthening impulse control. Repeatedly, alienists stressed the positive value of hard work, education, self-discipline, and thrift. As Dr. Thomas Mayo complained in 1829:

> It is one of the most pernicious effects of the study of novels and romances, so widely permitted to our youth, that in such works they generally see success and its rewards attendant on action prompted by passion, without any intermediate stage of self-control.[114]

Most early Victorian alienists recommended a regime of self-discipline to restore the mind's control over a person's animal side. They were unsparing in their criticism of the personal excesses that led to insanity and quick to praise the values of foresight and self-restraint.[115]

Even in the field of public health, built on the acceptance of the necessity of collective measures transcending what any individual could do for himself, personal responsibility for health was far from forgotten. Explanations of disease causation frequently intermixed environmental and behavioral factors. In cataloguing the predisposing causes of epidemic disease, medical writers normally cited a wide spectrum of influences ranging from the purely impersonal to the purely personal. One typical listing in 1831 in *The Lancet* of the factors predisposing to cholera noted "grief, fasting, want of cleanliness, innutricious and irregular diet, the depression which succeeds the excitement from drinking ardent spirits, utero-gestation and parturition: in short, whatever produced diminished energy of the nervous system, and lessened vascular action to the surfaces."[116] From this standpoint, control over one's habits, and thus over one's physical state, became of the first importance.

Consequently, the energy of public health activists was devoted not only to

have happy, healthy, intelligent children – children able to control *their* own will and thus destiny, able to grapple successfully with the ominous and often unmanageable tendencies towards moral entropy and lack of control that seemed to lurk within almost all individuals." ["The Bitter Fruit: Heredity, Disease and Social Thought," in C. Rosenberg, *No Other Gods: On Science and American Social Thought* (Baltimore: Johns Hopkins University Press, 1976), p. 233.]

[113] Quoted in K. Figlio, "Chlorosis and Chronic Disease in Nineteenth Century Britain: The Social Construction of Somatic Illness in a Capitalist Society," *Social History 3* (1978), 188.

[114] Thomas Mayo in a review of G.M. Burrows, *Commentaries on the Causes, Forms, Symptoms and Treatment, Moral and Medical, of Insanity* in *London Review I* (1829), 208.

[115] For example, see Hayward, p. 78.

[116] Dr Henry Dodds, quoted in R.J. Morris, *Cholera 1832: The Social Response to an Epidemic* (New York: Holmes & Meier, 1976), pp. 174–5.

identifying and publicizing external causes of disease, but also to finding ways to reform personal behavior. Along with drainage and ventilation, most activists promoted the extirpation of bad and the inculcation of good habits – of diet, cleanliness, and orderliness. The success even of physical and environmental sanitary reforms depended after all on mass conformity, on a personal level, to new behavioral norms. Public sanitation required not only drains and garbage removal, but the dependable and universal use of such services – a greater regulation than ever before of intimate personal habits of ingestion, excretion, and home management.[117] Moreover, even crusaders for drains like Edwin Chadwick (often accused of an engineering fetish) saw the new system of public health institutions as a great educational instrument for the general improvement of character, aiding in the diminution not only of ill health but of poverty and crime as well.[118]

For early Victorians, then, the need to build popular character permeated virtually every field of understanding of human nature, society, and public policymaking. The problem of crime and punishment was approached in such a context.

[117] See Richard L. Schoenwald, "Training Urban Man," in *The Victorian City: Images and Realities*, ed. H. J. Dyos and Michael Wolff (London: Routledge, 1973), Vol. 2, pp. 669–92; M. J. Cullen, *The Statistical Movement in Early Victorian Britain* (New York: Barnes & Noble, 1975), pp. 62–4, 68–9, 106–7, 135–7.

[118] Chadwick, with his influential schemes for reforming welfare and policing, among other areas, was as interested in the moral fitness as in the physical fitness of the population. While composing his landmark report on public health, Chadwick told Thomas Spencer, a leading antidrink reformer, that he rested his hopes for the recovery and permanent improvement of the laboring classes not on government but on the temperance societies. [B. Harrison, *Drink*, p. 96.]

2

Victorian criminal policy I: reforming the law

"The law is the most powerful of all teachers in showing men their social duties, and in compelling their performance."

Report of the Commissioners of Bankruptcy and Insolvency, 1840

"It is the business of the law to prevent wrongdoing, and not simply to patch up the consequences of it when it has been committed."

J. S. Mill, *Principles of Political Economy*, 1848

"Men ought to command their passions; and if they fail to do so, they ought to suffer for it. The object of the criminal law is to control the passions which prompt men to break it."

J. F. Stephen, "Capital Punishments," 1864

From acts to character: new conceptions of crime, new tasks for criminal policy

During the early decades of the nineteenth century, in the minds of those in Britain who shaped social policy, a particular construction of human nature and its dangers and a corresponding set of approaches to dealing with those concerns moved to center stage.

Underneath the well-known controversies that emerged in the 1830s and raged for the next generation over forms of punishment – the death sentence, public hangings, transportation, and separate versus silent and, later, the Irish versus the English systems of prison regimes – an unspoken consensus was taking shape on the nature and meaning of crime and the purposes of punishment. It was less the actions than the characters of offenders on which attention came to focus. Although want and mistreatment were acknowledged as contributing factors, crime was essentially seen as the expression of a fundamental character defect stemming from a refusal or an inability to deny wayward impulses or to make proper calculations of long-run self-interest. As the religious Prison Discipline Society had already concluded in 1818, what most needed dealing with were not criminal deeds per se, but "the habits and inclinations" of criminals that, if uncorrected, would only generate more future offenses.[1] Despite his deep appreciation of the critical influence of environment on public health, Edwin Chadwick had been at pains in the report of the 1839 Constabulary Commission to refute the claim that much property crime stemmed directly from want: "in the great mass of cases," he wrote, crime "arises from the temptation of obtaining property with a less degree of labour than by regular industry."[2] Mayhew similarly defined criminals as "those who will not work."[3]

Why did they so refuse? No doubt, it was usually admitted, an element of rational, if unattractive, self-interest was involved. Yet at root such behavior was seen as irrational, and the ultimate source of the problem was traced to defective socialization, to the lack of conformation, as Mayhew put it, "to civilised habits."[4] Civilization was coming to be seen in terms of the new character ideal – that of the *self-distancing individual* capable of disciplining his impulses and planning his life – taking shape across the spectrum of social action and policy as a liberal solution to an apparently rising tide of passion and willfulness. The historic movement of emancipation and empowerment of the individual could only continue without disaster, as long as every effort was simultaneously made to reshape both personal life and social institutions to foster the widespread development of such a character that would embed firmly within itself a principle of order.

Thus, despite their sometimes heated differences on methods of treatment of criminal offenders, several groups – reformers, administrators, and judges – participated to a large degree in a common discourse of moralization. In the task of establishing new forms of discipline compatible with the liberalization of society, the law was to play a crucial role. "What education is to an individual," wrote the reforming magistrate, Patrick Colquhoun, as he called in 1795 for a thorough overhaul of the law and its administration, "the laws are to society."[5]

Through this century of rapid change, law was expected more than ever to educate people in new standards of behavior. In a similar fashion, the law was expected to do more than deal with the consequences of people's behavior; it was also to give people guidance before they acted. Even civil law, less directly concerned with social morality than criminal law, came to serve educational and disciplinary purposes, giving new "character-building" meanings to gen-

---

[1] Society for the Improvement of Prison Discipline, *Report of the Committee* (London, 1818), p. 7.

[2] *Report of the Royal Commission on the Constabulary 1839*, 181 [P.P. 1839 v. 19].

[3] Henry Mayhew, *London Labour and the London Poor Vol. 4: Those That Will Not Work* (New York: A. M. Kelley, 1967).

[4] Henry Mayhew, *Criminal Prisons of London* (London: Griffin, Bohn & Co., 1867), p. 386.

[5] *A Treatise on the Police of the Metropolis* [1795] (Philadelphia, 1798), p. 205.

eral terms like "intent of the parties," "negligence," and "the reasonable man."
Criminal law, like civil law, was increasingly expected to uphold and advance
the age's central myth of the responsible individual. Since crime was a central
metaphor of disorder and loss of control, criminal laws occupied what might
be called cultural high ground. As in civil law, the interpretation of criminal
law came to reflect the new reigning assumption that the members of the general public were to be considered more rational and responsible than they had
hitherto been. In part this assumption was believed to be true, but, as in other
areas of social policy, it was believed that treating men and women thus would
have the effect of making them more so in fact. A crucial supposition underlying early Victorian attempts at law reform was that the most desirable way
of making people self-governing was to hold them, sternly and unblinkingly,
responsible for the consequences of their actions. High and expansive legal
standards of personal liability – even strict liability – were thus not alternatives to a standard of personal fault, but part of a moral agenda. These standards were, in part, an expression of a faith in individual will power, but also an
instrument to apply increasing pressure on the individual to develop and
strengthen such powers of self-regulation.

The purpose of criminal laws was to deter through a clear tariff of efficiently
enforced penalties that could be counted on by potential offenders, while also
moralizing by rewarding their exercise of self-discipline and punishing their
surrender to impulse. This program depended upon assuming criminals to be
people subject to varying degrees of temptation, who nonetheless chose to
commit crimes and who could have, and might have, chosen otherwise. The
power of circumstances external to the will had to be played down. Thus the
effort at mass character reform that the law aided insisted upon the existence
of a popular capacity to stand back from impulse and take a longer view of
one's own interest. It was a capacity somtimes undeveloped, sometimes
damaged, but, it was insisted, it was there to be called upon and encouraged.
As Bentham had declared, "Men calculate some with less exactness, indeed
some with more: but all men calculate."[6] A system of clear and predictable
penalties proportioned to the seriousness of the offense would provide that
such calculations of self-interest generally produced socially harmless behavior. Even more important in the long run, such a rationale for criminal policy
promised to provide a lever to foster a farsighted and calculating character by
increasing the material and symbolic incentives to reflect more clearly and to
regulate oneself more thoroughly. As we have seen Bentham's disciple, James
Mill, argue, the principle of utility "marshalls the duties in their proper order,
and will not permit mankind to be deluded, as so long they have been,

[6] *Jeremy Bentham's Economic Writings* (London: Published for the Royal Economic
Society by Allen & Unwin, 1952–54) III, p. 434.

sottishly to prefer the lower to the higher good, and to hug the greater evil, from fear of the less."[7]

Most crime thus signaled not only a generalized social disorder, but one particularly linked to defective self-management. Its remedy would increasingly be seen as involving efforts at reforming and developing the characters of offenders and potential offenders. With most criminals seeming to emerge from a world of imperious impulses and short mental horizons, criminal policy – as other fields of social policy – was enlisted in the effort to advance the civilizing process by fostering personal discipline and foresight. For this end, inherited institutions of criminal justice would not do. Hanoverian justice seemed fatally flawed not only by its inequality, inhumanity, and inefficiency (all of which, there is now much reason to believe, were exaggerated by Victorian reformers),[8] but also by its unsuitability to address the new fears that had crystallized around the images of savagery and social demoralization. Early Victorian reformers and progressive administrators thus worked to replace unsystematic and overly flexible forms of justice that at the time seemed counterproductive in their effects on character with a more defined and impersonal, and thus more predictable, criminal law. This reformed criminal policy was to be carried out by overhauling the institutions of police, trial, and punishment, creating a visible force for social surveillance, a more predictable and systematic hearing process, and a prison system subjecting its inmates to a discipline that would without violence both deter and build character. It was to serve not only the immediate practical aim of crime control, but even more importantly the ultimate goal of public character development by reinforcing a new structure of values. Given prevailing views of human nature and of the role of law, the aims of deterrence and moralization seemed by no means incompatible.

Expanding the reach of the criminal law

Reformers and most authorities agreed that the first imperative for criminal justice was to become more active and to extend its reach over all lawbreakers.

[7] *Fragment on Mackintosh*, quoted in W. Thomas, *The Philosophic Radicals*, (Oxford: Clarendon Press, 1979) pp. 103–4.

[8] See John Beattie, *Crime and the Courts in England 1660–1800* (Princeton, N.J.: Princeton University Press, 1986); John Langbein,"Albion's Fatal Flaws," *Past and Present 98* (Feb., 1983), 96–120; J. Innes and J. Styles, "The Crime Wave: Recent Writing on Crime and Criminal Justice in Eighteenth-Century England," *Journal of British Studies* 25 (1986), 380–435; Clive Emsley, *Crime and Society in England 1750–1900* (London: Longman, 1987); the same applies to pre-Victorian policing and punishment: see for instance B. J. Davey, *Lawless and Immoral: Policing a Country Town 1838–1857* (Leicester: Leicester University Press, 1983); M. DeLacy, *Prison Reform in Lancashire. 1700–1850* (Stanford: Stanford University Press, 1986).

Revisionists are surely right to stress that early Victorian criminal law reform was rarely libertarian; we have become well aware of the fact that the first half of the nineteenth century saw a very large increase in the number of arrests, trials, and convictions. The numbers prosecuted in assizes and quarter sessions rose from 4,605 in 1805 to 31,309 by 1842; thereafter, more and more of the load began to be shifted to magistrates acting summarily.[9] Similarly, restriction of the promiscuous use of the death sentence was accompanied by a marked rise in the total amount of noncapital punishment meted out.

The reach of the law was extended through several means. The best known is the creation of professional police forces, urged and supported by most law reformers. Peel's Act of 1829 established the metropolitan police, providing a model of a force consisting of a larger number of constables, set apart from the population by uniform and discipline and pressed to be more active and less discretionary than their predecessors. Acts of 1835, 1839, and 1856 first encouraged and then required the creation of county and borough police forces on that model.[10] As police forces grew, the summary jurisdiction of magistrates also expanded, capped by a series of acts between 1847 and 1855 making it possible to process a much higher caseload without creating many expensive new courts. Enforced by professional police and harder working magistrates, the law became less discretionary and less tolerant, pulling in more and more lesser offenders – vagrants, drunkards, prostitutes, and disorderly juveniles.[11] Many of these offenses had traditionally been ignored by the authorities. A police commissioner reflected in the more settled situation of 1880 that "The Metropolitan Police in their early days were rather over-

---

[9] Gatrell, "Crime, Authority and the Policeman-State," (forthcoming).

[10] The tendency of recent scholarship to revise downward the contrast between old and new local policing has made the rise of the new police all the more intriguing, and perhaps culturally revealing. In addition to works cited above, see David Philips, " 'A New Engine of Power and Authority': The Institutionalization of Law-Enforcing in England 1780–1830," in V. Gatrell, B. Lenman, and G. Parker, *Crime and the Law: The Social History of Crime in Western Europe Since 1500* (London: Europa, 1980); Carolyn Steedman, *Policing the Victorian Community: The Formation of English Provincial Police Forces, 1856–1880* (Boston: Routledge, 1984); D. J. V. Jones, "The New Police, Crime and the People in England and Wales 1829–1888," *Transactions of the Royal Historical Society 1982* (London, 1983); *Policing and Prosecution in Britain 1750–1850*, eds. Douglas Hay and Francis Snyder (Oxford: Clarendon Press, 1989), pp. 151–68. The fullest account is Stanley Palmer, *Police and Protest in England and Ireland 1780–1850* (Cambridge: Cambridge University Press, 1988).

[11] Behind the growth of public order legislation and enforcement is evident a diminished tolerance for behavior labeled indecent and immoral. Examples are given in M. J. D. Roberts, "Public and Private in Early Nineteenth-Century London: The Vagrant Act of 1822 and Its Enforcement," *Social History 13* (1988), 273–94, and B. J. Davey, *Lawless*. "The increased readiness," Roberts has noted, "of respectable and official opinion [in the 1820s] to re-cast old liberty as new license is unmistakable" [p. 290].

enthusiastic in enforcing the law and dealing with minor offences."[12] This widened activity of the criminal law embraced not only apprehension and trial, but conviction and punishment for offenses that, as the first prison inspectors noted in 1836, "were formerly disregarded, or not considered of so serious a character as to demand imprisonment."[13] The sharpest rise in prison admissions came not for serious felonies, but for petty felonies and misdemeanors. Not only were more people being taken into custody, many more also were being summoned by magistrates for public order and nuisance offenses; the number of summonses issued in London rose faster than the population until the early 1870s.[14] Clearly, during the first half of the century and beyond, governmental intolerance for popular immorality and disorderliness, however minor, was on the rise.

The extended arm of criminal justice had its greatest effect on the "unrespectable" poor and the young – most of all those who were unrespectable, poor, and young. Despite emerging sentimentalization of childhood and the mounting practical interest in child welfare and in the provision of education, during the first half of the century juveniles were treated as being even *more* liable to criminal sanctions than earlier. Apparently the traditional common law doctrine that a child under 14 could not be presumed legally responsible was usually ignored.[15] Ursula Henriques has summed up the situation of juveniles at this time:

> Possibly on the theory that they should be deterred early, they were, in some ways, more harshly treated than adults.... Magistrates who believed in nipping crime in the bud would inflict a short sentence with a whipping to remember at the beginning and end, a practice officially sanctioned by the Larceny Act of 1847.[16]

Concerned about the loosening of traditional controls of family, community, parish, and apprenticeship, adult social observers and administrators saw young people (even those under age 14) as having become more independent – and thus more dangerous and more in need of the discipline of law – than ever before.[17] As late as 1852 a metropolitan police magistrate could

---

[12] Quoted in J. J. Tobias, *Crime and Industrial Society in the Nineteenth Century* (London: Batsford, 1967), p. 66.

[13] Quoted in Susan Magarey, "The Invention of Juvenile Delinquency in Early Nineteenth Century England," *Labour History 34* (Canberra) (1978), 13.

[14] Metropolitan police commissioner's report, cited by David Jones, *Crime, Protest, Community and Police in Nineteenth Century Britain* (London: Routledge, 1982), p. 118.

[15] See S. Magarey, "Invention," 14.

[16] Ursula R. Q. Henriques, *Before the Welfare State: Social Administration in Early Industrial Britain* (London: Longman, 1979), p. 185.

[17] For example, M. J. D. Roberts has found magistrates in the 1820s formally declaring the highly dubious proposition that public sexual harassment of women and girls was a modern and specifically urban trend. "Public and Private," 291, n. 80.

remark that "the characters of children brought up in town are so precociously developed that I should find it difficult to mention any age at which they should not be treated as criminals."[18] The worldly philanthropist Richard Monckton Milnes, whose suggestion that no child under 9 years of age should be regarded as accountable was swiftly rejected by his fellow members of an 1850 Parliamentary Select Committee, recalled late in his life that the usual term for juvenile offenders at midcentury was "infant felons."[19]

These developments in the administration of criminal law sharply increased the number of convicted criminals. As a recent student of nineteenth-century juvenile criminal policy has concluded, "at least half of the increasing number of juvenile prisoners, which so alarmed the property-owning classes, were in prison as a result of the creation of new criminal offences, an extension of the powers of justices of the peace, and a widespread readiness to treat children as young as nine or ten as fully responsible adults."[20] Less dramatically, the same trend held for other categories of minor offender, a higher proportion of whom were female than was true of serious felons.[21] As the century unfolded, then, criminal law reached further into British society. Many more persons – Artful Dodgers and Nancys now, as well as Sikeses – were being apprehended by police; of those charged, a higher proportion were being tried; and of these, a higher proportion were being convicted and sentenced to some form of punishment, increasingly imprisonment. Every year criminal law played a larger role in the regulation of social life.

Building character through the law

It has often been assumed that although the reach of the law may have been expanding in the early Victorian years, its content was becoming more morally neutral and thus more libertarian. In particular, utilitarianism, with its conception of law as an instrument for satisfying human needs, has been seen as underlining the distinction between law and morality. Certainly, it was often so stated. Macaulay observed in drawing up the Indian Penal Code that the criminal law was not a body of ethics, but must content itself with keeping men from doing positive harm, leaving to public opinion and to teachers of morality and religion the office of furnishing men with motives for doing posi-

---

[18] Quoted in Magarey, 19.

[19] Harcourt MS 94/173 (Letter to Harcourt, October 6, 1880), Bodleian Library, Oxford; *Report of the Select Committee on Prison Discipline 1850*, 13–19. [P.P. 1850 XVII.]

[20] Magarey, 16.

[21] See Gatrell, "Decline of Theft and Violence" in *Crime and Law*, eds., Gatrell, Lenman and Parker, and Gatrell, "Rise of the Policeman-State," (forthcoming).

tive good.[22] Such professional modesty, limiting the sphere of law, was often declared by nineteenth-century judges, jurists, and legislators. Yet, such professions were not a good guide to practice. In early Victorian England, law reform had Evangelical as well as utilitarian dimensions, while, as we have seen, utilitarians themselves usually held an implicit moral agenda rather distinct from the more permissive modern-day utilitarian philosophies. Indeed, despite the frequent anticlerical insistence on the distinction between law and morality, the law was nonetheless used to advance a program of broad moral reform. The increasingly middle-class composition of the judicial bench nurtured not only an inclination to look favorably upon the development of capitalism, as revisionist historians have argued, but also an inclination to see the fostering of middle-class character in the general population as an important purpose of the law.[23]

In his pioneering essay on Victorian judges, C. S. Fifoot perceptively remarked that their utilitarian frame of mind by no means precluded an "itch to moralise," indeed, he pointed to their susceptibility to what he derogatorily labeled a "moral contagion."[24] But it would be misleading to see concern with the moral function of law simply as an illogical weakness. The desire to improve public character was more than a capricious or irrational itch or fever; it structured much of the discourse of those making and administering the law in the nineteenth century.

The character-building task of law, usually left implicit, was brought into the open in regard to the criminal law by one of the rare nineteenth-century judicial intellectuals, James Fitzjames Stephen, who blended utilitarian and Evangelical influences in his thinking in a way characteristic of many. The criminal law, Stephen frequently insisted, was more than a pragmatic mechanism for dispensing justice and protecting the public from manmade harm; it was essentially an "organ of the moral sense of the community," giving expression to, and advancing, public morality.[25] Stephen, like most barristers rather scornful of sentimentalists, was careful to distinguish law from morality. Yet he also stressed that in practice criminal law could hardly

---

[22] John Clive, *Macaulay: The Shaping of the Historian* (New York: Knopf, 1973), p. 447.

[23] On the changing composition of the bench, see Daniel Duman, *The Judicial Bench in England 1727–1875: The Re-shaping of a Profession* (London, Royal Historical Society, 1982).

[24] C. S. Fifoot, *Judge and Jurist in the Reign of Victoria* (London: Stevens, 1959), pp. 55, 128.

[25] Leslie Stephen, *Life of James Fitzjames Stephen* (New York: G.P. Putnam's Sons, 1895), p. 333. On Stephen, see Leon Radzinowicz, *Sir James Fitzjames Stephen 1829–1894 and His Contribution to the Development of Criminal Law* (London: Quaritch, 1957); James Colaicaco, *James Fitzjames Stephen and the Crisis of Victorian Thought* (London: Macmillan, 1983); K. J. Smith, *James Fitzjames Stephen: Portrait of a Victorian Rationalist* (Cambridge: Cambridge University Press, 1989).

be dissociated from morality.[26] No social institution, Stephen argued in his characteristically brutal fashion, "can have a greater moral significance or be more closely connected with broad principles of morality and politics than those by which men rightfully, deliberately and in cold blood, kill, enslave or otherwise torment their fellow creatures."[27]

Stephen agreed with reformers that simple Beccarian deterrence based on acts was not enough. Conviction and punishment, he believed, should be based on a dual assessment of the consequences of the criminal action and the perpetrator's moral state. In this, Stephen stated clearly the rarely articulated operating principles of most judges. He particularly would search for evidence in an offender of three qualities he labeled especially "odious": "Malignity, lust and recklessness." "Combine any one of these tempers of mind," he declared, "with an act highly injurious to others, and the worst form of crime is the result."[28] Thus, he concluded, these qualities ought to be specially punished in offenders and discouraged in others.

Not only did lawyers and judges, like Stephen, frequently scratch their moral itch, in general through his century of rapid change the law was increasingly seen by both sentimentalists and realists as, in the words of one temperance reformer, "the most powerful national schoolmaster."[29] Despite a certain worldly detachment on the part of judges and barristers from the rhetoric of professional moralists, it was assumed that the law should not only uphold accepted moral standards but also educate the public in the new, higher, standards. Similarly, both civil and criminal law were expected not only to deal with the consequences of people's behavior, but also to give people guidance on behavior before they acted.

The ideal of the responsible individual came to stand ever more at the center of the law. Its administration was overhauled to better embody the assumption that the members of the general public were to be considered more rational and responsible than they had been hitherto. This principle of individual moral responsibility, however, was as much instrumental as declarative, as much interventionist as laissez-faire. For people were not necessarily believed to be responsible in fact; more important, it was accepted that treating men (and even women) thus was the best way of making them more so. A crucial supposition underlying early Victorian law reform was that

---

[26] *A General View of the Criminal Law of England* (London: Macmillan, 1863), p. 75; *History of the Criminal Law of England Vol. 2* (London: Macmillan, 1883), pp. 78–81.

[27] Quoted in Leslie Stephen, *Life of Sir James Fitzjames Stephen*, p. 204.

[28] "The Punishment of Convicts," *Cornhill Magazine VII* (Jan.–June, 1863), 195.

[29] William Shaen, *Suggestions on the Limits of Legitimate Legislation on the Subject of Prostitution* (1877), quoted in Brian Harrison, *Peaceable Kingdom: Stability and Change in Modern Britain* (Oxford: Clarendon Press, 1982), p. 400.

the most urgent need was to make people self-governing and that the best way to do so was to hold them, sternly and unblinkingly, responsible for the consequences of their actions. In this way, the more precise definitions and higher legal standards of personal liability declared a faith in the existence of individual free will and made use of a promising instrument for developing such capabilities of will.

This agenda of character building, shared by utilitarian activists and religiously motivated reformers, has not been sufficiently appreciated. Reformers were doing more than bringing the law into closer accord with human nature and social realities; they hoped to use the law to *change* that nature and those realities. As we have seen, Bentham's disciple, James Mill, described the principle of utility in normative rather than descriptive terms when he noted that it "marshalls the duties in their proper order." Utilitarian reform, Mill argued, would encourage and, if necessary, compel men to focus their minds on the long-run consequences of their acts and in the process come to defer gratification. Consequentialism would build character.[30]

As Patrick Atiyah has perceived, the utilitarianism of the founding generations focused on social education, not pragmatic administration. It was, in modern philosophic language, "almost certainly of the 'rule-utilitarian' variety. They believed in principles of behavior which, taken over all, would produce the greatest happiness; but they did not believe that each individual act should be weighed in the balance (at least by the common herd) to decide whether it would promote the greatest happiness or not."[31] John Austin, the great exponent of legal positivism, had nonetheless stressed the absoluteness of moral principles. Even if, he insisted, in the tenth or hundredth case, violation of the rule would do more harm than good, it must not be violated. For this would weaken the force of the general rule:

> In the hurry and tumult of action it is hard to distinguish justly; to grasp at present enjoyment, and to turn from present uneasiness, is the habitual inclination of us all, and thus, through the weakness of our judgments and the more dangerous infirmity of our wills, we should frequently stretch the exception to cases embraced by the rule.[32]

[30] *Fragment on Mackintosh*, quoted in Thomas, *The Philosophic Radicals*, pp. 103–4. His son's continuation of this moral agenda is evident in Bernard Semmel, *John Stuart Mill and the Pursuit of Virtue* (New Haven: Yale University Press, 1984). The role utilitarian consequentialism has played in modern philosophic argumentation as the antagonist of the explicitly moral positions of intuitionism and retributionism has obscured its own original moralizing ambitions.

[31] P. S. Atiyah, *The Rise and Fall of Freedom of Contract* (Oxford: Clarendon Press, 1979), pp. 354–6.

[32] Austin, *The Province of Jurisprudence Determined* (1861), quoted in Atiyah, p. 356. Recent closer scrutiny has revealed the early Austin to have invested law with very clear

To teach people how to behave required general rules. As Atiyah has explained:

> If the only object of a rule is to enable a Judge to decide *after the event* whether the right act was done or not, rules would be largely unnecessary and could be replaced by giving a discretion to the Judge to decide what he thinks fair in all the circumstances. [But in the nineteenth century] the function of law was not seen as merely that of deciding, after some event, whether a person had acted wisely or morally. The function of law, as the function of morality, and of social or commercial principles, was to give people guidance on their behaviour in advance of the necessity for action.[33]

In this way, much legal reform during the first three-quarters of the nineteenth century aimed to encourage and enforce the growth of a more self-restrained character type in the general public, one that deferred immediate gratification and looked toward the distant consequences of actions. This implicit moral agenda was quite compatible with the emerging professional distinction of law from morality and with the growing judicial reluctance to reach decisions solely on the morality of a particular action.

If public character was to be developed, however, more would have to be done to the law than simply expand its reach; its character would have to alter. Thus, most change in law and in its administration involved qualitative as well as quantitative changes. This was true even of the growth of police. Professional police forces were envisioned by few as simply, or even chiefly, apprehenders of criminals. More important, they were to be deterrents to the commission of crime and to disorderly and immoral behavior in general. In the short run, people were not to be deprived beforehand of the widest freedom of action, but rather to be clearly presented with both the penalties and the certainty of their application if they used freedom harmfully; the police were there to discourage antisocial choices and to provide an external restraint on impulse and self-will. In the longer run, however, they had a positive role to play as well. By their constant presence, the police would encourage people to form moral habits and to reshape their characters to become more self-disciplined and aware of consequences of their actions before taking them. As the Benthamite magistrate Patrick Colquhoun had put it at the turn of the

---

moral functions. "The triumphant Austinianism of the last 100 years," John V. Orth has noted , "is not necessarily to be identified with the Austin of the . . . 1830s." "Casting the Priests Out of the Temple: John Austin and the Relation Between Law and Religion," in *The Weightier Matters of the Law: Essays on Law and Religion*, ed. John Witte, Jr., and Frank S. Alexander (Atlanta, Ga.: Scholar's Press, 1988), p. 236; see also W. Morrison, *John Austin* (Stanford, Calif.: Stanford University Press, 1982).

[33] Atiyah, p. 357.

century, the police should do more than seek out wrongdoers; they should be always present as a deterrent to crime, and, even further, they should supervise popular recreation and other such activities "to give the minds of the People a right bias."[34]

Law reform aimed at qualitative as well as quantitative change even more than police reform did. Indeed, the deepest discontent with the law during the first half of the century centered not on its limited scope but on its apparently disorderly nature; with the erosion of older forms of authority, the inner logic of eighteenth-century justice had become unintelligible. Eighteenth-century Britain, as a number of historians have recently reminded us, was in many ways still an "old regime" in its "face-to-face" social relations and personalistic modes of governing. J. C. D. Clark has stressed in particular the persistent power of hierarchy and an aristocratic code of honor,[35] and William Rubinstein has highlighted the significance of the abolition during the first half of the nineteenth century of "Old Corruption." Rubinstein has argued that the existence as the century opened of a vast number of lucrative offices without practical duties, offices obtained through personal relations, was "indicative of a pre-modern, non-Weberian conceptual mode, which lacked at least an element of the modern notion of merit, individual responsibility, and organizational rationale." Indeed he claimed that such a system – like more visible "non-rational survivals" like the unreformed House of Commons itself – was "antithetical to whatever we mean by Victorian consciousness, which identified individual reward strictly with individual merit and voluntary agreement – from status to contract – according to rational and 'modern' criteria of merit."[36]

Compared to the system in place by the late Victorian period, "Old Regime" criminal justice was particularistic, discretionary, and personalistic.[37] Criminal law was not then intended to apply uniformly to classes of crime and criminals. "Eighteenth-century parliaments," Clive Emsley has

[34] Quoted in Philips, " 'A New Engine,' " 177.

[35] *English Society 1688–1832* (Cambridge: Cambridge University Press, 1985). His argument, untenable in its full terms, is helpful in correcting the excesses of an historiography that since the 1950s has stressed the modernity of the eighteenth century. For related, if more judicious, modifications of that historiography, see John Cannon, *Aristocratic Century: The Peerage of Eighteenth Century England* (Cambridge: Cambridge University Press, 1984) and Lawrence and Jeanne Stone, *An Open Elite? England 1540–1880* (New York: Oxford University Press, 1984). Clark is well criticized in Joanna Innes, "Jonathan Clark, Social History and England's 'Ancien Regime,' " *Past and Present 155* (May, 1987), pp. 165–200.

[36] W. D. Rubinstein, "The End of 'Old Corruption' in Britain 1780–1860," *Past and Present 101* (Nov., 1983), pp. 68, 70.

[37] Such contrasts do not deny the many lines of continuity in criminal justice practices between the two centuries, lines that will be noted below.

stressed, "did not legislate for species of crime.... Legislators never attempted to codify capital legislation, indeed they did not think in terms of general codification or going back to first principles."[38] This lack of concern with a system left wide scope for discretion. Thomas Green has pointed to the lack of formal rules of evidence, a lack obscured by the mystique (not necessarily a false one) of judicial solicitude for the accused. Such solicitude operated in a highly particularistic manner, relatively unconstrained by general rules, "manipulat[ing] the framework of protections surrounding the defendant ... in accordance with the defendant's offense, bearing, and background." English criminal justice before the nineteenth century, Green concluded, "was not mainly a matter of the application of abstract rules. The threshold of proof required for capital punishment was flexible."[39]

The well-known nominal severity of Hanoverian criminal statutes was merely a point of departure. All the major published studies of the administration of criminal law have stressed the wide gap between the rigid letter and the highly flexible practice of the law. "At every stage of the trial and in the administration of punishment," John Beattie has concluded, "the system was shot through with discretionary powers."[40] Although many hundreds of men and women each year faced a possible death sentence, comparatively few were actually hanged. "It is clear," states Beattie, "that few men thought that all these laws needed to be rigidly enforced to serve their purpose.... The instruments of mitigation were at hand in the jury and in the royal prerogative of pardon [largely in the effective hands of the judges], and together they made it possible for the law to be applied with rigor or leniency as conditions seemed to require."[41] Both jurors and judges possessed wide discretionary powers in regard to whether, and to what degree, the provisions of the law would be applied, and they generally concurred in tailoring the law to each specific situation and offender. Indeed, the development of the sanction of

---

[38] Emsley, *Crime and Society*, p. 204.

[39] Thomas Andrew Green, *Verdict According to Conscience: Perspectives on the English Criminal Trial Jury, 1200–1800* (Chicago: University of Chicago Press, 1985), pp. 286–7.

[40] J. M. Beattie, *Crime and the Courts in England, 1660–1800* (Princeton: Princeton University Press, 1986) p. 406.

[41] *Ibid.*, p. 420. Douglas Hay's path-breaking stress on the discretionary power of the judiciary ["Property, Authority and the Criminal Law," in Douglas Hay, Peter Linebaugh, John G. Rule, E. P. Thompson, and Cal Winslow, *Albion's Fatal Tree: Crime and Society in Eighteenth-Century England* (New York: Pantheon Books, 1975)] has been more recently balanced by scholars highlighting the discretionary powers of the jury: see Peter King, "Decision-Makers and Decision-Making in the English Criminal Law, 1750–1800," *Historical Journal* 27 (1984), 25–58, esp. 52; and Green, *Verdict*, esp. Ch. 7. Both Hay and his critics, however, agree on the highly flexible nature of virtually all facets of the era's criminal justice, and indeed the controversies set off by Hay's work have underlined that very characteristic.

transportation early in the century expanded both sorts of discretionary powers, stimulating the flowering of the partial verdict, a largely jury-administered scheme of mitigation,[42] and further encouraging the use of royal pardons, largely determined by judges. Thus, juries were allowed very wide scope in deciding who was to be given a death sentence, and judges gained an almost free hand to choose who of those convicted of capital offenses would actually be hanged and who sent to the American colonies and later to Australia.[43]

Such flexibility and variability were closely related to the law's "personalism." Eighteenth-century Englishmen, Douglas Hay has argued, "tended to think of justice in personal terms" and saw authority "embodied in direct personal relations."[44] As Peter King has more sympathetically put the same point, eighteenth-century justice was "a private and negotiable process involving personal confrontation rather than bureaucratic procedure."[45] The legal system placed great reliance on personal initiative and knowledge of the protagonists, presupposing a "face-to-face" society of persons acquainted with each other, or at least bearing reputations.[46]

The personal relationships of those brought before the courts often overshadowed formal principles of law. "Who the prisoner was – his character and reputation – was as critical a question as what he had done (and even in some cases whether he had done it), and it was centrally the business of the trial to find the answer."[47] The criminal court thus served in many ways as a theater for acting out social dramas, in which the disturbance that had disrupted order was assessed and either resolved or removed, and order reaffirmed. As befits theater, it was an expressive process in which personal confrontation and interaction were central. The most distinctive aspects of trial, as they had been in the sixteenth century, were still, as Green has noted,

> the defendant's self-representation in full sight of the jury and the presentation of witness testimony largely ungoverned by rules of admissibility.

[42] See Green, *Verdict*, p. 280.

[43] See Beattie, p. 432, pp. 506–9.

[44] Hay, p. 39.

[45] King, p. 25.

[46] This was not new; Anthony Fletcher and John Stevenson have described English criminal justice for several centuries at least before the nineteenth century as "a system whose logic was based on close social relationships," giving wide scope to personal considerations and the discretion of judges, juries and victims. "Introduction," *Order and Disorder in Early Modern England*, eds. Anthony Fletcher and John Stevenson (Cambridge: Cambridge University Press, 1985), p.17. See also Cynthia Herrup, *The Common Peace: Participation and the Criminal Law in Seventeenth-Century England* (Cambridge: Cambridge University Press, 1987).

[47] Beattie, p. 436. "Men were not all equal before the law," Beattie observed, "nor was that sought as an ideal" [p. 440].

The most dramatic moments of trial were those of relatively unmediated confrontation between the accuser, who still bore the expense and responsibility of setting forth the case for the prosecution, and the accused, who, until late in the century only occasionally had the advantage of counsel.[48]

It had in fact many characteristics of an intimate family or communal drama, with injured directly confronting injurer, the jury functioning as relations or neighbors, and the judge as father or lord, both treating the counsel-less accused with a paternal blend of solicitude and sternness.[49]

Such intimate dramas, however, became increasingly inappropriate to the "society of strangers" emerging in the new century.[50] With its foundation in a stable localized and personalized structure of social relationships eroding, criminal justice was coming to appear both arbitrary and ineffectual. The criminal laws, the reformer Samuel Romilly typically complained, were the "fruits of no regular design but of sudden and angry fits of capricious legislators."[51] Unclear and inconsistent laws, only occasionally enforced, with penalties alternately overlenient and bloody, could hardly build a new internalized moral order. "How long," the youthful Macaulay wrote to his father, "may a penal code at once too sanguinary and too lenient, half written in blood like Draco's, and half undefined and loose as the common law of a

---

[48] Green, p. 270.

[49] The stress placed here on change should not be taken as denying the continuation of these traditional characteristics of law into, and, in some respects, through the Victorian period. Two valuable studies which highlight the discretionary and non-uniform aspects of Victorian justice are Carolyn Conley, "Crime and Community in Victorian Kent," unpublished Ph.D dissertation Duke University, 1984, and G. R. Chadwick, "Bureaucratic Mercy: The Home Office and the Treatment of Capital Cases in Victorian England," unpublished Ph.D. dissertation, Rice University, 1989. Also, the persistence of private prosecution has recently been highlighted by Douglas Hay and Francis Snyder [*Policing and Prosecution in Britain 1750–1850*, "Introduction"].

[50] Significantly, it had been in the rapidly growing metropolis of London, so unlike the rest of the kingdom, that eighteenth-century justice had been found most wanting. As John Beattie has noted, "a system that suited a society in which men were known – or were at least known to be strangers – and in which their dispositions and characters could easily be enquired into was less satisfactory, however, for those who had to deal with crime and disorder in the metropolis of London." [p. 624]. Toward the end of the century, other rapidly growing areas were the sites of similar growing discontent with the administration of criminal justice: see DeLacy, Chs. 2, 3 and John Bohstedt, *Riots and Community Politics in England and Wales 1790–1818* (Cambridge, Mass.: Harvard University Press, 1983), pp. 72–5, 87, 94–6.

[51] Quoted in John A. Hostettler, "The Movement for Reform of the Criminal Law in England in the Nineteenth Century," unpublished Ph.D. thesis, University of London 1983, p. 12.

tribe of savages, be the curse and disgrace of the country?"[52] Reformers consequently trained their guns on this uncertainty and willfulness in the law. The vast scope for discretion built into the eighteenth-century system had created, Romilly charged in 1810, a "lottery of justice," and introduced, Wilberforce put it the following year, "a sort of gambling into vice," teaching men just the wrong lessons – to take a chance, yield to impulse, and not think about consequences.[53] Persons convicted of the same offense were punished in widely varying ways, and widely differing offenses had the same penalties attached to them. When a sentence was pronounced it was far from clear that it would be carried out. When a person was finally executed, it was often not on account of the specific offense for which he was convicted, but because of personal reputation or government policy. What clear lesson, what raw material for personal calculation and planning, did all this offer the public?

Both deterrence and popular character building required that the sanctions of the criminal law should be clear, consistent, and certain. The task of the law was more and more seen as that of laying down clear and reliable rules of behavior in all areas of social life that individuals increasingly cut loose from the moorings of tradition, hierarchy, and community could then confidently rely upon in planning their actions.[54] Rationalization would thus promote both social order and social reform. Indeed, across the spectrum of legal activity, in civil as in criminal areas, a rationalizing trend was underway. During the late eighteenth century, the reporting of decisions became more regular, thorough, and reliable. By 1800, as A. H. Manchester has noted, there was among lawyers and observers "a general belief that the public interest required that the principles according to which the law was administered should be made known."[55] Moreover, during the first half of the nineteenth century, lawyers were increasingly exposed to (and themselves beginning to write) a new kind of legal treatise that stressed general principles rather than the listing of precedents that had been customary.[56] The enthusiastic acceptance of Pothier's Law of Obligations when it appeared in English translation

---

[52] November 9, 1818, quoted in Clive, *Macaulay*, p. 436.

[53] *1 Parliamentary Debates 19* (Appendix), c. 12 (February 9, 1810); *19*; c. 744 (April 8, 1811). On the reformist assault upon discretion, see Randall McGowen, "The Image of Justice and Reform of the Criminal Law in Early Nineteenth Century England," *Buffalo Law Review 32* (1983), 89–125.

[54] For an interesting interpretation of Bentham as providing a system of rules as a more useful guide to behavior in the new "society of strangers," see D. J. Manning, *The Mind of Jeremy Bentham* (London: Longman, 1968), pp. 4–6.

[55] A. H. Manchester, *A Modern Legal History of England and Wales 1750–1950* (London: Butterworth, 1980), p. 24.

[56] Manchester, p. 268.

in 1806, a moment when national chauvinism might have been expected to run high, seems a sign of a new spirit, searching for "objectivity" and uniformity in the law.[57]

The growing legal insistence on inflexibly enforcing private agreements and promises cannot be fully explained as either the progress of civilization or the satisfying of the demands of business interests. In fact, in particular cases this insistence could be inhumane, socially inconvenient, or burdensome to businessmen.[58] It had another function – a moral and educational one – that could and did override the claims of immediate practicality. As Atiyah noted, "the rule that a person ought to keep his promises, observe his contracts, be faithful to his engagements, was a most important rule of behavior in nineteenth-century life. It is obvious that the message would have been greatly weakened if it had been qualified as the reality might have required."[59]

This same need to deliver a clear message, which Atiyah has examined in contract law of the period, is even more evident in criminal law. Reformers attacked the arbitrariness of the law at least as much as they denounced its cruelty. Legal reform was pressed to reconstruct the criminal law on a consistent and reliable basis. As he had early learned to be disgusted by the apparent inconsistency of English law, Macaulay applied himself with determination to the task of rationalization. He set forth in 1833 the principle that was to guide his development of a law code for India: "Uniformity where you can have it, diversity where you must have it; but in all cases certainty."[60] That such legal certainty would assist the progress of society was a lesson that was drawn even from Scripture. A year before Macaulay's statement, Harriet Martineau portrayed human government following "an analogy with the divine": "The divine government ordained arbitrary punishments in the infancy of the peculiar people, and afterwards withdrew its ordinances when they became capable of recognizing and anticipating natural consequences."[61] Arbitrary law was appropriate, she argued, like Macaulay, only to savages and children. Indeed, also like Macaulay's, Martineau's strong feelings against arbitrariness suggested a stronger objection than inappropriateness: that the uncertainty of the law sustained social savagery and obstructed social maturation.

As such objections were raised to the irrationality of the Old Regime, commissioners were appointed in 1833 with the brief of making recommenda-

---

[57] Atiyah, p. 351.

[58] As John Adams and Roger Brownsword point out in their lucid introduction, *Understanding Contract Law* (London: Fontana, 1987), "what had emerged [from the early nineteenth-century crystallization of contract law] was surprisingly out of touch with the world of commerce whose tool it might have been supposed to be" [p. 37].

[59] *Rise and Fall*, p. 431.

[60] Quoted in Clive, p. 427.

[61] *Monthly Repository VI* (1832), 579.

tions for digesting and clarifying criminal law.[62] The commissioners spent fifteen years producing thirteen reports and many bills. They sought clearer definition of offenses, not primarily for the convenience of the legal profession, the government, or the public, but to make the law a more effective influence upon popular behavior. The commissioners stated in their first report that the looseness in the existing definitions of offenses had produced "great uncertainty in the application of punishment, whereby the motive to abstain from the commission of offences is weakened."[63] In discussing capital punishments, they noted that it was "of the very essence of a law that its penalties should be definite and known; how else are they to operate on the fears of offenders, or to afford a practical guide of conduct?"[64]

Along with making legal prohibitions and penalties clearer and more certain, the commissioners urged that they should correspond as closely as possible to moral distinctions to maximize their contribution to public character formation. Criminal law, they argued, "ought to recognize and impress [moral distinctions] because nothing can be more certain, as nothing is more natural, than that neglect of moral distinctions should cause the laws to be disregarded." The gravity of crimes and the severity of punishments were to be brought into better relation; they complained that "crimes bearing little moral resemblance to each other, are, by sweeping definitions, frequently classed together without discrimination as to penal consequences."[65] They aimed at reconstructing legal prohibitions to correspond as closely as possible to moral distinctions, so that they could work to improve rather than deteriorate public character. Citing examples where due moral distinctions were ignored by the law, they argued that it was "impolitic and dangerous that offences of so widely different a character should be treated as legally identical.... Great risk is incurred lest wrongdoers should regard such offences to be as undistinguishable in point of morals as they are in law."[66]

As part of their hope to make law a more effective instrument of moral education, the commissioners continually stressed the indispensability of a subjective test of criminal liability. In their second report they asserted that no degree of likelihood of an injurious consequence whatsoever could serve as a test

---

[62] George Fletcher has described the commission as a response to "the newly felt chaos of the common law rules." "The Metamorphosis of Larceny ," *Harvard Law Review 89*, no. 3 (Jan., 1976), 504.

[63] *First Report of His Majesty's Commissioners on Criminal Law*, p. 152 [P.P. 1834, v. 26] . For an analysis of the philosophy of the commissioners, see Radzinowicz and Hood, pp. 723–31; the most thorough, if not particularly penetrating, account of their work is Hostettler's.

[64] *Second Report of His Majesty's Commissioners on Criminal Law*, p. 24 [P.P. 1836, v. 36].

[65] *Second Report*, p. 205.

[66] *Seventh Report*, p. 102 [P.P. 1843, v. 19].

of criminal responsibility. Criminality required not only that an act should cause peril to life or property, but that the offender should also be aware of the peril. Though the commissioners were utilitarian, they were not modern consequentialists; their attention was focused just as much on consciousness as on consequences. Much of what in their discussions appears to a modern sensibility to be consequentialism can perhaps better be seen as a more extended notion of intent than was later to prevail. For example, they rejected the notion of degrees of culpability in regard to willful injuries leading to death, whatever the motive of the injurer; where death resulted from acts done with full knowledge that they exposed the lives of others to danger, there could be no distinction regarding various shades or degrees of risk. The offender's knowing exposure of life to danger satisfied the test of implied malice, whether or not he actually intended death or even serious harm. As one scholar has put it, "[T]he offender's motive or ultimate object was immaterial. The willful doing of that which was likely to produce evil and suffering itself constituted the mens rea."[67] This broad construction of intent was not necessarily a privileging of consequences over intent as much as a heightened disapprobation of recklessness and a minimizing of the distinction between recklessness and specific evil intent. Recklessness in knowingly incurring risk of harm to others was for them generally included, along with conscious intent, in "willfulness," although to a modern legal mind this seems a stretching of language and blurring of critical distinctions.[68] In other words, they read into intent a good deal more than a later legal mind would tend to.

The commissioners did not want to do away with capital punishments, but rather to restore their effectiveness by making them predictable; to salvage punishment by breaking its associations with accident and personality. They looked for ways for the law to encourage rather than discourage popular inclinations and abilities to calculate and plan. They thus worked out a system of carefully defined gradations of seriousness of offense, an effort that proved extremely difficult in practice, indeed, that could seem ludicrously pedantic and was to be adopted only in small part. Nonetheless, although they failed to attain their largest aim of codifying the criminal law, the commissioners did move it a long way in the direction of certainty. Legislation in following years tended to restrict judicial discretion. For example, in limiting the death penalty essentially to murder alone, the Offences Against the Person Act of 1861 also did away with the traditional power of the trial judge to commute that sentence. Henceforth, only the home secretary, exercising the royal prerogative, could commute death sentences. The tendency of Victorian legal change

---

[67] Hostettler, p. 417.

[68] As Hostettler complained, such inclusion of recklessness in mens rea "is, however, not far removed from constructive malice" [p. 417].

was toward establishing a more uniform and nondiscretionary body of laws and an explicit system of gradations of offenses and penalties in closer correspondence with accepted moral rules.

Justice, it was coming to be accepted, required presenting the individual with clear guidance as to the likely consequences of his actions and leaving him, so informed, to draw the necessary conclusions. Following from this, the criminal trial also evolved toward greater impersonality and predictability. From a ritual show reaffirming the social and religious order, the trial was to become a new sort of educational process; from the court as participatory and expressive theater was to be shaped the court as reflective and instructive schoolroom. During the first half of the nineteenth century, criminal justice was pressed to move from a series of expressive semipersonal confrontations, personally directed by an involved judge and with highly variable results, to a more restrained, rule-governed, predictable, depersonalized process. Reformers sought, as Randall McGowen has put it, to "rout the personal from the courtroom" so as to make justice more expectable and respectable.[69]

Even reforms that have been attributed to simple libertarian motives played their part in the project of depersonalizing the law. Although the proposal to grant defense counsel in felony cases the right to address juries might appear to us long overdue, this reform was sharply resisted, for it challenged basic assumptions of Old Regime English justice.[70] "At present," one Tory observed, "the court [is] counsel for the prisoner," a beneficial situation in the eyes of conservatives. As with the wide scope for discretion in the award of punishment, the usual absence of effective counsel established the personal authority, and freedom of action, of the judge as the sanction to see that justice was done to the accused. This created a personal connection between judge and accused that humanized the law. Defenders cited "that presiding spirit of humanity, as active as it was benevolent, which from the bench itself, when the life of the accused was risked, so frequently tended to rebuke the severity of the law." Permitting defense counsel to address the jury, some believed, would remove this protective role from the bench and actually make the treatment of accused criminals harsher. But to reform advocates, the evil of the existing system was not removed by particular instances of judicial concern for defendants. What was most offensive was not the severity but the arbitrariness of the personalized justice. While Sir James Mackintosh was adamant that "the safety of the prisoner was not to be left to the casual feelings of a judge," reformers did not necessarily seek to increase the chance of

---

[69] "The Image of Justice," 116.
[70] The argument in this paragraph is based on McGowen, "Image of Justice," and the quotations are taken from there.

acquittals or even lighter sentences; they equally stressed the "undue leaning in [the prisoner's] favour" that could result from this personalized system.

In 1836, as the reformers' ideas gained acceptance, the assumptions of criminal law were altered with the passage of the Prisoner's Counsel Act. This act supplemented the efforts of the Criminal Law Commissioners by relocating the representative of the law above the personal drama being enacted, as the commissioners sought to remove from the law itself openings for the exercise of personal sentiment and prejudice. Instead of being a feeder of emotion *into* the trial, the judge would become a monitor *against* it; as Mr. Baron Parke observed in an 1845 murder case, the new scope for defense counsel now made it a central part of the judge's duty to counter irrelevant appeals to the "fears and passions" of the jury and continually to remind them of their duty to the public as well as to the prisoner.[71] Thus, it was felt, the removal of judicial paternalism would confront the individual, despite his increased access to professional assistance of counsel, more directly with responsibility for his actions. By this confrontation, individuals would morally improve themselves and society. In addition, removing the personal element from the workings of the law would, it was hoped, lower the emotional intensity of the subject's relationship to the law. In place of the metaphors of family, which encouraged both unpredictability and excessive release of the passions by plaintiffs and accused, the law and its courts were to be imbued with the character of a market, a meeting place of self-contained, self-disciplining individuals rationally pursuing their own interests under the impersonal arbitration and discipline of the unvarying rules of law. Passionate contest was to be placed in the professional hands of lawyers, for whom passion was an instrument of calculation, and confined by the rules of law, presenting no danger to society. Out of their contest, as out of a noisy but rule-governed marketplace or stock exchange, justice would emerge.[72]

Even in the judicial realm that lawyers did not enter, the expanding sphere of magistrates' summary jurisdiction, the dominion of rules advanced. Legislation in 1847 that dealt with a rapidly rising criminal case load by sharply extending summary jurisdiction was immediately followed by a series of acts that set out for the first time in detail a uniform procedure for magistrates to follow.[73] "The relaxed, relatively informal magistrates' tribunals of the eighteenth century," Clive Emsley has observed, "had little place in the in-

---

[71] *Morning Post*, March 15, 1845, p. 5.

[72] This is not to say that this act was not at the same time a needed counterbalance to the enhanced effectiveness of the prosecution.

[73] See David Freestone and J. C. Richardson, "The Making of English Criminal Law (7) Sir John Jervis and his Acts," *Criminal Law Review* (Jan., 1980), 5–16.

creasingly urbanised England of the nineteenth century with its emphasis on decorum and bureaucratic formality."[74]

The law increasingly aimed at fostering public character building, not only indirectly – by the spread of legal uniformity and certainty – but also more directly through specific expressions of this implicit moral agenda. As facilities for surveillance, apprehension, trial, and incarceration of offenders expanded, so definitions of criminality in case law and legislation also expanded. As police were more thoroughly scrutinizing popular behavior, judges and magistrates became readier to use criminal law against behavior seen as immoral or disorderly. The most familiar examples of this tendency relate to conflicts between employers and workmen in the defining as theft of many appropriations traditionally seen by workmen as perquisites of employment and of much trade union activity as intimidation.[75] But these well-studied judicial intrusions into the workplace – notable instances of law as class interest – gain a new dimension when placed in the more subtle context of a contemporaneous inclination to both pass new law and to read new, more stringent, moral standards into a wide range of existing common law dealing with harms both to property and to persons. These intrusions suggest a growing administrative and judicial concern with encouraging development of what could be called bourgeois character in the population.

Criminal and civil law relating to property relations underwent important alterations. One area of change was in what constituted unlawful appropriation. In the later eighteenth and nineteenth centuries, judges extended the law by reinterpreting the definition of larceny. As A. H. Manchester has noted, judges showed "a readiness to classify as criminal, conduct which formerly they had regarded as no more than sharp practice."[76] By 1860, with minimal parliamentary intervention, the structural principles grounding larceny had been altered, with the effect of greatly enlarging the ordinary individual's potential criminal liability.[77] Mere attempts to steal and immoral but

---

[74] Emsley, *Crime and Society*, p. 157.

[75] See John V. Orth, "The Law of Strikes, 1847–1871," in *Law and Social Change in British History*, eds. J. A. Guy and H. G. Beale (London: Royal Historical Society, 1984); David Sugarman, J. N. J. Palmer, and G. R. Rubin, "Crime, Law and Authority in Nineteenth-Century Britain," *Middlesex Polytechnic History Journal* (1983), 28–141.

[76] A. H. Manchester, *Modern Legal History*, p. 204.

[77] This has been most thoroughly examined and forcefully argued by George Fletcher, in "The Metamorphosis of Larceny," 469–530, and *Rethinking Criminal Law* (Boston: Little, Brown, 1978). Though Fletcher gives a class explanation for this development – the desire to afford greater protection to property – the shift of attention from harm to intent had many undertones and ramifications, not always supportive of business or capitalist

not manifestly larcenous appropriations were more thoroughly criminalized.[78] Cases of 1784 and 1801 began the formal doctrine of criminal attempts; thereafter, liability began earlier – one did not have to complete one's plans or efforts to be open to criminal prosecution.[79] Similarly, the nineteenth century spelled out the liability of finders and of receivers by mistake, and relatively invisible acts of misbehavior – such as appropriating lost goods when "reasonably believing" that the owner could be found or making no effort to return a bank overpayment – became criminal for the first time during the first two-thirds of the century.[80] In other words, outwardly innocent preparations and takings, which the law had previously ignored, could now, if accompanied by a prohibited state of mind, turn out to be criminal.

This expansion of the criminal law of theft has been interpreted as "re-equipping the medieval law of larceny to play an appropriate role in the new industrial Britain."[81] Revisionists have acutely challenged the question-begging obscurity of terms such as an "appropriate" role, seeing that role as the use of the traditional authority of the law to underpin the new power of capitalists. We may inquire, with the revisionists, into what new roles were sought for the law, but without halting our inquiry at the advancement of capitalist class interests. Judicial (and legislative) constructions of unacceptable behavior seem to have been changing for a number of reasons in response to a number of needs, not all of them material or political. The heightened concern we have seen with the control of impulse found one outlet in these changes in the law of larceny, which, by lowering the threshhold of illegality and

interests (except through rather convoluted reasoning). Judges, magistrates, and others exhibited an attachment to the concept of intent that went beyond its instrumental value for the existing property system.

[78] The shift from harm to intent can be seen in the reinterpretation noted by Fletcher of the rules relating to temporary takings: "The traditional text writers concurred that in the common law, as distinguished from Roman law, a temporary taking was not felonious. As Blackstone put it, if a neighbor takes another's plow that is left in the field and uses it upon his own land and then returns it ... [cases like this] are misdemeanors and trespasses but not felonies. When Archbold returns to this hypothetical case in 1812, in the first edition of his influential manual on criminal evidence, it is apparent to him that the issue is not whether the goods are in fact returned, but whether at the time of the taking there was an intent to return" ["Metamorphosis," 509].

[79] Fletcher, "Metamorphosis," 503. This pushing of criminal liability earlier in time, to the stage of conception and preparation of the act, parallels the rise of the executory contract in civil law. As Atiyah has described this latter development, "all contracts came to be seen as consensual ... binding in their inception. The focal point of contract law shifted from the performance back in time to the 'making' of the contract," in the agreement of the parties, before anything was done about it. [*Rise and Fall*, p. 420.]

[80] Fletcher, "Metamorphosis," 514–17.

[81] Manchester, p. 204.

moving it earlier in time, provided new incentives for more self-disciplined and foresightful behavior throughout society.

A similar pattern is discernible in the law of debt. On the one hand, imprisonment for the simple condition of debt was abolished in 1869, but, as revisionist historians have pointed out, the sanction of prison remained and was readily used against fraudulent debt or willful refusal to repay debt.[82] Even as imprisonment of faultless debtors was being done away with, willful debt was being more stigmatized than ever before.[83] Here, as in larceny, liability to penal sanction was more closely tied to the existence, not simply of the fact of debt, but of disapproved states of mind and bad character. As Baron Bramwell observed in an 1887 case, a commitment to prison under the 1869 act was no longer imprisonment for debt, but "imprisonment for past dishonesty."[84] The Master of the Rolls, Sir George Jessel, had declared a few years before that the power of imprisonment was now given not merely as a means of enforcing payment, but as a punishment for a fraudulent or dishonest debtor.[85] In line with this aim, the 1869 act removed the exemption from most forms of prison discipline hitherto enjoyed by debtor prisoners. The law was now intended to go easier on men like Dickens's William Dorrit but harder on the Harold Skimpoles.

If the thrust of legal change bore most heavily upon working-class behavior, the middle classes were not unaffected. At the same time that blue-collar

[82] See O. R. Macgregor, *Social History and Law Reform* (London: The Hamlyn Trust, 1981), pp. 54–55; G. R. Rubin, "Law, Poverty and Imprisonment for Debt, 1869–1914," in *Law, Economy and Society 1750–1914*, eds. G. R. Rubin and D. Sugarman (Abingdon: Professional Books, 1984), pp. 241–99.

[83] Indeed, as literary scholars have shown, the man who more than any other dramatized the plight of imprisoned debtors, Charles Dickens, was rigid in his insistence on the overriding moral obligation to repay debts, not only in his personal affairs but throughout his writing. Any reluctance of a character to repay, regardless of its difficulty, is considered at best tainted (as the feeling of the otherwise admirable Amy Dorrit). The moral law here was inflexible; as William Myers pointed out, although Dickens considered the forgiveness of debts to be a virtue in creditors, he was far from thinking that debtors have any human right to be forgiven. [William Myers, "The Radicalism of 'Little Dorrit,'" *Literature and Politics in the Nineteenth Century: Essays*, ed. John Lucas (London: Methuen, 1971), pp. 77–104; see also N. N. Feltes, "Community and the Limits of Liability in Two Mid-Victorian Novels," *Victorian Studies* 17 (1973–4), 335–69; George H. Ford, "Self-Help and the Homeless in *Bleak House*," *From Jane Austen to Joseph Conrad*, eds. Robert C. Rathburn and Martin Steinmann, Jr. (Minneapolis: University of Minnesota Press, 1958), pp. 92–105; C. R. B. Dunlop, "Debtors and Creditors in Dickens' Fiction," unpublished paper presented to the conference on Legal Fictions: Dickens, Victorian Society and the Law, University of California at Santa Cruz, August, 1988.]

[84] Quoted in William Holdsworth, *A History of English Law* Vol. 15 (London: Sweet and Maxwell, 1965), p. 499.

[85] *Marris* v. *Ingram* (1882) 13 Ch.D. 338, cited in G. R. Rubin, "Imprisonment for Debt," 253.

offenses of appropriation were being more expansively defined, white-collar offenses were being given greater judicial and legislative attention.[86] If economic development required that laws governing bankruptcy be less restrictive, this facilitation, like the easing of the sanction on debt, was accompanied by a heightened zeal for drawing moral distinctions. The Bankruptcy Act of 1849 established an unprecedented system of classifying the bankrupt's certificate of discharge into three categories according to the amount of fault involved. Though the law was repealed in 1861 as unworkable, it testified to the same desire on the part of lawmakers for a way of distinguishing and labeling degrees of moral responsibility for middle- and upper-class insolvency, as the reformed debt laws were doing for popular insolvency.[87]

Civil law changes in regard to property also can be illuminated by being viewed from the vantage point of the Victorian character-building enterprise. Here, too, developments like the growth of contract law provided new or intensified forms to regulate the relations among middle-class men. The nineteenth-century expansion of contract law involved much more than a freeing of capitalists; it carried with it an implicit moral agenda. The new salience of contract law did not always underpin the existing distribution of power and wealth, for it tended to substitute one form of property right for another and was accompanied by a rising judicial intolerance of a person's failure to foresee consequences and fulfill one's promises.[88] As a society in which moral duties arose largely out of stable and specific social relationships gave way to a mobile, individualist society of strangers, so contract law, like criminal and tort law, offered a way to publicize and enforce universal and impersonal standards of behavior. In particular, the law could assist in erecting internal barriers to the tug of impulse, to build gratification-deferring and future-oriented character throughout the general population.

As Atiyah has observed, the growing inclination of judges in the early nineteenth century to award damages for loss of expectation was often "a reward for diligence, skill, and foresight," and a penalty for their lack. This inclination can be seen therefore as expressing a growing valuation of these characteristics, a deep shift of social mores.

> In the eighteenth century (as, perhaps, today) there were many who viewed these qualities with some distaste rather than with admiration. To

---

[86] See R. S. Sindall, "Middle-Class Crime in Nineteenth-Century England," *Criminal Justice History 4* (1983), 23–40.

[87] See the account in Barbara Weiss, *The Hell of the English: Bankruptcy and the Victorian Novel* (Lewisburg, Pa: Bucknell University Press, 1986), pp. 23–47. One of the chief objects of the influential National Association for the Promotion of Social Science, founded in 1857, was further reform of the bankruptcy laws to distinguish more clearly and treat differently "honest misfortune" and "fraud, extravagance and recklessness."

[88] Atiyah, p. 138, passim.

make a contract to buy at less than the market price was to outwit your contracting partner, perhaps to take advantage of his ignorance or foolishness or necessitous circumstances. Was this to be encouraged? Or again, to make a contract for future performance, and then to insist on performance at the contract price when the market had changed, was hardly gentlemanly.[89]

Intentions and promises – expressions of the will – were increasingly held to create liability in contract law. A man was to be held to what he willed – wills were in this case to be the same as action; thus would the quality of that will – its caution, care, and foresightfulness – be improved. In this way,

> the principle of the due observance of promises fitted in very well with the ethic of self-discipline and self-reliance. To perform a promise was usually like doing labour – to the classical economists and the utilitarians this was a painful exertion, a 'dis-utility' – but in the long run, good would come of it to the promisor. If the promisor had not yet received any benefit from his promise – if some counter-performance was due afterwards – the reward for performing the promise would be direct and immediate. But even if the promisor had already received his due, he would still gain in the long run from performing his own promise. His credit would be maintained, he would be trustworthy in future; he would find others willing to deal with him, to trust his word.[90]

The moral agenda, however, was more deeply rooted even than Atiyah argues. In contract, as in larceny law, a covert moral agenda – an expectation of reasonable and proper behavior and the readiness to punish its absence – can be detected acting through (and on occasion contradicting) an overt philosophy of laissez-faire and non-paternalism.[91] Even in judgments apparently dealing purely with will and the voluntary incurring of obligations, an implied set of rules of behavior is often apparent. As Steven Hedley has persuasively argued, in the mainstream discourse of Victorian lawyers and judges, intent – to modern lawyers essentially a legal fiction – was *not* a fiction:

> They took a very wide view both of the 'intention of the parties', and of their own ability to divine it. Large chunks of this 'intent' are what we would now regard as part of the judge's own opinion, which he was foisting on the parties. This is particularly so in matters of morality: the

---

[89] *ibid.*, p. 202.

[90] *ibid.* p. 354.

[91] When the free market and the covert moral agenda clashed, the market usually gave way. For example, growing inclination to require the fulfillment of promises did not prevent the passage of the Gaming Act of 1845, which made gambling contracts unenforceable at law. Other sorts of contracts deemed immoral were regularly voided, with or without statutory sanction, by Victorian judges.

[Victorian] bench would read in all sorts of moral injunctions, on the ground that 'all reasonable men' must intend them.

Thus what might appear to be the moral neutrality (or class-interested hypocrisy) of laissez-faire was not necessarily so. The constant assertions of Victorian judges, Hedley has pointed out, "that No-one Should Be Placed Under An Obligation Not Voluntarily Assumed [sic] were not mere cant. But to make sense of them today we have to realise the ease with which the judges would find an obligation to have been assumed."[92] "Victorian notions of interpretation," Hedley has reminded us,

> differ substantially from modern notions. . . . The Victorians . . . did not draw so sharp a distinction between 'what the parties intended' and 'what all reasonable people in the parties' position would have intended'. They were well aware that texts contain ambiguities which cannot be resolved from the text itself but only by reference to background custom and understandings; and they were not in the least self-conscious or apologetic in filling the gaps with whatever 'all reasonable people may be taken to have intended' to fill them. All in all this gave them a much freer hand in interpretation generally, leaving them free to bring in background policy or considerations of morality as seemed appropriate.[93]

Central to reasonable behavior were foresight, self-discipline, and reliability, which clearly were valued by the judges independently of the intentions of the contracting parties. These expectations were often read into their intentions and thus enforced in the name of enforcing intentions. Through such an interpretative process, the Victorian courts were engaged in their own sort of legal modernization.

The implicit agenda of character development extended beyond property law. It can be discerned in the setting of new moral standards and the deterrent-educational aims increasingly in evidence in many legal areas bearing on crimes and harms of all sorts against the person. Like contract, the law of marriage has been seen as moving in libertarian or market directions in this period toward greater personal freedom of action; yet, also like contract, this very movement harnessed it to use as an instrument of character building. The 1857 Divorce Act provided a new nonecclesiastical, nonparliamentary, and less expensive procedure and also enlarged the grounds for divorce, thus making it more generally accessible. Yet the number of divorces never rose during

---

[92] Steve Hedley, "Where Anson Went Wrong (and Why We All Followed Him)", paper, 1986.

[93] Hedley, "From Individualism to Communitarianism? The Case of Standard Forms," in *Legal Record and Historical Reality*, ed. Thomas G. Watkin (London: Hambledon Press, 1989), 229–42.

the century above the level of a few hundred per year. One reason for this is that neither the act nor its administration was meant to generally encourage divorce, but rather to allow the most blatant victims of marital misconduct an avenue of escape while punishing those who had offended against them, thus morally strengthening marriage as an essential social institution. Divorce remained difficult and expensive and, most significant, was more than ever rooted in notions of fault, now extended, though not equally, to both parties. Criticizing the act for enshrining the double standard, important as that was, obscures the equally important fact that the measure made possible for the first time divorce of a husband by a wife by establishing the first statutory standard of what constituted unacceptable husbandly behavior.[94]

Though a civil institution, the divorce court was (like bankruptcy court) in tone not unlike a criminal court, punishing the guilty party not through imprisonment but through public denunciation. It was also suggestive of a criminal court in the secondary aim of deterring, through its stigma, others from falling into guilt and educating the public, through its proceedings and decisions published in the newspapers, in the rules of respectable conjugal behavior. The centrality of fault in divorce law reinforced the norm of personal responsibility; if a marriage failed, someone was responsible and that person must be called to the bar of justice. Relief from a failed marriage came very much behind punishment of those responsible for the failure; if both parties had committed adultery, regardless of the circumstances, no divorce could be granted. Similarly, not only relief but even punishment without deterrence or public education did not suffice the lawmakers; the provisions of the law were directed not only toward punishing adulterers and relieving their victims, but more generally toward reducing adultery in English society. Suggestions for facilitating judicial separations as a substitute for divorces and for barring remarriage of the guilty party were both handily rejected as having a demoralizing social influence – the first for not sufficiently stigmatizing adultery, the second for encouraging further illicit sexuality. A divorce, in the case of clear fault, that permitted remarriage was seen as the best means of reducing the incidence of adultery. In this way, the law, through the new divorce court,

---

[94] For such criticism, see Margaret K.Woodhouse, "The Marriage and Divorce Bill of 1857," *American Journal of Legal History 3* (1959), 260–75, and Mary Lyndon Shanley, "'One Must Ride Behind': Married Women's Rights and the Divorce Act of 1857," *Victorian Studies 25* (1981–82), 355–376. Despite the very restricted grounds for suits on the part of the wife, between 1859 and 1909, 42 per cent of divorce judgments were issued against husbands; see Gail L. Savage, "The Operation of the 1857 Divorce Act, 1860–1910: A Research Note," *Journal of Social History 16* (1983), 103–110. Perhaps the most significant fact about Lord Cranworth's statement in 1854 that it would be too harsh to bring the law to bear against a husband who was "a little profligate" was not its blatant double standard but the fact that it provoked a good deal of outraged comment in the press, including a rebuke from *The Times* [cited in Shanley, 364–5].

took on the task (hitherto left to the church) of the moral improvement of husband-wife relations. The divorce court remained focused upon this new role well into the twentieth century.[95]

Other areas of private law[96] also were giving heightened attention to character by now more clearly locating and punishing fault for harms. Despite the perennial judicial fear of explosions of litigation, civil liability for injuries caused by negligence was rapidly developing, as was liability for injuries caused by defective goods or premises.[97] These legal trends suggest that in the conduct of everyday life, more rigorous standards both of care for others and of self-management were appearing. One cause of this movement in law was economic; technological development, in the form of factories and railways, was increasing the dangers of inadequate carefulness and foresight. But more was involved than new practical needs. An adherent of this sort of technological determinism must assume, in the absence of such actions from the law reports of earlier times, that preindustrial laborers did not suffer accidents at work, "an assumption," as J. L. Barton has dryly observed, "which can hardly be shared by anyone who has perused a medieval coroner's roll."[98] Increasingly in the nineteenth century, workplace accidents were seen as preventable by an achievable degree of foresight and care, and thus as someone's responsibility. If the growth of the concept of negligence was not merely an inevitable practical response to technical change, as Morton Horwitz has usefully reminded us, it was also (like the stricter enforcement of promises) more than simply a tool for advancing economic interests.[99] Gary T. Schwartz has found in the nineteenth-century negligence standard "a highly expansive quality."[100] And J. L. Barton has concluded that rather than limiting an earlier more absolute liability (thus protecting the interests of capital and property), the history of the concepts of negligence and of defective

---

[95] A suggestive argument along these lines is Allen Horstman, *Victorian Divorce* (New York: St. Martin's Press, 1985); also see Savage, "Operation." Not until 1937 were grounds other than adultery accepted for divorce, and only in 1969 was divorce without the establishment of fault made possible.

[96] Something of a misleading designation in this period, when public deterrence and education were functions, as is argued here, by no means limited to criminal law.

[97] See Manchester, pp. 281–301; Christopher Tomlins, "A Mysterious Power: Industrial Accidents and the Legal Construction of Employment Relations in Massachusetts, 1800–1850," *Law and History Review* 6 (1988), 375–438; J. L. Barton, "Liability for Things in the Nineteenth Century," *Law and Social Change in British History*, eds. J. A. Guy and H. G. Beale (London: Royal Historical Society, 1984), pp. 145–55.

[98] Barton, "Liability for Things," 154–55.

[99] See Morton Horwitz, *The Transformation of American Law, 1780–1860* (Cambridge Mass.: Harvard University Press, 1977).

[100] "Tort Law and the Economy in Nineteenth-Century America: A Reinterpretation," *Yale Law Journal* 90 (July, 1981), 1759.

goods and premises shows that "the judges of the nineteenth century were engaged in extending liability rather than in restricting it."[101]

The new contexts of behavior set by factories, mines, and railways, although in the long run to undermine faith in the possibility of personal responsibility, initially provoked an intensified effort to reinforce that responsibility, through both civil and criminal legal sanctions. As P. W. J. Bartrip and S. W. Burman have brought out, the concern shared by all judges and nearly all legislators, even Liberal ones, as they faced the growing problem of industrial accidents in the 1840s, was neither to mandate safety directly nor to compensate for injuries, but rather to deter careless and encourage careful behavior; the chief difference between liberals and conservatives was how this instruction should be distributed between employers, employees, and consumers. Edwin Chadwick, for example, in 1846 urged the parliamentary Select Committee on Railway Labourers to propose legislation granting automatic compensation from employers for the families of railway workmen killed in accidents, unless the employer could "establish the fact of gross and wilful misconduct on the part of the deceased."[102] Chadwick's aim in suggesting this striking expansion of social provision was less to meet the needs these families than to improve safety through better behavior; the main thrust of his argument was that imposing this liability would cause employers to take care to select careful workmen, to employ safer materials, and to superintend the works. It would also, he felt, have a secondary educational effect upon the public and the working classes in teaching greater respect for the value of life.[103] The parliamentary Select Committee indeed recommended such legislation. Most legislators were not willing to go so far in imposing liabilities upon employers, and nothing was done to implement these recommendations. However, the alternative mode of dealing with industrial accidents – Lord Campbell's act (the Fatal Accidents Act) of that year, which gave a right of legal action to the dependents of fatal accident victims – if much less generous to workmen, similarly stressed legal sanctions as mechanisms for encouraging careful behavior. Though commonly known as it moved through Parliament as the Compensation Bill, the Fatal Accidents Act, Bartrip and Burman concluded, "would appear to have been passed mainly *as a deterrent measure*, with

---

[101] "Liability for Things," 155. Barton's essay traces this tendency through a large number of nineteenth-century cases on defective goods and premises. He acknowledges a growing sympathy on the part of many judges with the problems of businessmen and manufacturers (encouraged, no doubt, by the increasingly middle-class composition of the bench), but Barton shows this sympathy struggling with and frequently failing to outweigh rising expectations of careful behavior.

[102] Bartrip and Burman, *The Wounded Soldiers of Industry: Industrial Compensation Policy 1833–1897* (Oxford: Clarendon Press, 1983), p. 70, n. 63.

[103] *ibid*, n. 69.

compensation of the injured an incidental rather than the prime consideration."[104] Lord Campbell had expressed his desire to induce greater caution
and care through the rapidly growing economy, and this is generally how the
measure was seen at the time.[105]

The newly elaborated doctrine of the assumption of risk, which came in
practice to remove the teeth from Lord Campbell's act, in fact drew its justification from this same standard of character development. In 1837 Lord
Abinger, in denying a workman's suit for damages for injury against his
employer, made the novel assumption that an employee on taking employment
implicitly agreed to accept all the risks incident to that employment of which
he was aware or that were obvious. Abinger justified this assumption not by
appeal to precedent, but by general considerations of policy:

> If the master be liable to the servant in this action, the principle of
> that liability will be found to carry us to an alarming extent. . . . In fact,
> to allow this sort of action to prevail would be an encouragement to the
> servant to omit that diligence and caution which he is in duty bound to
> exercise on behalf of his master, to protect him against the misconduct or
> negligence of others who serve him, and which diligence and caution,
> while they protect the master, are a much better security against any
> injury the servant may sustain by the negligence of others, engaged under
> the same master, than any recourse against his master for damages could
> possibly afford.[106]

Gradually, Abinger's doctrine was extended by other judges to the doctrine
of common employment – that one of the risks voluntarily accepted by an employee was the risk of his fellow-servants' negligence – and in this form became a notorious weapon against workmen's claims against employers. Later
in the century, when the political setting had shifted, these sorts of arguments
began to be applied against employers along the lines Chadwick had marked
out. Lord Justice Brett in 1883 turned this deterrent shaft against the employer, drawing out the general "duty of care" implicit in it. Summarizing a
number of relevant cases, he concluded that

> the proposition which [they] suggest, and which is therefore to be de-
> duced from them, is that whenever one person is by circumstances placed
> in such a position with regard to another that everyone of ordinary sense
> who did think would at once recognise that if he did not use ordinary care

---

[104] *ibid.*, p. 102 [authors' italics].

[105] *ibid.*, pp. 97–103.

[106] Quoted *ibid.*, p. 104. Similarly, a leading U.S. decision, *Farwell* v. *Boston and
Worcester Railroad* (1840), turned each employee, as defendant's counsel had advocated,
into "a form of superintendent," not only of others but also of himself. See Tomlins,
"Mysterious Power," 414.

and skill in his own conduct with regard to those circumstances he would cause danger of injury to the person or property of the other, a duty arises to use ordinary care and skill to avoid such danger.[107]

His fellow Appeals judges concurred in finding for the plaintiff, but shied away from such dangerous and uncharacteristic generalizing, preferring to cite specific duties.[108] Thus, whether the burden of proof of fault was placed upon masters or men, the justifications were much the same – the fostering of greater foresight, self-discipline, and care in individuals as the proper route for remedying social ills. Of course, it made very great practical difference whether such demands for care were laid upon employers or employees; the political uses of this discourse were various and shifting. Yet it *was* a coherent discourse within which the issue of industrial safety was normally addressed.

By the 1890s, lawyers' and judges' preference for cautious particularization tended to obscure the degree to which moral judgment had been built into nominally value-neutral tort law. As the leading U.S. jurist, James Barr Ames, reflected contentedly in 1908, "the ethical standard of reasonable conduct had replaced the unmoral standard of acting at one's peril."[109] In England, C. S. Kenny remarked in 1904 on

> the change which has passed over the conception of the legal liability for tort. The older decisions paid more regard to the fact that the plaintiff had sustained a loss through the defendant's conduct than to the question whether there was anything in that conduct so blameworthy as to justify them in shifting this loss from one man's shoulders to another's.[110]

In the modern era, he was happy to report, "the idea of culpability had become judicially associated with that of liability for torts."[111]

---

[107] *Heaven v. Pender* (1883) 11 Q.B.D. 503.

[108] Eventually, professional caution won out, and Brett "recanted" in 1893, observing that all that the earlier case had established was that "under certain circumstances one man may owe a duty to another even though there is no contract between them" [*Le Lievre v. Gould* (1893) 1 Q.B. 491]. By then the preference of the lawyers for particulars had been reinforced by the appearance in 1889 of Beven's *Principles of the Law of Negligence*, which took 1,200 pages to catalogue specific duties.

[109] James Barr Ames, "Law and Morals," included in James Barr Ames, *Lectures on Legal History* (Cambridge, Mass.: Harvard University Press, 1913), p. 437.

[110] *Cases on the Law of Torts* (1904), (Cambridge, Mass: Harvard Law Review Publishing Association, 1909–1910), p. 146. Kenny, Downing Professor of Law at Cambridge, was a Gladstonian Liberal best known for his *Outline of Criminal Law* (1902).

[111] This is not to gainsay the continuation right through the Victorian era of the sort of strict and even absolute liability judgments characteristic of earlier (and later) periods. Philosophical consistency is not to be expected of English case law. If for no other reason, the reverence for precedent in the English judicial ethos prevents, for good or ill, the attainment of either the intellectual tidiness of the treatise writers or the comparatively di-

In the criminal, as in civil, law, the principle of fault, although it limited personal liability in some directions, expanded it in others, particularly as it was often subjected to broad readings to attain moral ends.[112] The notion of intent was on the whole enlarging. Even if specific harm was not intended, reckless behavior was ever more likely to be punished; not necessarily by overriding the rule of intent, but (as in civil cases) by reinterpreting it. Reasonable care was being read into a growing number of situations. Already in the second half of the eighteenth century, John Beattie has discovered a tendency for the proportion of convictions in murder prosecutions to rise, and even more strikingly, for persons charged with manslaughter, who would earlier have been released or been punished very lightly, to be convicted and imprisoned. He attributed this trend to both the availability of new forms of secondary punishment – transportation, the prison – and to "a change in attitude towards forms of behavior that might once have been overlooked but were increasingly condemned." In particular, he perceived "a tougher attitude in the courts toward carelessness that led to death and an anxiety to condemn forms of violence that earlier might have been entirely excused."[113]

Judicial attitudes toward recklessness hardened further in the nineteenth century. In 1822, the penalties for manslaughter were substantially increased.[114] Moreover, a wider variety of circumstances was being taken to allow an inference of intent to kill – if a deadly weapon were used, if a killing took place in the course of other criminal activity, if a representative of authority (such as a policeman) were attacked, or if death resulted directly from wildly reckless behavior.[115] Tolerance for drunkenness in the courts also diminished. Drunkenness had traditionally been viewed indulgently by

---

rect expression of social values possible for legislators. Nonetheless, both a coherent ideal of behavior and a consistent conception of the role of law in promoting that ideal did come increasingly to shape the thinking of Victorian courts in questions of tort as in contract or crime. John G. Fleming has summarized the Victorian position on the law's role: "In company with the criminal law, the primary function of tort recovery was seen in its admonitory or deterrent effect. An adverse judgment against the tortfeasor served at once as punishment for him and a warning for others." [*Introduction to the Law of Torts* (Oxford: Clarendon Press, 1968), p. 7.]

[112] Indeed, moralism held even greater sway in criminal matters. While, as Fifoot noted [p. 126], "in tort [the judges'] response to the equation of fault and liability was fitful . . . in the criminal law they received it as axiomatic."

[113] Beattie, pp. 89, 91.

[114] James Fitzjames Stephen, *History of the Criminal Law of England* Vol. 3, pp. 78–9.

[115] See Chadwick, "Bureaucratic Mercy." Crime against the person, even without the use of a deadly weapon, could produce the presumption of intent. J. F. Stephen records a typical such case, that of a would-be rapist who stuffed a girls shawl into her mouth to stifle her cries for help. She suffocated and he was hanged despite his plea that he had not intended to kill her and that, in Stephen's words, "by doing so he frustrated his own object." [*History of the Criminal Law of England* Vol. 3, p. 83.]

magistrates (particularly in the countryside) and was often treated in criminal proceedings as a practical, though not formal, excuse or mitigation. However, with the rise of the temperance movement, it began to be taken more seriously.[116] Drink became perhaps the leading explanation for crime. Prison inspector Herbert Voules claimed in 1857 that "drunkenness is the source of almost all crime ... destitution arising from want of employment acts far less prejudicially on the working classes than this monster vice of our large towns."[117] The reforming chaplain of Preston jail, John Clay, similarly reported three years earlier that "if every prisoner's habit and history were fully inquired into, it would be placed beyond all doubt that nine-tenths of the English crime requiring to be dealt with by the law arises from the *English sin* which the same law scarcely discourages."[118] As Clay's terminology indicated, even when one advocated (as did Clay and Voules) various sorts of social reform, the problem tended to be perceived in a voluntaristic frame, as ultimately a personal moral failing. The craving for drink, which could be stimulated or discouraged by social policy, was usually seen by temperance supporters as inherent in sinful human nature or, as Samuel Smiles put it more secularly, "the hereditary remnant of the original savage," always ready to break out and wreak havoc.[119] Such a craving, however, men (and women) could learn to master, substituting "moral will" for "impulsive will."[120]

In 1849, Mr. Justice Coleridge reaffirmed an ancient but often disregarded rule, declaring that "drunkenness is ordinarily neither a defense nor an excuse for crime.... Juries ought to presume a man to do [sic] what is the natural consequence of his act."[121] In homicide, mid-Victorian judges, a recent

---

[116] Urbanization and the growth of central government's influence in the local administration of justice also seem to have contributed to a tougher attitude toward drunkenness. On attitude and activities concerning drunkenness, see Brian Harrison, *Drink and the Victorians: The Temperance Question in England 1815–1872* (London: Faber and Faber, 1971) ; A. E. Dingle, *The Campaign for Prohibition in Victorian England: The United Kingdom Alliance 1872–1895* (London: Croom Helm, 1980); R. M. Macleod, "The Edge of Hope: Social Policy an Chronic Alcoholism 1870–1900," *Journal of the History of Medicine 22* (1967), 215–45; on the vexed issue of drink and criminal responsibility, see Nigel Walker, *Crime and Insanity in England, Volume One: The Historical Perspective* (Edinburgh: Edinburgh University Press, 1968), pp. 177–181 and Roger Smith, *Trial by Medicine: Insanity and Responsibility in Victorian Trials* (Edinburgh: Edinburgh University Press, 1981), pp. 85–88.

[117] Quoted in Sean McConville, *A History of English Prison Administration, Volume 1 1750–1877* (Boston: Routledge, 1981), p. 330.

[118] Quoted in W. L. Clay, *The Prison Chaplain: A Memoir of the Reverend John Clay* (London, 1861), p. 554.

[119] Quoted in A. E. Dingle, "The Rise and Fall of Temperance Economics," *Monash Papers in Economic History 3* (1977), 8.

[120] F. R. Lees, *United Kingdom Alliance Prize Essay* (3rd ed., 1857), p. 27.

[121] *R. v. Monkhouse* (1849), quoted in Chadwick, "Bureaucratic Mercy," 409.

student of their behavior has noted, "were reluctant to see even chronic alcoholism as precluding malice. . . . Even prisoners with delirium tremens were considered to have retained sufficient reason and self-control to be liable for the consequences of their acts."[122] Given the assumptions that so much crime was related to drink and that its cravings could generally be resisted, any serious war on crime had to involve a stern attitude toward drunkenness. Even a medical man acknowledged in 1865 that it was "obvious that if drunkenness were to be readily admitted as a defence, three-fourths of the crimes committed in this country would go unpunished."[123] Indeed, it was often argued by temperance activists like Clay, and by moderate reformers like Lord Brougham, that rather than being taken as a mitigation or excuse, drunkenness should be considered an aggravation of an offense. Even that apostle of noninterference, John Stuart Mill, supported increased criminal sanctions against drunken offenders. Mill urged making drunkenness, in an offender previously convicted of any act of violence under the influence of drink, an aggravating rather than a mitigating factor. "The making himself drunk," Mill pronounced, "in a person whom drunkenness excites to do harm to others, is a crime against others."[124]

Yet another form of recklessness was also receiving greater legal attention. Although suicide (continuing a trend that had begun in the seventeenth century) was being treated with ever less theological horror and ever more sympathy,[125] arrests and prosecutions for the new offence of *attempted* suicide

---

[122] Chadwick, 410. Of course, while denied the status of an excuse voiding criminal liability, drunkenness was nonetheless frequently taken (by magistrates more than by judges) to be a mitigating factor in awarding punishment. However, those convicted of murder who claimed drunkenness as an excuse or mitigating factor were very unlikely to be saved from hanging, unless the victim was also drunk. The case of Joseph Bannister is suggestive. In 1877, Bannister killed his wife with a coal axe that he had taken to bed with him and pleaded insanity. Although the Home Office acknowledged that he had delirium tremens, he was convicted and executed; he presumably demonstrated intent by carrying his axe to bed. By comparison, see this instance reported in the *Gentleman's Magazine* for 1748: "At a Christening at Beddington in Surrey the nurse was so intoxicated that after she had undressed the child, instead of laying it in the cradle, she put it behind a large fire, which burnt it to death in a few minutes. She was examined before a magistrate, and said she was quite stupid and senseless, so that she took the child for a log of wood; on which she was discharged." [Quoted in Roy Porter, "The Drinking Man's Disease: The 'Pre-History' of Alcoholism in Georgian Britain," *British Journal of Addiction* 80 (1985), 387.]

[123] A. S. Taylor, *The Principles and Practice of Medical Jurisprudence* (1865), quoted in Smith, *Trial*, p. 51.

[124] *On Liberty* [1859], ed. David Spitz (New York: Norton, 1975), p. 90. On the sharp rise in criminal prosecution of drunkards in the decade after Mill wrote, see below.

[125] See Michael Macdonald, "The Secularization of Suicide in England 1600–1800," *Past and Present* no. 111 (May, 1986), 50–101.

steadily rose from 1830 to the end of the century.[126] Although few of these persons, who could not be tried summarily and against whom evidence of their intention was unusually difficult to assemble, were actually sent for trial, most spent a week or two behind bars. In cases of suicide pacts that failed, the survivor was usually charged with murder.[127]

Similarly, although a dramatic eighteenth-century fall in prosecutions and, especially, executions for infanticide continued in the nineteenth century, new legal efforts were made to deter and prevent this act. As elsewhere in the criminal law, horrific but rarely employed sanctions were replaced or supplemented by less harsh but more consistently enforced ones. In recognition of the reluctance of juries to convict women of a crime requiring the sentence of death, in 1803 an alternative offense of concealment of birth, bearing a maximum sentence of two years' imprisonment, was provided and soon became the preferred legal weapon against maternal killing of infants.[128] In 1861, in the midst of an infanticide panic, a further step toward more effective deterrence was taken by making it a misdemeanor for any person, not just the mother, to conceal a birth, whether the baby was born dead or alive.[129] Although no woman was hanged after 1849 for killing her own child under a year old, by the 1850s, about 100 women per year were being convicted of concealment of birth and imprisoned for periods of up to two years.[130]

Criminal liability for dangerous behavior grew in negative as well as positive forms. Judges found it less acceptable for defendants simply to refrain from the positive doing of harm — more and more, duty was being extended to the taking of necessary precautions and care. Many strict liability judgments around midcentury can be understood as not dispensing with the notion of intent, but, like in contract, expanding it to embrace an understood duty of care.

---

[126] Olive Anderson, *Suicide in Victorian and Edwardian England* (Oxford: Clarendon Press, 1987), pp. 263, 282–6. Here as in other matters the advent of the new police facilitated expanded intervention in private life.

[127] Chadwick, "Bureaucratic Mercy," pp. 136, 202.

[128] Indeed, for the killing of newborns it virtually replaced murder convictions; on prosecutions for concealment of birth, see Ann R. Higginbotham, "The Unmarried Mother and Her Child in Victorian London, 1834–1914," unpublished Ph.D. dissertation, Indiana University, 1985, 218–56; also see Lionel Rose, *The Massacre of the Innocents: Infanticide in Britain 1800–1939* (London: Routledge, 1986), pp. 70–78. Commitments for concealment of birth rose from an annual average of about 45 in the 1830s to 66 in the 1840s to 100 in the 1850s, continuing to rise for some years thereafter [Annual criminal statistics].

[129] On this panic, see George Behlmer, "Deadly Motherhood: Infanticide and Medical Opinion in Mid-Victorian England," *Journal of the History of Medicine and Allied Sciences* 34 (Oct., 1979), 403–27; on the 1861 act and its purpose, see Smith, *Trial*, p. 145.

[130] In addition to one or two each year who were convicted of murder, reprieved from the gallows, and committed to long terms of penal servitude. On convictions and sentences for child murder, see Cathy S. Monholland, "Infanticide in Victorian England 1856–1878," unpublished M.A. thesis, Rice University, 1989.

In 1846, a tradesman's lack of knowledge that the tobacco he was selling was adulterated proved insufficient to prevent his conviction. "A prudent man who conducts this business," Chief Baron Pollock observed, "will take care to guard against" such prosecution by examining his goods or by taking a guarantee from his supplier.[131] Henceforth, tradesmen had greater incentive to become "prudent men." Where the standard of intent was kept, broader standards of behavior (as in contract and tort) were frequently read into it. In an 1848 case, Mr. Justice Coleridge found a neglect of duty by a railway signalman grave enough to constitute a proper charge of manslaughter; the man was convicted.[132] Similarly, two years later, Chief Justice Lord Campbell found that, in a case of a coalpit lift operator, "an act of omission, as well as of commission, may be so criminal as to be the subject of an indictment for manslaughter."[133]

The criminalization of harmful behavior was also beginning to reach into the domestic sphere. As legal stigmatization of adultery and desertion (when combined with adultery) was about to be applied through the 1857 Divorce Act, the physical abuse of wives and children was statutorily recognized in 1853 in the Act for the Better Prevention of Aggravated Assaults upon Women and Children, popularly known as the "Good Wives' Rod."[134] The significance of this act has been dismissed because comparatively few cases of domestic violence were prosecuted under it.[135] Yet, as in the case of the Divorce Act, this measure is important for its symbolic, not necessarily its pragmatic, meaning; namely, the intent to strengthen an existing rule of behavior by adding the threat and the solemnity of legal sanction, not just a practical policy meant to afford immediate relief to a class of sufferers.

As the beating of good wives was being condemned, so the sorts of killings most common when women were the victims – in the heat of passionate reaction to insult or while intoxicated – were less readily excused by the bench. Judges were coming to expect a greater degree of self-control by men. In

---

[131] *R. v. Woodrow* (1846), 15 M. & W. 404.

[132] *R. v. Pargeter* (1848), 3 Cox Crim. Cases 191; clearly, however, the defendant was not felt to be as censurable as if he had possessed some more straightforward intent to harm – his sentence was three months' imprisonment.

[133] *R. v. Lowe* (1850), 4 Cox Crim. Cases 449; this man, too, was found guilty.

[134] This act, England's first statutory prohibition of violence against women and children, provided a maximum prison term of six months or a fine of up to £20 for attacks on all females and on males under fourteen that resulted in actual bodily harm.

[135] Margaret May, "Violence in the Family: An Historical Perspective," in ed. J. P. Martin, *Violence and the Family* (New York: John Wiley, 1978). If it proved only a slender rod for "good wives," it was of no help for those deemed to have fallen short in their wifely duties. At least until the 1880s, punishment of violence against wives depended very much upon moral evaluation of the victim. See Chadwick, "Bureaucratic Mercy," 381–90, and Conley, "Criminal Justice."

1852, Mr. Justice Cresswell, rejecting an accused wife murderer's plea for reduction of the charge to manslaughter by reason of provocation by taunting language, observed that not only did words form no justification, but death produced by a willful and unprovoked blow was murder, although the blow may have been given in a moment of passion or intoxication.[136] Mr. Justice Keating reiterated the point in an 1869 murder case with a male victim: "mere [taunting] words, or gestures . . . will not, in point of law, be sufficient to reduce the crime to manslaughter." He rejected the defense that "the prisoner was under the influence of ungovernable passion at the time he struck the blow." Keating observed that

> when the law says that it allows for the infirmity of human nature, it does not say that if a man, without sufficient provocation, gives way to angry passion, and does not use his reason to control it – the law does not say that an act of homicide, intentionally committed under the influence of that passion, is excused or reduced to manslaughter. The law contemplates the case of a reasonable man, and requires that the provocation shall be such as that such a man might naturally be induced, in the anger of the moment, to commit the act. . . . I can discover no proof of such provocation in the evidence.[137]

Thus, across the spectrum of law can be discerned a new moralizing subtext, a hardly questioned acceptance of the importance of strengthening the self-discipline, foresight, and reasonableness of the public and of the suitability of law as a medium for expressing and furthering these values.

Containing the specter of irresistible impulse

One indication of the heightened interest in building character and assigning responsibility was a growth in concern about the criminally insane. As criminal law extended and increased its emphasis upon personal responsibility, attention was drawn to the hitherto minor problem of those incapable of living up to this heightened demand, in particular to mentally disordered offenders. Their erratic behavior could less easily be left alone, as they kept now bumping up against the more ubiquitous law and against similarly expanding

---

[136] *R. v. Noon* (1852), 6 Cox Crim. Cases 137; the jury, probably focusing on the defendant's apparent drunkenness, found manslaughter. In this area, however, practice was slow to come into line with principle: the taunts of "bad" wives or tavern fellows were frequently allowed as provocation in assault and homicide cases. Nonetheless, the trend through the Victorian era was clearly in the direction of more severe prosecution of such violence.

[137] *R. v. Welsh* (1869) 11 Cox Crim. Cases 336; the prisoner was found guilty and sentenced to death.

standards of respectability. At the same time, since the criminal law's sanctions and methods of disposition of offenders were revolving more than ever around the presumed rationality and autonomy of the subject, a new degree of scrutiny was focused on the offender's powers of reason and self-government. These developments made the perennial phenomenon of irrational and impulsive offenders into a new problem.

During the first half of the century, rising fears of instincts breaking their bounds promoted a stereotype of the criminal lunatic as violent and danger-ous.[138] As we have seen, the emerging profession of psychiatry was develop-ing definitions of insanity based on defects of will and emotion, rather than intellect. These definitions directed attention to the breakdown of inner mechanisms of control. The upshot was a series of celebrated early and mid-Victorian trials whose impact was far out of proportion to the minute numbers of offenders involved.[139]

The special verdict of insanity had been created by statute in 1800. Its immediate cause seems to have been the desire for a general rule to ensure that men like James Hadfield – who had fired a pistol at George III, and subsequently been acquitted "as being under the influence of insanity" – did not go free.[140] In the longer run, the establishment of the special verdict marks the confluence of a growing interest in the phenomenon of insanity and the moral unease it produced about subjecting madmen to criminal sanctions, with the intensified concern for order we have already noticed. The Criminal Lunatics Act of 1800 removed from juries the alternative, commonly taken in the eighteenth century, of simply acquitting an offender whom the jury was satisfied was insane at the time of his crime. Henceforth the only permissible verdict in such cases was one making it clear that the acquittal was on the ground of insanity, and in such verdicts the court was required to order the accused "to be kept in strict custody, in such place and in such manner as to the court shall seem fit, until His Majesty's pleasure be known"; whereupon it would be for His Majesty to give orders for his custody.[141]

---

[138] See Janet Saunders, "Institutionalized Offenders: A Study of the Victorian Insti-tution and Its Inmates, with Special Reference to Late Nineteenth Century Warwick-shire," unpublished Ph.D. thesis, University of Warwick 1983, pp. 227–8.

[139] See Smith, *Trial*. In its concentration on conflict between law and medicine, however, this excellent study neglects the extent to which early and mid-Victorian psychiatry participated in the concerns about character formation and impulse control that were also shaping law.

[140] Richard Moran, "The Origins of Insanity as a Special Verdict: The Trial for Treason of James Hadfield (1800)," *Law and Society Review 19* (1985), 487–519. Like the legis-lation three years later making available the alternative verdict of concealment of birth, this act joined motives of humanity and deterrence.

[141] See Walker, *Crime and Insanity*, Ch. 4 and passim.; also Joel Peter Eigen, "Intentionality and Insanity: What the Eighteenth-Century Juror Heard," in eds. W. F.

This procedure held out a middle path between cruelty and laxity. It satis-fied emerging humane sensibilities by offering a safe and easily understood alternative to convicting and punishing an offender suspected of mental dis-turbance. At the same time, it provided new legal means to incarcerate an offender who might otherwise escape control. As Nigel Walker observed, it paid "lip service to his innocence but use[d] the law to make sure he remained in custody."[142] The importance of the desire for more certain custody is suggested by the additional provisions of the 1800 act. One provision applied the same procedure to persons about to be discharged for want of prosecution who appeared to be insane, and another made it possible for the justices to confine certain insane persons without the possibility of private bail, so that only two justices, or a higher judicial authority, could release them.[143] Of course, insane offenders had not necessarily been released before 1800; after acquittal they could be civilly committed as dangerous lunatics under the Vagrancy Act of 1744. Yet until the 1800 act, most insanity acquittees had been sent home; some had been placed under the care and protection of friends and relatives; only a few had been confined.[144] The 1800 act thus introduced not so much a major new escape route from criminal conviction for offenders suspected of mental disturbance, but rather a more systematic means of containing them within a voluntarist legal system and a more automatic and thorough method of ensuring their custody thereafter. Indeed, concern with security and even with deterrence (few men were so mad, suggested the sec-retary of war that year, as not to be influenced to some extent by the fear of punishment) seemed the most prominent reasons for the passage of the act. In fact, it might even be said, as Richard Moran has claimed, that the trial of James Hadfield marked the abolition of the insanity defense, not its origin, since a successful defense of insanity now led to automatic confinement for an indefinite period of time.[145]

As we would expect if the motives of the 1800 act were more those of security than humanity, we do not find in the years following a rise in the use of the insanity defense. Indeed, when Nigel Walker compared the frequency of insanity defenses in the 1830s with that of the mid-eighteenth century, he found they had done little more than keep pace with population growth and had in fact fallen *behind* the rapid rise in criminal prosecutions.[146] Nor were

---

Bynum, Roy Porter and Michael Shepherd, *The Anatomy of Madness: Essays in the His-tory of Psychiatry* (New York: Tavistock Publications, 1985), II, 35–49.

[142] Walker, p. 81.

[143] Walker, p. 80.

[144] Moran, 488 (though neither Moran, Eigen, nor Walker provides figures on the pre-1800 disposition of insanity acquittees).

[145] Moran, 489, 517.

[146] Walker, pp. 67, 88.

insanity pleas in general more successful after 1800; chances of acquittal
remained at about even, improving for crimes against the person while actually worsening for property crimes.[147] Down to the 1840s, then, the question
of lunacy caused barely a ripple in the course of English criminal justice.

The issue of criminal lunacy emerged for the first time into the spotlight of
public debate in the 1840s. By then, both professional and literary interest in
abnormal psychology had markedly developed, the general problem of insanity seemed to be growing, and the state was for the first time assuming
some responsibility for its treatment.[148] In 1842, efforts to improve the state
of asylums and to secure state action culminated in parliamentary sanction
of a detailed inquiry into the subject; this produced two years later a comprehensive report that examined the condition of every asylum in England, discussed the nature and forms of insanity, and made specific recommendations
for reform. The report was enthusiastically taken up by Lord Shaftesbury and
led to the two Lunatics Acts of 1845 establishing a permanent national lunacy
commission to inspect all asylums and requiring building of county and
borough asylums for the rising numbers of pauper lunatics.[149] Where the first
official inquiry, the 1807 Commons Select Committee on Criminal and Pauper
Lunatics, had identified as insane 2,248 persons, the 1844 report listed the
number of insane at over 20,000, and this figure continued to outpace population growth, almost doubling by 1860.[150] While this plague of insanity
seemed to be spreading, voluntarist-minded judges and legislators, as we have
seen, were reinterpreting the law to stress the individual's responsibility for
assessing the consequences of his behavior. These disparate trends joined to
heighten interest in the mental powers of offenders, which had not been an
important issue in the eighteenth century. This new interest was further
reflected in the growing use of medical evidence in trials, evidence that began
to draw from the new specialty of psychiatry.[151]

Two trials in the early 1840s brought the issue to a head: the case of
Edward Oxford, who fired at the Queen in 1840, and the case of Daniel
McNaughten, who killed Sir Robert Peel's private secretary in 1843. Medical
witnesses at Oxford's trial diagnosed hereditary moral insanity; Oxford was

[147] Walker, p. 74; Eigen p. 41.
[148] Prisons and asylums were beginning to develop a formal relationship. The Insane
Prisoners Act of 1840 laid down rules for the transfer of insane prisoners to asylums.
[149] Andrew Scull, *Museums of Madness: The Social Organization of Insanity in Nineteenth
Century England* (New York: St. Martins Press, 1979), pp. 107–113. One reason for rising
numbers of pauper lunatics may have been the higher standards of personal self-government now expected.
[150] Scull, pp. 222–3.
[151] See Smith, *Trial*, p. 3. In 1840, the special verdict of insanity was extended to
misdemeanors. [Walker, p. 80.]

acquitted and committed to Bethlem Asylum. McNaughten also was found not guilty by reason of insanity, the victim of irresistible impulses (though this was not a proper legal concept), and committed, on the unusual, if not unprecedented, basis of the evidence of nine medical men, and his counsel's appeal to the growing authority of science to exculpate him of guilt. Alexander Cockburn, one of the most brilliant lawyers of the day, signaled a new era in urging the court to "listen with patient attention to the evidence of men of skill and science." He argued that:

> The mistake existing in ancient times, which the light of modern science has dispelled, lay in supposing that in order that a man should be mad – incapable of judging between right and wrong, or of exercising that self-control and dominion, without which the knowledge of right and wrong would become vague and useless – it was necessary that he should exhibit those symptoms which would amount to total prostration of the intellect; whereas, modern science has incontrovertibly established that any one of these intellectual and moral functions of the mind may be subject to separate disease, and thereby man may be rendered the victim of the most fearful delusions, the slave of uncontrollable impulses impelling or rather compelling him to the commission of acts such as that which has given rise to the case now under your consideration.[152]

The McNaughten case in particular, coming while the unease resulting from Oxford's case was still fresh and with its novel talk of "uncontrollable impulses," produced considerable public alarm; many called for the clarification, and restriction, of the law. All the current efforts at rationalizing the law, which were supposed to enhance its effectiveness, seemed to run aground on the matter of criminal lunacy. The young Queen herself was one of the alarmed:

> The law may be perfect [she complained to Peel], but how is it that whenever a case for its application arises it proves to be of no avail? We have seen the trials of Oxford and MacNaughten conducted by the ablest lawyers of the day – and they *allow* and *advise* the Jury to pronounce the verdict of not guilty on account of insanity, whilst *everybody* is morally convinced that both malefactors were perfectly conscious and aware of what they did.[153]

To allay this anxiety the Lord Chancellor led a movement to formulate a set of questions to be answered by the judges appearing together before the House of Lords. The judges' answers to these questions, restating the knowledge of right and wrong test and pulling back from the wider and vaguer

---

[152] Quoted in Smith, pp. 102–3.
[153] Quoted in Walker, p. 188.

language employed in the Oxford and McNaughten trials, constituted the famous McNaughten rules. Essentially a man was not responsible for his criminal act only if, at the time of committing it, he was unable to know that the act was illegal and wrong. The rules, though not formally binding on the courts, established a clear and voluntarist legal principle, not officially altered until well into the twentieth century.

During the decade following McNaughten's trial in 1843, the percentage of special verdicts remained the same, and for several decades it rose slowly.[154] Judges, supported even by many medical doctors, normally refused to countenance pleas explicitly or implicitly based on uncontrollable impulses – the McNaughten specter they were determined to lay to rest. In rejecting such a plea in 1848, Mr. Baron Parke noted that "the excuse of an irresistible impulse, co-existing with the full possession of reasoning powers, might be urged in justification of every crime known to the law – for every man might be said, and truly, not to commit any crime except under the influence of some irresistible impulse."[155] As J. F. Stephen observed to the Juridical Society in 1855, "[T]here may have been many instances of irresistible impulse of this kind, although I fear there is a disposition to confound them with unresisted impulses."[156] For Parke, Stephen, and nearly all their fellow jurists of the early and mid-Victorian period, the question of a particular offender's capabilities of self-control was overshadowed by the dangerous moral implications of even allowing such a question to be asked.

Baron Bramwell, perhaps the most outspoken critic of irresistible impulse in criminal cases,[157] rebuked a juror in 1859 who suggested that a seemingly disturbed murderer might have suffered from an uncontrollable impulse:

[154] Walker, p. 88. A higher number of pleas was countered by a lower rate of success [Walker, p. 69]. One reason may have been sharpened judicial vigilance against feigned lunacy; as Mr. Justice Williams typically cautioned, "while on the one hand it would be a serious thing to put a man on his trial, when incapable of properly instructing his counsel for his defence, yet on the other hand, the jury should carefully guard against giving prisoners the opportunity, by simulating madness, to pervert the course of justice even for a single day" [*R.* v. *Davies* (1853) 6 Cox Crim. Cases 328].

[155] *R.* v. *Barton* (1848), 4 Cox Crim. Cases 276. Parke pointedly endorsed the view of his colleague, Mr. Baron Rolfe, who had recently rejected defense arguments of irresistible impulse and of motivelessness in a case where a well-known eccentric suddenly shot a woman right in front of her husband and other witnesses. In that case Rolfe had warned that "it is dangerous ground to take to say that a man must be insane because men fail to discern the motive for his act ... as if the perpetration of crimes was to be excused by their very atrocity." [*R.* v. *Stokes* (1848), quoted in Smith, p. 122.]

[156] J. F. Stephen, "On the policy of maintaining the limits at present imposed by law on the criminal responsibility of madmen," in *Papers Read before the Juridical Society, 1855–8* (London, 1858). For further examples of legal concern about this defense, see Smith.

[157] Bramwell also, not coincidentally, was probably the most outspoken judicial proponent of economic individualism.

That did not make the offence the less murder. Malice was implied when there was a deliberate cruel act committed, however sudden it might be. It was no matter how sudden the impulse – whether it was the result of long previous deliberation, or whether it was the impulse of an instant – it would be as much murder in one case as in the other. No jury could properly acquit on the ground of insanity, if they believed the accused was conscious of the act he was committing, and that he knew that act was contrary to law. If they gave a verdict contrary to this, the result would be to increase the number of cases of uncontrollable impulse.[158]

Bramwell went beyond enforcing the McNaughten Rules to repeatedly argue, in court and out, that the appearance of uncontrollable impulse called for even stronger and more certain punishment: "The unhappy madman is a person who requires the threat more than anybody else, because, from the condition of his mind, he is more likely to have some temptation to commit the offence, and less intelligence to deter him from doing it."[159] In short, "I would control it by the fear of hanging, mad or not mad."[160] Stephen summed up in a similar fashion in his *General View of the Criminal Law* (1863):

> If the impulse was resistible, the fact that it proceeded from disease is no excuse at all. If a man's nerves were so irritated by a baby's crying that he instantly killed it, his act would be murder. It would not be less murder if the same irritation and the corresponding desire were produced by some internal disease. The great object of the criminal law is to induce people to control their impulses, and there is no reason why, if they can, they should not control insane impulses as well as sane ones.[161]

Not only did insanity pleas venturing beyond the strict confines of the McNaughten rules very rarely succeed through the mid-Victorian years in preventing conviction, but few capital convictions were reprieved on the ground of insanity. Sir George Grey, a Whig-Liberal and devout Evangelical who headed the Home Office for most of the two decades between McNaughten and the Royal Commission on Capital Punishment, and his permanent under-secretary, Horatio Waddington, were not inclined to excuse offenders from culpability. Though he hated the burden of rejecting pleas for mercy, Grey rarely allowed the claim of insanity to draw a reprieve from the gallows, particularly if the insanity of the accused had been disputed at any

---

[158] Reported in J. G. Davey, "Insanity and Crime – Communication by Dr. Davy," *Journal of Mental Science* 6 (1859), 34.
[159] *Report of the Capital Punishment Commission* 1866 Q. 152 [P.P. 1866 v. 21].
[160] See Smith p. 105, n. 48, 49.
[161] *ibid.* p. 95.

time during the course of his trial.[162] In the case of a 69-year-old man who had killed his wife, Grey rejected a plea by Worcester magistrates for commutation, supported by a jury recommendation to mercy; he noted that the trial record showed "ample evidence of the determination with which the prisoner acted" and the "wanton and unprovoked" nature of the assault. At the same time, he rejected the claims of "previous character": "Character may be entitled to much weight where doubt exists as to the facts but not so where the crime is clearly proved to have been committed."[163] Grey's uncompromising stance was in tune with public opinion, for he was most fiercely criticized when he uncharacteristically did grant a reprieve on grounds of insanity to the notorious George Victor Townley, who had stabbed his fiance to death in 1863 when she informed him of her desire to marry another man. Grey's hand was forced by the coup of Townley's attorney, who took advantage of a loophole in the law and persuaded two justices and two medical doctors to sign a certificate that the man was insane. Townley's reprieve was denounced in press and Parliament as a miscarriage of justice produced by the influence of money. After this public outcry, Grey appointed another commission to report on Townley's state of mind. This commission found him sane, and Grey then changed the sentence to penal servitude and had Townley returned from Bethlem to prison.[164] As a result of Townley's case, the law was changed (at Grey's instigation) to prevent a defendant from choosing the justices to certify his insanity and to require that if a prisoner sentenced to death and then reprieved on grounds of insanity were later certified sane, he must be returned to prison from the asylum and face the punishment.[165]

In general, therefore, just as new legislation recognized divorce or bankruptcy but hedged them round with moral discriminations and stigma, the McNaughten rules acknowledged insanity while serving to seal the criminal floodgates that the Queen, and many others, had feared the McNaughten verdict would open. The subversive effect of expanding medical knowledge upon the newly established standard of personal responsibility was thus contained.[166]

[162] *Report of the Capital Punishment Commission 1866*, Q. 1512. Grey's severity did not stem from callousness; on at least one occasion he was reduced to tears before a deputation that was pleading for a man's life. A. Gathorne-Hardy, ed. *Gathorne-Hardy, First Earl of Cranbrook, Vol. 1* (London: Longmans Co., 1910), p. 162.

[163] Public Record Office (hereafter PRO), Home Office (hereafter HO) 13/107, Waddington to Sir Edmund Lechmere, Dec. 27, 1862.

[164] Townley concluded the matter by committing suicide. See the accounts in Walker, pp. 207–8, and Smith, pp. 131–3.

[165] See David Smith, "Sir George Grey at the Mid-Victorian Home Office," unpublished Ph.D. thesis, University of Toronto 1972, p. 102.

[166] Significantly, the misnomer "criminal lunatic" was universally used to denote those acquitted and committed to asylum from 1800 on; the language, as Bethlem's archivist,

By the 1860s, therefore, both criminal and civil law were placing greater stress upon impersonal rules defining, and insisting upon, individual responsibility. Law was being employed with increasing consistency as an instrument for developing self-disciplining and gratification-deferring personalities in the population at large. To counter the crime wave and immorality wave of the first half of the century stood a newly character-building law.

Patricia Allderidge, has pointed out, was "wrong" but little challenged and not formally dropped until 1938. ["Bedlam: Fact or Fantasy," *The Anatomy of Madness* Vol. 2, eds. W. F. Bynum, Roy Porter and Michael Shepherd, (London: Tavistock Publications, 1985), pp. 17–34.]

3

Victorian criminal policy II: reformed punishment

Dangerous punishments: against lotteries and spectacles

As in law reform, the new preoccupations with checking and purging impulse and building popular character first showed themselves in the realm of penalty in unhappiness with the Georgian inheritance. The repulsion reformers felt for the personalism, the uncertainty, and the disorderly mixture of cruelty with tolerance of traditional justice, they similarly felt for such qualities in the treatment of offenders. They saw the morally pernicious effects these qualities had on prisoners and the onlooking public alike. In particular, reformers concentrated their fire upon the balancing of lax enforcement by the resort to brutal exemplary punishments.

The early nineteenth-century movements against violent public punishments were rehearsed in the criticism of dueling that arose several decades earlier. Those attacks, though strictly speaking not dealing with a penal question, were powered by many of the same sentiments and values that soon were turned against public whipping and hanging. In both cases, reformers were appalled by the sanctioning of personal violence, the stimulus given by the practice to the venting of aggressive impulses. One critic of dueling, William Hunter, typically argued in 1792, that the confirmed duelist was no noble figure but rather, like the confirmed criminal, a bullying savage:

> The systematic duellist is one of those monsters, whom Nature, in her wrath, now and then produces, in order to exhibit the height of human profligacy. He is a wretch, without shame, without morality, without religion; in whose breast every degrading passion is constantly in action, and propelling him to the vilest and most nefarious purposes.[1]

The resurgence of dueling during the militaristic era of the Napoleonic wars, like the attraction to it of young, socially ambitious middle-class men,[2]

---

[1] William Hunter, *An Essay on Dueling* (London, 1792), p. 36.
[2] See Anthony Simpson, "Dandelions on the Field of Honor: Dueling, the Middle Classes, and the Law in Nineteenth-Century England," *Criminal Justice History 9* (1988), 99–155.

seemed to give substance to the specter of the contagiousness of savagery and the precariousness of civilization; such vices were not going to wither away of their own accord. Finally, in 1842 an Evangelically-colored association for the suppression of dueling, numbering distinguished aristocrats, military officers and M.P.s among the members of its steering committee, was founded. The following year a notorious prosecution for murder placed the institution in the dock of public opinion, and shortly thereafter the military code was amended, making severe the penalties for military men caught dueling. The last publicly recorded duel in England took place in 1852.[3]

By this time, similar sentiments and arguments were deployed against corporal and capital punishment. Already the late eighteenth century saw the pillory – where the criminal was subject to unpredictable and uncontrollable amounts of popular violence – falling into disuse. Moreover in the last decade of the century a notable decline took place in public whippings, at least in the Home Counties.[4] These practical changes, however, did not prevent a movement for national reform from arising. In the following decades the use of publicly inflicted bodily punishments, in and out of the armed forces, emerged as a national political issue.

The deepest objection to flogging or hanging was not to the suffering inflicted upon the convicted offender, but rather to the effects on those inflicting and watching the punishment. Public violence, corporal or capital – like the violence of the duel – was increasingly perceived to be working against the civilizing process, worsening popular character by legitimizing the open expression of dangerous passions. Whatever the public view of the recipient of such punishment, its effect was deleterious: if hostile, the punishment roused deep feelings of gratification at the sufferings of others; if sympathetic, it weakened the moral authority of the law and encouraged popular desires for revenge. The whipping post and especially the gallows, by their pornographic spectacle of violence, were seen as stimulating rather than subduing the passions, disordering the minds of spectators and calling forth just such scenes of saturnalia as would confirm the fears of character reformers. The American Benjamin Rush claimed that public physical punishments spread violence through society: "[H]as not every prison door that has been opened, to conduct criminals to public shame and punishment, unlocked, at the same time, the bars of moral obligations upon the minds of ten times the number of

---

[3] See Robert Baldick, *The Duel* (London: Chapman and Hall, 1965).

[4] J. M. Beattie, *Crime and the Courts in England 1660–1800* (Princeton: Princeton University Press, 1986), pp. 614–16. Beattie noted the rise from midcentury of criticism of "a punishment that encouraged the fury of the crowd and allowed them in effect to impose on the prisoner a sentence the law had not intended." [p. 614.]

people?"[5] As Dickens later remarked, "[I]t is bad for a people to be familiarised with such punishments.... The whip is a very contagious kind of thing, and difficult to confine within one set of bounds."[6] The use of the pillory was seriously restricted by statute in 1816 and abolished in 1837. In 1820, an act restricted corporal punishment to men. The use of public whipping steadily diminished until it was abolished in 1862, while the remaining corporal punishment was for the first time subjected to specific statutory regulations governing the number of strokes that could be ordered and the manner of their infliction.[7]

The leading reformer Samuel Romilly declared in 1813, that a public execution, even more than public floggings, was "a disgusting spectacle ... *shocking* to humanity."[8] Cruelty in the law, it was argued, encouraged cruelty in people. "We are," Romilly declared, "so constituted by nature, that such spectacles of horror are seldom beheld by any person with impunity." Public execution was a sentence whose "inevitable tendency" was "to corrupt and harden the heart." For the truth of this charge, he appealed to his fellow members of Parliament: "Is there a father in this assembly who would wish his child to be present at such a sad scene?"[9] If an upper-class child could not

---

[5] *An Enquiry into the Effects of Public Punishments Upon Criminals, and Upon Society* (Philadelphia, 1787), pp. 8–9.

[6] "Lying Awake," *Household Words*, Oct. 30, 1852, quoted in Philip Collins, *Dickens and Crime* (New York: St. Martin's Press, 1962), p. 255. Similarly, some criminal law reformers who had themselves experienced inflicting corporal punishment, as parents or teachers upon children, feared the dangerous attractions they had felt in themselves. The American reformer Cyrus Peirce, who had as a young schoolmaster regularly beaten his pupils, turned into a campaigner against all forms of beating; he "could not," he later privately admitted, "administer corporal punishment without awakening or yielding to emotions of a doubtful character." [Quoted in Myra Glenn, *Campaigns Against Corporal Punishment: Prisoners, Sailors Women, and Children in Antebellum America* (Albany, N.Y.: State University of New York Press, 1984), p. 21.]

[7] Sir Leon Radzinowicz and Roger Hood, *A History of English Criminal Law and Its Administration from 1750, Vol. 5: The Emergence of Penal Policy* (London: Stevens and Sons, 1986), p. 689. Military flogging, traditionally very harsh, began to diminish in the 1820s and fell rapidly in the 1830s [John Dinwiddy, "The Early Nineteenth-Century Campaign Against Flogging in the Army," *English Historical Review* 97 (1982), 308–31]. In the ancient public schools the frequency and public character of flogging began in the 1830s to abate. At Eton, John Chandos has noted, "gradually flogging ceased to be a literally public entertainment. From crowding into the library to witness the fun, intending spectators had to view or hear the proceedings from outside the door. Then, from about the 1860s, the door was shut and execution became a private event." [*Boys Together: English Public Schools 1800–1864* (London: Hutchinson, 1984), p. 245.]

[8] *1 PD 27*, c. 102–3, 179 (Nov. 22, 1813). On the reformist assault upon the gallows, see Randall McGowen, "A Powerful Sympathy: Terror, the Prison, and Humanitarian Reform in Early Nineteenth Century Britain," *Journal of British Studies* 25 (1986), 312–34.

[9] *1 PD 27*, c. 108.

but be moved in the wrong direction by such an overpowering spectacle, many feared its effect upon the lower classes, often likened to children in the relative weakness of their reasoning powers and their impressionability by sensual stimuli.

Executions were enormously popular events, a fact that deeply frightened reformers.[10] The Quaker J. J. Gurney described in 1816 his reaction to the execution of three men. He reported seeing "vast flocks of people" of all ages crowding along the streets toward the execution. He was pained at the thought that they seemed to possess "feelings of a pleasurable nature" for an event that he found to be "the most dreadful and melancholy." To Gurney, the most frightening aspect of this response was the eclipse of human sympathy by "a feeling of pleasure in the excitement itself." Thus, the "spectacle" of the gallows only strengthened "criminality in its roots!"[11] Reformers repeatedly denounced "the love of excitement" nourished by the gallows.[12] Even conservatives were becoming uneasy about this; the highly respectable *Morning Post* noted unhappily (though while recounting the day's events at considerable length) that most of the more than twelve thousand spectators present in 1845 at the execution of William Howell were "females and boys."[13]

What were the crowds so fascinated by? Reformers hammered on this psychological question. One American argued in 1833:

> If the sight of one capital execution creates an inhuman taste to behold another; if a curiosity, satisfied at first with terror, increases with its grati-fication, and becomes a passion by indulgence, we ought to be extremely careful how ... we lay the foundation for a depravity the more to be dreaded, because, in our government, popular opinion must have the greatest influence ... and this vitiated taste would soon be discovered in the decisions of our courts and the verdicts of our juries.[14]

Another American, a novelist, observed at the same time that:

---

[10] On the popularity of public hangings down to their abolition, see J. M. Golby and A. W. Purdue, *The Civilization of the Crowd: Popular Culture in England 1750–1900* (London: Batsford, 1984), p. 83, and Thomas Laquer, "Crowds, Carnival and the State in English Executions, 1604–1868," in A. L. Beier, David Cannadine, and James M. Rosenheim, eds., *The First Modern Society: Essays in English History in Honor of Lawrence Stone* (Cambridge: Cambridge University Press, 1989), pp. 305–55.

[11] *Memoirs of Joseph John Gurney* (1849), quoted in McGowen, "Sympathy," 319.

[12] Basil Montagu, *Thoughts Upon the Abolition of the Punishment of Death in Cases of Bankruptcy* (1821), quoted in McGowen, "Sympathy," 313.

[13] *Morning Post*, Jan. 27, 1845, p. 8.

[14] Edward Livingston, *A System of Penal Law, for the State of Louisiana* ... (1833), p. 27, quoted in David Brion Davis, *Homicide in American Fiction 1798–1860* (Ithaca: Cornell University Press, 1975), pp. 294–5.

the same motive which provokes this desire in the spectator, is the parent, to a certain extent, of the very crime which has led to the exhibition. It is the morbid appetite, which sometimes grows to madness – the creature of unregulated passions, ill-judged direction, and sometimes, even of the laws and usages of society itself, which is so much interested in the promotion of characteristics the very reverse.[15]

Some of the leading English writers of the age joined the assault. Perhaps the most enduring piece of reportage of the time on public execution was that by W. M. Thackeray, who in his early years at Charterhouse School had been abused by both other boys and the headmaster. In his 1840 essay, "Going to See a Man Hanged" – the victim being the valet Courvoisier, being hanged for the murder of his master, Lord William Russell – Thackeray gave classic expression to a revulsion not so much at the possible injustice done to the prisoner, but at the psychological effect on the spectators. He described with the power of a great novelist the "hideous debauchery" of a public hanging in terms of a pornographic exhibition:

> The sight has left on my mind an extraordinary feeling of terror and shame. It seems to me that I have been abetting an act of frightful wickedness and violence, performed by a set of men against one of their fellows; and I pray God that it may soon be out of the power of any man in England to witness such a hideous and degrading sight. Forty thousand persons (say the Sheriffs), of all ranks and degrees – mechanics, gentlemen, pickpockets, members of both houses of Parliament, streetwalkers, newspaper-writers, gather together before Newgate at a very early hour; the most part of them give up their natural quiet night's rest, in order to partake of this hideous debauchery, which is more exciting than sleep, or than wine, or the last new ballet, or any other amusement they can have. Pickpocket and Peer each is tickled by the sight alike, and has that hidden lust after blood which influences our race.[16]

Here was a carnival, a public loss of control over the passions incited by government itself. Moreover, it was a pornographic invasion of the integrity of the body, carried out in public by the agents of the state. Such spectacles pandered to the worst instincts of human nature and identified government in the popular mind with willful violence. They worked directly against the aim of criminal justice reformers of promoting "civilization" by encouraging a general acceptance and internalization of an authority seen to be rational and

[15] W. G. Simms, *Guy Rivers* (1834), quoted in Davis, p. 223.
[16] "Going to See A Man Hanged," in *Works* (London: J. M. Dent, n.d.) *23*, pp. 106–7. Later, like Dickens and many other early Victorian opponents of hanging, Thackeray shifted to oppose only public executions, substantiating the suggestion here that the dominating motive for most opponents of hanging and whipping was the fear of psychological harm to spectators.

dispassionate. Only such an authority, itself restrained, could nurture self-mastery in the people.

Thackeray's fellow novelist, Dickens, also denounced "the frequent exhibition of this last dread punishment."[17] "He was haunted," Philip Collins has observed, "as much by the bestiality of the crowd as by the obscenity of hanging."[18] "I believe," Dickens wrote *The Times* about the execution of Mr. and Mrs. Manning in 1849,

> that a sight so inconceivably awful as the wickedness and levity of the immense crowd collected at that execution this morning could be imagined by no man, and could be presented in no heathen land under the sun. The horrors of the gibbet and of the crime which brought the wretched murderers to it faded in my mind before the atrocious bearing, looks, and language of the assembled spectators. When I came upon the scene at midnight, the *shrillness* of the cries and howls that were raised from time to time, denoting that they came from a concourse of boys and girls already assembled in the best places, made my blood run cold.... I am solemnly convinced that nothing that ingenuity could devise to be done in this city, in the same compass of time, could work such ruin as one public execution, and I stand astounded and appalled by the wickedness it exhibits. I do not believe that any community can prosper where such a scene of horror and demoralisation as was enacted this morning outside Horsemonger Lane Gaol is presented at the very doors of good citizens, and is passed by unknown or forgotten.[19]

In *Barnaby Rudge* (1841), Dickens had shown the extremes meeting, as Dennis, the public hangman, became a leading rioter. The bestial mob of the Gordon Riots was intertwined with and intimately related to the brutal, impulsive aristocratic state. His letter to *The Times* raised again this specter of the state positively nurturing moral disorder, of the licentious bonds between corrupt high and barbaric low.

The number of hangings fell sharply in the 1830s, and the movement against capital punishment steadily gained strength into the 1860s. In 1868, six years after the abolition of public whipping, the spectacle at the apex of traditional punishment, the public hanging, was ended (though executions continued undiminished in private).[20]

Transportation of convicts overseas, attracting less intense emotions than

---

[17] *Barnaby Rudge* (1841), Ch. 74.

[18] Collins, *Dickens and Crime*, p. 240.

[19] *The Times*, Nov. 14, 1849, quoted in Collins, 236–7.

[20] See Radzinowicz, *History of English Criminal Law and its Administration IV* (London: Stevens, 1968), pp. 343–53; David D. Cooper, *The Lesson of the Scaffold: The Public Execution Controversy in Victorian England* (London: Allen Lane, 1974).

flogging and hanging, nonetheless gradually became unpopular with reformers, and eventually with most of "respectable opinion," for many of the
same reasons as those punishments. Transportation was both lottery and spectacle. Like corporal and capital punishment, it was arbitrary and uncertain in
application, and at the same time, although it did not involve such dramatic
public corruption as floggings and hangings, it nonetheless was frequently
both brutal and brutalizing – with not only prisoners, but even more important, as with public corporal and capital punishments in England, the free
population looking on. Like the old penal regime at home, transportation
could be either too severe or too permissive, harsher than its subjects might
deserve or positively attractive, depending on the particular, unpredictable
circumstances of its administration and the personalities of its administrators.

The assignment system, whereby most transported convicts in Australia
were lent out to settlers, was denounced by the reformist Select Committee
chaired by Sir William Molesworth in 1837 as a "strange lottery" ranging between "extremes of comfort and misery." Drawing an analogy with the hated
arbitrariness of slavery, the report announced that "as the lot of the slave
depends upon the character of his master, so the condition of the convict
depends on the temper and disposition of the settler to whom he is assigned."[21]
While the arbitrary cruelties of bad masters reduced English justice to the
degraded level of slavery in the United States, good masters – and good fortune when one's sentence was up – posed a problem of their own, for they
could undermine transportation's deterrent function. Convict letters home
often sent word not only of tribulations but of good fortune and opportunities

---

[21] *Report from the Select Committee on Transportation* 1837, pp. 8, 19–21. [P.P. 1837–8,
Vol. 22.] This was a committee "of exceptional standing," as Radzinowicz and Hood put it
[p. 478], including among its members Lord John Russell, Sir George Grey, and Sir
Robert Peel. It was also a highly biased committee. On the system of transportation to
Australia, see Robert Hughes, *The Fatal Shore* (New York: Knopf, 1987); for the system
as viewed from Whitehall and Westminster, see Radzinowicz and Hood, pp. 465–89. Re-
cent Australian scholarship from A. G. L. Shaw, *Convicts and the Colonies* (Melbourne:
Melbourne University Press, 1968) to J. B. Hirst, *Convict Society and Its Enemies* (Sydney:
G. Allen & Unwin, 1983) and Michael Sturma, *Vice in a Vicious Society: Crime and
Convicts in Mid-Nineteenth Century New South Wales* (St. Lucia, London, and New York:
University of Queensland Press, 1983), effectively drawn upon by Hughes, has demonstrated how inaccurate was the Molesworth report's tendentious characterization of
Australian society as locked in a downward spiral of "viciousness." Sturma, for example,
showed that the committee's claim that New South Wales had an exceptionally high crime
rate was exaggerated. He concluded that a large part of the colony's contemporary reputation for criminality could be attributed to an obsession with respectability and a confusion of convict vices with what were in fact working-class mores. Such a massive
misreading suggests powerful domestic motives and concerns shaping early Victorian
images of the novel convict society run by Old Regime methods as necessarily
demoralizing.

in the new labor-hungry land; there were instances of prisoners receiving or hearing of such letters and subsequently petitioning to be transported. Such occurrences caused much middle- and upper-class concern. By the 1830s, complaints were becoming common of transportation's growing attractiveness to the criminal classes and even to the (as yet) honest poor. By no means, as Radzinowicz and Hood found it "surprising" to note, were these complaints only from hardliners.[22]

At the same time, while the "lottery" face of transportation was seen to be producing one sort of moral harm, its "spectacle" aspect seemed to be wreaking another sort, equally bad. Although transportation removed the sight of demoralizing punishment to the other side of the earth, there it worked its evils on convicts and free population alike with even less check than ever it had in England. Molesworth himself declared that in Australia

> [e]very kind and gentle feeling of human nature is constantly outraged by the perpetual spectacle of punishment and misery – by the frequent infliction of the lash – by the gangs of slaves in irons – by the horrid details of the penal settlements; till the heart of the [free] immigrant is gradually deadened to the sufferings of others. . . . The whole system of transportation violates the feelings of the adult, barbarizes the habits, and demoralizes the principles of the rising generation; and the result is, to use the expression of a public newspaper, "Sodom and Gomorrah."[23]

Moreover, the committee argued, the convict system's reliance upon physical punishments only confirmed the convict's existing enslavement to "animal indulgences." Such reliance "rendered him mentally incapable of looking beyond the present moment, and confined his ideas to the feelings of the next instant." Yet because it was "precisely this habit . . . of disregarding the distant consequences of their actions, which chiefly lead men into the commission of crimes," the existing system was counterproductive.[24]

The main characteristics of transportation, the committee concluded, were "inefficiency in deterring from crime, and remarkable efficiency . . . in still

---

[22] Radzinowicz and Hood, p. 474.

[23] Extract from Molesworth's notes on the Select Committee Report, quoted in Hughes, p. 494.

[24] *Report . . . on Transportation* 1837, pp. xxii–xxiii, Instead, the government of convicts should aim at "teaching them to look forward to the future and remote effects of their own conduct, and to be guided in their actions by their reasons, instead of merely by their animal instincts and desires" [p. xliv]. The committee consequently praised the suggestions of Captain Alexander Maconochie for maintaining discipline by a system of earned and forfeited marks that would determine the degree of remission of sentence and urged that it be given a trial. For Maconochie's views, and their circulation in England over the next several decades, see below.

further corrupting those who undergo the punishment."[25] Indeed, it painted a lurid – and inaccurate – picture of rapidly rising crime and vice in Australia and claimed to find there a progressive demoralization of both the bonded and the free inhabitants.[26] In 1838 assignment was abolished in favor of a more uniform and impersonal system characterized by progressive stages.[27] But even this new system failed to satisfy critics, and transportation itself began to be squeezed by the twofold pressure of rising colonial discontent and continued denunciation by reformers at home. The government backed away from transportation step by step, until in November 1867 – a few months before the last public hanging – the last convict ship departed English shores for western Australia.

By the 1860s, then, all the traditional penalties that had made up nearly the entire arsenal of Georgian criminal sentences – the pillory, the whipping post, the gallows, and the convict ship – were extinguished. All had come to appear demoralizing in their arbitrariness and their tendency to incite dangerous passions. In their place were being put new, more measured forms of secluded punishment that would calm rather than inflame.

Once the public character of the penalties was done away with, the movements against both corporal and capital punishment rapidly lost strength. Private bills to abolish hanging invariably failed and soon ceased. Even government-introduced measures to modify the law of murder so as to diminish the number liable to the gallows died in Parliament in 1879 and 1881. Executions were carried out at a remarkably constant rate of about fifteen per year from midcentury to World War I.[28] Whipping as a penalty actually revived after its public administration was prohibited in 1862, starting with the Carroters Act of the following year. This turn of events powerfully suggests that what had been most widely upsetting about these penalties (beyond the ranks of committed humanitarians) had not been so much the fact of infliction of bodily pain or death upon malefactors, but its visibility and the psychological consequences that were felt to flow from that act of witness. Once out of sight, such penalties fell out of mind: corporal punishment was inflicted for a variety of offences until 1948;[29] capital punishment continued until 1965.

Similarly, of course, the ending of transportation purposefully did not lessen either the severity or the duration of the penal experience. The new

---

[25] *ibid.*, pp. xxii–xxiii.

[26] See *ibid.*, p. xxxiii.

[27] See Radzinowicz and Hood, p. 470.

[28] Annual criminal statistics. On the subsiding of the movements against corporal and capital punishment and the continued use of the penalties, see Radzinowicz and Hood, Chs. 20–21.

[29] See Radzinowicz and Hood, pp. 692–719.

sentence of penal servitude replaced periods of bondage in Australia with equivalent or longer periods of incarceration in England. These sentences, however, like private whippings and hangings, carried different meanings and associations than those they replaced. In the discourse surrounding these practices, we may find a fresh path into some distinctively mid-Victorian preoccupations.

A new language of punishment: reading the Victorian penal system

What the Whigs of the 1830s had begun, the Whig-Liberals of the 1860s brought to completion, closing the book on all the chief forms of pre-Victorian punishment. A few months after the departure of the last convict transport, the last public execution took place, that of the Fenian, Michael Barrett, implicated in the Clerkenwell explosion that had killed twelve persons. The reporter for *The Times* at Barrett's hanging expressed gratitude for deliverance from this spectacle. "Most assuredly," he wrote, "the sight of public executions to those who have to witness them is as disgusting as it must be demoralizing, even to all the hordes of thieves and prostitutes it draws together."[30] So too the sight of public floggings; six years earlier, the administration of corporal punishment in public had been prohibited.

What replaced the comparatively open Hanoverian mode of penality was the new closed regime of reformed prisons. Those who were hanged or whipped were now so treated behind prison walls; those who would have been shipped overseas or publicly punished and then released were now incarcerated. Existing prisons lost their comparatively open character, as the high degree of access of the public to them, and even of their inmates to the outer world, was removed.[31] Prison walls came for the first time to mark a clear divide between criminality and lawful society.

Although they exaggerated the thoroughness of the transformation and read its meaning in a too narrowly political fashion,[32] Michel Foucault and Michael Ignatieff were right to direct attention to this fundamental shift. In a

---

[30] *The Times*, May 27, 1868, p. 6.

[31] See Michael Ignatieff, *A Just Measure of Pain: The Penitentiary in the Industrial Revolution 1750–1850* (New York: Pantheon, 1978); Margaret DeLacy, *Prison Reform in Lancashire, 1700–1850: A Study in Local Administration* (Stanford: Stanford University Press, 1986); and Robin Evans, *The Fabrication of Virtue: English Prison Architecture 1750–1840* (Cambridge: Cambridge University Press, 1982).

[32] As DeLacy and others have demonstrated and as Ignatieff himself has partially acknowledged. [See M. Ignatieff, "State, Civil Society, and Total Institutions: A Critique of Recent Social Histories of Punishment," *Crime and Justice 3* (1981).]

more gradual and less complete manner than they suggested, the focus of punishment did move, in Britain as in France and the United States, from the public arena to a private sphere and from direct assault upon, or removal of, the body of the criminal to a new focus on restructuring his environment and reorienting his mind. However, this profound alteration in the treatment of the criminal bespoke more than an extension of state power or an establishment of bourgeois class interests. The new modes of punishment were bourgeois or capitalist in both a wider and a narrower sense than that argued by revisionists. Narrower, in that it is stretching the common usage of the term to the snapping point to see modes of punishment as constituting a strategy for domination; but wider in that they can reasonably be read – like the new forms and interpretations of law – as encoding and representing distinctive modes of constructing social reality, of envisaging human nature and social priorities – and the tensions and dilemmas that these modes carried with them – that had gained plausibility and force through the social transformations of the first half of the nineteenth century.

In the rising dissatisfaction with the modes of punishment inherited from the eighteenth century lay certain widely shared conceptions of the penal task. All but the most extreme participants in the fierce debates that raged between reformationists and punishers and between religious and secular approaches to the treatment of criminals drew upon the common moral vocabulary of perpetual struggle with impulse and the project of character building. The mode of punishment that seemed best suited to advance this project, among convicted criminals and for society in general, was the prison. From penalties of either public violence and humiliation or else banishment, reformers and most practical men turned toward a reliance on imprisonment within Britain in uniform disciplinary institutions isolated from the outside world. Already possessing a long history,[33] the prison was to prove a suitable instrument for the new purposes with which punishment was being imbued. The question of what specific form prison discipline should take proved highly contentious, leading to polemical battles between rival systems – first separate versus silent and later the Irish, with its series of graduations versus the more uniform English – but all these disputes presupposed certain shared concerns.

First of all, imprisonment, more than any other method, promised to be much more amenable to the felt need for certainty and uniformity in punishment. Terms of imprisonment could be allotted with arithmetical precision, and the conditions under which they were spent could be precisely calculated and controlled. At least potentially, prison sentences could be uniform, proportionate to moral guilt, and certain. Prisons themselves were to be run in a

[33] See Christopher Harding, Bill Hines, Richard Ireland, and Philip Rawlings, *Imprisonment in England and Wales: A Concise History* (London: Croom Helm, 1985).

rational, rule-governed manner. As in reformed policing and trial, predictable and uniformly applied rules were to circumscribe the scope of personal spontaneity. At the same time, imprisonment would privatize punishment, withdrawing it from public gaze, and abolish the irregularity of life on hulks and in penal colonies, which had entrenched the existing corruption of felons and spread it to others. Once rationalized and privatized, punishment could foster reform, both among prisoners and in society at large. Prison would become a school of moral discipline, that is, a training ground for, and a social representation of, the overcoming of immediate impulses and passions and the reconstruction of character.

From lottery to certainty

Perhaps the most persistent motor pushing Victorian penal policy was the imperative to remove elements of uncertainty and variability from punishment. This "fetish of uniformity,"[34] as the Webbs termed it, was triggered neither by the "pressure of circumstances," as historians of the pragmatic school have assumed, nor a misguided, even perverse, Gradgrindian obsession (as the Webbs saw it), nor even an inevitable corollary (as Radzinowicz believed) of belief in classical criminological tenets of universal free will and individual responsibility.[35] Much of this motor's power was drawn from psychic and social sources that were in a sense beneath both practicality and rationality, sources that must be understood rather than ignored or condescended to. Variety and uncertainty in penal conditions were perceived as impractical or unjust in an altered ideological climate that was coming to equate legitimacy with equality and morality with predictability. On the one hand, as formal social distinctions were losing their authority, variation in treatment for similar acts was coming to seem unfair and oppressive. On the other hand, if the uncontrolled vagaries of personal passions were feared, if moral order required conquest of impulse – if, in short, consequentialism were to become a psychic reality rather than only a moral philosophy – the future had to be made as foreseeable as possible. In particular, negative consequences had to follow as inexorably from antisocial acts as could be arranged. There was little point in reducing the uncertainties in apprehension, trial, and sentencing if disposal thereafter were to continue to be random. To produce the effect now sought on criminal and public character, sentences had to be carried out, and uniformly from jail to jail. In the early decades of the century, with the historical

[34] *English Prisons Under Local Government* (London: Longmans, 1922 [1963 ed.]), p. 204.
[35] See Radzinowicz, *Ideology and Crime* (New York: Columbia University Press, 1966), pp. 20–28.

inheritance of a heterogeneous array of local and county jails and convict hulks, no two quite alike, this was hardly the case. Even within a single jail, experience varied enormously and often unpredictably. Indeed, as John Bender has put it, "randomness was one of the rules in the old prisons."[36]

More than a mere corollary of uniformity, impersonality was a central premise – and promise – of such policies. Uniformity would banish personal vagaries from criminal justice. Penal reformers of all shades concurred in seeking less impulsive forms of punishment. The late Georgian Evangelical magistrate reformers John Howard and Sir George Onesiphorus Paul had sought to replace, in Paul's phrases, the "unregulated discretion" of the Hanoverian jails with "government by rule."[37] From the 1780s, one prison after another adopted fixed rules,[38] many of which were directed at gaolers.[39] After 1839, personal relations, whether friendly or hostile, between prisoners and staff were reduced to a minimum; warders were forbidden to talk to prisoners (other than to give orders) or to get closer than six feet to them. Nor were even warders to talk among themselves.[40] Like prisoners, prison staff members were to be constrained by new institutional rules. A new, self-disciplining character ideal was set for them:

> The humanity of the gaoler [Paul urged] should rather be the result of coldness of character than the effect of a quick sensibility.... He should be endowed with a patience which obstinacy the most pertinacious could not overcome; a sense of order which is method, rather mechanical than reflective.[41]

Bentham similarly sought to remove personality from punishment to the point of envisaging a whipping machine, a rotary flail made of canes and

---

[36] John Bender, *Imagining the Penitentiary: Fiction and the Architecture and Mind in Eighteenth-Century England* (Chicago: University of Chicago Press, 1987), p. 27.

[37] Paul, *An address to His Majesty's Justices of the Peace* ... (1809), quoted in Ignatieff, p. 77.

[38] On the replacement of discretion by rules, see Ignatieff, p. 77; Sean McConville, *A History of English Prison Administration, Vol. 1: 1750–1877* (London: Routledge, 1981), Ch. 4; DeLacy, Ch. 4.

[39] Prison staff members were ever more important, as the once large role of prisoners in running the gaols was steadily reduced, culminating in the prohibition in 1839 of any use of prisoners in the administration of prison discipline.

[40] See Philip Priestley, *Victorian Prison Lives: English Prison Biography 1830–1914* (London: Methuen, 1985), pp. 255–6, passim.

[41] Paul, *Considerations on the Defects of Prisons* (1784), p. 54, quoted in Ignatieff, 104. Reverend Daniel Nihil praised the separate system that, "by taking way the danger of collision [between warders and prisoners]," reduced the need for fear-inducing warders and was thus "calculated to raise up a new class of prison officers, both men and women, whose chief qualifications will be rather of a moral than of a physical order" [*Prison Discipline in its Relations to Society and Individuals* (London: Hatchard, 1839), p. 63.]

whalebone, which could be made to lash the backs of each offender with the same unvarying force to a preset number of strokes.[42] As Michael Ignatieff observed, "in his conception of pain ... what was rational was impersonal, and what was impersonal was humane."[43]

By the time prison reorganization got under way on a national level, such assumptions, alien to the Old Regime, had become ingrained. Power was now generally seen as most legitimate and most effective when least personal, most humane when least human. As in the courtroom and the police (and, indeed, the self-acting New Poor Law), the element of personality was in retreat in the penal world. Uniformity – which one scholar has called "an accepted axiom for all [early- and mid-Victorian] reformers,"[44] began to be brought to the realm of punishment by the same Whig government that was seeking both to introduce greater uniformity and to restrict the sway of personal discretion across a wide array of English institutions, from elections to welfare. The Prisons Act of 1835 – "An Act for effecting great Uniformity of Practice in the Government of the Several Prisons in England and Wales" – created the position of prison inspectors to bridge the gap between uniform central precept and varying local practice and set them to work to reduce the enormous differences from one jail to another.[45]

The senior prison inspectors, William Crawford and Whitworth Russell, in their influential reports between 1836 and 1846, insisted in a variety of ways that, as Sean McConville has put it, "prison management approached perfection in the same measure as it succeeded in eliminating the human element."[46] These urgings stemmed not from inhumanity, but from a deep distrust of human nature; these prison inspectors feared all discretionary power and sought to circumscribe and delimit it as far as possible. They insisted that discipline must not be influenced, either toward strictness or lenity, by the character of

---

[42] "Principles of Penal Law: Part II: Rationale of Punishment" [1830], *Works of Jeremy Bentham* (Edinburgh: William Tait, 1834), p. 415.

[43] *Just Measure*, p. 76.

[44] M. Heather Tomlinson, who thus found it "impossible to identify one person as being responsible for the policy of [penal] uniformity." ["Victorian Prisons: Adminstration and Architecture 1835–1877," unpublished Ph. D. thesis, University of London, 1975, p. 65.]

[45] The most thorough account of the inspectorate is S. G. Frouxides, "The English Prison Inspectorate 1837–1877," unpublished Ph. D. thesis, University of London, 1983.

[46] McConville, p. 246. Crawford and Russell set the pace, for although all five regional inspectorates were formally equal, the Home District (to which they were appointed) was in practice more prestigious and influential. Of course, their view was not universally agreed with: The Unitarian radical inspector, Frederic Hill, continued to insist, at the cost of much friction with other inspectors and the Home Office, that the ability and judgment of prison managers outweighed questions of prison architecture or rules. [Frederic Hill, *Frederic Hill: An Autobiography of Fifty Years in Times of Reform* (London: Bentley & Son, 1894), p. 182]. One can, however, say that in this era greater stress than before or after was laid on architecture and rules, even by men like Hill.

the persons by whom it was administered. A good penal system, they argued in 1838, possessed the "capacity of being administered with *exact uniformity* in every prison, unaffected by the diversity of character and disposition which must be expected in the keepers and subordinate officers of the various establishments."[47] Uniformity was of course an ideal as Benthamite as Evangelical and not confined to adherents of the separate system like Crawford and Russell. Opponents of separation did not disagree with the need for less variation and less personalism in punishment. Even the Radical inspector Frederic Hill, who looked somewhat askance at the senior inspectors' religious zeal, and expressed concern about too prolonged solitude, tirelessly pressed local authorities and his Whitehall superiors for greater legal certainty and penal uniformity.[48]

Change of government from Whig to Tory did not slow the push for uniformity. In 1843, Home Secretary Sir James Graham circularized the magistrates with a list of no fewer than 195 rules drawn up by the inspectors with the aim, as he put it, of introducing "consistency and the utmost practicable uniformity into the regulation of different prisons."[49] Yet even with the generally energetic inspectors at work, the goal seemed ever to recede. In 1849 Lord Brougham complained in Parliament that

> There are now no two gaols in England where the tried and untried, the juvenile and the adult offenders, where the prisoners under sentence of transportation for felony and the prisoners under sentence of imprisonment for misdemeanour, were not treated, in most essential particulars, with perfect diversity.[50]

As a result, Brougham complained, a judge did not know what punishment he inflicted or the community what penalty was administered. Each case was always different.

If changes in government mattered little, neither did swings in public temper. While public sentiment toward lawbreakers hardened as the ending of transportation drew near, little serious thought was given to reappraising the Hanoverian modes of dealing with offenders so scorned by the previous generation of reformers. The members of the Grey Committee on Prison Discipline

[47] Quoted in McConville, p. 246, n. 90.

[48] On Hill, see David Roberts, *Vicorian Origins of the British Welfare State* (New Haven, Conn.: Yale University Press, 1968), esp. p. 182, and Deborah Gorham, "Victorian Reform as a Family Business: the Hill Family," in *The Victorian Family*, ed. Anthony Wohl (New York: St. Martin's Press, 1978). Hill's interests and activities, like those of his even more influential brothers, were wide, going beyond the prisons to embrace education, poor law administration and industrial relations.

[49] Quoted in Frouxides, p. 260.

[50] 3 PD 106 (July 6, 1849), 1367.

(1850), striking a rather tougher tone, made no suggestions to reverse or even slow the trend to uniformity. The committee divided over the rival systems of separation versus silent association, but agreed on urging the maximum possible uniformity. They saw their task as carrying on the intent of their predecessors, the Select Committees of 1822 and 1835, in seeking to establish such a uniform system of prison discipline "as would ensure the sentences of the Courts of Justice being strictly carried into effect, and which would at the same time tend to improve the morals of convicted offenders."[51] They recommended still more uniformity in the joint interests of deterrence and reformation.[52]

By midcentury, uniformity "had become the watch-word for prison administrators at all levels. . . . No aspect of prison administration was to escape the imposition of the principle of uniformity, even if in practice, the results were sometimes disappointing."[53] Indeed, as we have seen, the chief point of domestic complaint about the long-established and arguably highly successful policy of transporting felons overseas was not its systemic cruelty or inattention to reformation, but its unpredictability. By 1856, Major-General Joshua Jebb, director of Convict Prisons, could assure former Colonial Secretary Earl Grey that the new system of penal servitude – incarceration in new national prisons that combined separation and associated labor – promised to provide "a more certain and deterring punishment" than transportation, while being "at the same time . . . more efficacious and economical."[54] Throughout the early and mid-Victorian years, particular penal policies – hanging, transportation, remissions of sentence – were rarely supported or attacked without reference to their supposed psychological effects on prisoners and the public. In particular, government policies were almost always justified in terms of advancing the clarity, consistency, and certainty of punishment.[55] This almost universally accepted aim underpinned the growth of central government through the century, and the chief practical means of reducing variation between and within prisons was by increasing the discretionary power of the Home Office, which could then act more effectively in reining in subordinate and local officials.[56] Sir George Grey, home secretary for most of the years be-

[51] *Report of the Select Committee on Prison Discipline 1850*, p. iii. [PP 1850 v. 17.]

[52] *ibid.*, pp. iv–vi.

[53] Tomlinson, p. 66.

[54] (1856), quoted in McConville, p. 197.

[55] The debates on hanging are well-known; on transportation and remission in relation to these principles, see for example 3 PD 144 (1857), c.382–97; 3 PD 145 (1857) c. 140–6, 161–4, 347, 353, 360–2, 370–5.

[56] See McConville, pp. 197, 246–7, 375, 379. In any event, the appeal to increased certainty of punishment continued in official discourse at least as late as 1879: see the *Report of the Commissioners on the Penal Servitude Acts 1878–79*, p. xxix. [P.P. 1878–79, Vol. 57.]

tween the governments of Peel and Gladstone, characteristically justified his request in 1857 for a substantial increase in central administrative discretion in the treatment of convicts on the grounds that such discretion would "produce a greater certainty of punishment."[57]

Certainty and uniformity were seen as important not only for convicts, but also for local prisoners. The variety of conditions in local prisons, until their nationalization in 1877, was greater and therefore more difficult to erase than that of centrally run convict prisons. The 1863 recommendations of the Carnavon Committee on local prisons, and the parliamentary debate on them the following year, show an even further intensified insistence upon certainty and uniformity. The Tory M.P. Charles Adderley (author of the Security Against Violence Bill of that year, which imposed a sentence of whipping in addition to imprisonment for robberies with violence) strongly supported the recommendations, arguing, surprisingly for a Tory, against the claims of localism:

> Any gaol of any size which refused to carry out the [separate] system was injuring the prison discipline and the beneficial effects of confinement throughout the country, because such a refusal would only tend to foster in the minds of criminals that speculation on uncertainty and that gambling on crime which tended to paralyze the power of all law.[58]

With successive prison acts in 1864, 1865 and 1877, the principles of uniformity and predictability were enshrined throughout prison administration. A prison became an extremely, almost minutely, regulated environment, in which each inhabitant, prisoner, or staff member would know the rules, applicable to all, by which life was governed.[59] By 1885, the head of the now-unified prison system could observe that "a sentence of penal servitude is, in its main features, and so far as it concerns the punishment, applied on exactly the same system to every person subjected to it."[60] The Victorian transformation of the prison experience was complete.

Yet at the same time that uncertainty and variability were seen as the enemy of character formation, an important place remained for certain kinds of nonuniformity. Both administrators and ideologues found some structured,

---

[57] 3 PD 145 (May 15, 1857), c. 375.

[58] 3 PD 175 (June 20, 1864), c. 2057.

[59] One provision of the 1865 act was for each cell to contain an approved abstract of the many regulations and a copy of the dietary. A prisoner unable to read was to have these documents read to him within 24 hours of his admission. "There was no excuse," W. L. Burn has observed, "for anyone in any prison not to know his duties, rights and obligations." [*The Age of Equipoise: A Study of the Mid-Victorian Generation* (London: Allen and Unwin, 1964), p. 185.]

[60] Edmund Du Cane, *The Punishment and Prevention of Crime* (London: Macmillan, 1885), p. 155.

one might say uniform, variations in conditions and length of sentence desirable. These variations would be self-acting incentives – not to be attained by subjective criteria, but only by the actions of the prisoner, thus serving both as a valuable aid to discipline and smooth working of the institution and, as a teaching tool, inculcating the lesson that only personal effort and self-mastery bring benefits.[61] Proponents of such structured variation, whether administrators or reformers, took pains to reconcile it with the overriding principle of uniformity and certainty. What developed to fill the place of transportation was a system of progressive stages that incorporated administratively convenient and ideologically necessary rewards for good behavior within a penal system based, more than ever before or since, on the overriding importance of uniform, certain, and predictable punishment.

From public spectacle to private struggle

Along with becoming predictable, punishment was to be removed from the overly exciting public stage. The prison was also well suited for this aim. All reformers and most policymakers could agree, whatever their preferred system, that "promiscuous mingling" had to be done away with; condemnation of its evils, Philip Priestley has noted, "was so widespread as to constitute an almost unanimous expression of enlightened opinion in the early part of the nineteenth century."[62] Both the separate and the silent systems were

[61] The issue became a site of prolonged struggles within as well as without the administration. As transportation began to be replaced by penal servitude in Britain, Sir George Grey refused Sir Joshua Jebb's requests for a scale of uniform remissions for well-behaved prisoners. Jebb, struggling with massive convict discontent over the loss of the tickets of leave in Australia that transportation had provided, was primarily concerned with managing his new penal system. However, Grey both feared releasing men who would return to crime and was concerned – as a serious Evangelical – with the moral effects of punishment and thus insisted that remission was always a matter of mercy on the part of the Crown, "to be granted only in 'exceptional cases'" where "conduct distinguished [the prisoner] from others." [HO 22/10, H. Waddington to Jebb, Nov. 24, 1856.]

Although the Home Office did eventually issue a standardized scale of remission, to prevent the period of incarceration under the new sentences of penal servitude from being substantially longer than that under transportation, it continued to guard against what it saw as the tendencies of prison administrators to employ early release as a tool for minimizing inmate discontent, insisting that a prisoner was never *entitled* to remission, but had to *earn* it. [HO 22/13, Waddington to J. H. Burton, Dec. 4, 1862.] By its lights, the Home Office, with the judiciary, had to maintain the twin principles of deterrence and moralization, which prison administrators, with their immediate managerial concerns, were always in danger of neglecting. [HO 22/7, Fitzroy to Jebb, Oct. 19, 1853; HO 22/13, Waddington to Jebb, Dec. 27, 1862.]

[62] *Victorian Prison Lives*, p. 34.

praised for their isolating and calming of prisoners, although for this aim separation had the stronger case. Though he was on the whole fearful of the psychological harshness of prolonged separation, Mayhew agreed that in the rival silent system

> the mind of the prisoner is kept perpetually on the fret by the prohibition of speech, and it is drawn from the contemplation of his own conduct and degraded position, to the invention of devices for defeating his overseers, or for carrying on a clandestine communication with his fellow-prisoners, deriving no benefit meanwhile from the offices of religion, but rather converting such offices into an opportunity for eluding the vigilance of the warders, and being still farther depraved by frequent punishment for offences of a purely arbitrary character.[63]

The search for means of diminishing the distractions and disruptions of the distrusted personal element in punishment gave a new importance to architecture. Bentham's Panopticon is well known as the archetype of the prison as a carefully designed machine. More generally, proponents of separation like the Reverend Daniel Nihil, chaplain and governor of the first national penitentiary, Millbank, turned enthusiastically to physical design, arguing that correct prison design allowed the prison building itself to provide the necessary discipline and take the place of naked force, thus calming rather than inflaming its inmates. Walls would take the place of guards: "Let the hindrances to enjoyment consist of passive and inanimate obstacles, which cannot be made subject to hostility."[64] At the same time, architecture offered aid to solving the new dilemma of how to deter without demoralizing. As Nihil put it, the pains of imprisonment had to be "sufficient to imbue the mind of the community with an abiding consciousness that crime drags punishment after it; and if all the details of suffering be not exposed to public gaze, enough at least should be unveiled to set the imagination at work, and to awaken mysterious and salutory awe."[65] Architecture was especially suited to setting the imagination at work; the necessary pain of punishment, rather than being publicly displayed with the ensuing moral dangers, could be *represented* by gloomy, forbidding prison design, especially in exteriors evocative of bastilles. Thus could punishment be internalized and secluded from public passions and yet operate on the public imagination. In such ways, the combination of architecture and machinery, rules and careful staffing, would circumvent the uncertain human factor and produce justice, deterrence, and reformation. In particular,

---

[63] Henry Mayhew and John Binny, *Criminal Prisons of London* (London: Griffin, Bohn & Co., 1862), p. 101.

[64] Nihil, *Prison Discipline*, p. 59. On how architecture was made a significant part of penal policy, see Evans, *Fabrication of Virtue*.

[65] Nihil, p. 6.

just as punishment would be separated from vindictiveness, so reformation would be separated from sentimentality and be seen as a rational and calm process of strict moral education.

The painfulness of reformation

That pain was required for reformation was rarely questioned. J. F. Stephen had appealed to this moral axiom in his critique of John Stuart Mill's *On Liberty*: "There is hardly a habit which men in general regard as good which is not acquired by a series of more or less painful and laborious acts. The condition of human life is such that we must of necessity be restrained and compelled by circumstances in nearly every action of our lives."[66] Put this way, even Mill himself would agree, at least for the sort of person who was likely to otherwise become a criminal offender. As he had written Florence Nightingale a year after publishing *On Liberty* (1859), in objecting to her determinist arguments:

> retaliation from others for injuries consciously and intentionally done them is one of these natural consequences of ill doing, which you yourself hold to be the proper discipline both of the individual and of the race. With many minds, punishment is the only one of the natural consequences of guilt, which is capable of making any impression on them. In such cases, punishment is the sole means available for beginning the reformation of the criminal; and the fear of similar punishment is the only inducement which deters many really no better than himself from doing acts to others which would not only deprive them of their own happiness, but thwart all their attempts to do good to themselves and others.[67]

Whether they inclined to stress deterrence or reformation, almost all early and mid-Victorians thought the latter should be as painful as the former. The revulsion against public and violent infliction of physical suffering did not yet generally extend to suffering administered privately and, especially, indirectly, through isolation and deprivation. Indeed, pain had not yet become a pure evil; as Gladstone, a founder of the Church of England Penitentiary Society, reflected in 1830, "pain is not in its nature an evil in the proper sense, nor is it invariably attended with evil as a consequence." Indeed, the most common

---

[66] James Fitzjames Stephen, *Liberty, Equality, Fraternity* (London: Smith, Elder, & Co., 1873), p. 59.

[67] J. S. Mill, *Collected Works*, XV, eds. F. E. Mineka and D. N. Lindley (Toronto: University of Toronto Press, 1972), pp. 711–12 (Oct. 4, 1860). Again, speaking a few years later in Parliament in support of continuing the death penalty, Mill warned (in terms reminiscent of Stephen) against "bringing about . . . an enervation, an effeminacy, in the general mind of the country. . . ." 3 PD 191 (Apr. 21, 1868), c. 1051.

effect of pain was to "energize … feelings of self-mortification and self-sacrifice," the harbingers of dawning virtue.[68] Gladstone carried this valorization of pain with him through his career. In 1843, he wondered to himself whether it had been "sufficiently considered how far pain may become the ground of enjoyment. How far satisfaction and even an action delighting in pain may be a true experimental phenomenon of the human mind."[69] As late as 1894, he was insisting on a "kind of joy" to be found "in salutory pain."[70]

For most reformers, the most basic distinction was not between the infliction of pain and its lack, but between purposeful and useless suffering. The reformationist Prison Discipline Society, founded in 1817, had described a good prison as:

> a school of moral discipline, where incentives to vicious propensity …
> are superseded by abstinence, order and restraint; where by personal
> seclusion and judicious classification, the evils resulting from con-
> tamination are prevented – where the refractory are subdued by punish-
> ment, and the idle compelled to labour until industry becomes a habit.[71]

For Crawford and Russell, reformationists though they were, the indispensable object of a prison was "to deter, not only the criminal himself, but others, by the endurance of hardship and privation."[72] They strongly rejected charges of psychic harshness leveled against their favored separate system:

> We scruple not to avow that we regard this severity as one of the
> excellencies of the System. It is necessary to guard against that mistaken
> humanity which shrinks from the infliction of adequate punishment, is
> prone, in its sympathy with the sufferings of the guilty, to forget the evil
> effects of impurity on others, and that misplaced lenity to the criminal is
> cruelty to the honest portion of the community.[73]

In this vein Nihil insisted that not sternness but vindictive passions were inimical to reclamation of criminals: "It is not the just severity applied to guilt, but the harsh and vindictive spirit of the agents who inflict it – it is the employment of ferocity to quell ferocity, which jars with the aim of Christian reformation."[74] Thus, one chaplain could note that "no punishment is more

---

[68] Gladstone, "On the Mediation of Christ," written in 1830 but not printed until 1896; quoted in Boyd Hilton, "Gladstone's Theological Politics," in *High and Low Politics in Modern Britain*, eds. M. Bentley and J. Stevenson (Oxford: Clarendon Press, 1983), p. 35.
[69] Quoted in Hilton, *ibid.*, p. 52.
[70] "True and False Conceptions of the Atonement," *Nineteenth Century 36* (1894), 327.
[71] *Third Report of the Society for the Improvement of Prison Discipline* (1821), p. 54.
[72] *First Report of the Inspectors of Prisons (Home District)*, p. 24. [P.P. 1836, Vol. 25.]
[73] *Second Report of the Inspectors of Prisons (Home District)*, p. 17 [P.P. 1837, Vol. 32.]
[74] Nihil, p. 30.

poignant than the infliction of Christian truths, which, if plainly and power-fully applied will carry deadly war into the heart of their pride and sin."[75] And Dr. Daniel Ritchie – a naval surgeon, penal administrator, and enthusiast for reclaiming criminals – observed to his charges in 1852 that "as it is often necessary to inflict pain to remove or remedy a physical complaint, so is it sometimes required to restore the morally diseased to health." He explained to them that the offender must be forced by solitude, by deprivation, and by exhortation to appreciate the heinousness of his acts. In Ritchie's words, "That callous depravity which spreads a sea of ice over every ennobling senti-ment, and congeals into selfish apathy every hallowing sympathy, must be thawed, before the eye can see truly the mass of revolting impurities which lies hidden."[76] Or, as the Earl of Chichester, a member of the 1835 Select Com-mittee on Gaols and one of the commissioners appointed to superintend Pentonville Model Prison, stated his opinion less religiously in 1856:

> Human nature is so constituted that when a man has been long addicted to a life of crime or sensual indulgence it requires a severe affliction to force him to reflect – he must be providentially deprived of those sources of animal pleasure and excitement which have hitherto enabled him to silence his conscience and to shut out from his mind all thoughts of the future – there must be something external to afflict, to break down his spirit, some bodily suffering or distress of mind, before the still small voice will be heard and the man brought to himself.[77]

Nor was the theme of moral healing as a painful struggle with self limited to advocates of the separate system. Supporters of silent association often called upon the same ideal, claiming their system's superiority precisely in its pro-motion of self-struggle. Whereas isolation offered little bar to prisoners' abandoning all effort and collapsing into either mental breakdown or in-dolence, silent association stimulated exertion. The prison inspector W. J. Williams, who was often at odds with Crawford and Russell, noted the "superior quality" of the silent system to lie in "the placing men under trying circumstances where they are compelled to exercise, and may acquire, the valuable habits of self-control."[78] Thus, advocates of separation and silent association, much as they jousted with each other, shared a view of prison as a demanding school of moral discipline. Out of this common stock of values, the

[75] Chaplain of Bridewell, in *Gaol Reports 1844*, p. 494. [P.P. 1845, Vol. 37.]

[76] Daniel Ritchie, *The Voices of Our Exiles, or Stray Leaves from a Convict Ship* (Edinburgh: John Menzies, 1854), p. 262.

[77] Earl of Chichester to the home secretary, Sept. 23, 1856, quoted in Ignatieff, *Just Measure*, p. 199.

[78] *Third Report of the Inspectors of Prisons (Northern and Eastern District)*, p. 6. [P.P. 1837-8, Vol. 31.]

1850 Grey Committee, which contained advocates of each system, proposed with no sense of incompatibility both greater efforts at reformation and greater attention to prevention of any slackening of discipline or softening of the conditions within jails.[79]

Such images of disciplinary reform permeated even the proposals of perhaps the most humane of early Victorian penal administrators, Captain Alexander Maconochie. Maconochie, who has recently been called "the one and only inspired penal reformer to work in Australia throughout the whole history of transportation,"[80] had run the penal settlement of Norfolk Island with a humanity hitherto unheard of in that grim locale and had given much praised evidence to the Molesworth Committee. His aim, as he put it to the Grey Committee in 1850, was to "create virtue, as well as merely keeping the men from vice." However, he was sceptical of the separate system so strongly urged by many Evangelicals; in isolation, he was convinced, prisoners deteriorated. Maconochie looked for reformation not to religious conversion, but instead to the workings of a rational system of "exertion and self denial."[81] Such a system was to be created by replacing time sentences with sentences of a fixed amount of (associated) labor and by further making all needs in prison obtainable only by such labor.

Against simple "punishers," Maconochie sought to stimulate moral improvement by providing room for choice – "moral influences" rather than "direct coercion." Although, as he put it to the Home Office, "undue indulgence is not thus contended for,"[82] "*unnecessary* restraint, regulation, degradation, or other source of gratuitous irritation" ought be eschewed. In his system, convicts were to "be induced to perform what is required of them, and to abstain from what is forbidden them, *in the first instance* by the loss or gain of Marks [which would purchase both material needs and time towards release], not by the use of direct force unless the method by Marks fails." The mark system, he argued, offered a realistic yet liberal approach to prison discipline:

> Instead of working on the fears of those subjected to it, it seeks to call out their manly exertion and emulation. Instead of unnecessarily depressing, it seeks to raise them. Instead of subjecting them to a minute discipline which leaves them nothing to think of but to obey, it desires to give them a sphere of free agency, even while in prison, which shall exercise their powers of thought and self-command against the hour of their discharge. It is thus not content with making them good prisoners (though this is

---

[79] *Report of the Select Committee on Prison Discipline 1850*, pp. iv–vi.
[80] Hughes, *The Fatal Shore*, pp. 488–9.
[81] *Select Committee on Prison Discipline 1850*, Q. 6551, 6532.
[82] "To that criminals have no right in any case and it is only to be rarely tolerated in peculiar circumstances."

also among its objects), but it desires still more to train them to be good free men.[83]

This humanitarian liberalism of Maconochie's has often been cited as a forerunner of milder twentieth-century approaches to criminal rehabilitation.[84] However, Maconochie's liberalism had a sterner side, which he shared with nearly all his contemporaries, one that did not eschew "purposeful" pain. Such pain, necessary and useful, was – and here he concurred with the advocates of separation – as far as possible not to be directly inflicted by human hands but built into the penal situation. Maconochie sought to create through his mark system a self-acting mechanism of punishments and rewards that would mimic the difficulties of ordinary life and in this way stimulate convict self-improvement. As he observed, "Adversity, the discipline of Providence in society, is not deteriorating, but the reverse – and if we study its forms there is little doubt but we may give our discipline the same character."[85]

Existing prisons, he complained, often provided better for inmates' physical wants than many of them had been used to in free life, while paying little attention to their moral needs, "regard for which need not wear any aspect of indulgence."[86] Instead, his system was based on:

> the inflexible principle of giving nothing for nothing.... No rations, or other supplies of any kind, whether of food, bedding, clothing, or even education or indulgences, to be given gratuitously, but all to be made exchangeable, at fixed rates, at the prisoners' own option, for marks previously earned; it being understood, at the same time, that only those shall count towards liberation which remain over and above all so exchanged; the prisoners being thus caused to depend for every necessary on their own good conduct; and their prison-offences to be in like manner, restrained by corresponding fines imposed according to the measures of each.[87]

Those who would not work, would not eat. Those who would work only to eat would get nothing else and would remain in prison for a long time, perhaps for life. The chief object of punishment thus was "*to reform by means of*

---

[83] HO 45/OS 1840, Maconochie to Le Marchant, Aug. 5, 1847.

[84] See, for example, Mike Selby, "Captain Alexander Machonochie RN, KH," *Prison Service Journal* n.s. no. 73 (Jan., 1989), 23–6.

[85] *Crime and Punishment: The Mark System* (London, 1846), p. 5. This tract was reprinted and more widely read in 1850 as *Principles of Punishment on which the Mark System is Advocated.*

[86] *ibid.*, p. 26.

[87] Maconochie quoted in Herbert Spencer, "Prison-Ethics," [1860], in Spencer, *Essays: Scientific, Political and Speculative*, Vol. 3 (London, 1891), p. 175.

severity . . . . The idea of punishment should be indissolubly allied with that of suffering." "What improves," he declared, is neither cruelty nor indulgence, but:

> a condition of adversity from which there is no escape but by continuous effort – which leaves the degree of that effort much in the individual's own power, but if he relaxes his suffering is deepened and prolonged, and it is only alleviated and shortened if he struggles manfully – which makes exertion necessary even to earn daily bread – and something more, prudence, self-command, voluntary economy, and the like, to recover prosperity.[88]

Maconochie was warmly embraced by Liberals and reformers, who were pleased to find a military officer concerned with prisoners' minds as well as bodies, with the possibilities for improving them and not merely keeping them in line.[89] None objected to his stress on struggle and adversity, on giving nothing for nothing, for it was the common coin of the era's liberalism. The vital distinction for most Maconochie's supporters was not between sternness and kindness, but between a severity that served a reformative purpose and a severity that was sterile.

One of them, Mary Carpenter, who established her reputation for the treatment of child offenders as children, drew a sharp line between child and adult criminals. For those past the age of majority, she urged a penal system of "well organized adversity" to "make [the prisoner] feel the consequences of his conduct." Essential to their reformation, she held, was "the penal element of suffering as the consequence of sin." Strict discipline was required to "enable the criminal to perceive the necessity for his punishment, and the amount of his guilt."[90]

Similarly, her fellow Unitarian, the Radical prison inspector Frederic Hill, a strong critic of purely punitive penal methods like the treadmill and generally of public capital and corporal punishment, assumed the need for painfulness of character reform and of struggle for lasting improvement – inside and outside prison walls. "In all cases," he observed to the 1850 Select

---

[88] *Crime and Punishment: The Mark System*, pp. 26, 43. Of course, this is not to deny the great differences, heatedly argued, between Liberals like Maconochie and conservatives who did not believe in the possibility of criminal reformation or who felt it should take a very subordinate place behind the need to terrorize and degrade criminals. This study bypasses the well-known debates between reformers and punishers, as it does the also important, if secondary, arguments between advocates of penal separation and silent association, in order to bring into relief neglected common ground.

[89] Maconochie, Dawn Roberts has noted, was "a much revered individual." "The Scandal of Birmingham Borough Gaol 1853: A Case for Penal Reform," *Journal of Legal History* 7 (1986), 332.

[90] *Our Convicts*, Vol. 1 (London, 1863) I, p. 102.

Committee, "it is quite necessary, in order to effect reformation, that the person to be acted upon should have received a great deal of pain in the process."[91] Like many other secular reformers, Hill supported Maconochie's view of the reformative benefits of steady adversity against both many religious enthusiasts' hopes for dramatic conversions of prisoners and the cynical disbelief of many hardened magistrates and prison officers in the possibility of rehabilitating criminals.[92]

The appeal of Maconochie's message of reformation through compelled "voluntary" labor reached beyond the ranks of those, like Carpenter and Hill, who were often criticized at the time as sentimentalists. The leading journalist William Hepworth Dixon[93] enthused in 1850, in a widely read survey of London prisons, that labor sentences would develop instead of deteriorate character:

> Not the least deplorable result of the present system is the absolute disregard for the value of time which it creates. Time becomes associated only with the idea of suffering and constraint. The criminal learns to regard it as a foe to be got rid of – not as a friend to be cherished. 'Time was made for slaves' – aye, and for prisoners too, he thinks. Soon he learns to hate it. Think of a man who for years has cultivated a habit of regarding time as an enemy to be avoided!
>
> How can time be murdered? Can it be murdered innocently? This is an important question. Let any one consider how *he* has ever killed a day – even an hour! According to present arrangement the criminal is placed in a position where he has nothing to do but stand aside – and watch the great stream flow past him. . . .
>
> The labour-sentence . . . would call out the more manly and hardy virtues. . . . A man has no power over the progress of time, but he has over the progress of work. In the one case he is a slave to a necessity outside of himself; in the other he is a free agent, with a task before him but freedom at the end. As he puts forth his energies, he feels that he is conquering his own freedom – and at the same time, whether he knows it or not, he is developing the virtues which will make him worthy of it. . . .

[91] *Report of the Select Committee on Prison Discipline 1850*, Q 1423.

[92] Hill, on the radical wing of prison administrators, looked forward to prisons becoming "schools of industry and morality." These "schools," or "moral hospitals," were to be highly structured, if not regimented, institutions, not unlike Florence Nightingale's model hospitals. Reformation would occur through the inculcation of moral order by a disciplined, rule-governed regime that centered on useful work. The prisoner-pupil's sentence would follow the course of a gradual approximation to the conditions of life in the society at large, from separation to association, from forced to paid labor, from infantlike helplessness to increasing control over his circumstances.

[93] Editor of the *Atheneaum*, 1853–69.

Such a discipline must be, in an eminent degree, healthy and invigorating. The individual subjected to it, is in a measure cast upon his own resources; he is required under it to act for himself; and if he have not yet acquired, will soon learn, the art of self-control. Under the present system, everything is done *for* the criminal. All responsibility is taken from him. He is unmanned, put into swaddling bands again, and done for, like an infant. He is made incapable of taking care of himself – with what results our gaol returns and tables of re-commitments only prove too fatally.[94]

In his own survey of prisons a few years later,[95] Mayhew followed Dixon's lead and lined up firmly behind Maconochie, arguing in particular against the purely punitive use of labor. As we have seen, work was crucial to Mayhew's social philosophy. It was in the treatment of work that he found existing penal methods most defective – "they one and all make labour a *punishment* to the criminal." Sentences of hard labour, whether separate or silent, "tend ... to confirm [the criminal] in his prejudice against regular labour." Yet, without a positive attitude toward work, the criminal would remain a criminal throughout life. To break this trap, personal benefit must be associated with proper work habits; criminals must be given a purpose to labor:

It is the presence of some such purpose that sets the more honest portion of the world working for the food of themselves and their families; and it is precisely because your true predatory and migratory criminal is *purposeless* and *objectless*, that he wanders through the country without any settled aim or end, now turning this way, now that, according to the mere impulse of the moment. Nor is it possible that he should be other than a criminal, the slave of his brute passions and propensities, loving liberty and hating control, and pursuing a roving rather than a settled life, until some honourable motive can be excited in his bosom.[96]

Mayhew thus urged that the prisoner's labor should be made the basis of his treatment, through a "purchase" system: all comforts above a punishment diet of bread and water[97] were "to be proportionate to the amount of labour done," preparing the prisoner for the world outside prison where, he assumed, reward was proportionate to effort.[98]

[94] William Hepworth Dixon, *The London Prisons* (London: Jackson & Walford, 1850), pp. 15–17.
[95] Although John Binny was listed as coauthor, Mayhew seems to have written the great bulk of it in 1856, with Binny completing it, adding accounts of several more prisons, in 1861–2. [Anne Humpherys, *Travels into the Poor Man's Country: The Work of Henry Mayhew* (Athens, Ga.: University of Georgia Press, 1977), pp. 115, 134.]
[96] *Criminal Prisons*, p. 108.
[97] In itself a practical compromising of Maconochie's purist "nothing for nothing."
[98] *Criminal Prisons*, pp. 302, 351–2.

Even within legal circles, which were generally resistant to schemes of reformation, the mark system had its strong proponents. One was the well-known barrister Joshua Williams, author of enormously successful books on the law of real property and of personal property and an influential voice in mid-Victorian discussions on the reform of property law.[99] Williams urged Maconochie's plan on his fellows as constituting the penal system most in harmony with everyday moral ideas. Its "great object" was "to place the criminal as far as possible in the same circumstances as those in which he would be placed in ordinary life." Since only God could see into the human heart,

> in judging of men generally there is but one rule for us, 'By their fruits ye shall know them.' It is the essence of this system, accordingly, to do nothing by recommendation, to take no heed of mere expressions of penitence ... [but] *open an account* against each criminal, to be gradually worked off by his own labour, and against which is to be set off, not only every punishment he may incur, but also every gratification in which he may be allowed to indulge. When this score is cleared off, however soon it may be, but never till then, though it may last the man's lifetime, the criminal is to be free.[100]

Charles Dickens was another hardnosed liberal impressed with Maconochie. Dickens befriended the captain very soon after the latter's return to England in 1846, and used his ideas as the basis for the discipline of Urania Cottage, the home for "fallen women" which Angela Burdett Coutts set up at Dickens's suggestion. "I do not know of any plan," Dickens wrote Miss Coutts in 1846, "so well conceived, or so firmly grounded in a knowledge of human nature, or so judiciously addressed to it, for observance in this place, as what is called Captain Maconochie's Mark System."[101] This system of *earned* betterment – as Dickens summarized it, "the principle of obliging the convict to some exercise of self-denial and resolution in every act of his prison life" – appealed to him as affording a practical path to the improvement of criminal character. It avoided both the destructive "tampering with the mind" he abhorred in separation and the "pampering" of bad men he detested in the proposals of unworldly chaplains. Although he felt Maconochie had a regrettable tendency to softness – "rigid silence [which Maconochie would dispense

---

[99] Williams's works on these subjects, written in 1845 and 1847, continued to be used well into the twentieth century; in the late 1840s and the 1850s he was active and influential in the discussion of schemes for reform of property law.

[100] Joshua Williams, "On the Union of the Mark System with Associated Labour in the Management of Criminals," *Papers Read Before the Juridical Society: 1855–1858* (London: Stevens & Norton, 1858), p. 134. [Read Dec. 3, 1855.]

[101] Quoted in Philip Collins, *Dickens and Crime*, p. 166. As Dickens's attitudes towards criminals hardened in the 1850s and 1860s, Maconochie's ideas probably held diminishing appeal for him; however, he never repudiated them.

with] we consider indispensable"[102] – Dickens found the mark system as a whole the only approach to dealing with adult criminals that, without damaging social morale, held any practical hope of rehabilitation.

Maconochie's vision of rational discipline exerted great appeal upon many other reformers, such as the influential solicitor for the City of London and Radical M. P., Charles Pearson. Pearson, an opponent of capital punishment and an advocate of juvenile reformatories, claimed a system of industrial prisons based on sentences of labor rather than time would not only support itself, relieving taxpayers of a growing burden, but would also "supply criminal offenders of all classes with motives and means to deliver themselves by their own industry and continuous good conduct from the consequences of their own crimes." Within the prison, a basic moral drama would be continually reenacted:

> Labour should be made to feed the appetite, or the appetite should be made to enforce the labour. Nine times out of ten the irregular indulgence of appetite will be found either the proximate or the remote cause both of the commission of crime and the suffering of punishment amongst our prison population. Appetite has been to the criminal outside of the prison both a tempter and a traitor; within the walls it should be made his teacher or his tormentor. The criminal should be practically taught to balance accounts between the organ of appetite and the organ of labour; the right hand of industry, long neglected and despised by the idle criminal, will then be taken into his confidence as the only friend that can save him in the hour of distress. . . . [It] shall be the instrument of his restoration to freedom, not by being put forth by fits and starts of exciting activity, but by constant and continuous exertion, cancelling hour by hour the sentence under which he is confined.[103]

[102] Quoted in Collins, p. 164.
[103] *What Is to Be Done with Our Criminals?* (London: A. Hall and Virtue, 1857), pp. 21, 26. Pearson had been making this argument since 1849, when he made a parliamentary speech that helped bring about the appointment of a Select Committee on Prison Discipline (the Grey committee). He also argued similarly to the National Association for the Promotion of Social Science: see "Labour and Appetite: The Basis of a Self-Supporting and Reformatory System of Prison Discipline," *Transactions N.A.P.S.S. 1858* (London, 1859), pp. 383–90. This image of the criminal as a person swept away by appetite was well entrenched by midcentury. As the later head of the prison system, Edmund Du Cane, remarked, "rather idleness and love of pleasure (which includes intemperance) are at the bottom of most of the misfortunes which lead a person into the ranks of the 'disinherited,' improvidence and mental or bodily incapacity bring others there. These became criminals, not from absolute want of necessaries of life, but because their desire for the gratification of their appetites, whatever they may be, is strong while their willingness to endure labour is weak; so that they set themselves to obtain the results of labour, in the only way it is possible to do without it, by stealing, or plundering of some sort." ["Review of Criminalite et Repression, Essai de Science Penale, par Adolphe Prins," *Law Quarterly Review* 11 (1986), 228.]

Although Maconochie's proposal raised insuperable legal and administrative objections, and thus was never tried in full, the rhetorical appeal of its themes of the power of work to reform character and of an impersonal mechanism to self-shape through struggle attracted wide attention inside as well as outside government, to moderates as well as to reformers. Despite his suspicion of remission, Home Secretary Grey held that "subject to certain restrictions . . . the principle of the Mark System may be usefully applied to convicts."[104] But a variety of obstacles arose. In particular, judges and politicians objected that it would remove the power to determine sentences from the courts and the legislature into the hands of prison administrators, while many of those administrators feared its divisive effects within the prisons.

Yet, though the labor sentence was never adopted, aspects of it were incorporated in the "Progressive Stages" system. Sir Walter Crofton, head of Irish convict prisons, proudly described in 1862 the Maconochie-like system of disciplinary stages he had recently instituted as one in which prisoners, through measured labor, "co-operated in their own amendment": "The convict is perpetually climbing a ladder the steps of which, difficult and toilsome at first, become easier and easier in ascent as self is overcome."[105] Two years later, a mark system was instituted in English convict prisons (together with a reduction in dietaries and gratuities), followed the next year by its partial introduction into local prisons as well. These reforms were meant to ensure that prisons were feared institutions where bleak and rigid discipline prevailed, but in which all prisoners could earn improved conditions and convicts early release also by "steady, hard labour, and the full performance of . . . allotted tasks."[106] M. D. Hill, a prominent Birmingham Unitarian magistrate, brother of the prison inspector, and the first Englishman to use the term "moral hospital," hailed this reform as simultaneously advancing reformation and discipline, producing harder-working and less mutinous prisoners. The great principle was at last established that any comfort and any remission of sentence would have to be *earned*.[107]

By 1873, Crofton could celebrate the triumph of his Irish methods in England; under the new administration of Edmund Du Cane, English prisons were at last approaching "that middle and wholesome condition where health and life are cared for, where all facilities for moral and religious improvement

---

[104] HO 13/93, Le Marchant to Hawes, Feb. 7, 1848.
[105] Quoted in Radzinowicz and Hood, p. 516.
[106] Standing Order no. 146: "Regulations — Mark System," July 22, 1864, quoted in McConville, p. 404.
[107] M. D. Hill, *On the Recent Improvements in the Treatment of Criminals* (London: Longmans, 1865).

are cared for, but where labour is exacted from all, and where a disagreeable sense of personal restraint and real punishment is brought home to each offender."[108] The penal system worked out by the time of nationalization of local prisons in 1877, though it never found a direct place for sentences of fixed amounts of labor, did thus embody the widely shared ideal of a uniformity blending motives of deterrence and reform, through the path of a strenuous ladder of labor to freedom and the restoration of character. As the prison commissioners noted with satisfaction in 1888, the system had proved itself a deterrent to criminal action while "provid[ing] that the rigour of the discipline to which each prisoner will be subjected shall be in some degree in his own hands."[109]

Dealing with special cases

Disability and the prison: medical officers and character building

As the penal system was gradually reconstructed, doctors were becoming important figures in prison life. Peel's reforms in the 1820s had included the appointment of surgeons or physicians to most gaols, and the centralizing Prisons Act of 1865, which sought to make conditions and discipline as uniform as possible, provided for the weekly medical inspection of all prisoners. The rising prominence of the prison doctor (which was paralleled by the decline of the chaplain) brought with it a potential alternative source of moral categorization; the doctor was invested with the power to declare a prisoner unfit, physically or mentally, for ordinary penal discipline and by so declaring present him with an immediate benefit, while removing him (at least temporarily) from the category of responsible moral agent. This power placed the medical officers in a difficult situation, potentially at odds with the prison administration. As one historian has critically put it.

> the doctors patrolled the narrow straits that separate hunger from starvation and punishment from outright cruelty, hauling aboard the life raft of their dispensations this drowning soul or that, and repelling, with brute force if necessary, the efforts of the others to climb to safety. In so doing, they lent to the work of preserving their employers' reputations whatever dignity and authority their emerging profession possessed – and lost it.[110]

[108] Quoted *ibid.*, p. 534; their attention fixed on the fierce rivalry during the 1860s between the uniform English and staged Irish system, Radzinowicz and Hood found this praise "most surprising."
[109] *Prison Commissioners' Report for 1887–88*, p. 9.
[110] Priestley, *Victorian Prison Lives*, p. 190.

Often, however, government officials found it necessary to caution medical officers against too readily excusing prisoners from embarkation for the voyage to penal colonies or from penal work or discipline.[111] Yet, although tension can be found, twentieth-century assumptions of an inherent and irreconcilable conflict between medicine and the criminal law are misleading in this era. While careerist interests sometimes may have led prison and convict ship doctors to compromise their medical judgment, their support of the system did not have to be at the expense of their professional outlook or personal values. Although the process of professionalization was eventually to draw the loyalties and ambitions of most prison doctors away from government administration, such a development still lay in the future. In the early and mid-Victorian years, as we have seen, professional medical discourse had not separated itself from common moral discourse and had not become significantly deterministic. Penal and medical discourse had many points of contact.

One such point was in the valuation of pain. The close association of character and health that we have noted encouraged a belief in pain's therapeutic benefits. If it was often thought good for the soul, it was also seen as frequently good for the body. Thus, the discovery of anesthesia produced hesitations within the medical profession as to how readily it should be used. As the vice president of the American Medical Association observed in 1849, "pain is curative – the actions of life are maintained by it – were it not for the stimulation induced by pain, surgical operations would more frequently be followed by dissolution."[112] Medical officers proceeding within this frame of discourse could accept a great deal of suffering in their charges without the crisis of conscience that would be provoked in the twentieth century.

In a similar fashion, early Victorian alienists had often seen a role for strict discipline and even deterrence in the treatment of the mentally disturbed. Insanity was often traced to indulgence in drink, irregular sex, and other vices; cures were seen as obtainable by systematic moral discipline. "Insane persons," Dr. Samuel Tuke, one of the founders of "moral treatment" of lunatics, had already argued in 1813, "generally possess a degree of control over their wayward propensities."[113] Even when asylum inmates were not cured (and the

---

[111] In 1850, for example, upon Home Office request Jebb cautioned all convict ship surgeons superintendent "against the rejection except on very strong grounds of convicts who have been reported by the medical officer of the convict service fit for embarkation" and required them "to make a specific report of the reasons" leading to any such rejection. [HO 121432, Jebb to Waddington, Nov. 4, 1850.] Such cautions recurred over the following decades.

[112] Quoted in Martin Pernick, *A Calculus of Suffering: Pain, Professionalism and Anesthesia in Nineteenth Century America* (New York: Columbia University Press, 1985), p. 44.

[113] *A Description of the [York] Retreat* [1813] (London: Dawsons of Pall Mall, 1964), p. 133.

difficulty of cure was by midcentury becoming depressingly clear), they could at least respond to the rewards and punishments of institutional rules, thus demonstrating a degree of rational responsibility. Criticizing an insanity finding in an 1843 trial, Dr. Thomas Mayo pointed out that it was well-established that "insane persons may be intimidated by example."[114] The opening of Broadmoor Criminal Lunatic Asylum in 1863 has usually been interpreted as marking official recognition of and provision for this category of offender apart from normal penal discipline. However, it also marked the end of the practice of removing all such offenders found by a jury to be insane out of the criminal justice system entirely. Out of concern for maintaining moral order in society, Dr. Mayo had urged such an institution years earlier. For many of the criminal lunatics confined in Bethlem Hospital, he had noted, "the enduring confinement is in itself a dreadful punishment. But in these cases there is a sad expenditure of unfruitful suffering; for the confinement being entirely and sedulously deprived of the character of a punishment operates unpreventively."[115]

If early and mid-Victorian prison doctors could reasonably see their disciplinary and healing roles as compatible, some could even take as enthusiastic an interest in moralizing their charges as did chaplains. Dr. Daniel Ritchie, surgeon superintendent of a convict ship in 1852, saw the voyage as a great moral opportunity. By his own lights a reformer and humanitarian, Ritchie deeply believed that nearly all criminals were reclaimable. To achieve this end he sought to organize the most effective possible moral regime for them during the voyage. Indeed, he later published extracts from a weekly ship journal, which he had established with contributions from convicts, to demonstrate how supposedly hardened felons could be improved. The journal is an illuminating document, less of "the moral and intellectual condition of our convict population," as Ritchie presented it, than of the mind of reformers like himself. While the modern mind questions how much of the uplifting contributions by the convicts was shaped by a natural desire to please those who controlled their daily life, one cannot doubt the sincerity of Ritchie himself in his own contributions.

"No error can be more erroneous," Ritchie argued in introducing this journal to the British public, "than that which considers all crime a natural sequence of a particular constitution, or mental formation." In particular, as a man of science he heaped scorn upon phrenological ideas, denying any perceptible physical difference between criminals and others. However, he agreed

[114] Quoted in Roger Smith, *Trial by Medicine: Insanity and Responsibility in Victorian Trials* (Edinburgh: Edinburgh University Press, 1981), p. 118.
[115] 1847, quoted in *Daniel McNaughten: His Trial and the Aftermath*, ed. Donald J. West and Alexander Walk (London: Hendley, 1977), p. 118.

there was mental difference, for in criminals the powers of reason and conscience were defective in one form or another. "Every convict could be
arranged," he noted, "in some degree, as the inmates of a lunatic asylum, according to their mental defects. There is this important difference, however,
that while a majority of the patients in the one case are incurable, in the other
they are nearly all susceptible of being restored to a correct frame of mind, by
restraint and education." And, indeed, to a great extent, he was convinced that
such had been accomplished on his voyage:

> By rendering every individual responsible for all the duties or obligations
> required of him; by establishing a system of order, regularity, obedience,
> cleanliness, and attention to personal appearance, a physical education
> was inculcated, that, reacting on their minds, might imbue them with
> sentiments of self respect, and teach them to feel, in the performance of
> the duties they owed themselves, their obligations to others. They were
> thus taught to view every act in their daily life as attended with fruitful
> consequences in relation to their present comforts or future prospects, in
> this way practically convicing them that the road to happiness runs par-
> allel with that to heaven.

When to this practical moralizing regime was added a program of direct
moral instruction ("daily admonitions, addresses on moral duty ... morning
and evening prayers, with a short practical scriptural lesson"), daily school instruction, and "the healthful stimulus created and sustained by a weekly
Journal, conducted by themselves.... [I]t appears impossible to construct a
more efficient system for the object in view – the moral reformation of the
criminal." Ritchie claimed "most favourable" results, presenting his convicts
as a group that, under his tutelage, had made great strides in self-control and
intellectual capabilities.[116]

Even after Evangelical fervor had cooled, most Victorian prison doctors
showed little discomfort with moralizing discourse. If they evinced decreasing
faith in the reformability of their charges, they continued to see them as responsible moral agents. After the early arguments over the psychological
effects of separation dissipated, insanity or mental weakness among prisoners
received little attention for several decades.[117] Feigning was much feared, and
examples of detected feigning appeared regularly in reports until the early
1890s. "The unpleasant topic of malingering," sighed the medical officer of
Portland in his 1870 report, "will, I fear, always have its place in the medical
return of a convict prison."[118] As Frederick Robinson noted in 1863, doctors

---

[116] Ritchie, pp. 10–11, 15.

[117] The first comment in the annual reports of medical officers was in 1870, in response to
Fenian charges of men being driven mad.

[118] *Report of the Directors of Convict Prisons for 1869*, p. 144.

were so reluctant to risk being thus deceived "that many really mad are regarded with suspicion ... and are treated like the rest of the prisoners if their conduct be not too glaringly outrageous."[119] Conscious of the danger of the power they wielded and sharing the concern of governors, magistrates, and civil servants to maintain institutional authority, prison doctors tended to use that power very cautiously and sparingly.

Typical of this post-Evangelical but pretherapeutic generation was John Campbell, who had begun his career as a naval surgeon and become medical officer at a succession of convict institutions between 1850 and 1880. In his memoirs, Campbell stressed how difficult was the task of the prison doctor charged with the duty of safeguarding the health of the inmates without weakening moral order within the prison. Prison doctors had to spend every day interpreting behavior as they faced the continual problems of distinguishing true illness or disability from malingering and deciding at what point illness or disability was sufficiently overpowering to exempt the prisoner from penal discipline.[120] Malingering was a constant concern for him; Campbell recalled "imposters [sic] of the most determined description ... the prisoners carried out their deception with a cunning and a persistency which rendered them very difficult of detection." Even a great many true invalids tended to become spoiled by their condition and required the strictest discipline consistent with health. In his first report from Woking Invalid Prison in 1860, Campbell had observed:

> Some of them, having been long under treatment in other prisons, appear to think that on coming to an invalid establishment they are to be allowed medical extras in abundance, to be exempt from labour of any kind, and, in short, to conduct themselves in a way most agreeable to their tastes, unrestrained by any kind of discipline. In these expectations they must be

---

[119] [Frederick Robinson], *Female Life in Prison, Vol.1* (London: Hurst & Blackett, 1863), p. 239. Typical observations on the problem are in *Report of the Directors of Convict Prisons 1859*, p. 471, and *Report of the Directors of Convict Prisons 1863*, p. 181. In the latter report, the medical officer of Dartmoor discussed one "remarkably cunning and obstinate" prisoner whose "efforts to deceive [through voluntary starvation] were finally rendered abortive by persevering observation ... he returned to the penal class from which it was his object to escape." In his study of prison medicine, Stephen Watson has remarked that in the later nineteenth century the detection of malingerers was felt to be such an important aspect of the prison medical officer's duties that it was "invariably mentioned in pleas for better pay and conditions of service." [Stephen Watson, "The Moral Imbecile: A Study of the Relations Between Penal Practice and Psychiatric Knowledge of the Habitual Offender," unpublished Ph.D. thesis, University of Lancaster, 1988, p. 135.]

[120] Grey and Waddington were ever wary of early release of sick convicts, warning Jebb on several occasions to be very cautious because so many of those offenders were recommitted. [HO 12/2432, Grey to Voules, Sept. 25, 1850; Jebb to Waddington, Nov. 4, 1850.].

undeceived, for although they meet with every kindness and comfort consistent with their situation and requirements, misconduct and acts of
insubordination cannot be overlooked.

It therefore appears to me very desirable that some means should be
devised for showing the invalid prisoners that if their illness does not prevent them from misconducting themselves, neither will it exempt them
from paying the penalty awarded to their offence.

Not only did invalidity not exempt a prisoner from moral liability, the condition itself in many cases was a product of moral disorder: "Some of these
men," he reflected, "are weakened both in body and in mind, as the result of
vicious and depraved lives."

Weak-minded prisoners presented yet another difficult problem for Dr.
Campbell. On the one hand, "the utmost caution is required to discriminate
between the really weak-minded and those cunning miscreants who feign
mental peculiarities as a cloak for their misdeeds. These men belong to the
worst description of criminals, and are proper subjects for the most deterring
punishments." On the other hand, even with genuine imbeciles, the question
of the degree of responsibility for misbehavior was always open: "each case
would require to be taken on its own merits." Campbell was particularly sus-
picious of violent behavior:

Such men, when guilty of assault, would sometimes say, "You can't
touch me; I am a lunatic." One of the worst and most treacherous was
discovered with a small stiletto made out of a piece of the steel spring of
his truss. This weapon was supposed to be intended for me; yet he would
ask me for indulgences in the most bland and obsequious manner. The
conduct of some of these dangerous men appeared inconsistent with
genuine lunacy, and to be more allied to wickedness of the worst description. It rendered them more fitted for the strict discipline of a prison than
for the indulgent treatment of an asylum. But having been invalided as
lunatics, they were treated accordingly, until we had good indications to
the contrary.

Campbell hardly questioned the need for strict discipline wherever possible,
for it was equally required by justice and reclamation. Of the latter, he
observed in 1884 that "the habits of order, cleanliness, and regularity which
the prisoners had acquired during their confinement were of immense advantage; and I deem these three items of prison discipline of far greater importance in the reclamation of prisoners than any of the new ideas so often
advanced by people wanting in practical experience."[121]

---

[121] *Thirty Years' Experience of a Medical Officer in the English Convict Service* (London:
T. Nelson, 1884), pp. 50, 57, 82, 80, 92, 91.

As evidence to official inquiries attests, Campbell spoke for many medical officers in his watchfulness for malingering and his disciplinary conception of his role.[122] The 1878 Committee on Prison Dietaries, which consisted of two medical officers and an inspector, rejected prison critics' complaints of undue harshness. The report noted that:

> in a large number of cases, imprisonment, as now generally conducted, is a condition more or less akin to that of 'physiological rest.' The struggle for survival is suspended; and the prisoner appears to feel that the prayer for daily bread is rendered unnecessary by the solicitude of his custodians. Tranquility of mind and freedom from anxiety are leading characteristics of his life. From the moment that the prison gates close behind him, the tendency, in most cases, is to lessened waste of tissue; he lives, in fact, less rapidly than before.... He is 'insensibly subdued to settled quiet'; and finds in many instances, a peace and repose to which, as a law-abiding citizen, he was perchance a stranger.

> Most prison medical officers, when first appointed, experience a certain fluttering when called upon to see one of the inmates at night, and are oppressed with the thought of conscious criminals tossing upon troubled beds.... [B]ut they soon find that the prisoners nestle very comfortably on their hammocks, and that however guilty their consciences may be, they do not trouble them.[123]

The committee report recommended a graduated dietary, based upon duration; the shorter the term of imprisonment, "the more strongly should the penal element be manifested in the diet." With time, prisoners would graduate to ampler diets.[124] The following year one of the committee members, Dr. R. M. Gover, now promoted to the post of chief medical officer, even recommended greater use of the treadwheel and crank.[125]

---

[122] Although he seems to have distinguished himself in his suspicion of malingerers, the swindler, George Bidwell, recalled his examination: "the doctor [Campbell] wound up the interview with the clincher, in his high squeaking tones: 'Well, my man, you know you were sent here to die, so you must not make any trouble, for there is nothing I can do for you.' This was his stereotyped reply, no matter what the case on the nature of the disease, which had usually been aggravated or brought on by hard work with insufficient food." [George Bidwell, *Forging his Chains: The Autobiography of George Bidwell* (Hartford, Conn: S. S. Scranton, 1888), p. 485.] For similar views of other medical officers, see *Report of the Commission on the Operation of the Penal Servitude Acts 1878–79*, Q. 8974–5, 10,615–29, 10,636–45.

[123] *Report of Committee on Dietaries of the Prisons of England and Wales 1878*, p. 5. [P.P. 1878, Vol. 42.]

[124] *ibid.* p. 7. They took for "self-evident" that "imprisonment should be rendered as deterrent as is consistent with the maintenance of health and strength." There was no change in dietary between 1865 and 1899.

[125] *Second Report of the Commissioners of Prisons*, Appendix 15.

In the same year also, the man who was to become superintendent of Broadmoor, the institution for criminal lunatics, warned against an emerging tendency to shrink the sphere of criminal responsibility. Dr. David Nicolson urged his fellow alienists not to lend their authority to loose generalizations by "people of a philanthropic turn" that the criminal is but "a moral invalid" or "moral imbecile." Medical doctors, he concluded, were (or should be) "always alive" to the interest of public security and moral order.[126]

As historians have highlighted in recent years the disciplinary face of Victorian public medicine – its support for compulsory vaccination, for the compulsory examination of prostitutes and incarceration of those infected with venereal diseases, and of habitual drunkards – we can better appreciate how medical service in prisons did not pose the conflict of values or of world views that would later come to the fore. Victorian medicine and Victorian punishment had many points of affinity and contact.

Women

The early Victorian expansion and intensification of criminal prosecution to embrace many more "disorderly," "immoral," and petty thieving offenders than hitherto brought a growing number of women into prisons.[127] Women prisoners presented a newly felt dilemma for policymakers by bringing into focus a latent tension between two sets of waxing attitudes. On the one hand, the differences between the sexes – in particular, women's physical weakness, even vulnerability, together with their greater moral sensitivity – were being ever more insisted upon; on the other, the universalizing struggle against instinct saw similar dangers in all human nature and demanded similar remedies of character building. The treatment of female criminals thus brought two faces of Victorianism into conflict.

This conflict was resolved (as with disabled, and as we shall see, juvenile offenders) by making special provisions for this group of criminals, but at the same time containing this special treatment within the general ideals of building character that guided the treatment of male criminals. Female prisoners were to be dealt with separately, somewhat less harshly, and with somewhat greater responsibility placed upon the authorities to achieve their

[126] "The Measure of Individual and Social Responsibility in Criminal Cases," *Journal of Mental Science* 24 (1878), 1–25, 249–73.
[127] It is difficult to be precise about this development, since in general separate breakdowns by gender were not made in official statistical reports until later in the century. It is certain that the number of women prisoners was rising, and very probable that their proportion was also rising, at least until the 1850s.

reformation, yet this was not to make their experience any less disciplined or, indeed, punitive.

Women were no longer whipped, as men continued to be until the end of the century, for infractions of penal discipline, and penal reduction in diet was much more sparingly applied to them than to men.[128] On the other hand, they were punished by removal to dark cells about as often as were men, and by passive restraints, such as handcuffs and straitjackets, with even greater frequency.[129] At first generally housed in separate wings of the same jails, and beginning in 1853 in separate, purpose-built prisons, their prison lives were in essentials the same as men's – under similar regimes, whether separate confinement, silent association, or a mixture of the two, receiving religious exhortation and, most importantly, laboring long hours to earn their upkeep, to possibly learn a useful skill, and to certainly acquire permanent "habits of industry."

Women received somewhat shorter sentences on average,[130] and, if convicts, had greater opportunity to gain time off their sentences than did men.[131] Moreover, women convicts released on license had no obligation, as was imposed upon men, to report regularly to the police. On the other hand, women were newly liable to modes of institutional control not applied to adult men. The early- and mid-Victorian period saw the establishment of a variety of semipenal institutions for wayward and criminal women. In part, these institutions – called variously homes, hospitals, refuges, and penitentiaries – were meant as alternatives to, and preventives of, imprisonment, but of course they were also extensions of most of the characteristics of prison to cases of less-than-full criminality. Moreover, in 1856 a new kind of refuge was created for the reception of convict women. Fulham Refuge in England and Golden Bridge Reformatory in Dublin received women required to enter them as a condition of early release from convict prison and kept them for an indeterminate term until they were judged reformed. In these institutions, though their manifest purposes were more reformatory than punitive, and

[128] For example, in 1870, women made up 21 percent of average daily local prison population, but received only 12 percent of the dietary punishments [annual criminal statistics].

[129] In addition to the annual criminal statistics and prison inspectors' reports, see Russell Dobash, R. Emerson Dobash, and Sue Gutteridge, *The Imprisonment of Women* (Oxford: Blackwell, 1986), p. 86, passim, and McConville, pp. 413–15, 425–28. McConville dwells on the difficulty prison officials faced in managing women prisoners without the sanction of corporal punishment, and in general on the various distinctions in prison discipline in favor of women, whereas Dobash, Dobash, and Gutteridge argue the hollowness of the supposed "gentler" treatment of women.

[130] As is shown by their consistently making up a somewhat smaller proportion of average prison populations than of commitals.

[131] Legislation in 1853 and 1857 providing for remission of sentences of penal servitude allowed women a higher maximum remission.

though admission was often (in theory) voluntary, inmates (especially of Fulham and Golden Bridge) were subjected to much the same regime – various forms of degradation (like the shaving of heads), strict discipline, extensive religious indoctrination, and long hours of labor – as in jails proper. To a twentieth-century eye, their similarities with contemporary prisons seem much more apparent than their differences. This is not surprising, since their aim – character reform for demoralized subjects – was felt to require a highly disciplined regime. As the superintendent of Golden Bridge, Sister Kirwan, put it in 1863, her charges had to be "untaught and then retaught since females of the criminal class are essentially idle and ignorant to helplessness."[132] Thus, for women, a network of semipenal institutions under private management was developed to supplement and in part replace the work of jails and prisons. Their relationship to the general principles of criminal treatment being worked out and applied in these years, like that of the treatment of women within prisons, was one of simultaneous qualification and extension; in the treatment of wayward and criminal women, in and outside prisons, the disruption threatened by new sentiments about women's nature was contained within a universalizing theme of instinctualism and character building.

Juveniles

As more expansive standards of social behavior and the accompanying growth of state instruments to enforce these standards had been bringing ever more juveniles before the courts, new fears for order and new hopes for the improvement of criminal character came to focus upon juveniles. For several reasons, juveniles became more of a problem for criminal policy. Their guilt (like that of lunatics) was more questionable than that of adult offenders, although (also like lunatics) they seemed more ruled by impulse and thus in the long run even more of a social danger. Like disability and even femininity, youth posed a problem for the insistence upon personal responsibility and self-mastery. In response, new policies emerged that sought to mediate between images of youthful malleability and the demands of character building. As with the mentally ill, and abandoned women, the early-Victorian period saw new optimism about reforming juveniles. In both cases, as a mode of reform that was quite compatible with the insistence upon imputing the maximum feasible responsibility, "moral management" seemed to offer great possibilities, even if to modern observers it seems characterized by what

---

[132] Quoted in Dobash, Dobash, and Gutteridge, p. 75.

one historian has described as a "morbid obsession with infant sin and sinners."[133]

The first major penal reform organization gave the young prominence in its title: the Society for the Improvement of Prison Discipline and the Reformation of Juvenile Offenders (1817). One of the society's basic tenets was the need to separate more malleable juvenile criminals – defined variously as up to 16 or 17 years of age – from hardened adult criminals to protect the young from moral contamination. Another was the desirability of providing a thoroughly controlled environment in which their characters could be reclaimed. These two principles guided efforts to reform both the transportation and the imprisonment of juvenile offenders.

Beginning in the 1840s, the treatment of boys exiled to the colonies was given special attention. Repeated instructions came from the Home Office that boys on convict ships were to be kept separate from both adult criminals and the crew; to have regular prayers, religious services, and religious literature; and to practice good language and bodily cleanliness.[134] In 1838 the first penal institution solely for juveniles, Parkhurst Prison, was opened. Yet, as with the regimes prescribed for juvenile exiles, prison itself was not intended to be in any way attractive to its charges. Few of those involved in creating separate facilities for juveniles meant to do away with responsibility of juveniles for their behavior, but only to enable these more hopeful offenders to be reformed more effectively. Thus, Parkhurst's administration followed the prescription of William Crawford, who had lobbied for its creation, that it should be "decidedly of a penal character." Once the prison had opened, Crawford watched over it, guarding against inclinations toward laxity. "Without a rigid system of habitual restraints," he warned the home secretary in 1839:

> I do not believe that the reform of the Juvenile Prisoners [at Parkhurst] would be generally attainable. Unless the prison be stern in its aspect, and obnoxious from its penal features, it will produce no deterring impressions upon those who are engaged in the commission of offences. Nor is this all. A prison for boys ought never to be viewed apart from the consideration of its influence on the minds of their parents and connexions. If the idea of privation during imprisonment, and of eventual banishment, be not associated with such an institution, its efforts will be most prejudicial upon parents, as also with reference to the more honest, as to the less principled, classes. Large numbers in the humble walks of

[133] Jo Manton, *Mary Carpenter and the Children of the Streets* (London: Heinemann Educational, 1976), p. 174.
[134] See HO 21/22, H. Waddington to Edward Simpson, July 2, 1849., and HO 13/95, G. C. Lewis to Tekuseh, Oct. 19, 1848.

life would rejoice at being relieved from the burden of supporting their children by obtaining for them admission into an asylum in which they would be lodged, subsisted, educated and taught a trade, at the public expense. These advantages would have a natural tendency to render parents indifferent to the rising vicious propensities of their children, well knowing that the commission of crimes would qualify them for admission into a comfortable asylum and confer on them benefits which they would not otherwise derive. Other parents, of a depraved class, would regard without dread an institution which inflicted no severe correction, and from which they would calculate on receiving back their children at the expiration of their sentences. A prison conducted on these principles would be a direct bounty on parental improvidence and neglect, and operate most unjustly upon those who, disdaining to have recourse to public aid, strive to bring up their families by prudent habits, and honest industry.

Though Crawford placed deterrence at the head of penal objectives, he assured the Home Office that there was "no reason to doubt that a strict system of penal discipline is quite compatible with the means requisite for the moral and religious improvement of the offender."[135]

The regime established at Parkhurst was thoroughly penal. For the first two years, each boy wore an iron manacle on one leg, and prison officials considered it unwise to establish an infirmary "in consequence of the temptation such would afford to the idle and deceitful to feign sickness for the enjoyment of a fireside and other comparative luxuries, not attainable in the wards."[136] Following the pattern of penal reform for adults, when leg irons were removed and an infirmary was built, the discipline was compensatingly tightened further. During his first four months, each prisoner was confined to his cell except for brief periods spent in the chapel, the schoolroom, and the exercise area; silence was enforced during times of association; diet was sparse; and a refractory class was established, in which boys were kept in their cells, let out only to march. Parkhurst's severity was explained as philanthropic. "Every punishment which we give," its governor insisted in 1849, "is shown to them to be a weapon drawn from the armoury of truth and love, that it is in accordance with the Divine administration, and directed for their real happiness."[137] Although its regime came under much criticism later, it was generally supported by the early generation of reformers. Elizabeth Fry, who visited the prison just before manacles were abandoned, recorded that its regime gave her much satisfaction and felt that it put into practice some of the things she her-

[135] HO 20/8, letter to Phillipps, Oct. 11, 1839.
[136] Quoted in John Stack, "Deterrence and Reformation in Early Victorian Social Policy: The Case of Parkhurst Prison, 1838–1864," *Historical Reflections VI* (Winter, 1979), 392.
[137] Quoted in *ibid.*, 397.

self had in part begun. Important newspapers like *The Morning Chronicle* and *The Times* were full of similar praise.[138]

Like the reformed prisons generally, Parkhurst followed the principle of "less eligibility," which rested on the simultaneous affirmation of personal responsibility and the sense of the urgent need to protect and develop that responsibility. Less eligibility was considered essential to prevent parents from succumbing to the temptation to allow their children to be supported at public expense.[139] In general Crawford and Russell observed, "The interests of society render it indispensable that a broad line of distinction should be observed between the treatment of the children of poverty, and those of crime."[140] When the state had to intervene, it had to be severe, many felt, both to assist the (essentially internal) process of reformation and to prevent the moral deterioration of either offenders or potential offenders. In an age of hard living conditions and minimal public welfare provision, one always had to be aware in dealing with juvenile, like adult, criminals that one did not create temptations to further crime. Prison inspector W. J. Williams, giving evidence to the Select Committee of 1850, conceded under prodding by Richard Monckton Milnes that he would have liked to ease the conditions of youthful inmates it was his duty to oversee, but "there is this great difficulty, that if you treat them otherwise than penally, you are giving a premium for the commission of crime, of which I am persuaded the injurious consequences will manifest themselves in times of distress, and lead you into very great difficulty."[141] Milnes himself, though a philanthropist and critical of Parkhurst's severity, introduced juvenile offender bills that provided for a second offense of vagrancy or petty theft ten weeks' hard labor in solitary confinement as a prelude to between one and three years in an industrial school, and for a third offense, five or seven years in a juvenile prison under a regime of "constant and severe labour."[142]

After midcentury, the focus of juvenile offender policy shifted from Parkhurst to new, privately run reformatory schools. Parkhurst came to be reserved for boys at least 14 years of age who had committed serious crimes; younger and more hopeful cases began to be passed to the Philanthropic So-

---

[138] See Radzinowicz and Hood, p. 151.

[139] *First Report of the Inspectors of Prisons [Home District]*, pp. 97–8. Their view of these parents can be seen in Crawford's proposal (not accepted by the Home Office) to abolish the privilege of letter writing and receiving: "[C]onsidering the character of too many of the parents of juvenile offenders no counteracting advantage can fairly be anticipated from allowing any such intercourse with them to be kept up." [HO 20/8, letter to Phillipps, Oct. 11, 1839.]

[140] *Second Report*, quoted in Radzinowicz and Hood, p. 149.

[141] *Select Committee on Prison Discipline 1850*, Minutes of Evidence, Q. 776.

[142] Quoted in Radzinowicz and Hood, p. 175.

ciety at its new school at Redhill. As Parkhurst's clientele became ever less distinguishable from ordinary convicts, the prison began to diminish in population and prestige. The 1852 Select Committee on Criminal and Destitute Children rejected it as a model for future reformatories because it was insufficiently reformative.[143] Its administration ceased to even speak of reforming their charges, and finally in 1864 Parkhurst was converted into a female convict prison.

If the midcentury reformatory movement marked a new acknowledgment of juvenile weakness and need for special help, this did not entail the repudiation of early Victorian moralism that historians once assumed. The dominant position in the movement until late in the century supported the need to first subject juvenile offenders to a term of penal imprisonment before placing them in reformatories. The Youthful Offenders Act of 1854, passed in response to the pressure of this newly organized movement, allowed the courts to commit convicted offenders under 16 years of age for two to five years in a reformatory school after a minimum of 14 days' imprisonment. This important act provided the first institutional alternative to prison for young offenders and also made a period of imprisonment a required preliminary to this alternative. It thus marked both the beginning of a new path for the treatment of juvenile lawbreakers, incorporating reformatories into the criminal justice system, and the simultaneous reaffirmation of the need to maintain the presumption of personal responsibility and consequent liability to punishment of these offenders.

Supporters of the principle of necessary punishment, usually in the form of preliminary imprisonment, felt the need to make a clear moral statement visible to all. The Reverend Sydney Turner, secretary of the Philanthropic Society, who became the first inspector of reformatory schools in 1857, called prior imprisonment essential for the "moral health of society at large."[144] He continued to believe throughout his career that preliminary imprisonment was needed both "for the moral impression to be made on the offenders themselves" and for "the impression made on the public feeling of the community." He urged "that all wrong doing however originally suggested, or afterwards encouraged by external influences, should be punished, and that vice and mischief should not seem to be rewarded and encourage." Preliminary imprisonment contributed to this especially by involving "the disgrace of a public conviction."[145]

---

[143] *ibid.*, p. 154.
[144] Quoted in Susan M. Magarey, "The Reclaimers: A Study of the Reformatory Movement in England and Wales," unpublished Ph.D. thesis, Australian National University, 1980, p. 162.
[145] Quoted in Radzinowicz and Hood, pp. 202–3.

Arguments for prior imprisonment for juveniles also tended to stress the high degree of rationality and free will possessed even by these children for whom they sought to create special institutions. Jelinger Symons could speak of criminal children as "diseased" and "to be dealt with as patients,"[146] and yet vigorously support preliminary imprisonment on the grounds that punishment was a necessity "which society requires in its defence, in order to deter the future commission of crime by others as well as the offender." Moreover, he found convicted juveniles to be "in a very large proportion, older children, who are perfectly conscious of their faults nad deserts."[147] Symons's friend, Thomas Barwick Lloyd Baker, a magistrate and reformatory founder, insisted that punishment was essential "to impress on a boy's mind the feeling that he has done wrong."[148] Punishment was also necessary to deter others and to preserve and strengthen the moral fabric of society. "Were punishments withdrawn from crime," Baker warned the British Association in 1854, "not only the numbers of legal criminals would increase but ... this very fact would increase the number of criminals at heart and give us a greater number to reform (if we trusted to reformation solely) than we could possibly undertake."[149]

Harsh penal conditions played a role in attaining the milder aims of reformatories. "The stricter the diet and the more effectual and real the labour have been in the prison from which the boy comes," Sydney Turner argued, "the more rapidly and easily his improvement can be effected."[150] Similarly, the reformist prison chaplain, John Clay, thought the minimum period of fourteen days established by the 1854 Reformatory Schools Act *"far too short a term"*; he suggested that "three months' discipline in a separate cell would make a lad attach a proper value to the more active life and advantages of a school."[151] Even Mary Carpenter, the foremost critic of prior imprisonment, came very soon, after experience running reformatories, to see its value in "preparing the child to receive with more thankfulness the contrasted condition of the school."[152] Not only did prior imprisonment receive general support within as well as outside the reformatory movement, there was even greater practical consensus on the reformatory regime to follow the punishment phase. The "moral hospital"[153] that was to treat morally diseased youth was to be not much less strictly organized than Parkhurst. At the French

---

[146] Jelinger C. Symons, *Tactics for the Times* (London: John Ollivier, 1849), p. 147.
[147] "Reformatory Discipline," *Journal of the Society of Arts 3*, 524 (June 8, 1855).
[148] Barwick Baker, *War with Crime* (London: Longmans, 1889), p. 223 [May 16, 1881].
[149] *ibid.*, p. 165 (Sept. 26, 1864).
[150] *Select Committee on Prison Discipline 1850*, Q. 8286, 8289.
[151] W. L. Clay, *The Prison Chaplain* (Cambridge: Macmillan, 1861), pp. 464–5.
[152] 1857, quoted in Radzinowicz and Hood, p. 203.
[153] This term seems to have been first used by Matthew and Frederic Hill in the 1840s.

reformatory at Mettray, important as the chief model for early English reformatories, self-denial was the order of the day.[154] The basis of the Mettray regime was hard physical labor, which Turner cited as the "backbone of reformation."[155]

The Home Office vigorously rebuffed early suggestions to put reformatory schools under the Committee of Council on Education. Home secretaries of both parties were convinced that the moral health of society and of the reformatories' inmates would be undermined if these institutions were severed from the necessary associations with crime and punishment. While reformatories had been introduced under Whig governments, Tory Home Secretary Spencer Walpole warned that it would be a grave mistake to intro- duce into criminal circles the notion that the reformatory had no penal charac- ter. A moral stigma, he insisted, appropriately attached to the subjects of the reformatory "not the effect of the detention but of the crime which has caused it." Certainly, reformatories ought not to be put

> on a level with ordinary schools.... The vast distinction between Re- formatory and primary schools is that the latter are for those who have done no wrong, who seek instruction, and who come and go at their own will, or at the will of their parents but reformatories are for those sent there under the criminal law by courts of justice and compulsorily detained for a definite period and partly no doubt for purposes of edu- cation but partly for correction also.

Crime, detention, and "the nature of the education itself," he noted, "draw a broad line between the inmates of the reformatories and untainted children of the poor" that could not and should not be obscured.[156] Walpole's opposite number on the Whig-Liberal benches, Sir George Grey, encouraged the creation of new reformatories and frequently praised their work, but was at one with Walpole on the need to maintain moral distinctions. Grey cautioned magistrates that "reformatories ought as much as possible to be reserved for children of confirmed criminal habits.... It is undesirable to commit to those establishments comparatively innocent children on a first conviction, to be maintained and educated at the public expense, when they have friends who are able and anxious to take proper charge of them."[157]

Though they tended to press for greater use of these institutions than cost-

---

[154] Radzinowicz and Hood, p. 157.

[155] Quoted in Radzinowicz and Hood, p. 190. Barwick Baker knew "of no employment which will allay the excitement and tranquillise the mind, so as to prepare it to be acted upon by a firm kindness, like steady hard digging." ["On Reformatory Schools" (1854), in Baker, *War with Crime*, p. 167.]

[156] HO 25/7, Gathorne Hardy to C. B. Adderley, Jan. 10, 1859.

[157] HO 13/107, Waddington to the Clerks of the Magistrates, Sept. 5, 1862.

conscious governments were ready to approve, most reformatory founders and managers had little difference with the moral outlook of the mid-Victorian Home Office. Since 1841, Sydney Turner had operated a reformatory regime at Redhill that was puritanically strict: "We do not recognize," he noted to the 1850 parliamentary committee, "anything like recreation beyond the few minutes that he may get from his meals, or from his schooling being over." He proposed for new reformatories a regime of

> exposure to weather and cold ... diet studiously plain ... no hot slops, cocoa, soup or gruel ... no attractive dress, but plain rough clothing. Let there be no high education with "lectures on chemistry illustrated by experiments", no formation of bands and glee-singing classes, but only plain, useful instruction.[158]

Or, as he put it in his capacity as inspector of reformatories (a post he held for eighteen years), the

> tone of discipline, dietary, industrial occupation, lodging, habits or rec-reation etc. etc. must have something of the hardness which Saint Paul prescribes as an essential element in the Christian's training.... Self-will, disorder, idleness, and sensual indulgence have more or less been the causes of their perversion. A manly training to obedience, regularity, in-dustry and self-control is the needful remedy.[159]

The two leading politicians in the reformatory movement, Sir Charles Adderley, later Lord Norton,[160] and Lord Shaftesbury, known as "the chil-dren's Peer," were at one in essentials with Turner. Both men, Evangelical Tory landlords, fused moralization with humanitarian reform; they were dedicated to reclaiming through a stern regime those whom Adderley referred to as "the young outcasts of society."[161] Both had independently introduced juvenile crime bills in 1852 and 1853 and had met to reconcile their mea-sures.[162] The resulting government bill, which became the Reformatory Schools Act of 1854, owed much to each man's efforts. Shaftesbury's pro-found dedication to helping children was accompanied by a conviction of the

---

[158] [Sydney Turner], "Juvenile Delinquency," *Edinburgh Review 94* (Oct. 1851), 421.

[159] *General Report of the Inspector of Reformatories & Industrial Schools 1859*, pp. 2, 15. [P.P. 1859, 2nd Session, Vol. 13.]

[160] Like Barwick Baker, Adderley was a Tory squire devoted to horse riding and tobacco, as well as a serious Evangelical, but a good deal wealthier, having inherited vast estates round Birmingham on which he created the model town of Saltley. Adderley sat as Tory M. P. for North Staffordshire for 37 years.

[161] In his tract *Transportation Not Necessary* (1851), quoted in William S. Childe-Pemberton, *Life of Lord Norton 1814–1905: Statesman and Philanthropist* (London, 1909), p. 96.

[162] Childe-Pemberton, p. 136.

overriding need to insist upon placing blame and providing moral discipline. His bill proposed both heavier sanctions for parents and a wider scope for disciplinary institutions than the government was ready to support; it gave the police power to arrest vagrant children, put them into the workhouse, and educate them compulsorily at the expense of their parents.[163] Adderley, second only to Shaftesbury in political weight, took on for four decades the first role in reformatory legislative work.[164] "The gaols would have been full," a Home Office official was later to declare, fulsomely but generally accurately, "if it had not been for the efforts of Mr. Adderley in Reformatory work."[165] After the success of 1854, Adderley went on to carry the Industrial Schools Bill of 1857, enacting aspects of his and Shaftesbury's earlier bills. The act of 1857 established for the first time nonpenal but highly disciplined institutions to which magistrates or Boards of Guardians might send vagrant, but noncriminal, children aged 7 to 14 for moral and vocational training.

Through the following decades, despite their passionate desires to relieve suffering, both men frequently supported restrictions upon demoralizing assistance, as when in 1871 Shaftesbury attacked a proposal to have commitment to industrial schools include children of women convicted of crime, arguing that to allow these children to be "fed, clothed and lodged at the public expense" would be "a direct encouragement to crime."[166] He believed throughout his career that, as he put it in 1872, "laws may remove obstacles, and sympathisers may give aid, but it is by personal conduct, by sobriety, by order, by honesty, by perseverance that a man, under God, becomes 'the architect of his own fortunes.'"[167] It was the task of reformatories, like ragged and industrial schools, to inculcate these saving virtues.

Liberals and radicals in the reformatory movement spoke in similar terms. As M. D. Hill exhorted: "The three great lessons to be taught [in reformatories] are religious convictions, industry and self-control. If prosecuted with perseverance, success is *certain*."[168] Even Mary Carpenter, the most prominent figure in the soft wing of the movement, who insisted that "child-

---

[163] See Geoffrey B. A. M. Finlayson, *The Seventh Earl of Shaftesbury* (London: Eyre Methuen, 1981), p. 349. This bill illustrated, Finlayson pointed out, Shaftesbury's desire "to discipline and restrain" as well as to reform.

[164] See Childe-Pemberton; also Manton, *Mary Carpenter*, p. 122. Adderley had become an opponent of convict transportation in the 1840s and in 1849 persuaded Home Secretary Grey not to send Irish political prisoners to the Cape Colony. This involvement in the transportation question gradually led him to take an interest in young offenders, some of whom were among the transportees.

[165] Quoted in Childe-Pemberton, pp. 197–8.

[166] 3 PD 207, c. 1933.

[167] Speech reported in *The Times*, Dec. 6, 1872, quoted in Finlayson, p. 602.

[168] Quoted in Manton, p. 122.

hood is a condition absolutely distinct from manhood,"[169] treated her young outcasts in a highly authoritarian manner in order to reclaim them from "depravity."[170] Although she urged that wayward children needed love, she assumed without question that they equally needed training in order and self-denial. Carpenter's administration of her best-known institution, the female reformatory, Red Lodge, reveals an intense concern for moral discipline. Although her most recent biographer, Jo Manton, made great efforts to explain away unpalatable aspects of life there, she acknowledged that "many difficulties at Red Lodge arose from [Carpenter's] determination to regulate the smallest details of everyday life." Minute, strict rules were promulgated for the girls' moral improvement, leaving them virtually no freedom of action. Nor were they coddled materially; Red Lodge, Manton notes with surprise, "was the cheapest girls' reformatory.... In particular, the expenditure on food seems very low, and the school was censured for this after Mary Carpenter's death."[171]

Carpenter proudly claimed the title of disciplinarian. At Red Lodge and Kingswood, the other reformatory school under her supervision, she observed in 1864, "though these are not regarded as penal establishments, we endeavour to maintain in them such *steady discipline* as may appear right and best to attain the end [of reformation], without considering whether our scholars regard our restrictions or treatment as irksome, and without endeavouring to lead them to obedience by indulgence of their appetites."[172] Moreover, despite her urgings upon Parliament to employ "kindness," at Red Lodge when discipline broke down Carpenter resorted, albeit with sorrow, to solitary confinement and even corporal punishment.[173]

Although after 1854 steadily fewer children were imprisoned,[174] those who were continued to be treated in most essentials as adults until 1896.[175] "Less

---

[169] Quoted in Radzinowicz and Hood, p. 168.

[170] Mary Carpenter, *Reformatory Schools for the Children of the Perishing and Dangerous Classes and for Juvenile Offenders* (London: C. Gilpin, 1851), p. v.

[171] Manton, pp. 128, 169.

[172] Mary Carpenter, *Our Convicts, Vol. 1* (London: Longman, Green, 1864), pp. 114–15.

[173] One "strong case of hysteria ... feigning" whom she put in the solitary cell died a few days later. Cited from Carpenter's Red Lodge journal, F. B. Smith, *Florence Nightingale: Reputation and Power* (London: Croom Helm, 1982), p. 151. Smith, pausing momentarily in an indictment of Florence Nightingale's character to quote some choice passages from Carpenter's journal, found there "sadism, deceit and self-righteousness' and a personality "domineering, sentimental and cruel" (pp. 1, 31). However unfair and even misogynist Smith's analysis is, he was perceiving a true "hardness" within the "humanitarianism", one however less due to personal defects of Carpenter (or Nightingale) than to the cultural context in which she worked.

[174] Between 1857 and 1877, the proportion of persons aged 16 years or less in the total of prison committals fell from 10 to 4 percent [Radzinowicz and Hood, p. 624.]

[175] See Magarey, 251.

eligibility" remained a vital moral principle for the treatment of juveniles, as well as adults. Nor, as we have seen, did reformatories present a radical cultural break with the prison regime. The honorary secretary of the Reformatory and Refuge Union observed with equanimity in the House of Commons in 1872 that, though privately run, reformatories were quite properly "quasi-penal" institutions because they dealt with many "hardened criminals."[176] The humanitarian rhetoric of reclamation, with rare exceptions, linked arms with the voluntarist rhetoric of personal responsibility and disciplinary, character-building reform.

Punishment and Victorian liberalism

... by this I mean liberty in the English sense, liberty under rule, and the whole question is what rule is admissible or desirable.

W. E. Gladstone to H. E. Manning, 1849[177]

Our Almighty Father is continually, aye day and hour, calling upon us, almost compelling us, to act. Now acting is not the mere discharge of an outward function. It is a continuing process, in which we are reponsible throughout. What is meant by being responsible? It is meant that we expose ourselves to consequences flowing from our actions. These are (say) of two kinds. First, there is alteration of environment; which implies that in the future actings, which cannot be escaped, we shall have to cast our account anew with circumstances. The second cuts deeper still. It is that our action modifies, that is to say progressively but silently alters, from time to time, and eventually shapes, our own mind and character.

W. E. Gladstone, *Studies Subsidiary to the Works of Bishop Butler*, 1896

The tide of disciplinary moral reform, as regards criminals and others considered unrespectable, crested during the 1860s. The flowering of liberalism brought with it a burst of penal legislation – prison acts in 1864 and 1865, and prevention of crime acts in 1869 and 1871 – and of disciplinary social measures on pauperism, drink, education, and related questions. In recent writings on nineteenth-century criminal policy, the coercive tone of the 1860s has been attributed almost exclusively to fears induced by the ending of transportation of convicts.[178] This was no doubt the most important short-run

---

[176] 3 PD 211, c. 622 (Stephen Cave).

[177] Quoted in Perry Butler, *Gladstone: Church, State and Tractarianism* (Oxford: Clarendon Press, 1982), p. 226. Gladstone was referring to the liberty of the Church of England, but the statement is applicable in a wider sense. As Butler observed, "He did not conceive of liberty as the opposite of authority, discipline or order."

[178] See Jennifer Davis, "The London Garrotting Panic of 1862: A Moral Panic and the Creation of a Criminal Class in mid-Victorian England," in eds. V. A. C. Gatrell, B.

influence that shaped policy. Yet leading policymakers made a point of noting that the crime rate (and even the total number of criminals at large) was overall declining.[179] There is little evidence of a reluctant Liberal government being stampeded by a crime wave and public hysteria into ideologically repugnant action. Liberal leaders expressed few reservations about their stricter criminal measures, and in fact were prepared to go further in applying legal sanctions against criminals and related classes than was the majority of either house. These pieces of criminal legislation illuminate fundamental, if neglected, inclinations of mid-Victorian liberalism. In particular, a closer look at the criminal concerns and activities of Gladstone's Liberal ministry of 1868 to 1874 suggests that this government saw the fullest development of the disciplinarian concerns with popular character formation that had been developing through the nineteenth century.[180]

Through its many clashes of philosophy and interest, early- and mid-Victorian social discussion and policymaking possessed an overarching frame of reference – what one historian has recently called "an embracive, wide-ranging and unitary political culture."[181] However heatedly they argued with one another, many publicists, politicians, and administrators shared a common language, bridging the divide between the religious- and secular-minded that was both highly moralistic and surprisingly interventionist.[182] As J. P. Parry has observed:

Lenman, and G. Parker, *Crime and the Law* (London: Europa 1980); P. Bartrip, "Public Opinion and Law Enforcement: The Ticket-of-Leave Scares in Mid-Victorian Britain" and H. M. Tomlinson, "Penal Servitude 1846–1865: A System in Evolution", in ed. V. Bailey, *Policing and Punishment in Nineteenth Century Britain* (New Brunswick, N.J.: Rutgers University Press, 1981); Radzinowicz and Hood, p. 231.

[179] See 3 PD 198, c. 1254 (Aug. 4, 1869) [Home Secretary Bruce]; 3 PD 194, c. 336 (Feb. 26, 1869). [Lord Kimberley, who introduced the Prevention of Crime Bill.]

[180] Most recent studies of Gladstone and mid-Victorian Liberalism have brought out their conservative and religious aspects. "Gladstonian Liberalism," as Derek Schreuder has suggested, "was, in the last resort, a force for stability and order in an age of acute destabilizing transition." [D. M. Schreuder, "The Making of Mr. Gladstone's Posthumous Career," in *The Gladstonian Turn of Mind*, ed. Bruce Kinzer (Toronto: University of Toronto Press, 1985), p. 234.]

[181] Lawrence Goldman, "The Social Science Association, 1857–1886: A Context for Mid-Victorian Liberalism," *English Historical Review 101* (Jan. 1986), 96. From a very different angle than Goldman, stressing the importance of religious rather than social science concerns, J. P. Parry has also argued for the existence of a common culture in the "political classes" in these decades [*Democracy and Religion: Gladstone and the Liberal Party, 1867–1875* (Cambridge: Cambridge University Press, 1986)].

[182] In this light Gladstone appears a most appropriate leader for the liberalism of the time, linking moral and administrative as well as religious and scientific strands. He was

The Victorian age was a moral age, and one task of politicians was held to be educative: to guide public opinion; to teach citizens, many of them newly enfranchised, the basic tenets of good political behaviour; and to establish the conditions in which spiritual progress could be generated.

Politics, consequently, was to a high degree "disciplinary, educative and uplifting."[183] As George Watson observed some years ago, "The duty of the state to promote a moral society" – despite Nonconformist suspicions – was "part of the common change of Victorian political debate."[184] Whig-Liberal approval of a specific social policy, Parry has insisted, depended less on whether it was (to use anachronistic terms) individualist or collectivist, but "above all, on its moral effect: whether it encouraged or attacked 'materialism',"[185] whether, as we might put it here, it nurtured or obstructed the development of character.

Nor was the discourse of character confined to the religiously minded politicians in whom Parry was interested. The Social Science Association (SSA), founded in 1857, which exercised a powerful influence upon the policies of the Liberal government,[186] defined itself (against classical political economy) by its concern with the moral dimension of social life. G. W. Hastings, its very active secretary and a Liberal M.P., stressed this attribute in 1861:

> The Association sprang out of the belief that many of our political economists have illogically narrowed their investigations by ignoring all view of moral duty, and that a union was needed between the moral and

not only intensely religious, he was also, as Goldman notes, the science-minded and reformist Social Science Association's "favourite statesman." [p. 118.] Gladstone combined an executive-minded readiness to use government with a preoccupation with "seriousness": "We want, most of all," he declared in 1856, "that a character of seriousness and earnestness should be once more impressed upon the proceedings of Parliament." [Quoted in Goldman, p. 118.] In July 1868, Gladstone presided over an important SSA meeting, [Goldman, p. 121.]

[183] Parry, *Democracy*, pp. 5, 53.

[184] George Watson, *The English Ideology: Studies in the Language of Victorian Politics* (London: Allen Lane, 1973). p. 75.

[185] Parry, p. 113.

[186] See Goldman. Home Secretary Bruce in particular was a very active member of the Social Science Association, presiding over its Education Department in 1866 and over the entire congress in 1875. For the association's influence on criminal policy, see Michael W. Melling, "Cleaning House in a Suddenly Closed Society: The Genesis, Brief Life and Untimely Death of the *Habitual Criminals Act, 1869,*" *Osgoode Hall Law Journal 21* (1983), 326; and Goldman, 104. The association crystallized many aspects of mid-Victorian Liberalism. Its membership was mostly Liberal (three-quarters or more of its many M.P.s were Liberal), and, founded in 1857 and winding up in 1886, it rose and fell with the fortunes of that form of liberalism.

economic sciences, in order to constitute a philosophy which should embrace in its inquiries alike the conditions of social prosperity and the rights and obligations of citizenship.[187]

Members of the association were concerned about the obligations of citizenship as much as about its rights. Like Jelinger Symons, a reformist professional man very much in the SSA mold, its members found a root evil of the age in the "relaxation of moral restraint" and a model for social policy in the new reformatory schools.[188] "In a well-regulated reformatory school," Hastings declared to the opening session of the association, "may be seen the effect of moral and religious discipline, combined with good sanitary conditions, and a proper union of industrial and intellectual education, upon wayward, ignorant and hardened natures. Such an institution is a type of the great work before us, for there is nothing done in a reformatory school which might not, with proper appliances, be effected for society at large."[189]

That archetypal Liberal reform, extension of the franchise, was rarely seen as an unqualified right. Not only was it to severely limit the number of voters, it was almost always thought of as conditional in character, linked to demonstrated moral fitness for the exercise of this power. Such fitness involved, in Gladstone's famous phrasing, "self-command, self-control, respect for order, patience under suffering, confidence in the law, regard for superiors."[190] Almost all participants in mid-Victorian political discussion accepted that character – the constantly reinforced disposition to restrain one's animal instincts – was the prerequisite for responsible independent behavior. Thus the argument over extending the franchise revolved to a large extent over the question of how widely and how thoroughly the working classes had developed character.[191] Even for young radicals urging franchise reform in 1867, concern with popular character was at the forefront, as they spoke anxiously of working class "brutes," of "the sensual herd," of "unbridled sensuality and riotous animalism."[192]

This concern gave prominence to the vision of the "respectable workingman" as social salvation – a vision (the photographic negative of the member of the "criminal classes") that could reconcile the claims, equally dear, of wider political citizenship with those of moral order. Thus, many of the younger generation of Liberal M.P.s, whether oriented primarily toward sci-

[187] "Introduction", *Transactions NAPSS 1861*, p. xviii.

[188] *Tactics*, p. 15.

[189] *Transactions NAPSS 1857*, p. xxiv.

[190] 3 PD 175, c. 325 (May 11, 1864).

[191] This point is deftly explored in Stefan Collini, "The Idea of 'Character' in Victorian Political Thought," *Transactions of the Royal Historical Society* (Fifth Series) *35* (1985), 29–50.

[192] See Collini, *ibid.*

ence or religion, sought to accompany franchise extension by administrative and social improvements designed to help such men help themselves, such as by extending the education system, expanding savings facilities and reducing indirect taxation. But, at the same time, most shared Gladstone's conviction that these measures would avail little without a reinvigorated public religiosity.[193]

Fears of encouraging materialism and license, and the consequent desire to set clear and strict moral conditions for the exercise of rights, were as characteristic of mid-Victorian Liberalism as the quests to stimulate material progress and to empower the individual. As Gladstone, in criticizing the Divorce Bill of 1857, had warned his colleagues: "Take care, then how you damage the character of your countrymen. You know how apt the English nature is to escape from restraint and control: you know what passion dwells in the Englishman."[194] Years after he had shucked off much of the conservatism of the 1850s, Gladstone's standard of liberty remained quite firmly "of the English type . . . under rule." Gladstone himself was one of the founders, in 1848, of the Church of England Penitentiary Association, and for thirty years was a visitor at Millbank Prison.[195] He was more familiar with the penal system than most politicians or social thinkers, but betrayed no feeling that it was in need of any softening or loosening. His deeply rooted religious beliefs provided him with a lifelong faith in the reality of sin, the necessity of retribution, and the validity of reformation through suffering and repentence.

Gladstone's first home secretary, Henry Austin Bruce, one of "the work horses of the liberal party in the 1870s,"[196] faced crime with a similar sternness. A magistrate for five years before entering Parliament, Bruce's attitude toward violent offenders in general was unsympathetic; in rejecting memorials for a reprieve from hanging in 1869, he noted that "the recent frequency of these murderous assaults, and the reckless indifference to human life they

---

[193] See Parry, pp. 31–2.

[194] 3 PD 147, c. 854 (July 31, 1857). This highly restrictive and moralistic measure was as far as divorce was allowed until 1922. Although he was outvoted in 1857, Gladstone spoke for most of his generation when he observed in later life that the modest rise in divorce that followed "marks degeneracy and the increasing sway of passion." [(1889) In *Correspondence on Church and Religion of W. E. Gladstone*, ed. D. C. Lathbury (London, 1910), vol. II, p. 361.]

[195] Herbert Gladstone, *After Thirty Years* (London, 1928), p. 66.

[196] H. C. G. Matthew, ed., *The Gladstone Diaries V: 1855–1860* (Oxford: Clarendon Press, 1978), p. xlvii. Locating Bruce's precise political position has been something of a puzzle for historians; most recently he has been called a "Peelite" by J. P. Parry [*Democracy and Religion*, p. 76], while Colin Matthew has placed him as one of a key a group of men "of a moderate but nonetheless firmly held radicalism" [*The Gladstone Diaries*, vol. 5, p. xlvii]. Taken together, this would seem to place him as close as anyone to the heart of Gladstonian Liberalism; indeed Bruce has recently been sited "at the center of the social reforms of the Liberal administration." [Goldman, p. 104.]

exhibit, call for severe and unfaltering repression."[197] Nor was Bruce amenable toward requests for remissions of lesser sentences. In refusing the recommendation of a chairman of Quarter Sessions to reduce a sentence of twelve months imprisonment imposed on two sailors for sheepstealing, he noted that the grounds for mitigation proposed – that they acted under the instigation of their captain – rather than helping them, "might be good ground for prosecuting the captain." Such instigation, however, afforded "no sufficient justification for advising the mitigation of a sentence, not in itself excessive, passed upon two grown men."[198]

Under Bruce's administration, the 1864 and 1865 prison acts were vigorously implemented. During his first year in office he ordered more frequent inspection of prisons, to uncover "any laxity of discipline" or "irregularity," that is, failure to comply with the provisions of the law. He also requested more communication and "occasional personal conference and interchange of opinions" between inspectors, the surveyor general, and the directors of convict prisons, to "promote the uniformity of system which it is so desirable to establish in all prisons."[199] There is no evidence that he sought to mitigate any of the severity of the prison system; indeed, the tough director of convict prisons, Colonel Edmund Henderson, was a "close friend" of his.[200] As he remarked in replying to Irish complaints about the treatment of Fenian prisoners:

[197] HO 13/110, Liddell to Jacob Bright, M.P., March 27, 1869. In another case, this one of a 17-year-old who had clearly murdered with premeditation, he resisted a unanimous jury plea for mercy, as well as petitions and personal appeals from influential persons and only gave in and commuted the sentence to life after a file search revealed that no person under age 18 had been hanged in the past eighteen years. [HO 144/9236, Dec. 23, 1871–Jan. 6, 1872.] Bruce's sternness was shored up by his permanent under-secretary, Alphonsus Liddell. Liddell reported in the latter case that his clerks "cannot find any case of commutation on the grounds of youth only. The rule of Law is that on the attainment of 14 years the criminal actions of infants are subject to the same modes of construction as those of the rest of society for the law presumes them at those years to be 'doli capex' and able to discern between good and evil and therefore subjects them to a punishment as if they were." [*ibid*, Jan. 4, 1872] This supported the conclusion Bruce had already reached in his first reaction to the case ("no ground for commutation. His youth alone affords no justification. Everything else is against him."). A later Conservative government turned to Bruce in 1888 to chair a committee on the most suitable methods of carrying out death sentences; the committee heard without remark a great deal of testimony that Radzinowicz and Hood found "repellant." [p. 664.]

[198] HO 13/111, Liddell to Lord Newborough, March 1, 1871. In one case he did reverse an initial refusal to interfere with a sentence, stressing however that this was *only* due to the forwarding of new information about the crime from local officials. [HO 13/110, Liddell to Henry Angus, Feb. 3, 1869.]

[199] HO 22/16, Liddell to Inspectors of Prisons, Dec. 23, 1869.

[200] Henry Austin Bruce, *Letters* (Oxford: Printed for Private Circulation, 1902) vol. I, p. 265.

though penal servitude could not be prolonged beyond many years without danger to health and life, yet within certain limits it was comparatively a lenient sentence. It involved labour, undoubtedly, but a life of labour was better than a life of inactivity.[201]

Not surprisingly, petitions from prisoners met a cool reception. Soon after taking office, seemingly irritated by demands of a convict for both remission of his sentence and compensation in consideration of an injury sustained in prison, Bruce set out as a general rule that no remission or compensation be granted "for ordinary accidents occurring to convicts on public works, or which may be occasioned by their own negligence."[202] As had Sir George Grey, Bruce repeatedly denied requests from visiting justices for early release by reason of illness or disability. Statements by medical officers that further imprisonment "would be prejudicial to [the prisoner's] health" were not considered sufficient; what was necessary was a certification that "further confinement would endanger the prisoner's life."[203] Even medical claims that a prisoner's life might be prolonged by release would not do; such a claim, he complained, was "a most vague and indefinite assertion." The Home Office insisted that medical certificates as to the danger arising from prolonged imprisonment "should be precise and distinct."[204] Similarly, it cautioned prison officials that inmates who had a history of insanity must nonetheless be treated as sane until duly certified to be of unsound mind.[205]

The area of criminal policy in which Bruce took greatest personal interest related to juveniles. As vice-president of the Committee of Council on Education from 1864 to 1866 he developed close relations with managers of reformatory and industrial schools[206] and helped pass Adderley's 1866 Industrial Schools Act, which widened the definition of children eligible for commitment to include orphans, children of a surviving parent who was undergoing penal servitude or imprisonment, and refractory children or children of criminal parents who were regarded as unsuitable to be kept in work-

---

[201] 3 PD 179, c. 809 (June 29, 1869).

[202] HO 22/16, Liddell to Lieutenant Colonel Henderson, Feb. 9, 1869. The only cases in which the question of remission might be considered were "those where the accident occurs through the negligence or default of the prison officers." Bruce's assumption here was apparently that by breaking the law, the criminal voluntarily assumed the normal hazards of prison life, much as a free workman did by accepting a contract of employment.

[203] HO 22/16, Knatchbull-Hugessen to the Visiting Justices of Nottingham Prison, Jan. 27, 1869.

[204] HO 22/16. Knatchbull-Hugessen to Lord Beauchamp, Sept. 30, 1869.

[205] HO 13/110, Liddell to E. W. Barnwell, May 17, 1869.

[206] As displayed later in his supportive activity as chairman of the 1884 Royal Commission on Reformatory and Industrial Schools and in private defenses of managers to his more critical successor, Harcourt.

houses. The act multiplied committals to industrial schools,[207] dramatically
expanding state control over the children of "the criminal classes." Even as industrial school admissions were rapidly rising, the proportion of reformatory
committals continued to grow, and, more strikingly, the proportion of such
committals for the maximum term of five years was sharply on the rise.[208]
Bruce, eager to remove children from bad influences, seems to have supported
all these trends. As he observed in 1869, "the evil of crime was not so much in
the direct loss it occasioned, by the plunder committed, as in the fact that the
offenders constituted schools of crime in which the young and ignorant were
entrapped."[209] In cases of disputed committal, the home secretary usually
supported magistrates and managers against parents.[210] He was ready to support committal in any case where what he considered "proper guardianship"
was lacking.[211] Even when he ruled against an overeager magistrate, morality
was the test: proper guardianship referred not to material but to moral factors.
Poor parents could not have their children taken from them, unless their
character was called into question.[212] Where character was wanting, parental
rights could be overridden and children compulsorily incarcerated.

Similar to these new powers of committing juveniles were the new powers
for control and punishment of habitual offenders given by acts of 1869 and
1871.[213] In his election speech at Glasgow in January 1869, Bruce cited control of the increasing number of criminals at large as the chief task facing the

---

[207] Admissions rose from 170 in 1865 to 1,465 in 1868, and continued rising thereafter
until 1879 [annual criminal statistics].

[208] Maximum term reformatory committals rose from about 40 percent in 1857 to 65
percent at the end of the 1870s [annual criminal statistics].

[209] 3 PD 179, c. 1259 (Aug. 4, 1869).

[210] See for example HO 13/110, Liddell to clerk of Coventry Justices, Dec. 3, 1869; HO
13/110, Knatchbull-Hugessen to James Hall, Oct. 20, 1869; HO 13/110, Knatchbull-
Hugessen to clerk of Middlesbrough Justices, Jan. 22, 1870.

[211] Thus, that parents come forward and declare their readiness to support their child
picked up as vagrant was not enough to prevent its committal: "If the child's parents are
habitual drunkards, or of known vicious or criminal character, or tramps, or if they continually [abuse?] or neglect the child, and are thus the cause of its wandering and destitution, and are leaving it to grow up in the habits of vice and beggary, they cannot be said
to be *proper* guardians of it." [HO 13/110, Knatchbull-Hugessen to James Hall, Oct. 20,
1869.]

[212] HO 22/16, Liddell to Sydney Turner, Dec. 3, 1869. This reversal was suggested by
Turner.

[213] Urgings for habitual criminal legislation came from across the political spectrum,
from Liberals and radicals as well as conservatives. In his early days in office Bruce
received two delegations urging this—one headed by Sir Walter Crofton, the chief of the
Irish prison system, and a second led by three Liberal London members of parliament.
The leading agitators for such a measure—Crofton, Barwick Baker, M. D. Hill—were all active (as was Bruce himself) in the Social Science Association. As Hill declared in 1866, habitual criminals should be held in a special prison whose regime would be "harsher by

Home Office.[214] His mind was set, he declared, "upon preventing the spread of crime at once – first by cutting off the source of its supply, and next by devising a good system of punishment."[215] He was true to his pledge; the Habitual Criminals Bill was introduced the following month, one of the first measures put forth by the new government. Although its appearance on a Liberal legislative agenda strikes twentieth-century eyes as anomalous, this criminal justice legislation formed a natural continuation of the measures enacted under Palmerston to tighten penal discipline, strengthen the deterrent force of sentences, and expand police supervision of the criminal classes.[216] The legislation of 1864 and 1865, in addition to making prison conditions more severe and more uniform, had increased the difficulty of earning early release, provided a higher minimum sentence of penal servitude for repeat offenders, and authorized police supervision of convicts released before expiration of their terms. The 1869 bill took this disciplinary effort even further by reaffirming and extending the application of the principle of progressively heavier sentences for repeated offences, by expanding the scope of police supervision to embrace absolutely released prisoners as well as those on license, and by giving magistrates new powers to imprison summarily these former offenders and vagrants on suspicion only.

The bill sought to apply the principle of cumulative sentencing that was strongly advocated by both reformers and conservatives in the 1860s and already recommended by the 1863 Royal Commission.[217] It set a mandatory sentence of seven years penal servitude for a third conviction of felony.[218] This provision was, however, dropped, after a number of members pointed out, not that it was too harsh, but that it might be so perceived by juries, leading them to acquit unjustly.[219] Though the provision for a mandatory minimum sentence failed to make it through the legislative process, the act contained enough enhancements of criminal liability and police power, further extended by the 1871 Prevention of Crimes Act, to break significant new ground in the extension and intensification of the exercise of state power. The act was directed, as the parliamentary under-secretary at the Home Office put

many degrees" than the already highly severe regular prisons, and which would never reach "a condition which even the humblest member of society would esteem one of even tolerable welfare." [Quoted in Radzinowicz and Hood, p. 233.]

[214] *The Times*, Jan. 26, 1869, p. 9.

[215] *The Times*, Jan. 15, 1869, p. 9.

[216] On the passage of this bill, see Melling, "Cleaning House," 315–362; Radzinowicz and Hood, pp. 231–265.

[217] See D. A. Thomas, *Constraints on Judgment* (Cambridge: Institute of Criminology, 1979), p. 12.

[218] If the second conviction had been within the previous five years.

[219] See Melling, 338.

it, at "restraining [detected offenders] from lapsing into their old habits of crime. For this purpose greatly increased powers have been intrusted to the police."[220] These expanded police powers were not meant, however, to impinge upon the lives of the general population. A line was drawn in these measures between those to whom the rights of "free-born Englishmen" applied and those to whom they did not, and a charter was set out for a sweeping regulation by the agents of the state of the everyday lives of the latter. As Lord Kimberley, who introduced the 1869 bill in the upper chamber, argued, there was nothing repugnant to justice in placing one group of persons, twice-convicted felons, "under a disability.... Men who by repeated crimes have shown that they set the laws of society at defiance should be placed under a different code."[221] Such a code was to consist of police supervision and the shift of the burden of proof from the state to the accused. It was time, Bruce stated in Parliament, "that society should arm itself with more effectual weapons against habitual crime.... What they ought to aim at was to give assistance and encouragement to the reclaimable, but with respect to the hopelessly irreclaimable to hunt them down without mercy."[222]

At the same time, tolerance for lesser forms of deviance was also evaporating; as this bill was making its way through Parliament, apprehensions and prosecutions of public order or moral offenders, including prostitutes, beggars, and drunkards, were setting new records.[223] The 1869 bill did not limit its expansion of state disciplinary power to serious, or even repeated, offenders. Vagrants – "more properly styled, rogues and vagabonds," noted Kimberley – were "a class which has hitherto escaped being regarded in the eye of the law as criminal."[224] This unfortunate gap in the law was remedied by a provision making such persons, who might never have been convicted of a criminal offense, for the first time liable to criminal sanctions without the need to prove an unlawful act. All that would be required would be "sufficient evidence to convince a magistrate that the vagrant was [in a dwelling house or public place] with an unlawful purpose" and he could be summarily sentenced to imprisonment. Criminal intent was to be inferred from the circumstances of the case and from the person's known character.

The 1869 bill also gave new powers for dealing with another disreputable group – receivers of stolen goods. The original version provided that any

---

[220] E. W. Knatchbull-Hugessen to the lord mayor of London, Nov. 20, 1869. Reported in 48 *Law Times* 52.

[221] 3 PD 194, c. 340 (Feb. 26, 1869).

[222] 3 PD 198, c. 1258–9 (Aug. 4, 1869).

[223] *Report of the Police Commissioner for the Metropolis for 1869*, p. 6. The commissioner observed that the numbers of arrests and convictions of prostitutes (for public annoyance) in particular "greatly exceeds that of any former year."

[224] 3 PD 194, c. 343 (Feb. 26, 1869).

person previously convicted of an offense punishable by imprisonment and subsequently discovered to have stolen goods in his possession was deemed to have known them to be stolen until he proved the contrary. This definition was amended to replace the words "punishable by imprisonment" by "involving fraud or dishonesty," so as to focus the application of the presumption of guilt in such cases upon the intended target, professional fences. Such determination to bring the force of law to bear to root out the receivers of stolen goods was heartily endorsed by no less a libertarian than John Stuart Mill, who indeed urged that the effort be stepped up, since receivers were "the solid support and foundation of all professional theft, and without them a criminal class, as a class, could not exist."[225] The act also made criminal the known harboring of thieves or reputed thieves, thus notably extending the criminal liability of yet another group – innkeepers and public house owners (whose legal liability was soon to be further extended by the 1872 Licensing Act).

Rather than making reluctant concessions to right-wing public pressure, Bruce seems to have inclined to even more severity and use of state power than was politically feasible. Though he did not press it, Bruce personally endorsed Henry Taylor's argument for life sentences of imprisonment for irreclaimable offenders; moreover, he sympathized with Susanna Meredith's desire to extend control of released female offenders beyond the provisions of the bill, but accepted that those provisions went "quite as far as public feeling at present admits."[226] He also was gratified to see that most proposed amendments were in the direction "not of narrowing or weakening but of enlarging the principle of the Bill."[227] Nor was Bruce ever subject to second thoughts after the passage of the act. Several years later he noted that its workings "had given great satisfaction."[228] To make it "work more smoothly and effectually," he put through a supplementary act in 1871. This measure clarified the language of the 1869 measure and responded to police complaints of excessive work load by removing the requirement for supervision of repeat offenders and leaving it to the discretion of the courts.[229]

Such criminal legislation brings into sharp relief a coercively activist face of Victorian liberalism long ignored by historians. From the turn of the twentieth

[225] (1870), 48 *Law Times* 167.

[226] 3 PD 179, c. 1259 (Aug. 4, 1869); HO 13/110, Liddell to Mrs. Meredith, March 25, 1869.

[227] 3 PD 179, c. 1260 (Aug. 4, 1869).

[228] *The Times*, Oct. 14, 1875, p. 10.

[229] Radzinowicz and Hood, pp. 256–7. Administration moved in tandem with legislation. In 1870, the criminal branch of the Home Office was upgraded to a department, and by the 1880s, Jill Pellew has observed, "the status of criminal work had risen so much" that it was "clearly the superior department of the office." [*The Home Office 1848–1914: From Clerks to Bureaucrats* (London: Heinemann, 1982), p. 57.]

century onward, images of philosophical laissez-faire, a minimal state, and Gladstonian libertarianism have overlaid and obscured these facial features. Conservatives like Dicey and Socialists like Webb, each for his own reasons, entrenched such images in the historical imagination. When the collectivist tide had crested and this face began to be noticed, it was seen as peculiar, peripheral, and atypical of true liberalism. In a path-breaking study in the 1960s, W. L. Burn rescued the criminal legislation of the 1860s from obscurity and linked it with other neglected legal disciplines of the time. Yet even Burn failed to notice the affinities his mid-Victorian disciplines had to the liberalism of the time. Indeed, his only reference to the latter in his discussion of criminal policy was to note that Bruce's argument for the Habitual Criminals Bill "came, perhaps, a little oddly from a member of a Liberal Government whose chief business that session had been that liberalizing measure, the disestablishment of the Church of Ireland."[230]

Yet we can now see the penal legislation of the 1860s and early 1870s not as a peripheral anomaly, but as an expression of the disciplinary subtext of Gladstonian liberation. It was characteristic of this form of Liberalism to accompany virtually every conferring of benefit with a demand for better behavior. Social policy was to foster active self-discipline – replacing, in the phrase of a temperance activist, "impulsive will" by "moral will."[231] Excepting the views of a small minority of laissez-faire doctrinaires, self-help and self-discipline were more than the residual result of a policy of not doing things for men that they might do for themselves (or their families); this aim involved also a positive commitment to *make* men self-governing by enforcing new standards and obligations upon them. As Frederic Hill observed with satisfaction in 1868 to the Social Science Association, social affairs were increasingly based on the principle that "if error be committed or wrong done there may be no doubt with whom the chief blame rests."[232] Everyone, high or low, must be held accountable for his actions. The imposing of blame and penalties upon those who failed to meet the obligations of citizenship, who misused freedom, rather than being alien and exceptional, was rooted deeply within mid-Victorian liberalism.

The wider liberty individuals were granted, the more liable to blame and punishment they became for misusing that liberty. The consequent linkage of the expansion of individual rights with the enforcement of new standards of personal behavior was exhibited throughout the social policies of the first

---

[230] W. L. Burn, *The Age of Equipoise* (London: Allen & Unwin, 1964), p. 193.

[231] F. R. Lees, *United Kingdom Alliance Prize Essay* (3rd ed., 1857), p. 27.

[232] *The Principles and Functions of Government* (London: National Association for the Promotion of Social Science, 1868), p. 3.

Gladstone government. The administration of the Poor Law and of elementary schools and the regulation of the drink trade, housing, public health, and public morals were all given greater disciplinary force through the more extensive and stricter application of legal penalties.

Throughout the Victorian era, the Poor Law was "educational machinery," expected to help shape popular behavior.[233] This instructive purpose reached a culmination in the later 1860s and the 1870s. By 1868, the time seemed ripe to many policymakers for a full-scale assault upon pauperism as upon crime.[234] In that year the Poor Law Board launched a "crusade against out-relief." By strictly enforcing the workhouse test, by widening its applicability to all able-bodied men and women, by denying out-relief to the "undeserving" disabled, by maintaining the stigma associated with the acceptance of relief,[235] and by providing such assistance as was given solely according to clear, consistent and published rules,[236] poor relief would, as its chief inspector put it, "offer the minimum of discouragement to the formation by the poor of provident and independent habits"; indeed, it would even positively "encourage providence."[237] In 1871, the workhouse labor test was introduced for able-bodied single women.[238] At the same time, the board also began to encourage criminal prosecution of fathers for deserting or neglecting

[233] As E. P. Hennock has put it: "Those who made Poor Law policy ... thought of it not as machinery for the provision of needs only, but also as educational machinery designed to transform the attitudes of the labouring poor towards social change. Much modern writing on the nineteenth century Poor Law is vitiated by a failure to take this into account." [Review of Derek Fraser, ed., *The New Poor Law, Social History 2*, no. 6 (Oct., 1977), 829.]

[234] See Gareth Stedman Jones, *Outcast London* (Oxford: Clarendon Press, 1971); Parry, p. 115; Michael Rose, "The Crisis of Poor Relief in England 1860–1890" in W. Mommsen, ed., *The Emergence of the Welfare State in Britain and Germany* (London: Croom Helm, 1981).

[235] The workhouse pauper, like the prison inmate, was seen as providing an instructive social lesson; as the organizer of a regular national conference of Poor Law Guardians put it in 1875, "paying the penalty of their misfortunes or faults, they serve the useful purpose of warning the young and careless of the need of making provision against the possibilities of ill-health and the certainties of old age." [Albert Pell, M.P., in *Reports of the Poor Law District Conferences 1875*, p. 298.]

[236] Karel Williams has suggested that the new requirements for published (and largely moral) criteria of eligibility were meant to give members of the working class an educational opportunity to reflect on the reasons (their personal shortcomings) why an application for out-relief would not be successful. [*From Pauperism to Poverty* (London: Routledge, 1981), p. 99.]

[237] Henry Longley, *Report to the Local Government Board on Poor Law Administration in London* (1874), quoted in Karel Williams, pp. 198, 195.

[238] See Pat Thane, "Women and the Poor Law in Victorian and Edwardian England," *History Workshop* no. 6 (Autumn, 1978), 29–51.

to support their families, a trend that rose steadily to a peak in 1876.[239] After the passage in 1872 of amendments to the bastardy clauses of the Poor Law Act, fathers of illegitimate children faced new legal responsibilities and legal sanctions; criminal sanctions even began to be applied to adult children who refused to support their destitute parents.[240] Increased benefits for those who met the criteria of citizenship – free medical treatment in new Poor Law dispensaries and infirmaries – were coupled with intensified penalties for those who failed the test.[241]

[239] George Behlmer, *Child Abuse and Moral Reform in England, 1870–1908* (Stanford: Stanford University Press, 1982), p. 92.

[240] See U. R. Q. Henriques, "Bastardy and the New Poor Law," *Past and Present 37* (July, 1967), 103–29; David Thomson, " 'I am not my father's keeper': Families and the Elderly in Nineteenth Century England," *Law and History Review 2* (1984–85), 265–86.

[241] Many reformist Liberals, not chiefly motivated, as politicians and even civil servants often had to be, by the desire to hold down taxes, supported these policies of selective and discriminatory welfare on moral grounds. The distinguished academic radicals, Arnold Toynbee and Henry Sidgwick, for instance, each served on Oxford and Cambridge Boards of Guardians, respectively, and helped introduce there more discriminating relief policies. See Christopher Harvie, *Lights of Liberalism* (London: Allen Lane, 1976), pp. 195–6.

The "anomaly" of the failure of the 1869 act abolishing imprisonment for debt to actually do so [see Chapter 2] makes sense in light of the purposes of other contemporaneous Liberal reforms; like these other measures, that act sought to draw a clear moral line, prohibiting imprisonment for debt except in cases of moral fault, that is, of "wilful refusal to pay" when adjudged to have the means to do so; in the latter cases, reformers were as ready as traditionalists (perhaps readier) to come down hard.

Similarly, the Charity Organization Society (COS), founded in 1868, supported in its work by many academic and professional Liberals, was intended to further this dual task of assistance and punishment by developing more scientific methods of discriminating between deserving and undeserving. To the first it could provide more effective assistance than the state often could do; the second it would more surely consign to their merited penalties. [See Rose, "Crisis," 61–2; E. P. Hennock, "Poverty and Social Theory in England: The Experience of the Eighteen-Eighties," *Social History 1* (1976), 67–92; G. Stedman Jones, *Outcast*, pp. 262–80.] The COS worked closely with Poor Law officials, central and local, and its discourse, like that of both Poor Law and penal policymakers, was profoundly moralist. "If one sentence could explain the principle of our work," the Reverend Samuel Barnett put it, "it is that we aim at decreasing, not suffering but sin." [Henrietta Barnett, *Canon Barnett: His Life, Work and Friends* (London, 1918) vol. I, p. 75.] Sin could hardly be decreased without disciplinary methods. As the COS's leading housing reformer, Octavia Hill, observed of her system of philanthropic landlordism, "It is a tremendous despotism, but it is exercised with a view to bringing out the powers of the people and treating them as responsible for themselves within certain limits." [Quoted in David Owen, *English Philanthropy 1660–1960* (Cambridge, Mass.: Harvard University Press, 1964), p. 390.] She argued early on that "the inexorable demand for rent (never to be relaxed without entailing cumulative evil in the defaulter, and setting a bad example)" for other tenants, conferred "a dignity and glad feeling of honourable behaviour which has much more than compensated for the apparent harshness of the rule." ["Cottage Property in London," *Fortnightly Review VI* (November, 1866), 683.]

Drunkenness, often seen as pauperism's twin and as a dissolvent of character and a cause of crime, was more energetically attacked after 1868 on two fronts. On the one hand, criminal prosecutions for public drunkenness markedly rose,[242] and sentences for this offense and more serious ones involving drink became heavier.[243] As we have seen, even that notable opponent of prohibition, John Stuart Mill, supported raising criminal sanctions against drunken offenders. At the same time that criminal treatment of drunkards was toughening, calls for licensing restrictions were becoming insistent. Prodded by temperance activists, but reflecting a wide sentiment that something needed to be done, Bruce introduced in 1871 a licensing bill that sharply tightened legal penalties on public drunkards and, more novelly, on public house owners for breach of regulations, with the explicit purpose of morally improving the public. Indeed, Bruce described the bill as "a necessary supplement" to the Education Act passed the previous year, which had made elementary education available to all.[244] To render the increased penalties effective, the bill provided new methods of enforcement. Licenses were henceforth to be taken out in the name of the owner rather than of the resident manager, and offenses were to be automatically endorsed on the license. Thus, there would be no evading of responsibility and the deterrent principle could operate. Moreover, Bruce envisaged a substantial new force of public house inspectors, financed by license charges. However, on this question the government ran into a storm of opposition led by the liquor interest – with the Paris Commune having just erupted, Bruce was called both a communist and a spymaster – and a much weakened bill finally passed into law the following year. Yet the government compromised only after exhibiting once again the disciplinarian face of liberalism.

Underneath these various policies lay a compelling vision of all of society as,

[242] From 1857 to 1861 such prosecutions in England and Wales had averaged about 84,000; from 1862 to 1866, 100,000; from 1867 to 1871, 122,000; from 1872 to 1876 (after passage of the Licensing Act) they peaked at about 186,000, leveling off thereafter (from 1897 to 1899, they averaged about 203,000). *Criminal Statistics for 1899*, p. 16. The Metropolitan Police commissioner pointed out in 1877 that "much of the apparent increase of late years is due to the increased activity of the Police under recent legislation" and not to a real rise in drunkenness. *Report of the Metropolitan Police Commissioner for 1876*.

[243] Both directly and indirectly these prosecutions were increasingly leading to imprisonment. Sentences of imprisonment rose from about $4\frac{1}{2}$ percent of proceedings in 1860 to about 11 percent in 1876, while the proportion imprisoned in default of payment of fines was also rising. Perhaps most significant, the proportion discharged without penalty fell dramatically in these years from more than one-third to less than one-tenth. See the table, drawn from the annual criminal statistics, in Brian Harrison, *Drink and the Victorians* (London: Faber and Faber, 1971), p. 398.

[244] *Alliance News* May 6, 1871, quoted in Harrison, *Drink*, p. 271.

in Hasting's phrase, a "well-regulated reformatory." Given such a vision, and its practical influence, it is not surprising that one disgruntled Tory complained in 1872 that "the tendency of recent measures . . . was to subject all of mankind to penal legislation." "If anybody," J. H. Scourfield continued, "were called on to portray the advancing civilization of England, it might be fitly conveyed by the representation of a large prison."[245]

[245] 3 PD 211, c. 2013 (June 20, 1872).

Figure 1. *Newgate Prison Discipline* by George Cruickshank, 1818. Unregulated association condemned. *Source:* British Library.

Figure 2. *Execution Scene Outside of Newgate* by Thomas Rowlandson, circa 1810. Public executions were surrounded by a circuslike atmosphere until their abolition in 1868.

Figure 3. *The Solitary Prisoner* (uncredited). *Source:* Charles Dickens, *American Notes*, 1850, Cheap Edition.

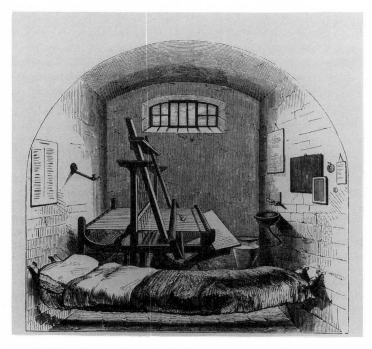

Figure 4. Uniform "industrious isolation" was the essence of the new penal regime. *Source:* Henry Mayhew and John Binny, *The Criminal Prisons in London and Scenes of Prison Life* [1862], reprinted in 1968 by Frank Cass & Co. Ltd.

4

A changing human image

The mysterious citadel of the will

Interwoven with its practical functions, Victorian social policy also had an expressive role, that of enacting strongly held voluntarist aspirations and concerns centering on the vision of the individual struggling to master nature, without and within.[1] Through the many turns and twists of nineteenth-century history, this vision (however qualified, complicated, and even disregarded at times) gave a certain coherence to social discourse and social policy. In no area of social concern was this more true than with crime and criminals. However, the symbolic realm was no more fixed than the practical. Even while social and intellectual changes had been heightening concern about the control of impulses, the same developments were paradoxically foreshadowing a different, almost opposite, crisis, in which the most pressing problem of human nature was seen as stemming from its weakness rather than its powers.

A "block universe"?[2]

Scientific and social change combined forces in the later decades of the century to reshape perceptions of human nature and agency.[3] The Darwinian revolution and contemporaneous developments in physics and astronomy began to shrink the individual in an ever vaster cosmos. Similarly, within the

---

[1] By now it should be clear that voluntarism does not mean a simple belief in free and autonomous individuals, but a trope of continual *struggle* to actualize a potential of autonomy and self-governing freedom, a trope that could encourage a wide array of interventionism and interferences with liberty.

[2] The phrase is from William James, a late Victorian very much concerned with the threat of determinism.

[3] Particularly useful studies of the impact of scientific ideas on mid- and later Victorian images of man and society are Alan W. Brown, *The Metaphysical Society: Victorian Minds in Crisis, 1869–1880* (New York: Columbia University Press, 1947); J. D. Y. Peel, *Herbert Spencer: The Evolution of a Sociologist* (London: Heinemann, 1971); Frank M. Turner, *Between Science and Religion* (New Haven: Yale University Press, 1974); and Greta Jones, *Social Darwinism and English Thought: The Interaction between Biological and Social Theory* (Brighton, Sussex: Harvester, 1980).

social world, the ever-increasing scale and complexity of life was, after the first flush of liberation from custom, coming to leave the individual feeling smaller and less effectual. In particular, as novel technology and the expanding market extended the effective reach of actions, the first psychic effect – a sense of expanded powers and potentialities – gradually was giving way to growing uncertainty about one's own autonomy. As the effective reach and force of the individual's actions grew, so too did the reach and force of others' actions grow to impinge upon the individual. The giddy sense of unleashed powers that had excited, and frightened, middle-class early Victorians, was being countered as the century progressed by a sense of subjection to the actions of remote others, actions that became increasingly crystallized into impersonal forces. By the turn of the century, it was becoming widely recognized, as the social analyst Graham Wallas put it, that "each man's life depends on causes he can't understand."[4]

This paradoxical message of multiplied power neutralized for each individual by diminished autonomy that was embodied in the rise of what Wallas called the "Great Society" was underlined by the rapid advance of science. Every day science seemed to be making it clearer that natural phenomena exhibited predictable regularities and that causation in nature followed invariant laws. In physics and biology, the dominant paradigms reinforced a sense of a determined system of mechanical causation in which there might be much room for chance, but not for conscious will, a system of large forces and units in which the individual counted for little.[5]

At the most fundamental level, new scientific theories were making it harder to imagine the human world as exempt from the sway of natural law. Individuals, however free and effective they might feel themselves, were seen to be dependent upon the operation of forces and the constitution of structures beyond the control of their will. Although Samuel Smiles might

---

[4] Notes for a lecture on "The Decay of Liberalism" given in October 1901, quoted in Martin Wiener, *Between Two Worlds: The Political Thought of Graham Wallas* (Oxford: Clarendon Press, 1981), p. 104. See also Thomas L. Haskell, *The Emergence of Professional Social Science: The American Social Science Association and the Nineteenth-Century Crisis of Authority* (Urbana: University of Illinois Press, 1977).

[5] We must bear in mind that recent work has shown how *many* implications, not necessarily compatible with one another, there were in Darwin's work and in Darwinism. See for example, Robert C. Bannister, *Social Darwinism: Science and Myth in Anglo-American Social Thought* (Philadelphia: Temple University Press, 1979) and Peter J. Bowler, *Evolution: The History of an Idea* (revised ed.; Berkeley: University of California Press, 1989). Darwin's work repays study as a literary text, as Gillian Beer, *Darwin's Plots* (Boston: Routledge, 1983), has demonstrated; the complex and partly contradictory strands of meaning even at the very heart of Darwin's theory have been unravelled in Robert M. Young, "Darwin's Metaphor: Does Nature Select? in *Darwin's Metaphor: Nature's Place in Victorian Culture* (Cambridge: Cambridge University Press, 1985), pp. 79–125.

insist, in the year of *The Origin of Species*, that "in every moment of our life, conscience is proclaiming that our will is free,"[6] Darwin's work was fundamentally subversive of such a notion.[7] In the succeeding decades (despite a certain revival of Lamarckianism),[8] reflective persons found it harder to believe Smiles without ever more qualification.

Perceptions of growing social complexity and interdependence reinforced Darwinian modes of thinking. This convergence of sociological and biological mental models is strikingly illustrated in the thinking of Herbert Spencer. In 1860, he was already arguing that the main features of social organization "are neither supernatural, nor are determined by the wills of individual men ... but are consequent on general natural causes."[9] It was impossible, he insisted, for any individual to step outside the ever-growing social organism: "The individual citizen [is] embedded in the social organism as one of its units, moulded by its influence and aiding reciprocally to remould it."[10]

Naturalistic liberals like Spencer and even Darwin himself (at least in public) bridged their two sets of beliefs by claiming that natural selection necessarily favored all the character traits of which they approved and thus was bringing about moral evolution. As Darwin put it:

> Man prompted by his conscience, will through long habit acquire such perfect self-command, that his desires and passions will at last yield instantly and without a struggle to his social sympathies and instincts, including his feeling for the judgment of his fellows.... It is possible ... even probable, that the habit of self-command may, like other habits, be inherited.[11]

Or, as Leslie Stephen argued a few years later, personal self-command was an evolutionarily valuable trait, as moral conduct was ultimately efficient, useful

---

[6] *Self-Help* [1859] (London: J. Murray, 1925), p. 198.

[7] This point has been most recently reiterated by George Levine, *Darwin and the Novelists* (Cambridge, Mass.: Harvard University Press, 1989). Darwin wrote his wife as early as 1848 that "Hensleigh [Wedgwood, her philosopher brother] thinks he has settled the Free Will question, but hereditariness practically demonstrates that we have none whatever" [*The Correspondence of Charles Darwin, Vol. 4: 1847–1850*, ed. F. Burkhardt and S. Smith (Cambridge: Cambridge University Press, 1989), p. 143].

[8] Peter Bowler, *The Eclipse of Darwinism* (Baltimore: Johns Hopkins University Press, 1983), has brought out the vigor of this resurgent Lamarckianism, but also shown it sharing Darwinism's "impersonalism," flowing at least as much into "collectivist" racist and eugenic channels as into any reinvigorated individualist voluntarism. For our concerns, most of the fierce scientific disputes of the later nineteenth century were irrelevant; both sides tended to accept and advance the erosion of voluntarism.

[9] Herbert Spencer, "The Social Organism" (1860), quoted in Peel, *Spencer*, p. 175.

[10] *ibid.*, p. 188.

[11] Charles Darwin, *The Descent of Man and Selection in Regard to Sex* [1871] (New York: D. Appleton, 1896), p. 115.

conduct. For society's evolution, "incontinence of feeling is a source of weakness, though it may at times cause a superficial appearance of vigour."[12] Yet the development of continent character through natural selection was a form of moral progress that operated by impersonal compulsion, without room for individual choice, thus saving the skin of Victorian Liberalism only by gutting its innards.[13]

Paradoxically, as the power of mankind over nature soared, the sense of the limits of one's power over the self and one's own actions grew with ever greater force. Although this could appear to enthusiasts for a science of man as opening unprecedented vistas of human power – if it were collective, expert, and guided by science – in shaping human life, as time went on it seemed to pose a mortal threat to the deep-rooted need to believe in autonomous individuals morally responsible for their actions. The scientific world view shifted attention from acts to contexts, from the conscious human actor to the surrounding circumstances, whether in one's environment or one's constitution. Such an outlook did not sit easily with notions of free will or personal autonomy, for its thrust was always to go behind the immediate situation – the apparently free choice, for instance – to the forces operating on that choice. Its basic tendency, desired or not, was toward determinism.

As scientific naturalism entered the process of constructing the human world, it began to influence conceptions of human nature and narratives of social action. It supplied a language in which agency could be relocated and simultaneously spread uneasiness with holding individuals fully responsible for their actions or assuming them free to change their behavior. Scientific developments suggested two forms of limitation upon personal freedom and power: environmental and constitutional. Advancing sociological and medical discourses combined to render problematic the feasibility of setting as a goal such a high degree of personal mastery over one's circumstances or one's constitution. Yet for many, this meant a dangerous loss of bearings. The poet Laureate Alfred Tennyson warned, "Take away the sense of individual responsibility and men sink into pessimism and madness."[14] Oscar Wilde later underlined this fear by his very acquiescence in the loss:

---

[12] Leslie Stephen, *The Science of Ethics* (London: Smith, Elder & Co., 1882), p. 422.

[13] As became apparent in the writings of the influential turn-of-the-century social Darwinist, Benjamin Kidd. See D. A. Crook, *Benjamin Kidd* (Cambridge: Cambridge University Press, 1984).

[14] Hallam Tennyson, *Alfred Lord Tennyson: A Memoir by His Son*, Vol. 1 (New York: Macmillan, 1905), p. 317. It must be remembered, however, that determinism could be not only a specter but a great relief. Personal responsibility is after all a burden. It is interesting that social psychologists have found that "subjects who attribute their inability to control an aversive outcome to their own inadequacy appear to experience considerably more stress than subjects who attribute it to factors in the environment or situation." Wortman, Panciera, Shusterman, and Hibscher, "Attributions of Causality and Reactions

By revealing to us the absolute mechanism of all action, and so freeing us from the self-imposed and trammelling burden of moral responsibility, the scientific principle of Heredity has become, as it were, the warrant for the contemplative life. It has shown us that we are never less free to act than when we try to act. It has hemmed us round with the nets of the hunter, and written upon the wall the prophecy of our doom. We may not watch it, for it is within us. We may not see it, save in a mirror that mirrors the soul. It is Nemesis without her mask.[15]

The belief in free will had already faced its first challenge in the early Victorian period with the appearance of a science of statistics. The Statistical Department of the Board of Trade was founded in 1832, the Manchester Statistical Society in 1833, and the Statistical Society of London (later to become the Royal Statistical Society) in 1834. As Theodore Porter has pointed out, statistics held great appeal for liberals, for like political economy it derived order from the free movement of individuals, revealing that society had its own organizing principles that depended little upon government.[16] Yet the order it uncovered seemed to dispense with individual free will. As the greatest statistician of the era, the Belgian Alphonse Quetelet (who assisted in the creation of the London society) put it, "the more the number of individuals is great, the more the individual will effaces itself." As a prime example of this process, Quetelet repeatedly cited crime rates. As he put it in 1835:

This constancy with which the same crimes are annually reproduced in the same order and receive the same penalties in the same proportions, is one of the most curious facts that the statistics of tribunals have taught us. . . . Sad condition of the human species! We are able to enumerate in advance how many individuals will stain their hands with the blood of their fellows, how many will be forgers, how many prisoners, much like one can enumerate in advance the births and deaths that must take place. Society contains within itself the seeds of all the crimes that are to be committed, and at the same time the facilities necessary for their development. It is society that, in some way, prepares these crimes, and the criminal is only the instrument that executes them.[17]

to Uncontrollable Outcomes," *Journal of Experimental Social Psychology* 12 (1976), 301, 311.

[15] (1891). Quoted in Peter Morton, *The Vital Science: Biology and the Literary Imagination 1860–1900* (London: Allen & Unwin, 1984), p. 149. This aspect of Wilde seems to have provided a key subtext for the seemingly irrational anti-Wildean "moral panic" at the time of his trial.

[16] Theodore Porter, *The Rise of Statistical Thinking 1820–1900* (Princeton: Princeton University Press, 1986), pp. 5–6.

[17] Quoted in Theodore Porter, "The Calculus of Liberalism: The Development of Statistical Thinking in the Social and Natural Sciences in the Nineteenth Century." unpublished Ph.D. dissertation, Princeton University 1981, pp. 109, 110.

Quetelet's striking remark was often cited to support social reforms; yet even those citing it disavowed any exculpation of immorality or criminality. Dickens, for all his denunciations of uncaring society for allowing conditions that foster crime, provided in *Hard Times* a biting attack on the use of statistical science to evade moral duty. There, Tom Gradgrind justifies his thievery by his father's doctrine of statistical law:

> So many people are employed in situations of trust; so many people, out of so many, will be dishonest. I have heard you talk, a hundred times, of its being a law. How can *I* help laws? You have condemned others to such things, Father. Comfort yourself![18]

Neither Quetelet nor most British statisticians were ready to follow Tom Gradgrind. Determined to help in the great task of strengthening popular character, they took this revelation of regularity not as a counsel of resignation, but as a call to action. Indeed, by its very uncovering of the apparent lawfulness of social behavior, statistics opened new vistas for scientifically assisting human progress. The economist Nassau Senior happily noted in 1860 that statistics taught that "the human will obeys laws nearly as certain as those which regulate matter."[19] And Henry Thomas Buckle made many of the implications of statistical science explicit and commonplace in his widely read *History of Civilization in England* (1857). "In the moral world," he declared, "as in the physical world, nothing is anomalous, nothing is unnatural, nothing is strange. All is order, symmetry, and law."[20] For all these men, eager to make use of the new knowledge for improvement of their fellows, scientism led not to fatalism but to social activism. As natural science's discovery of nature's laws had led to unprecedented material progress, perhaps then the uncovering of society's laws could do the same for moral progress. Thus, Edwin Chadwick, the foremost crusader for deterrent police, was also the foremost crusader for public health reform. His belief in the calculative nature of individuals coexisted with his tracing of a large part of the serious character deficiencies of the modern urban population to the deficiencies in the environment. The latter were correctable by organized and scientific effort; a population exposed to "noxious physical agencies" was, he argued, "less susceptible of moral influences, and the effects of education are more transient than with a healthy population."[21]

Yet although Chadwick's successors continued to stress how much ameliorative efforts could alter the effects of natural laws, as statistical thinking

[18] Bk. III, Ch. 7.
[19] "Opening Address," *Journal of the Statistical Society of London 23* (1860), 359.
[20] Quoted in Porter, *Rise*, p. 61.
[21] Edwin Chadwick, *Report on the Sanitary Condition of the Labouring Population of Great Britain*, M. W. Flinn, ed., (Edinburgh: Edinburgh University Press, 1965) p. 423.

became commonplace it undermined the sort of interest in character that had come naturally to Chadwick himself. The statistical outlook drained apparent causal power away from the individual toward impersonal forces. Even as they set forth inspiring vistas of social advance, statistical and sociological thinkers were propagating a weakened image of the individual. In place of the individual, the subject of the human sciences became society or nature.

Medical thought, like social science, moved from personal and moral modes of explanation toward more impersonal and deterministic ones. Not only were spiritual explanations of illness being banished, explanation by general states was replaced by the principle of disease specificity (which was much less supportive of the importance of character), and the focus on internal constitution yielded to a stress on external influences, whether infectious or environmental.[22] The advance of medical materialism went hand in hand with the rapid development of the study of psychology, based on a growing preoccupation with the biological conditions shaping character. During the first half of the nineteenth century, physiologists moved ever further into the study of psychological phenomena.[23] The "science" of phrenology was an early indication of the growing interest in physicalist explanation of human behavior. Stimulated by the physiological work of Gall and Spurzheim between 1800 and 1820, which treated mental faculties as localized brain functions, an English school of phrenology developed wide influence in the following generation. As Roger Smith has noted, it "supplied a language for talking about mental faculties and brain activity simultaneously. It served as a linguistic and conceptual bridge in the transition to physicalist views [of human behavior]."[24] Physiological psychology touched fundamental issues concerning free will and the nature of moral action – as did the alternative, introspective, movement in psychological inquiry that was to culminate at the turn of the century with the reception of Freud. While in many ways sharply at odds with physiologists, depth psychologists concerned with penetrating the unconscious shared their impatience with the image of the rational, self-commanding self underlying so much public and even professional

---

[22] Karl Figlio has pointed out that after 1866, when E. Greenhow became the first appointee to the newly established lectureship on public health at St. Bartholomew's Hospital, his criticisms of the individualized and moralized perspective of sanitary investigators like Chadwick began to gain sway within the emerging public health profession; Greenhow stressed in detailed studies the occupation dependence of illness in his *Papers Relating to the Sanitary State of the People of England ... General Board of Health (1858)*. See K. Figlio, "Chlorosis and Chronic Disease in Nineteenth-Century Britain," *Social History 3* (1978), 189n.

[23] See Roger Smith, *Trial by Medicine* (Edinburgh: Edinburgh University Press, 1981), p. 3.

[24] *ibid.*, p. 44.

Victorian discourse.[25] Thus, the attitude that this image of the self was problematic was not the work of one school of social or psychological thought, but rather a general tendency that reached across the barriers of scientific dispute.

A particularly strategic position, straddling the worlds of science of practical affairs, was occupied by medicine, and no part of it more so than the growing specialty of psychiatry, or, as it was then known, alienism. During the century, alienists, like social statisticians, were steadily widening the range of behavior they claimed for their jurisdiction. Also like the social statisticians, these very efforts of alienists to advance the usefulness of their profession served to undermine the moralism they continued to enact in their therapeutic work. In 1835, J. C. Prichard, influenced by the French alienists Pinel and Esquirol, had distinguished two types of insanity, one corresponding to the intellect and the other to the will, using for the latter the term "moral insanity." In cases of moral insanity, he wrote,

> the moral and active principles of the mind are strangely perverted and depraved; the power of self-government is lost or greatly impaired; and the individual is found to be incapable ... of conducting himself with decency and propriety in the business of life. His wishes and inclinations, his attachments, his likings and dislikings have all undergone a morbid change.[26]

Moral insanity, Prichard admitted, presented new problems of definition and delimitation, for there was "in this disorder no discoverable *illusion* or *hallucination*." Thus, it was often "very difficult to pronounce, with certainty, as to the presence or absence of moral insanity, or to determine whether the appearances which are supposed to indicate its existence do not proceed from natural peculiarity or eccentricity of character."[27] This new sort of insanity, in other words, was continuous with eccentricity and deviance; the old sharp division between sanity and madness was blurring. Moreover, its sufferer, though perhaps less visibly mad, was even more helpless than the hallucinating madman, for if he might still be able to reason, he no longer controlled his own will. At first, as we have seen, this redefinition of madness had supported intensified concern with self-government and efforts to promote such self-government by moral treatment. The problem of insanity was redefined as one of loss of self-control, not loss of reason or intellect, and the task of alienists was to stimulate personal efforts of will to regain self-mastery. But now a growing trend to trace behavior to physical sources gradually

---

[25] See Frank Sulloway, *Freud: Biologist of the Mind* (New York: Basic Books, 1979).

[26] J.C. Prichard, *A Treatise on Insanity* (London: Sherwood, Gilbert, & Piper, 1835), p. 4.

[27] J. C. Prichard, *On the Different Forms of Insanity, in Relation to Jurisprudence* (London: H. Bailliere, 1842), p. 31.

shifted the terms of interpretation of this problem to a plane on which the power of efforts of will carried far less conviction.

From what source proceeded the disturbance of the will called moral insanity? Writing in the 1840s, Prichard, like his peers, located it in the body, without being able to be very specific.[28] Prichard was followed in such imprecise physicalism by other alienists. As J. C. Bucknill declared in the first issue of the *Asylum Journal* in 1855, "all diseases are organic," even if we are unable to discover the underlying pathological changes.[29] Since physicalism provided a powerful justification for medical claims to expertise and authority over mental disturbance, it is not surprising, as several scholars have argued, that it became in the second half of the century almost a professional article of faith.[30] However, while the physicalist paradigm may have led to confidence in the eventual understanding and mastery of the self by a developing medical profession, it also underlined the uncertainty of present remission or cure, as well as the tenuousness of complete normality. As Bucknill and Tuke put it in their widely used 1858 textbook:

> The brain, like every other organ of the body, for the performance of its functions, requires the *perfect* condition of its organization, and its freedom from all pathological states whatever. Consequently, the existence of *any* pathological state in the organ of the mind will interrupt the functions of that organ, and produce a greater or less amount of disease of the mind – that is of insanity.[31]

Anything less than perfection of organization might doom an individual to some form of mental disease about which at present little could be done with much promise of cure. The therapeutic implications of physicalism, at least in the near term, were rather pessimistic, particularly as it was associated with an increasing role in human affairs being assigned to inheritance. The French psychologist Ribot noted that, "since the direct cause of insanity is some morbid affection of the nervous system, and as every part of the organism is transmissible, clearly the heredity of mental affections is the rule."[32]

[28] See Smith, *Trial*, p. 43.

[29] J. C. Bucknill, in *Asylum Journal 1* (1855). quoted in W. Bynum, "Theories in British Psychiatry: J. C. Prichard (1786–1848) to Henry Maudsley (1835–1918)," in *Nature Animated*, ed. Michael Ruse (Boston: D. Reidel, 1983), p. 234.

[30] Smith, *Trial*; Andrew Scull, *Museums of Madness: The Social Organization of Insanity in Nineteenth Century England* (New York: St. Martin's Press, 1979), Chs. 4–5; L. S. Jacyna, "Somatic Theories of Mind and the Interests of Medicine in Britain, 1850–1879," *Medical History 26* (1982), 233–58.

[31] J. C. Bucknill and D. H. Tuke, *A Manual of Psychological Medicine* (London: Blanchard & Lea, 1858), p. 353 (my italics).

[32] T. Ribot, *Heredity: A Psychological Study of its Phenomena, Law, Causes, and Consequences* (1875), quoted in Smith, p. 55.

Alienists, and physicians generally, were increasingly trained as the century wore on to look to specific defects in one's physical constitution, both inherited and acquired, to understand one's state of mind and behavior. As human behavior was thus naturalized, blame and responsibility became seriously problematic notions. Although medical metaphors and models were familiar in early and mid-Victorian discourse on crime, to call crime the product of disease or disability and to look to medicine for a treatment model gradually began to carry increasingly deterministic and disturbing implications and associations.

This trend was epitomized by Henry Maudsley, who emerged in the 1870s as the leading English psychologist of his time. *The Physiology and Pathology of the Mind* (1867), his first important book, enumerated "the disturbing causes which may affect the activity of the spinal cord both as a conducting path and as an independent centre of the generation of nerve-power." He then concluded,

> When we reflect upon the great proportion of the daily actions of life that are effected by its unconscious agency, we cannot but perceive how most important is the due preservation of its integrity. No culture of the mind, however careful, no effort of the will, however strong, will avail to prevent irregular and convulsive action when a certain degree of instability of nervous element has, from one cause or another, been produced in the spinal cells. It would be equally absurd to preach control to the spasms of chorea, or restraint to the convulsions of epilepsy, as to preach moderation to the east wind, or gentleness to the hurricane. That which in such case has its foundation in a definite physical cause must have its cure in the production of a definite physical change.[33]

Thus, a lunatic was described by Maudsley as an "organic machine automatically impelled by disordered nerve-centres." Six years later he extended his naturalization of madness and linked it closely to inheritance: "Multitudes of individuals come into this world weighted with a destiny against which they have neither the will nor the power to contend; they are the step-children of nature and groan under the worst of all tyrannies – the tyranny of a bad organization."[34] Heredity set immovable bounds to the operation of moral forces: "Great as is the power of education," he argued, "it is yet a sternly limited power; it is limited by the power of the individual in nature, and can

[33] Henry Maudsley, *The Physiology and Pathology of the Mind* (London: Macmillan 1867), pp. 83–4.

[34] *Body and Mind* (London: Macmillan, 1873), p. 43. He urged a few years later that "if man will but make himself the subject of serious scientific study, he shall find that [the] working out of degeneracy through generations affords him a rational explanation of most of those evil impulses of the heart which he has been content to attribute to the devil." [Henry Maudsley, "Materialism and its Lessons," *Fortnightly Review 26* (1879), 255–7.]

only work within this larger or smaller circle of necessity; no training in the world will avail to elicit grapes from thorns or figs from thistles." Thus,

> it would be quite useless to inculcate rules for self-formation upon one whose character had taken a certain mould of development; for character is a slow and gradual growth through action in relation to the circumstances of life; it cannot be fashioned suddenly and through reflection only.... The fixed and unchanging laws by which events come to pass hold sway in the mind as in every other domain of nature.[35]

Or, as Maudsley dramatically put it on another occasion:

> in consequence of evil ancestral influences, individuals are born with such a flaw or warp of nature that all care in the world will not prevent them from being vicious or criminal, or becoming insane.... No one can escape the tyranny of his organisation; no one can elude the destiny that is innate in him, and which unconsciously and irresistably shapes his ends, even when he believes that he is determining them with consummate foresight and skill.[36]

The growing professional links between psychology and neurology were institutionalized in 1878 by the founding of the journal *Brain*. The new physiological psychology raised fears within and without the profession over its moral implications – in particular, as one historian of psychology has noted, over "the possible encouragement it might lend to materialist or fatalist theories of human conduct."[37] The leading older figure in the field, W. B. Carpenter, argued in 1874 that the distinction between automatic and volitional activity was necessary both intellectually and morally, for it had "long appeared to me the only sound basis ... for Education and self-discipline."[38]

---

[35] Henry Maudsley, *Responsibility in Mental Disease* (London: King, 1874), pp. 20, 272.

[36] *Body and Mind*, p. 76.

[37] Lorraine J. Daston, "British Responses to Psycho-Physiology, 1860–1900," *Isis 69* (1978), 192. Indeed, Daston went on, "This perceived tension between the moral necessity of free will and a law-governed mental science played a central role in the selection of the topics, approaches, and explanations which dominated psychological discussion. The sovereign position which psychological treatises of the period assigned to theories of volition reflects this concern, as does the emphasis placed on the clinical applications of these theories to problems of moral responsibility such as alcoholism, the legal defense of insanity, and child rearing."

[38] W. B. Carpenter, *Principles of Mental Physiology* (London: H. S. King, 1874) Preface, p. ix. Carpenter, L. S. Jacyna has noted, was "horrified" by T. H. Huxley's claim that the physiology of reflexion provided the basis for a thoroughgoing automatism in which consciousness was allowed no part in the determination of bodily movements. In his own psychology, Carpenter insisted upon a hierarchy of faculties. While the lower functions were performed reflexively, the highest were the result of the determinations of an imma-

As scientific intellectuals like Maudsley, T. H. Huxley, and W. K. Clifford drew out the implications of the new biology and physiology for a wider audience in the 1870s, moral fears spread. "If Conscience be, as Dr. Maudsley assures us, only a function of physical organization," the Gladstonian Liberal W. L. Courtney complained even in the scientifically inclined *Fortnightly Review*, "it is more than ever difficult to see whence will be derived the power of ethical sanction."[39]

Another Gladstonian Liberal, Henry Sidgwick, Professor of Moral Philosophy at Cambridge, identified the core of the problem:

> The belief that events are determinately related to the state of things immediately preceding them is now held by all competent thinkers in respect to all kinds of occurrence except human volitions. It has steadily grown both intensively and extensively, both in clearness and certainty of conviction, and in the universality of explication, as the human mind has developed and human experience has been systematized and enlarged. Step by step, in successive departments of facts, conflicting modes of thought have receded and faded, until at length they have vanished everywhere, except for the mysterious citadel of the will.[40]

Now the citadel itself was under siege – not by a few philosophic advance scouts making bold forays as in the past, but by the massed infantry of scientific naturalism, appearing daily more natural in light of the ever-tightening interdependence of modern life. The issue was more than simply philosophic; it was social and personal. The U.S. periodical, *The Century*, noted fearfully in 1883 "the close relation between what is sometimes called the 'advanced' thought of the day and the rude notions of the lowest stratum of society" and warned that "a doctrine that ... makes of man only a bundle of

---

terial principle. It was essential to preserve the power of the will, Carpenter insisted, "If the formation of individual character upon proper lines was to be assured," [See L. S. Jacyna, "The Physiology of Mind, the Unity of Nature, and the Moral Order in Victorian Thought," *British Journal of the History of Science 14* (1981), 125.] As Carpenter's generation passed from the scene, this distinction became ever harder to maintain within the profession. Moreover, ethical questions themselves were becoming marginalized in scientific discourse. Whereas all the major debaters of the 1870s – materialists and antimaterialists – accepted the problems of ethical conduct and value as appropriate questions for a scientific psychology, by the turn of the century the realms of facts and values had separated, and professional communication between them was ever more tenuous. The very issue of moral responsibility, it has been observed, "was losing some of its emotional charge for British psychologists." [Danston, "British Responses," 207.]

[39] *Fortnightly Review 82* (1879), 328.
[40] Henry Sidgwick, *The Method of Ethics* (London: Macmillan, 1874), p. 47.

appetites and impulses and propensities whose law is in themselves destroys . . . religion and morality . . . and makes discipline a solecism."[41]

A running-down world?

As if the extinction of free will were not enough, science seemed to be raising a second specter, that of an eventual and inevitable extinction of energy, and thus of life, itself. The second law of thermodynamics, set out in 1851, and the development of astrophysics during the second half of the century provided compelling images of a universe inexorably running down. By the last years of the century, the educated public understood that the nature from which the individual was now seen as inseparable was itself irreversibly losing organization.[42] Of course, the tendency toward equalized energy flows was only a tendency, ultimately triumphant only after billions of years, and thus logically entropy had no direct message for the life of humanity and society. Symbolically, however, it had a dramatic impact, subverting, as did determinism, assumptions of a universe indefinitely open to human will. Entropy placed an inexorable principle of decay within nature, life, and humanity. In his growing pessimism, in part fed by his own mental decline, John Ruskin seized upon it. His 1884 lecture on *The Storm-Cloud of the Nineteenth Century* interpreted that year's bad weather as symptomatic of a secular deterioration and fiercely expressed his disillusion with a nature that was no longer benignly Wordsworthian. In his slide toward madness Ruskin here tapped wider intellectual anxieties. In the 1890s, the specter of universal decay became a common property of imaginative writers like Thomas Hardy or Joseph Conrad, who privately decried "the curse of decay – the eternal decree that will extinguish the sun, the stars one by one, and in another instant shall spread a frozen darkness over the whole universe."[43] Even a radical scientist like T. H. Huxley came later in life to place his philosophy within the frame of an inevitably decaying universe. In his 1894 "Prolegomena" to his Romanes lecture of the year before on "Evolution and Ethics," Huxley made his own gardern into a parable of man versus nature, describing it as a carefully maintained artificiality carved from a wilderness to which it will revert unless attention is unremitting. As Peter Morton has observed, this parable became

[41] Quoted in T. J. Jackson Lears, *No Place of Grace: Antimodernism and the Transformation of American Culture 1880–1920* (New York: Pantheon, 1981), p. 39.

[42] See P. M. Harman, *Energy, Force, and Matter: The Conceptual Development of Nineteenth Century Physics* (Cambridge: Cambridge University Press, 1982), pp. 64–9.

[43] Ian Watt, *Conrad in the Nineteenth Century* (Berkeley: University of California Press, 1979), p. 153.

a vivid expression not so much of Huxley's belief that men should combat the natural order but, rather, of his fear of degeneration transformed into a homely image. . . . As his train of thought runs on it emerges that what really interests and appals the retired Huxley as he looks out upon his newly laid-out flowerbeds at Eastbourne is not how the garden may best be weeded, nor what it looked like in a state of nature before Caesar first came to Britain, but what would happen almost instantaneously if the hands of Caesar's modern descendents were withdrawn.[44]

As Huxley wrote,

The walls and gates would decay; quadrupedal and bipedal intruders would devour and tread down the useful and beautiful plants; birds, insects, blight, and mildew would work their will; the seeds of the native plants, carried by winds or other agencies, would immigrate, and in virtue of their long-earned special adaptation to the local conditions, these despised native weeds would soon choke their choice exotic rivals. A century or two hence, little beyond the foundations of the wall and of the houses and frames would be left, in evidence of the victory of the cosmic powers at work in the state of nature, over the temporary obstacles to their supremacy, set up by the art of the horticulturist.[45]

All life, whether the product of nature, horticulture or human culture, here seems only an example of entropy running backward for a while, merely a temporary bulwark against the universal decay.

What did such a view of nature mean for the image of human life? Despite the generally progressivist outlook of Darwin's *Origins* and his *Descent of Man*, they provided a basis for the new prospect of degeneration. With purpose banished from evolution and the backdrop now one of ultimate universal decay, it was only a short step to fears of a downward turn to human development.[46] As Charles Kingsley's Mrs. Bedonebyasyoudid had warned in his Darwinian fantasy, *The Water Babies*:

Folks say now that I can make beasts into men, by circumstance, and selection, and competition, and so forth. . . . But let them recollect this,

[44] Peter Morton, *The Vital Science* (London: Allen & Unwin, 1984), p. 87.
[45] T. H. Huxley, "Evolution and Ethics: Prolegomena," *Evolution and Ethics and Other Essays* (New York: D. Appleton, 1902), pp. 9–10; also see O. Stanley, "Huxley's Treatment of Nature," *Journal of the History of Ideas 18* (1957), 120–7.
[46] Robert Nye has observed that "the idea of degeneration had a powerful appeal to British men and women in the period after 1885 no matter what their politics or their views on genetics. This was so because the basic concept had become part of both social science lore and popular culture for sound historical reasons. It appeared to account for developments in British life about which there was widespread public concern." [In J. Edward Chamberlain and Sander L. Gilman, *Degeneration: The Dark Side of Progress* (New York: Columbia University Press, 1985), p.64.]

that there are two sides to every question, and a downhill as well as an uphill road; and, if I can turn beasts into men, I can, by the same laws of circumstance, and selection, and competition, turn men into beasts.[47]

Even more likely than a return to the beasts, indeed, an ultimate certainty, was a general devitalization, a running-down of human energies paralleling universal entropy. From Darwinism the entropic metaphor gained a particular twist. Within Darwin's vision of nature lay a romantic valuation of natural energies sharply at variance with the Malthusianism that otherwise exerted so much influence upon him. Darwin's theories mirrored his naturalist's love of the overwhelming energy and generativeness of nature; in them the role of reproductive energy is not only central but creative. This contrast was first noted by Gillian Beer: "Whereas Malthus sought to curb and curtail human hyperproductivity, Darwin speaks of 'slow-breeding man'."[48] But when this more positive description of natural instincts flowed together with an entropic cosmology, a changed attitude to the future prospects of the human race was suggested. Civilization itself, whose task had so regularly been seen as one of bringing those natural impulses under check, became problematic. Whereas Tennyson (an excellent barometer of conventional educated sensibilities) could confess that "the lavish profusion ... in the natural world appals me, from the growths of the tropical forest to the capacity of man to multiply, the torrent of babies,"[49] concerns began to surface late in the century that progress might have more to fear from an insufficiency than an overabundance of sexual and, by extension, other natural impulses. If so, their control would have to be rethought, as would the nature of civilization itself.

Thus, scientific naturalism was doubly Janus-faced. It held out new vistas of power for mankind collectively (under the guidance of scientific experts) while carrying within it a diminished image of the ordinary man and woman. And it stimulated fantasies of indefinite progress while nurturing specters of a degenerating humanity in a running-down universe.

Scientific naturalism was in a sense the natural philosophy of the emerging great society. As the growing complexity of society and the length, in time and space, of chains of causation sank into and became part of normal consciousness, the place of individual will receded. At the same time, fears of uncontrolled impulse and social anarchy were on the wane, so that such imagination of weakness became less threatening. As the establishment of a working norm of public order and of respectable behavior, accompanied by the process of peaceable democratization, promoted a shift in the professional

[47] Charles Kingsley, *The Water Babies* [1863] (London, 1888) pp. 276–7.
[48] Beer, *Darwin's Plots*, p. 124.
[49] Quoted in Hallam Tennyson, *Tennyson* 1, p. 314 [no date given].

class from social fears of anarchic turmoil to feelings of popular inertia,[50] the new images associated with science became more plausible. Along with these developments, a bureaucratic machinery developed and took on tasks that could less and less be left to individuals in an increasingly complex society, thus further allowing society's *expectations* of individuals to diminish. Thus, by the last decade of the century, images of human nature and social agency among the intellectual, professional, and administrative classes had significantly altered from Victorian models; this was to have important consequences for social and criminal policy.

"A shallow, feeble, and vague abstraction"

I believe in a degeneracy of man, in the Fall – in *sin* – in the intensity and virulence of sin.

W. E. Gladstone, to Mrs. Humphrey Ward 1888

I think the modern who believes in God and cherishes the dear memory of a human Christ will learn humbly ... 'to accept himself,' and life, as they are, at God's hands.

Mrs. Ward, replying to Gladstone 1888[51]

The sea change in constructions of human nature and social agency encouraged both a relaxation of moralizing pressures on the individual and a new anxiety about individual ineffectuality. A profound indicator of this change was the gradual but decisive alteration in conceptions of the workings of divine justice. During the second half of the nineteenth century, divine severity of the sort taken for granted by countless generations of Christians became unacceptable to all but a relative handful. The focal point of both Anglican and Nonconformist faith increasingly moved from judgment to salvation, from the Atonement to the Incarnation.[52] As part of this growing stress on divine compassion and forgiveness, the traditional core of the doctrine of the Atonement – that God the Father had inflicted pain on an innocent party, his Son, and that this innocent suffering was the source of human salvation – was more and more glossed over. By this "evasion," Gladstone objected in 1894, the redemptive value of suffering was being forgotten, and

[50] As evident in three important works written closely together: Walter Bagehot, *Physics and Politics* (1872), Fitzjames Stephen, *Liberty, Equality, Fraternity* (1873), and Henry Maine, *Popular Government* (1886).
[51] Quoted in Janet Penrose Trevelyan, *The Life of Mrs. Humphrey Ward* (London: Constable, 1923), pp. 59,61.
[52] See Boyd Hilton, *The Age of Atonement*. (Oxford: Clarendon Press, 1988).

the sensibility to "corrective" justice was dulled, making it harder for men to feel that "kind of joy in salutory pain" that had played a significant role in Gladstone's own life.[53]

If the reformative function of suffering was moving off the center stage of religious belief, even more precipitous was the fall of that ultimate deterrent, eternal punishment. Gladstone pointed out in 1896 the great contrast with the days of his youth; the idea of future punishment of the wicked, with which he had been early familiar, had now been relegated "to the far-off corners of the Christian mind ... there to sleep in deep shadow as a thing needless in our enlightened and progressive age." He explained:

> It is not now sought to alarm men by magnifying the power of God, and by exhibiting the strictness and severity of the law of righteousness. The anxiety now is to throw these subjects into the shade, lest the fastidious-ness of human judgment and feeling should be so offended as to rise in rebellion against God for his harshness and austerity.[54]

The reality and the moral necessity of hell, so distant from modern sensibilities, had been taken for granted by many nineteenth-century reformers as well as by conservatives. Their evaporation was a portentous cul-tural event indeed.[55] The evaporation was in part owing to the strengthened inclination to apply human standards of justice to the deity. Yet it was more than this, for God has always been interpreted through human lenses. It was also that, as we have been seeing, those lenses were being reground – those standards of justice themselves were in flux. "Shall not the Judge of all the earth do right?" cited Dean Farrar in 1877, in arguing against orthodox conceptions of hell. "Judicial terrorism" could not be an attribute of "the crucified Redeemer."[56] This recoil from a harshly punitive divine image was intertwined with changes in conceptions of human responsibility and in attitudes toward pain and suffering. Farrar's controversial *Eternal Hope* (1878), which humanely denied the eternity of divine punishment, was at-tacked by a perceptive if pitiless Oxford cleric, H. R. Bramley, for degrading the image of man. Farrar, Bramley charged, neglected the voluntary character

---

[53] "True and False Conception of the Atonement," *Nineteenth Century* 36 (1894), 327.

[54] William Gladstone, *Studies Subsidiary to the Works of Bishop Butler* (Oxford: Claren-don Press, 1896), pp. 201, 206.

[55] See Geoffrey Rowell, *Hell and the Victorians* (Oxford: Clarendon Press, 1974). Of course this evaporation was a long process that had begun in the seventeenth century. On its origins, see D. P. Walker, *The Decline of Hell* (Chicago: University of Chicago Press, 1964), and on some eighteenth-century aspects as they bear on criminal punishment, see Randall McGowen, "The Changing Face of God's Justice," *Criminal Justice History* 9 (1988), 63–99.

[56] F. W. Farrar, *Eternal Hope* (London: Macmillan, 1878), p. 70 (sermons preached in Westminster Abbey 1877–8).

of sin and the centrality of choice in each human life.[57] Farrar's neglect, we can now see, was not a personal quirk; the drama of individual choice was in fact being so qualified as to begin to recede from center stage in the dominant understanding of human life.

Oxford's clerical Tories were joined by political leaders in denouncing Liberal Anglican interpretations of doctrine like Farrar's, interpretations that reduced hell to at most a purgatorial interlude. In 1879, Gladstone himself criticized the tendency of Evangelicalism toward a view of grace as unconditionally available.[58] Later he warned of the grave consequences of "mental errors" that banished hell:

> These inventions are revolutionary not only as towards the dispensation we live under, but as towards human nature itself, and all the modes in which it is rationally impelled to action, or guided in pursuing it. It is remarkable that this scheme [of ultimate universal salvation] does not present the prospect of a plan for the reformation of character, with cessation of penalty as its natural consequence; but it is rather a repeal or exhaustion of penalty, with reformation of character set in the shade, and playing a secondary part: at the very best a reformation brought about arbitrarily, and in defiance of all known laws. And those stern denunciations of Holy Scripture, which on a long course of trial have been found none too strong for their purpose, it is deliberately sought to relax by promising to every sinner of whatever inveteracy, audacity, and hardness, an endless period of immunity from suffering; after a period spent in [punishment], which they have no means of defining, and which every offender is therefore left to retrench at his own pleasure, on his own behalf. What is this but to emasculate all the sanctions of religion, and to give wickedness, already under too feeble restraint, a new range of license?[59]

It is not surprising that Gladstone described in 1893 the sense of sin as "the great want in modern life," or that he had been deeply saddened, four years earlier, to note throughout society a "decline ... in the sense of sin which, instead of being, as under the Christian system it ought to be, piercing and profound, is passing with very many into a shallow, feeble and vague abstraction."[60] From this vantage point, we can appreciate that the rise in these years

[57] Rowell, *Hell*, p. 151.

[58] Gladstone, "The Evangelical Movement," *British Quarterly Review 70* (1879), 14.

[59] Gladstone, *Studies*, p. 223. He warned that it was not only "everlasting punishments in particular" that were in danger of being lost from sight, but "all and any punishment intelligibly enforced." [*ibid.*, p. 206.]

[60] Gladstone to Lionel Tollemache, Dec. 30, 1893, in *Gladstone's Boswell: Late Victorian Conversations*, ed. Asa Briggs (New York: St. Martin's Press, 1984), p. 96. See also Gladstone's responses to Tollemache's "modern" arguments on moral responsibility, pp. 82–6; Gladstone to B. M. Malabari, July 20, 1889, in *Correspondence on Church and Religion of William Ewart Gladstone*, Vol. 2, ed. D. C. Lathbury (London: Macmillan, 1910), p. 118.

of what Beatrice Webb called the consciousness of social sin was made possible by a decline of a consciousness of personal sin.[61]

Once the old harsh religious beliefs had faded, their instrumental value for building character was nostalgically remembered. Shortly after Gladstone's death, the American *Scribner's Magazine* mourned "The Passing of the Devil":

> The old doctrine was stern and terrible enough in principle, and trivial enough in some of its workings out; but it encouraged the idea that each man must bear his own burden and fight his own fight. It developed the martial virtues; it trained a race of men, austere and narrow, but so virile, so indomitable and forceful, that their impress is even yet stamped deep upon our national character. Will the new attitude do as much? The man who believes that he is tempted by a definite spirit of evil whom he may resist and ought to resist may yield, or even take sides with the tempter and sin with a high hand, and yet be of heroic mould; but what hope is there for the man who holds himself blameless because his course is shaped by a power too strong for resistance? Is there for him any possibility of brave living or genuine effort?[62]

The language of moralization was being redefined. For early and mid-Victorians, religious and nonreligious alike, the moral value of suffering had been so accepted that metaphors such as cleansing fires had become cliches. "For gold must be tried by fire, as a heart must be tried by pain!" wrote Adelaide Proctor in her widely read poem, "Cleansing Fires." "The actual redemptive fires," John Reed has observed, "that occur in such works as *Jane Eyre, Aurora Leigh, The Adventures of Harry Richmond,* and *Great Expectations*, indicate how familiar this attitude was, and how open to literary exploitation."[63] "Deep, unspeakable suffering," declared the unbeliever George Eliot, "may well be called a baptism, a regeneration, the initiation into a new state." Such reflections were increasingly challenged: Wilkie Collins objected in his novel *Armadale* (1866) that "Suffering can, and does," develop the latent evil that there is in humanity, as well as the latent good," and this counter argument became the theme of much of George Gissing's work.[64]

For a weaker, less responsible humanity, the positive role of discipline and even suffering in character development was losing relevance. Such a trend was strengthened by the easing of the conditions of everyday life. An early

---

[61] Beatrice Webb, *My Apprenticeship* [1926] (New York: Longmans, Green & Co., 1950), pp. 155–7.

[62] (1899), quoted in Lears, *No Place*, p. 46.

[63] John R. Reed, *Victorian Conventions* (Athens, Ohio: Ohio University Press, 1975), p. 18.

[64] Quoted in *ibid.*, pp. 18, 19–20.

Victorian innovation like anesthesia, making the infliction of pain more cruel and unusual, could only lower the threshold of public sensitivity to pain.[65] At the same time, medical resistance to the wide use of anesthesia, partly rooted in a conviction of the positive value (physiological and moral) of pain,[66] was itself eroded with erosion of that world view. In the later 1880s and early 1890s, while selective salvation was giving way to universal, selective anesthesia also gave way to universal anesthesia[67] – the same period in which the Humanitarian League was founded in Britain (1891), antivivisection sentiment became a movement to be reckoned with, and, as we will see, the Victorian penal system also began to be radically criticized.[68]

As life lost much of its harshness, tolerance for the bearing or inflicting of pain shrank. The young Fitzjames Stephen, at the same time that he was castigating those who would erode personal responsibility through such means as the insanity defense, was pointing out the historic novelty of the emerging intolerance for physical pain:

> That anybody should be in pain [he observed in 1860], and not be immediately relieved – that sharp pain should ever be inflicted on any one under any circumstances – that physical discomfort, in the shape of bad health, or habits tending to produce it, or in almost any other shape, should ever be allowed to exist undisturbed – shocks and scandalizes people in these days.

This intolerance, he felt, was not so much of all suffering, but of direct and observable physical pain. "We shrink not from the notion that a fellow creature is unhappy, but from the idea of cutting, tearing, or bruising flesh and limbs like our own." Stephen regretted this delegitimization of physical pain, for, as he reflected, "the lessons which are taught by discomfort and suffering are wonderfully valuable. There is no other school in which things are set in their true light and rated at their true value so completely."[69]

---

[65] On the development and application of anesthesia, seen from a rather Whiggish standpoint, see A. J. Youngson, *The Scientific Revolution in Victorian Medicine* (New York: Holmes and Meier, 1979).

[66] See Martin Pernick, *A Calculus of Suffering: Pain, Professionalism and Anesthesia in Nineteenth Century America* (New York: Columbia University Press, 1985), and James Turner, *Reckoning with the Beast: Animals, Pain and Humanity in the Victorian Mind* (Baltimore: Johns Hopkins University Press, 1980).

[67] The phrase is Pernick's [p. 237] to characterize the medical practice of the period from the 1840s through the 1880s.

[68] See Richard D. French, *Antivivisection and Medical Science in Victorian Society* (Princeton: Princeton University Press, 1975) and Coral Lansbury, *The Old Brown Dog: Women, Workers and Vivisection in Edwardian England* (Madison, Wisconsin: University of Wisconsin Press, 1985).

[69] James Fitzjames Stephen, *Essays by a Barrister* (London: Smith, Elder, 1862), pp. 142–49.

For many, the value of pain seemed intertwined with the question of free will. The U.S. philosopher William James, who like Stephen wrestled with the challenge that modern scientific and philosophic ideas presented to a belief in free will, was similarly fascinated by the contrast between past and present attitudes to pain. In 1902, he remarked on the "strange moral transformation" that had during the previous century swept over the Western world: "We no longer think that we are called upon to face physical pain with equanimity. It is not expected of a man that he should either endure it or inflict much of it, and to listen to the recitals of cases of it makes our flesh creep morally as well as physically."[70]

This rising intolerance of pain went together with a general relaxation of moral disciplinarianism among the upper middle classes that became apparent after about 1870.[71] "The culture of the late Victorian middle classes," F. M. L. Thompson has remarked, "had shed the husk of earnestness and self-righteousness, and embraced the notion of fun."[72] While moralization continued its advance down the social scale, the prosperous new generation that adopted the less severe Queen Anne style of architectural design in the 1870s was, as Mark Girouard has observed, one that "could afford to relax." This generation's "views grew less dogmatic, their manners smoother, their prose lighter, and their morals easier. They looked with distaste at much that their parents had taken for granted. They needed a new life style."[73] Their new domestic environment gave expression to this need. As another architectural historian has argued,

> Queen Anne, in all its multifarious forms, meant the final end of Puginian discipline: decoration no longer expressed structure; it was simply *decoration*. The puritan focus of Puginian theory – the attempt to equate function and propriety ... had finally been abandoned in favour of the aes-

---

[70] William James, *The Varieties of Religious Experience* [1902] (New York: Collier Books, 1961), p. 239. Like many late Victorian members of the upper middle class, James suffered from symptoms of the "new" illness of neurasthenia, a malady its leading analyst, G. M. Beard, saw characterized by "lack of nerve force" and paralysis of the will. Beard saw neurasthenia as a disease of "over-civilization," and, foreshadowing Freud, noted as one of its causes "repression of emotion." Too much success in moral control was, in the minds of concerned observers like Beard, undermining the vitality of man. [Lears, pp. 50–1 passim.]

[71] Especially upon its male members, for with the acceptance of "separate spheres" ideology, moralism became more gender-specific. However, this fascinating subject is too large to explore here.

[72] F. M. L. Thompson, *The Rise of Respectable Society: A Social History of Victorian Britain 1830–1900* (London: Fontana, 1988), p. 260.

[73] Mark Girouard, *Sweetness and Light: The Queen Anne Movement 1860–1900* (Oxford: Clarendon Press, 1977), p. 3.

thetics of hedonism. . . . The attempt – by Pugin and Ruskin – to control
. . . historicism by means of morality had been abandoned.[74]

While middle-class architecture was turning away from moral discipline,
a parallel movement was occurring in the reading of middle-class children.
In boys' literature, in particular, the highest approbation was changing from
"purity" to "healthiness." With the appearance in 1879 of the highly influential *Boy's Own Paper* (published by the Religious Tract Society in a shift
of tactics), the policy of direct preaching to youth began to be abandoned in
favor of one of accepting "boy nature" and attempting to co-opt it into the
support of established values. Juvenile novels show at the same time a move
away from an earlier war on child nature. "It almost seems," one scholar of
juvenile fiction has observed, "to paraphrase Virginia Woolf, that in or about
January, 1880, human character changed. . . . While for early Victorian
rationalist and evangelical authors alike the mark of childish and indeed adult
virtue had been the ability to conquer human nature, later Victorians and
Edwardians generally agreed that to be good was to be 'normal'."[75]

A related shift took place in the higher reading in the universities, where
classical culture received successively less puritan interpretations. Whereas for
Dr. Arnold the study of the Greeks was the best form of moral instruction
outside chapel,[76] his son began to turn such study against Victorian
"Hebraism." However, even Matthew Arnold's advocacy of Hellenism, from
which Girouard took the title of his work on Queen Anne style, was by later
standards highly moral. Frank Turner has pointed out how Arnold's
unquestioning confidence in "the moral rationality of the Greeks" allowed
him "to embrace a moral spirit more flexible than that of Christianity without
seeming to encounter moral license." Arnold could sound so confident about
the wisdom of Hellenism because he "assumed the permanence of the Hebraic
moral achievement."[77] Later versions of Hellenism increasingly challenged
that achievement, raising anxious concerns among reviewers and moral
commentators. J. A. Symonds' "radiant, adolescent" Hellenic genius had little
moral content; in place of narrowing "conscience," the Greeks had "true artis-

---

[74] J. Mordaunt Crook, *The Dilemma of Style: Architectural Ideas from the Picturesque to the Post-Modern* (London: Murray, 1987), p. 179.

[75] Claudia Nelson, "Sex and the Single Boy: Ideals of Manliness and Sexuality in Victorian Literature for Boys," *Victorian Studies 32* (Summer, 1989), 526.

[76] See Richard Jenkyns, *The Victorians and Ancient Greece* (Oxford: Blackwell, 1980), pp. 60–2.

[77] Frank Miller Turner, *The Greek Heritage in Victorian Britain* (New Haven: Yale University Press, 1981), pp. 23, 31.

tic sensibility," facilitating a "free expansion of personality."[78] And Walter Pater's Plato was the first aesthete:

> Plato is ... unalterably a lover. In that, precisely, lies the secret of the ... diligent eye, the so sensitive ear. The central interest ... of his profoundly impressible youth ... gives law and pattern to all that succeeds it ... the experience, the discipline, of love, had been that for Plato; and, as love must ... deal above all with visible persons, this discipline involved an exquisite cultivation of the senses. It is 'as lovers use', that he is ever on the watch for those dainty messages ... to eye and ear.[79]

As Victorian Hellenism became more morally "relaxed", Hebraism – in the upper middle classes – also softened. In the university world of the latter decades of the century, Turner has argued, "religion came to be regarded as a manifestation of human culture, and Hebraism became tempered ... the liberal theological examination of the Old Testament as a document exemplifying only one of many possible modes of religiosity and morality ... permitted the two elements of Arnold's dichotomy to shade off into each other."[80]

Indeed, along with this relaxation and growing impatience with tight moral constrictions came a new fear of the devitalization of life and a yearning to recapture the spontaneity and intensity of experience associated with both childhood and earlier stages of history.[81] For some this led again to Greece or to Renaissance Italy. Contemplation of both eras led Pater to preach a new gospel of experience. In his famous "Conclusion" to *Studies in the Renaissance* (1873), he wrote, "not the fruit of experience, but experience itself is the end." In one's life, he continued, one should seek to "pass most swiftly from point to point, and be present always at the focus where the greatest number of vital forces unite in their purest energy." Against this quest for intensity, "the theory, or idea, or system, which requires of us the sacrifice of any part of this experience, in consideration of some interest into which we cannot enter, or some abstract morality we have not identified with ourselves, or what is only conventional, has no real claim upon us."[82] Others, led by William Morris,

---

[78] John Addington Symonds, *Studies of the Greek Poets* (London: Smith, Elder, 1877), pp. 431, 429. The essence of the Greek spirit for Symonds was "the harmony of man with nature ... cheerfully accepting the world as we find it, acknowledging the value of each human impulse" [pp. 429, 437]
[79] Walter Pater, *Plato and Platonism* (London: Macmillan, 1893), p. 120.
[80] Turner, *Greek Heritage*, pp. 32–3.
[81] On this subject the most illuminating work, although dealing only with America, is Lears, *No Place of Grace*.
[82] Walter Pater, *Studies in the History of the Renaissance* (London: Macmillan, 1873), pp. 210–12; "Failure," he observed in deliberate opposition to the Victorian consensus, "is to form habits." [pp. 210–11.]

turned to Norse sagas and to a different, more sensual Middle Ages than that which had enthralled the generation of Pugin. Late Victorian medievalists sought now not order but vitality and spontaneity. Now it was the childlike, direct, and primitive qualities of the Middle Ages that were favorably juxtaposed to the present. And many who had no brook with aestheticism, medievalism, or primitivism nonetheless were finding their age disturbingly marked by progress in prosperity and decay in intensity. The rising popularity of the exotic adventure literature of Haggard, Kipling, Stevenson, and many lesser "masculine world wanderers" was traced by one perceptive critic from the United States to a deep social need. "We had become so over-nice in our feelings, so restrained and formal, so bound by habit and use in our devotion to the effeminate realists," Bliss Carman observed in 1894, "that one side of our nature was starved."[83]

All of these cultural moves, to aestheticism, medievalism, primitivism, or exotic adventure, were bulwarks against a spreading disbelief in the power and autonomy of the individual will. Already in the novels of Dickens the fear of disorder – of individual desires unchecked – so evident in the early novels *Oliver Twist, Barnaby Rudge*, and *Martin Chuzzlewitt*, was yielding to his fear for "the death of feeling,"[84] and after that to an even more drastic sense of the collapse of personal efficacy in a vast and inhuman society. From *Dombey* onward, social problems in Dickens's work became more intertwined with each other and with large impersonal processes and less amenable to individual or moral solutions. Enveloping metaphors of disease, fog, prisons, and machines multiplied in his work and dissipated the earlier sense of a human world.[85] On the basis of this development, Dickens was to be rediscovered as a profound social critic by Bernard Shaw and subsequently by Edmund Wilson and others, who took for their theme Shaw's 1911 claim that the later novels showed that "it is not our disorder (as the Victorian thought) but our order that is horrible."[86]

[83] Quoted in Lears, p. 106. Another form taken by the quest for vitality was a growing romanticization of gypsies and even tramps. Whereas in 1880 the 20,000 gypsies in England were decried as "black spots upon our horizon," dangerous vestiges of precivilization, by the turn of the century that same "animalism" was being idealized as a valuable tonic for an overcivilized society. As Arthur Symons put it admiringly in 1908, gypsies possessed "the lawlessness, the abandonment, the natural physical grace in form and gesture, of animals." [Quoted in George Behlmer, "The Gypsy Problem in Victorian England," *Victorian Studies* 28 (1985–6), 247, 251. A similar point is made by M. A. Crowther, "'The Lure of the Open Road': Vagrancy, Literature and Policy in Britain 1800–1914," unpublished paper to the Social History Society, 1987.]

[84] See Steven Marcus, *Dickens From Pickwick to Dombey* (New York: Basic Books, 1965), pp. 338–43, 348.

[85] The best discussion of this pattern is Alexander Welsh, *The City of Dickens* (Oxford: Clarendon Press 1961).

[86] Introduction to Charles Dickens, *Hard Times* (London: Waverley, 1911).

More generally, Patrick Brantlinger has noted that whereas early Victorian literature is much preoccupied with the individual, good or evil, after midcentury society comes to bulk larger in literature, as "the fictional realism of Thackeray, Trollope, and Eliot displaces the power of social amelioration from human agency to the slow growth of the social organism." Even social institutions could seem possessed of little power in an overwhelming universe. Brantlinger characterized as "one of the final avatars of this process" the operation of fate or chance in Thomas Hardy's novels, "in which human agency, stripped of all rational control over circumstances, is viewed as existentially absurd."[87] A similar cosmic pessimism permeated the early scientific romances of Hardy's younger contemporary, H. G. Wells. Standing at the confluence of the currents of later Victorian Darwinism and literary naturalism, and acutely sensitive to the flow of ideas and sentiments around him, Wells created in the 1890s a series of visions of human beings caught in the meshes of an overdeveloped society and an implacable nature. *The Time Machine* (1895), for instance, joined images of the running-down universe with more specific concerns about middle-class effeteness and working-class brutalization. Both Eloi and Morlocks – the surviving types of humanity his Time Traveller discovers in the distant future – are degenerated, each by carrying forward certain present trends. From such diagnoses it was a short step for Wells, and others to advocate social policies aimed no longer primarily at enhancing personal responsibility but, increasingly, at more directly regenerating the nation's human material.

Considering the great material advances achieved over previous generations, English social thinking at the end of the Victorian age was unexpectedly gloomy. In the vistas provided by determinism and entropy ever less scope was left for individual will or human vitality and thus ever less point in the ideal of character. In his youth in the 1870s and 1880s, Havelock Ellis (who was to do much to demolish that ideal) later recalled, he

> had the feeling that the universe was represented as a sort of factory filled by an inextricable web of wheels and looms and flying shuttles, in a deafening din. That, it seemed, was the world as the most competent scientific authorities declared it to be made. It was a world I was prepared to accept and yet a world in which, I felt, I could only wander restlessly, an ignorant and homeless child.[88]

Such sentiments, like the speculations of literary artists and popular scientists on degeneration, fed into the official classes' social discourse. Anthony Wohl has observed with surprise that despite improving mortality and mor-

[87] Patrick Brantlinger, *The Spirit of Reform: British Literature and Politics, 1832–1867* (Cambridge: Harvard University Press, 1977), p. 234.
[88] Havelock Ellis, *The Dance of Life* (London: Constable, 1923), p. 199.

bidity rates, discussions of public health at the turn of the century were "dominated by the vision of a lethargic, sickly people."[89] Edwardian social discourse, with its preoccupation shared by left and right with race deterioration and with external, collective, and statist intervention, was pervaded by images of the ineffectiveness and devitalization of ordinary individuals.[90] A "sense that the uncontrollable was upon them"[91] was never far from the thoughts of Edwardian social analysts.

[89] Anthony S. Wohl, *Endangered Lives: Public Health in Victorian Britain* (London: Methuen, 1983), p. 330.

[90] See Samuel Hynes, *The Edwardian Turn of Mind* (Princeton: Princeton University Press, 1968), esp. Chs. 2–3, and G. R. Searle, *The Quest for National Efficiency* (Oxford: Basil Blackwell, 1971) and *Eugenics and Politics in Britain 1900–14* (Leyden: Noordhof International, 1976); and Richard Soloway, "Counting the Degenerates: The Statistics of Race Deterioration in Edwardian England," *Journal of Contemporary History 17* (1982), 137–64. It was characteristic of this climate of opinion that in discussing the relation between alcoholism and crime, a physician could take it for granted (erroneously) that the average height of the British population was declining. [Albert Wilson, "Alcoholism and Crime," *British Journal of Inebriety* (1910), p. 187.]

[91] Standish Meacham, *Toynbee Hall and Social Reform* (New Haven: Yale University Press, 1988), p. 86.

5

Late Victorian social policy –
a changing context

The revival of social pessimism in the 1880s and the increasing gloom of social descriptions at the turn of the century masked the broad and striking success of Victorian efforts at social moralization. "By 1900," Robert Roberts recalled in his penetrating memoir of working-class life, "those cherished principles about class, order, work, thrift, and self-help, epitomized by Samuel Smiles and long taught and practised by the Victorian bourgeoisie, had moulded the minds of even the humblest."[1] Most indexes of disorder, irregularity, and vice – among them crime, bastardy, pauperism, drunkenness, and even disease and accidental death – were firmly in decline, and respectability commanded at least the nominal allegiance of nearly all.[2] Yet in spite of these triumphs, indeed in part, ironically, *because* of these triumphs, social policy was by the turn of the new century jettisoning ever more Victorian ballast and setting its course in a different direction away from deterrence and moralization.

The change in direction of social policy was also fed by the steady advance of democracy. The ever-greater political power of the poorer classes stimulated in the governing classes ever-greater sympathy for the difficulties facing the weak and steadily diminished both the perceived justice and the practical feasibility of insisting on maximal personal responsibility and self-improvement. Deterrence was thus to play a steadily smaller part in social policy, and its place was to be filled by more direct methods of state intervention, regulation, and assistance. A similar influence was exerted by the other great political trend of the age – the steady advance of professionaliza-

[1] *The Classic Slum: Salford Life in the First Quarter of the Century* (Baltimore: Penguin Books, 1974), p. 30.
[2] Despite a strenuous and not unsuccessful effort to show the lack of middle-class influence upon the working classes, in his recent *Rise of Respectable Society* (London: Fontana Press, 1988), F. M. L. Thompson demonstrates very effectively the triumph throughout society by 1900 of a broadly similar set of attitudes, however varied their sources and however distinctive their specific class and subclass forms. Within British society, the distinctions between modes of respectability may have appeared (and may still appear) large, but by contrast with the state of society a century earlier, or with many other contemporaneous societies, they pale before what was shared.

tion and bureaucracy.[3] This second trend, by increasing the capabilities and the self-confidence of the state and the professions, also diminished reliance upon popular deterrence and education in favor of direct administration. And where general social policy headed, so too moved criminal policy.

Social policy and will power

As the erection of Victorian modes of punishment had taken place within a wider context of social policy, so their transformation that began around 1880 must also be set in a policy context. Social policy was a broad field that centered on deliberate public legislation and administration, but embraced as well on the one side the meliorist activities of voluntary societies and on the other the less overtly value-laden but no less ultimately value-shaped workings of the civil law. Moreover, this wide field of policy itself was irrigated by still broader, if yet more diffuse, cultural streams.

Running through late Victorian and Edwardian social policymaking can be traced a mental thread of diminishing faith in the rationality, freedom, and efficacy fo the will power of the ordinary individual. The policy historian José Harris has observed in the last three decades of the century "a marked decline in that confident belief in universal human rationality that had been such a hallmark of the Chadwick era."[4] The concepts of unfitness and social wreckage[5] were ever more pervasive, sometimes in environmental dress, sometimes in biological dress.[6] The claim was increasingly made that, as the scientific rationalist Furneaux Jordan put it in 1890, "character rests primarily on [physiological] organization.... It is organization – a sad and erring organization – which, for the most part, decides who shall be criminals, or paupers, or drunkards, or libertines, or lunatics."[7] Others preferred to stress environmental determinants, but in either form character was becoming more

---

[3] See Harold Perkin, *The Rise of Professional Society 1880–1980* (London: Routledge, 1989).

[4] "The Transition to High Politics in English Social Policy, 1880–1914," in *High and Low Politics in Modern Britain*, ed. Michael Bentley and John Stevenson (Oxford: Clarendon Press, 1983), p. 71. This decline is traced among a number of social thinkers in Martin J. Wiener, *Between Two Worlds: The Political Thought of Graham Wallas* (Oxford: Clarendon Press, 1971).

[5] See for example, Francis Peek, *Social Wreckage* (London: W. Isbister, 1889). Peek was the chairman of the penal reform organization, the Howard Association.

[6] This has been ably analyzed for the later Victorian years in Gareth Stedman Jones, *Outcast London* (Oxford: Clarendon Press, 1971) and from the 1890s in Michael Freeden, *The New Liberalism: An Ideology of Social Reform* (Oxford: Clarendon Press, 1978).

[7] *Character as Seen in Body and Parentage* (London: Kegan Paul, 1890), p. 85.

and more perceived as a constraining cage limiting the individual rather than as something created by the individual's efforts.

This shifting perception of human nature was accompanied by a corresponding shift in the view of the role of the state. Individual moral improvement remained the goal of nearly all reformist intervention, but many felt it increasingly unlikely to be produced by simple evangelism or even by the discipline of adversity.[8] Indeed, adversity might crush rather than stimulate the individual's moral energies. Reformers increasingly argued that adversity must be scaled, if necessary by state intervention, to what ordinary human beings could manage. As the radical J. A. M. Macdonald insisted in 1893 about the problem of the unemployed:

> [W]e allow, of course, the truth of the general proposition that strength of character is the result of struggle with circumstance. And we further admit that, as a general proposition, it is true that any attempt to interfere with the free action of circumstance is a mistake. But ... it is not ... true as to every circumstance of our life. Before circumstances can operate as a real discipline in life, before they can become the means of evoking the reason in us, they must themselves be in their nature reasonable.[9]

It was not only that adversity could easily be too overpowering to yield any moral benefit. It was also that moral improvement seemed now to require not only less adversity, but more of something outside the individual that operated more directly and surely than either exhortation or threat – in short, means that did not depend on the individual's response. By the 1890s, Michael Freeden has argued, moral improvement was becoming a question of "reforming the framework in which the individual functioned."[10] Reforming the framework meant more direct, if less moral, intervention in the social environment and within the individual himself, than the pattern of Victorian reform had normally allowed.

---

[8] This is not to deny the persistence of both individualism and moralism in the attitudes of policymakers and general public. Rachel Vorspan and Standish Meacham, among others, have highlighted such lines of continuity in Edwardian social thinking and policy. [Vorspan, "Vagrancy and the New Poor Law in Late-Victorian and Edwardian England," *English Historical Review* 92 (1977), 59–81; Meacham, *Toynbee Hall and Social Reform* (New Haven: Yale University Press, 1988).] However, the recognition of continuities should not blind us to deep if gradual alterations in the prevailing meanings of traditional terminology. See Freeden, *New Liberalism*, Stefan Collini, *Liberalism and Sociology: L.T. Hobhouse and Political Argument in England 1880–1914* (Cambridge: Cambridge University Press, 1979), and A. W. Vincent, "The Poor Law Reports of 1909 and the Social Theory of the Charity Organization Society," *Victorian Studies* 27 (1983–4), 343–63.

[9] Quoted in Freeden, p. 171.

[10] Freeden, p. 171.

The drunkard becomes a patient

One of the first social problems to begin to be reconstructed along these new lines was drunkenness. The late 1880s and the 1890s formed a watershed in efforts against drink, as in so many areas of social discourse and policy. On the one hand, both fear and its accompanying moral fervor were waning, as the evil of drunkenness seemed at last to be in retreat. Alcohol consumption in England had peaked in the mid-1870s. From over 15 percent of total working-class family expenditure at the crest in 1876, spending on drink declined to under 9 percent in 1910.[11] Arrests for drunkenness similarly declined from a mid-1870s peak.[12] Public intoxication and drink-related violence became less common, and, correspondingly, support for drastic remedies like prohibition (and official hostility to popular fairs and amusements) began to erode. By the turn of the century, A. E. Dingle has noted, the dominant aim among Liberal temperance reformers "was no longer to prohibit, but to improve drinking habits and ensure the 'maximum prevention of mischief.' "[13]

On the other hand, remaining hard-core drunkards began to appear to be the prisoners of their habit, less able to change their ways by their own efforts and more of a menace (through the inheritance of alcoholism) to succeeding generations. Not only prohibitionist zeal, but also faith in voluntarist temperance evangelism, began to wane as faith in the power of an awakened will dimmed.[14] Reformist discourse on drink ceased to be structured moralistically by the polar alternatives of voluntary evangelism and prohibition. Instead, late Victorian and Edwardian discussion and policy began to move in two complementary new directions: greater regulation of the drink trade and of the general environment of drinking[15] and, beginning with the Habitual

---

[11] A. E. Dingle, "Drink and Working-Class Living Standards in Britain," *Economic History Review 25* (1972), 611–12.

[12] David Woods, "Community Violence," in *The Working–Class in England 1875–1914*, ed. John Benson (London: Croom Helm, 1985), p. 173.

[13] A. E. Dingle, *The Campaign for Prohibition in Victorian England* (London: Croom Helm, 1980), p. 224. Quotation from N. Buxton and W. Hoare, "Temperance Reform," in *The Heart of the Empire*, ed. C. F. G. Masterman (London 1900). See also A. E. Dingle, "The Rise and Fall of Temperance Economics," *Monash Papers in Economic History*, No. 3 (Monash University, Victoria, Australia 1977).

[14] On shifting views of the relation of drink to poverty, see J. B. Brown, "The Pig or the Stye: Drink and Poverty in Late Victorian England," *International Review of Social History 18* (1973), 380–395.

[15] For an example of the shift of blame from the drinker to brewers and pub owners, see J. O. Bairstow, *Crime and Vice: Their Suppressors and Abettors* (London: Blenkinsop, 1902). The 1899 Royal Commission on the Liquor Licensing Laws recommended establishing in law a virtually absolute liability for selling drink to someone already intoxicated (a principle introduced, but only in a weak form, in the 1872 act). It proposed

Drunkards Act of 1879, more direct custody and medical treatment of habitual drunkards.[16]

Greater regulation of the sale and consumption of drink involved both diminishing scruples against state intervention and increased readiness to disregard rather than reinforce distinctions between the sober and the intemperate. In 1887 the young radical R. B. Haldane observed that considerations "of expediency" might lead to regulation of all consumers of drink, including many who had no need of it. Yet the considerations might well be "so strong as to justify, in the general interest, the subjection of the sober section to some inconvenience for the sake of those whose motives are not enduring enough to save them from intemperance."[17] By 1911, Leonard Hobhouse could describe the Liberal state's relation to the drunkard very differently than had Mill, with his dual approach of general libertarianism and severe criminal sanctions for drunken offenders. Hobhouse's Liberalism no longer placed the struggle against temptation at the core of moral development. Instead, he saw an "obvious and elementary duty [on the part of the state] to remove the sources of temptation, and to treat as anti-social in the highest degree every attempt to make profit out of human weakness, misery, and wrong-doing." This argument, he added, went beyond the problem of drink, and "applies to all cases where overwhelming impulse is apt to master the will."[18]

The drunkard as Hobhouse described him – "beset with a fiend within" while subjected to ceaseless temptation from without by those seeking their own gain – could hardly be expected to save himself. The purchase of drink by such a person, Hobhouse argued, "is not unlike that of a very unequal contract." As the state would void a contract made with a minor, a lunatic, or a feebleminded adult, so it should refuse to allow the drunkard to consummate his own ruin. Hobhouse argued that the *true* liberty and moral progress of the individual would be furthered by directly taking charge of him, "so far as he is the victim of an impulse which he has allowed to grow beyond his own control." The question "whether he should be regarded as a fit object for tutelage or not is to be decided in each case by asking whether such capacity of self-control as he retains would be impaired or repaired by a period of tutelar restraint."[19]

to shift the burden of proof from the police or prosecutor to the publican, who "should be required to prove that he and his servants were ignorant of the drunkenness, or that if they knew it they did not permit the offender to remain on the premises." [*Royal Commission on the Laws Relating to the Sale of Intoxicating Liquors, Final Report 1899*, p. 21.] This recommendation was enacted in 1902.

[16] On the medicalization of habitual drunkenness, see Chs. 7 and 9.

[17] R. B. Haldane, *Life of Adam Smith* (London: W. Scott, 1887), p. 156.

[18] L. T. Hobhouse, *Liberalism* [1911] (New York: Oxford University Press, 1964), pp. 80–1.

[19] *Liberalism*, p. 81.

Regulation of the environment of drinking culminated in the 1914 Intoxicating Liquor Act and 1915 Defense of the Realm Act, many of whose wartime controls on pub opening hours and other aspects of public drinking survived into the peace. Direct control of the habitual drunkard culminated in the 1913 establishment of the Board of Control, which absorbed habitual drunkards into the category of the mentally deficient and disabled.

Treatment for the pauper

The problem of pauperism was undergoing similar redefinition in the late nineteenth century.[20] As they looked back over the long reign, late Victorians saw that, like drunkenness, both pauperism (the state of dependence upon public authorities) and poverty (absolute material deprivation) were diminishing. Of course, the extent of pauperism was largely defined by policy decisions; in particular, the "war against out-relief" instituted at the beginning of the 1870s had sharply reduced that form of assistance without increasing indoor (or institutional) relief. Persons receiving outdoor relief fell from 37.5 per thousand in 1871 to 23.6 in 1876, thereafter drifting further downward to 17.2 by 1893. The smaller number on indoor relief initially also fell, then began in the 1880s a slow rise; by 1893, though, it remained as a percentage of total population below that of 1871.[21] The severe Liberalism of the early 1870s had in fact succeeded (with the aid of rising real wages) in reducing pauperism. However, as often occurs in the history of social policy, this success was accompanied by a gradual reconceptualization of the problem. The focal concept for welfare policy gradually shifted from pauperism to poverty, from the state of dependence to the state of deprivation. In this development as in so many others, the 1890s were a watershed.

As the proportion of paupers and vagrants in society diminished, those remaining came increasingly to be seen as a hard core, perhaps incapable of raising themselves to respectability and unable to respond to the sticks and

---

[20] This necessarily brief discussion of welfare policy (like that of drink policy above) makes no claims to completeness. In particular, in examining cultural aspects of such policy it presumes both the persistence of great local variation in policy implementation and the importance of a variety of practical influences upon the development of policy. These administrative, financial, and political pressures are explored in *The New Poor Law in the Nineteenth Century*, ed. Derek Fraser (London: St. Martin's Press, 1976); M. A. Crowther, *The Workhouse System 1834–1929* (Athens, Ga.: University of Georgia Press, 1982); *The Foundations of the Welfare State*, ed. Pat Thane (London: Longman, 1982); and José Harris, "The Transition to High Politics in English Social Policy, 1880–1914," in *High and Low Politics*, eds. Michael Bentley and John Stevenson (Oxford: Clarendon Press, 1983).

[21] Karel Williams, *From Pauperism to Poverty* (London: Routledge, 1981), p. 102.

carrots of Victorian policies of poor law-cum-philanthropy. In the light of rising national income and solidifying public order, the aura of dangerousness invested in the poorer classes during the Chartist era and thereafter, faded; no revolt was going to spring from such lumpen. At the same time, the expansion of the electorate – nationally in 1884 and, most significantly, locally in 1894 – constricted the ability of government to employ deterrent methods against large numbers of paupers.[22] Yet it was also becoming unacceptable to leave them be; rising national income and spreading respectability made the lack of regular employment and residence more anomalous. Moreover, with the international arena becoming ever more competitive, militarily and economically, there was heightening concern for increased national fitness and efficiency. Whereas Mayhew's street children had appeared to overflow with vigor, however misdirected, late-Victorian street children now seemed more pathetic than dangerous, but just as problematic. As Mary Tabor noted in her contribution on "London Children" to Charles Booth's *Life and Labour*:

> Puny, pale-faced, scantily-clad and badly shod, those small and feeble folk may be found sitting limp and chill on the school benches in all the poorer parts of London. They swell the bills of mortality as want and sickness thin them off, or survive to be the needy and enfeebled adults whose burden of helplessness the next generation will have to bear.[23]

As images of the poor increasingly stressed their weakness,[24] paupers and vagrants threatened the social fiber as well as the social conscience. More direct action seemed called for, whether of a helping nature for the deserving or of a frankly coercive and segregative nature for the undeserving. The state would have to take a more assertive hand in both preventing the deterioration of character and building it up among the weaker elements of the community.[25]

This shifting interpretation of need and capability fostered two developments in poor law thinking. One was a slow softening (gradually and in piecemeal fashion, varying from place to place, often without revising formal

---

[22] This changing political context was reflected in the novel decision of the 1895 Royal Commission on the Aged Poor to include a pauper among its witnesses.

[23] Charles Booth, *Life and Labour of the People of London*, Vol. 3 (1902 coll. ed.; London: Macmillan) p. 207.

[24] Nearly every review of the strongly selling "New Liberal" volume of essays, *The Heart of the Empire* (London: T. F. Unwin, 1901), remarked upon the description by Charles Masterman of the "new city type" of person, a weedy, weak, worthless specimen, hardly fit to maintain a world empire. See Bentley Gilbert's introduction to the 1973 reprint edition, esp. p. xxiv.

[25] The literature on the Edwardian issue of 'national inefficiency' is large; see G. R. Searle, *The Quest for National Efficiency* (Oxford: Basil Blackwell, 1971); Aaron Friedberg, *The Weary Titan: Britain and the Experience of Relative Decline 1895–1905* (Princeton: Princeton University Press, 1988).

principles) of the twin pillars of deterrence – resistance to relief outside the workhouse and the rigor and stigma of the workhouse regime itself. The other was a growing interest in classification and specialized treatment, therapeutic or coercive, for particular types of paupers. The first official step to separate unemployment from pauperism, and in consequence make possible centrally sanctioned state relief outside the poor law, was taken in Joseph Chamberlain's 1886 circular to local authorities urging relief work for the un-employed. Although this policy change, as José Harris has pointed out, had little immediate effect, in the long run it did mark a major watershed.[26] In the same year the Charity Organization Society abandoned the classification "un-deserving" in its administration of relief.[27] Although the pace of change in this area was slow, eventually legislation like old age pensions in 1908, national insurance in 1911, and their extensions after World War I drastically expanded nonworkhouse state assistance to the poor and the incapacitated.

Within the poor law, resistance to outdoor relief began to soften in the 1890s. Already, from 1882 on, the treatment of vagrants was easing. A series of circulars between 1882 and 1888 allowed local boards to dispense with de-tention and provide alternative forms of diet and labor for persons honestly seeking work. When boards too eagerly took up these new powers, renewed central efforts at tightening up followed in 1888 and 1897, but they formed merely momentary halts in a long-term trend toward a loosening of the prin-ciple of less eligibility. It was coming to be questioned whether penal methods were appropriate for vagrants. Responding to an influx into the prisons of vagrants committed for misbehavior in the workhouse (apparently an unfore-seen consequence of prison reform), the head of the Edwardian prison system, Evelyn Ruggles-Brise, noted that this problem could not be solved simply by restoring the previous harshness of prison life:

[26] See José Harris, *Unemployment and Politics* (Oxford: Clarendon Press, 1972). Chamberlain justified this policy in private, as did almost all policymakers of the period, as a way of separating deserving and undeserving poor and allowing unimpeded severity to be applied to the latter. Temporary public employment of the unemployed, he wrote the future Mrs. Webb, "will remove one great danger, viz., that public sentiment should go wholly over to the unemployed, and render impossible that state severity to which you and I equally attach importance. By offering reasonable work at low wages we may secure the power of being very strict with the loafer and confirmed pauper." March 5, 1886, in Harris, p. 76. Nonetheless, though Harris puts the circular in perspective, she does not challenge its status as the first move by the central government away from simple uniform deterrence of the able-bodied, a move with significant long-term consequences. See, for example, Harris, p. 90.

[27] Meacham, *Toynbee Hall*, p. 73. Though this shift was significant, it of course did not mark a dramatic conversion; Meacham points out the term "not likely to benefit" was sub-stituted, continuing to stress that, as he put it, "*present* character remained foremost among the criteria employed to weigh the potential benefit of any program of social better-ment." [p. 73.]

The question is much broader than that of the comparative comfort or attractiveness of the Prison and of the Casual Ward, and has a wider administrative significance. It is, in fact, the question whether 'penal' methods, based upon the analogy furnished by Prison regime, e.g., separate cells, dietary and task, can properly be adopted in the case of vagabond persons coming to Casual Wards for shelter and rest on account of destitution.[28]

If less was now being expected of vagrants, it was coming to seem especially unreasonable to expect the poor to have fully provided for their old age. Public sentiment was moving toward dispauperizing the aged. Charles Booth's 1894 study, *The Aged Poor*, marked something of a turning point, for it challenged conventional presuppositions about the relation between relief practice and pauperism.[29] Comparing different local relief practices and relief loads, Booth found that placing strict conditions on allowances outside the workhouse did not in fact promote independence among the old, nor did unconditional allowances promote greater dependence. Booth's findings encouraged him to pursue his recent advocacy of old-age pensions,[30] but also of course raised questions for his readers about whether severe discouragement of out-relief was necessary.[31] The royal commission set up the following year urged Poor Law officials to treat the aged poor with more consideration, and subsequently the Local Government Board recommended outdoor relief for the elderly, wherever suitable.[32] In circulars in 1890, 1910, and 1911, the Local Government Board (LGB) recommended that "adequate" relief be given, although it made no effort to define adequacy.[33] After many of the aged were removed from Poor Law rolls by state pensions

[28] (1911) Quoted in Leon Radzinowicz and Roger Hood, *History of English Criminal Law Vol. 5* (London: Stevens and Sons, 1986), p. 354. Also contributing to the growing reluctance to employ penal methods on vagrants was probably the developing literary idealization of tramp life. [see Chapter 4.]

[29] See Williams, *Pauperism*, pp. 341–4.

[30] *The Aged Poor* immediately followed Booth's equally neglected 1892 inquiry, *Pauperism and the Endowment of Old Age*, which presented pauperism among the old as a disturbing problem requiring radical solutions and then made the first serious and respected argument for universal, noncontributory old-age pensions.

[31] His findings of course could be, and were, challenged on methodological grounds; perhaps their chief significance was not scientific but in legitimizing a shift of public opinion already underway.

[32] Pat Thane, "Non-Contributory Versus Insurance Pensions 1878–1908," and M. A. Crowther, "The Later Years of the Workhouse 1890–1929," in *The Origins of British Social Policy*, ed. Pat Thane (London: Croom Helm 1978), pp. 96, 45.

[33] M. A. Crowther, *Workhouse*, p. 86; Williams, *Pauperism*, p. 130. Williams has stressed that there is no evidence that adequacy was meant to be more generous than existing standards. A better fit with particular need (i.e., more scientific treatment), not generosity per se, was what seems to have been chiefly sought.

and insurance, new regulations in 1914 encouraged more generous outdoor relief for the largest remaining group, widows.[34] Finally, postwar unemployment led to a rapid rise in out-relief, as well as the legislative extension of
national insurance. By 1927, out-relief rolls were almost three times the level
of 1913.[35]

By this time, the workhouse had become politically and culturally unacceptable as a way of dealing with unemployment. Already by the late nineteenth
century, most workhouse inmates were elderly or disabled, a result made inevitable by the very success of efforts to deter the able-bodied from applying
for assistance. This disabling of the indoor poor was further accentuated by
relaxing standards of what constituted able-bodiedness. As early as 1878 a hint
of a new image of paupers appeared in discussion within the Local Government Board on the classification of workhouse inmates. A departmental inquiry had drawn attention to the fact that existing policy categorized all
inmates between the ages of 16 and 60 as able-bodied, regardless of their
physical condition. But as medical provision grew and the mental climate of
the policymakers changed, this homogeneous categorization appeared peculiar.
An official observed that "this report shows very conclusively that if the Poor
Law Statistics are to inform and not to mislead the public, it is high time that
. . . the blind and the halt and the lame are no longer called 'able-bodied'
simply because they are under 60 years of age."[36] In 1880 new draft rules
were drawn up to ensure that disabled paupers were not lumped in with the
truly fit.[37] Further official distinctions followed in 1895, and, finally, in 1911
the LGB gave up any attempt to classify the able-bodied.[38]

The disappearance of the able-bodied from the workhouses through deterrence and recategorization (with the exception of the vagrant casual wards)
encouraged a rise in inmate numbers (from 1883) and a softening of rules on
workhouse discipline (after 1885). As the LGB acknowledged in 1895:

> Whilst workhouses were in the first instance provided chiefly for the
> relief of the able-bodied, and their administration was therefore
> intentionally deterrent, the sick, the aged, and the infirm now greatly
> preponderate, and this [has] led to a change in the spirit of the
> administration.[39]

[34] Crowther, *Workhouse*, p. 91. Here as elsewhere, however, as recent scholars have
stressed, moral distinctions remained. Even in 1914 ampler outdoor provision for "deserving" widows went along with the continued threat of the workhouse for the undeserving.
[35] Crowther, "Later Years," p. 48.
[36] P. R.O., Ministry of Health (hereafter MH) 32/93, Dec. 23, 1878.
[37] MH 32/93, Nov. 22, 1880.
[38] Crowther, *Workhouse*, p. 100.
[39] Circular quoted in Crowther, *Workhouse*, p. 74.

In the early 1890s guardians were permitted to furnish a variety of little comforts – books, newspapers, tobacco, and snuff for the aged, toys for the children, and dry tea with sugar and milk for deserving inmates to brew at will.[40] These small relaxations reflected a larger movement away from reliance upon general deterrence. By 1895, an inspector could describe with disapproval the new comfort of workhouse life and blame it for a creeping return of some able-bodied men to dependence – a dangerous trend that he urged be nipped in the bud.[41] Despite such resistance, the discarding of deterrence continued. After 1900 therapeutic and welfarist justifications for the workhouses were increasingly articulated by guardians and civil servants, and in 1913 the term workhouse was officially replaced by Poor Law Institution.[42]

While deterrent severity was relaxing, a trend toward classification and specialized treatment was becoming more pronounced. Although classification can be traced back to Edwin Chadwick and the Poor Law Commission of 1834, early and mid-Victorian workhouses had been almost always comprehensive institutions whose "blind, repressive discipline" took little account of variations among their subjects.[43] At first hesitantly and indirectly (through regulations on workhouse construction) from 1868 and then more decisively (through explicit policy pronouncements) in the 1890s, central government began to encourage distinctions in treatment by category of pauper.[44] In the infirmaries and dispensaries built during the latter decades of the century the principle of "scientific treatment" began to replace that of "less eligibility."[45] The proliferation of Poor Law infirmaries distinct from workhouses was followed by the building of separate specialized institutions for the old and children, which were staffed by specially trained personnel,

---

[40] Crowther, *Workhouse*, p. 82.

[41] MH 32/93, Sept. 21, 1895.

[42] Crowther, *Workhouse*, p. 87. She notes, however, that officials continued in their private correspondence to use the old term, suggesting that one purpose of this and related shifts in terminology was conservative, to "save the Poor Law" in a time unfriendly to it. Yet, the very need to employ euphemisms, here as elsewhere, suggested a change in public attitudes.

[43] Williams, *Pauperism*, p. 113; see also Crowther, *Workhouse*, Ch. 2.

[44] See in particular Williams's analysis of memoranda and circulars on workhouse construction, *Pauperism*, pp. 107–28.

[45] See Michael Rose, "Crisis of Poor Relief in England 1860–1890," in ed. W. Mommsen, *The Emergence of the Welfare State in Britain and Germany* (London: Croom Helm, 1981), pp. 60–2; Crowther, *Workhouse*. Mary MacKinnon has pointed to "a massive increase in capital construction" of poor law hospital facilities starting in 1895 in "Poor Law Policy, Unemployment, and Pauperism," *Explorations in Economic History*, 23 (July, 1986), 327.

and by efforts within workhouses to separate and treat differently deserving and undeserving inmates.[46]

As faith in the continued effectiveness and legitimacy of general deterrence waned, classification could justify both gentler treatment and more precisely focused harshness. It would distinguish between those for whom rigor was not appropriate, because of their incapacity (the sick, the aged, the very young) or their character (the deserving poor), and the undeserving able-bodied remainder who could justifiably be subjected to it. Indeed, since Poor Law rigor had not forced them out of dependence, this remainder apparently needed the even more coercive regime proposed from the 1890s for compulsory labor colonies. Classification would allow the replacement of uniform deterrence operating both directly on paupers and indirectly on the general population by specialized administration operating purely directly upon its charges. It would make possible the provision of a range of treatment appropriate to each case.

Despite their conflicts, both the majority and the minority of the 1909 Royal Commission on the Poor Laws agreed that general mixed workhouses should disappear in favor of specialized institutions. Although workhouses remained for many years thereafter, the trend to specialization did accelerate. Specialization held many attractions. As Anne Crowther has observed:

> Specialized institutions appealed to humanitarians who felt that the helpless would be "better off" inside them; to eugenists who hoped incarceration would prevent the unfit from breeding; to the medical elite who were themselves becoming more specialized; and to a vague public sense of propriety which disliked mixing the deserving with the disreputable poor.[47]

This shift from uniform deterrence to specialized treatment could mean greater helpfulness but at the same time even less liberty.[48] Appropriate treatment could range from assistance to protection to complete control, like that being proposed at this time for drunkards. Proposals for public works, labor exchanges, and social work assistance for the unemployed were accompanied by plans for labor colonies. As one official of the Poor Law Unions Association explained in 1903, echoing the rationale of recently created Inebriate Reformatories:

> What we have to do is to subject the [vagrant] to a treatment that is likely to assist in the formation of regular and industrious habits. To do this we must keep him from drink, give him plain but suitable food, enforce reg-

[46] Crowther, *Workhouse*, Ch. 3.

[47] Crowther, *Workhouse*, p. 90.

[48] See, among others, Williams, *Pauperism.* pp. 130–6; most of the contributions to *The Origins of British Social Policy*, ed. Pat Thane; David Garland, *Punishment and Welfare* (Aldershot: Gower, 1985).

ular hours, and make him work. We must take complete control of the man for a time, because his mind and will are *so diseased that he is incapable of controlling himself,* and that time must be long enough to give good hopes of the eradication of the disease.... The vagrant's laziness is very much a matter of habit, and industry must be made habitual instead.[49]

In 1904 the Inter-Departmental Committee on Physical Deterioration had, significantly, been called into existence by alarms over the high rate of enlistment rejections during the Boer War. In its report the committee concluded that it might be necessary for the state to take charge of the lives of persons who were "incapable of independent existence up to the standard of decency which it imposes." As a last resort, the committee endorsed the idea of compulsory labor colonies for such persons. Other official endorsements of compulsory labor colonies followed, from the Report of the Departmental Committee on Vagrancy in 1906 and, most enthusiastically, from the 1909 Minority Report of the Royal Commission on the Poor Laws. The latter saw the work-shy as suffering from "a morbid state of mind, which makes them incapable of filling a useful place in the industrial world," and urged labor colonies not as a last resort but as a place for all vagrants.[50] However, for all its appeal among the policymaking classes, the idea of compulsory labor colonies for the hard-core unemployed failed to be translated into practice by 1914, and the rapid draining of the "stagnant pools" of unemployment during the war, together with the granting of universal suffrage at its end, foreclosed the possibility of implementing such institutions and indeed permanently altered discussion of this problem.

Nonetheless, by the end of the Edwardian period, while most of the new coercive proposals toward the disreputable poor had been sidetracked, welfare policy as a whole, like policy toward drink, was moving along new lines. These new developments, sometimes presenting the gentle face of humanity and sometimes the severe one of social efficiency, were in either guise patterned by the same deep alteration in conceptions of human nature and social agency.

Education as welfare

In similar fashion, educational policy was highlighting weakness and incapacity. Mary Tabor's picture of the children of the poor as "small and feeble folk" growing up to inevitably pass on their "burden of helplessness" to the

---

[49] *Poor Law Conferences*, 1902–3, 581, quoted in Vorspan, "Vagrancy and the New Poor Law," 76. [My italics.]
[50] Quoted in Radzinowicz and Hood, pp. 367, 371.

next generation was repeated over and over by other reformers of all shades, from socialist to eugenicist. In 1907, Reginald Bray, a member of the London County Council Education Committee, made a typical argument; the families of the poor did not have sufficient strength to cope with modern life without state assistance. The parental instinct, "like other instincts . . . at its inception is frail and easily destroyed. It must be cherished by exercise or it will die at its birth." But, he stressed, simply leaving the family to itself, as had been done in the past, would not nurture this instinct:

> [I]f the struggle to maintain the family is too exacting, either the struggle will cease, and the family as a unit disappear, or the struggle will go on, because it is the least of many evils, but the sentiment of family affection will be quenched and its place taken by a sense of weariness or a feeling of active irritation at the harassing ties involved. . . . Parents are human beings, and in consequence share the frailties which are the heritage of the race. Humanity is hedged in on all sides with limitations. Up to a certain point it is no doubt true that the pleasure of attainment is to some extent proportionate to the degree of effort expended. But when that critical point is reached, the tide of pleasure changes, ebbs rapidly, and may easily be transformed into a current of vigorous pain. . . . Few people seem to realise how nearly the lives of the poor reach the limits of human endurance.[51]

Policymaking in state education, like that relating to drink and poverty, was increasingly recognizing these limits and manifesting heightened sensitivity to human weakness. The spreading net of educational provision was meshing with the development of neurology and psychiatry to encourage concern about mental strain in schoolchildren. The introduction in 1880 of national compulsory attendance at school gave impetus to emerging dissatisfaction with the uniformity and discipline encouraged by Robert Lowe's 1862 Revised Code and its system of "payment by results."[52] This system made state grants to elementary schools conditional upon pupils' performance in examinations on the 3 Rs.[53] In education as in poor relief, recipients of benefits were required to meet specific standards of performance.[54] Now this demand was seen as

---

[51] Reginald Bray, *The Town Child* (London: T. Fisher Unwin, 1907), pp. 305–9.

[52] See the discussion of mental strain among schoolchildren carried on in the correspondence columns of *The Times*, April 8, 9, 10, 13, 15, 19, 1880. On criticism and reform of the system of "payment by results," see Gillian Sutherland, *Policy-making in Elementary Education 1870–1895* (London: Oxford University Press, 1973), Chs. 7–9.

[53] Sutherland, *Policy-making*, pp. 8–9, 193.

[54] The character of early Gladstonian Liberalism is illuminated by recalling that, in framing the landmark Education Act of 1870, two reforms that are usually conjoined in modern minds – compulsory attendance and the abolition of school fees – received very different attention. Both W. E. Forster and his second-in-command, Lord Ripon, urged

unrealistic and an obstacle to social progress. From 1883, what the secretary of the National Union of Elementary Teachers termed "the attempt to force all scholars at an equal pace to the same standard" was attacked from many quarters, and a campaign began against "over-pressure" in the schools, backed by a heterogeneous coalition of interests and philosophies.[55] Dr. James Crichton-Browne, a leading psychiatrist, examined children in fourteen schools in the worst areas of London and declared that the existing intense system of education was the major cause of a national rise in mental illness. Although his arguments were knowledgeably rebuted by the Education Department, the general campaign continued unabated and forced the problem of educational demands to governmental attention. A royal commission on elementary education set up in 1885 led to, among other changes, the effective abolition of payment by results. Once freed from the strictures of the code, educational policymakers at all levels in the 1890s – prodded by A. H. D. Acland, the energetic Liberal head of the Education Department between 1892 and 1895 – shifted their attention to increasing the flexibility of the sys-

compulsion; even Robert Lowe, now chancellor of the Exchequer and obsessively concerned about costs, accepted that compulsion must follow the assumption of responsibility for education by the state. Although compulsion was rejected by the cabinet as too politically contentious in an area already overburdened with strong feelings, the act did grant school boards the power to compel attendance if they wished (and compulsion was included in the Scottish Education Act two years later). Lowe's well-known remark after the Reform Act of 1867 has usually been revealingly misquoted: rather than "we must educate our masters," Lowe's observation was that "we must compel our future masters to learn their letters." Significantly, the first English group to be universally required to send their children to school, in 1873, were recipients of poor law out-relief. However, while compulsion was very much on the agenda, making schooling free was not seriously considered by anyone in authority. "Few people in 1870," Gillian Sutherland has pointed out, "paid even lip service to free education as an objective." [pp. 118–25, 163.] Obviously, in this the interests of church schools and of ratepayers bulked large; but there were widely shared moral considerations also at work. Even the radical crusader for educational provision, A. J. Mundella, opposed free schools. Among radicals, perhaps the leading critic of free education was Henry Fawcett, ably supported by his feminist wife Millicent. In his tract, *Pauperism: Its Causes and Remedies* [1871], Fawcett argued for compulsion while denouncing free education; the advancing social conscience of the age, he claimed, was coming to recognize rudimentary education as one of the duties of parenthood, along with food and shelter, which the state could and should enforce under threat of punishment.

[55] Described by Gillian Sutherland, in *ibid*, pp. 245–60, and in her subsequent *Ability, Merit and Measurement: Mental Testing and English Education 1880–1940* (Oxford: Clarendon Press, 1984), pp. 7–10. Quotation in Sutherland, *Policy-making*, p. 248. Sutherland brings out clearly the political context of this movement, which drew from the resistance of voluntary schools to state encroachment, and thus led a newly returned Conservative government to set up a Royal Commission on Elementary Education. The existence of this special interest enabled a rising sensitivity among professionals to childhood incapacity to gain a more ready political hearing than might otherwise have been the case.

tem, and new ideas and methods of teaching that encouraged less structured and less uniform activities were advanced.

Meanwhile, public attention was being drawn to the exploration of mental deficiency. A second royal commission was created in 1885 to deal simply with the education of the blind, but its scope was soon extended to cover the deaf and dumb and then also "such other cases as from special circumstances would seem to require exceptional methods of education." Its report in 1889 referred for the first time to "educational imbeciles." As Gillian Sutherland has observed, "The health and capacities of elementary schoolchildren seemed now established as a continuing topic for investigation and concern."[56] Between 1888 and 1894, a committee of the British Medical Association examined 100,000 schoolchildren for mental abnormalities. The distinguished medical man who supervised many of these examinations concluded that 15 percent of the schoolchildren examined were defective in some respect.[57] Charles Booth's classic *Life and Labour* (1891) gave much attention to "School Life," denouncing the stultifying effects of payment by results. Mary Tabor, Booth's research worker, observed: "The buildings, the staff, the educational appliances, the requirements of the Code, are the same for every class. It is the children alone who vary."[58] Concern with variation and incapacity led to legislation creating new kinds of state-funded special schooling – the 1886 Idiots Act and the 1893 Blind and Deaf Act, addressing easily defined problems, and, after a good deal more intellectual and political wrangling, a measure with wider implications, the 1899 Elementary Education (Defective and Epileptic Children) Act. This measure opened up a field of a continuum of deficiency that had no sharp dividing line and required specialized expert diagnosis and treatment. In recommending such a measure, the Education Department had noted the previous year that:

> From the normal child down to the lowest idiot, there are degrees of defi-ciency of mental power; and it is only a difference of degree which distinguishes the feeble-minded children ... on the one side from the backward children who are found in every school and, on the other side, from the children who are too deficient to receive proper benefit from any teaching which the School Authorities can give.... Though the difference in mental powers is one of degree only, the difference of treat-ment which is required is such as to make these children, for practical purposes, a distinct class.[59]

[56] *Ability*, p. 9.
[57] Nikolas Rose, *The Psychological Complex: Psychology, Politics and Society in England 1869–1939* (London: Routledge, 1985), p. 100.
[58] Quoted in Sutherland, *Ability*, pp. 9–10.
[59] Quoted in N. Rose, Psychological Complex, p. 99.

Following a common pattern in the history of social policy, this permissive act was later superseded by a compulsory one, passed shortly after the 1913 Mental Deficiency Act, aimed at providing institutional care and detention for adult defectives. As time went on, educational incapacity, pauperism, and drunkenness were increasingly linked to the emerging concepts of social deficiency and a problem population. The moral problems of the nineteenth century were becoming the administrative ones of the twentieth century.

Civil law: character-building ebbs

Social values were also expressed and solidified and policy made, if less directly than in legislation, through case law. Despite its formation in a more fortuitous and piecemeal process than that of parliamentary legislation, case law still, in the main, exhibited elective affinities for particular social assumption and values – even when, as the nineteenth century drew to a close, judges were increasingly claiming to be simply logical technicians applying the law and eschewing moral and policy concerns.

In the long run moving along similar lines as Westminster legislation and Whitehall administration,[60] High Court case law was nevertheless much slower to change. This was perhaps inevitable, for it was the province of a politically insulated legal fraternity whose task – to resolve specific contemporary problems by applying the rules of earlier cases and statutes – made it necessarily more backward looking. Thus, the sort of shifts in social perceptions and assumptions that appeared in a variety of public policy areas from the later 1870s on only had a major effect upon case law, civil or criminal, in the twentieth century. The last decades of the nineteenth century, indeed, brought to full flower classical principles of contractual liability based on free consent and tort liability based on personal fault, though these were ever more removed from the cultural context in which they had developed. New text writers, seeking to show each branch of the law as a rational system, elaborated and reinterpreted consent and fault as self-sufficient and value-free deductive logical principles from which the entire body of contract and tort law could be built up.[61] In so doing, of course, as critics from the Legal Realists of the 1930s to recent adherents of Critical Legal Studies have pointed out, these

[60] The homogeneity of the English governing elite has often been remarked upon; Westminster, Whitehall, and the Royal Courts of Justice in the Strand were not only geographically close to one another, but more significantly, closely connected by ties of family, school, club, and business.

[61] Most important among these were Sir Frederick Pollock on contract (1876), Sir William Anson on contract (1879), and Pollock on torts (1882); a latter influential work in this tradition was Sir John Salmond on torts (1907).

legal principles entrenched Victorian cultural values and interests within a nominally scientific body of thought.

Nonetheless, by the turn of the century the now fully opened blooms of consent and fault as the bases of liability began to be affected by a chill in the judicial air. Both the fundamental concepts of consent and fault drew sustenance not only from a philosophy that assumed that society was made up of autonomous individuals, but also, as we have suggested, at an even deeper level from a widespread frame of mind in which that conception was less an assumed reality than an idealized goal. In this frame of mind, society was seen as endangered by an individual's lack of self-government, in whose development the law had a central role to play. As we have seen, because the rethinking of human nature was associated with the rise of natural and social science when Victorian efforts were successfully establishing order and diffusing respectability through society, the legal principles of consent and fault lost much of their authority. Holding out longer in the courts perhaps than elsewhere, the image of a population both desperately in need of, and readily capable of profiting from, deterrent training in prudence and self-discipline began to fade too and weakened an openly moralizing notion of the role of law. The rationale of the law as a character-building force, as an institution for producing responsible individuals, began to lose its urgency.

As this happened, the hortatory and deterrent functions of law began to yield center stage to its functions of adjusting conflicts and compensating for harms. Gradually, less came to be expected of the ordinary citizen, while the power of circumstances was more highly rated. The time horizon of judicial decision making began to shorten, diminishing judicial tolerance of current pain and suffering. Allowing individuals to suffer harms they might have avoided with greater prudence came to seem both less just and less useful. Instead, more direct remedies gained approbation. Allotting blame and punishing fault seemed ever less adequately to provide for the efficient allocation of social risks, and use of the law to prevent directly harmful behavior and compensate harm sufferers was increasingly accepted. In short, civil law began to shed some of its educational character and take on more of an administrative aspect.

Perhaps the most visible change was in contract law, which saw its newly dominant position in the civil law begin to erode. From the 1890s on an ever-wider range of circumstances was allowed to mitigate or erase consensual obligation, whereas obligations arising apart from consent were more expansively defined and insisted upon. The power of consent alone to create binding obligation or to abrogate obligation arising elsewhere was increasingly restricted.[62] In such cases, the educational purpose – and presumably, the

---

[62] The classic work on the decline, as on the earlier rise, of consent-based liability, is

effect – of contract law ("As you make your bed, so shall you lie in it") was diminished at the expense of its administrative function (smoothing economic and social life). Similarly, twentieth-century tort law[63] – expanding as contract law has narrowed – found much greater place for strict liability.[64] This development was made possible by the growth from the later nineteenth century of liability insurance[65] and the limited liability form of company legal organiz-

Atiyah, *The Rise and Fall of Freedom of Contract* (Oxford: Clarendon Press, 1979). See also Atiyah, *From Principles of Pragmatism* (Oxford: Clarendon Press, 1978). Also see John Adams and Roger Brownsword, *Understanding Contract Law* (London: Fontana, 1987).

[63] There exists no single dominating work for the history of English tort law like Atiyah's on contract, but see John G. Fleming, *An Introduction to the Law of Torts* (2nd ed. Oxford: Clarendon Press, 1985); P. H. Winfield, "The Law of Tort [1885–1935]," *Law Quarterly Review 51* (1935), 249–62; T. Hadden, "Contract, Tort and Crime: Forms of Legal Thought," *Law Quarterly Review 87* (1971), 240–60; Manchester, *A Modern Legal History of England and Wales* (London: Butterworths, 1980) pp. 280–301; Carol Harlow, *Understanding Tort Law* (London: Fontana, 1987). The most illuminating work on parallel developments across the Atlantic is G. Edward White, *Tort Law in America: An Intellectual History* (New York: Oxford University Press, 1980). Also see Atiyah, *Rise and Fall*, Chs. 21–22.

[64] This despite the well-known "rise and rise of negligence" [Harlow, p. 35.]. As it was increasingly called upon by the courts, the tort of negligence altered its focus from individuals to institutions and in the process explicitly became a device for redistributing risk in a complex and interdependent society. As Harlow has observed, "over the course of time, courts found themselves lengthening the chains of damage for which defendants were liable", and thus attenuating the once close link between negligence and fault. The result in many areas was what she has called a "movement towards strict liability within the law of negligence" [pp. 47,51].

[65] "The natural tendency," Tom Hadden has argued, "in a system where insurance and the common law are combined is towards strict liability." As this tendency develops, "status takes precedence over actual performance. It is for the law to decide which party should normally be held responsible, rather than who if anyone was to blame in the particular circumstances. The insurance industry may then assess how much the party should pay for cover against that risk. The need for a new approach to the question of defining duties of care in this light should be obvious. Predictability will be more important than foreseeability. . . . The law must formulate new principles of responsibility to meet modern practice." Hadden, "Contract, Tort and Crime," 255–6. As G. Edward White has observed of U.S. law, the massive infiltration of liability insurance into the field of torts marked a fundamental change in the social role of tort law. Beginning as a device to idemnify employers against the risks of lawsuits from employees, it became a means for using tort law not to "admonish currently undesirable civil conduct" but to "compensate injured people." "By the 1930s . . . the presence of liability insurance was now regarded as creating an opportunity to compensate injured parties in Torts suits. . . . A paternalistic state, rather than letting losses 'lie where they fell,' was intervening, through its lawmaking officials, to distribute losses among society generally, with the criteria for distribution being prevailing notions of efficiency or fairness." White, *Tort*, pp. 147–8. This change

ation.[66] Under these conditions, stricter liability meant not greater but lesser focusing of responsibility upon individuals. Remedies for harms became surer and swifter, while responsibility was diffused throughout society, first to those with the greatest power and ultimately, through insurance, to all consumers, shareholders, and taxpayers.

These somewhat parallel tendencies in contract and tort law[67] exhibit a shift in reliance in dealing with harms from personal character to impersonal institutions guided by statistics.[68] Pulled along in the wake of acts of Parliament and actions by the bureaucracy, judges and juries in civil law cases gradually gave less weight to the possession of good character (as denoted by such traits as thinking carefully about future consequences of actions and being prudent about making promises and reliable in fulfilling promises made), as they also penalized less the possession of a bad one. All this did not of course necessarily reflect a denial of the desirability of good character; it did reflect a declining belief in it as the necessary bedrock of social life and policy.

One of the first areas in which this shift was noticeable was the highly contentious and quickly politicized issue of liability for industrial accidents. Legal rulings through the early and mid-Victorian period had interpreted employment as a contract implying an acceptance by the workman of liability for most industrial accidents. This interpretation had been widely justified as a necessary discipline to ensure employees' "diligence and caution," as Lord Abinger had put it in a landmark decision in 1837, and in any event as a cost that would be taken account of in the wages bargain. However, with the extension of the franchise to many skilled workmen in 1867 and the formation of

proceeded faster and further in the United States than in Britain, but a similar tendency was at work in both countries.

[66] Although midcentury legislation made this possible, it only developed to a significant degree in the late nineteenth century. See P. W. Ireland, "The Rise of the Limited Liability Company," *International Journal of the Sociology of Law 12* (1984) 239–60, and David Sugarman and G. R. Rubin, "Towards a New History of Law and Material Society in England 1750–1914," in eds. Rubin and Sugarman, *Law, Economy and Society, 1750–1914* (Abingdon: Professional Books, 1984), p. 6.

[67] Hadden noted the similarity between main lines of twentieth-century development in tort and contract; in contract also "it is normally more important that the risk should be precisely allocated than that the merits of each case should be investigated in detail. The shift from agreement to status which this implies, of course, necessarily detracts from the absolute freedom of contract. . . . The same body of law will be applicable in all cases in which loss or injury arises from bad luck or bad judgment in the normal course of events." [p. 256.]

[68] As Winston Churchill remarked in 1909, in arguing as president of the Board of Trade for the unconditionality of unemployment insurance, "I do not like mixing up moralities and mathematics." Quoted in Bentley Gilbert, *The Evolution of National Insurance in Great Britain* (London: Michael Joseph, 1966), p. 272.

the Trades Union Congress (TUC) the following year, this question moved from the cloisters of case law into the hurly-burly of politics. Through the 1870s the TUC regularly denounced this aspect of the law, and from 1876 on had bills to revise it introduced into Parliament. During 1876 and 1877 a select committee heard evidence on the issue. The outspoken individualist Baron Bramwell lamented this "agitation" to the committee:

> Why does he not leave the employment if he knows that it is dangerous? To my mind, it is a sad thing to hear men come into court, as I have heard them, and excuse themselves for not having done that on the ground that their bread depended upon it, or something of that sort. I should like to see a more independent feeling on the part of workmen, so that they would say, 'I will have nothing to do with a man who employs dangerous things or dangerous persons.'[69]

Nonetheless, doubts about the adequacy of the law were penetrating official circles. In 1878, the idea of compulsory insurance for both employers and workmen was seriously broached for the first time in a paper by a leading barrister delivered before the Social Science Association.[70] The proposal provoked intense debate, at the association and, later that year, within the Home Office. The assistant under-secretary for legal affairs at the Home Office, Godfrey Lushington,[71] observed, favoring the suggestion made by the Scottish Judge Lord Shand, that employers should insure their workmen as a body:

> The workmen . . . are unable (except where the danger is obviously great as in a gunpowder mill) to secure a higher rate of wages to meet the risk of the work, and it is absurd to expect each working man to insure. It is in this helplessness of the working man that the practical injustice of law consists.[72]

Thus, in the same year that a civil servant at the Local Government Board questioned the undiscriminating application of the term "able-bodied" in

[69] Quoted in Manchester, *Modern Legal History*, p. 297.
[70] See P. W. J. Bartrip and S. B. Burman, *The Wounded Soldiers of Industry: Industrial Compensation Policy 1833–1897* (Oxford: Clarendon Press, 1983), pp. 140–5.
[71] Lushington was the son of a reformist Whig judge and had been one of the first English positivists when a student at Oxford in the 1850s. He was known as a friend of workmen's causes, having argued against the existing law of master and servant and for legalizing trades unions in a contribution to the radical *Questions for a Reformed Parliament* in 1867. He was to become permanent under-secretary at the Home Office in 1885.
[72] Godfrey Lushington, memorandum on Employers' Liability, July 30, 1878, HO 45/9458/72731A. In 1892, Lushington went further, putting the case for full employer liability. He argued that "the great majority of accidents set down to negligence ought more properly to be attributed to the dangerous nature of the industry". [HO 45/9865/B13816/123 (Feb., 1892).]

categorizing paupers, another civil servant at the Home Office was calling attention to the law's unjustified assumption of working-class capability of self-protection against occupational accidents. However, in the latter as in the former matter, the still dominant deterrent paradigm only slowly admitted of change. The Conservative government put forth a half-hearted bill making a few exceptions in existing law; it drew the opposition of the TUC and expired. The issue became important in the 1880 general election, and Gladstone's second government quickly passed an Employers' Liability Act that left to the side the new issue of insurance, rather allowing workmen greater grounds of recovery against an employer. Gladstone's measure was as deterrent in intent as the law it replaced, but, more important, it sought to shift the subject to be deterred from the workman to the employer. However, this meant that the need to prove fault remained, and, together with the many specific limitations upon recovery incorporated in the act by employers' interests, this in turn meant that relatively few claims were brought and little money changed hands.[73] The act's effects seemed to have been less compensatory than symbolic – relieving workmen of what they perceived as an unfair onus of responsibility, while, as one factory inspector put it in 1891, "making employers feel their responsibilities more fully."[74]

Despite the symbolic victory for the unions, year by year dissatisfaction mounted with the effectiveness of the employers' two remaining legal defenses – the principles that either negligence on the part of the plaintiff or his consent to undertake a risk erased a claim for damages. By the later 1880s, the view even from the bench shifted so that arguments like Bramwell's moved from the center toward the margins of professional debate. In a series of cases between 1887 and 1891, judicial opinions began to restrict the definition of the employee's "consent." In the landmark case of *Yarmouth* v. *France* (1888), the plaintiff won on appeal, the court recognizing that the mere continuance to work even in a situation known to be dangerous was not proof of consent to the danger. Lord Esher observed that "to say that a master owes no duty to a servant who knows that there is a defect in the machinery and, having pointed it out to one in authority, goes on using it . . . seems cruel and unnatural, and in my view utterly abominable."[75] With Yarmouth the modern view that the fact of continuing to work while knowing of a danger was not enough to bar from recovering damages emerged.[76] In the same year another judge stated the same argument from the viewpoint of the revisionist

---

[73] Bartrip and Burman, p. 188.

[74] M. Johnson, quoted in Harry Smith, "Judges and the Lagging Law of Compensation for Personal Injuries in the Nineteenth Century," *Journal of Legal History 2* (1981), 268.

[75] Quoted in Bartrip and Burman, *Wounded Soldiers*, p. 183.

[76] A careful examination of the case law on this issue is provided in Terence Ingman, "A History of the Defence of *Volenti Non Fit Injuria*," *Juridical Review 26* (1981), 1–28.

economics that was gaining ground with the new prominence of the problem of unemployment. Mr. Justice Hawkins observed in *Thrussell* v. *Handyside & Co.*:

> It is true that he knows of the danger, but he does not wilfully incur it.... If the plaintiff could have gone away from the dangerous place without incurring the risk of losing his means of livelihood, the case might have been different, but he was obliged to be there; his poverty, not his will, consented to incur the danger.[77]

The most recent and most thorough students of the issue have concluded that the High Court was at last "showing a marked tendency to make allowances for the weak bargaining position of the workman."[78] Another 1888 decision (a year before the passage of the first Prevention of Cruelty to Children Act) held that the employer had a duty to warn an employee of tender age (17 years) of the dangers involved in the work and to insist on the worker making use of protective devices supplied; the court, in other words, accepted an age-graduated standard of personal responsibility to work rather than a uniform one for all mentally competent persons of legal age.[79] Finally, in *Smith* v. *Charles Baker & Sons* (1891), the House of Lords went beyond modifying and graduating the mid-Victorian doctrine of implied consent; it decisively rejected it. The Liberal peer Lord Herschell spoke for the majority:

> If the employed agreed, in consideration of special remuneration, or otherwise to work under conditions in which the care which the employer ought to bestow, by providing proper machinery or otherwise, to secure the safety of the employed, was wanting, and to take the risk of their absence, he would no doubt be held to his contract, and this whether such contract were made at the inception of the service or during its continuance. But no such case is in question here. There is no evidence that any such contract was entered into.... I must say, for my part, that in any such case in which it was alleged that such a special contract as that suggested had been entered into I should require to have it clearly shewn that the employed had brought home to his mind the nature of risk he was undertaking and that the accident to him arose from a danger both foreseen and appreciated.[80]

The Liberal government's Employers' Liability Bill of 1893 sought to eliminate the loopholes in the 1880 act, whereby employers had been able in

---

[77] Quoted in Bartrip and Burman, p. 183.

[78] *ibid.*, p. 182.

[79] *Crockler* v. *Banks* [1888], summarized in Bartrip and Burman, p. 184.

[80] Quoted in Atiyah, p. 707. Between 1891 and 1944, when Lord Goddard declared it virtually dead, the defense of *volenti* appears to have succeeded only twice in master-servant cases. [Ingman, 23.]

practice to escape responsibility for most injuries to their workmen.[81] However, the bill was rejected in the Lords because of its radical ban on the much used practice of "contracting out" of this liability. The issue was resolved by the Unionist government's adoption of the principle of insurance in its Workmen's Compensation Act of 1897. This measure cut the Gordian knots of rival attachments to blame-fixing and rival interpretations of free contract that had dominated discussion of the issue through the Victorian era. Under this essentially no-fault scheme, all occupational injuries in the covered industries – regardless of cause, and regardless of consent to risk them – would be compensated by the employer, who in turn would be insured against this risk.[82] In the following decade, coverage was extended to most occupations, and with it the Victorian use of the civil law to encourage workmen's carefulness came virtually to an end.[83] In its place was an administrative mechanism for distributing the risks of economic activity throughout society.

As the inadequacy of relying on employee (or even employer) prudence to prevent occupational accidents was thus acknowledged, the practical weakness of persons in many other everyday economic and social relations was coming to be more recognized by the law. For example, the waning of faith in the power of character made the continuing imprisonment of many small debtors ever more difficult to justify. As early as 1873, a select committee had criticized the harsher treatment of small debtors than large ones (who could go into bankruptcy and void the threat of imprisonment) and recommended that the power of county court judges to imprison for debt be abolished.[84] Out of fear for the loss of any sanction over the economic behavior of those without distrainable property, judges blocked this change. Yet, judicial arguments

---

[81] In this bill, Bartrip and Burman point out, deterrent ideas persisted, only now turned fully against employers rather than employees; "Underpinning the activities of the reform movement which pushed for the Employers' Liability Act [of 1880] and subsequent legislation was the assumption that if only the legal rules could be suitably restructured, industrial accidents could be virtually eliminated. The fallacy of such thinking had long been appreciated by the industrial inspectorates and in 1893 Joseph Chamberlain pointed out in the Commons that most accidents were just that and not foreseeable or the result of negligence." [p. 189.]

[82] Even here, fault was not entirely banished. A stipulation was included that compensation was not payable for injuries where the accident was caused by "the serious and wilful misconduct of the workman." [Quoted in Bartrip and Burman, p. 205.] However, this stipulation was severely restricted in 1906. [P. W. J. Bartrip, *Workmen's Compensation in Twentieth Century Britain* (Aldershot: Gower, 1987), p. 52.]

[83] Although the continuing availability of action under the Employers' Liability Act meant that the negligence of management remained subject to legal penalties (but with any influence on behavior greatly cushioned by the insurance system). See Bartrip, *ibid.*

[84] See O. R. McGregor, *Social History and Law Reform* (London: Published under the auspices of the Hamlyn Trust by Stevens, 1981), pp. 36–38.

such as Bramwell's for the deterrent usefulness of the law were, like Bramwell's other pungent views, becoming less fashionable and less frequently voiced without qualification.

Parliament also began to step into the field of consumer credit. Legislation was passed in 1882 to restrict the kinds of property that could be put up to secure small debts and thus limit enforcement of debt payment by seizure of chattels. This measure, which aimed to protect small borrowers against unpopular small-time usurious moneylenders, "aroused," as Atiyah notes, "the wrath of Bramwell," because it limited the contractual freedom of the prudent borrower in order to protect the imprudent borrower from his own folly.[85] The 1882 act was followed by one in 1900 that gave the courts power to reopen moneylending transactions if the rate of interest were excessive and the transaction harsh, unconscionable, or otherwise of the sort for which a court of equity would give relief.[86]

While recalcitrant debtors adjudged capable of paying were not regarded even by reformers with much sympathy,[87] concern was growing to separate real willful defaulters from the many overwhelmed by circumstances. Just as the limitations of moral solutions for poverty were becoming more apparent, the viciousness of defaulting was being reappraised. Clementina Black of the Women's Trade Union League voiced a growing sentiment when she insisted that

> the sad truth is that thrift, like cleanliness, is a virtue which can only be exercised upon a certain level of prosperity ... you cannot save when you have barely enough money to keep a shelter over your head and to get a reasonable average of meals during the day.[88]

One lawyer, discussing the treatment of petty debt the following year, agreed:

> The frequent strikes, bad weather, holidays, and illnesses, etc., make an ordinary working man's lot a very unenviable one, and the most industrious and thrifty amongst them must have a very difficult task to keep all straight. The enormous amount spent by the improvident workmen and their wives on drink, betting, etc., make their cases almost hopeless.[89]

[85] Atiyah, p. 710.
[86] Atiyah, pp. 711–12.
[87] 4 PD 3 (April 17, 1892), 837–8. The reformist Howard Association and even the sharp critic of criminal law, Reverend W. D. Morrison, agreed in his earlier writings with the Home Office that debtor prisoners (assuming they were indeed capable of paying) should cease receiving more lenient treatment in prison than ordinary criminals. W. Tallack, *Penological and Preventive Principles* (London: Wertheimer, Lea; 2nd ed., 1896), pp. 402–3; W. D. Morrison, *Crime and Its Causes,* (London: S. Sonnenschein, 1891), p. 140; *Report of the Departmental Committee on Prisons 1895,* pp. 287–9.
[88] Clementina Black, "Thrift for the Poor," *New Review 7* (1892), 667.
[89] "Pro Bono Publico," *Law Journal 28* (March 4, 1893), 161.

By the Edwardian period, moral condemnation of petty debtors was being replaced by a picture of them as either "weak" and "unfortunate," or, less sympathetically, "degenerate."[90] The 1906 Liberal government (as had its predecessor of 1892) set up a select committee on the imprisonment of debtors. The committee rejected by one vote a recommendation for the complete abolition of imprisonment as a penalty, but proposed a number of restrictions upon its use.[91] The numbers annually jailed gradually diminished in the last prewar years, fell sharply during World War I, and never regained their prewar level thereafter. Finally in 1970, following another inquiry whose report described many imprisoned debtors as "inadequate; incapable of managing their own affairs . . . irresponsible or feckless . . . [but] not dishonest"[92] all imprisonment for debt was abolished.

Greater allowance for the power of circumstances was of course also being made higher up the social scale. In particular, bankruptcy law was losing its punitive character. In 1883 bankruptcy was placed under the jurisdiction of the Board of Trade, reducing the power of creditors. The new system, as *The Times* noted a few years later, "certainly seems, directly or indirectly, to have dimished the total volume of insolvency." But, it suspected that this advantage had been purchased too dearly, for the lessened control it provided over the debtor might have "weakened the obligations of straightforward dealing and lowered the standard of trading morality."[93]

Even monetary punishment was coming to seem inappropriate for most cases of failure to fulfill a promise. Atiyah has called attention to an increasing tendency in a variety of contract law areas "away from penal damages or results, and a like tendency to insist that the function of the Court is purely to compensate for actual losses." The decline of imprisonment for debt between 1869 and 1970, he went on to note,

[90] First quotation from a reformist County Court judge, Edward Parry in 1906, quoted in Rubin, "Law, Poverty and Imprisonment for Debt, 1869–1914," In Rubin and Sugarman, p. 289; second quotation from Commander Lionel Sanders (RN), governor of Wakefield Prison, to the 1909 Select Committee on Imprisonment of Debtors (Q. 2814.).
[91] *House of Commons Select Committee on Debtors (Imprisonment), Recommendations 1909*, pp. vi–x.
[92] 1969, quoted in Rubin, p. 289.
[93] It quoted the report of the Inspector-General in Bankruptcy: "The interest of the debtor in providing a substantial dividend for his creditors having been materially lessened, his inclination to prevent individual creditors obtaining a preference over others is correspondingly lessened, and the consequence, as shown in a large number of instance during the past year, has been that many debtors only come into Court after they have disposed of very available asset, and make use of the Bankruptcy Act simply as a means for being 'white-washed." *The Times* concluded that "it will occur to many that this is one of the worst tendencies that bankruptcy legislation could exhibit." *The Times*, Sept. 11, 1888, p. 9.

has been matched by a general whittling away of penal damages in contractual cases. In 1909, indeed, the House of Lords decided [*Addis* v. *Gramophone Co.*] that contractual damages should not generally include any penal element, so that it may be said that the law of contract is now concerned primarily to patch up disputes, or pick up the pieces after a conflict, rather than to guide behaviour in the future.[94]

So too, Atiyah observed that businessmen are most unlikely today to sue for breach of contract merely to teach someone a lesson, as not uncommonly happened in the Victorian period.[95]

Another sort of contract whose breach or abrogation became less penalized with time was the marriage contract. The prevailing Victorian view – that, as one modern lawyer put it, "maintenance of the institution of marriage was so essential to human society that nothing should be done to impair it whatever hardship might be caused to the parties themselves"[96] – was challenged first by legislation from 1878 on that made judicial separation more available[97] and second by arguments that divorce ought to be allowed upon grounds other than adultery. This new phase of divorce law history was opened by Samuel Smith's 1892 bill to make desertion a ground for divorce. Though doomed by Gladstone's opposition, the bill significantly drew the support of younger Liberals like Asquith. Other grounds that began to be included in proposed legislation were cruelty and insanity. Incurable insanity posed a greater problem for moral approaches to marriage law than did either desertion or cruelty, which were voluntary acts and might be regarded broadly as matrimonial offenses. As one lawyer has observed,

> Divorce for desertion and cruelty could be justified upon a contractual conception of marriage; the contract might be regarded as broken by misconduct and an action for dissolution of the marriage treated as a common law action for breach of contract. But divorce for incurable insanity required a conception of marriage as a continuing human relationship which the accident of insanity had determined involuntarily.[98]

By the Edwardian era such a conception had taken hold at least within mainstream Liberal opinion. A majority of the Royal Commission on Divorce reporting in 1912 recommended a number of new grounds for divorce, includ-

---

[94] *Rise and Fall*, p. 677.
[95] On such suits, see Lord Alverstone, *Recollections of Bar and Bench* (London: E. Arnold, 1914), pp. 20–1.
[96] C. E. P. Davies, "Matrimonial Relief in English Law," in *A Century of English Family Law*, eds. R. H. Graveson and F. R. Crane (London: Sweet & Maxwell, 1975), p. 319.
[97] From 1897 to 1906, only 5,700 divorces were granted, but over 87,000 orders for separation and maintenance. [MacGregor, *Divorce*, Ch. 1.]
[98] Davies, "Matrimonial Relief," 320.

ing the above-mentioned three, citing the great hardships the existing law produced, most especially for the poor. The commission majority was ready "to recognize the deficiencies of human nature" and cease upholding an unrealistic demand for maintenance of a legal relation that no longer corresponded to a human relation.[99] Such views seemed to be widely accepted in upper-middle-class circles, yet, lacking a political constituency[100] and facing tenacious Church resistance, efforts to broaden the grounds for divorce took another generation to succeed.[101] And it was yet another generation before the guiding concept of matrimonial fault was abandoned, to be replaced by the language of "irretrievable breakdown" in the Divorce Reform Act of 1969. This measure essentially completed the erosion of the hortatory and deterrent roles of marriage law.

With the broadening of avenues of escape from marriage, whether by judicial separation or divorce, lawyers and M.P.s were coming to question the appropriateness of penalizing with legal damages what might be called a pre-emptive escape from marriage. In 1878 the first of many bills was introduced into the Commons to abolish the increasingly employed action of breach of promise to marry. Since, it was argued, a marriage without affection was likely to produce much suffering and little good, the ending of such affection, for whatever cause, *before* the marriage union ought to be allowed to end the relation. Legal penalties, it was urged, had no place in such delicate, intimate relations. Feelings could not be compelled, and thus it was absurd to punish "the man who refuses to make two lives miserable."[102] One leading advocate of repeal argued that "the welfare of the community can only be attained by elevating men's views of the marriage bond, and making it absolutely free from any coercion or avoidable restriction."[103] This thinking suggested, though hardly anyone as yet carried it this far, that intimate personal behavior was not to be improved by sanctions. As they were in regard to the hortatory and deterrent functions of divorce law, feminists were divided on breach of promise suits, but as they gradually became more critical of marriage, they

---

[99] *Report of the Royal Commission on Divorce and Matrimonial Causes 1912*, p. 94.

[100] Feminist divisions over the divorce issue are described in Dorothy M. Stetson, *A Woman's Issue: The Politics of Family Law Reform in England* (Westport, Conn.: Greenwood Press, 1982).

[101] In the meantime, however, the deterrent function of divorce court was becoming less central, as shown by the restriction of press coverage in 1926, which removed that check upon "the violation of the marriage vows" that the fear of publicity had been meant to supply.

[102] 3 PD 245, c. 1886 (May 5, 1879). [Sir Henry James.]

[103] Charles MacColla, *Breach of Promise: Its History and Social Considerations* (London 1879), pp. 61–2. My discussion here owes much to the as yet unpublished research of Ginger Frost.

began to favor change of the existing law. As Clementina Black observed in 1890, "surely, at the worst, the broken courtship will cause less pain than the unhappy marriage."[104] Defenders of breach of promise suits borrowed the language of both contract and criminal law in stressing the need to punish men who disregarded the standards of gentlemanly conduct. Solicitor-General Sir Hardinge Giffard complained in 1879 that abolition would be "a complete inversion of our jurisprudence; a breach of any contract, according to our ordinary rules of law, gave a right of action."[105] An earlier writer in the *Law Times* had argued for retention on the ground that

> the law is bound to take cognisance of any willful injury inflicted by one person on another, and what injury is more willful than that of engaging the affections of a woman, exciting her expectations and hopes, and then disappointing them?

The threat of a lawsuit, he went on, raised rather than lowered the moral tone of courtship, for it

> makes an engagement what it ought to be, a serious affair.... Young men can not be too deeply impressed with the serious nature of the step they take in making a marriage engagement; and anything which would induce greater levity in such matters would be a danger to public morals.[106]

Repeatedly, defenders cited the deterrent value of legal liability for matrimonial promises. Sir John Eardley Wilmot cited the existence of many men "who would otherwise, from mere wantonness, trifle with the affections of women."[107] H. T. Cole noted that "in most of the cases of seduction that came before the Courts, the injury had been done under a promise of marriage. Make such a promise of no value, and men would not hesitate to give it."[108] As the editors of the *Solicitor's Journal* argued in 1881,

> It is all very well to say that it is better to break the promise than to keep it in such cases. We say that it is better not to make the promise in such cases, and our suggestion is that the existence of the action causes fewer promises to be made which it is afterwards better to break.[109]

---

[104] Clementina Black, "On Marriage: A Criticism," *Fortnight Review 53* (April, 1890), 593.
[105] 3 PD 245, c. 1884.
[106] "Breach of Promise Actions," *Law Times 45* (August 15, 1868), 299.
[107] 3 PD 245, c. 1875–6 (May 5, 1879).
[108] *ibid.*, c. 1882.
[109] "The Action for Breach of Promise of Marriage," *Solicitor's Journal 25* (Aug. 20, 1881), 792.

Although a resolution to abolish action for breach of promise to marry passed the Commons in 1879, after a debate that revealed much sentiment against the practice, bills to accomplish this end repeatedly failed. With juries as well as most judges, breach of promise actions remained acceptable for a long time. The strengthening sentiment that legal sanctions were inappropriate when used to deter and punish intimate behavior together with the weakening of the chivalric impetus behind such deterrent vigor by the gradual improvement in the status of women seem to have been counterbalanced by a rising appreciation of the unfairness of women's remaining disabilities and the consequent need to protect and compensate them for mistreatment. Only much later, in the altered circumstances of 1970, in the wake of the ending of fault-based divorce, were legal penalties for breach of promise to marry abolished.

Thus, across a broad spectrum of civil law matters, a pattern of values and attitudes began to emerge at the turn of the century that was not dissimilar from the pattern more obvious in state social policymaking. In both cases, moral discourse was giving way to administrative or welfarist discourse; common law modes of proceeding yielded to equitable ones. Principles were retreating before pragmatism, and long-term considerations before shorter-term ones. How this discursive shift would affect criminal policy is the subject to which we must now turn.

6

The de-moralizing of criminality

Criminal policy was very much a part of general social policy. As with other subjects treated earlier, our approach to late Victorian and Edwardian criminal policy begins by the pathway of discourse – not what actions were taken, but what was perceived and what constructions were put on these perceptions. On this pathway the fictional and the factual intersect. The fiction of crime – embracing sensational stories, detective writing, and realist fiction of low-life criminality – shared key images and tropes with factual writing, both the journalistic genre and the scientific body of writing known as criminology that emerged in this period. These different forms of constructing crime reveal in many ways similar concerns and similar procedures. Particularly now, when the artificial barriers long established between fictional and factual or programmatic cultural work have been lowered and we have come to appreciate both the hidden agenda in fiction and the fictive element in nonliterary discourse, it is time to juxtapose these two modes of discourse. In this chapter we will explore common elements of a criminology latent in late Victorian crime fiction and a story latent in late Victorian police memoirs and criminology. Perhaps the crucial link between the two modes of discourse was produced by the interaction of the rise of scientific naturalism and the simultaneous success of Victorian criminal policy – a dissolution of the sharply focused contest between character and criminality.

The professionals take over

A turning point in public concern about crime came in the 1870s. The ship of criminal policy entered calmer waters, as the threat of criminality seemed to ebb. Yet, ironically perhaps, success not only eased the problems facing such officials, but helped to redefine their nature, interacting with a shifting culture to encourage changes in the construction of crime and alter the public faces of criminality. In the decades after midcentury, the police established their dominance over the streets, and ever more thoroughly invaded the "rough" and "dark" parts of town, setting up new stations and fifteen-minute patrols.[1]

---

[1] See D. J. V. Jones, "The New Police, Crime and People in England and Wales, 1829–1888," *Transactions of the Royal Historical Society, Fifth Series, Vol. 33*, 1983. pp. 151–68, and *Crime, Protest, Community and Police in Nineteenth-Century Britain* (London: Routledge, 1982).

Recent historians of the police have noted a watershed in the late 1860s and early 1870s, during which more stringent standards of public order were established and a new sense of public security began to emerge. "By the mid-1870s," D. J. V. Jones has observed, "police reformers registered a marked improvement in city life; respectable residents now rested more comfortably in close proximity to those three great 'moral teachers': the jail, the workhouse and the police station."[2]

By the mid-1870s, expressions of relief were beginning to predominate over statements of anxiety, becoming ever more widespread and confident as the downward trend of crime statistics continued. In 1876, one of the first serious historians of crime, L. O. Pike, could observe that, compared to earlier decades, "the sense of security is almost everywhere diffused."[3] The uniform professional policing and the uniform and increasingly professional prison discipline developed through the early and mid-Victorian years seemed, even more than most other social policies, to have worked. The meetings of the Social Science Association, in earlier years filled with arguments about the best form of penal system and modes of dealing with juveniles, habitual offenders, and other types of criminals, now heard little of questions relating to crime. As its secretary reflected in 1879, this was chiefly because "they had been so successful in impressing their views upon the Home Office and Parliament."[4] "Property," even the once-nervous *Times* observed in 1881, "is safer than it has ever been against depredations of every sort."[5] Normally cautious civil servants began to make bold assertions. The director of Scotland Yard's Criminal Investigation Department insisted in 1883 that "London . . . is the safest capital for life and property in the world."[6]

Official statistics by the 1880s more and more strongly supported these claims. Falling particularly dramatically were the estimated numbers of members of the "criminal classes at large," who had so frightened the mid-Victorians, from almost 78,000 in 1869 and 1870 to about 31,000 in 1889 and

---

[2] D. J. V. Jones, "New Police," p. 160.

[3] L. O. Pike, *A History of Crime in England* (London: Smith, Elder, 1876), p. 480.

[4] G. W. Hastings, in *NAPSS Transactions 1879*, 337.

[5] Aug. 8, 1881.

[6] *Report of the Commissioner of Police of the Metropolis for 1882*, p. 342. [P.P. 1883 v. 31] Looking back on the half century since the Molesworth Committee, *The Times* reflected with satisfaction that "it would not have seemed credible to [the members of that Committee] that fifty years later, with a population almost double that of 1836, the persons sentenced to transportation, instead of being doubled, which would bring them to 7,222, should be represented by 1,027 persons sentenced to penal servitude, and that the transported prisoners on the hands of this country in Australia should be represented by 38 men." *The Times*, Dec. 28, 1886, p. 10.

1890.[7] By the year of Victoria's Diamond Jubilee, the criminal registrar at the Home Office threw bureaucratic qualification to the winds and flatly announced that "crime has immensely decreased since 1836."[8] In 1896, he reported that the number of persons tried for indictable offenses was the lowest, excepting one year, since 1860, despite a large increase in the nation's population.[9] And the decline, the Home Office noted three years later, seemed to extend beyond strict criminality to embrace the broader realm of social behavior. The report for 1899 concluded that "on the whole, the facts seemed to indicate a great change in manners: the substitution of words without blows for blows with or without words; an approximation in the manners of different classes, a decline in the spirit of lawlessness."[10]

The growing sense of security from the threat of public de-moralization and society's slide into anarchy, joined with an advancing scientism to encourage the bifurcation of the dominant image of criminals into two quite different, and even in some ways opposite types, yet both detached from Victorian moral discourse. On one hand, the traditional working-class criminal was seen to be in retreat – not only quantitatively, but qualitatively. The new police presence and control of the streets diminished respectable persons' fear and awe of the criminal. Increasingly, ordinary criminals were depicted in both fictional and factual discourse as enervated of vital energies, not so much choosing crime but shaped by their heredity and their environment into persons who were barely conscious of the moral significance of their actions. Felons, carrying less moral baggage for law-abiding society, were cutting less awesome figures and were portrayed more as "social wreckage" than as social outlaws. On the other hand, at the same time that the bulk of lawbreakers were being deprived of their terrors and their moral significance for law-abiding citizens, a second image of some among them as skilled professionals was being developed, chiefly by the spokesmen, real and fictional, of the new professionals charged with carrying on the war on crime. Rather than restoring to criminals their wider moral significance, however, this image of professional lawbreakers posed an

[7] *Introduction to the Criminal Statistics for 1869–70*, p. 8; *Introduction to the Criminal Statistics for 1889–90*, p. 8.

[8] *Introduction to the Criminal Statistics for 1896*, p. 18. Historians have endorsed this claim: See Gatrell, "Decline of Theft and Violence," in *Crime and the Law*, eds. V. A. C. Gatrell, B. Lynman, and G. Parker (London: Europa, 1980); David Peirce, P. N. Grabosky and T. R. Gurr. "London: The Politics of Crime and Conflict, 1800 to the 1970s," in eds. Gurr, Grabosky and R. Hula, *The Politics of Crime and Conflict* (Beverly Hills, Calif: Sage, 1979), pp. 33–213, and L. Radzinowicz and R. Hood, *History of English Criminal Law*, *Vol. 5* (London: Stevens and Sons, 1986), pp. 113–17.

[9] *ibid*, p. 13.

[10] *Introduction to the Criminal Statistics for 1899*, p. 37.

intellectual rather than a moral problem and was an accompaniment to the rise of professional crime fighters, whose social stature was growing as the threat of crime retreated. First the policeman and then the detective – first police and later private – were taking on aspects of the social vitality and power once possessed by criminals.[11]

Whereas Regency and early Victorian popular crime writing had centered on the criminal, with the rise in the status of all sorts of professional men, the professional crime fighter, both public and private, emerged as the hero of fictional and factual crime literature.[12] Literary appreciation of the police detective had begun to develop around midcentury, with the path blazed by Dickens, who became fascinated by the newly established Detective Department of the Metropolitan Police. Dickens's work registered a watershed in the literary reputation – moral even more than intellectual – of the police. In *Bleak House*, where Mr. Tulkinghorn's detective work is in the older mode, in support of blackmail, Tulkinghorn's death and his replacement as central intellectual figure by Inspector Bucket cleanses detection of this moral taint. Bucket turns detection to the support of society and moral order. Henceforth, not only in Dickens's writings, but in works like Tom Taylor's popular melodrama *The Ticket-of-Leave Man* (1863), the detective, in Ian Ousby's phrase, "is very like the Victorian philanthropist. In the complex and perilous world of the metropolis he acts as the defender of embattled innocence and champion of the dominant social morality."[13]

In a series of articles from 1850 on in his magazine, *Household Words*, and then in his fiction, Dickens created compelling images of acute and commanding investigators of wrongdoing. Whereas in *Oliver Twist* (1839) the Bow Street Runners Blathers and Duff are no help, indeed appear only as a comic interlude, in *Bleak House* (1853), both ordinary constables and, of course, Inspector Bucket, are described with admiration. Bucket, the first

---

[11] Professionalism was advancing in trials as well as in apprehensions; during the second half of the century there was a steady increase in the use of medical and technical witnesses (especially by the prosecution) in murder trials and, in G. R. Chadwick's assessment, "a marked improvement in the coherence" of their evidence. ["Bureaucratic Mercy," Ph. D. dissertation, Rice University, 1989," p. 118.]

[12] A parallel "torrent" of books in the United States "purporting to reveal the secret life of the real detective" between 1870 and 1900 has been analyzed in Larry K. Hartsfield, *The American Response to Professional Crime 1870–1917* (Westport, Conn.: Greenwood Press, 1985), p. 44 passim. Hartsfield also finds in this literature a shift from a moral frame to an aesthetic or scientific frame.

[13] Ian Ousby, *Bloodhounds of Heaven: The Detective in English Fiction from Godwin to Doyle* (Cambridge, Mass.: Harvard University Press, 1976), p. 74. Before Dickens, the literary detective had played a morally dubious role; for example, Ousby noted, "in the work of Defoe and Harrison Ainsworth, Jonathan Wild had appeared as the corrupter and destroyer of innocence and youth in the big city." [p. 74.]

police detective hero in English fiction, is a marvel of presence and penetration, speaking a language that combines vigor with unimpeachable respectability. Dickens, ever fascinated by professional life, brought the embryonic
profession of police detective to public attention and, with questionable justification, helped invest it with the image of silent efficiency that it was long to
hold in the public mind. As he wrote in one of his articles in *Household Words*:

> [T]he Detective Force organised since the establishment of the existing
> Police, is so well chosen and trained, proceeds so systematically and
> quietly, does its business in such a workmanlike manner, and is always so
> calmly and steadily engaged in the service of the public that the public
> really do not know enough of it, to know a tithe of its usefulness.
>
> Such . . . is the peculiar ability, always sharpening and being improved
> by practice, . . . for which this important social branch of the public ser-
> vice is remarkable! For ever on the watch, with their wits stretched to the
> utmost, these officers have, from day to day and year to year, to set them-
> selves against every novelty of trickery and dexterity that the combined
> imaginations of all the lawless rascals in England can devise, and to keep
> pace with every such invention that comes out. . . . These games of chess,
> played with live pieces, are played before small audiences, and are
> chronicled nowhere. The interest of the game supports the player. Its
> results are enough for Justice.[14]

Power was felt to be flowing from unorganized criminals to these new
professionals, both individually and collectively. The perception of this new
source of social power exhilarated Dickens. Putting himself in the shoes of the
offender, he thrilled: "And to know that I *must* be stopped, come what will.
To know that I am no match for this individual energy and keenness, or this
organised and steady system!"[15] "How complete the power of the police!"
exclaimed another social observer some years later. "The strong arm of the
law has bent their [offenders'] strong and obstinate wills."[16]

The policeman's power was highlighted by his ability to defend society with
a minimum of violence. By contrast to the earlier broadsheet, melodrama, or
Newgate novel, the emerging detective story – both in factual accounts[17] and
in fiction, from the sensational fiction of midcentury to Sherlock Holmes and

[14] "The Detective Police," [1850] in *The Uncommercial Traveller and Reprinted Pieces*
(London: Oxford University Press, 1958), pp. 485, 502–3.
[15] "On Duty with Inspector Field," [1851] *ibid.*, p. 520.
[16] Junius Junior (Johnson), *Life in the Lower Parts of Manchester* (Manchester: Heywood,
n.d.), p. 8.
[17] See, for example, Andrew Landsdowne, *A Life's Reminiscences of Scotland Yard*
(London: Leadenhall Press, 1890); Major Arthur Griffiths, *Mysteries of Crime and Police*
(2 vols.; London: Cassell, 1899).

beyond – displayed comparatively little physical violence. Crimes tended to take place before the story began, or offstage, and even denouements typically saw little bloodshed;[18] nor were punishments administered in view (or, often, at all; Sherlock Holmes frequently allowed culprits to escape the law, if its penalties would be excessive). In this fiction, little sense remained of a backdrop of general social disorder or of a beleaguered and thus violent authority. Social order was no longer threatened. The "liberal myth of political stability as the fruit of long progress and constitutional development," which A. E. Dyson has pointed out was "not allowed us" in *Barnaby Rudge* – or, one might add, in *Oliver Twist* and the Newgate novels to which they are related – was now not only allowed, but established.[19] Violence tended to be associated with the imperial fringes or the rural backwaters, not with the metropolitan van of modern life; violence existed in the India of *The Sign of Four* or the Dartmoor of *The Hound of the Baskervilles*, not in Baker Street or even the East End. "It is my belief, Watson," Holmes avers, "founded upon my experience, that the lowest and vilest alleys in London do not present a more dreadful record of sin than does the smiling and beautiful countryside."[20]

By the close of the century, the detective, whether police or private, had taken over the imaginative center stage from the criminal. G. K. Chesterton noted this shift, arguing that the policeman was the new form of the romantic hero appropriate to modern civilization:

> It is the agent of social justice who is the original and poetic figure, while the burglars and footpads are merely placid old cosmic conservatives, happy in the immemorial respectability of apes and wolves. The romance of the police force is thus the whole romance of man. . . . It reminds us that the whole noiseless and unnoticeable police management by which we are ruled and protected is only a successful knight-errantry.[21]

The police and the detective promised, however, not only a modern form of romance that the criminal was no longer providing, but also a modern efficiency demanded by the increasing complexity of society. In the age of professionalization a new profession had taken form, one with great imaginative appeal. Major Arthur Griffiths, inspector of prisons and a prolific author of both factual and fictional crime accounts, assured his readers:

---

[18] In his important work on crime fiction, Stephen Knight noted with surprise Sherlock Holmes's scant contact with violence. [*Form and Ideology in Crime Fiction* (Bloomington: Indiana University Press, 1980), p. 88.]

[19] In *The Inimitable Dickens* (London: Macmillan, 1970), p. 51.

[20] "The Copper Beeches," (1892) *The Complete Sherlock Holmes*, (New York: Doubleday, Doran & Co., 1932), vol. 1, p. 299.

[21] 1901, quoted in Julian Symons, *Bloody Murder*, (Harmondsworth: Penguin, 1972) p. 76.

Society, weak, gullible and defenceless, handicapped by a thousand conventions, would soon be devoured alive by its venomous parasites; but happily it has devised the shield and buckler of the police.... The personalities, the finer achievements of eminent police officers are as striking as the exploits of the enemies they continually pursue. In the endless warfare, success inclines now to this side, now to that; but the forces of law and order have generally the preponderance in the end. Infinite pains, unwearied patience, abounding wit, sharp-edged intuition, promptitude in seizing the vaguest shadow of a clue, unerring sagacity in clinging to it and following it up to the substantial capture, these qualities make constantly in favour of the police.[22]

Moreover, Griffiths pointed out, the personal abilities of the police were magnified by "the machinery and organisation of modern life":

The world's 'shrinkage,' the facilities of travel, the narrowing of neutral ground, of secure sanctuary for the fugitive, the universal, almost immediate, publicity that waits on startling crimes, all these are against the criminal. Electricity is his worst and bitterest foe, and next rank the post and the Press. Flight is checked by the wire, the first mail carries full particulars everywhere, and to an ubiquitous international police, brimful of *camaraderie* and willing to help each other.[23]

Yet the new dominion of the forces of law and order, particularly in the context of the naturalization of social discourse, though it helped weaken the image of the criminal, did contain new sources of moral unease. If crime was less physically threatening and social order less imperilled, this release from fear carried with it a new concern. The growing power of society vis-à-vis the individual did not leave the law-abiding citizen untouched; he now seemed less capable of fighting crime and uncovering criminals than previously. Detection accounts and stories suggested not only that traditional street criminality had indeed become less threatening, but at the same time that ordinary, law-abiding citizens were less capable of defending themselves against the crime that remained without calling in professional assistance. Professionals were every day more needed in the struggle with crime, as in other areas of modern life. Dickens's enthusiasm for police, for example, had mounted just when his vision of ordinary human beings, and especially the poor, was increasingly highlighting their comparative helplessness in the emerging "great society". As the Bow Street Runners are quite incompetent compared to Inspector Bucket so, contrariwise, Jo, the crossing-sweeper of Bleak House is pathetic compared to Fagin's resourceful street boys.

If the police were now no longer problematical, but ranged fully as

[22] Griffiths, *Mysteries*, vol.1 pp. 7–8.
[23] *ibid.*, p. 8.

supporters and defenders of morality, their support was increasingly integral to a moral order that was less capable of relying upon personal character alone. The personal moral drama stressed earlier was now to be structured by organized intelligence. Individual action was to be aided by scientific knowledge, character to be guided by intelligence. In this regard Dickens's detectives were still as much early Victorian as late because he gave equal attention to their intellectual and moral facets. Along with their ability to penetrate mysteries Dickens stressed the real-life Inspector Field's perfect self-discipline and easy establishment of personal mastery in a den of criminals or the fictional Inspector Bucket's self-effacing yet sure authority, symbolized by the omnipresent thrusting forefinger. However, as the need for social knowledge came to be felt more acutely than the need for character building, the intellectual facet of the police detective – the image of watchful penetration and efficiency – was to gain ever more attention at the expense of the detective's qualities of character. Tom Taylor took this image, and its intellectual apotheosis of the police detective, a step beyond Dickens in his figure of Hawkshaw, "the 'cutest detective in the force" in *The Ticket-of-Leave Man*. Hawkshaw is a master of disguise who can penetrate the criminal world with ease, defeating the villains out to ensnare and use a paroled convict.

However, with growth and routinization, the Detective Department lost its novelty and glamour. Gradually, both the character and the competence of fictional police detectives declined. The typical police detective in late Victorian fiction, as Ousby remarked (despite Griffiths's paeons), "is a stolid and unimaginative bureaucrat, faithfully but mindlessly applying a simple set of official rules to the cases that come his way."[24] With the arrival of Sherlock Holmes, the now boring police detective yielded literary center stage to the private detective.

Making his appearance in 1887, Holmes combined the extraordinary acuteness of Bucket or Hawkshaw with the freedom of a private citizen, unbound by rigid legal or institutional rules. The combination yielded a virtual superman – "the most perfect reasoning and observing machine that the world has seen"[25] – but one dedicated to protecting the values of the ordinary, respectable world. With Holmes, the battle against crime becomes truly scientific. Like Darwin vis-à-vis nature, he offers through scientific method a sense of control over the complex and overwhelming detail of social life, in particular its deviant corners. As he puts it in his first appearance:

> Like all other arts, the Science of Deduction and Analysis is one which can only be acquired by long and patient study. Before turning to those moral and mental aspects of the matter which present the greatest diffi-

[24] Ousby, p. 131.
[25] "A Scandal in Bohemia," (1891) *Complete Sherlock Holmes, Vol. 1*, p. 161.

culties, let the inquirer begin by mastering more elementary problems. Let him, on meeting a fellow mortal, learn at a glance to distinguish the history of the man, and the trade or profession to which he belongs. Puerile as such an exercise may seem, it sharpens the faculties of observation, and teaches one where to look and what to look for. By a man's fingernails, by his coat sleeve, by his boot, by his trouser knees, by the callosities of his forefinger and thumb, by his expression, by his shirt-cuffs – by each of these things a man's calling is plainly revealed.[26]

Holmes's scientific method is underpinned, like that of Griffiths's real police detectives, by modern technology. All his investigations are carried out by means of the new mechanisms of transportation and communication. As Franco Moretti has observed,

Carriages, trains, letters, telegrams, in Conan Doyles's world, are all crucial and *always* live up to expectations. They are the tacit and indispensable support of the arrest. Society expands and becomes more complicated; but it creates a framework of control, a network of relationships, that holds it more firmly together than ever before.[27]

Representing modern science and technology, Holmes is an assurance that the criminal cannot stand up against modern authority. Indeed, he suggests a continued devitalization of the criminal. "Man, or at least criminal man," he remarks, "has lost all enterprise and originality."[28] As Griffiths insisted, "criminals continually 'give themselves away' by their own carelessness, their stupid, incautious behaviour."[29] Yet in this incapacity, the criminal may stand in for ordinary humanity. For neither Griffiths nor Conan Doyle presents scientific method as available to all; beneath its democratic guise, it requires either the organization of the state or the irreproducible genius of Holmes. In particular, Holmes's science has attributes of magic and Holmes of a magician. Dickens' inspector Bucket, despite his homely name and unpretentious manner, nevertheless had exuded "an aura of mysterious power which at times hints at the supernatural."[30] Now, Conan Doyle's Holmes suggests the special power of the expert and underlines the lack of competence of ordinary human beings in the face of the mysteries of modern society. Sherlock Holmes is part social physician, part magician; the one thing he is not is like his readers. Watson (ironically, a doctor) stands in for them, and he can solve nothing.

As both factual and fictional stories constantly demonstrated, the pro-

---

[26] "A Study in Scarlet," (1887) *Complete Sherlock Holmes, Vol. 1*, pp. 18–19.
[27] Franco Moretti, *Signs Taken For Wonders: Essays in the Sociology of Literary Forms* (London: NLB, 1983), p. 143.
[28] "The Copper Beeches," (1892), *Complete Sherlock Holmes, Vol. 1*, p. 290.
[29] *Mysteries, Vol. 1*, p. 23.
[30] Ousby, p. 99.

fessional, scientific detective would selflessly resolve mysteries that endangered or disturbed middle-class moral order. In this genre, moralization had become irrelevant to the struggle against crime. Analytic intelligence of the specialized few rather than character widely diffused becomes the prime weapon against disorder. As Griffiths looks to the agents of the state, so Conan Doyle and his imitators look to the exceptional individual. Sherlock Holmes is presented as detached from moral feeling, as a scientist and a professional man, but also one with pronounced artistic and Bohemian traits. As John Cawelti has observed, the detective story shows that "aesthetic and scientific attitudes toward crime are by no means irreconcilable, since both depend on a certain detachment from intense moral feeling."[31] This detachment became ever more pronounced as the genre developed, setting the new detective story apart from its early and mid-Victorian precursors. The battle of wits replaced the struggle of passions and wills. Crimes were intellectual puzzles, no longer moral ones. In imagination, as in fact, the fighting of crime was professionalized or, rather, the crime-fighting professional changed (as other professionals were changing) from a model of character to a model of intelligence, from a knower of the human heart to a master interpreter of circumstances.

Criminals as "manufactured articles"

The success of the Victorian war on crime not only elevated the image of the new professional crime fighters, but at the same time weakened the criminal image and diminished its moral meaning. If even the most skilled professional quarry of the forces of law and order were neither a moral challenge nor ultimately an intellectual match for their hunters, so much less so were the bulk of ordinary offenders. Less and less was crime seen as either posing a general threat to society or possessing a general moral significance. Rather, crime was either, as Holmesiana suggests, an intellectual game or, as we will see here, a scientific and administrative problem. The problem was one of poor human material, rather than a moral problem of deliberate declaration of war on society, whether produced by inherent sin or by failure in character development.

The daring outlaws of old had been replaced, it was frequently lamented, by crude garroters and skulking burglars. Nor, as Leslie Stephen was already mockingly complaining in 1869, were even modern murderers up to their predecessors' mark: "the style of the act is in a state of perceptible decline." Stephen blamed this on the social triumph of respectability:

---

[31] John Cawelti, *Adventure, Mystery, and Romance: Formula Stories as Art and Popular Culture* (Chicago: University of Chicago Press, 1976), p. 58.

If, to make a liberal allowance, half of our income is spent for our pleasure, the other half is invariably spent in obedience to a code of rules tacitly marked by general consent.... No man has the courage to live apart from his kind like a savage dog in a farmyard. A Commission of Lunacy would be taken out against him, and he would be ordered, on pain of imprisonment, to live with other people.

Thus, "our modern heroes are marked by an absence of the ancient energy. One man is more and more like his neighbour.... Nobody rises very far above the general average, or sinks much below it." While the aristocracy had become hopelessly embourgeoised, Stephen allowed a partial, if temporary, exception to this uniformity to those lower levels of society where respectability had yet to make its impact: "We have amongst us large masses of a population who have escaped the enervating polish of civilization. To them we may still look occasionally for vigorous passions and decided actions. They have the rude energy along with the brutal propensities of a more animal existence." Yet, he suggested, this remaining bastion of primitive and childish vigor was doomed (fortunately for human happiness if not for the intensity of life) to fall before the inexorable assault of civilization.[32]

Such observations on the banality of modern crime became common in the later decades of the century. *The Spectator* noted in 1882, regarding several recent murders, that "there is hardly a trace of overpowering emotion of any sort." Instead, their most striking characteristic – "much more than the wickedness involved" – was "the deadness of all the passions which seem to have been involved." *The Spectator* linked this new prosaicness of modern murder not with the reign of respectability but with the decline of hell:

[T]he more the genuine belief in a divine judgment fades away, the more likely it must be that exceptionally wicked criminals will be able to fit their crimes into a self-satisfied view of life, and to reconcile themselves both to the criminal intent and the criminal recollection.

The fading of "the sensitiveness of conscience to evil" was, the paper concluded, heralding

a new phase in the history of moral evil – the phase in which evil has much fewer terrors, much fewer guilty starts, much fewer auguries of the intolerable misery of self-knowledge, than it used to have – the age in which evil is stolid, and careful, and prudent, and obtuse, and far better disposed to live the small life of petty animal enjoyments, than it has ever been during the past.[33]

[32] A Cynic [Leslie Stephen], "The Decay of Murder," *Cornhill Magazine 20* (1869), 722–33. He may have had in mind De Quincey's well-known Regency essay, "On Murder Considered As One of the Fine Arts."
[33] "The Fenayrou Trial," *Spectator 55* (August 19, 1882), 1078–9.

This diminution of the criminal was much accentuated by the advance of
scientific naturalism, which pushed the fundamental issue of determinism and
free will out of the theologian's and philosopher's study and into the public
square. In the understanding of criminality – placed as it was at the crossroads
of moral philosophy and everyday social policy – both practical and theoretical
sea changes converged. Determinism and devitalization advanced together
through both fictional and factual discourse. Representations of criminality
and deviance were increasingly associated with weakness and degeneration
rather than inadequately controlled energies and with a relative lack of autonomy rather than a willful rejection of social limitations.

As with images of the poor, drunkards, and other subjects of Victorian
social policymaking, the literary image of the working-class criminal had by
the 1890s been reshaped by the diminishing sense of the power of the individual will into a new form; the criminal was no longer a wicked individual but
rather a product of his environment and heredity. In contrast to both the
melodramatic Newgate and the more serious industrial novels of the early
Victorian years, the urban novels of the 1880s and 1890s allowed much less
role to individual conscience and character. However much they were inflamed by fears of working-class violence and revolt, the earlier social novels –
of Dickens, Gaskell, Kingsley, and others – complemented these fears with
the hope of personal regeneration among the denizens of this underworld.
However harshly pressed by circumstances – and such pressures were often
vividly described and insisted upon – the thieves in *Oliver Twist* or the violent
workmen in *Mary Barton* retained the germ of conscience within, the possibility of character development in the future. Crime had been seen as leading
not only to punishment, but to an acceptance of responsibility and often to
repentance. Though impelled by powerful external forces, crimes had not
been pictured as inevitable. With changes of heart among both the poor and
their powerful superiors, such horrors could have been avoided and could be
so in the future. John Barton's murder of Harry Carson, for example, was
characteristically used by Elizabeth Gaskell to indict society without
detracting from Barton's own guilt, which, overwhelmed by conscience, he
came to fully acknowledge. By the end of *Mary Barton*, the portrait of John
Barton had turned from that of a life buffeted by large external forces to that
of a life with much potential for good, but whose moral struggle against great
odds had ended in a succumbing to evil – a fall, however, that was neither inevitable nor irredeemable.[34]

---

[34] Catherine Gallagher, as part of a rather different argument, has also stressed the importance of Gaskell's treatment of John Barton's criminality in *The Industrial Reformation
of English Fiction: Social Discourse and Narrative Form 1832–1867* (Chicago: University of
Chicago Press, 1985), pp. 83–7.

By contrast, late Victorian serious social novelists – most notably Gissing, Hardy, and Kipling – tended to locate individuals tightly embedded within larger structures, with little room to maneuver either physically or morally. As Noel Annan pointed out some years ago, Kipling's Indian stories contain a sociological subtext about the power of environment and institutions, indeed, even an "assumption that morality is an entirely social product."[35] Such late Victorian naturalism could be at the same time progressive in indicting society and suggesting institutional change and more direct social intervention and conservative in viewing ordinary persons as products rather than producers of the circumstances of their lives, beings with limited moral potentialities. Very few of George Gissing's figures, for instance, undergo major changes in character; they go on much as they began. They may become wiser, but rarely better. Strong willpower is rarely exhibited by characters who move through life like debris on a river; when effort and will are evidenced, they rarely bring the sort of benefit they would have in the fiction of the preceding generation (or in the more popular literature of Gissing's adventure story contemporaries). In his stories, responsibilitity for individuals' failings tends to fall upon their environment or their inheritance. In particular poverty is again and again shown as depressing and disabling its victims. In *New Grub Street* (1891), Alfred Yule's vindictiveness is explained by his poverty: "I am all but certain that, if he became rich, he would be a much kinder man, a better man in every way. It is poverty that has made him worse than he naturally is; it has that effect on almost everybody."[36] The villain of that novel, Milvain, explains himself similarly: "Selfishness – that's one of my faults. . . . If I were rich, I should be a generous and good man; I know I should. So would many another poor fellow whose worst features come out under hardship."[37] "Poverty," Gissing remarks in the *The Nether World* (1889), "makes a crime of every indulgence."[38]

At the beginning of the 1890s, criminal characters were particularly in evidence in the new literary realism. Kipling's East End story, "Record of Badalia Herodsfoot" (1890), like another influenced by him, Arthur Morrison's "Lizerunt" (1894), shocked readers by its blunt insistence upon individual helplessness. Both stories recounted the grim lives of slum women abused by brutal husbands, deliberately challenging Victorian conventions by offering no hope. If the stories portrayed the victims as without inner resource, the perpetrators of violence were shown not as true villains, but rather

[35] Noel Annan, "Kipling's Place in the History of Ideas," *Victorian Studies 3* (1959–60), 347.
[36] George Gissing, *New Grub Street, Vol. 1* (London: Smith, Elder, 1891), Ch. 5.
[37] *ibid.*, Ch. 8.
[38] *Vol. 3* (London: Smith, Elder, 1889), p. 106.

as animalistic brutes, less responsible, less reflective even than Dickens' famous brute, Bill Sykes. Where even Sykes, irredeemably bad though he was, felt the horror of his murder of Nancy, Kipling's and Morrison's characters feel nothing. Nor does one feel that the world around them – roused into a storm of vengeance in *Oliver Twist* – will take much notice of such routine crime.[39] For dealing with such criminals, if neither moralization nor deterrence offered a solution, a different tack would be required. One could optimistically set about changing the environment, even the heredity, by social reform and eugenics, or one could pessimistically see little to be done beyond quarantine and perhaps gradual extinction.

A science of criminology began to take shape during the second half of the century, and particularly its last quarter, that sought to apply the apparent advances being made in the natural sciences to practical knowledge of human behavior. Two things were implied by this naturalization of deviant human behavior: that it had become less morally threatening, but that it had also become more opaque. Where criminals came from and what they were like were no longer questions generally addressable, but now required a science and trained experts to discover and understand. During the early and middle Victorian period, as we have seen, the new social science of statistics and the physiological one of phrenology had appealed partly because they seemed to offer new tools for reform, handles for the continuing effort to improve human beings. They could be used, in other words, as fresh instruments of moralization. But such use slowly began to alter the terms of discourse. Criminal offenders, as we have also seen, came increasingly to be described in terms of the external forces acting upon their will – their social environment, their physical and psychic constitution, or a mixture of the two. They were less likely to be portrayed by reformers (despite rebuttals such as Chadwick's of explanations of crime as the natural consequence of poverty) as simply people who deliberately chose to break the law, but more likely to be described as problem personalities that manifested pathologies.

In short, scientific approaches to crime led gradually to a subtle weakening of moral judgment of the individual.[40] If the criminal was only "the instru-

---

[39] Similarly, Larry K. Hartsfield has described a shift in "criminal autobiography" in the United States from a nineteenth-century "picaresque" mode, emphasizing a strong central character and action turning on choices, to a turn-of-the-century "sociological" mode, stressing background and the role of developmental processes in shaping human personality. Post-Victorian thieves "began to adopt a role that stressed the persona of the helpless victim, without choice or alternatives. The dominant image in the presentation of their lives became a vision of something 'wrecked' or destroyed, of a loss of control." [*American Response*, pp. 14–16, 25, passim.]

[40] However, this was not a simple or complete process; rather, as we have already seen in Chapter 1, moral and scientific discourse reached a variety of accommodations and partial

ment . . . of society" or the victim of defective physiology, the early-nine-teenth-century effort (fueled by anxieties about personal and social disorder) to reinforce the traditional role of criminal justice in apportioning blame and punishing misdeeds would be called into question. What would happen to the aim of clearly locating responsibility for all offenses if free choice was to dis-solve upon inspection into myriad lines of social and biological influence? The Unitarian Radical, Harriet Martineau, flushed with enthusiasm for a science of man, already criticized as early as 1838 "the pernicious notion that there is a line drawn for human conduct, on one side of which all is virtue, and on the other all vice" and recommended instead what she called "the more philosophical and genial belief that all wickedness is weakness and woe" and its implication that "the guilty need more care and tenderness in the arrangement of the circumstances under which they live than those who en-joy greater strength against temptation, and an ease of mind which criminals can never know."[41] As long as moralization remained the prime social task, this conclusion remained latent in respectable Britain. However, as respect-ability came to be ever more widely accepted as a norm, the new implications for conceptions of the individual contained in the development of the natural and social sciences began to be acknowledged. With these implications redrawing policymakers' maps of social reality, discourse about criminals began to exhibit signs of a paradigm under strain.

As we have seen, in both factual and fictional criminal discourse, character-izations of deviance and crime moved from moral to natural categories. They came to appear more deeply rooted within the offender's nature than in the moral consciousness or the rational intellect. What had once been assumed to

incorporations with each other during the Victorian era, particularly in the practice of medicine and most especially in the rapidly growing field of psychiatry. Nevertheless, in these successive accommodations the clarity of personal responsibility was dissolving. See Michael J. Clark, "The Rejection of Psychological Approaches to Mental Disorder in Late Nineteenth-Century British Psychiatry," in *Madhouses, Mad-doctors, and Madmen: The Social History of Psychiatry in the Victorian Era*, ed. Andrew Scull (Philadelphia: Univer-sity of Pennsylvania Press, 1981), pp. 271–312; Janet Oppenheim, "The Diagnosis and Treatment of Nervous Breakdown: A Dilemma for Victorian and Edwardian Psychiatry," in *The Political Culture of Modern Britain*, ed. J. W. M. Bean (London: Hamilton, 1987), pp. 75–90.

[41] *How to Observe Morals and Manners* (London: C. Knight, 1938), p. 126. In a similar fashion, across the Atlantic, E. W. Farnham, head of the Female Prison at Mount Pleasant, New York, argued in 1846 that society throughout history had falsely judged "all persons equally capable, and had consequently erected one standard, which none may fail to reach, however they may be incapacitated, without being judged guilty, not only of the offenses they have committed, but of the infinitely greater one of having acted in defiance of the decisions of higher powers, powers which they never possessed." [Quoted in D. B. Davis, *Homicide in American Fiction 1798–1860* (Ithaca: Cornell University Press, 1957), p. 24.]

be the result of either sin or miscalculation was increasingly seen as being tied
to constitutional defects in the offender or to defects in social institutions
shaping him. This perception of the natural rootedness of deviance had two
sorts of immediate consequences for constructions of the criminal. First, the
determined character of criminality implied a reconstruction of its boundaries;
if the criminal was to be understood and studied as, in Havelock Ellis' term, a
"natural phenomenon,"[42] he or she would come to appear more distinct from
the noncriminal majority. Criminality would be seen as belonging to a world
that in comparison to the moral world of will and choice was a fixed one – a
criminal class whose members were shaped by their conditions of life. In
Henry Maudsley's phrase, they were "step-children of nature," morally handicapped by their physical organization.[43] Second, along with an isolating
reconstruction of criminality's boundaries went a shrinkage of its image. The
more rooted criminality or other deviance was perceived to be in the sphere of
nature, the less power the deviant himself was assumed to have over his own
deviance. As faith in the power of the individual will waned, the image of the
criminal deviant – hitherto the archetype of individual will unchecked – weakened. If will now had a diminished role in causing crime, it presumably also
had an equally reduced role in curing it. For this task, less came to be
expected of the criminal and more of experts and professionals who had studied the genealogy and nature of criminality.

The subjects of Charles Booth's late Victorian social survey afford an
illuminating contrast ot earlier models. Whereas Mayhew's subjects, like those
of the early Victorian social novelists, were individual actors who told their
stories through his many interviews, each unique life possessing the dramatic character that stemmed from the possibility of moral choice, Booth's
were less individualized. Whereas Mayhew kept returning from social
categories to individual life stories, Booth, seeking generalizations serviceable
in social administration, relied wherever he could on statistical criteria. And
whereas Mayhew's first-person accounts often establish (in a Dickensian
fashion) a personal vitality that countered his own negative generalization
about the poor and criminal, Booth's impersonality (like that of much naturalistic fiction) reinforced a pessimism about the capacities of these subjects and
their consequent need of outside intervention.

Those in Booth's bottom classification of working-class London, consisting
of "some occasional labourers, street sellers, loafers, criminals and semi-
criminals," he saw as largely "hereditary in . . . character." He was pessimistic about their possibilities, for they "render no useful service, they create
no wealth; more often they destroy it. They degrade whatever they touch and

---

[42] *The Criminal* (London: C. Scribner's Sons, 1890), p. 231.
[43] *Body and Mind* (London: Macmillan, 1873), p. 43.

as individuals are perhaps incapable of improvement." But if Mayhew feared that such persons would always exist, Booth was more sanguine. They posed no real danger to civilization: "There are barbarians, but they are a handful, a small and decreasing percentage; a disgrace but not a danger."[44] The slums in which they lived were being torn down and their children being taken away to be reared in pauper or industrial schools or Dr. Barnardo's homes. Thus, though they might not be reformable, the progress of social administration was diminishing their numbers and even held out the prospect of their extinction.

While Booth and others were carrying further the gathering and analysis of social statistics, the biological impulse begun in phrenology also was being followed up. Throughout the second half of the century, physiological psychologists and alienists were staking out new claims for both understanding and treating social problems. An expanding range of social problems seemed to require medical expertise. In professional journals after midcentury, arguments were increasingly being put forth that more and more forms of deviant behavior could be regarded as physically rooted and analogous to insanity, and therefore within their province. In 1865 the Asylum Officers' Association changed its name to the Medico-Psychological Association. W. A. F. Browne, as president, announced the change of title indicated "a wider and more legitimate destiny" for them. Browne attached great importance to the role of psychology in preventing the spread of mental defects in the population; he described the "conservative mission of our science in anticipating, preventing and modifying mental maladies." Browne claimed that psychiatric science had revealed an affinity between crime and such debilitative disorders as insanity, alcoholism, and epilepsy. Physiological roots had been revealed for a wide array of moral defects. Moreover, science had powerfully suggested that these defects were fundamentally hereditary, a contention that opened the door to a program of intervention to reduce their incidence.[45] By 1883, the Association's president, who was also director of Broadmoor Criminal Asylum, could readily speak of society's "duty" to diagnose and treat lunatics *before* they committed crimes.[46]

Through the later nineteenth century, physicalist models of mental malfunctioning tended to expand to explain various sorts of deviance, most obviously crime. As William Guy, professor of medicine at King's College, London, and secretary of the Royal Statistical Society, had observed in 1869,

---

[44] Charles Booth (ed.), *Life and Labour of the People in London*, Vol. 1, (1889), pp. 39, 594–5.
[45] See Jacyna, "Somatic Theories of Mind and the Interests of Medicine in Britain, 1850–1879," *Medical History 26* (1982), p. 255.
[46] W. Orange, "Presidential Address," *Journal of Mental Science 91* (1883), pp. 329–54.

"those who have experience of the insane show a growing disposition to attribute many acts of cruelty, violence and fraud to unsoundness of mind; while those who have no such experience turn from these views with suspicion and aversion."[47] Such widespread mental unsoundness was increasingly seen as deeply rooted in physical structures and past generations – what Thomas Laycock, professor of medicine at Edinburgh, had called in 1862 the "inexorable . . . law of hereditary transmission of mental and moral qualities."[48] At the very time when the threat of serious crime was beginning to recede, a naturalistic image of the criminal was spreading out from physiologists and doctors to a wider public.

This emerging scientific conception of the criminal was stated most effectively by the most prominent psychologist of the later Victorian period, Henry Maudsley. In 1867, as we have seen, he had provided the most readable statement of physiological determinism and coined the vivid phrase, "the tyranny of organization." During the following decade, he pursued some implications of such thinking for social thought and policy. In 1874, after attacking already discredited moral theories of insanity and reiterating the indispensable nature of medical skills in the treatment of the mad, Maudsley proceeded to question whether *any* form of deviance could be understood on purely moral premises. The "wicked" he declared, "are not wicked by deliberate choice . . ., but by an inclination of their natures which makes the evil good to them and the good evil." In other words, criminal acts, like lunatic acts, did not issue from the will of their perpetrators, but were the outcome of physical causes over which they had no conscious control.[49] Maudsley insisted that

> It is certain . . . that lunatics and criminals are as much manufactured articles as are steam engines and calico-printing machines, only the processes of the organic manufactory are so complex that we are not able to follow them. They are neither accidents nor anomalies in the universe, but come by law and testify to causality; and it is the business of science to find out what the causes are and by what laws they work.[50]

Specifically, Maudsley explained the "evil propensities" of habitual criminals as "veritable instincts." "We may take it then," he concluded, "that there is a class of criminal formed of beings of defective physical and mental organization; one result of the defect, which really determines their destiny in

---

[47] Quoted in Roger Smith, *Trial by Medicine* (Edinburgh: Edinburgh University Press, 1981), pp. 29–30.

[48] Quoted in Radzinowicz and Hood, p. 10 ; see also Jacyna, "Somatic," p. 252.

[49] *Responsibility in Mental Disease* (London: King, 1874), p. 24.

[50] *Responsibility*, p. 28

life, being an extreme deficiency or complete absence of moral sense; that an absence of moral sense may be a congenital vice or fault of organization."[51]

From the later 1860s on, such "faults of organization" began to be probed by medical men who had contact with criminals – prison doctors who (thanks to the provision in the 1865 Prisons Act mandating regular medical examination of all inmates) were becoming a more significant and active presence in the penal system. From the first, these inquiries took a pronounced physicalist form. In 1869, Dr. George Wilson set out to the British Association for the Advancement of Science his findings derived from measuring the heads of 464 convicts. Wilson reported well-marked signs of cranial underdevelopment, and talked of widespread "moral imbecility" among criminals. Moreover, he concluded, "the cranial deficiency is associated with a real physical deterioration. Forty percent of all criminals are invalids more or less."[52]

The following year, James Bruce Thomson, resident surgeon to the Scottish state prison at Perth since 1858, published an influential article, "The Psychology of the Criminal." "The physical organisation of the criminal," he announced, "is marked by . . . a singular stupid and insensate look." Diseases of the nervous system were unusually prevalent among convicts; moreover, half of those who died in prison were below 30 years of age, and postmortems uncovered the striking fact that nearly every organ in the body was diseased, "few dying of one disease but generally 'worn out' by a complete degeneration of all vital organs." Thomson also noted the low intellectual state of prisoners and a tendency on their part to violence without any distinct purpose, which he saw as a "symptom of weakmindedness." Indeed, he estimated that 12 percent of prison inmates were "mentally weak in different degrees." He interpreted his observations through the lens of current medical thinking, arguing "that crime is [often] hereditary in the families of criminals . . ., and that this hereditary crime is a disorder of mind, having close relations of nature and descent to epilepsy, dipsomania, insanity and other forms of degeneracy. Such criminals are really morbid varieties, and often exhibit marks of physical degeneration." Thomson identified "a distinct and incurable criminal class, marked by peculiar low physical and mental characteristics."[53]

After this efflorescence of scientific reinterpretation of criminality in the later 1860s and early 1870s, theoretical criminology, and the advance of criminological naturalism in particular, came to a standstill in England just as the positivist school was appearing on the Continent.[54] Indeed, the rise

---

[51] *Body and Mind*, pp. 128–131.

[52] Quoted in C. H. S. Jaywardene, "English Precursors of Lombroso," *British Journal of Criminology 4* (1963), p. 168.

[53] J. B. Thomson, "The Hereditary Nature of Crime," *Journal of Mental Science 15* (1870).

[54] See Radzinowicz and Hood, p. 11.

abroad of such a thoroughgoing physicalist and hereditarian thinker as Lombroso may have weakened rather than strengthened interest in criminology in England by associating it with what could readily be seen as the latest form of Continental intellectual extremism.

The massive task of reorganization and rationalization of prisons embarked upon after their 1877 nationalization by the firm hand of Sir Edmund Du Cane left little scope for prison doctors to pursue investigations not part of their required duties. In fact, the very institutionalization of medical officers in the administration of prisoners reinforced their sense of responsibility for maintaining good order in the prisons and supporting the official aims of deterrence and reformation. As Dr. David Nicolson, assistant head of Broadmoor, reassured the public in 1878, medical men were not by any means inclined to treat all or even most criminals as "moral invalids"; they were, Nicolson insisted, "always alive" to the interests of public security and moral order.[55]

Nicolson exemplified the more practical blend of moralism and naturalism that flourished under the Du Cane regime. Having served since 1867 as a medical officer at a series of convict prisons, Nicolson wrote a series of articles between 1873 and 1875 on "The Morbid Psychology of the Criminal," in which he sorted inmates into two types, the habitual criminal who "possesses an unmistakeable physique with rough and irregular outline and a massiveness in the seats of animal expression," and the accidental criminal who "differs little or nothing from the ordinary run of mortals."[56] The former he characterized as representing "the very lowest form of mental sanity."[57] A few years later, now with greater practical knowledge and administrative responsibilities as deputy medical superintendent of Broadmoor, Nicolson dissociated himself from the oversweeping claims of the physicalists, arguing that physical distinctions were characteristic only of a minority of criminals and stressing that most offenders were not constitutionally distinct from the general population, but essentially responsible and suitable objects of penal discipline and prospects for reformation. Medical attention, Nicolson was at pains to establish, did not challenge the moral tasks of deterrence and reformation of the penal system, but was properly to be focused upon a minority of criminals.[58]

Such accommodation of Victorian moral discourse with naturalistic

---

[55] See Chapter 3.

[56] Quoted in Jayewardene, p. 168.

[57] *Journal of Mental Science 19* (1874), p. 224.

[58] "The Measure of Individual and Social Responsibility in Criminal Cases," *Journal of Mental Science 24* (1878–9), pp. 1–25, 249–73. On the development and dominance of this English "middle way" in criminology, see David Garland, "British Criminology Before 1935," *British Journal of Criminology* 28 (1988) 131–47.

language did not, however, prevent criminology's new form from gradually reshaping its content – the character of this old wine was not untouched by its new naturalistic bottles. Declining fear of crime and rising administrative professionalism joined to bring the incapable minority of offenders more attention than ever before. The characteristically English incorporation of alienists and medical men generally into criminal administration,[59] as opposed to their more independent role on the Continent, diminished their inclination to theoretical radicalism, but it also enhanced their practical influence and their professional interest in criminals. During the 1880s, that organ of English psychiatry, the *Journal of Mental Science*, devoted increasing attention to questions of criminal psychology. English criminal administration had not only domesticated and to some extent moralized naturalism, it had also introduced a naturalistic frame of mind within its daily workings. Physicalist speculation was checked, and indeed was to some degree recanted by men like Maudsley, who conceded that "assuredly external factors and circumstances count for much in the causation of crime."[60] Yet such recantations did less to restore the place of moral judgment than to simply widen the sphere of determining agencies to embrace the social as well as the biological. The tendency to look beyond moral interpretations of criminal behavior and to discover in it various forms of incapacity continued to develop and, indeed, began for the first time to affect criminal administration. In the 1880s, as we will see, prison doctors and medical men interested in deviance were exhibiting greater readiness to reclassify offenders as primarily medical cases rather than criminal ones, as representing natural failures, as well as, or more than, moral failures.

At the beginning of the 1890s, such questions returned for the first time since the 1860s to the wider sphere of public discourse. The phenomenon of Jack the Ripper had revived concern about the criminal nature, a concern that experts now stepped in to calm. The Ripper was not, they insisted, the sort of "symptom of a moral disease" that the previous generation had read in the newsworthy crimes of its day. He was rather a sign of a limited and professionally manageable abnormality, a born criminal. Even in detective fiction

---

[59] As in the regular employment of alienists after midcentury to determine criminal responsibility of accused capital criminals. The more general English peculiarity of allowing access to the world of the governing elite to intellectuals and experts in the human sciences at the price of their "practicality" and sensitivity to the interests and concerns of administration has been noted in Noel Annan, "The Curious Strength of Positivism in English Political Thought," *L.T. Hobhouse Memorial Lecture no. 28* (London, 1959)]; Philip Abrams, *The Origins of British Sociology 1834–1914* (Chicago: University of Chicago Press, 1968); and Lawrence Goldman, "The Social Science Associatian," *English Historical Review 101* (Jan. 1986).

[60] Quoted in Griffiths, *Mysteries, Vol. 1*, p. 2.

– a genre at root incompatible with determinism – the power of inheritance and the sway of constitution were often cited. Sherlock Holmes referred to an hereditary criminal strain in the blood of his chief opponent Professor Moriarty.[61] By the turn of the century he was generalizing that

> There are some trees ... which grow to a certain height and then suddenly develop some unsightly eccentricity. You will see it often in humans. I have a theory that the individual represents in his development the whole procession of his ancestors, and that such a sudden turn to good or evil stands for some strange influence which came into the life of his pedigree. The person becomes, as it were, the epitome of the history of his own family.[62]

The central theme of new criminological writing was the constitutionally rooted weakness of the powers of self-government among many criminals and the consequent uselessness of moral approaches to crime. As the *Journal of Mental Science* noted with satisfaction in 1890 in reviewing Havelock Ellis's *The Criminal*, "a strong feeling is spreading that there are certain physical or physiological criminals to whom short punishments are of no use."[63] Indeed, Ellis went further, arguing for the importance of constitutional influences upon the majority of criminals. Similarly, the Reverend William Morrison, a modern-minded prison chaplain who was to become a leading critic of the penal system, argued in his *Crime and Its Causes* (1891) for shifting attention from criminal acts in themselves to the biological and social forces that shaped criminals. In such ways, the will and personality of the criminal offender had faded into the impersonal conditions from which he was manufactured. He became less a moral actor and more a point of conjunction of forces larger than individuals, a sign of weak spots in the human (and, to a lesser degree, social) constitution.

Gordon Rylands, one of the new generation of criminological writers, summed up the new directions in 1889: "Two influences which determine above all others the amount of crime ... to one or the other of which indeed all others may be ultimately reduced ... [are] Heredity and Environment."[64] He concluded his book on crime with this analysis:

> Many unfortunate persons have bequeathed to them by their parents morbid affections of the brain which compel some to homicide, some to suicide, some to drunkenness and its consequent vicious and degraded mode of life, reducing others to idiocy or raving madness. In this sad

[61] "The Final Problem," (1893), *Complete Sherlock Holmes, Vol. 1*, p. 247.
[62] "The Empty House," (1903), *ibid., Vol. 2*, p. 23.
[63] *Journal of Mental Science 36* (1890), 411.
[64] L. Gordon Rylands, *Crime: Its Causes and Remedy* (London: T. Fisher Unwin, 1889), p. 29.

class of cases it is obvious enough to any one that the criminal should be no less an object of our deep commiseration than the man who has been seized by a loathsome and painful disease. The words punishment and vengeance are tragically ludicrous in such a connection.[65]

When constitution was not at fault, Rylands indicted society. Noting that the largest number of first convictions occurred before the age of twenty, he saw much of this as avoidable by altering social conditions:

> The children of the very poor playing in idleness about the slums will, out of natural childish mischief and thoughtlessness, do things which their more fortunate richer brother does almost daily with no more serious consequences to itself than a slapping, and not always that, but which will lodge the friendless gutter-child in prison, and thereby start it on the way to a criminal career.... Now it cannot be denied that these unfortunate boys were all the victims of circumstances; and that, so far from the acts which brought them into trouble being essentially immoral, in some of the cases a really generous disposition and loftiness of purpose was evinced, albeit obscured and misdirected by lack of training.[66]

Thus, neither natural nor accidental criminality was at root a question of personal responsibility. This argument was repeated by Morrison in 1891, but was made most forcefully and with greatest influence in 1890 by the young Havelock Ellis, at this time still a medical student. In *The Criminal* – the first widely read scientific work on criminality in England, revised and expanded several times over the next two decades – Ellis sought to bring Continental analysis to an English audience. As in his later, better-known sexology, Ellis here aimed at detaching his subject from the constricting jurisdiction of common moral discourse, instead treating criminality, as he would later sexuality, "as a natural phenomenon."[67] Also, like his sexology, Ellis sought to expose the unrealism of purely moral demands unrelated to scientific understanding of the shaping conditions of human character. He offered a detailed quasi-medical classification of criminal psychological types, a gallery of specimens exhibiting physical and/or psychological abnormalities and malfunctions existing (at least in latent form) from birth. He categorized criminals as occasional, habitual, professional, or instinctive. While only the last category (the rough counterpart of Lombroso's born criminal) was fully abnormal, all the others partook of varying (and difficult to delimit) degrees of abnormality. Individual cases were always liable to slide from a lesser category to a more serious one:

[65] *ibid.*, p. 35
[66] *ibid.*, pp. 37, 42,
[67] Havelock Ellis, *The Criminal* (London: C. Scribner's Sons, 1890), p. 231.

Such are the slow steps by which the occasional criminal becomes the habitual criminal or the professional criminal. It must be remembered that
the lines which separate these from each other, and both from the instinctive criminal, are often faint or imperceptible. 'Natural groups,' as Mr.
Galton remarks, 'have nuclei but no outlines.'[68]

Since Ellis suggested a number of times that organic malfunction lay at the
root of the "moral monstrosity" of instinctive criminals ("It may well be," he
mused, "that if we possessed a full knowledge of every instinctive criminal we
should always be able to put our hands on some definite organically morbid
spot."[69]), the ease sliding into this category implied widespread, if unrecog-
nized, organic "morbidity." By the third edition of the work, even "the average criminal" appeared to him to be a "more or less congenitally abnormal
person."[70]

Occasional criminals, the majority of offenders, while not as radically disordered as either lunatics or instinctive criminals, showed even more evident
constitutional problems. Ellis called attention to "the great class of vagabonds
among men, who also live on the borderlands of criminality, and who also
present a larger proportion of abnormalities than even criminals."[71]

Of 250 recidivists condemned five times at Paris nearly all have begun by
vagabondage. Mendel has examined 58 vagabonds in the workhouse at
Berlin. He found 6 absolutely mad; 5 weak-minded; 8 epileptics; 14 with
serious chronic disease; in the remaining 25 there was without exception
pronounced mental weakness. We see here the organic root of the hopelessly idle, vicious character of the vagabond class.... It is not sufficiently known that these poor creatures, who form such an extensive
recruiting field for crime, are already, by the facts of their physical organisation, cut off from the great body of humanity.[72]

In the female sex, the counterpart of vagrants were prostitutes:[73]

One is inclined on first approaching the subject to make the clear line of
demarcation between crime and vice, which is necessary in practical life.
From the anthropological point of view, however, it appears on closer
examination impossible to draw this clear line.

[68] *ibid.*, p. 21.
[69] *ibid.*, pp. 16–17.
[70] 3rd edition, 1901, p. xvi.
[71] 1st edition, p. 222.
[72] *ibid.*, pp. 222–3.
[73] Eric Trudgill has noted the waning moral fervor against prostitutes: "The bad woman
in 1849, wrote Charlotte Bronte, was for most men a fiend; but by the 1890s neither those
striving to control her with few exceptions, let alone those seeking to defend her, would
have considered using any such description." [*Madonnas and Magdalens: The Origins and
Development of Victorian Sexual Attitudes* (New York: Holmes & Meier, 1976), pp. 127–8.]

... it is a remarkable fact that prostitutes exhibit the physical and psychic signs associated usually with criminality in more marked degree than even criminal women. While criminal women correspond on the whole to the class of occasional criminals, in whom the brand of criminality is but faintly seen, prostitutes correspond much more closely to the class of instinctive criminals. Thus their sensory obtuseness has been shown to be extreme, and it is scarcely necessary to show that their psychical sensitiveness is equally obtuse.[74]

In this way Ellis's study of criminality led to the more basic problem of unfitness; this was the fundamental characteristic shared by the criminal and the noncriminal "vicious." Lawbreaking and immorality were both manifestations of organic incapacities:

We must be careful not to confuse vice and crime. At the same time we have to recognise that they both spring from the same root. The criminal is simply a person who is, by his organisation, directly anti-social; the vicious person is not directly anti-social, but he is indirectly so.... They are both anti-social because they are both more or less unfitted for harmonious social action, both, from organic reasons, more or less lazy. Criminals and prostitutes, as Féré remarks, have this common character, that they are both unproductive. This is true also of vagabonds, and of the vicious and idle generally, to whatever class they belong. They are all members of the same family.[75]

The common characteristic of criminals was "arrested development," or "atavism". He observed that criminals "constantly reproduce the features of savage character – want of forethought, inaptitude for sustained labour, love of orgy, etc."[76] Such equations of criminals with savages were, as we have seen, a stock Victorian simile. Now, however, these uncivilized characteristics appeared rooted in the tyranny of organization. The criminal was, as W. D. Morrison put it the following year, "the offspring of degeneration and disease."[77]

Such physiological determinism was complemented (not always logically) by social determinism. Although Ellis noted that the instinctive criminal was the most dramatic criminal type, he argued that more attention should be paid to the occasional criminal, who was

a much commoner and more normally constituted person. In him the sensual instincts need not be stronger than usual, and the social elements, though weaker than usual, need not be absent. Weakness is the chief

[74] *ibid.*, p. 221.
[75] *ibid.*, p. 223.
[76] *ibid.*, p. 209.
[77] *Crime and Its Causes* (London: S. Sonnenshein, 1891, p. vii).

characteristic of the occasional criminal; when circumstances are not quite favourable he succumbs to temptation. Occasional crime is one of the commonest forms of crime; it is also that for whose existence and development society is most directly responsible; very often it might equally be called social crime.

Many of these persons were themselves victims: "society was the criminal." Society's guilt was not that of creating criminality *de novo*, but of turning existing weaknesses into much more serious ones, in providing just the wrong kind of intervention. Through misguided criminal policy, the occasional criminal is "recklessly flung into prison" and "ruined for life.... We have, as well as we are able, manufactured him into what is called the *habitual criminal*."[78]

Whether organically doomed or socially mistreated, the predominant fact about criminals was their weakness — indeed, even occasional criminals were, Ellis remarked, "congenitally weak-minded person(s)."[79] Ellis felt little of the sense of danger so manifest a generation earlier; for him, the danger posed by both criminality and "viciousness" was not immediate, but a long-term eugenic one that indicated a gradual weakening of the physiological fiber of the population through both the reproduction of the unfit and the failure of society to treat their diseases and malfunctions. As in the sexology he was about to develop (where the difficulties of sexual arousal were newly seen as a problem),[80] the early Victorian specter of instincts overwhelming the defenses of civilization was nowhere to be seen; in its place was a less intense and essentially opposite concern about the dangers of organic enervation and insufficient natural energies.

Such dispowering of the image of the criminal was exemplified in two quite independent works appearing in 1896, both focusing on the juvenile crime of the slums. The Reverend W. D. Morrison's criminological text, *Juvenile Offenders* and Arthur Morrison's novel, *A Child of the Jago*, offered visions of

---

[78] *ibid.*, pp. 17–19. [Ellis's italics.]

[79] 3rd edition, 1901, p. xv.

[80] See Paul Robinson, *The Modernization of Sex* (New York: Harper & Row, 1976): "Ellis considered that sexual arousal [was not an automatic function but] had to be pursued in a conscious and artful manner." Thus he stressed courtship and techniques of arousal, a major break with nineteenth-century sexology. As Robinson put it (while ahistorically fusing the nineteenth century with all previous eras in the unhelpful term "traditional"): "In traditional theory it was not the stimulation but the control of sexual activity that posed difficulties: satyriasis and nymphomania rather than impotence or frigidity seemed to represent the great threats to sexual equilibrium. All modern theory, by way of contrast, makes exactly the opposite assumption ... Ellis's work stood at the beginning of this revolution in sexual perspectives ... what the world needed, in Ellis's view, was not more restraint but more passion." [pp. 16, 28.]

a population of "step-children of nature" and of a society, if not doomed, then at least destined for failure and transgression. The criminologist Morrison (no relation to the novelist) concluded, after examining official statistics on and medical inquiries into the physical inheritance and condition of juvenile offenders, that heredity and environment together determined nearly all their crime. The most striking characteristic of juvenile offenders was their weakness:

> Whether we look at these juveniles from the point of view of parentage, or from the point of view of actual physical condition, the conclusion is in each case forced upon us that a high percentage of the youthful delinquent population is more feebly developed on the physical side, and more liable to succumb to the attacks of disease than juveniles of a similar age in the general community. In other words, the physical basis of mental life is in a worse condition amongst juvenile offenders as a body than amongst the ordinary population at the same stage of existence.[81]

This physical weakness not surprisingly produced a tendency to moral defect; in addition, moral weaknesses were also directly inheritable. The "doctrine of heredity," he observed, "teaches us to believe this mental inertia, this defect of will and character, is transmissible, and is frequently transmitted from the parents to the child.... [T]he weakness of will in the parent reappears in the child in the form of an absence of power to resist criminal instincts and impulses."[82]

The language of will so evident earlier in the century has here taken on a different meaning. Whereas will had been opposed to impulse and had meant the moral power to resist temptation and choose the right, it now referred to a natural endowment, an energy that was not distributed in equal proportions to the entire population.[83]

> We may ... say on the grounds of heredity that a considerable proportion of juvenile offenders come into the world with defective moral instincts, and that their deficiencies in this respect, combined with external circumstances of a more or less unfavourable character, have the effect of making these juveniles what they are.[84]

These "external circumstances" included not only poverty, but more directly, "parental example, social surroundings, social habits, the presence of temp-

[81] W. D. Morrison, *Juvenile Offenders* (London: T. Fisher Unwin, 1896), p. 105.

[82] *ibid.*, p. 111.

[83] Randall McGowen, "Rethinking Crime: Changing Attitudes towards Lawbreakers in Eighteenth and Nineteenth Century England," unpublished Ph.D. dissertation, University of Illinois 1979, p. 305. I am indebted to this pioneering work for important insights on W. D. Morrison and Havelock Ellis.

[84] Morrison, *Juvenile Offenders*, pp. 109–10.

tation and opportunity."[85] The weaknesses cruelly bestowed by nature were by these conditions nurtured and fostered. Perhaps they could even (like others concerned with reform, Morrison never systematized his explanations) outweigh one's biological inheritance:

> As a rule a man is shaped by the surroundings in which he has been born and is obliged to live. If these surroundings are all calculated to injure him and to degrade him he will sooner or later degenerate, and become a drunkard, a pauper, a lunatic, or a criminal, or, as not infrequently happens, a combination of all.[86]

Whatever the precise weightings of influence, under these twin pressures of heredity and environment, juveniles had in fact little freedom of action; when the pressures were unfavorable, the product was a criminal.

While Reverend Morrison was examining the juvenile offender, the fiction writer Arthur Morrison followed his story, "Lizerunt," with the most important literary work of the 1890s focusing on criminality, *A Child of the Jago* (1896). This work echoed and yet profoundly contrasted with *Oliver Twist*; instead of Dickens's illustration of "the principle of Good surviving through every adverse circumstance,"[87] Morrison's *Jago* hammered home the lesson of the tyranny of circumstance and the mirage of moral freedom already foreshadowed in "Lizerunt." As Morrison explained the following year in his preface to the third edition, the Jago was a description of a real part of the East End "where children were born and reared in circumstances which gave them no reasonable chance of living decent lives; where they were born foredamned to a criminal or semi-criminal career."[88] The book's central character, Dicky Perrot, is enveloped by the criminal ghetto, the Jago, and is dragged down to criminality and destruction. The Jago has energy aplenty, but it is all wasted, turned to random violence and self-destruction; it is the energy of putrefaction. The forces of Victorian moralization, philanthropy, education, even the police, make little impact on the amoral (not immoral) world of the Jago. The police do succeed, at least, in confining it physically, and turning it inward on itself. The Jago "rats" (the vermin imagery is pervasive) fear the force of the police and the law and consequently prey chiefly on themselves and the weaker inhabitants of their world. For all its amorality, the Jago poses no threat to the respectable world, as had the underworld in *Barnaby Rudge* or *Oliver Twist*; it is now contained, a ghetto (which one could not have called Dickens's criminal world) with no effect outside its borders.

[85] *ibid.*, p. 37, also see pp. 170–4.
[86] *ibid.*, p. 283.
[87] Dickens, *Oliver Twist*, Preface.
[88] Arthur Morrison, *A Child of the Jago* (London: MacGibbon and Kee, 1969), p. 39.

As Morrison describes the Jago, its criminality runs far deeper than being the spawn of bad social conditions. Even large environmental remedies prove insufficient; slum clearance – the physical destruction of the Jago and its replacement by new council housing – does not provide a fresh start, but only seems to spread the plague:

> The dispossessed Jagos had gone to infect the neighborhoods across the border [of urban renewal], and to crowd the people a little closer. They did not return to live in the new barrack-buildings; which was a strange thing, for the County Council was charging very little more than double the rents which the landlords of the Old Jago had charged. And so another Jago, teeming and villainous as the one displaced, was slowly growing.[89]

Yet the impresssion from the entire novel is of such a deeply rooted way of life that one feels little hope that, even had council rents been sufficiently low, many "Jago rats," with their primitive "clan" pattern of living, would have wished to dwell in such housing or that any could have been reformed by new housing. Morrison's picture of criminality is of a rooted culture, resistant to efforts at either reform or deterrence. Thus, while Morrison could indict society ("For the existence of this place, and for the evils it engendered, the community was, and is, responsible" [p. 39]) and support public housing and other environmental reforms, he also pessimistically urges the creation of penal settlements where habitual criminals must be quarantined for life.[90] The nearest to a prescription for criminality offered in the novel is that of a tough-minded surgeon who abhors sickly "sentiment." He indicts society's unconcern: "Think how few men we trust with the power to give a fellow creature a year in gaol, and how carefully we pick them! Even damnation is out of fashion, I believe, among theologians. But any noxious wretch may damn human souls to the Jago, one after another, year in year out, and we respect his right; his sacred right." Yet, brutally, he offers no hope save destruction and sterilization: "Here lies the Jago, a nest of rats, breeding, breeding, as only rats can; and we say it is well. On high moral grounds we uphold the right of rats to multiply their thousands. Sometimes we catch a rat. And we keep it a little while, nourish it carefully, and put it back into the nest to propagate its kind."[91]

The "degeneration" of slum life became a keynote of the burst in the later 1890s of fiction modeled on Morrison's working-class stories, books that were pervaded by a fatalism that accepted vicious and immoral behavior as

[89] *ibid.*, p. 179.
[90] P. J. Keating, "Biographical Study," *ibid.*, p. 32.
[91] *ibid.*, p. 171.

inevitable in such a setting.[92] Here imaginative literature met realistic social investigation in creating images of unfitness. Even the radical novelist Jack London described the people of the East End in extremely depressing terms in 1903:

> They are stupid and heavy, without imagination . . . a stupefying atmosphere of torpor, which wraps about them and deadens them. . . . Mind and body are sapped by the undermining influences. . . . Moral and physical stamina are broken . . . the children grow up . . . without virility or stamina, a weak-kneed narrow-chested, listless breed, that crumples up and goes down.[93]

If change were to come, it would have to come from outside.

The criminal within respectability

In a number of ways, then, the once close relation between criminality and moral choice was distanced in late Victorian imaginations. However, a tendency even more subversive to the moralizing enterprise was being manifested at this same time – a tendency that would not simply distance crime from questions of character, but even suggest that criminality and respectability, rather than being opposites, had hidden affinities. Such radical suspicions did not affect policy very quickly, but they had a great deal to do with shaping the climate of opinion in which twentieth-century policy would be made.

As crime detection, in both fact and fiction, was being removed to an expert and esoteric realm, suspicions appeared that there existed much hitherto unsuspected expert and esoteric crime. The increasing sense of conquest of the external criminality of the streets combined with the blurring of the stark moral certainties of the early nineteenth century to turn middle-class attention inward, from the streets to the home, from the public house to the counting house, and in general from the unruly populace to persons and scenes of apparent respectability. In the process this shift in perceptions probed new, hitherto hidden, forms and locales of criminality.

As the police, courts, and prisons dealt ever more thoroughly with known crimes, concern was increasingly expressed about crimes that might not be coming to light, crimes that were secretive by nature, committed by persons that a patrolling police force was ill suited to either deter or apprehend – such

---

[92] P. J. Keating, *The Working Classes in Victorian Fiction* (London: Routledge, 1971), p. 196.
[93] Jack London, *The People of the Abyss* (London: Journeyman Press, 1977), pp. 25–6.

as poisonings, embezzlement, fraud,[94] and blackmail.[95] All these new crimes implicated the respectable classes in a way that traditional crimes rarely had and, even more, cast suspicion on respectability itself; these crimes even depended upon the appearance of respectability and character, which was truly upsetting. One pamphlet writer of the 1870s could remark that even murders nowadays "are very easy of concealment, and that they are probably more frequent than anybody has hitherto believed. In a very material sense it is deemed possible that there may be, roughly speaking, a 'skeleton in every house'."[96] Indeed, the houses of the respectable had the room, so to speak, to store skeletons. The fading of the riotous and openly menacing old Hogarthian underworld was thus not only making public life more secure and traditional criminals less feared, but at the same time was raising questions about what might lie underneath the surfaces of respectability and normality. The conquest of the antisociety of crime, while on one level rendering society itself more transparent, on another made it less so, by throwing into relief the remaining elements of nontransparency in social life, particularly among the middle and upper classes. There, criminality had become in some ways more, rather than less, mysterious.

The discourse of murder reflected not only the weakening of common criminality, but a new concern for criminality hidden within the respectable world. On one hand, less fear of murder was expressed, and newspapers, popular pamphlets, and even street literature treated it in a less heated, melodramatic fashion than earlier in the century. Even among the poor, it was, as Leslie Stephen had predicted, losing both a degree of horror and of grandeur, coming to be seen as often nothing more than (to quote the registrar of criminal statistics in 1905) an "incident in miserable lives."[97] On the other hand, certain murders – planned, concealed ones – were gaining new interest as signs that lit up for a brief moment an unseen and opaque dark underside of modern life. Thus, Jack the Ripper, the most celebrated criminal of the age, was often suggested to be not a denizen of the Jago but a medical doctor (implying a certain distrust, even fear, of the growing power of professionals and scientific experts). In this way, a double image of murderers – as both irresponsible brutes but also, at times, carefully premeditating and

---

[94] See R. Sindall, "Middle-Class Crime in Nineteenth-Century England," *Criminal Justice History 4* (1983); Norman Russell, *The Novelist and Mammon* (New York: Oxford University Press, 1986).

[95] See Alexander Welsh, *George Eliot and Blackmail* (Cambridge, Mass.: Harvard University Press, 1985).

[96] *The Whitechapel Mystery*, quoted in Kalikoff, *Murder and Moral Decay* in *Victorian Popular Literature* (Ann Arbor: University of Michigan Press, 1986), p. 59.

[97] See Chapter 7.

dissembling members of respectable society – came to flourish in the late Victorian era.

With the increasingly problematic nature of personal responsibility and of character as a solution to crime, fictional images of the criminal were becoming not only less passionate, but also blurred, socially and morally. The satisfying clarity of good and evil and the certainty of cathartic punishment for villainy that characterized most early Victorian popular literature and theater gave way in the second half of the century to a diffusion of evil and to more incomplete resolutions. If a certain crudity and violence of feeling were in retreat, so too was an assurance of the complete defeat of evil. Villainy was appearing in more unexpected social locales and in more complex and unpredictable forms that were less clearly distinguishable from good. The domestic family, the professional classes, and even (as with *Dr. Jekyll and Mr. Hyde*) the respectable individual himself, were becoming the loci of fictional criminal behavior. At the same time, outcomes were becoming less sure. Mysteries were replacing melodramas, and chance and fate were ousting providence from the controls of the machinery of popular art. Sweeney Todd was giving way to Professor Moriarty, and the public gallows to repeated eludings, and the final uncertainty of Reichenbach Falls.

Not only was society becoming more complex through population growth, urbanization, mobility, and economic and technological development, but even, ironically, the very advance of knowledge, as it spread light into dark corners, at the same time seemed to heighten the sense that respectable social life was permeated by buried secrets. Indeed, in a Foucaultian sense, secrets can be seen to be *produced* by the very explosion of information and public scrutiny of personal life. "As publicity in general enhances the value of privacy," Alexander Welsh has argued, "a police force enhances secrecy, or the deliberate enactment of privacy," as the innocent as well as the guilty strive to avoid questioning by keeping their affairs as private as possible.[98] An awareness was spreading that the instruments developed and extended by the early Victorians to push back social disorder – police, press, public opinion – could also rebound upon the respectable middle class; along with an emerging feeling of social security came a complementary sense of domestic and personal insecurity, of potential exposure – and explosion – of the previously private. The new, safer policed and investigated society was also a world of heightened surveillance.[99] The creation of the Detective Department and the nationwide establishment of police forces, which were capable of not only keeping the

---

[98] Welsh, *Blackmail*, p. 91.
[99] See D. A. Miller, "Discipline in Different Voices: Bureaucracy, Police, and Bleak House," *Representations* no.1 (1983), 59–89.

working class under surveillance but also (if, of course, less routinely) invading middle-class privacy[100] were accompanied by the rise of the modern popular newspaper, for which police reports and (after 1857) divorce court proceedings became staples. The enhanced social capacity for information gathering and distribution increased public safety, as Major Griffiths and other officials insisted, but also increased everyone's vulnerability to the exposure, inadvertent or deliberate, of discreditable secrets (more damaging than they would have been before the early Victorian heightening of moral standards), secrets buried in the past or within the castle of the home or family business. Thus, it is not surprising that blackmail – the threatened destruction of apparent respectability by the exposure of secrets – became for the mid- and later Victorians a greater preoccupation in law and in fiction than either before or since.

The first form of fiction to exploit anxiety about secrets was the sensation novel that flourished in the 1860s, just as the national crime rate was beginning to fall. As a reviewer for *Fraser's Magazine* complained in 1863, "a mystery and a secret are the chief qualifications of the modern novel."[101] The mysteries of sensation fiction, however, were not exotic ones, but close to home. This new fiction juxtaposed the excitement of earlier genres of melodrama, romance, and gothic with the factuality of everyday middle-class settings and thus registered a movement of the sense of the menacing unknown from the social and physical fringes of respectable society into its domestic core, providing "a middle-class Newgate."[102] Although the term was first used in 1860 to refer to Wilkie Collins's *Woman in White*, the genre could be considered to begin with a number of works of Collins's friend and mentor, Dickens, notably *Bleak House* (1853) and especially *Great Expectations* (1860).[103] In sensation fiction the clear distinction in most early Victorians a greater preoccupation in law and in fiction than either before or and even vanishes. As a replacement for this lost social division, often a psychic division opens up or sharpens within the villain or criminal, with his or

---

[100] Anthea Trodd has found in both many novelists of the 1860s and in public reactions to a real case, the Road Murder, "deep fears about the threat to the world of domestic innocence posed by the new police world of subterfuge and surveillance." ["The Policeman and the Lady: Significant Encounters in Mid-Victorian Fiction," *Victorian Studies* 27 (1984), 435–60.]

[101] Quoted in W. Hughes, *The Maniac in the Cellar* (Princeton: Princeton University Press, 1980), p. 5.

[102] *ibid.*, p. 16.

[103] Ousby, *Bloodhounds*, p. 90, cited *Bleak House* as the "sensational novel par excellence." Indeed, Hughes observed, sensation novelists "proclaim[ed] Dickens as their prototype." [p. 5.]

her identity seeming to blur or fragment. The sensation novel turned melodramatic conflict inward, into middle-class domesticity and indeed into the
middle-class personality. Thus, not only villains and villainesses, but heroes
and heroines were often morally ambiguous and divided selves.

The appearance of the sensation novel among the middle-class, novel-read-
ing audience suggested a saturation with the discourse of moralization. These
exciting stories offered, in Winifred Hughes's phrase, an "antidote to a surfeit
of prosaic respectability."[104] Outraged critics accused the authors of subverting moral distinctions. The limits of the faith in character were hinted at
through these works' questioning of not only the possibility but even the desirability of total control of impulse. Moralistic critics were outraged by the
suggestion that the passionate instincts (even in women) were as human as
they were bestial and liable to come to the surface even in the best families.
Although, as some critics also complained, sensation fiction brought the vulgar
excitement of melodrama to a respectable audience, the most disturbing aspect
of the new genre was that it dissolved the moral clarity that melodrama had
shared with more genteel forms of fiction. Where melodrama created a daylight world of moral order to vanquish the nightmare of anarchy and evil triumphant, sensation fiction interpenetrated the two worlds. In embedding
aspects of gothic in actual domestic settings, thus domesticating the wild, sensation fiction also gothicized the normal. Typically in a sensation novel, a respectable person is gradually revealed to be a criminal; for example, Lady
Audley, the fragile, childish, upper-class wife, turns out to be a secret bigamist
who has unceremoniously disposed of her first husband by pushing him down
an abandoned well. "The final import of the sensation novel," concluded
Hughes, "is that things are not what they seem, even – in fact, especially – in
the respectable classes and their respectable institutions."[105]

Whereas, for example, much of the force of Dickens's *Oliver Twist* derives
from the juxtaposition and struggle between separate (if linked) criminal and
respectable worlds, in *Bleak House* and his later novels the two worlds are inseparable; they merge into an all-embracing but indistinct society, symbolized
variously by London's fog, its river, prisons, and diseases. Most obviously in
Great Expectations, through the characters Magwitch and Estella, criminality
and refinement turn out not to be warring opposites but intimately bound
together. Unraveling these hidden connections becomes a pervasive activity in
these later novels, moving Dickens and some of his contemporaries toward the
genre of detective fiction. In the theater, also, the "lurid excess" of melodrama
gradually gave way to more subtle evil. Instead of the protracted, bloody
crimes of such early Victorian popular plays as *The String of Pearls* and *The*

---

[104] *Maniac*, p. 36.
[105] *ibid.*, p. 190.

Murder in the Red Barn, stage crimes after midcentury, Beth Kalikoff has observed, "are secret and shameful, desperate, not demonic. Stealth and deceit mark criminal behavior."[106] Popular theater followed sensation fiction in raising questions about respectability. Stage murderers now came from all ranks and stations and acted out of a wide variety of motives, sometimes even almost creditable ones. The line between good and evil motives was also blurring. In a number of plays of the 1870s, Kalikoff has argued, the motives for being respectable and prosperous were the same as those for committing crimes. Stage murderers, then, "no longer kill only through madness or passion. They kill with the same motives that make members of the audience consider themselves good citizens."[107]

Sensation villains tended to be more complex than those of melodrama and often indeed were self-divided. As scholars have noted, Bradley Headstone, the sexually enflamed murderous schoolteacher in *Our Mutual Friend* (1865), contains much of the later Dickens himself, torn between the restrictions of respectability and his own passionate nature. Indeed, Dickens's later villains tend to have elements of good mixed with evil. His last, John Jasper, makes a striking contrast with his earliest. The final chapters of *The Mystery of Edwin Drood* (1870) were to be "in the condemned cell,"[108] and if written would have satisfyingly completed this movement from the London slum thiefmaster to the Cloisterham choirmaster. Instead of "Fagin's Last Night Alive," Dickens would do Jasper's – a significant rewriting of one of the most renowned scenes from his early work. As Jerome Meckier has noted,

> Having moved back and forth between Cloisterham and an East End opium den, Jasper combines in his experience, and internalizes within his dual personality, Fagin's den and the Brownlow-Maylie world. Originally, doubleness through self-division in Dickens was a potentially curable sociological matter, which the opposing tugs Fagin and Brownlow exert on Oliver's pliant nature crudely externalized. When Jasper replaces Fagin in the death cell, he also subs for Oliver as a representative of all earthbound pilgrims. Unlike Oliver, however, Jasper cannot choose one place over another because the murderer-choirmaster carries heaven and hell inside himself.[109]

The sensation story had introduced detectives and detection into respectable society in a psychological climate of anxiety. The genre's sense of pervasive mystery and explosive buried secrets had set its characters to detective

---

[106] *Murder and Moral Decay*, p. 81.
[107] *ibid.*, p. 155.
[108] Dickens, quoted in Jerome Meckier, *Hidden Rivalries in Victorian Fiction* (Lexington, Kentucky: University of Kentucky Press, 1987), p. 155.
[109] *ibid.*

work.[110] When sensation fiction fell out of fashion after 1870, detection continued in the form of the detective story per se. As we have seen, this genre developed the reassuring face of sensation's insistence that secrets will out, while downplaying sensation's other doubtful and subversive face. Yet anxieties about the dark secrets within respectability did not simply evaporate; they were continued and developed within other fictional forms.[111] The classic vision of the criminal within the respectable man was to be provided just one year before the reassuring appearance of Sherlock Holmes, in Robert Louis Stevenson's *Strange Case of Dr. Jekyll and Mr. Hyde*. This is not a story of multiple personalities, but of the flaws and fractures in Jekyll's personality. "Like many characters in late-century popular genres," one critic has argued, "he is his own monster."[112]

Jekyll and Hyde have entered popular culture as a mythic embodiment of man's divided nature and the eternal war between the good and the bad sides of man – a traditional framework that has allowed for the discovery of a broad range of interpretive meanings. Upon the book's publication, *The Times* provided the basic Victorian interpretation when it described the story as one of "a feeble but kindly nature steadily and inevitably succumbing to the sinister influences of besetting weaknesses. With no formal preaching, and without a touch of Pharisaism," *The Times* observed approvingly, Stevenson "works out the essential power of Evil which, with its malignant patience and unwearying perseverance, gains ground with each casual yielding to temptation, till the once well-meaning man may actually become a fiend, or at least wear the reflection of the fiend's image."[113] In this form, it was a simplistic cautionary tale, easily parodied by later literary critics: "If you weren't careful, the evil in you would swallow up the good, as the wicked Hyde does Dr. Jekyll. And you'd be lost. So be careful!"[114] Yet although such an interpretation has always been popular, this Victorian reading obscures much in a text that seethes with anti-Victorian feelings.

Jekyll and Hyde reveals much about the cultural situation of the professional middle classes to which Stevenson belonged. His exploration of the dark secrets of the eminently respectable Dr. Jekyll uncovers problems not so

---

[110] In *Bleak House*, for instance, J. Hillis Miller has noted not only the prevalence of mysteries, but the active response of characters, many of whom seek "some kind of clarity, some knowledge about themselves or about one another, some revelation of a mystery," and it is from this activity that much of the plot arises. [Miller, *Charles Dickens: The World of His Novels* (Cambridge, Mass.: Harvard University Press, 1958), p. 168.]

[111] See Meckier, p. 155 passim., on connections between Edwin Drood and Dracula.

[112] Kalikoff, *Murder and Moral Decay*, p. 131.

[113] *The Times*, Jan. 25, 1886.

[114] Charles Keith, quoted by Edwin Eigner, *Robert Louis Stevenson and the Romantic Tradition* (Princeton: Princeton University Press, 1966), p. 149.

much of insufficient resistance to temptation, but within respectability itself, with the process of personal moralization. *Jekyll and Hyde* seems to have had a very personal dimension, for the author had struggled in his own life against an overdisciplined puritanical upbringing and with the strain and hypocrisy such excessive demands upon human nature engender. Jekyll is far from a purely good man who through the desire to help mankind carelessly releases an evil force from its chains. Instead, as Stevenson maintained shortly after the story appeared, the harm was in Jekyll precisely because he was *too* careful, "because he was a hypocrite. . . . The Hypocrite let out the beast of Hyde."[115] The closer one looks, the more one sees flaws in Jekyll's own character and the more Jekyll and Hyde seem intimately related.

Edwin Eigner pointed out some years ago that the first draft of the story, destroyed by Stevenson because his wife found it not meaningful enough, seems to have made this point more straightforwardly.[116] In it the physical change the chemicals wrought in Jekyll was intended simply as a disguise; there was no attendant moral or temperamental transformation. With his altered face and stature, the respectable Dr. Jekyll was enabled merely to indulge his nighttime passions without fear of discovery or embarrassment. Even in the published version, Jekyll had been living two lives for many years past. Long before the physical appearance of Hyde, Jekyll admits, "I concealed my pleasures; and . . . when I reached years of reflection, and began to look round me and take stock of my progress and position in the world, I stood already committed to a profound duplicity of life." Moreover, the final version retained elements of the disguise motif. After the experiment, as Jekyll writes:

> I began to profit by the strange immunities of my position. Men have before hired bravos to transact their crimes, while their own person and reputation sat under shelter. I was the first that ever did so for his pleasures. I was the first that could thus plod in the public eye with a load of genial respectability, and in a moment, like a schoolboy, strip off these lendings spring headlong into the sea of liberty. But for me, in my impenetrable mantle, the safety was complete. Think of it – I did not even exist!

Jekyll's goodness, as we see it in the story, is not expressed in spontaneous human warmth or affections, but solely in pious statements and public charities, springing, as he confesses, chiefly from an "imperious desire to carry my head high, and wear a more than commonly grave countenance before the public." He is unable to accommodate the impulsive, sensual child in him and

[115] Quoted in Eigner, *Stevenson*, p. 150.
[116] *ibid.*

attempts instead to segregate once and for all the two sides of his life and thus to relieve the unbearable strain of the struggle to present perpetually one face only to the world. Jekyll's chemical experiment is thus less an error that proved fatal than a culmination of a lifelong effort to polarize instead of reconcile the tendencies of his nature.

Once released, Hyde is portrayed, rather surprisingly, as younger and smaller than Jekyll – a wicked youth, from the standpoint of Jekyll's respectable morality, but perhaps simply an uncivilized, animal-like ("ape-like") boy. Becoming Hyde, Jekyll feels "younger, lighter, happier in body," at one with the "sensual" impulses he had been unable to accept and thus had distilled and separated from his public face.[117] As Jerome Charyn has suggested, "Hyde is a timid monster, who is more child than killer man ... that unredeemed child in Jekyll (and Stevenson himself), that dwarf who stays asleep until Jekyll pushes him out and gives birth to Edward Hyde, his shrunken twin."[118]

At the beginning, Hyde is simply without conscience; as he provokes hatred from those respectable persons who encounter him, he becomes more positively evil; impersonal indifference to others finally develops into malicious hatred. Hyde, now the feared criminal, is produced not by relaxing moral vigilance, but by Jekyll's polarizing rejection, assisted and encouraged by the rest of society in the persons of the bystanders and other narrators of the story who find Hyde revolting. From this standpoint, then, *The Strange Case of Dr. Jekyll and Mr. Hyde* is less an allegory of the evil in man swallowing up the helpless good than "a story of a whole man driving one part of his nature to depravity until the entire ego is destroyed."[119] This work, Edwin Eigner concluded, was intended by Stevenson as a story of the pathetic waste produced by the rejection of one's full nature.

Another theme even more subversive of Victorianism can be discerned in *Jekyll and Hyde*: beneath its deliberate critique of Victorian character building lies a perhaps unconscious gothic questioning of the era's very concept of character.[120] Stevenson has Jekyll himself wonder whether "man will be

---

[117] *The Strange Case of Dr. Jekyll and Mr. Hyde* (New York: Bantam, 1981), pp. 79, 82, 86, 102.

[118] "Afterword," *ibid.*, pp. 110, 107.

[119] Eigner, p. 160.

[120] This is the collective theme of a recent collection of critical essays, *Dr Jekyll and Mr. Hyde After One Hundred Years*, eds. William Veeder and Gordon Hirsch (Chicago: University of Chicago Press, 1988). As Ronald Thomas put it in his contribution to this volume, *Jekyll and Hyde* launches "an elaborate assault on the ideals of the individual personality and the cult of character that dominated the nineteenth century, striking at the heart of that ideology: the life story." ["The Stange Voices in the Strange Case: Dr. Jekyll, Mr. Hyde, and the Voices of Modern Fiction," p. 74.]

ultimately known [not for his duality, but] for a mere polity of multifarious, incongruous and independent denizens."[121] This question is never answered, this specter never exorcised. If this were to be realized, the ideal of character would stand exposed as not simply misguided but fantastical. Thus, if the detective story moved away from character building by stressing intellect and expertise, such neogothic fiction carried the deconstruction of Victorianism a step further, by interiorizing crime and providing no solution. If the Sherlock Holmes stories mark one path of development from sensation fiction and its anxieties about Victorianism, Stevenson's powerful and influential tale marks a complementary, and darker, one, using the image of crime and criminality to convey more general middle-class fears.

Even within the new criminology, a similar unravelling of Victorian clarities was taking place. As a work like Stevenson's both continued and challenged the assumptions of Victorian moralizing fiction, the criminological work of Havelock Ellis contained, in addition to its manifest naturalizing of Victorian moral distinctions, a subversive subtext based on an undermining of the fixity of moral boundaries. The natural world lacked the clear distinctions of the moral world, the sharp divide provided by choice; a universe of action that could be located as good or evil was being replaced by one of constitutions and dispositions that differed from one another only in degree. "Natural groups," as Francis Galton put it, "have nuclei but no outlines."[122] Thus, while initially naturalizing discourse served to conceptually (and emotionally) isolate the criminal offender, in the long run it tended to blur the dividing lines between degrees of criminality and, more important, between criminality and respectability, as more generally between the normal and the abnormal, because both categories were now being derived from a naturalistic continuum rather than the either-or typology of moralism.

Thus, although focusing on the deep-rooted pathologies of criminals deepened pessimism about their moral rehabilitation or prevention and also encouraged medical and administrative approaches to their treatment, at the same time the fading clarity of the old boundaries slowly diminished the sense of profound difference between deviance and normality. As a result, the abnormal was increasingly discovered within the normal, while the sphere of normality itself began to reclaim some of the territory hitherto declared abnormal. Even the sternly moralistic secretary of the Howard Association, William Tallack, a lifelong supporter of the Charity Organization Society, came to reflect in 1889 on the variety and ubiquity of "physical and mental mal-devel-

[121] *Strange Case*, p. 82.
[122] Quoted in Havelock Ellis, *The Criminal* (3rd. revised ed., 1901), p. 21.

opment" and was struck by the extent to which "all mankind are, more or less, the subjects of hereditary weakness and defect."[123] The war against crime was beginning to turn into the administration of abnormality, simultaneously expanding social control and relaxing moral judgment.

Despite his frequent citation of Lombroso and his belief that ultimately organic causes would be found for virtually all criminality, Ellis did not find criminals for the most part easily recognizable on sight. The signs of their criminality were more hidden, requiring practical and scientific expertise to uncover. If criminals might not be recognized by others, they might not recognize themselves. Individuals might possess organic flaws predisposing them to crime or vice unawares, until they began to manifest themselves. Moreover, despite his professed aim of providing the foundations of a natural taxonomy of criminality, Ellis returned again and again to the point that this subject did not admit of hard and fast distinctions. Categories blended into one another – the different types of criminals, of criminality and insanity, of criminality and vice, and, most unsettling of all, of criminality and apparent normality. All his criminal categories existed, as he put it, in the broad and uncharted "borderland" between sanity and lunacy. Moreover, seen as malfunction and maladaptation, rather than willful evil, criminality was not a fixed category, but depended upon changing social roles. Signs of a growing criminality of women, being cited by many as evidence of modern moral decline, Ellis argued were:

> but the inevitable accident of a beneficial transition. Criminality, we must remember, is a natural element of life, regulated by natural laws, and as women come to touch life at more various points and to feel more of its stress, they will naturally develop the same tendency to criminality as exists among men, just as they are developing the same diseases, such as general paralysis. Our efforts must be directed, not to the vain attempt to repress the energies of women, but to the larger task of improving the conditions of life, and so diminishing the tendency to criminality among both sexes alike.[124]

Struggling within Ellis's evolutionary images of criminality as "regression" and "atavism" was an incipient cultural relativism (incipient, indeed, in all evolutionary social philosophies), which emerged more clearly in his sexology, particularly in relation to homosexuality.[125] He believed that one could not define crime except in relation to prevailing social norms; criminality was ex-

---

[123] William Tallack, *Penological and Preventive Principles* (London: Wertheimer, Lea, 1889; 2nd ed. 1891), pp. 258–9.

[124] *Criminal*, p. 218.

[125] In his sexology, it has been observed, "Ellis seemed to enjoy liquidating distinctions." [Robinson, *Modernization of Sex*, p. 26.]

plicitly defined as "a failure to live up to the standard recognised as binding by the community."[126] While criminals, he agreed, could be compared to savages, Ellis was at pains to insist that it was not their savagery (no longer felt to be the social threat the early and mid-Victorians had seen in it) but their nonconformity to the nonsavage standards of their society in which their criminality lay:

> That the criminal often acts like a savage who has wandered into a foreign environment – it is scarcely necessary to remark that a savage in his own proper environment is not an anti-social being – is true. But we must be cautious in arguing that this necessarily means a real atavistic revival of savage traits. The criminal acts like the savage, for the most part, merely because a simple and incomplete creature must inevitably tend to adopt those simple and incomplete modes of life which are natural to the savage.[127]

Citing the new French sociologists, Ellis stressed that "savage" modes of life had their functions in their own social context:

> To say . . . that among savages criminality is the rule rather than the exception, is to introduce confusion. Among many savages infanticide, parricide, theft and the rest, far from being anti-social, subserve frequently some social end, and they outrage, therefore, no social feeling. These acts are not anti-social . . . there is under the conditions a certain reasonableness in them, although among us they have ceased to be reasonable, and have become criminal. On the other hand, many acts which the needs or traditions of a barbarous society have caused to be criminal become in a higher phase of society trivial or beneficial.[128]

Moreover, he questioned the moral superiority of civilization. Indignation, he remarked, was easy to arouse "against the social habits of lower races," but these were often little more to be censured than "civilized" practices like war and commercial fraud.[129] If criminality was relative and if every society had its forms of criminality, the distinction between criminality and "respectable morality" becomes difficult to ascertain.

Ellis's ambivalence toward the "primitivism" of criminals stemmed not only from criticism of the excessive pride of "civilization" in its distance from savage vices, but from his admiration – shared with *Jekyll and Hyde*'s author – of primitive peoples' strength, sensuality, and forcefulness. In such ways, as crime ceased to be an imminent danger or a critical moral issue, the image of

---

[126] *Criminal*, p. 206.
[127] *Criminal*, 1901; pp. xv–xvi.
[128] *Criminal*, 1890, p. 205.
[129] *ibid.*, p. 206.

the criminal changed from being a support for to becoming a subverter of moralization. With this changing view of crime and deviance, older forms of repression appeared to be neither effective nor desirable. More positive means would have to be devised to deal with crime and other social threats.

7

Prosecution and sentencing: the erosion of moral discourse

The "administratization" of criminal law

"After 1890 the tocsin ceased to sound . . . the slums and their inhabitants were no longer viewed as a violent threat to the state – just centres of vice, degeneracy, and criminality. . . . The age of social administration had dawned."[1]

In the last three chapters we have seen the cultural underpinnings of early and mid-Victorian criminal policy changing. In the latter decades of the nineteenth century, the meanings of criminality and punishment were being gradually, and to a large degree unintentionally, reshaped. At the heart of this reformulation was a new sense of the diminished power of the individual will. Nurtured, ironically, by the advances of science and moralization, this new image of humanity raised questions about assessing responsibility, and thus guilt, and consequently about how much suffering could be deserved. At the same time it rendered the existing penal regime more subjectively burdensome and less clearly productive, because offenders were seen to be weaker and less able to bear punishment. This shift was part of a general shift of social policy. As Victorian moral interventionism had presumed an individual who was at least potentially autonomous and responsible, post–Victorian interventionism, increasingly welfarist and administrative, arose with the diminution of the mid–Victorian image of the moralistic individual.

From the later 1870s, into the 1890s, while each annual report from the criminal registrar and from the Prison Commission was more self-congratulatory than the last, pressures were building that would force changes in the criminal justice system. All the developments we have examined in previous chapters – the increasing effectiveness of all sorts of social regulation and the spread of self-discipline, the percolation of naturalistic and social scientific modes of thinking, an emerging democracy and an increasingly meritocratic civil service – were at work through the period to alter both attitudes and possibilities of action. By the early 1890s, they were coming together to render

[1] David Englander, *Landlord and Tenant in Urban Britain 1838–1918* (Oxford: Clarendon Press, 1983), p. 33.

questionable the basic Victorian paradigm of deterrent and moralizing punishment.

The very success of Victorian criminal policy created pressures for change; criminal justice and social policy in general had been reshaped by the Victorians to exorcise the specter of license by insisting on and promoting the social ideal of self-discipline and personal responsibility, with as little room as possible for exceptions. With the fading of the fear of license, however, the ideal of the disciplined, responsible individual became less attractive (and less believable). At the same time, as the divine severity that Christians had taken for granted for centuries became unacceptable to all but a relative handful, and with sin, guilt and hell losing their former clarity, penal policy could hardly remain unaffected. New views of human nature and criminality came together with the changing incidence of crime and the nature of the prison population to alter, silently but dramatically, the context in which criminal justice operated. Even as the system's mid-Victorian form was being brought to perfection, its ideological and social underpinnings were crumbling away.

The consequences of success

Failure is usually seen as a motor of change; success is not. Yet, contrary to this bit of common sense, the Victorian criminal justice system was rendered ideologically vulnerable far more by its successes than by its failures. The increasing mastery of police, courts, and other agencies of the state over the criminal classes lessened the felt need for further deterrence or for the clear fixing of responsibility and dispensing of punishment for criminal acts. As *The Times* observed in 1896, "We treat the criminal better when he is caught; but he is caught oftener."[2] Such relaxation of the need to deter or punish undermined gradually, if unintentionally, the plausibility and, in the end, the legitimacy of the Victorian penal system. Success in the war on crime softened the fervor of the campaigners; the metaphor of war itself fell into disuse after the early 1870s. One index of a lower emotional temperature was the gradual mitigation of sentences. The average length of sentences fell, and fines replaced many short jail sentences.[3] "The knowledge that crime is diminishing," observed the criminal registrar in 1894, "encourages judges and magistrates to deal with crimes more leniently."[4]

---

[2] *The Times*, Dec. 21, 1896, p. 9.

[3] The average length of a sentence of imprisonment declined from 48.3 days in 1880 to 34.4 in 1894. [*Report of the Departmental Committee on Prisons 1895*, Appendix III, graph IV] The number of fines issued by magistrates sitting summarily was 248,542 from 1869 to 1870, 367,334 from 1880 to 1881, and 451,957 from 1889 to 1890 [annual criminal statistics].

[4] *Criminal Statistics for 1893*, p. 80.

With the fear of crime waning, members of the governing class became more receptive to scientific and humanitarian ways of thinking that highlighted the complexities that were involved in locating responsibility in an ever more complicated world, which had been glossed over by the previous urgency of the threat of crime. Waning fear and moral certainties also encouraged an emerging discomfort with the infliction of suffering by the state, for ends were now seen as less urgent and less clear. By the mid-1890s, there had clearly developed, as *The Times* itself (rather grumpily) observed, "a feeling of distrust of the efficacy of severe sentences and . . . a conviction as to their mischievousness in many cases, and pity or tenderness towards a large class of criminals as the victims of circumstances."[5]

Social problems were increasingly being defined in terms of heredity and environment, in which the criminal justice system had not been designed to operate. At the same time, success was encouraging the extension of legal sanctions and institutions to altogether new fields of behavior, whose less directly criminal nature reflected back upon the law and gradually loosened the bonds that previous generations had tightened between personal character and social harm. And as these bonds relaxed, the discourse of criminal policy became less moral and more administrative.

Extending the reach of criminal law

Although serious crime was diminishing, the criminal justice system's clientele was nonetheless widening. Since the law and its institutions were succeeding in combating serious and traditional crime and were also becoming more efficient through professionalization and administrative reform, they were increasingly applied by legislators, administrators, and magistrates, urged on by reformers, to many lesser, but more extensive tasks of social regulation. Streamlining the process of apprehension and trial enabled greater numbers to be processed. Police forces grew in numbers and improved in efficiency and became increasingly publicly accepted. Alongside this growth in police went a series of acts, beginning in 1820 and running throughout the century, that transferred jurisdiction over many categories of offenses and offenders from jury trial to magistrates courts.[6] An 1899 act made all offenses committed by juveniles (except murder) as well as most adult offenses triable summarily. By

---

[5] *The Times*, Dec. 21, 1896, p. 9.

[6] L. Radzinowicz and R. Hood, *History of English Criminal Law and its Administration, Vol. 5* (London: Stevens and Sons, 1986), pp. 618–24, describe these measures. This was no professional secret; reviewing the annual judicial statistics, *The Times* in 1882 stressed "the enormous growth of summary jurisdiction as compared with proceedings by indictment and with trial by jury." Aug. 25, 1882, p. 7.

1900, the proportion of offenses tried summarily had risen to a record high of 81 percent.[7] Both these Victorian developments – the rise of the police and the dispensing with juries for an ever longer list of offenses – expanded the state's net, enabling a higher proportion of all offenders and, most strikingly, more minor offenders to be apprehended and prosecuted. Indeed, the increasing effectiveness of the police was a key social fact of Victorian Britain. *The Times* recalled near the close of the reign that

> in great towns it is not long since they had often to walk warily and to be very discreet in their operations. They were not always strong enough to apprehend those whom they suspected, or, if they dared to do so, they knew that a conviction was out of the question by reason of the inability to procure evidence from people who feared the law or feared even more the vengeance of its enemies.

> And in villages before the police, there had often been a licensed bully who, as long as he stopped short of the worst crimes, was suffered to do what he liked. His reign is over. Those who would have submitted to his tyranny do not hesitate now to seek redress, and he goes to prison for offences of which he would once have openly boasted.[8]

But the rise in convictions, especially for nonindictable offenses, was produced not simply by the greater efficiency of the criminal justice system in carrying out its traditional tasks. Social ambitions were fed by success. Through the Victorian era, despite the steady removal from the statute books of obsolete crimes and, after the early 1870s, a more lenient pattern of sentencing, an ever wider range of behavior was brought within the active purview of the criminal law. In part, this development betokened a rearrangement of social regulation, the replacement of private and informal modes of control by public, legal ones. *The Times* also noted: "The lads who plunder an orchard do not have their ears boxed, as in primitive times, by the owner. That domestic forum is closed, and they are prosecuted."[9] At the same time, this expanded role for the law also represented some real expansion of social regulation. Through the Victorian and Edwardian eras, a variety of new crimes were created, in two areas in particular: commercial, as definitions of larceny, fraud, adulteration, embezzlement, and official corruption were broadened[10]

---

[7] *Criminal Statistics for 1902*, p. 37.

[8] *The Times*, Dec. 21, 1896, p. 9.

[9] Dec. 21, 1896.

[10] The head constable of Liverpool observed in his report for 1905: "The tendency of legislation for the past 25 years, tardily following the development of crimes of dishonesty, has been to extend the remedies of criminal law; commercial dishonesty has been dealt with by Acts imposing penalties upon adulteration, fraud in the supply of food and drugs, the imitation or misuse of merchandise marks, offences against the Bankruptcy Acts, and

and public order, morals, and welfare, including such disparate offenses as public drunkenness, soliciting for or into prostitution, cruelty to animals, cruelty to children, failing to send one's children to school, and even "neglecting to maintain one's family."[11]

One can interpret this extension of criminalization as a sign of "the progress of civilization," as did U.S. sociologist A. C. Hall in 1902. His paradoxical thesis, widely noted in Britain, was that "society's conflict with its criminal members, due to the enforcement of new social prohibitions, is one of the chief means by which humanity, in every age, has risen from a lower to a higher plane of civilization." Focusing upon nineteenth-century British criminal statistics, Hall argued:

> Is not crime clearly a social product, and has it not been increasing with giant strides in this enlightened and humane nineteenth century? Is not this increase due to growth of intelligence and social morality, realizing the new needs of a rapidly progressing civilization, causing the enactment of prohibitions increasing crime and making criminals? . . . . The most civilized and progressive nations have the most criminals, and more abundant crime as they ascend higher in the scale of social development.[12]

Recent revisionists see this process as a less benign indicator. V. A. C. Gatrell, who shares Hall's view of the rising numbers of convictions as a sign of changing social standards rather than of any sort of deterioration in public behavior, nonetheless interprets this rise in more sinister terms as the growth of a policeman-state. Focusing upon the unequal social impact of this tightening discipline, Gatrell has listed among the new, later Victorian tasks given the criminal law:

> the policing of industrial relations; the policing of the nation's drunks, vagrants, paupers, prostitutes, homosexuals and aliens; the policing of those who might service allegedly deviant cultures, like publicans and

kindred matters, [while] the Larceny Act has been extended to cover abuse of certain fiduciary relations formerly outside its scope." [*Criminal Statistics for 1905*, p. 18.] The Office of Public Prosecutor was created in 1879 in response to a series of complex banking and insurance company frauds. In part, no doubt, commercial criminalization was a response to real rises in dishonesty, taking advantage of the greater opportunities afforded by economic development; it also seems to have been promoted by a more critical view of such dishonesty and a greater readiness to employ the sanctions of criminal law against it. This question calls for more thorough investigation.

[11] The table of nonindictable offenses, which, though "technically criminal . . . are not to be regarded as criminal in the full sense" for selected years from 1858 to 1898 in the *Criminal Statistics for 1898*, p. 26, is illuminating; see also the remarks of Radzinowicz and Hood, p. 118.

[12] A. C. Hall, *Crime in its Relations to Social Progress* (New York: Columbia University Press, 1902), pp. vi, 274.

pawnbroker-receivers and sellers of pistols or of obscene publications; or the policing of those whose practices subverted an increasingly rigid ideal of urban order, whether they be street-traders, street-betters or traffic offenders, or those who merely beat carpets in the highway.[13]

Our purpose here is neither to approve nor condemn such trends, but simply to note the general agreement, by contemporaries and by recent historians, that a significant widening of the scope of the criminal law was taking place. As the criminal law, in part responding to success, extended its reach to a wider range of behavior and "a bewildering array of social groups,"[14] new sorts of offenders – both middle-class and working-class – were taking the place of old.[15] In addition to explicit extensions of summary jurisdiction, both the proliferation of licensing acts and statutes and bylaws to regulate street order and the increasing use of the summons raised the number of summary prosecutions.[16] The pronounced, long-term decline in the number of prosecutions for serious traditional crimes[17] was thus masked for much of the latter half of the century by the rise on the number of lesser prosecutions, both within the category of indictable offenses and, especially, in the category of nonindictable offenses. Whereas the total number of indictable offenses prosecuted began to turn down in the 1880s, nonindictable offenses (particularly minor ones) continued to climb until the end of the century; the average number from 1892 to 1896 was almost double that from 1857 ot 1861, when such statistical recording began.[18] In this shift we can see a greatly widening role in social regulation for criminal justice system. "As the century wore on," Gatrell argued in an earlier essay, "the English judicial system came very near to as total a regulation of even petty – let alone serious – deviance as has ever been achieved."[19]

---

[13] V. A. C. Gatrell, "Crime, Authority and the Policeman-State," in ed. F. M. L. Thompson, *Cambridge Social History of Britain 1750–1950* (forthcoming).

[14] *ibid.*

[15] On the widening range of working-class convictions, see Gatrell, "Decline of Theft and Violence" and "Policeman-State." On the nonetheless growing proportion of middle-class convictions for more serious offenses, see Rob Sindall, "Middle-Class Crime in Nineteenth Century England," *Criminal Justice History 4* (1983), 23–40.

[16] See Gatrell, "Policeman-State."

[17] Such as manslaughter, prosecutions for which fell from 227 in 1870 to 172 in 1900. [annual criminal statistics].

[18] *Criminal Statistics for 1896*, p. 16. The largest contributors to this rise were drunkenness, breach of the education acts, highway acts, and police regulations (which included the rapidly extending codes of county and borough bylaws.) The Home Office's criminal registrar stressed through the 1890s the significance for these totals of "the creation of new offences." See for example the table of nonindictable offences, 1858–1898, in the *Criminal Statistics for 1898*, p. 26.

[19] "Decline of Theft and Violence," p. 244.

As criminal law expanded into more social spaces, however, it also was attenuated. For the inflation of criminal regulation did not only signify growing state power, as Gatrell and others have argued; at the same time it betokened an alteration in the character of the criminal sanction. One consequence of inflation is to depreciate the currency being inflated. In this case, the depreciation was in the moral currency of the criminal law, diluting the gravity of an encounter with it and the stigma its sanctions carried. As the criminal registrar noted in 1900, "the idea of vindicating the law and executing justice prevails less [than formerly]."[20] The expansion of criminal sanctions thus, ironically, contributed to loosening the bonds between social harm and moral condemnation and to turning the discourse of criminal policy in a civil or administrative direction. By 1904, indeed, the criminal registrar was encouraging the use of civil proceedings: "for certain offences the civil courts afford a preferable remedy."[21] With a growing proportion of indictable offenses being tried without juries, and a growing proportion of all prosecutions being for nonindictable offenses,[22] the perceived seriousness of crime tended to diminish. Moreover, as persons became liable to an increasing number of regulatory offenses for which mens rea did not need to be proved, the symbolic divide between the typical criminal defendant and the private law defendant narrowed.[23] One indication of a fading moral stigma upon criminal offenders is the frequency of remarks on the not really criminal character of various sorts of offenses and offenders. The criminal registrar observed in his report for 1898 that the offenses that were rising in number were for the most part "technically criminal, but . . . not to be regarded as criminal in the full sense of the term."[24] Another related indication is the falling scale of punishment. Not only were jail sentences steadily shortening, but alternatives to imprisonment – fines and recognizances – were increasingly employed; in-

---

[20] *Criminal Statistics for 1898*, p. 25. [C.E. Troup.]

[21] *Criminal Statistics for 1902*, p. 36. [John Macdonnell.]

[22] Within the category of nonindictable offenses, serious offenses were making up a steadily smally proportion: the only classification growing per capita was noncriminal offenses. See Radzinowicz and Hood, p. 119.

[23] W. T. S. Stallybrass, in an important 1936 essay, ascribed what he provocatively called "the eclipse of mens rea" largely to "the steady advance made by criminal law into regions in the past outside its territory." "The Eclipse of Mens Rea," *Law Quarterly Review 205* (Jan., 1936), 63.

[24] Page 26. Earlier, the imposition of criminal penalties upon the use of inaccurate weights and measures had led to much discussion in the 1870s among magistrates as to whether such offending tradesmen, when jailed upon nonpayment of fines, were to be subject to the same prison rules as real criminals; the Home Office insisted that they were and that "all persons convicted of any offence are criminal prisoners." [HO 45/9384/4529 (June 9, 1875, and June 18, 1875).] The issue was to recur, in a variety of forms, with increasing frequency.

deed, a growing proportion of prison commitments – by 1894, a majority – was the result not of incarcerative sentences but of nonpayment of fines.[25]

Although the extension of summary jurisdiction was primarily a change of procedure, it nonetheless promoted a change in the penalties attached to many offenses.[26] Since nonjury proceedings had traditionally been restricted to very minor offenses and consequently limited in the punishments that they could award, the transfer of more serious offenses to this level tended, even without statutory alteration, to reduce the penalties inflicted for these offenses. Similarly, nonjury proceedings had sometimes dispensed with the need to prove criminal intent, and this dispensation tended to spread to more cases. Moreover, the reduction of penalties (which accompanied the shift from incarcerative to monetary form) and the lessened attention to intent (traditionally the hallmark of moral guilt) tended to reinforce one another.[27] In this way, while creating a new offense to be tried without jury further blurred the distinction between criminal and civil harms, making an existing offense triable summarily both made a statement that it was regarded less seriously and institutionalized a process that would further diminish its seriousness. Trial by jury was not only a "bulwark of English liberty" but also, as Fitzjames Stephen and many others realized, a traditionally effective instrument for ratifying and reinforcing public moral standards – for, in short, blaming. As trial by jury became rarer, so did the moral function of the law; in turn, as the need for the moral function of the law was less felt, so was the need for the jury.

In a similar way, the growing readiness to contemplate a Court of Criminal Appeals in part reflected the movement of criminal law toward the realm of civil law, where such proceedings were already allowed. In civil law the tendency to replace public trial by jury with review by professionals had gone much further,[28] and denunciation and deterrence were already much less important. Opponents of criminal appeals repeatedly cited the threat to the jury and the

[25] The major acts from 1847 on extending summary jurisdiction also made provision for certain offenders to enter into recognizances to come up for judgment when called upon and meantime keep the peace and be of good behavior. On imprisonment for nonpayment of fines, see Sean McConville, *History of English Prison Administration, Vol. 1: 1750–1877,* [London: Routledge, 1981] p. 331, and Radzinowicz and Hood, pp. 649–50.

[26] See William McWilliams, "The Mission to the English Police Courts 1876–1936," *The Howard Journal 22* (1983), 131.

[27] Mr. Justice Wills indeed suggested in 1889 that the nature and extent of the penalty attached to an offense was a proper element in determining whether or not mens rea is required. [*R. v. Tolson* (1889) 23 QBD 172–7.]

[28] As *The Times* noted in 1882: "Few things ... are more characteristic of our time than the partial discredit into which trial by jury has fallen. The old eulogies upon it seem in these days curiously strained and even ridiculous ... For the present, however, this distrust takes distinct shape only in regard to civil disputes." Feb. 3, 1882, p. 9.

swiftness and the certainty of legal sanctions.[29] Nonetheless, as time went on such objections were less persuasive than the equitable considerations put forth by proponents, and successive bills were introduced, resulting in the establishment of such a court in 1907.[30]

The elaboration of the apparatus of criminal law and its wider application not only helped to diminish the seriousness of the perception of the criminal offender, but also provided new possibilities and facilities for general social administration. The Convict Supervision Office of Scotland Yard, created in 1880, had in its first six years, the police commissioner claimed, not only kept track of most habitual offenders and convicts released on license, but had helped several thousand persons find work and assisted the emigration of many others.[31] In that year its creator, Howard Vincent (by then a Conservative M.P.), began a campaign to extend that model to the treatment of less serious offenders, substituting police-supervised probation for imprisonment.[32] Between 1887 and 1907, indeed, such a welfarist function did emerge.[33] As police roles widened, the divide between criminals and other persons supervised, regulated, or assisted by the police narrowed another bit.

In the last decades of the nineteenth century, the operation of criminal law became a locus for conflict between, on the one hand, a new inclination, encouraged by science, success, expanding social ambitions, and the difficulties encountered in practice in precisely locating legal responsibility,[34] to replace the moral fixation of the law by an extending administrative role and, on the other hand, a continuing anxiety on the part of many about the social dangers of the law's losing its moral bearings. This confrontation often

---

[29] As *The Times* warned, "unlike the procedure administered in civil courts, the criminal law has been certain as well as expeditious ... [With such a change] the uncertainty and delay which we associate with civil proceedings may appear in criminal also." March 19, 1883, p. 9; see also *The Times*, Aug. 17, 1889.

[30] On the debate over and eventual establishment of a Court of Criminal Appeal, see D. A. Thomas, *Constraints on Judgment* (Cambridge: Institute of Criminology, 1979), pp. 75–93, and Radzinowicz and Hood, pp. 758–70.

[31] HO 144/184/A45507, Metropolitan Police Commissioner, "Report on the History of the C.S.O."

[32] See his letter to *The Times*, July 26, 1886, citing as the chief obstacle to his plans the prejudice of parliamentary and civil service Liberals against further growth of the police. More acceptably to these Liberals, the great expansion of summary jurisdiction was already promoting the employment of Church of England Temperance Society missionaries as semiofficial probation officers. [See W. McWilliams, "Mission," 135.]

[33] See Radzinowicz and Hood, pp. 633–47.

[34] In part Victorian voluntarist ambitions in practice subverted themselves. The determination to locate precisely the responsibility for all disapproved behavior opened up a Pandora's box of difficulties. A kind of uncertainty principle came to attach itself to this aim; the more one attempted to locate it precisely, the more it diffused. Yet this difficulty only promoted redoubled efforts to do so.

focused on the role of the law in fixing personal responsibility for social harms and the corresponding role of deterrence in social regulation.

Killing and responsibility

The slippage of denunciation and deterrence from center stage in criminal policy, although it went furthest, as we will see, in regard to lesser offenses, nonetheless made itself felt even in the realm of the most serious of crimes – nonaccidental killings. In these offenses the definition of the extent of personal responsibility bore the weightiest consequences and was thus of extreme importance.

An unsound state of mind: self-murderers and murdering mothers

Among homicides, the concept of personal responsibility was most readily dispensed with in killings of self. Particularly from the turn of the 1880s, medical opinion coalesced around a picture of suicide as the product of mental defect, inherited or acquired. A leading Bristol alienist, J. G. Davey, argued in 1878 for a reduction in the severity of criminal, civil, and ecclesiastical law relating to suicide.[35] Three years later, Enrico Morselli's *Suicide: An Essay on Comparative Moral Statistics* was translated into English and stirred much discussion. Morselli, believing that the "old philosophy of individualism" was dead, argued for studying suicide no longer in terms of individual cases but rather as "a social phenomenon." He interpreted suicide Darwinistically, as "an effect of the struggle for existence and of human selection."[36] For Morselli, the only way to prevent suicide was somehow to diminish the severity of the stuggle for existence among large numbers of the populace. The influence of both Davey and Morselli was evident in the first full-length English study of suicide in half a century by the deputy coroner for central Middlesex, W. W. Westcott.[37] In this work, published in 1885, Westcott criticized the overreliance of Morselli and other continentals on a statistical approach, but agreed that it was time, once and for all, to decriminalize suicide. Westcott urged greater attention to melancholia, despair, and misery

[35] J. G. Davey, "On Suicide, in Its Social Relations," *Journal of Psychological Medicine*, n.s. 4 (1878), 230–55.
[36] Quoted in Barbara T. Gates, *Victorian Suicide: Mad Crimes and Sad Histories* (Princeton: Princeton University Press, 1988), p. 19.
[37] William Wynn Westcott, *Suicide: Its History, Literature, Jurisprudence, Causation and Prevention* (London: H. K. Lewis, 1885).

in an effort to diminish the number of deaths by suicide. By 1887 even *The Times* was denouncing as "absurd" the indictment of the survivor of a suicide pact for murder: "there could be no more convincing proof," it concluded, "of the necessity for an amended definition of murder."[38] The naturalization of suicide was completed in the early 1890s by two members of the Medico-Psychological Association. S. A. K. Strahan, who was also a barrister (and a fellow of the Royal Statistical Society), saw it as linked with a variety of psychological and social ailments and called for decriminalizing its attempt.[39] Henry Maudsley observed pessimistically in a paper on depression that suicide "considered objectively, as a physical event . . . is a natural event of the human dispensation, just a necessary incident from time to time of the course of its organic evolutions and dissolutions."[40]

Radical and conservative observers in the 1890s agreed that moral condemnation of suicide had largely disappeared outside the ranks of professional moralists.[41] The *Daily Chronicle* noted in 1893 that "the idea of suicide as a sin hardly exists [anymore] in popular consciousness. Pity, or the conviction that the act was a rash one, represents the nearest approach to moral reprobation."[42] From the other political side, the conservative clergyman H. H. Henson four years later lamented the fact that "suicide is now regarded with sympathy rather than with abhorrence. It is spoken of as a 'misfortune' rather than a crime. Partly the change arises from a better understanding of the conditions of suicide; partly from that almost extravagant sympathy with wretchedness, as such, which characterizes [the] age."[43] In such a mental climate, the law no longer had much of a role to play in regard to suicide. In 1879 suicide ceased to be classed as homicide and the maximum penalty for attempted suicide was reduced to two years' imprisonment; three years later all penalties imposed by common and statute law for the crime of self-murder

---

[38] Feb. 5, 1887, p. 9.

[39] S. A. K. Strahan, *Suicide and Insanity: A Physiological and Sociological Study* (London: Swan Sonnenschein, 1893), and "The Necessity of Legislation re Suicide," *Journal of Mental Science 40* (1894), 605–9.

[40] Henry Maudsley, "Suicide in Simple Melancholy" (1892), quoted in Gates, *Victorian Suicide*, p. 22.

[41] Olive Anderson is sceptical that there was any pronounced shift in popular opinion about suicide in the second half of the century, finding it already quite sympathetic to the perpetrator at midcentury. [*Suicide in Victorian and Edwardian England* (Oxford: Clarendon Press, 1987).] However, her own evidence suggests important movement among officials, professionals, and clergymen, who appear in the early Victorian period to have been markedly less tolerant of suicide than was the general populace.

[42] *Daily Chronicle*, Aug. 19, 1893, p. 4. This article was probably written by W. D. Morrison, who was soon to write an influential series of prison exposes for that paper. [Anderson, *Suicide*, 249n.]

[43] H. H. Henson, *Suicide* (London: Oxford House, 1897), quoted in Gates, p. 166.

were removed.[44] Civil and ecclesiastical law followed suit. Suicide exclusion clauses in life insurance policies, upheld in several court cases of the 1840s, gradually stopped being enforced by companies sensitive to their public image. By 1885 Westcott found that most insurance companies confined this exclusion to a limited initial period after the grant of a policy, and even then rarely enforced it.[45] Even in the church, condemnation was waning: in 1879, Convocation proposed to exclude from the Anglican burial service not "any that have laid violent hands upon themselves", but "any who having laid violent hands upon himself, hath not been found to have been of unsound mind."[46] Although attempted suicide, unlike the successful act, remained a criminal offense until 1925, it was steadily downgraded. In 1889 its trial was removed in most cases from assizes to the lesser court of quarter sessions. The proportion of prison sentences for this offense steadily fell after 1870 (especially in London), along with the length of those sentences. By the Edwardian period, the outcome of most trials was, as Olive Anderson has noted, "a solemn undertaking not to repeat [the] attempt, porbably reinforced by the giving of sureties and perhaps supervision by an officer of the court for six months."[47]

Meanwhile, with the subsiding of the mid-Victorian panic about infanticide,[48] the last obstacle was removed to the general acceptance of a psychiatric view of women who killed their infants.[49] Judges were increasingly ready to admit privately the inapplicability of the principle of personal responsibility in such cases. As Mr. Justice Keating (a former attorney general) confidentially observed to the Home Office in 1872: "All cases of infanticide (confining the term to newly born children) involve the great difficulty of properly estimating the state of mind of the mother, in the midst of unaided physical suffering, of the most agonizing character, producing necessarily a certain amount of mental disturbance." While, he went on, "the purposes of justice" might require "applying to the acts of a woman in that state, the strict rule which should govern other cases of an ordinary character . . . in considering the pun-

---

[44] Gates, *Victorian*, p. 152; Anderson, *Suicide*, p. 264. In 1882 also, suicides were granted the right of burial in daylight hours. [Gates, p. 152.]

[45] Anderson, pp. 266–8.

[46] *ibid.*, p. 274.

[47] *ibid.*, pp. 305–6.

[48] See Behlmer, "Deadly Motherhood: Infanticide and Medical Opinion in Mid-Victorian England" *Journal of the History of Medicine and Allied Sciences 34* (Oct. 1979), p. 406.

[49] The medicalization of infanticide had been developing since the eighteenth century. Indeed, infanticide cases had followed suicide ones in pioneering the use of medical evidence, and infanticide played an important role in the emergence of a forensic medical specialism in the early nineteenth century. [Roger Smith, *Trial by Medicine* (Edinburgh: Edinburgh University Press, 1981), p. 143.]

ishment due to such a crime, all the circumstances may be properly looked at."[50]

"All the circumstances" was coming to embrace not only medical but social considerations; it was increasingly evident that infanticidal women, usually poor, uneducated, and unmarried, were step-children of society as well as of nature. Prosecutions for concealment of birth fell steadily from their mid-1860s peak,[51] and sentences for infanticide grew shorter; whereas women convicted in the 1850s and 1860s received sentences of penal servitude ranging from ten years to life, by the 1880s sentences averaged less than seven years. In 1886, the first suggestion was made within the Home Office to "reconsider the question as a whole," and by 1899 it had become the policy there to consider automatically for release anyone serving longer than the average length of sentence for infanticide (as for abortion).[52] A woman who killed her child at or immediately after birth, the Home Office now acknowledged, could "hardly be said [to be] in her right senses."[53] Although the law was not amended until 1922, by the close of the Victorian era bureaucrats, judges, and juries all considered the killing of a newborn by its mother (like suicide or its attempt) as prima facie evidence of mental illness.

The insanity plea

This increasing tendency to construe some killers as mentally unsound also was evident outside these special forms of taking life in the more general treatment of murder itself. Arguments for and against the insanity plea had, as we have seen, exploded after the McNaughten case and the rules that case provoked. Since the question of where to draw the boundaries of personal responsibility was at the heart of Victorian culture, it is not surprising that the insanity plea took on after mid–century a symbolic importance above and beyond the actual frequency of its use, an importance the issue had not possessed in the more fluid pre-Victorian criminal justice system.

The chief proponents of the insanity plea were, of course, medical doctors, particularly alienists. The more alienists identified with physicalist modes of explanation, and the more ambitious they became for their profession, the less

[50] HO 45/9314/14,725, case of Ann Hawkins.
[51] From 143 in 1865 to 82 in 1880. [Annual criminal statistics.]
[52] See Monholland, "Infanticide in Victorian England 1856–1878," unpublished M.A. thesis, Rice University 1989; pp. 242–44, and Chadwick, "Bureaucratic Mercy: The Home Office and the Treatment of Capital Cases in Victorian England," unpublished Ph. D. dissertation, pp. 194–5. In 1899 this average was four years and eight months for infanticide at birth; by 1910, it was down to three years.
[53] 1899, quoted in Radzinowicz and Hood, p. 671.

tolerable they found existing criminal law. Criticism of the restrictive definition by the McNaughten rules of legal insanity as an essentially intellectual
impairment (ascertainable by laypeople) of the ability to distinguish right from
wrong became a rallying point for professional self-definition. Alienists were
soon denouncing the McNaughten guidelines for creating "artificial lines, un-
true to Nature."[54] Nature's lines ran deeper than intellect; legal definitions of
insanity, they argued, should focus on impairments of will brought about by
bodily disorders. And those best suited to make such determinations were
alienists, not lawyers or juries. The assertion of professional expertise carried
with it, necessarily, a constriction of the realm of moral discourse. This was
clearly implied in the remarks of J. G. Davey in 1859 and 1860 to the annual
meetings of the Association of Medical Officers for Asylums. Davey, calling
for a professional agitation to change the law, noted that "the peers and judges
who framed the law of lunacy . . . failed in their estimate of the indications of
the disordered mind, its promptings to morbid movements, and to criminal
acts, because they were no physiologists." He complained that lunatics were
allowed to be free until, "neglected and borne down by the pressure of disease
of the brain, they were impelled – having lost their volition . . . to the commission of crime." Then the error was compounded by treating them as ordinary criminals, instead of subjecting them to "wholesome and necessary treatment."[55] As one member of the association noted in 1859, after Davey's first
address, "ignorance, gross and dark, pervaded the mind of the public upon
these matters, and with regard to the results of physical disorder on mental
acts."[56]

The previous year had seen the drastic legal implications of physicalist psychiatric theory first set out explicitly. Joshua Burgess, medical superintendent
and proprietor of a lunatic asylum, had published a treatise presenting the
concept of the cerebrum as a mass of cells that "secreted nerve force and
thought" as grounds for rejecting the existing legal definition of insanity.
Since, he argued, insanity was revealed by modern physiological anatomy to
be "an abnormal condition of the organic structure," lawyers or juries were
incompetent to determine it. They should, therefore, "hand it over to a
physiological inquest." Burgess argued that a system of tribunals separate
from the criminal courts should be established to decide whether or not
individuals were insane; the tribunals would examine minor offenders for signs
of insanity before they could commit more serious crimes. These courts would

[54] 1872, quoted in Smith, *Trial,* p. 16.
[55] J. G. Davey, "Relations between Crime and Insanity," *Journal of Mental Science* 5
(1859), 86, and "Insanity and Crime," *ibid.* 6 (1860), 31.
[56] *ibid.* 5 (1859), 37.

remove insane persons entirely from the ambit of the criminal law and instead ensure proper therapy for them.[57]

Yet, as we have seen, such arguments were resolutely rebuffed by the courts. They received their most official hearing in the proceedings of the Royal Commission on Capital Punishment from 1864 to 1866. Several medical witnesses insisted that the definition of insanity devised by the judges had led, in Dr. Harrington Tuke's words, "to great error in the administration of the law."[58] Nonetheless, Baron Bramwell pronounced that definition "perfectly right" and in the eyes of Lord Wensleydale it "could . . . not . . . be made more clear."[59] The commissioners could find no way to bridge this professional chasm and refused to make any recommendation on the grounds that the law on insanity in criminal cases went far beyond the question of murder. The effect was by omission to ratify the existing state of the law.

After the 1860s, however, movements in the climate of educated opinion began to percolate into the discourse of criminality. Even some clerics – custodians of moral discourse – were becoming more hesitant about fixing blame for offenses. If highly unlikely to go whole hog with materalist medical men like Henry Maudsley or James Thomson, prison chaplains nonetheless were moving away from clear moral judgments. One chaplain had already observed before the National Association for the Promotion of Social Science in 1868 that "the degree of moral responsibility of persons acting under strong natural propensities is very difficult to determine. . . . [A] man may possess a disposition and a temperament which may lead him to commit certain crimes with a certainty which is perhaps only partially recognized."[60]

Increasingly, violent behavior was being connected to mental abnormality. The most influential medical advisor to the Home Office, Dr. William Guy, stressed again and again between 1869 and 1882 that the mentally abnormal or deficient were unusually addicted to violent and destructive crimes, and those "indicating a preponderance of the animal nature."[61] He argued from convict evidence that weak minded people were four times more likely to commit sexual offenses and three and a half times more likely to commit arson than "the

[57] Joshua Brugess, *The Medical and Legal Relations of Madness; Showing a Cellular Theory of Mind, and of Nerve Force, and also of Vegetative and Vital Force* (London; John Churchill, 1858), discussed in Jacyna, "Somatic Theories of Mind and the Interests of Medicine in Britain, 1850–1879," *Medical History 26* (1982), p. 251.

[58] *Report of the Capital Punishment Commission 1866*, Evidence, Q. 2394.

[59] *ibid*, Qs. 150, 360.

[60] Reverend Henry Lettsom Elliot, "What Are the Principal Causes of Crime, Considered from a Social Point of View?," NAPSS, *Transactions 1868*, pp. 335–6.

[61] W. A. Guy, "On Insanity and Crime; and on the Plea of Insanity in Criminal Cases," *Journal of the Statistical Society 32* (1869), 171–5.

healthy."[62] Such associations were said to operate in reverse as well, coloring violence with the hues of psychic abnormality. The proportion of offenders certified as criminal lunatics who had been charged with murder, serious assault, or rape (the definition of which in this era required a good deal of violence) rose from only one-third in 1857 to over one-half in 1881 and to two-thirds by 1890; leaving aside those who became insane while serving their prison sentence, the proportion in 1890 was over three-quarters.[63]

In most cases, of course, violent offenders were not adjudged insane; they were, however, viewed more and more as noncalculative. *The Times* reflected in 1881 on the change in patterns of crime that had made violence much more rarely a deliberate part of theft and more the province of passion and impulse. "Instead of knocking a man down and rifling his pockets afterwards, the better instructed operator brings out a bubble company or a mine with no very certain whereabouts." If property offenders were less likely nowadays to employ violence, the paper similarly cited recent murders to argue that the motive for contemporary brutality was rarely "greed for gain. [Rather] rage, or jealousy, or the lust for revenge has been the impulse.... It is clear that with all our boasted progress in civilisation we have not yet got rid of the brute. In these days the creature who figures most frequently as the murderer does not belong to what are known as the criminal classes. Whether he does or does not is very much of an accident.... His neighbour's purse may be in no danger from him, but for life or limb, when passion stirs him, he has absolutely no regard." In a "passing moment of madness" he takes away a life. "Murder done for gain," the article concluded, "is an act quite distinct from murder done at the instigation of anger or of settled hatred. Its modern type has been changed from what it used to be."[64]

The more thorough collection and publication of criminal statistics after 1857 supported this perception. What emerged from the thumbnail sketches of capital sentences and reprieves in the annual judicial statistics was the rarity of premeditated murder as compared with killing by impulsive brutality. If such was the case, then the law would have to deal with impulse killing differently than it would with the calculated, planned use of violence. One alternative urged by a growing number of commentators (including *The Times*) was to intervene earlier against lesser acts of violence (usually against women or children) that might eventually lead to murder. Such activist calls also indirectly influenced the image of the murderer, diminishing its autonomy and rationality. An unreflective brute, neither calculating nor freely choosing his behavior, was hardly susceptible to deterrent or denunciatory penalties.

---

[62] *ibid*, 172.

[63] Annual criminal statistics; see in particular *Criminal Statistics for 1889–90*, p. lvii.

[64] *The Times*, Aug. 8, 1881, p. 7.

Some judges did become uneasy with the McNaughten rules. E. W. Cox, a prominent barrister, magistrate, and legal editor, criticized them early, declaring in 1855 that they had been "repudiated by physiologists as opposed to science, [and] rejected by the common sense of juries, as inapplicable to the cases that come before them."[65] Cox suggested instead that the inquiry should be whether the prisoner was laboring under a delusion on the subject of the crime or had committed the crime under an impulse over which he had no control.[66] Though, as with many of his colleagues, the concern he showed at the time of these remarks later waned, Cox never retracted his critical views on the McNaughten rules.

Another leading legal figure, James Fitzjames Stephen, had initially been a strong supporter of the McNaughten formula, since he feared "any course of proceeding which would enlarge the immunities at present extended to madmen."[67] But, more of an intellectual than most of his fellow barristers, he seriously grappled with the newer currents of medical thinking and gradually changed his opinion. In 1855 he conceded the existence of "instances of irresistible impulse" that the McNaughten rules did not recognize, but warned against the "disposition to confound them with unresisted impulses."[68] By 1863, his tone was less hostile as he acknowledged that such a defect of will might be relevant to the criterion set out by the rules:

> The only question which the existence of such impulses can raise in the administration of criminal justice is, whether the particular impulse in question was irresistible as well as unresisted. If it were irresistible a person accused is entitled to be acquitted because the act was not voluntary and was not properly his act. If the impulse was resistible, the fact that it proceeded from disease is no excuse at all.[69]

Yet to find any place for such a defect of will in the intellectualist wording of the McNaughten rules was to strain the language, which went against Stephen's grain. He was thus led in the 1870s to put aside his fear of permissiveness and urge the extension of the formula in order to recognize explicitly the concept of irresistible impulse. Stephen embodied this later view in his draft Homicide Law Amendment Bill of 1874 and his draft Criminal Code of 1879, and repeated it in his *History of English Criminal Law* (1883). Here

---

[65] 26 *Law Times* 145 (1855). See Peter Spiller, *Cox and Crime* (Cambridge: Institute of Criminology, 1985).

[66] 27 *Law Times* 258 (1856).

[67] "On the Policy of Maintaining the Limits at Present Imposed by Law on the Criminal Responsibility of Madmen," *Papers Read before the Juridical Society* (London: Stevens & Norton, 1855), p. 69.

[68] See above, Ch. 2.

[69] *General View of the Criminal Law of England* (London: Macmillan, 1863), p. 95.

again, however, he carefully qualified his argument; not only must an impulse be truly irresistible, but its domination must not be the sufferer's own fault.

> I think that the general rule that a person should not be liable to be punished for any act done when he is deprived by disease of the power of controlling his conduct should be qualified by the words, "unless the absence of the power of control has been caused by his own default."[70]

Despite these qualifications, his desertion of the McNaughten rules was criticized as opening up the Pandora's box of indeterminacy and setting the law on a slippery slope of exculpation; just how could the resistibility of an unresisted impulse be demonstrated? And even the simpler criterion, of prior default, was subject to an infinite regress; how could one be confident that that default was not the result of defects that made the impulse already irresistible? Because of such concerns, Stephen's bill and code did not succeed. Baron Bramwell voiced a widely shared opinion about the bill when he wrote the home secretary to object to introducing the capacity for self-control as a criterion of legal responsibility. "What is the meaning," he fiercely asked,

> of a man being prevented from controlling his conduct? When he is prevented, it is because the preventing motives are strong enough. When he is not prevented, it is because they are not strong enough. The effect of this would be to lessen the preventing motives. A. wishes to commit a rape. Disease of mind weakens his power of acting on motives of chastity, religion, morality, goodness, etc., but fear of the law added to those motives makes him able to resist. The proposal is to take away one of his good motives.[71]

Similarly, if less pungently, an 1879 royal commission concluded:

> The test proposed for distinguishing between such a state of mind [of irresistible impulse] and a criminal motive, the offspring of revenge, hatred, or ungoverned passion, appears to us on the whole not to be practicable or safe, and we are unable to suggest one which would satisfy these requisites and obviate the risk of a jury being misled by considerations of so metaphysical a character.[72]

---

[70] *History of the Criminal Law of England, Vol. 2* (London: Macmillan, 1883), p. 177.

[71] *Special Report from the Select Committee on Homicide Law Amendment Bill,* Q. 183 [letter quoted in evidence]. [P.P. 1874, Vol. 9.] Another high court judge, Lord Blackburn, was less argumentative in his evidence and acknowledged the need for tempering the rigidities of the law. However, he much preferred to leave this task, as traditionally, to the discretion of judges and home secretaries in conducting trials and reviewing capital sentences and keep such qualifications of strict liability out of the formal law.

[72] *Report of the Royal Commission on Indictable Offences 1878–79,* p. 18. [P.P. 1878–79, Vol. 20.]

Most legal authorities, whose practical views on the matter ranged somewhere between Bramwell's and Stephen's, were content to leave the McNaughten rules unamended. They would rely on the discretion of judge and jury to do justice in specific instances. Stephen had spelled out what most of his colleagues preferred to leave unsaid.

Legal practice, if not legal principle, began to reflect these concerns. As Radzinowicz and Hood have noted, "Under the pressure of criticisms in the light of advances in medical science, the interpretation of the McNaughten rules in individual cases often departed from their rigid enunciation."[73] Gradually, the use and the success of the insanity plea and the recognition of insanity by the authorities before and after pleading increased. By 1882, *The Times* was complaining that the insanity plea had become virtually automatic for educated offenders.[74] It traced this corruption of the law to the notion that seemed to be spreading "that there must be something wrong in a man's mental organization before he could have committed a certain crime in certain circumstances."[75] Similarly, Mr. Justice Wills complained to the Home Office in 1890 of "the extreme and growing frequency of the [insanity] defence in cases of murder." His response to this, however, was not to try to rule medical evidence out of court, but to ask the Home Office to supply such evidence to the judge well before the trial to allow sufficient time to evaluate it.[76]

In the late 1870s, under R. A. Cross, the Home Office came to rely upon a number of regular medical advisers, and under his successor, W. V. Harcourt, gathering of medical evidence became routine in all capital cases. Harcourt was readier than his predecessors to transfer prisoners without trial to Broadmoor Criminal Lunatic Asylum and also put through a provision in the Criminal Lunacy Act of 1884 that provided for medical examinations of prisoners under sentence of death to ensure that no lunatic was executed.[77] Soon after he

[73] Radzinowicz and Hood, p. 684.
[74] April 12, 1882.
[75] *ibid.* Later that year, and again the following year, the paper fulsomely praised Old Bailey juries who resisted the medical onslaught and rejected insanity pleas: *The Times*, Nov. 22, 1882, Oct. 20, 1883.
[76] HO 144/236/A51751 (Aug. 12, 1890).
[77] See Nigel Walker, *Crime and Insanity in England, Vol. 1; The Historical Perspective* (Edinburgh: Edinburgh University Press, 1968), pp. 204–10, 228–9. The number administratively diverted to asylums is unclear, except that Harcourt encouraged it until an 1885 judicial protest. For those committed for trial on indictment for murder, the finding of "unfit to plead" jumped in the 1880s (totaling 37 in the decade from 1861 to 1870 and 51 in the decade from 1871 to 1880, it reached 94 in the decade from 1881 to 1890). In addition, the number respited to Broadmoor after sentence of death, less than 10 in earlier decades, reached 21 in the 1880s. [Annual criminal statistics.] Also see Walker, pp. 86, 226–31, 264–65; Nigel Walker and Sarah McCabe, *Crime and Insanity in England, Volume Two: New Solutions and New Problems* (Edinburgh: Edinburgh University Press,

left office, Harcourt observed in Parliament about the commuting of death sentences:

> [T]he fact of a man not being completely master of his actions, through his mind being disturbed, it might be, by some hereditary taint by insanity, was a matter that ought to be taken into account. Neither he nor his immediate predecessors in office had thought that they were bound by the strict legal interpretation of insanity as laid down by the judges in the House of Lords [the McNaughten rules], which he had always thought was much too narrow; and he believed that a much more liberal interpretation had been adopted in all cases where the prerogative of mercy was to be exercised.[78]

Despite the lack of formal alteration of the law, then, a significant change in its administration was occurring. Stimulated by the new climate for penal reform, the Medico-Legal Association set up a committee in 1894 to investigate possibilities for amending the McNaughten rules. Its chairman found that the case for amendment was now more difficult because injustices had become rarer: "Imperfect as the wording of the law is," Dr. Charles Mercier told his colleagues, "we have to look to its practical effect and the practical effect is that justice is done."[79] As Dr. Turnbull observed the following year in presenting the committee's full report to the association, "the McNaughten rules are dying a natural death. . . . Perhaps our best plan is to let them."[80]

Limiting the liability of killers

Even when the quagmire of insanity was avoided, the law's assumptions concerning responsibility were being increasingly scrutinized. Once the death penalty had been practically restricted by 1861 to the crime of murder, murder law itself began to be more carefully examined and consequently it appeared, not only to humanitarian reformers but also to administrators and

---

1973), pp. 23–4, 58–9; Janet Saunders, "Institutionalized Offenders: A Study of the Victorian Institution and Its Inmates, with special reference to Late Nineteenth Century Warwickshire," unpublished Ph.D. thesis, Warwick University, 1983, Ch. 7; Radzinowicz and Hood, pp. 676–85.

[78] 3 PD 305, c. 780–1 (May 11, 1886).

[79] Dr. Charles Mercier, *Journal of Mental Science 41* (1895), 665–74. As *The Times* had observed in 1894, criminal law had become more "flexible . . . in [the] presence of exceptional circumstances" than might be supposed. "The legal view and the medical view of criminal responsibility appear very widely divergent when set forth polemically. In practice they approximate much more closely." Sept. 1, 1894, p. 9.

[80] *Journal of Mental Science 42* (1896), 217. Thus, the Committee on Criminal Responsibility recommended no action to press for new legislation.

jurists, to be in need of revison. At the very moment when the movement for rationalization and uniformity had triumphed in the Criminal Law Consolidating Acts of 1861 and the Prison Acts of 1864 and 1865, more and more persons involved in the criminal justice system began to exhibit uneasiness over the law's rigid conceptions of behavior and its causation, and the unrealistic demands it consequently placed upon many offenders' powers of calculation and will. The 1866 Royal Commission on Capital Punishment criticized the law's overstrict presumptions of responsibility:

> It has been established by the decision of our courts, that no provocation by words, looks or gestures, however contemptuous and insulting, nor by any trespass merely against lands or goods, is sufficient to free the party killing from the guilt of murder, if he kills with a deadly weapon, or in any manner showing an intention to kill, or do grievous bodily harm. In these cases, though the suddenness of the provocation may rebut in point of fact the *express malice aforethought*, it is not allowed, on account of its supposed insignificance, to overcome the *general malice aforethought*, which is implied by the *law*, by the wickedness and cruelty of the deed.... The practical results of this state of things is most unsatisfactory. A man who, in a sudden fit of passion, aroused by insult to himself or his wife, kills the person who offers the insult, is, by law, guilty of the same crime, and liable to the same principle, as the assassin, who has long meditated and brooded over his crime.[81]

The commission recommended establishing two degrees of murder, as had been done in some American states, in order to separate unpremeditated from premeditated homicide and to void the former's liability to the penalty of death. The thrust of such revision would be to diminish formal criminal liability; this was the source both of much of its appeal and of the suspicion with which the proposal was treated. Whereas the other chief recommendation of the commission – abolition of public execution – was promptly enacted, on the question of amending the law of murder the government, now a Conservative one, responded by introducing a bill but letting it die, and the Liberal government that followed had more pressing concerns. Radzinowicz and Hood have recounted the long series of unsuccessful attempts subsequently made by private members, and, finally, by Sir William Harcourt as home secretary in 1882, to bring in bills either instituting two degrees of murder or introducing more scope for extenuating circumstances. These authors ascribe the bills' repeated failure to the practical difficulties of formulating precise distinctions that would not themselves create new anomalies and to the obscurantist resistance of most of the judiciary, which exaggerated the real but not insuperable

---

[81] *Report of the Royal Commission on Capital Punishment*, 1866, p. xlix.

practical problem.[82] All this is true, but this issue points as well to a deep-rooted reluctance to let go of the image of criminal offenders as essentially, or normally, autonomous and responsible. Judges might be ready to do this in particular cases, but they balked at acknowledging such a change in principle.

In 1866 Stephen summed up the dilemma when he noted to the Capital Punishment Commission that juries were not turning against the death penalty, but had become increasingly reluctant to convict in cases they did not consider real murder.[83] Some years later, the Murder Law Amendment bill (1874) he drafted for the Liberal M.P., Russell Gurney, explicitly noted a variety of extenuating conditions and circumstances often allowed for by judges and juries but that had never been statutorily acknowledged. Though a fierce critic of sentimental humanitarianism, Stephen, a good utilitarian, was made most uncomfortable by what he saw as the growing dissonance between strict principle and flexible practice. "The object of the Bill," he told a select committee, was "to express, in definite language, what I understand ot be the unexpressed ... the working, law of the day." He particularly hoped to remove the scandal created by the sentencing of many persons to death without any serious intention of carrying out the penalty; he feared this undermined popular respect for the law. The statutory simplicity of the law of murder, he argued, by being so different from its administration, actually made the law appear to a thoughtful citizen, who was ever more aware through newspapers and public discussion, to be in actual practice "a kind of chaos."[84] Stephen's bill, like those of some others, sought to formally limit the liability of persons not in full command of themselves, by reason of either pressures from within (particularly, by intolerable provocation) or, as we have seen, from within (overpowering impulses). But some judges – and most vociferously, Baron Bramwell – feared in both recognitions the weakening of social control. Judicial opposition proved too much, and the 1874 bill was dropped.

Efforts to amend the law of murder continued, however, and came closest to success when Home Secretary Harcourt had a bill drafted and circulated to the cabinet in 1882. This bill would have made it necessary to prove willful intent to kill in order to apply the death penalty, thus expanding the grounds for limiting liability. But, again, nothing came of this initiative, which raised objections even from Harcourt's own officials as too drastic a revision of voluntarist principles. As his chief legal adviser complained, "semi-insanity, not enough to justify acquittal, but enough to modify the criminality of the offence, is altogether a new principle in our law."[85] After this failure, murder

---

[82] Radzinowicz and Hood, pp. 661–71.

[83] *Report of the Royal Commission on Capital Punishment*, 1866, Q. 1995.

[84] *Special Report from the Select Committee on Homicide Law Amendment Bill*, 1874, Qs. 17, 13, 88 [P.P. 1874, v. 9].

[85] Memorandum from Godfrey Lushington, 1882, HO45/9643/A35731/5.

law remained unamended until 1957. Yet if voluntarist principles had been preserved and statutory reform of murder law rebuffed, the idea of semi-responsibility was becoming ever more rooted in practice. From the late 1870s, a rising proportion of those indicted for murder were found mentally incompetent at some stage of the criminal justice process.[86] The taking of life was increasingly associated with unsoundness of mind.[87]

Below the grave level of liability to the death sentence, and particularly in the lesser realm of crimes against property rather than person, acknowledgment of limitations upon responsibility was even more readily gaining ground. For one category of offender after another, qualifications to the norm of personal responsibility were increasingly being noted and distinctions drawn between the shrinking number of offenders for whom deterrent sanctions were seen as just and effective and the growing numbers for whom they were not.

Theft

In the diminishing insistence upon personal responsibility, the treatment of theft paralleled that for most forms of homicide. As with the latter, the statistics showed that the amount of traditional theft was in decline; the proportion of trials to population began to fall in the mid-1860s and continued to do so down to World War I.[88] With a relaxation of fear of crime and the spread in the 1880s of social conscience, the responsibility of society was increasingly stressed. The argument was made by criminals as well as by social reformers. Michael Davitt recounted to the 1895 Departmental Committee on Prisons a conversation he had had with a Dartmoor burglar. "Put yourself in my position," the convict had told him.

> I never knew my father or my mother. My first recollection is of being turned out of a workhouse. I fell among thieves. I got educated in crime. I learned to read and write in prison. Unlike you I have had no moral

[86] See Walker, *Crime and Insanity*, pp. 86–7, 122–3, 226–31, 264–5. Whereas in the mid-Victorian years, about one in seven of those brought to trial for murder were either declared unfit to plead, acquitted as insane, or certified by a Home Office inquiry after conviction, by the years immediately preceding World War I the proportion had risen to more than one in three. [Chadwick, "Bureaucratic Mercy," p. 477 (Table 5).]

[87] In tension with the overall trend to perceive mental incapacity behind the taking of life was a mounting intolerance – expressed in parliamentary legislation and also (it would appear) in prosecutions, verdicts, and sentencing – of violence perpetrated against women or nonnewborn children. This tension has indeed increased through the twentieth century; the subject very much needs further exploration.

[88] See the table drawn from annual criminal statistics in Gatrell, "Decline of Theft and Violence," p. 282.

training. I hold that man is naturally a thief. Take for instance a child in
its mother's arms; anything that excites its fancy it wants to get, and if
that natural feeling is not corrected by parental training and moral
influence and education it gets stronger as the child grows older. I am
such a product of your civilisation. You allowed me to grow up with these
animal instincts uncorrected, and then you send me to prison when I
exercise them.[89]

Toward a related form of misappropriation of property – that of debt
default, both elite and popular – the law, as we have seen, was gradually
adopting a less punitive attitude. Bankruptcy was losing its harsh stigma and
nonwillful debt default had been relieved in 1869 of penal liability. The
continued imprisonment, as willful defaultors, of substantial numbers of small
debtors after 1869 began to draw increasing fire, and though the courts
resisted formal change in the law the length of time such persons spent in jail
steadily fell.[90]

In the same years, complaints rose in press and Parliament about the
traditionally harsh sentencing practices for theft.[91] In fact, from midcentury
through the 1870s, most criticism of sentencing had been of its excessive
leniency. Now, despite the fact that sentences were shortening, the opposite
charge began to proliferate and predominate. Indeed, when the humane trend
was noticed, it was seen as misapplied to the least merited types of cases –
those committing violent offenses but less than homicide. Liberal, and
occasionally Conservative, M.P.s and reformers pejoratively contrasted the
lenient sentences given to wife beaters and other offenders with the harsh
sentences imposed on those convicted of crimes against property, especially
comparatively petty offenses. Although complaints continued to mount of undue judicial leniency shown to acts of violence against the weak (women and
children), they were now increasingly linked with arguments for shorter
sentences for petty property offenders. Street criminals were rarely now being
described as dangerous beasts or self-willed villains, but rather as almost pathetic incompetents. In this context, current sentencing practices seemed
misdirected and, for the first time since the abolition of capital sanctions for
property crime, official interest reappeared in realigning penalties for offenses
against the person and offenses against property. From 1880 on, the Liberal

---

[89] *Report of Departmental Committee on Prisons*, 1895, 389 (Q. 11,393).
[90] G. R. Rubin, "Law, Poverty and Imprisonment for Debt, 1869–1914" in eds. G. R.
Rubin and David Sugarman, *Law, Economy and Society 1750–1914* (Abingdon: Professional Books, 1984), p. 264. However, the numbers did not fall; indeed, from 1891 to
1906 they rose markedly. [Rubin, Table B.] Two competing explanations are an intensification of social control in an age of expanding consumer credit, and a diminishing fear and
stigma of imprisonment in an age of penal reform; probably both factors were operating.
[91] See examples cited in Radzinowicz and Hood, pp. 741–47, and Thomas, *Constraints*.

M.P. D.H. Macfarlane kept before the public eye the lack of seriousness with which the courts treated assaults against women and children as compared to offenses against property; he called for both greater judicial protection of the helpless and more lenient sentencing of petty property offenders. In 1889, the House of Commons debated the issue of sentencing, with several Liberals denouncing the continuing imbalance between the severity meted out to property offenders and the leniency enjoyed by perpetrators of violence, particularly in offenses against women and children. The debate even produced calls for a royal commission.[92]

Underneath this divergence in concern about these two categories of objectionable offenses lay several broad developments: the increasingly successful control of street crime, which relaxed fears; the spread of material prosperity (and the appearance of insurance against theft), which lessened the economic importance of the offenses; a growth of democratic sensitivities, which raised concern for the weaker members of society, disproportionately the victims of violence more than of theft (as Macfarlane pointed out, all had a person but only a minority had significant property); and, not unconnected with democratization, a weakening belief in the chosen, willed character of deviant behavior. The advance of democracy from 1867, and particularly after 1884, was certainly making it more difficult for the state to judge sternly offenders who might now be members of the body politic (or, more likely, friends, relations, and neighbors of members) and to consign them to increasingly repellent punishments. Just as the entry of growing numbers of the poor into the status of citizen gradually and indirectly weakened the punitive thrust of the Poor Law, so criminal policy similarly came to show this influence. And alongside an emerging sympathy for the difficulties of working class life went a diminishing assumption of the efficacy of deterrence. For a consistent deterrent philosophy, there need be no disparity in severely punishing a calculated offense like theft, with the aim of preventing future occurrences, while leniently treating uncalculated crimes unlikely to be repeated or imitated, such as that of men murdering their wives, usually in fits of rage. Indeed, defenders of judicial severity against thieves and burglars stressed the need to keep punishments high enough to overcome the powerful temptation to steal.[93] As the civil servant C. E. Troup observed to the Depart-

---

[92] 3 PD 336, c. 1003–39 (May 24, 1889). The previous year this argument had been made by the former director of Criminal Investigation at Scotland Yard, Howard Vincent, who urged the home secretary to impress upon the judges "the importance attached by the public in the interest of general safety to the treatment of offences against the person on a scale of punishment at least equal to that adopted in offences against property." [3 PD 325, c. 755 (April 27, 1888).]

[93] See "Judges and Police," *Saturday Review 53* (1882), pp. 288–9, an argument that the temptation to steal made more severe sentences necessary.

mental Committee on Prisons in 1895, the tendency to punish property offenses more severely than offenses involving violence without theft

> arises simply from the fact that offenses against property are those by which a person can gain his living, and there is, therefore, a temptation to go on committing them; whereas in the case of offences against the person they are generally committed in hot blood, and are not at any rate the sort of thing one would ever get his living by.[94]

However, as perceptions of the potential power of individual will and the consequent efficacy of deterrence diminished, such differences in penalties were losing functional justification and becoming ever more widely perceived as unjust disparities.

In this new climate of opinion the practice of cumulative sentencing, which had spread among judges and magistrates since the decline of transportation and was intended to make deterrence more effective against repeat offenders, was appearing pointlessly cruel. Not only reformers, but even the chairman of the Prison Commission, Edmund Du Cane, in 1884 criticized excessively long sentences. Home Secretary Harcourt took up Du Cane's suggestions and pressed the issue within the government. He was eager to reduce the length of sentences, since the success of efforts to moralize the populace now allowed, in his judgment, a relaxation of penal sanctions. He passed on Du Cane's memorandum on sentencing to the Lord Chancellor, with a strong endorsement on wider grounds than Du Cane's. Citing "a solid and stable improvement in the moral staple and fibre of the population" and the increasing ease in managing prisoners, he argued that "it may . . . be safely concluded, that we have successfully tapped the fountains of crime, and that the labour and the expense to which we have gone in the improvement of the social soil, has not been without its results." With the crime rate steadily falling, he proposed that it was time "to consider whether severity may not be relaxed," particularly in "ordinary cases."[95] Again and again, arguments from both sides of the political aisle attacked the disproportion between punishments awarded to repeated petty offenders and to those guilty of violent personal crimes; the brutal ruffian who abused his mistress, wife, or children was now seen as a more serious threat to society than the pickpocket, thief, or burglar who stole from strangers. As fear of street violence and street theft was fading away, domestic violence was moving to center stage; the discovery of domestic violence was the obverse of the growing sense of public security. Similarly, early advocates of cumulative sentencing, like William Tallack of the Howard Association, began in the 1880s to criticize the excesses of magistrates in dealing with petty

[94] *Report of the Departmental Committee on Prisons*, 1895, 410 (Q. 11,614).
[95] Correspondence on the Administration of Criminal Law, *Sentences and Punishments— Memoranda*, HO 45/18479/565861 (1884).

offenders. In 1889, Tallack cited some outrageous examples, such as that of one man who

> for stealing a piece of canvas, was sentenced to twelve years' penal servitude, to be followed by seven years' supervision. He had already undergone six minor detentions in jail and three sentences of penal servitude, amounting to twenty-two years, and including one of ten years for stealing a shovel. So that this poor weak creature has been committed to thirty-four years of imprisonment, with seven years' supervision, all for petty thefts; whilst few of the most atrocious ruffians, violators, or burglars, of England, have had half such an amount of punishment meted out to them![96]

The feared depredators of the early and mid-Victorian years had become the "poor weak creature(s)" clogging up the courts and jails.

Criticisms of the misapplication of cumulative sentencing to pathetic rather than brutal offenders yielded center stage during the later 1880s and 1890s to outright attacks upon cumulative sentencing itself, as applied to the mass of ordinary property offenders. C. H. Hopwood, a sometime Liberal M.P. and recorder of Liverpool, mounted a personal campaign against the cumulative principle. He claimed by 1889 to have dealt with nearly 2,000 prisoners without once imposing penal servitude and argued that the lack of any subsequent crime wave in Liverpool demonstrated that "severity shown in long imprisonment, in cumulative punishment, is unnecessary, and if unnecessary then obviously wasteful of the public means and resources, and therefore cruel." Listing a number of "painful and unjustifiable" sentences passed by adherents of the cumulative principle, Hopwood characterized those judges who imposed such "gross and successive sentences for comparatively harmless thefts" as, ironically, "men who would shrink from inflicting the slightest pain upon a fellow-creature, themselves merciful in other relations of life," but they "consider themselves bound in obedience to a cold hard theory to blot out from existence for five, ten, twelve or more years, poor wretches whose offences are in themselves of slight gravity."[97]

Hopwood heralded release from such bondage, though many magistrates were not eager to throw off their chains and regarded Hopwood askance.[98] Yet his activities forced the issue into consideration at the highest levels. In 1890 the House of Lords, with Hopwood clearly in mind,[99] debated the cumulative

---

[96] W. Tallack, *Penological and Preventive Principles* (London: Wertheimer, Lea, 1889), p. 171.
[97] Address to the grand jury at Liverpool Quarter Sessions, Oct., 1889, quoted in Thomas, *Constraints*, pp. 8–19.
[98] See for example 3 PD 336 (May 24, 1889), c. 1041.
[99] See the remarks of Lord Herschell, quoted in Thomas, p. 19.

principle on a motion for an inquiry into the principles followed by judges in sentencing offenders.[100] Hopwood's views drew support from a powerful quarter, that of Lord Chief Justice Coleridge. Coleridge observed that, while he "would never dream of acting upon such fallacy as that prior convictions of the criminal are not to be taken into account in passing sentence," agreed that the cumulative principle had been taken too far:

> I have known a woman to be sent to penal servitude for fifteen years for stealing a shovel. It may be quite true that she had previously stolen six-teen or seventeen shovels, and it may appear to some that that would jus-tify the fifteen years penal servitude; but I do not think so, and nothing will ever persuade me that I ought to punish an offender such as that woman as I ought to punish a person who has inflicted gross and detest-able cruelty on man, woman or child. In cases like this the punishment and the offences are not correlative, and whenever there is an excess of punishment, the minds of intelligent men are set against the law instead of being enlisted on its side and against the criminals.[101]

Although this debate, like later ones in Parliament and the press, led to no consensus and no legislation, the practice of awarding heavy cumulative sentences to petty property offenders seems to have become less common. While courts continued to pass sentences of penal servitude on offenders convicted of minor larcenies, the length of such sentences was diminishing. Between 1894 (when the revision of the criminal statistics affords for the first time some evidence on this point) and 1900, an average of 95 persons convicted of minor larceny were sentenced to penal servitude, but less than five sentences in excess of five years were passed on average in each year, and only three sentences in excess of seven years were imposed for this offense during the whole period.[102]

Thus, like so much else of the voluntarist apparatus of Victorian criminal policy, cumulative sentencing was not formally repudiated but as the urgency behind it evaporated and its objects came to be seen as less threatening and more needful of help rather than retribution, it came to be seen as ever less necessary and thus ever harsher and more repugnant. By the debates of the early 1890s, this method of enhancing deterrence was clearly on the defensive, ever more purely strictly the weapon of last resort for exasperated magistrates who did not know what else to do with chronic small-time thieves. Indeed, de-terrence itself seemed less and less an answer to the persistent petty property crime that took up so much of the time and effort of criminal justice.

[100] 3 PD 343 (Apr. 21, 1890), c. 924–55.
[101] *ibid.*, c. 942.
[102] See Thomas, p. 23, summarizing the annual criminal statistics.

Juvenile offenders

Juveniles had traditionally constituted a disproportionate share of petty thieves, and this group also was to make up the largest category of offenders of diminished responsibility. During the Victorian era, the public conceptualization of childhood and youth evident in social policy passed through a watershed that took two related forms – greater protectiveness and lessened legal responsibility. In the first half of the century, driven by both fear and the desire to promote moralization, magistrates had actually held juveniles if anything *more* liable to criminal sanctions than earlier, frequently ignoring the traditional informal common law presumption that a child under 14 was not legally responsible.[103] This tide of juvenile criminalization crested in the 1840s. Age distinctions entered the criminal justice process with an 1847 act making some petty juvenile offenders triable without juries; that measure, however, did not touch the question of responsibility. Similarly, the 1854 Reformatory Schools Act, which began the diversion of juveniles from jails to reformatories, dealt only with disposition and not with formal legal liability. The reformatory school pioneers of the 1850s, as we have seen, concerned themselves with making the treatment of juvenile offenders more reformative, for the most part leaving to one side the more contentious questions of legal responsibility; even the treatment they espoused retained much of the moralistic severity accepted for adult offenders.

By the 1870s, however, juvenile crime seemed to have been tamed. In his last report, in 1875, Inspector of Reformatory Schools Sydney Turner struck a new note, pointing to a dramatic change that had come over his charges:

> In addition to this mere falling off in number [of juvenile criminals], the marked amelioration in the character of the offence and the criminal status of the offender must be taken into account. The mass of the boys and girls now sent to Reformatories have very little of the old thorough viciousness and premature depravity which had to be encountered in the earlier stages of the Reformatory movement. I have taken pains to ascertain the views and consult the experience of most of our more important schools on this point, and find them pretty unanimous in their testimony, that the inmates of their schools are now much more remarkable for their dull, neglected condition, than their active wickedness, and that though not so apprehensive for purposes of instruction, they are far more easy and submissive to manage.[104]

[103] See Chapter 2.
[104] Quoted by H. A. Bruce, "Address on Crime, Delivered at the Opening of the Congress of the National Association for the Promotion of Social Science, Brighton, 1875," in *Lectures and Addresses by the Rt. Hon. Henry Austin Bruce, First Lord Aberdare* (London: C.J. Thynne, 1917), pp. 250–1.

While Turner was declaring victory in the first war on juvenile crime, members of the next generation of reformers were already beginning to describe juvenile offenders as true victims – of their parents' mistreatment, their slum environments, and even their biological constitutions. From this angle, the moral and social distinctions of Turner's generation were no longer visible; dangerous children were not clearly distinguishable from deprived or defective children, who had not (as yet) run afoul of the law. As J. A. Picton, M.P., observed in 1888, reformatory children "have indeed been convicted of crime, but they are really of the same character as those sent to industrial schools."[105] The clarion call of the new approach was Benjamin Waugh's 1873 tract, *The Gaol Cradle – Who Rocks It?* A Congregational minister who was serving on the first London School Board, and was thus deeply involved in getting parents to allow their children schooling, Waugh attacked the application of the criminal justice system to children and in particular their imprisonment. He sought instead a system of juvenile courts and mitigated treatment that would allow for childish weakness. "Ignorance," he declared, "is the secret of harsh judgment, as it is of blundering legislation also. On acquaintance even the gravest cases appear to be partially excusable."[106] Waugh's arguments were taken up by other reformers. The Howard Association, whose chairman was also serving on the London School Board, in 1875 sent a deputation that included Waugh to the home secretary complaining of the imprisonment of children as young as 7 and 8. As the association noted in its annual report the following year, many children, "wretched little victims of poverty and neglect," were jailed for "mere peccadilloes which the children of the middle and upper classes generally commit with impunity."[107]

Seeking understanding rather than condemnatory treatment of juveniles, Waugh (perhaps influenced by experiences on the London School Board) and his supporters in the Howard Association redirected the need to place blame and to punish by targeting the parents (as at the same time calls were growing to place more liability for industrial accidents upon employers, for drunkenness upon brewers and publicans, and for domestic conflict upon the husband and/or father). Waugh simultaneously urged removing children from the criminal justice system and extending criminal sanctions to a wide range of parental misbehavior – both parental encouragement or tolerance of their offspring's criminal activities and, more widely, parental mistreatment and neglect. In 1884, the London Society for the Prevention of Cruelty to Chil-

---

[105] 3 PD 327 (June 13, 1888), c. 65. Industrial schools had been established to train compulsorily vagrant and destitute children.
[106] *The Gaol Cradle – Who Rocks It?* (London: Strahan & Co., 1873), p. 26.
[107] Howard Association, *Annual Report*, 1876, pp. 11–12. The association distributed 300 copies of *The Gaol Cradle* at the expense of its chairman.

dren was founded, and Waugh soon became its director. The society made parental neglect its central cause, and its prime method under Waugh was the use of the criminal law. Parental malefactors were detected and prosecuted with great fervor, and legislation extending criminal sanctions was sought and, in 1889 and 1893, achieved. Indeed, the transference of children into a category of diminished responsibility was made more politically and emotionally feasible by a simultaneous heightening of blame directed at bad parents. Similarly, this stigmatization of parents made more acceptable the removal of working-class children from their parents to reformatory or industrial schools or other forms of welfarist supervision, whose expansion Waugh and other crusaders for the decriminalization of children generally supported. The new child protection movement was thus able to draw strength from both the excusatory implications of the newer social and medical perspectives and also the earlier denunciatory and deterrent traditions of the criminal law.

The number of children and young people under 17 years committed to prison was already declining when these calls were made, from about 10 percent of committals in 1857 down to about 4 percent twenty years later (reflecting in part the growth of reformatory schools).[108] But the issue of child imprisonment was only directly taken up in the late 1870s. In 1878, as a new Factory Act was raising the ceiling of childhood for the purposes of employment to age 14, Home Secretary Cross's parliamentary under-secretary assured the Howard Association that his chief "felt an especial interest with regard to the subject of the punishment of children, which was in such an unsatisfactory condition at the present time, and with regard to which the Government hoped shortly to be able to effect some improvements."[109] The Summary Jurisdiction Act of the following year extensively altered the definition and treatment of juvenile offenders. The act encouraged a lowering of penalties for first offenders and also formally limited for the first time children's liability to trial (though only under age 12); henceforth, not only children but juveniles between ages 12 and 17 were to be categorized apart from adults.[110]

Cross's successor, Sir William Harcourt, strongly endorsed this measure, declaring it "altogether improper" to imprison a child even for a few days for offenses like breaking windows, however often repeated; from such treatment "neither he nor others can derive any possible benefit."[111] Harcourt went much beyond his predecessor, however, delivering a series of speeches against

---

[108] Annual criminal statistics, cited in Radzinowicz and Hood, p. 624.

[109] Howard Association, *Annual Report*, 1878, p. 6.

[110] See S. Magarey, "The Reclaimers: A Study of the Reformatory Movement in England and Wales," unpublished Ph.D. thesis, Australian National University, 1980, 255.

[111] Correspondence in *The Times*, Sept., 1880, quoted in Radzinowicz and Hood, p. 625.

juvenile imprisonment, and ordering the review of all committals of children under 15.[112] He used favorable public response to his campaign to place pressure upon magistrates, observing to one bench that "recent discussion" had shown that "it seems to be all but universally admitted ... that imprisonment in the common gaol is not the best form of punishment to be applied in the case of petty offences committed by very young children." It was not necessary, he reminded the magistrates, to reconstruct the law formally: "Although the letter of the Law in many cases makes no distinction between the treatment of the same offence by an adult and a child, most persons will recognize that in the administration of that Law it is proper that a difference should be made not only in the quantity but in the quality of the punishment to be awarded in the two cases."[113] By remitting sentences on children in particular cases that had gained press attention and pressuring magistrates to find alternatives to jailing, Harcourt achieved a sharp decrease in the number of juveniles imprisoned. The number of offenders under 12 years of age jailed fell from 866 in 1879–80 to 528 the following year and to 250 in 1885–86; those between the ages of 12 and 16 dropped less dramatically, from, 6,550 to 5,051, and to 4,563 by 1885–86.[114]

Harcourt's determination to reduce the imprisonment of children made him the first home secretary to oppose the long-standing requirement for a brief preliminary imprisonment of convicted juvenile offenders before committal to reformatory schools. In this, he sided with the position long held by the humanitarians within the movement, and he now claimed to be speaking for most of the magistrates and other authorities whose views he had canvassed.[115] Yet his own Royal Commission on Reformatory and Industrial Schools, chaired by his Liberal predecessor H. A. Bruce, only went so far as to recommend for offenders under 14 years of age replacing preliminary imprisonment by whipping in the case of boys and 7 to 14 day's solitary confinement for girls.[116] Although the resistance of most reformatory managers preserved this requirement until 1893, contemporaries attributed much of the gradual fall after 1879 in the population of reformatory schools (while that of industrial schools, which had been established for noncriminal offenders, continued to rise) to growing magisterial reluctance to impose the prison taint.[117]

[112] 3 PD 256, c. 1279 (Sept. 4, 1880).

[113] HO 43/134, G. Lushington to Oxfordshire Clerk of the Peace, Nov. 6, 1880.

[114] Annual criminal statistics. Once in prison, however, juveniles continued until 1896 to be treated in most respects as adults. [Magarey, 251.]

[115] 3 PD 260, c. 1820 (May 5, 1881). In this, he seemed to be reflecting the trend of enlightened opinion. The Social Science Association at its 1880 meeting had voted with only one dissentient for abolition of preliminary imprisonment. [NAPSS, *Transactions 1880*, 399.]

[116] See Radzinowicz and Hood, pp. 204–5.

[117] See I. Fish, 1891, cited in Radzinowicz and Hood, p. 205.

As in murder law reform, so in juvenile offender reform, when Harcourt went beyond administrative scrutiny of individual cases to an apparent questioning of the principle of holding people responsible for their misdeeds, strong resistance was roused. His quoting in a speech the remark of a school inspector that "a child under fourteen years of age can hardly be considered responsible for his actions," drew a sharp private protest from none other than the "children's Peer," Lord Shaftesbury. "If that be so," Shaftesbury pointed out,

> no child should be punished.... But I am bold enough to hold an opinion diametrically opposite; and having been much among children all my life; and having no little acquaintance with the criminal, and embryo-criminal classes, I do not hesitate to affirm, that a judgment between right and wrong, and a sense of responsibility, may be imparted to children of very tender years; and that these sentiments form the only solid, and true, basis of real education.[118]

Yet Shaftesbury, ever sensitive to youthful suffering, supported most of Harcourt's practical efforts to diminish both the length of imprisonment and the harshness of prison discipline for law-breaking children.

Harcourt's plans drew a similarly ambivalent response from the other leading mid-Victorian parliamentary spokesman for reform in the treatment of juvenile offenders, C. B. Adderley, now Baron Norton. Norton supported diminished imprisonment of juveniles, but like Shaftesbury he had qualms about Harcourt's tendency to exempt juveniles from the application of voluntarist principles.[119] Norton urged Harcourt to consider greater recourse to corporal punishment instead of incarceration. This was not what Harcourt had in mind. But to Norton, whipping and reformation were not at all in conflict because before the process of reform could commence, "those convicted of actual crime must be punished." If reformatory and industrial schools were one of his enthusiasms, corporal punishment was another. As well as cosponsoring the Reformatory Schools Act of 1854, Norton had authored the Security Against Violence Act of 1863 (popularly known as the Garroter's Act), which instituted the penalty of whipping in addition to imprisonment for adults who committed robbery with violence. He had also supported

---

[118] Shaftesbury to Harcourt, Nov. 10, 1880: Bodleian Library, Oxford, Harcourt MS 94/195–6.

[119] Norton lived into the twentieth century, long enough to see his combination of humanitarian concern for neglected children with firm attachment to corporal punishment become a mark of eccentricity, giving him by then the appearance of a man who had survived his time; yet it was in the reformist mainstream of the 1860s and 1870s. The only work on Norton remains William S. Childe-Pemberton. *Life of Lord Norton 1814–1905: Statesman and Philanthropist* (London: J. Murray, 1909).

Governor Eyre in the great controversy over the latter's bloody suppression of a rebellion in Jamaica in 1866. Challenges to authority abroad and at home, he insisted, must be punished. Once punishment was carried out, Norton was quite advanced in his views; he urged Harcourt, for example, to merge the reformatory with the industrial schools established for noncriminal but vagrant children (a reform not accomplished until 1933). "The two," he argued, "have become practically assimilated." Both were in his view simply "schools for children not otherwise provided. They cannot differ in treatment, and the inmates of both are the same class of children – generally neglected and living in mischief or actual crime."[120] From 1881 on, he introduced bills to accomplish this merger. He remained insistent, though, about punishment, and his bills also provided for extending the use of the birch, which cost him the essential support of many Liberals. Norton's, and Shaftesbury's, responses to Harcourt's initiatives suggest that a sea change in the meaning and application of punishment could proceed gradually as long as the underlying issues were not made explicit.

In like fashion, Harcourt dismayed even those reformatory activists who supported his opposition to imprisonment when he went further, extending his criticism to reformatory and industrial schools as well. Harcourt did not confine himself to particular abuses, but rather showed himself highly sceptical of their very rationale. He questioned whether, as Bruce assured him, these institutions were clearly distinguishable from prisons and a boon to their inmates. Harcourt rejected the claim that they furnished the moral education that large numbers of the children of the poor were in dire need of and that their parents could not be relied upon to provide.

By the 1870s, the rapid expansion of reformatory and industrial schools promoted by mid-Victorian home secretaries had aroused governmental concern, in which were blended financial, moral, libertarian, and even humanitarian objections.[121] Richard Cross set stricter legal guidelines both to protect

---

[120] Lord Norton (C.B. Adderley) to Harcourt, Nov. 17, 1880: Bodleian Library, Harcourt MS 94/199–200.

[121] The permanent under-secretary of the Treasury joined financial and moral concerns in warning Harcourt against further developing the educational side of reformatory schools, which he feared would increase the attractiveness of these institutions, their charge upon the Treasury, and "tend to discourage independence and self-respect in classes above those from which the children are supposed to be drawn." [Ralph Lingen to Harcourt, Nov. 14, 1880, Harcourt MS 94/197–8.] Concern over the growing financial burden was heightened by the diminishing political acceptability of efforts to recover costs from parents. In 1877 parliamentary under-secretary H. Selwin Ibbetson cited "the disfavor with which the public view the pressure put on parents (more especially by school boards)" in refusing Reformatory School Inspector Col. Inglis's request for more funds for bringing actions against parents. [HO 137/1, Nov. 24, 1877.] Not surprisingly, the amount recovered from parents fell continually thereafter, until the effort was abandoned just before World War I. [Annual criminal statistics.]

parental rights and to prevent excessively severe treatment of the children; he also discouraged magistrates from committing children under age 13, which he called "almost . . . a miscarriage of justice."[122] His 1879 Summary Jurisdiction Act initiated a long-term decline in reformatory committals. Harcourt took this effort much further, seeing little difference between reformatories and jails. In his challenge to the reformatory movement Harcourt combined traditional Whig hostility to interference with "the rights of freeborn Englishmen" with a newer populist defense of working-class family life and a scepticism about the benefits of institutional disciplinary moralization. Noting in Parliament that "there are a great many cases of children sent to a reformatory for a long period for which there is no justification," he subjected these institutions to much closer Home Office scrutiny than ever before. More forcefully, Harcourt privately complained to Bruce (who was much more sympathetic to reformatories) that although the diminution of crime and immorality had lessened the need for them, these institutions had continued to expand, and were becoming instruments of "tyranny":

> Many if not most of the cases in these schools now are those of children who for some petty act of naughtiness (such as our own children commit every day) are seized upon, haled off by the Police before the Magistrate, who without any inquiry into the character of the home of the parents commits them to Prison and takes them away from good or happy homes for seven or eight years and then sends them off to sea or the Colonies without their parents being even allowed to know where they have gone . . . . The greatest of all offenders . . . are the School Board Managers. They get hold of children of the tenderest age who are simply truants and for mere non-attendance at School commit them to Prison for eight years and dispose of them just as they think fit without the knowledge and consent of their parents, often parents just as good as you or I.[123]

Such views, though not expressed publicly with such pungency, were

---

[122] HO 45/9394/49874/1, Circular to Reformatory School Managers, Dec. 1, 1875. Though a majority of managers seemed to agree, a vocal minority made a point of citing cases to show that, as one asserted, "the moral badness of children is very often irrespective of age." [*ibid*,/57.] Cross insisted on careful monitoring of punishments and disciplinary isolation; as his permanent under-secretary wrote the clerk of the Liverpool School Board in regard to their industrial school: "Children differ so widely in character and constitution that a degree of seclusion, not at all hurtful to some, might be productive of serious injury to others, and Mr. Cross thinks it essential that the utmost care should be taken to avoid all risk of the proposed treatment pressing too heavily upon a child without attracting the immediate attention of the authorities." [HO 137/1, Jan. 11, 1878.]

[123] 3 PD 287, c. 1149 (May 2, 1884); HO 45/9629/A22484: Harcourt to Lord Aberdare (Henry Bruce), Dec. 27, 1884; this letter was in reply to one by Bruce defending reformatory managers.

clearly communicated and roused much resentment among reformatory managers and their supporters. Harcourt was charged with casting unfair aspersions upon a dedicated body of men. "The tone of Sir William Harcourt's circulars throughout," typically complained one set of managers (just after Harcourt had left office), "seem[s] to infer that we Managers are a tyrannical and headstrong (if not interested) set of persons whom it is the duty of the Secretary of State to check and discourage as far as possible." More generally, Harcourt was charged with condoning and even encouraging social immorality. In protesting a Home Office circular prohibiting the enlistment or apprenticeship of reformatory boys without parental consent, a group of these managers noted that, contrariwise, the 1884 Royal Commission on Reformatory Schools, chaired by Bruce, had recommended extending their powers of control until 18 years of age "to prevent that interference on the part of worthless parents which the late Home Secretary has done so much to uphold and encourage."[124]

Nevertheless, while imprisonment of children was falling year by year, the reformatory schools actually were losing inmates.[125] Instead, ever more dependent on government financing, these institutions were becoming themselves tarred with the penal taint. Coming to be seen as "handmaids of the Prison system," reformatory school managers increasingly found themselves placed on the defensive, and indeed the very term "reformatory movement" fell into disuse during the 1880s.[126]

Home Office activism cooled under Harcourt's Unionist successor, Henry Matthews, a tough-minded barrister who took a jaundiced view of anything that smacked of softening in the criminal justice system.[127] Indeed, the government ceased supporting private efforts to amend the laws, including bills to abolish the requirement of preliminary imprisonment. Yet the tendency to attribute ever less responsibility to juveniles continued to develop, over a wide field of activities, the lead now being taken by backbenchers and philanthropic pressure groups. Despite Matthew's foot-dragging, Howard Vincent's Probation of First Offenders Bill passed in 1887, allowing

---

[124] HO 45/9629/A22484/37, letter from the Managers of the Essex Reformatory, July, 1885.

[125] Reformatory school population peaked in 1878 (although the numbers in nonpenal industrial schools continued to rise until 1891); few new reformatories were founded after 1876, and voluntary donations markedly declined. [Annual criminal statistics; Pellew, *The Home Office 1848–1914* (London: Heinemann, 1982), pp. 164–73.]

[126] See Magarey, "Reclaimers," 6, and J. E. Carlebach, *Caring for Children in Trouble* (London: Routledge, 1970).

[127] Matthews strongly supported preliminary imprisonment of juvenile offenders and blocked suggestions to institute juvenile courts. [Radzinowicz and Hood, pp. 205, 629.]

magistrates more alternatives to jail for juveniles and others. Under this act, the court was enjoined to have regard to "the youth, character and antecedents of the offender, to the trivial nature of the offence and to any extenuating circumstances under which it was committed."[128]

The Liberal victory in the general election of 1892 set the stage for further moves ot promote juvenile decarceration and diminish the penal character of reformatory schools. Home Secretary H.H. Asquith pushed reduction in the size of fines and increased use of bail to prevent children from being detained in jail awaiting trial.[129] Legislative efforts to allow magistrates to dispense with the practice of giving juveniles a brief taste of jail before they could be committed to reformatories finally succeeded. A private bill to accomplish this, now supported by the government, passed in 1893,[130] and was followed six years later by the full abolition of preliminary imprisonment. By 1902, only eight children under the age of 12 and only 1,073 between the ages of 12 and 16 were jailed.[131] In 1893, also, the minimum age for committal to reformatory schools was raised from 10 to 12,[132] and two years later an interdepartmental committee was set up to investigate the reformatory and industrial schools.[133]

These actions were not only of practical importance, but were also cultural landmarks. Ideologically, the removal of juveniles from prisons – and the simultaneous disenchantment with the severities of the reformatory schools – signaled the lasting defeat of reclaimers like Shaftesbury and Bruce, reformers whose moralistic views of the responsibility and treatment of juvenile offenders had dominated Victorian discussion and policy. The victory belonged to the child-savers who sought to rescue helpless juveniles from conditions beyond their control.[134] Moreover, these decriminalizing measures were complemented by new protective legislation.[135] Expanded workplace

[128] Quoted in Radzinowicz and Hood, p. 638. The use of probation thereafter greatly rose, although unevenly, since magisterial response varied; a continual theme in subsequent reports of the Howard Association was the unfortunately minimal use made of the act's provisions. After the reformist Ruggles-Brise took over the Prison Commission, similar complaints appeared in official reports. [See for example, the *Report of the Prison Commissioners for 1899–1900*.]

[129] See for example HO 43/180, Lushington to Aberavon Justices, Jan. 30, 1893.

[130] Many magistrates were clearly happy to be released from this requirement: 72 percent of those committed to reformatories the following year were not first imprisoned. [Magarey, 346.]

[131] Annual criminal statistics.

[132] By the act of 1893 that made preliminary imprisonment optional.

[133] For its report, and subsequent developments, see Chapter 9.

[134] This argument is presented in Magarey, "Reclaimers."

[135] As well as new and expanded rescue efforts, like Dr. Barnardo's institutions, and a movement for boarding out vagrant children.

regulation[136] and morals legislation[137] further distinguished children from adults. Even more important was legislation in 1889 and 1893 on prevention of cruelty ot children, which opened up a virtually new field of legal protection of children, criminalizing various forms of parental mistreatment and neglect.[138] The decriminalizing of juvenile offenses and criminalizing of parental mistreatment underlined the trend to diminished responsibility of juveniles. By the mid-1890s, the criminal justice system was clearly moving, from several directions, to deal with the young as constituting a distinct category of lessened responsibility.[139]

Habitual drunkards

In 1879, the same year that the criminal liability of juveniles was first limited, another category of diminished responsibility was legally noted for the first time: the habitual drunkard. At the very time when police prosecutions and prison commitments were reaching unprecedented heights, official attitudes about drunkards began to move away from moralistic voluntarism. As in the case of juveniles, changes in the treatment of drunkards began to be advocated during the 1870s when a new, less autonomous image of drunkards emerged. Moral tales of individual surrenders to and triumphs over the temptation of drink began to be challenged by more determinist stories of weakened men and (increasingly) women succumbing to their pathological environments and

[136] The 1878 act was followed after 1892 by greatly intensified factory regulation and new legislation that further protected and restricted juvenile employees.

[137] The Criminal Law Amendment Act of 1885, which attacked both organized prostitution and sexual deviance, was generally discussed in terms of child protection and drew support and opposition from many of the same quarters as the Prevention of Cruelty to Children Acts of 1889 and 1893. The act of 1885 raised the age of consent from 13 to 16 and instituted new penalties for procuring and maintaining a brothel; all this advanced the image of the prostitute – a young one at any rate – as a victim of persons and forces beyond her control (as with the drunkard – and, indeed, a disproportionate number of arrests for public drunkenness were of prostitutes).

[138] See G. Behlmer, *Child Abuse and Moral Reform* (Stanford: Stanford University Press, 1982).

[139] Another index of this lessening of responsibility was the diminishing proportion of young murderers who were executed. During the decade of the 1860s, 13 out of 21 death sentences on persons under the age of 20 were carried out, a higher proportion than that for all death sentences. In the first decade of the new century, by contrast, only 6 out of 19 were, and all of these prisoners were aged over 19 years. By 1888 a convention had been established in the Home Office that no one under 18 years of age should be hanged. By then, these deliberations show a "growing willingness to recognize the unbalanced and impressionable turbulence of adolescence," although the word had yet to come into use. [Chadwick, "Bureaucratic Mercy," 330–2.]

constitutions and by the encouraging entry of professionals to assist them in that struggle.

Benjamin Waugh's campaign for a new view of wayward juveniles as needy victims was paralleled for drunkards in the activities of Drs. Donald Dalrymple and Norman Kerr who argued that drunkenness was an affliction in which "self-control is suspended or annihilated."[140] Dalrymple, a Liberal M.P., started the reform effort in 1870, and each year thereafter introduced in Parliament a bill to acknowledge the impaired character of habitual drunkards, criminal and noncriminal, and to provide special incarcerative treatment for them modeled on lunatic asylums (of one of which he had been a proprietor)[141]. Dalrymple died before passing any legislation, but Kerr and the British Medical Association took up the cause, and by 1879, they had taken a first step toward the goal of full medicalization of dipsomania. The Habitual Drunkards Act of that year allowed the voluntary commitment of persons defined by magistrates as habitual drunkards to newly created asylums, wherein they could be confined against their will for a period of time to undergo a course of treatment. Bowing to opposition, however, the bill's proponents agreed to the exclusion of drunkards charged with criminal offenses and of any form of compulsory or free commitment.[142]

As with juveniles, this movement in the direction of diminished responsibility for drink brought anxieties of principle even to its supporters. Lord

[140] *Report of the Select Committee on the Control and Management of Habitual Drunkards,* 1872, 1. [P.P. 1872 v. 9.] There was no unanimous medical opinion on this matter: the distinguished physician, Sir John Bucknill, author of the standard textbook on psychiatry, strongly objected to discarding moral language in regard to drunkards. Some, he admitted, were truly "diseased," but these cases he attributed to prior insanity, not to drink; he found few inhabitants of private inebriate asylums to be truly mentally disabled. The rest should not be incarcerated, but neither should they be relieved of responsibility for their behavior. Most drunkards who were not insane, he held, were vicious: they could control their behavior but chose not to. John Charles Bucknill, "Habitual Drunkenness: A Vice, Crime or Disease?" *Contemporary Review 29* (1877), 431–47; also, Bucknill, *Habitual Drunkenness and Insane Drunkards* (London: Macmillan, 1878). Bucknill was, however, in the minority among his colleagues: at the annual meeting of the British Medical Association in 1876, only 10 supported his revolt against the petition for legislation organized by the association's Committee for the Reformation of Habitual Drunkards. [Radzinowicz and Hood, p. 292n.] His position seems to have become even more of a minority one in the profession as time went on.

[141] The most recent account of the late Victorian creation of a system of inebriate reformatories is Christopher Harding and Laura Wilkin," 'The Dream of a Benevolent Mind': The Late Victorian Response ot the Problem of Inebriety," *'Criminal Justice History 9* (1988), 189–207.

[142] "There are not a few," *The Times* had complained in 1870, "who would willingly get drunk every Sunday and Monday if they could be assured of being sent to an asylum and reformed during the week." [Quoted in A. H. Safford, "Habitual Drunkenness," *Law Magazine 30* (1870–71), 108.]

Shaftesbury was again centrally involved, since he carried the 1879 Habitual Drunkards Bill through the House of Lords. He held back from fully endorsing the medical conception of what he called a "great social evil." While many cases of habitual drunkenness, he agreed with the doctors, could only be considered as a disease that was frequently inherited; yet, he also agreed with the critics that "in many persons it was vice beyond all dispute" and went on to criticize magistrates who condoned offenses committed under the influence of alcohol. However, Shaftesbury observed that the difficulty of distinguishing cases of vice from cases of disease was not an argument against the legislation he was introducing on behalf of the BMA, since it provided only for voluntary commitment to inebriate asylums; a compulsory bill, desired by most of the doctors involved, would be a different matter. Even the issue of compulsory restraint *after* voluntary commitment made Shaftesbury uneasy, but, as he put it, he "bowed to the opinion of the learned men who gave such earnest and such scientific opinions" on its necessity.[143]

Meanwhile, reformers complained that the benefits of medical treatment in "Dalrymple Homes" were restricted under the 1879 act to the few rich enough to afford it and reasonable enough to agree to be committed. Unrealistic moral and libertarian prejudices, they argued, kept many from receiving the help desperately needed. As one former habitual drunkard explained his experience of illness and cure:

> [T]he effort of the will is a physical phenomenon, and is not entirely under the control of any man. It obeys fixed laws. Its strength or its weakness consists of the impulses which act upon it. There is a limit to its power.... The toxic agent acting upon the brain changes its organic composition and deteriorates its function. There is a weakening of the controlling power of the higher brain centres, a pollution by alcoholic poisoning of the source whence flows the dictates of the will. Indeed, there are structural alterations of the whole nervous system, until at length the nervous batteries become so feeble that not only is there no spontaneous over-flow of nervous power but no discharge whatever, and the will is paralyzed. When such is the case, every motive for prudence and restraint, all the force of dear-bought experience, is as nothing compared to the craving for drink.... To say to such a man, "Make an effort of the will," is as useless as to tell the fever-stricken patient to be quick and be cured.[144]

[143] 3 PD 245 (May 8, 1879), c. 1945–53. Existing accounts of Shaftesbury's role by Macleod and by Geoffrey Finlayson, *The Seventh Earl of Shaftesbury* (London: Eyre Methuen, 1981) pass over his stated reservations.
[144] "An Habitual Drundard," "Habitual Drunkenness," *Westminster Review 129* (1888), 605–6.

New terminology suggested the new construction of the problem. In 1884, the professional pressure group for further legislation, now headed by Kerr, changed its name from the Society for Promoting Legislation for Control and Care of Habitual Drunkards to the Society for the Study and Cure of Inebriety, and when an act was passed in 1888 making the original measure permanent, it substituted the Latinate term "inebriate" for the morally laden "habitual drunkard."[145] Gradually, official attitudes shifted. In the 1870s, Home Secretaries Bruce and Cross had refused to support legislation for habitual drunkards, the former objecting to giving doctors the power to indefinitely deprive a person of liberty, the latter citing the "great practical difficulties" in ascertaining membership in this ambiguous class lying between lunacy and criminality.[146] However, when the 1879 act was made permanent in 1888, the measure was government sponsored.

As the symbolic responsibility of respectable drunkards diminished, the strict punishment of intoxicated criminals began to be less insisted upon.[147] The common practice of criminally punishing public drunkards began to be questioned. Even the police were finding their expanded role in this regard uncomfortable. Metropolitan Police Commissioner Henderson complained in 1875 that "no more unsatisfactory or unpleasant duty" existed than arresting people for drunkenness. "The fact of a person being drunk is always a mere matter of opinion, in which the medical gentlemen who are called in to assist the Police are frequently as much at fault as the Police themselves. There is in fact no medical test for drunkenness, and among the immense mass of such cases mistakes will recur almost inevitably," creating embarassing incidents

---

[145] At the Social Science Association in 1881, Dr Barnardo noted in criticizing police supervision of exprisoners: "a policeman did not always draw the distinctions which a finer and more subtle agent would do with regard to convictions. Many offences were committed every year through drink, and a man once convicted for an offence whilst in a state of intoxication should not be regarded as so utterly criminal unless it could be proved that he afterwards relapsed into crime. Of course he did not mean to suggest that it was wrong to attach full responsibility to crimes committed under the influence of drink, but it would certainly be right to draw a difference between those acts and others." [*NAPSS Transactions 1881*, 315.] By 1886, an alienist, G. H. Savage, could criticize what he described as the recent trend toward treating drunkenness and insanity virtually "as if they were one & the same thing." ["Drunkenness in Relation to Criminal Responsibility," *Journal of Mental Science 32* (April, 1886), 23–30.]

[146] See Radzinowicz and Hood, pp. 294–5.

[147] C. E. Troup, whose Home Office career spanned the years 1880 to 1922, claimed that whereas Bruce and Cross had refused to interfere with capital sentences in cases of drunkenness "unless the effects of drink were such as to produce a condition of insanity in the legal sense," Harcourt was more receptive to considering the influence of drink as a possible mitigating factor. [*The Home Office* (London: G.P. Putnam's Sons, 1925), pp. 67–8.]

that undermined the authority of the police.[148] The subjectivity of the legal label of drunkenness was also noted by influential politicians, who began to raise their voices against the purely deterrent and punitive treatment of the problem. The Radical leader Joseph Chamberlain, speaking from his expertise in local government, told the 1877 Select Committee on Intemperance that the alarming criminal statistics were meaningless: "If to-morrow it was necessary for any purpose, I could undertake to have the statistics for Birmingham made ten times as bad as they were before; just one turn of the screw would bring in ten times the number." In fact, he opposed dealing with the problem as a criminal one; "drunkenness must be treated as a kind of lunacy, as a disease."[149]

From their peak in 1876, both per capita prosecutions and severity of punishments for drunkenness began a steady decline, as social fear eased and with it the assumption of personal responsibility and insistence upon punishment. Prosecutions fell from an annual average of 812 per 100,000 inhabitants from 1874 to 1878 to an average of 636 from 1884 to 1888 and 595 in 1894.[150] That substantial decline seems to have masked a still sharper fall in proceedings against simple drunkenness. Commissioner Henderson called attention in the early 1880s to the recent widespread questioning by magistrates of the very power of the police to arrest for drunkenness alone; the result was to shift the focus of prosecution from drunkenness per se to drunk and disorderly offenses:

> The uncertainty of the proper mode of dealing with persons found drunk and incapable, which has resulted from some magisterial decisions, has had the effect of largely diminishing the number of persons taken to police stations on this account. They are now discharged, when sober, on their own recognizances to appear before a magistrate; as a rule nothing more is seen of them.[151]

---

[148] *Report of the Metropolitan Police Commissioner for 1874*, p. 3. In 1877, the chief constable of Birmingham complained that public opinion was turning against criminal prosecution of drunkards. [*First Report of the Select Committee of the House of Lords on Intemperance*, 1877, Qs. 2119–23. (P.P. 1877 v. 11).]

[149] *First Report of the Select Committee of the House of Lords on Intemperance*, PO 234 (Qs. 2356–62). Even temperance attitudes were moving away from voluntarism; the select committee was told of a poll of members of the Church of England Temperance Society (which was just beginning to provide missionaries to police courts) that found the "general opinion [in regard to legislation] appears to be in favour of restraint in the case of habitual drunkards." Restraint had more support than proposals for stronger punishment of drunkards or of publicans. Reverend Canon Hopkins, in *Third Report*, PO 173 (Qs. 9486–7)

[150] *Criminal Statistics for 1894*, p. 16.

[151] *Report of the Metropolitan Police Commissioner for 1881*, p. 4. However, he noted, "it cannot be inferred that there is any less drunkenness than before – on the contrary, the

The tendency of the last two years, he noted in 1883, had been "to limit the number of drunken persons taken by the Police to cases of absolute incapacitation."[152] Thus, in the 1880s and early 1890s, growing approval of medical treatment of habitual drunkards was paralleled by diminishing zeal to punish the drunkard criminally and even perhaps by somewhat greater willingness to allow intoxication as a mitigating or excusing factor in criminal prosecution.[153] The result of these complementary trends was again, as with juveniles, to soften the hitherto sharp distinction between criminal and noncriminal character and treatment.

During the first years of the 1890s, at the same time that the views of child-savers were triumphing over more moralistic reclaimers of wayward youth, public opinion swung behind the British Medical Association's calls for incarcerative state medical treatment of inebriates. One historian has even detected in the volume and character of press comment a watershed around 1891.[154] By 1894, Kerr declared in the preface to the third edition of his treatise on inebriety that in the six years since the second edition had appeared there had developed "a consensus of intelligent opinion, that habitual and periodic drunkenness is often either a symptom or a sequel of disease."[155] Policymakers began to respond to this new consensus. In 1891, a Liberal leader, Lord Herschell, moved for an inquiry into the existing methods of dealing with common criminal drunkards.[156] The resulting Home Office departmental committee indeed marked a watershed in official positions, because it recommended compulsory commitment of noncriminal inebriates and the establishment of institutions for criminal inebriates. However, applying compulsory committal to persons who had not committed any crime stuck in most Conservative and many Liberal gullets.[157] Once that demand was

---

number of persons arrested for being drunk and disorderly increased from 16,520 in 1880 to 18,721 in 1881."

[152] *Report of the Metropolitan Police Commissioner for 1882*, p. 4. After the early 1880s, drunkenness is given much less attention than previously in these reports. Sentences for this offense, as for most others, seem to have been getting shorter; see Radzinowicz and Hood, p. 301. By 1894, the criminal registrar was making a point of denying drink to be a significant cause of most crime. [*Criminal Statistics for 1893*, pp. 76–7 (Troup).]

[153] See for example Stephen's sympathetic remarks in *R. v. Davis* (1881), 14 Cox C.C. 563, and *R. v. Doherty* (1887), 16 Cox C.C. 306.

[154] R. M. Macleod, "The Edge of Hope: Social Policy and Chronic Alcoholism 1870–1900," *Journal of the History of Medicine and Allied Sciences* 22 (July 1967), 233. He particularly noted the campaign that year of the *Daily Telegraph* for government action to "rescue" many from the "slavery of drink."

[155] N. S. Kerr, *Inebriety or Narcomania* (3rd ed., London: H. K. Lewis, 1894), p. vii.

[156] 3 PD 354, C. 1701–7 (June 5, 1891).

[157] There was also the very important practical objection of cost, whether to the Exchequer or to local authorities (just as Treasury resistance to increasing costs

dropped, in 1898, a statute was passed empowering magistrates to commit criminal offenders to reformatory inebriate asylums in lieu of the usual forms of punishment. Henceforth, the characterization of inebriety, which now cut across the line separating lawbreakers from law abiders, carried with it the practical recognition of diminished responsibility.

Habitual criminals

The increasing attention paid to habitual drunkards was only one aspect of a growing focus on the problem of the habitual criminal. The more successful Victorian criminal policy was, the more repeat offenders stood out among the clientele of the penal system. At the same time, the decline in the statistics of crime after 1871 was softening fears of a semiorganized criminal class,[158] while the spreading influence of medical and biological thinking was giving constructions of criminality a less moralistic, more naturalistic cast. In particular, the image of habitual criminals was bifurcating into a small group of hard-core professional outlaws and a much larger group of inadequates, misshapen by both nature and nurture, who generally committed petty offenses. The writings of medical men and physiologists merged in the general middle-class mind with Darwinian images to establish a picture of most repeat offenders as, indeed, habitual and of their illegality, like the inebriate's drinking, as not freely chosen and thus not responsive to rational deterrents. The behavior of the habitual criminal was seen as deeply rooted in his habits, even in his constitution, and thus susceptible (if susceptible at all) only to deep treatment.

Such repellent, but no longer frightening, images were appearing often enough to begin to affect policy. E. W. Cox, a leading barrister, magistrate, publisher of the widely read *Law Times*, and a strong supporter of maximum deterrence, nonetheless could describe habitual criminals as early as 1870 as "persons of very low mental and bodily organisation, with small heads and stupid aspect . . . nine-tenths of them really and truly were both mentally and

encouraged official scepticism about the value of reformatory and industrial schools). Unlike questions of principle, this issue could be compromised, but only by severely limiting the actual effects of the ensuing legislation.

[158] Content analysis of articles dealing with crime and punishment in a wide range of journals between 1855 and 1880 shows a steady growth in the use of the term "criminal class" from 1860 to 1869 and a marked fall thereafter. See S. J. Stevenson, "The 'Criminal Class' in the Mid-Victorian City: A Study of Policy Conducted with Specific Reference to Those Made Subject to the Provisions of 34 and 35 Vict., c. 112 (1871) in Birmingham and East London During the Early Years of Registration and Supervision," unpublished Ph.D. thesis, Oxford University, 1983, p. 32n.

bodily diseased."[159] A few years later, in his *Principles of Punishment*, he noted their characteristic "weak-mindedness."[160] Similarly, Sir Edmund Du Cane, chairman of the Prison Commission, and who in regard to normal criminals was a strict believer in rationality and personal responsibility, described in 1875 the common characteristics of habitual criminals as

> entirely those of the inferior races of mankind – wandering habits, utter laziness, absence of forethought or provision, want of moral sense, cunning, dirt, and instances may be found in which their physical characteristics approach those of the lower animals so that they seem to be going back to the type of what Professor Darwin calls 'our arboreal ancestors'.[161]

The constitutional deficiencies of habitual criminals were stressed by liberals as well as conservatives. We have seen even the sternly moralistic William Tallack urging attention to the "social or hereditary causes [of poverty and crime], uncontrollable by the sufferer"[162] and referring frequently to "the innate weakness of many criminals," particularly habitual ones.[163] His continuing moralism found one outlet in urging greater distinction between the dangerous minority of "wilfully brutal ruffians, and the other class of habitual offenders who are weak and indolent, rather than violent or cruel."[164]

Such sentiments eventually affected policy.[165] Deterrence for such persons appeared both less necessary and less effective. Thus, the three intertwined policies begun in the 1860s to deal with the threat of habitual criminality – tightened prison discipline, intensified prosecution increasingly employing cumulative sentencing,[166] and police supervision of repeat offenders and

---

[159] *49 Law Times* 458 (1870).

[160] E. W. Cox, *The Principles of Punishment as Applied in the Administration of the Criminal Law by Judges and Magistrates* (London: Law Times Office, 1877), p. 10.

[161] Edmund Du Cane, "Address on the Repression of Crime," *NAPSS Transactions* 1875, pp. 302–3.

[162] William Tallack, *Penological and Preventative Principles* (London: Wertheimer, Lea, 1889), p. 30.

[163] William Tallack, *Howard Letters and Memories* (London: Methuen, 1905), p. 202.

[164] *Penological*, p. 165.

[165] But more slowly than in regard to juveniles. As S. J. Stevenson has remarked ["The Criminal Class," 422], "like the 'feeble-minded' [habitual criminals] did not constitute or attract the support of any sizable political grouping and the degree of coercion inflicted by the statute laws bore no resemblance to the changing intellectual climate of the mid 1870s and early 1880s."

[166] Even if, in practice cumulative sentencing for misdemeanants was throughout the exception rather than the rule; unlike the case with felons, it had never been enshrined in legislation, and the ever heavier magisterial caseloads produced by the expansion of summary jurisdiction, together with continuing judicial attachment to classicist norms of equal sentences for equal offenses, were major obstacles to the general adoption of the sort of cumulative sentencing urged by many.

suspected habituals (working with sternly moralistic discharged prisoners' aid societies) – all began to unravel in the late 1870s.

First, as we will see in the following chapter, as soon as nationalization of the prisons had finally been attained, discomfort began to build with the uniform and severe disciplinary regime. Second, as we have seen, both repeated short jail sentences and their new alternative, cumulative sentencing, came under growing criticism in the 1880s and early 1890s. The former apparently neither deterred nor reformed, and the latter seemed increasingly cruel when applied not only to petty thieves but to drunk and disorderly offenders and habitual petty offenders in general. While Hopwood was campaigning against the whole practice in the late 1880s, even a persistent advocate of progressive sentencing like William Tallack, who saw in longer prison terms opportunity for training in industry and morality, came to urge a sharper distinction between serious and petty offenders, the latter to be dealt with less harshly. By 1889, while castigating foolish libertarians and "over-humanitarians," Tallack scaled down his earlier proposals to increments of detention of only a fortnight.[167] By then, discontent with existing sentencing practices had become quite vocal. The charges included inequality and inconsistency, overseverity, routine application of cumulative sentences, and lack of provision for appeal.[168] In 1889 and 1890, strong efforts were made to obtain a royal commission on sentencing; although rebuffed by Home Secretary Matthews, a stout defender of judicial autonomy, the efforts were symptomatic of a weakening confidence in the criminal justice system. In 1892, to deflect the growing criticism the judges met, acknowledged the existence of a problem, and recommended that a special court be set up to review sentences. Like so much else of the voluntarist apparatus of Victorian criminal policy, cumulative sentencing was never formally repudiated but, as the urgency behind it evaporated and the objects of this policy came to be seen as less threatening and more needful of help rather than retribution, it came to seem, unless carefully tailored to the history and character of the individual offender, less useful and thus harsher and more repugnant. In the debates of the early 1890s, this method of dealing with repeat offenders was clearly on the defensive, ever more purely the last ditch weapon of exasperated magistrates who did not know what else to do with habitual lawbreakers.

---

[167] In 1874 the Howard Association had recommended a scale of cumulation of three days, a week, fortnight, a month, three, six, nine, twelve, eighteen months, two years, all to be served in truly penal conditions of separate confinement. [*Annual Report* 1881, p. 12.] In 1889, Tallack now proposed a caution only for the first offense, succeeding sentences of two weeks, four weeks, six weeks, and so forth. [*Penological and Preventive Principles*, p. 181.]

[168] See for example 3 PD 336, 1003–56 (May 24, 1889). On this issue, see Radzinowicz and Hood, Ch. 23, and Thomas, *Constraints*.

A third policy – police supervision – had been meant to deter, but gradually this supervision became less serious and more nominal and was eventually less applied. The protective power of police supervision came to exist more as a useful myth than an ever present reality. The myth did continue to have its uses in soothing the middle-class mind and even perhaps in restraining anti-social behavior. But, as time went on and the criminal class was less in evidence, the image of a dangerous army of professional criminals faded from official, and public, discourse. Measured by the criminal statistics, the Habitual Criminal Acts of 1869 and 1871 proved a great success. The following decades were to see a fairly continuous decline in crimes reported and tried. Already in 1872, a "large and remarkable" decrease in crimes was attributed by the Home Office to the Acts.[169] Even years later, much was credited to supervision. Two journalists writing on the police noted in 1889, "The system has exercised a wholesome influence upon many clever thieves who ostensibly lived in London, but used to make frequent excursions into country districts to commit crime. The risk of recognition is now too great. Police officers have little or no difculty in discovering the haunts of suspected men."[170]

But, as Radzinowicz and Hood have convincingly argued, the attempt to convert the police into an effective agency of supervision failed from the outset. For one thing, there were simply too many persons to supervise for an institution on a tight mid-Victorian budget. Over 3,500 convicts who would be subject to supervision for seven years after their release were sentenced each year. This meant that eventually the police would be expected to keep under surveillance at least 25,000 persons.[171] Consequently, the 1871 act gave judges discretion as to whether to make habituals subject to supervision. It was hoped that supervision could be made effective for the most dangerous cases, while the threat of arrest and imprisonment for those found "gaining a living by dishonest means" or acting "suspiciously" in certain circumstances would be sufficient deterrents to other "habituals." In practice, the act of 1871 was interpreted to mean that only the chief officer of police had power to enforce supervision and to institute proceedings against habitual criminals found gaining a livelihood by dishonest means. Consequently, deterrent supervision was actually applied to relatively few of its potential subjects.[172] From 1879

---

[169] *Memorandum respecting the Decrease in Crime* ... (1872), cited in Radzinowicz and Hood, p. 258.

[170] Charles T. Clarkson and J. Hall Richardson, *Police!* (London: Scribner and Welford, 1889), p. 356.

[171] Radzinowicz and Hood, p. 258.

[172] Particularly as the fading of midcentury fears encouraged the revival of resistance to such an expanded role for the police and to the very idea of such close supervision of such large numbers; see for example the remarks of *The Times*, Sept. 10, 1882, criticizing French police excesses. The expenditure that effective supervision would require was also a growing objection.

on, prosecutions under the act first leveled off and then declined. With transportation no longer an option, the number of convicts on license subjcet to police supervision was growing (reaching over 21,000 by 1890), yet the number prosecuted each year was well under 100.[173] In 1893, only 55 of the vast mass of men liable to be prosecuted as twice-convicted persons were brought before the courts and only 326 were placed under police supervision by the courts compared with ten times that number in 1872.[174] Sir Robert Anderson, the head of the Criminal Investigation Department, exasperatingly pronounced in 1891 that the habitual criminal acts were "almost a dead letter."[175] Certainly, as Radzinowicz and Hood have argued, whatever the wish of legislators, the administrative means for thoroughgoing preventive and deterrent policing were hardly adequate. The police forces were still too small and inefficient to take on such a large program, particularly when the methods of identification were highly inaccurate (and would remain so until the advent of fingerprinting at the turn of the century). Moreover, the legislative proponents of police supervision in the 1860s did not fully appreciate the reluctance of magistrates and police officials to use these powers and the public's continuing suspicion of an "un-English" system of official spying. However, had the fears of the 1860s persisted or had the mid-Victorian faith in deterrence remained undimmed, much more would probably have been done.

As police supervision was used less than had been originally expected, the nature of its use, or at least its justification, shifted from a primary focus on deterrence. With public interest in crime fading, attitudes toward the functions of police supervision itself began to alter. The difficulties that faced convicts released on license and the added burden and stigma upon them of police supervision were increasingly recognized. After complaints by some prisoners' aid societies of harassment of ticket-of-leave men, the Metropolitan Police set up in 1879 a Convict Supervision Office, and plainclothes (rather than uniformed) officers began to work in closer association with these philanthropic bodies,[176] who were now receiving government subsidies. After complacently noting the success of supervision, the late-Victorian chroniclers of the police, Clarkson and Richardson, described its functions as twofold; in addition to easily "discovering the haunts of suspected men," police officers "are enabled to pick out new recruits, and by a helping hand prevent these first offenders from falling into the ranks of habitual criminals."[177]

Of course, such a characterization is too benign. The "helping hand" could be coercive and most unwelcome, and complaints continued of harassment

---

[173] Annual criminal statistics.
[174] Radzinowicz and Hood, p. 258.
[175] Quoted *ibid.*, p. 258.
[176] See Clarkson and Richardson, p. 356.
[177] *Police!*, p. 356.

and of men losing their jobs because police informed employers of their men's criminal past. Moreover, such constructive expansion of the policeman's role, ardently lobbied for by activist police administrators like Howard Vincent and Robert Anderson, drew resistance from a wide spectrum of opinion that included unreconstructed punishers, civil libertarians, cautious police bureaucrats, and governmental expenditure watchers.[178] Nonetheless, this policy change did mark a significant redefinition in the rationale of police supervision and apparently also some change in actual behavior. In the course of the 1880s, the role of the police in regard to former convicts was moving in principle, whatever the lag in practice, from one purely of deterrence and control to one with a broader conception of social aid. Together with the Summary Jurisdiction Act of 1879, which provided for less serious offenders a form of probation with police supervision, this police policy change gave impetus to a gathering shift in at least the *ascribed* role of the police, from a purely deterrent one to one that also expected them to perform constructive social tasks. In addition to now being expected to help old offenders to go straight, policemen were being given a wider range of noncriminal functions, from the finding of lost children and lost property to the regulation of traffic.[179]

At the same time, voluntary societies formed to rehabilitate discharged offenders were gradually being drawn into more expansive efforts and closer connection with state authorities. As their scope widened, these societies similarly began to soften their moral rigor. Whereas the shrinking ranks of

[178] Indeed, these attitudes could be found combined, as in Under-secretary Lushington's repeated objections – on moral, libertarian, administrative, and financial grounds – to extensions of the activity of the police. From this regard he had criticized provisions of the Criminal Law Amendment Bill of 1884 that gave police new powers over prostitutes, brothels, and homosexuals and also provisions of the Probation of First Offenders Bill of 1886. For instance, he found the proposal to apply police regulation similar to that already applicable to habitual criminals to first offenders, however benevolent the motive, "perfectly monstrous." [Memorandum, Aug. 26, 1886, *Home Office Printed Memoranda*, Vol. XVI, p. 251.] Even shortly before his retirement, he was objecting to the new practice of using police to take into custody persons judged to be suffering from delirium tremens and convey them to workhouses, and upon magistrates' committal orders, to asylums. "Their primary duty," he complained to the secretary of the Lunacy Commission, "is on the streets, and the less they are called off the better.... They represent *force*, and it is advisable that so far as may be they should not interfere in private or domestic life." [MH 51/70, Oct. 31, 1894.] Such anti-interventionism can as readily appear "reactionary" as "progressive" to modern eyes; using the same arguments, Lushington resisted through the 1880s pressures for what he termed "invasive" legislation against cruelty to wives and children.
[179] The Lost Property Branch of the Metropolitan Police, for example, established some time after 1869, began around 1890 to get more than nominal attention in the commissioner's annual reports.

convicts retained a powerful stigma, treatment of the far larger group of discharged petty offenders could more easily turn in an administrative or welfarist direction. The Church of England Temperance Society's (C.E.T.S.) mission to the police courts was established in 1876 with the purpose of reforming individual drunkards, but within a few years its agents were ranging much more more widely. The missionaries quickly made themselves generally useful to the magistrates by taking on tasks that were still felt to be best handled informally – acting in family and neighbors' quarrels, interviewing children who were beyond their parents' control, assessing applicants for the poor box, and so on. Most significantly for criminal policy, they began to be employed by magistrates in supervising offenders released on recognizances under the provisions of the 1879 Summary Jurisdiction Act. More acceptable in many places than policemen, the missionaries soon became an indispensable adjunct to the magistrates, greatly extending their effective range of action. If, after 1879 and even more after the Probation of First Offenders Act of 1887, the magistrates needed a new supply of supervisory agents to make the increased use of alternatives to incarceration workable, they similarly needed more information in order to decide who should receive this more lenient treatment; again the missionaries were turned to. Probably before, but certainly soon after the 1887 act, they were drawn into the process of inquiry before sentence. As Howard Vincent, author of the 1887 act, observed, "if [it] induces courts ... to inquire into the antecedents of prisoners, and into the collateral circumstances attending upon the offence before passing sentence, then it will have achieved its objectives."[180] Thereafter, in regard to petty offenders, the C.E.T.S. missionary "became the mediator of the court's mercy," the forerunner of the post-1907 probation officer.[181]

A "crisis in criminal law"?

"Often, of late," noted *The Times* in 1896, "it has been said that there has come a crisis in criminal law." It cited a group of proposals that had recently come before the public and Parliament for reform of trial, sentencing, and penal procedures, seeming to agree with their proponents that English justice, though praised many times over by that paper, was indeed gravely flawed. *The Times* now doubted that the existing system took sufficient regard for either the rights of the defendant or the protection of the public, or that it deterred or reformed offenders. Although the paper refused to commit itself in

---

[180] Letter to *The Times*, Sept. 5, 1887.
[181] William McWilliams, "The Mission to the English Police Courts 1876–1936," *Howard Journal 22* (1983), 137.

favor of any specific reform, clearly something was amiss. Despite its successes, in the 1890s Victorian criminal policy found itself in the dock, condemned among Liberals for its severity and across the political spectrum for its overly rationalistic and uniform approach to a clientele grown in number but diminished in frightfulness. Neither deterrence nor disciplinary moral education seemed as appropriate or as feasible as they once had to deal with a population of offenders that appeared less wicked, but also less rational and less autonomous than formerly. Increasingly, more and more scientific investigation, discrimination, and treatment were called for. "Anything is better," concluded *The Times*, "than a pedantic, mechanical administration of the criminal law without regard to the character or circumstances of the offender."[182] A new, more welfarist or administrative approach to crime was about to emerge.

[182] April 17, 1896, pp. 9–10.

8

Disillusion with the prison

After midcentury, imprisonment became the normal punishment for almost all crime. By the 1860s, more than 90 percent of those convicted of indictable offenses were sentenced to prison.[1] Between the Prisons Act of 1877, which sought (in Sir Stafford Northcote's words) to promote "uniformity of punishment,"[2] by placing all the jails in England and Wales under one central authority and the retirement in 1895 of Edmund Du Cane as chairman of the Prison Commission (a post that the act had created), the Victorian prison experience reached its fullest systematization. During this period, as several scholars have chronicled, mid-Victorian prescriptions were translated into national practice, as the local prisons were brought into line with the uniform bureaucratic regime previously established in the convict prisons.

Yet in these years wider forces – the naturalization of social discourse, the expansion of the range of the criminal law, and the easing of social fear – were also beginning to affect patterns not only of prosecution and sentencing, but of punishment. As they did, the cultural meaning of imprisonment began to alter. First, ever more exceptions to the disciplinary rule were discovered, and then, as multiplying exceptions fed back upon conceptions of the norm, the legitimacy of the standard of deterrent and moralizing imprisonment itself began to be questioned and then attacked. By 1895, the cultural substructure of the Victorian prison system had sharply eroded, and the result was wide support, for the first time since the early Victorian years, for a program of penal reform. A new era in punishment was opening.

Out of uniformity, multiplicity:
the discovery of exceptions to normal prison discipline

Ever more exceptions to the image of real criminality and its norm of full and equal liability to punishment began to be discovered not only at the stage of trial and sentencing of offenders, but within the prisons as well. Here again the utilitarian drive toward rationalization ultimately worked against its own

[1] Annual criminal statistics.
[2] 3 PD 230, 932 (July 3, 1876).

universalist principles. The very drive to subject all criminals to uniform discipline made prisoners who, for whatever reason, did not fit the criminal stereotype for which that discipline had been devised into a problem requiring new and special measures; ironically, a more lax, less single-minded regime, such as had existed before Victorian reform, would not have revealed these problems. Thus, hardly had the aims of underlining personal responsibility and promoting self-discipline by penal methods of certainty, uniformity, and severity been established than they began to be qualified, as the very aim of uniform treatment implanted in the system by prison acts from 1835 to 1865 increasingly drew the attention of administrators to prisoners who did not fit, to exceptional cases.

Exceptions came in several forms. The first to be noted was that of the juvenile prisoner. Beginning under Cross (1874 to 1880) and becoming much more pronounced under Harcourt (1880 to 1885) administrators not only saw juveniles as less responsible and less tough than earlier, they also began to lose faith in the value of imprisoning them. Harcourt declared that it was "altogether improper" to imprison a child even for a few days for offenses like breaking windows, however often repeated; from such treatment "neither he nor others can derive any possible benefit."[3] Meanwhile, both the prestige and the population of reformatory schools passed their peaks. For juvenile offenders, recognizances and parental fines were replacing the sanction of prison, and even of its handmaid, the reformatory school. Breaking with his mentor, Reverend Turner, the assistant inspector of reformatory schools reflected in 1895 that "we can do nothing with punishment."[4]

Women constituted a second exceptional category. Although they continued to be committed to prison at about the same rate per conviction as men, the length of time members of the "weaker sex" spent behind bars was diminishing more rapidly. Local prisons were becoming gradually, and convict prisons sharply, more male.[5] Other groups of inmates also began to gain special consideration. One was the politicals, few in total but often of a higher social class than most prisoners and prominent far out of proportion to their numbers – notably, the Irish Nationalists, or Fenians, whose revolutionary activities were in principle treated by the government as purely criminal. Another increasingly visible exceptional category, but more difficult to deal

[3] Correspondence in *The Times*, 1880, quoted in L. Radzinowicz and R. Hood *History of English Criminal Law and its Administration, vol. 5* (London: Stevens and Sons, 1986), p. 625.

[4] *Report of the Departmental Committee on Prisons 1895*, Qs. 2535–8: Henry Rogers.

[5] The female proportion of average local prison population fell from 22 percent in 1870 to 16½ percent in 1895, to 15¼ percent in 1912; for convict prisons the decline was from 14 percent in 1878 to 6¾ percent in 1895, to a little over 3 percent in 1912. [Annual reports of the Prison Commissions.]

with separately than the juvenile or the political, was that of the "gentleman" prisoner, of a higher social class and generally more delicate constitution and sensibility than a Fagin or a Sikes. With the rapid development of commerce and the heightening of legal sensitivity to white-collar crimes like commercial fraud, more embezzlers and swindlers seemed to appear among the prison rolls.[6] At a lesser level, the expansion of the use of criminal sanctions was bringing into the local jails growing numbers of fine defaulters – not only drunk and disorderly persons but householders, tradesmen, and workingmen breaking local bylaws. This sort of offender, like the debtor, had often escaped the application of full penal discipline,[7] and the promulgation of uniform rules in 1878 drew immediate protests and some official modifications.[8] Yet another group of exceptional prisoners was the apparently growing number of physically and, especially, mentally disabled inmates, those not fit for, or perhaps even deserving of, the full rigors of prison discipline. Despite the fact that nationalization had led to greater isolation of the prisons from public gaze, all these exceptions were much more noted after 1877 than they had been before.[9]

Gentleman prisoners

The debate over nationalization of the prison from 1876 to 1877 had revived interest in these institutions and was followed by a spate of prison memoirs.

[6] See R. Sindall, "Middle Class Crime in Nineteenth-Century England," *Criminal Justice History 4* (1983)] How far such growth was real awaits more thorough quantitative analysis.

[7] Before nationalization, even under pressure from Whitehall, many justices of the peace had been reluctant to apply full penal discipline to such persons. See HO 45/9384/45291 (1875) (correspondence between Oxford J.P.s and the Home Office concerning who was a criminal prisoner).

[8] See *The Times*, Aug. 12, 1878 ("The New Prison Rules and Plank Beds"), Aug. 15, 1878 ("The New Prison Rules"), and Sept. 11, 1878 ("New Prison Rules for Debtors"). The home secretary quickly withdrew the application of plank-bed discipline to women, children, and old men, leaving it standing however, as one Radical M.P. complained, for "persons committed to prison for the nonpayment of fines consequent on trifling breaches of the municipal law – such as cab-drivers littering in the streets, or carters carrying timber improperly loaded on their carts, or violations of the School Board or Cattle Plague Acts, and the thousand-and-one other offences which those who have not a full purse are compelled to expiate in person." *The Times*, Aug. 12, 1878. However the complaints continued, Mitchell Henry, M.P., making himself a gadfly in the cause of relieving short-term prisoners of some of the severities made uniform upon local prisons by the new regulations. See *The Times*, March 11, 1880 ("The Prison Regulations").

[9] As shown by the explicit modification of the new rules for women, children, and old men, *ibid.*

These criticized the failure of the system to make moral distinctions between prisoners, which led to the visitation of excessive, unnecessary, and counterproductive cruelties upon the less culpable and more reformable, while treating the hardened criminal too leniently. The first of these works, *Five Years' Penal Servitude*, by "One Who Has Endured It," published in 1877, quickly found a large audience. The author, a gentleman convicted of commercial fraud, described his "terrible ordeal" and criticized some of the humiliations and cruelties he encountered. In particular, he called for more attention to be paid to the aim of reformation, which, he suggested, should be pursued less sternly and more sympathetically. He wanted two types of criminal clearly distinguished, and the one separated from the other: "those who have deliberately and in cool blood ... set to work to rob or defraud, and those who have been led astray by others, or have given way to a strong temptation in a moment of difficulty [like himself]." He argued that men "unduly pressed by adverse circumstances" will sometimes fall, but such are readily reformable if punished with humanity and kept from the contaminating influence of "the thieving and swindling class of prisoners." These two classes "should be kept as much as possible distant, and men undergoing punishment for first offences should on no account be mixed up with hardened and confirmed rogues."

The prison experience, this exconvict felt, bore much harder on men from the higher classes: "To a large number of criminals it is merely so many years being shut up in prison, restricted from doing their own will, and being compelled to labour, to a certain extent whether they like it or not. To the man in a good position, it is moral death, accompanied with ruin and disgrace to his family and relatives." In order to argue for mitigating this unequal effect, "One Who Has Endured It" constructed a category of lesser culpability, numbering those first offenders, on the one hand, who were less able to endure the rigors of penal discipline and, on the other, those of readily salvageable character; this new category was one whose members were disproportionately to be found among middle-class prisoners. It was indeed an exceptional category that, like others, could and would in time be expanded. At the same time, the author carried on an essentially moralistic discourse and maintained, and in fact underlined, his belief in the need for the severely deterrent penal treatment of "real" criminals.[10]

A prison memoir published two years later by an embezzler reiterated many of these points. "A Ticket-of-Leave Man" similarly focused his attack on

[10] "One Who Has Endured It," *Five Years' Penal Servitude* (London: R. Bentley, 1877), pp. 2, 355–6, 373–5, 169, 377, 365. F. W. Farrar, while writing *Eternal Hope* (London: Macmillan, 1878), read and pondered *Five Years' Penal Servitude*, drawing from it the lesson of how morally varied was the population of the prisons. *Eternal Hope*, p. 103n.

the penal system's ineffectiveness at reforming, and at its major cause, the system's lack of moral discrimination. The particular evil that resulted from that lack and that most exercised the author, was the forcing of an erring but "respectable" man (himself) into long association with professional criminals. About the latter he had nothing good to say:

> [I]n the complaints I may make of the working of the present system, and the suggestions I may offer for its reform, I am actuated by no feelings of tenderness for that ruffian class, who, because they *will* drink and will *not* work, exist from childhood to old age, by committing outrages upon their fellow-creatures, and by filching from them the proceeds of honest labour and enterprise. . . . I have nothing in common with those who try to create any sympathy for thieves on account of the hideous dress they have to wear, or because their hair is cropped, or their beds hard, or their beef tough. I have lived among these thieves for six years, and for the future I shall close my ears to all such claptrap complaints. A man who lives for no other purpose and with no other object than to break the laws of his country has no right to expect 'kid-glove treatment.'

"A Ticket-of-Leave Man" urged greater recognition "of *degrees* of guilt," of the need for shorter and less rigorous sentences for most middle-class and many working-class offenders, "erring men, in nearly every case deeply sensible of their guilt, and deeply penitent." Repeat offenders, on the other hand, should be dealt with more sternly even than at present, since "it is a mistake to suppose that habitual thieves have any dread of penal servitude in its present form."[11]

Fenians, buoyed by a cause, even more forcefully inveighed against their treatment as common criminals. O'Donovan Rossa objected to being measured

> by the same rule as that by which they measured their thieves and pickpockets; . . . which made me wish to have the authorities learn they were mistaken in supposing that the application of this rule to Irish revolutionists was to have the same effect upon them as upon the garrotters and Sodomites of England.[12]

Similarly, *The Irishman* communicated to the public the prisoners' sense of outrage at being associated with what it called "the vilest criminals," at being forced to wear shirts and flannels worn by "those leprous outcasts of society."[13] Through the rest of the century, the Nationalists missed no opportunity to press for special treatment for political offenders, and thus, as we will

[11] "A Ticket-of-Leave Man," *Convict Life, or, Revelations Concerning Convicts and Convict Prisons* (London: Wyman & Sons, 1879), pp. 3, 5, 22, 243.
[12] 1874, quoted in Radzinowicz and Hood, p. 422.
[13] 1869, quoted in *ibid.*, p. 426.

see, to throw their weight on the scales against the mid-Victorian ideal of a penal discipline of uniform severity.

The unfit

While a growing proportion of local prisoners were appearing to be trivial offenders, more serious offenders – those in convict prisons – were becoming less threatening, not only in quantity but in quality. As the greater uniformity and universality of schooling had helped to bring the issue of unfit children to the fore, a similar process was underway in punishment, with the greater uniformity and universality of application of the sanction of imprisonment working to highlight the extent of unfitness of many prisoners. One indicator was that their literacy level (as measured by chaplains) was apparently barely improving in a period of rapid growth in the provision of primary schooling. Such revelations led both officials and newspaper editors to suggest that prisoners were becoming more anomalous as compared to the general population, remnants of an earlier, less civilized era being left behind by the progress of society.[14] Already in 1879, prison officials were agreeing that both local and convict inmates were becoming less formidable.[15] Prisoners were increasingly seen as the "residuum" of a one-time criminal world, in the phrase of the chairman of the Penal Servitude Commission, and distinct from the current working-class world – the "dregs of the towns," as the vice-chairman of the Irish Prisons Board put it.[16]

This shift in the perceived nature of the prison population was reinforced by the growing role of prison medical officers. As a complement to its provisions for uniformity, the Prisons Act of 1865 had required regular medical inspection of all prisoners. Prison doctors consequently began to play a larger role in managing and defining the nature of prisoners, a role that was further expanded by the 1877 Nationalization Act and the recommendations of the Penal Servitude Commission of the following year.[17] In the process, medical

[14] Whether and to what extent this shift in peceptions reflected actual changes in the nature of prisoners is difficult to establish.

[15] *Royal Commission on the Penal Servitude Acts 1878–79* (Kimberley Commission), Qs. 2546, 4527, 7426–37, 8872–6, 9964–5.

[16] *ibid*, Qs. 7426, 7437, 9964.

[17] Among the commission's proposals that were quickly adopted were the appointment of a superintending medical officer, which, McConville has noted, in effect added a medical member to the Board of Directors, and the opening of appointment of assistant prison surgeons to competition, which "provided a greater measure of professional independence for medical officers." [Sean McConville, *History of English Prison Administration Vol. 1: 1750–1877* (London: Routledge, 1981) pp. 452–3.] This enhanced role for doctors was also prodded by Irish Nationalist complaints. [See Beverly A. Smith, "Irish Prison Doctors – Men in the Middle, 1865–90," *Medical History 26* (1982), 377–8.]

doctors became, unwittingly, a potential source of challenge to the dominant moralist discourse of the system. The doctor was invested with the power in extreme cases to certify a prisoner as insane, removing him to Broadmoor, and less drastically, to declare a prisoner physically or mentally unfit for ordinary penal discipline. By declaring unfitness, he would present the prisoner with an immediate benefit, while removing him (at least temporarily) from the category of responsible moral agent. This potential threat was, however, for a long time only potential; by and large, as we have seen, the doctors were themselves committed to moralist discourse, a commitment reinforced by their official positions as part of the prison administration. Dr. John Campbell, whose memoirs of service from 1850 to 1880 we have explored, was in his never-ending watchfulness against malingerers and his belief in the physical and spiritual benefits of discipline typical of his generation of medical officers.[18]

Nonetheless, the institutionalization within the prisons of the authority of an ever more assertive and self-administering medical profession, whose discourse was becoming increasingly deterministic, introduced a new potential for divergence and discord within the administration, one that Du Cane would make intense efforts to control.[19] Although the change came slowly, the late Victorian generation of prison medical officers was beginning to play a less supportive role than had men like Campbell who had been shaped in the early and middle years of the reign. Despite such innovations as padded cells, which enabled the penal system to better tolerate irrational refractory inmates,[20] medical officers gradually became more ready to recognize physical and mental disability and to disassociate themselves from "weakening" modes of discipline.

This trend must be understood not simply as the result of the regularization of medical inspection by the 1865 act, but rather as the outcome of the broader changes we have noted in medical and criminological discourse. In 1869 insanity and weak-mindedness were first discussed in the reports of convict medical officers; thereafter, the subject was a perennial one. The medical officer of Millbank Prison, Dr. R. M. Gover, noted that "I have reason to believe that the proportion of convicts afflicted with mental and bodily diseases and infirmities is greater than would be found in any other section of the community." The following year he went further:

> It would be difficult to say in how many of these cases [of the 28 Millbank convicts certified that year as insane] offences against the law resulted

---

[18] See, for example, the evidence of Dr. Roone and evidence about his conduct to the 1878–79 Penal Servitude Commission: Qs. 7981–8078, 8211–17.

[19] After 1877, for instance, he replaced the full reports of prison medical officers in the prison commissioners' annual reports with selective summaries.

[20] On the introduction of padded cells in the 1860s see Saunders, "Institutionalized Offenders," unpublished Ph.D. thesis, Warwick University, 1983, p. 235.

from the working of a diseased brain, or in how many confirmed insanity was the natural termination of a life of self-indulgence and crime alternating with imprisonment; but that original defects will account for many of the crimes committed by the convicts who have passed through this prison I can entertain no doubt.[21]

Characteristic of the emerging tension between the needs of deterrence and moralization and the fear that the human material in the prisons was too weak were the ambivalent conclusions of the 1878 committee on prison dietaries (on which Dr. Gover had served). On the one hand, as we have seen, this committee of two medical doctors and an inspector endorsed the use of the treadwheel and the crank, as well as the legitimacy of a "penal element" in prison diet. Yet the committee also recommended (in contrast to its 1864 predecessor) no further reductions in diet, but instead opened the way for dietary improvements with length of incarceration and to greater authority for medical officers to order variances in individual cases.[22] The concern underlying this recommendation of flexibility was evidenced the following year in Dr. Gover's objection to bread and water as a form of punishment. Gover complained to the Penal Servitude Commission that such punishment was counterproductive, for it weakened the will and rendered the prisoner an "automaton."[23]

Overseen and edited by Du Cane, the medical officers' annual reports continued to express concern about the feigning of illness and disability. Yet discomfort was mounting. As Dr. Gover remarked, the prison doctor was faced over and over again with a ticklish problem: "In the majority of cases the malingering consists in an exaggeration of some existing ailment so that great care on the part of the medical officer is necessary in order (medically speaking) to do justice to each case on the one hand, and on the other hand, to discourage and prevent imposture."[24] Gradually, the balance came to shift between the relative importance of "doing (medical) justice to each case" as compared to doing legal justice.

The combination of a more uniform and rigorous penal regime with an expanding role for medical doctors thus came to uncover growing numbers of prisoners who, through mental or physical deficiency or other causes, seemed not to be amenable to the intensified penal discipline meant to deter and

[21] *Report of the Directors of Convict Prisons for 1868*, p. 49; *Report of the Directors of Convict Prisons for 1869*, p. 51. Gover became the medical inspector of the entire prison system after nationalization.
[22] *Report of the Committee on Dietaries of the Prisons of England and Wales 1878*.
[23] *op. cit.*, Q. 1631.
[24] *Report of the Directors of Convict Prisons for 1891–92*, Appendix No. 18, p. xl. Interestingly, however, this was part of the last discussion of malingering in these reports.

moralize.[25] These exceptions were a disturbing force within the prison, and administrators began to search for ways to preserve "normal" prison rule from disruption or erosion. Under the Lunacy Act of 1867 the only way of excluding from ordinary penal discipline those convicts who were discovered to be mentally disabled was by certifying them as insane. Such a drastic step was, however, repugnant to both the Broadmoor authorities (who objected, like most asylum managers, to the mixing of "lunatics of the non-criminal classes with those of the ordinary criminal convict type"[26]) and to Du Cane and his Home Office superiors (who disapproved of such radical decriminalization). Instead, despite the lack of legal sanction,[27] beginning in 1875 a lunatic wing was opened at Woking Invalid Prison where male "prisoner lunatics" were treated, as Du Cane phrased it in an internal communication, "with some reference to their condition as prisoners" – that is, with more "restraint" and fewer "indulgences" than if at Broadmoor, and certainly than if under the authority of the lunacy commissioners.[28]

The 1879 Penal Servitude Commission, the first inquiry to examine at length the question of inmates unfit for prison discipline, approved the arrangement at Woking, but urged that it be extended from insane convicts to those "known as the weak-minded or imbecile," prisoners who were "peculiarly subject to sudden and ungovernable outbursts" and who were "not amenable to the ordinary influences of self-interest or fear of punishment." These sorts of prisoners appeared, as one prison commissioner acknowledged, to be increasing.[29] The commission requested a census by the convict authorities on the precise number of such inmates[30] and recommended that they be removed from penal discipline, placed in a separate institution, and put under treatment suitable to their nature.[31] In the next annual prison commission report, Du Cane and his colleagues (taking their cue from the royal

---

[25] From 1868, the numbers of prisoners found unfit to plead begin to rise. See Walker, *Crime and Insanity in England, Vol. 1* (Edinburgh: Edinburgh University Press, 1968), p. 228. Similarly rising were the numbers of convicted prisoners found unfit for normal prison discipline.

[26] HO 45/9353/28292/1 (1873).

[27] As a later Home Office memorandum observed, "the whole arrangement was illegal from the first," PCOM 7/360/117516 (Aug. 2, 1898).

[28] HO 45/9353/28292, Du Cane to home secretary, Dec. 19, 1873. The number of convicts in that wing rose from 56 on Dec. 31, 1875, to 169 on March 31, 1881, by which time it was beginning to come under criticism. PCOM 7/360/117516 (Aug. 2, 1898).

[29] *Penal Servitude Acts Commission 1879*, Qs. 12,326–7 (Captain Stopford).

[30] This was immediately done. In 1879 there were by official count 541 imbecile prisoners. *Report of the [Departmental] Commission on Criminal Lunacy 1882*, Appendix A, p. 150.

[31] *ibid.*, p. xliii. However, this was only carried out after the Gladstone Committee's report in 1895.

commission) noted that in many cases, particularly among habitual offenders, "mental incapacity prevents [prisoners] from profiting by their experience" and supported devising some means "which should ensure proper care being taken" of such offenders.[32] Reformers seized upon the royal commission's report as evidence that, as the Howard Association put it, many prisoners were "semi-mad" and should be placed in Broadmoor or Woking or other asylums.[33]

In the midst of attacking the treatment of juvenile offenders in 1880, Home Secretary Harcourt also appointed a departmental committee on criminal lunacy. Two developments were behind this action: first, political pressure, from on the one hand asylum doctors who sought to get rid of dangerous patients, and on the other local authorities who sought, after the state takeover of the local prisons, to relieve local ratepayers of the burden of maintaining any "quasi-criminal" asylum inmates; and second, Harcourt's own unhappiness with the lack of allowance made by the criminal justice system for mentally incapable offenders and prisoners. The committee's charge included provision and treatment not only for criminal lunatics but also – for the first time in an official inquiry – for imbeciles who habitually broke the criminal laws. Its report, which in itself stimulated public and professional interest in the mental state of criminals, urged "wide discretionary powers" for the home secretary "in the disposal of criminal lunatics according to the requirements of their condition." At the same time, it expanded the definition of criminal lunatics by recommending (as a sop to local authorities) payment by the state of the costs of criminal inmates of asylums, a recommendation enacted into law in 1884, and by discussing at length the treatment of the weak-minded in prisons. Committee members begged off a full examination of this new category, instead suggesting that a fresh committee take up the subject, since this class of persons raised large new issues of policy; it was "a numerous class, and it is difficult to say how numerous it might become if the burden of [its] maintenance were borne by the State." The committee, however, did recommend that inmates of the lunatic wards at Woking "be distinctly recognized as criminal lunatics" subject to the authority of the lunacy commissioners and that existing law on removing mentally unfit inmates from prison discipline be enforced.[34] Of course, because the category of mental disability had expanded since the 1867 Lunacy Act (and was to expand further), such enforcement would really constitute an extension. Du Cane, fearing the intrusion of the lunacy commissioners onto his territory, dug in his heels against this interpretation of law and only after it was made explicit in the

---

[32] *Report of the Commissioners of Prisons for 1879–80*, pp. 7, 30.
[33] See Howard Association, *Annual Report 1880*, p. 9.
[34] *op. cit.*, pp. 17, 19, 20.

1884 Criminal Lunacy Act did Harcourt feel in a position to issue directions to discontinue the existing halfway procedure and certify its subjects.[35] The 1884 act also followed up the committee's call for flexible authority by giving the home secretary power to make, revoke, and vary prison regulations for the treatment of any prisoners "who appear ... to be from imbecility of mind either unfit for penal discipline or unfit for the same penal discipline as other prisoners."[36] Thereafter, the Home Office began to press for special provision for weak-minded prisoners.[37] But the prison administrators dragged their feet, placing as few convicts as possible in this category.[38]

At the same time, Harcourt was concerned about the subjection to penal discipline of not only the mentally weak, but also the physically debilitated. He strove to make the regular medical examinations of prisoners less perfunctory and more frequent, for he expected this would lead to more removals from prison (it did for as long as he was in office). As Harcourt complained to his officials in 1884, "there remain a considerable number of deaths in Prison, and there are probably a far larger number of persons who are permanently invalids and consequently not fit subjects for Prison Discipline." He asked for, and received, a return of the numbers of chronic invalids "with a view to their removal, either to their friends, or to the Workhouses."[39] Although the resulting increase in medical releases failed to outlast Harcourt's tenure,[40] this

[35] Even so, Du Cane's powers of delay were considerable: it was not until October 1888 that the lunatic wing at Woking was closed and the remaining inmates transferred to Broadmoor. PCOM 7/360/117516 (Aug. 2, 1898).

[36] "An Act to consolidate and amend the Law relating to Criminal Lunatics," 47 & 48 Vict. c. 64 (1884), s. 12.

[37] Under request from above, the prison commissioners established in 1884 in selected prisons arrangements for the care of weak-minded prisoners with sentences of over two months. [*Report of the Prison Commissioners for 1884–85*, p. 14.]

[38] A survey conducted for the Gladstone Committee on Prisons on a particular day in 1895 could find no more than 80 or 2.35 percent of the entire convict population. In the local prisons there were only 159 weak-minded prisoners or 1.24 percent of the population. [Radzinowicz and Hood, p. 538.]

[39] HO 45/9640/A34434/3a (Dec. 16, 1884). Du Cane urged caution, because it would add to the burden on medical officers: "Any person who has not been brought into contact with the subject would find it difficult to believe the ingenuity and perseverance by which prisoners succeed in feigning disease and baffling the doctor." Du Cane suggested requiring two medical opinions for release and that the release be conditional. With Du Cane's cautions accepted, henceforth every case of death in prison was examined by the medical inspector and an annual return was made of all prisoners who were ill and unlikely to survive until the termination of their sentences and of all prisoners "who, by reason of their mental or bodily condition, are unfit for any prison discipline and likely to be so during the whole of their sentences." [HO 45/9640/A34434/8.]

[40] See *Report of the Prison Commissioners for 1887–88*, Appendix B, p. 66.

fact may be owing as much to the clearing-out of a backlog of incapable inmates and the reduction in new committals as to any hardline backlash. Indeed, new and lasting requirements for medical examinations at time of committal and for more frequent and careful examinations periodically thereafter very likely permanently raised standards of what constituted mental and physical fitness for penal discipline; this, in turn, made magistrates more hesitant to incarcerate[41] and prison authorities more cautious to discipline persons of uncertain health. Significantly, fully half of the prisoners received at Pentonville from 1889 to 1890 with sentences of hard labor were found unfit for it and exempted.[42] More generally, as the number of prisoners throughout the system fell, the numbers judged fit for hard labor fell still faster, from 75 percent in 1881 to 56 percent by 1897.[43]

Harcourt's tenure at the Home Office marked a watershed in official discourse on crime and disability, a discourse that would be confirmed, extended, and translated into practice in the following decade.[44] In spite of a lack of sympathy on the part of many judges, the prison commissioners, and Harcourt's conservative successor, Henry Matthews, the issue of disability became ever more important within the penal system. Images relating to mental defect and crime moved away from the stereotype of the unusual violent madman or woman toward one of the much more common weak-minded habitual offender.[45] Policy was eventually to follow; for example, though the Criminal Lunacy Committee had recoiled (fearing for both the taxpayers' pockets and the liberty of the subject) from Dr. Guy's suggestion to create an entirely new class of institution to confine these persons permanently, the movement of

[41] It is difficult to quantify magisterial behavior in this regard, since the increased scrutiny of entering prisoners by medical officers by itself tended to raise the figures of unfit committals, counteracting any diminution in the magistrates' inclination to commit persons of questionable fitness. Fitness was therefore a moving target. Thus despite official policy directed at eliminating them, the number of such committals continued to rise until 1896 (the number of local prisoners found insane rose from 294 in 1889 to 1890 to 479 in 1895 to 1896). [Prison Commissioners' annual reports, medical appendices.]

[42] *Report of the Prison Commissioners for 1889–90*, Appendix pp. 18, 56.

[43] *Report of the Prison Commissioners for 1897–8*, p. 27.

[44] Similarly in Scotland, as Joy Cameron has noted, in the treatment of criminal lunatics "from 1881 the trend of public and scientific opinion laid greater stress on the mental state of the criminal and its scientific treatment rather than on the punishment of his crime. Real efforts were being made to discontinue the practice of locking all the doors all the time, and to present the attendants in the guise of nurses rather than of jailers." [Joy Cameron, *Prisons and Punishment in Scotland* (Edinburgh: Cannongate, 1983, p. 177.]

[45] This paralleled the shift in psychiatric thinking from a focus on a small number of extreme cases to a larger number of lesser cases; see L. J. Ray, "Priests of the Body: Professionalization and Medical Ideas about Insanity in Nineteenth Century England," unpublished D. Phil. thesis, University of Sussex, 1981.

opinion was in some such direction and Guy's proposal was to recur with greater authority in the decades to come.[46]

This growing awareness of weak-minded and weak-bodied criminals posed a dilemma for the Victorian criminal justice system.[47] It produced both ideological uneasiness and administrative conflict; although more weak-minded prisoners were being noticed, the managers of neither (local) asylums nor (state) prisons wanted them, seeing in them a threat of both administrative dislocation and incoherence of purpose. In the context of an increasingly self-confident central bureaucracy and a growing perception of the inadequacy of the nation's human material, the outcome of such struggles was an expanding assumption of responsibility by the state, in part within and in part without the penal system. The 1884 act provided on the one hand for removal to asylums of weak-minded persons already in prisons and on the other for continued state maintenance and responsibility for these persons. It also provided (somewhat obliquely) for keeping criminal lunatics in Broadmoor at the expiration of their sentence, rather than transferring them to local asylums, upon a medical officer's certification that they might be dangerous.[48] Yet in practice, reducing the number of unfit prisoners proved difficult; in spite of the act's provisions for transfer and its formal discouragement of magisterial committal of weak-minded offenders to prison, such committals and the census of mental unfitness within the prison population continued to rise.[49] Indeed, the 1884 act seems to have unintentionally encouraged such committals, as magistrates found it more convenient to send accused persons to prison for the careful medical observation now provided than to try to themselves determine such persons' mental state. The prisons thus took on a psychiatric role that had not been intended for them and that they did not want. Even a Home Office circular to magistrates in 1889, explictly disapproving such committals and providing for the first time an easy way of directly committing to asylum, failed to stem either the apparent rise in such committals or the growth in the labeling of prisoners as mentally unfit. By 1893, as Dr. Gover noted, the number of lunatics proportional to prison population was "larger than that of any year on record."[50] If this was due in part, as he argued, to magistrates com-

---

[46] See Saunders, 233.

[47] One sign of this was that instances of mixing of insane and weak-minded prisoners with normal ones became public scandals, such as at Derby jail in 1890: see 3 PD 343 (Apr. 19, 1890) and HO 45/9715/51407.

[48] See HO 144/63194603A/7–8 (1884).

[49] The consequent rising protest from medical officers and the prison commissioners helped produce the 1889 circular. [See Saunders, in ed. V. Bailey, *Policing and Punishment in Nineteenth Century Britain* (New Brunswick: Rutgers University Press, 1981), pp. 234–5.] However, as Saunders noted, even after 1889 findings of unfitness among prisoners continued to rise, suggesting other forces at work.

[50] *Report of the Prison Commissioners for 1892–3*, p. 6.

mitting persons to prison for observation, it was also in part the result, as he acknowledged the following year, of a change in official perceptions. "In former times," he told the Gladstone Committee on Prisons, "I have no doubt a great many prisoners who were insane were dealt with as if they were sane more than now."[51] Moreover, as the proportion of mentally or physically disabled prisoners seemed to rise inexorably, the government, in its effort to stop or slow this trend, took a critical step away from legalism. As Janet Saunders has noted, the 1889 circular for the first time officially stated that in the case of less serious offenders, "the primary issue was one of appropriate disposal in the interests of offenders themselves, regardless of their legal responsibility under the law for their crimes."[52] A new ideological era was dawning for the Victorian penal system.

"A huge punishing machine": the discrediting of the normal penal regime

Through the 1880s normal deterrent and disciplinary imprisonment, like the formal principles of criminal liability, continued to function; indeed, in many ways under Du Cane it was more fully realized than ever before. But while the norm was retained and perfected, it was becoming an ever less typical experience; the prison population was falling, modifications were being introduced into the prison regime to accommodate a growing range of exceptional cases, and around the prison grew up a number of nonpenal incarcerative institutions – for juveniles, there were the privately run refuges like those of Dr. Barnardo and also the publicly run industrial schools, both less penal than not only jails but also reformatory schools; for middle-class habitual drunkards, the private inebriate reformatories; for lunatics and imbeciles, public asylums; and finally, for a myriad of categories, the ubiquitous workhouses, casual wards, and infirmaries administered with widely varying levels of punitiveness. From none of these institutions were inmates simply free to depart, yet none of them saw their function as punishment. These developments, inside and outside the prison, were beginning to blur the once sharp line between penal and other forms of incarceration.

Along with the proliferation of alternative models of nonpunitive institutionalization, disillusion was setting in more generally with the supposed benefits of institutional routine itself. As early as a *Lancet* commission in 1877, psychiatric thinking had been moving away from the idea of simple incarceration in a general asylum in favor of a dual strategy of more medically

---

[51] *op. cit.*, p. 48 (Q. 1431).
[52] "Institutionalized Offenders," 251.

focused treatment of that minority of cases involving possible cure on the one
hand (in mental hospitals with no "associations of prison") and social prevention and early treatment on the other (what was later to be called social
hygiene).[53] Similar developments had been occurring with juveniles brought
in by the police, with the new "panaceas" of boarding-out and apprenticed
emigration gaining, from the 1880s on, at the expense of internal institutional
solutions. By 1890, even the Howard Association, a long-time supporter of
expanding the industrial schools, could criticize what it now called the
"institutional craze" and urge that deserted, orphaned, or pauper children be
boarded out rather than committed.[54]

Penal discipline was also placed in question by changes in the language of
moralization. As the focus of Christian thought moved from the Atonement to
the Incarnation, the positive role of adversity in character development – what
Gladstone had called "the redemptive value of suffering" – was losing relevance for a population seen to be weaker and less responsible. This was all
the more true as contemporaneous alterations in everyday life were underlining this shift in images of human nature and potential. The diminishing tolerance of pain through the nineteenth century, as life became more secure and
more comfortable and as anesthetics were discovered and gradually applied in
medical procedures, helped to form a new context for punishment. While
punishment's rationale was becoming less clear, its purposes were now also
clouding. What, after all, was the increasingly distasteful infliction of physical
pain supposed to accomplish? More than ever before, such infliction had to justify itself explicitly and thoroughly. In particular, as the century drew toward
its close, suffering in itself was increasingly seen as more likely to crush than to
stimulate the moral energies of ordinary individuals. Across a wide range of
social ills, reformers began to argue for intervention to *reduce* adversity to a
level with which human beings in their existing state could cope. Policymakers
were coming to expect less, not only from drunkards, vagrants, and paupers,

[53] On this commission, see L. J. Ray, "Priests," 351–5; on disillusion generally with the
asylum, see A. Scull, *Museums of Madness* (New York: St. Martin's Press, 1979). In the
United States also, the reputation of institutions for the insane was declining in the late
nineteenth century. See Gerald Grob, *Mental Illness and American Society, 1875–1940*
(Princeton: Princeton University Press, 1983), and David Rothman, *Conscience and Convenience: The Asylum and Its Alternatives in Progressive America* (Boston: Little, Brown,
1980), pp. 294–7. "Upon my word," scolded the eminent neurologist S. Weir Mitchell,
invited to address asylum medical superintendents at their fiftieth annual meeting in 1894,
"I think asylum life is deadly to the insane." [Rothman, p. 296.]

[54] Howard Association, *Annual Report 1890*, p. 15. The following year, reviewing progress
in keeping juvenile offenders out of jail, the association argued that even for the more
benevolent reformatory and industrial schools there was room "for a further application of
the principle of wiser *substitutes*" such as warnings, probation, or a few strokes with the
birch. *Annual Report 1891*, p. 3.

but even from ordinary citizens. In case law and in legislation that set conditions for the enforcement of contractual obligations, assessed liability for occupational and product safety, and in general distributed responsibility for harms, we have already noted the development of a twofold, interrelated shift. Reluctance to inflict or tolerate suffering on the part of ordinary citizens grew, while far greater recognition was accorded to the power of circumstances.

The rethinking of how character was built similarly came to redound upon penal attitudes, as prison memoirs became more expansive in their criticism of the system. Prison exposés of the 1870s, whether by gentlemen or politicals, retained much moralism, simply calling for greater distinctions to be made between men like their authors – men serving a higher cause, as the Irish saw themselves, or "men unduly pressed by adverse circumstances," as the author of *Five Years' Penal Servitude* put it – and the common run of criminals. The latter memoirist balanced his emotional call for society and the penal authorities to ease their "over-righteousness" about accidental offenders like himself with suggestions for cracking down on "real" criminals. "There is plenty of room for the discipline being made much more severe than it is," he argued. In some ways conditions were too good; at Dartmoor, for example, "a great many of the prisoners never slept in such good beds when free men. Men have told me repeatedly, especially men from agricultural districts, that they were better fed and had better beds in prison than ever they had in their lives before." He did not object to this comfort for prisoners of decent character, but he saw no reason why these should be provided for all. In particular, he proposed flogging for "all professionals who come for a second time into the convict prisons" and the prevention of all verbal communication between prisoners.[55] All these complaints were essentially with the administration of the system rather than with the system itself, let alone with the moral universe behind it. For instance, the pseudonymous "Bill Sykes," a City of London businessman sentenced to penal servitude, spent his time behind bars composing melodramatic poems describing the ruinous consequences of drink and gambling ("The Wife's Lament," "Kiss Me, Father!," etc.), and emerged from prison a temperance crusader. Yet, by their denuciation of the treatment meted out to them, these early middle-class prison memoirists challenged the moral legitimacy of the prison system. Again and again, they inveighed against the "absurd rules and regulations at present in force," the pointless restrictions and humiliations, the enforced silence, the brutalities, and the unchecked power of prison officers.[56]

[55] "One Who Has Endured It," *op. cit.*, p. 377. "Ticket-of-Leave-Man," in 1879, had much the same to say, and "D – S – ," author of *Eighteen Months' Imprisonment* (London: Routledge, 1883), went further. A former military officer discharged early by Harcourt on grounds of health, "D – S –" complained that "hardened criminals," many of them "wild beasts," were in fact treated too leniently.

[56] "Bill Sykes," *Prison Life and Prison Poetry* (London: Newman & Co., 1881), p. 75.

With even critics rarely taking issue with the principles of deterrence and character-building, policymakers, not surprisingly, reiterated them even as they made exceptions and qualifications. For the "normal" offender, the "real" criminal, the 1879 Penal Servitude Commission reaffirmed the principles and administration of deterrent punishment. It rejected suggestions to lower the minimum sentence for penal servitude; such a change, it feared, would weaken the special stigma of penal servitude, the "wholesome dread" of it in the public mind. Neither were its members agreeable to allowing the prison authorities to reduce in practice the maximum sentence, refusing to agree with Du Cane, no man for soft sentiment, that "twenty years is quite enough" even for life-sentence prisoners. In general, the commissioners resisted suggestions by both the Howard Association and some prison administrators to increase the amount of potential remission of sentence, as undermining the authority of judges and increasing the arbitrariness of the law. Similarly, they found that on the whole, discipline in prisons was not too severe. Hearing attacks by ex-convict witnesses on the brutality and absolutism of prison administration, the commissioners put forth a number of cautious suggestions for introducing greater due process into prison discipline and slightly tempering its severity; at the same time, they denied the existence of fundamental problems and saw no need for drastic change in the system or its principles. "The first object," they noted in opposing the exemption of printers from heavy manual labor, remained "the infliction, as nearly as may be, of equal punishment." From a variety of angles, then, the commissioners reaffirmed the importance of the principle of deterrence by means of uniform, severe, and inescapable punishment.[57]

Despite his concerns for exempting juveniles and the disabled and despite his readiness to consider removing particular cruelties,[58] Harcourt similarly reaffirmed in principle on a number of occasions the appropriateness of deterrent severity for the treatment of mentally competent adults. Although he acknowledged that the 1865 Prisons Act was "very severe," and that he was prepared, with his activist temperament, to review particular cases, he publicly supported Du Cane's administration of it, indeed defending the convict prisons of which Du Cane had most complete control as "perhaps, the best-conducted institutions in this country."[59] Harcourt upheld the value of deter-

---

[57] *Report of the Royal Commission on Penal Servitude 1878–79*, pp. xxviii–xxix; xxxiii; 237 (Qs. 2844–8); pp. li, xlvi.

[58] As in his instructing in 1884 the disuse of dark cells for punishment. [*Report of the Scottish Prison Commissioners for 1884–5*, p. 1.]

[59] 3 PD 253, c. 1121 (June 29, 1880); letter from Harcourt to William Tallack, secretary of the Howard Association, published in *The Times*, June 7, 1882, quoted in Radzinowicz and Hood, p. 572n.

rent punishment for rational and responsible lawbreakers, resisting pressures for letting off those rousing strong public sympathy (like the celebrated shipwrecked cannibals, Dudley and Stephens) or reducing sentences and easing treatment of those with particular constituencies (like Irish revolutionaries). Harcourt even rejected Du Cane's own suggestions (which would have taken the Prison Commission out of the line of fire) for allowing the Irish the status of political prisoners under special, less penal regulations. "I do not think," he firmly rejoined, "there will be any difficulty in treating these men as ordinary prisoners and I do not desire at present that any difference should be made."[60]

Yet, signs were multiplying of a waning confidence in the prison as a social tool. Almost as soon as the prisons were nationalized, the recourse to imprisonment began to be qualified, first in the diminishing length of terms behind bars and then as a proportion of sentences, as noncustodial alternatives like fines, recognizances, and probation began to be used more and more. Between 1883 and 1893, average daily local prison population fell by one-third and convict population by almost one-half.[61] The benefits of the prison experience to society – and to the prisoner as well – were appearing less obvious, if only slowly at first. A decentering of the prison in criminal policy, which has been attributed to the period after 1895,[62] was actually well underway in the heyday of Du Cane. Anticipatory tremors made themselves felt as early as the proceedings of the 1879 Royal Commission on Penal Servitude.

"One Who Has Endured It" had concluded his memoir by calling for a royal commission "to thoroughly investigate the whole convict system with a view to its reformation," and by urging that such a commission, unlike earlier ones, take the evidence of former and present prisoners.[63] Such a commission, was, indeed, soon created. In contrast to its predecessor of 1863, the Kimberley Commission worked in a new atmosphere of relative public security and of confidence in the manageability of the crime problem. That for the first time, substantial evidence was taken from convicts and ex-convicts (albeit usually gentleman prisoners) including the author of *Five Years'* himself, suggests both a relaxation of both fear and moralism and the influence of political democratization.

[60] HO 45/9624/A 19541 (1882).
[61] Annual criminal statistics, and annual reports of the prison commissioners. The falling convict population was chiefly due to fewer sentences of penal servitude (which had a fixed minimum period), whereas the decline in local prison population was almost entirely the product of shorter terms of imprisonment. Both seemed to be responses to a diminishing confidence in the prison and in deterrence as social tools.
[62] See D. Garland, *Punishment and Welfare* (Aldershot: Gower, 1985), pp. 23, 36.
[63] *Five Years'*, p. 384.

The author of *Five Years' Penal Servitude* had argued, both in his book and before the commission, that first offenders like himself, persons often led astray by circumstance or a momentary succumbing to impulse, should certainly be kept apart and treated differently from deliberate, professional lawbreakers. The commissioners, while defending the system against the emotional charges of cruelty, seemed to be influenced by this line of argument. They endorsed the differential treatment of prisoners who did not fit the image of real criminal. They acknowledged a need to distinguish between types of offenders and, by contrast with the continued deterrent treatment of "real" criminals ("professional" repeat offenders), to lessen the severity and length of imprisonment for juveniles and first offenders. In particular, they recommended placing in a distinct class prisoners who had not been previously convicted of any offense, a recommendation to which the prison administration reluctantly agreed. Even while reaffirming the mid-Victorian principles of the system, the commissioners were shifting their attention toward the growing problem of exceptional categories of prisoners. Henceforth as we have seen, the reports of the prison administration increasingly noted distinctions between regular prisoners and those special categories of offenders for whom regular prison discipline, or the prison institution itself, was no longer felt to be suitable. This ambivalence about the sanction of imprisonment, hesitantly expressed in the proceedings of the Kimberley Commission, came into the open after Harcourt arrived at the Home Office. While reaffirming the voluntarist principles of the criminal justice system, he promoted decarceration[64] and expanded alternative provisions for exceptional categories of offender, thus beginning an erosion of the existing system and its social meaning.

In the meantime, the prison system was facing a new practical problem for which it had not been designed, that of administering to a large number of political prisoners who for the first time possessed significant parliamentary support. In the forefront of complaints in the House of Commons about overly harsh sentencing and penal discipline were the Irish M.P.s who denounced the treatment of their compatriots convicted of treason-felony and sentenced to long prison terms. With its intensification in the 1880s, the Irish Question thus became also an issue for penal policy, as the Nationalist prisoners and their spokesmen demanded special status within the prisons. Many influential figures in government were prepared to concede such status. But, while allowing them various privileges and special treatment in practice, home secretaries, both Liberal and Conservative, refused either to meet all their

---

[64] He was later to urge his private secretary at the Home Office, when appointed to the Prison Commission at the beginning of 1892, to "continue the good work of diminishing [the prison] population." [Shane Leslie, *Sir Evelyn Ruggles-Brise* (London: J. Murray, 1938), p. 78; see also pp. 69–70.]

demands or grant them a formally distinct status for fear of eroding the moral and deterrent principles on which the existing system of criminal justice rested. Although this refusal turned back one kind of formal challenge to the system, it was a pyrrhic victory, because it meant that the normal world of the convict prisons had to absorb in significant numbers a new and much more difficult type of gentleman prisoner. This type of prisoner was extremely alienated from authority, particularly sensitive to mistreatment, and highly articulate about it; moreover, he had a body of supporters outside the walls to press his complaints. Indeed, the Irish Nationalists created in the 1880s the first antiprison lobby, a pressure group in whose interest it was to publicize anything about the convict prisons that might offend or disturb English public opinion. Even though through the decade their efforts seemed to produce little interest in England, the Irish political prisoners were contributing to a slow alteration in the mental landscape, making the image of the prison more problematic, a source of some discomfort for the public and certainly for the governing class.

Prison memoirs also began to reflect an erosion of the moral rationale of the prison. Where the authors of such works as *Five Years' Penal Servitude* (1877), *Convict Life* (1880), and *Prison Life and Prison Poetry* (1881) had complained of the lack of moral classification, of the lumping together of comparatively mild, reformable offenders like themselves with hard-core criminals, memoirs of former prisoners and of prison visitors from the mid-1880s on increasingly attacked the general character of the whole penal system. The Irish political prisoners of the 1860s and 1870s had made little criticism of the penal system in general, focusing their complaints – like those of English gentleman prisoners – upon the degradation of their being lumped together with common felons. However, in the 1880s this outrage began to spill over into more general criticisms. A new note was sounded in Michael Davitt's *Leaves From A Prison Diary* (1885). Davitt, an Irish Nationalist M.P., had been imprisoned from 1870 to 1877 and treated as a common convict. During his second imprisonment, from 1881 to 1882, he was, now a public figure, more respectfully dealt with in practice, if not in principle. Given a cell in the infirmary, a special diet, visits from friends, and, most important, the freedom to read and write, he turned his mind from the treatment of himself and his fellow politicals toward a dispassionate general critique of the penal system and of society in general. Davitt attacked the harshness and rigidity of the existing regime. "The discipline of convict prisons," he objected, "has been regulated by what is necessary to maintain the most insubordinate prisoner in constant subjection, and not by a standard of what is required to keep in order, and measure out a just and reasonable daily punishment to, the average type of fairly-conducted prisoners." Even for the worst prisoner, this discipline was counterproductive: "its merciless disregard of human passion and feeling, its exaction of implicit obedience to humiliating, minute, and ceaseless regulations . . . are calculated to keep in sleepless activity every incentive to rebellion of which the human mind is capable under the keenest provocation that could possibly be devised, short of systematical torture." Penal servitude was an utter failure on all counts, undone by its mechanical uniformity in dealing with criminal offenders. He concluded:

> Penal servitude has become so elaborated that it is now a huge punishing machine, destitute, through centralised control and responsibility, of discrimination, feeling, or sensitiveness; and its non-success as a deterrent from crime, and complete failure in reformative effect upon criminal character, are owing to its obvious essential tendency to deal with erring human beings – who are still men despite their crimes – in a manner which mechanically reduces them to a uniform level of disciplined brutes.

The root of this penal failure Davitt traced to a lack of understanding of the real causes of crime, which lay beyond the criminals themselves. He denounced

> the unreasonable, if not vindictive, severity of the law in dealing with a class of human beings for whose Ishmaelite propensities society itself is, in the main, responsible. . . . Given . . . a percentage of the population of Great Britain upon whom poverty and ignorance are allowed to exercise their demoralising influence, and upon whose perverted lives the accessory evils of intemperance and the solicitations of ostentatious wealth are permitted to have full play, how can the society that is responsible for such a state of things sanction the sentences that are now passed upon criminals who have been thus nurtured by its own neglect, and for crimes which are mainly the outcome of its own defective police organisation?[65]

Davitt devoted the second volume of his prison memoirs to examining the "social evils" that bred crime and what could be done about them.

The more Victorian demands upon "erring human beings" seemed unrealistic and unproductive, the more the existing penal system stood condemned as too harsh and too uniform for any useful purpose. Davitt's image of the prison as a machine became a leitmotif thereafter in the writings of reformers and former prisoners.[66] The very characteristics that had been deliberately striven for over the previous half-century – dispassionate impersonality, uniformity, predictability (as Major Arthur Griffiths, chief prison in-

---

[65] *Leaves From a Prison Diary* (London: Chapman & Hall, 2 Vols., 1885), Vol. 1, pp. 240–4, 249.

[66] As one prestigious committee of the newly formed American Institute of Criminal Law and Criminology noted in 1911, criminal justice could no longer be "indiscriminate and machine-like, but must be adapted to the causes, and to the man as affected by those causes." [Quoted in Rothman, *Conscience*, p. 57.]

spector under Du Cane, happily recalled, "everything worked with clock-like precision"[67]) – were now attacked for their oppressive negativism and their grinding denial of the individuality and variability of criminals. One reformer complained in 1889 that the prison system was "a complicated machinery" for the processing of criminals: "a rascal is put into a machine, a crank is made to revolve a definite number of times, and a virtuous man is supposed to come forth.... But human beings cannot be treated advantageously as if they were lumps of dead metal, or clay.... [T]he treatment of 1,500 men in one institution by means of a cast-iron system, under inflexible rules, is simply a modern revival of the bed of Procrustes."[68] One well-known gentleman prisoner, Austin Bidwell, put it more pungently in 1895:

> An English prison is a vast machine in which a man counts for just nothing at all. He is to the establishment what a bale of merchandise is to a merchant's warehouse. The prison does not look on him as a man at all. He is merely an object which must move in a certain rut and occupy a certain niche provided for it. There is no room for the smallest sentiment. The vast machine of which he is an item keeps undisturbed on its course. Move with it and all is well. Resist, and you will be crushed as inevitably as the man who plants himself on the railroad track when the express is coming. Without passion, without prejudice, but also without pity and without remorse, the machine crushes and passes on. The dead man is carried to his grave and in ten minutes is as much forgotten as though he never existed.[69]

Frederick Brocklehurst, a Radical Manchester city councillor who spent a month in Strangeways jail for refusal to pay a fine for illegal public speaking, similarly denounced "the machine-like character of prison administration" and "the mechanism and routine of prison life." "The prison system," he complained, "does its best to reduce its victims to a dead unthinking level, to the position of numbered cogs in a mighty Juggernaut wheel."[70]

By the time Bidwell and Brocklehurst were writing, penal reform had become a major public issue. The Liberal defeat in 1886 had allowed advanced Liberals, freed from pressures of loyalty to the government, to put an increasing number of parliamentary questions about excessive sentences and harsh treatment. In 1887 the general issue of penal reform emerged for the first time in Parliament. The Unionist government, with a new crimes act, had just

---

[67] Major Arthur Griffiths, *Fifty Years of Public Service* (London: Cassell, 1904), p. 166.

[68] L. Gordon Rylands, *Crime: Its Causes and Remedy* (London: T. Fisher Unwin, 1889), 219–20.

[69] *From Wall Street to Newgate* (Hartford, Conn.: Bidwell Publishing Co., 1895), pp. 459–60.

[70] *I Was in Prison* (London: T. Fisher Unwin, 1898), pp. 17, 69.

intensified coercion in Ireland, which put growing numbers of Nationalists in prison.[71] Irish members followed Davitt's lead and broadened their penal agenda from the issue of political status to demands for general reform. With political tempers high, the annual supply vote became the occasion for general criticism of the administration of prisons. The Irish Nationalist Arthur O'Connor, seconded by Radical English members, argued that "it is of the first consequence that the prison treatment should not only be punitive and deterrent, but that it should also be of such a nature as is likely to improve rather than to deteriorate the character of the persons so confined."[72] When, the following week, English members took up the cudgels, citing especially the prison policy of banning anything more than the barest communication between prisoners and their families, the protesters drew a promise from the unsympathetic home secretary, Henry Matthews, to consider, during the upcoming recess, "the whole question of Prison Rules."[73] It was now coming to be assumed, in the absence of countervailing influences, that deterrent punishment deteriorated its subjects.

The following year, when the government did nothing further, the attacks widened to embrace general conditions such as sparse diet, plank beds, and lack of heating. The pro-Irish Radical Henry Labouchere seemed to sense a sea change in public sentiment, declaring that "they did not put men in prison for the purpose of torturing them," and calling for an inquiry to clarify just what were the country's principles of prison discipline.[74] When the letters that the government had been relying on to link Parnell with terrorism were shown to be forgeries, public opinion swung against its policy of Irish coercion. Home Secretary Matthews felt compelled, against his inclinations,[75] to

[71] See L. P. Curtis, *Coercion and Conciliation in Ireland 1880–1892* (Princeton: Princeton University Press, 1963).

[72] 3 PD 319, c. 1485–89 (Aug. 22, 1887). Home Secretary Matthews, in private scornful of humanitarianism, was careful not to directly rebuff such complaints: Noting that it was too late in the session to "enter into the large subject of prison discipline," he acknowledged "the views enunciated by the honorable Member and by others, that when you catch a thief you are immediately to set about reforming him in order to make him into a good member of society—that is a growing belief, and I do not dissent from it. Since the year 1837 the number of prisons has been reduced from 115 to 60, so that not bad work has been done in the time, and I think we have almost reached the limit." [*ibid*, c. 1469–97.]

[73] 3 PD 320, c. 745–46 (Sept. 1, 1887).

[74] 3 PD 330, c. 1326–7 (Nov. 15, 1888). Du Cane seems to have been feeling pressure mounting, for he devoted several pages of the prison commissioners' report for 1887 to reprinting an 1882 speech by Harcourt praising the prison system. From this point on, the annual reports, always self-laudatory, devote a growing proportion of space to defense against actual or potential criticism.

[75] The only penal changes Matthews favored were to tighten up the system; he supported (but did not press) restoring corporal punishment and restricting loopholes that allowed criminals to escape conviction. He took little interest in the workings of the penal system

act on Irish prison complaints. Over Du Cane's objections about opening a can of worms[76] and over press objections that Irish prisoners already received treatment "better than that meted out to like offenders on this side of St. George's Channel,"[77] Matthews set up a departmental committee of inquiry into prison rules and discipline. The committee was chaired by Gladstone's first home secretary, Lord Aberdare. Though its work was directed at Irish complaints, particularly such symbolic issues as clothing and haircutting, the committee in making any changes would, as Matthews realized, "make similar changes in England inevitable."[78]

The report of the Aberdare Committee, while, as *The Times* gratefully noted, "giv[ing] no sign of tenderness for political offences," did suggest some penal relaxations for prisoners not sentenced "for offences of an immoral, dishonest, shameful, or criminal character,"[79] The report was followed by the Penal Servitude Bill of 1891, the first legislation for prisons since 1877; the bill removed a few of the most inflammatory minor facets of the regime, endorsed maximizing possibilities for remission, and lowered the minimum term of penal servitude from five to three years.[80] The bill passed with little discussion; most notable were complaints that it did not go far enough. Indeed, the Tory reformer Lord Norton, still active after more than forty years in Par-

---

except for such occasional interventions, such as suggesting to his officials that they might take advantage of the necessity of a bill modifying prison rules to "introduce a clause giving power to award whipping as part of the sentence for burglars or using deadly weapons." [HO 45/9767/B849/8 (April 5, 1889).]

[76] Du Cane claimed the time was not ripe for reviewing the law in regard to convict prisons: "this subject is one which is at this moment sure to fall into long and acrimonious discussions as to prison treatment [and] political offences and which would probably not result in an improvement of the prison administration or the more effective execution of the object of punishment." [Memorandum to the home secretary, Feb. 5, 1889. HO 45/9767/B849/6.]

[77] *The Times*, March 11, 1889, p. 9.

[78] Memorandum to G. Lushington, April 5, 1889. HO 45/9767/B849/8. This was true not only directly, in subsequent modifications of English convict prison rules on diet and dress, but indirectly, in removal of such stigmatizing rules as requiring convicts tried on new charges to appear in court in convict dress; from 1892, they were allowed to wear civilian clothing. [Radzinowicz and Hood, p. 548.]

[79] *The Times*, July 13, 1889, p. 11. As even a conservative official privately conceded a few years later, "a proper punishment for ... the thief and the burglar ... must from the nature of things bear with terrible force physically and mentally upon those who, however atrocious may be their crime, are of a superior class and education to the ordinary convict." PCOM 7/358/117516, C. S. Murdoch, November 1896.]

[80] In drawing up new rules for its administration, the Home Office increased the amount of remission earnable by including categories of convicts hitherto excluded. [HO 45/9731/A53188 (1891–2).] The bill also in effect abolished sentences of imprisonment above two years. [HO 45/9731/A53188B (1891–2).]

liament, made the first call from the government side of the floor for a royal commission to investigate the entire sphere of prison administration. "Everybody," he observed,

> is delighted with the undoubted fact that crime is being very much reduced in this country; and therefore many people are hastily thinking, if that is the case, what is the use of looking into the system. The system must be good under which crime has been reduced. But the reduction of crime, I think . . . is attributable not to the perfection of our penal system – I think that has been rather adverse to the reduction of crime – but it is attributable to the extension of education and the reformatory system, and to the Discharged Prisoners' Aid system in this country.[81]

Others seconded Norton's call, but the government, seeing it as a largely Irish and Radical issue, was loath to respond.

Yet just as the Irish political prisoners were being released from convict prisons in large numbers and their penal grievances appeased, public attention was drawn to the hitherto much less controversial regime inside local prisons. A new source of support for a rethinking of the concept of imprisonment was emerging in the form of another sort of political prisoner, the conscience offender. A campaign of resistance to compulsory smallpox vaccination had, since the mid-1880s, been bringing into the local prisons respectable offenders unused to penal treatment.[82] The Vaccination Acts were a particularly controversial example of the Victorian trend toward expanding the use of criminal sanctions to enforce public health and welfare regulations. This trend was leading to the conviction and, if they refused to pay their fine, the imprisonment of persons clearly not of the criminal type; these persons, faced with the normal prison regime created for an altogether different social class, were appalled by its degrading and inhumane aspects. At the same time also, members of the increasingly militant Salvation Army were being arrested for obstructing the streets in their evangelizing efforts, refusing on principle to pay the fine, and finding themselves imprisoned.[83] Members of both movements testified before the Aberdare Committee of the "needless indig-

---

[81] 3 PD 356, c. 388–90 (July 27, 1891).

[82] Vaccination acts dated from 1840, but effective compulsion from legislation of 1867 and 1871. Penalties were fines, but default either from lack of means or from principle resulted in jailing. The resistance movement took up civil disobedience in the 1880s and gained appointment of a royal commission in 1889, which sat until 1896. See R. M. Macleod, "Law, Medicine and Public Opinion: Resistance to Compulsory Health Legislation 1870–1907," *Public Law* (Summer–Autumn, 1967), 107–28, 189–211.

[83] See Victor Bailey, "Salvation Army Riots, the 'Skeleton Army' and Legal Authority in the Provincial Town," in *Social Control in Nineteenth Century Britain,* ed. A. P. Donajgrodszki (London: Croom Helm, 1977), pp. 231–53.

nity" inflicted by the prison regime.[84] As with Irish Nationalism, so too other movements having nothing to do with criminal policy came, as a by-product of their activities, to bring prison conditions to the attention of the middle classes and thus fueled dissatisfaction with the prisons. From yet another direction, the regime of the prisons was becoming an issue.

Like the Irish, the critics of compulsory vaccination, as they waited for their behavior to be decriminalized, sought to establish special status within the prison system. A private members' bill in 1891 proposed to create in effect, chiefly for anti-vaccinationists and also for overly enthusiastic Salvation Army missionaries, a new category of conscience prisoner to be exempted from some of the restrictions of ordinary imprisonment. To legal-minded civil servants at the Home Office this proposal, like Irish demands for special status, threatened both the moral legitimacy of the law and the law's deterrent power. Lushington observed that "it seems wrong or foolish to make imprisonment less deterrent or to weaken the public impression that it is a punishment for the doing of something mischievous to society."[85] When the Royal Commission on Vaccination in 1892 supported such a change, Lushington stubbornly noted that "my own view always has been that a person who willfully breaks the general law of the land should be treated as a criminal offender, and punished with a view to deter him from breaking it again (the punishment will of course vary in severity, but nothing should be done to show that the law-breaker is not a criminal). I do not see how conscience can be pleaded."[86] Civil servants felt that the solution was not to try, as some reformers were urging,[87] to calibrate penal regimes to assessments of offenders' motives rather than their deeds, but instead to narrow the overgrown reach of the criminal law so that it embraced only real criminals and provided noncriminal penalties for offenders against administrative regulations. C. E. Troup, a senior clerk later to fill Lushington's shoes as permanent under-secretary, suggested in 1891 drawing "a distinction between crimes and mere police offences."[88] Officials in the early 1890s, who noted that criminal

---

[84] *The Times*, July 13, 1889.

[85] Comments on memorandum on Prison Acts Amendment Bill 1891, HO 45/9840/B10768/1 (June 4, 1891).

[86] HO 45/9840/B10768B/2 (May 11, 1892).

[87] For example, William Tallack, *Penological and Preventive Principles* (London: Wertheimer, Lea. 1889) and Gordon Rylands, *Crime: Its Causes and Remedy* (London: T. Fisher Unwin, 1889).

[88] Comments on memorandum on Prison Acts Amendment Bill 1891, HO 45/9840/B10768/1. Troup was more exercised than was his chief by the inequity and inefficiency of uniform treatment, concluding that "much may be said for the view that a person sent to prison (on failure to pay a fine) for failing to sweep the snow from his doorway, or from failing to send his boy to school, or for breach of minor municipal or sanitary bye-laws, should not be imprisoned in the same way as a housebreaker or a forger." In fact, after a

liability had been continuing to expand even as crime rates fell and who were coming under political criticism because of this disparity, were led to suggest ways of limiting criminal liability. Increasingly, they came to make distinctions between real and not real criminals and consequently, paralleling that distinction, between prisoners suitable and not suitable for normal prison discipline.

As the distressing experiences of conscience prisoners were being recounted in press, pamphlet, and public speech, a number of scandals broke involving local prisons. The death of a prisoner in Strangeways Prison, Manchester, led to a parliamentary debate in March 1890, in which a Radical English member, E. H. Pickersgill, who had been repeatedly raising questions about cases of jail deaths and mental breakdowns,[89] for the first time leveled a general attack on the prison commissioners for their "policy of hushing up everything that may in any way bring discredit on the administration, and consequently on themselves."[90] The Strangeways scandal was followed the next year by a riot at Wormwood Scrubbs Prison, an event that kept public attention on prison conditions.[91] While these scandals were being discussed, a general shift in sentiment against the degradation of penal discipline also occurred. Complaints rose against even nonviolent public displays of degradation such as the conveying of prisoners by marching them handcuffed through the streets or transporting them in public railway carriages.[92] Such implicitly degrading ceremonies began to receive the outrage formerly reserved for public

royal commission in effect recommended it in 1891, prosecutions for refusal ot comply with the Vaccination Acts rapidly fell (while the number of children remaining unvaccinated rose), practically decriminalizing resistance. See *Criminal Statistics for 1896*, p. 18. Legislation in 1896 ratified this practical decriminalization.

[89] A few weeks earlier, he had cited the authority of Lord Chief Justice Coleridge, who had characterized a prison sentence as of "terrible severity." [3 PD 342, c. 1143 (March 18, 1890.)] Coleridge, a moderate Liberal in politics, also, as we have seen, criticized applying cumulative sentencing to petty offenders.

[90] 3 PD 343, c. 331–38 (March 31, 1890). An Irish member sardonically applauded the fact "that the prison discipline of this country is now beginning to attract the attention of English Members"; perhaps serious reforms, such as had not followed Irish complaints, might now ensue. [P. O'Brien, *ibid*, c. 339–42]

[91] See 4 PD 1, c. 196–7 (Feb. 11, 1892).

[92] For an increasingly common protest, see 3 PD 350, c. 468 (Feb. 12, 1891): Here, as in other such cases, the Home Office promised to discourage such practices. Complaints in the Home Office files about public handcuffing of women date from 1891. [See HO 144/A54980.] The practice was ordered ended in 1899 after a new wave of protests. [A conservative paper, the *Western Mail*, had noted on March 3, 1899, that the appearance of handcuffed prisoners, male and female, being moved from Swansea jail to the Cardiff Assizes, on a railway platform "jarred considerably upon the spectators, who had modern views upon the fitness of things. The girls, whose disgrace was thus unwisely, if not unnecessarily, forced upon the attention of the public, betrayed in their demeanour the

floggings and hangings. Alongside the new intolerance for the infliction of stigma was the rising intolerance for the infliction of pain, marked by the legislative success of the child protection movement and the emergence of the antivivisection movement at the turn of the decade. Indeed, 1891 saw the founding of the Humanitarian League, whose chief causes became the prevention of cruelty to animals, children, and prisoners.

All these pressures began to affect penal practice. While resisting legislation and public inquiries, prison administrators, under serious political fire for the first time, began to modify their regime. After Du Cane's post-1877 tightening up, the punitive thrust of the prison system began in the 1880s to soften. Given the large decline in the prison population – produced in part by the growing resistance to imprisoning juveniles, women, first offenders, trivial offenders, and the mentally or physically weak – one must presume that the proportion of hard-core offenders was rising, pushing discipline if anything toward greater severity. Yet, even as public objections to prison cruelties and indignities rose in the later 1880s,[93] the number of punishments per capita for disciplinary infractions fell, the provision for exceptional categories of prisoner status continued to expand, and the proportion of prison officers recruited from the military declined.[94]

By 1892, public and parliamentary opinion may have crossed a watershed. All three legs of midcentury penal policy – uniformity, long (and frequently cumulative) prison sentences, and severe penal discipline – had ceased to be generally accepted, although no alternatives clearly replaced them. The prison itself appeared to be of questionable value for most cases of lawbreaking. Even the great new fictional defender of law and order, Sherlock Holmes, was sceptical of the value of imprisonment. On at least fourteen occasions the great Holmes let caught felons go free; as he said of one such man, "Send him to

shame they felt. . . . The spectacle of handcuffed women in a public place is certainly unusual, and revolting to the feelings of most people."] Complaints also appear about 1890 about parish bell tollings and Newgate flag lowerings to mark executions.

[93] And as grievance petitions from prisoners to the home secretary seem to have been rising. [HO 45/9736/A54343B (1892–3)].

[94] Prisoners receiving corporal punishment in local prisons, as a percentage of average daily population, fell slowly from an average of 1.08 percent in the period from 1868 to 1877 to .80 percent from 1892 to 1893, and then rapidly to .50 percent from 1894 to 1895. [*Report of the Prison Commissioners for 1893–4*, p. 27; *Report of the Prison Commissioners for 1894–5*, p. 9]–a "remarkable" decrease, Legge pointed out to Gladstone while they were preparing the departmental committee report. [B.L. Add MSS. 45990/251 (Feb. 15, 1895.] After 1879, in most cases, floggings were carried out with the milder birch instead of the cat. In convict prisons per capita floggings remained steady until 1893, when they too began to fall rapidly. As for staff, Radzinowicz and Hood (pp. 549–50) note that whereas in 1876 two-thirds of prison officers came from the military, by 1894 this had fallen to 55 percent of recent recruits.

gaol now, and you make him a gaolbird for life."[95] Despite the growing frustration with short sentences, there was little broad sentiment to reverse the well-established trend of shortening sentences; if short sentences seemed useless, long ones seemed both useless and barbaric. One sign of the times came in 1892 when a Scottish bill providing for the length of sentences to increase with the number of convictions was crushingly defeated in the Commons. Reverend W. D. Morrison observed a year later to one of the growing number of committees of inquiry, "There is a strong feeling with regard to long sentences at the present time."[96] As the barrister and miners' M.P., Llewellyn Atherley-Jones, declared during the debate on the 1898 Prisons Bill, "A sentence of two years' hard labour is a sentence which no judge, in my judgment, and in the judgment of persons more capable than myself, should inflict upon a fellow-creature."[97] There was a similar feeling about harsh discipline. In the debate on the Strangeways death, another Radical, Handel Cossham, had stated that "all vindictive treatment" was a mistake, because it "tends to harden prisoners."[98] By 1894, even *The Times* was reassessing its outlook. "Modern controversies as to the chief ethical problems of life," that conservative newspaper reflected,

> have affected men's estimates of conduct as to which there was once an accepted opinion. We are not all so sure as we once were of the good effects of a residence in prison, or of the genesis of crime. We do not hang or imprison a man with the self-complacency and sense of self-righteousness of our fathers.[99]

The climate was ripe for a penal crisis and for an era of penal reform.

---

[95] Marcello Truzzi, "Sherlock Holmes: Applied Social Psychologist," in eds. Umberto Eco and Thomas A. Sebeok, *The Sign of Three: Dupin, Holmes, Peirce* (Bloomington, Indiana: University of Indiana Press, 1983), pp. 73–4; quotation from "The Blue Carbuncle" (1892), Arthur Conan Doyle, *Complete Sherlock Holmes, Vol. 1* (New York: Doubleday, 1930), p. 178. Suspicion of the Victorian prison was perhaps natural to Holmes, standing as he did for individualized solutions to crime over against the uniform routine of the police; indeed, the shift in interest from the police to the private detective his popular success exemplified may have been one facet of a more general disenchantment with uniform, institutional solutions.

[96] *Report of the Departmental Committee on the Treatment of Inebriates*, 1893, p. 60.

[97] 4 PD 55, c. 848 (March 24, 1898). He went on: "Nobody, who has not had the opportunity of observing the condition of the victims, can have any conception of the effect of a lengthened term of imprisonment, even on the most robust."

[98] 3 PD 343, c. 343–47 (March 31, 1890).

[99] *The Times*, Dec. 17, 1894, p. 9.

9

The outcome: social debility and positive punishment

From moralism to causalism

Placed in Victorian cultural context, the penal crisis of the 1890s takes on more complex and more resonant contours than if it is seen as a stage in the march of either humanitarianism or the disciplining state. Whiggish historians were not wrong to see a revival of ameliorative hopes, a new level of sensitivity to suffering, and a new distaste for incarceration in these years. On the other hand, revisionists were also right to point out that the reforms that followed reshaped rather than relaxed social control. Yet it was both more and less than either idealism or politics; to insist on one or the other interpretation as sufficiently explanatory is to impose modern moral parameters on a situation that they do not fit, forcing the texture of mental experience within the Victorian and Edwardian policymaking strata into alien terms of discourse. Instead, this study has sought to highlight a neglected dimension of social discourse and policy – the symbolic, even the aesthetic – the never-ending effort to construct a satisfying narrative of the relations of individuals to each other and to the state. This aspect tied into, but at the same time cut across, both the efforts to humanize and enlighten the treatment of criminals and efforts (often the same ones) to make that treatment a more effective means of social control. The crisis of the 1890s was also a crisis in the representation of the individual and the state; the penal reconstruction that followed was part of a reconstitution of these representations, a reconstitution that could promote simultaneously new forms of humanization and of control.

In the late nineteenth century a gradual but ultimately profound reshaping of the human image took place – normal as well as deviant. Even as the image of autonomous and effective, but self-restraining, Protestant man established in the first half of the century was strengthening its hold on social classes *beneath* them, members of the official classes were finding that image increasingly unconvincing intellectually and unsatisfying emotionally. Social and intellectual developments impinging first on the more educated and prosperous highlighted what Jackson Lears has described as "the need for profound

337

revision in the concept of the self."[1] A changing society provided fertile soil for the advance of biological and sociological perspectives that jointly subverted the intellectual foundations of the punitive but restrained Victorian state, thus opening the doors to more beneficent but more intensive state action. These revisions were practical as well as philosophical, because this gradual but profound reshaping helped alter not only British culture but also approaches to social welfare and punishment for much of the twentieth century.

As both the practicality and the humanity of insisting upon an individual's responsibility for his fate came into question, the once-dominant policy outlook of moralism – the distribution of benefits and penalties according to the moral deserts of the people involved in a situation – was losing its former consensual force. In its place was emerging a new outlook we might entitle *causalism*. Bypassing the questions of blame central to moralism, causalism aimed to minimize overall harm and suffering regardless of the moral status or past behavior of the parties involved. If moralism was associated with the Victorian state, causalism came to be associated with the more expansive but less punitive twentieth-century state. Indeed, a diminished estimate of the capabilities of the unaided individual both contributed to a more expansive appreciation of the need for and possibilities of state action and was itself more deeply established by the very growth of the state. The sociologist who coined these useful terms has argued that the causalist view emerges naturally in an increasingly bureaucratic society:

> Indeed, the causalist mode of tackling moral questions is one that developed originally because it was the most convenient way of governing the relationship between large bureaucratic organizations. Business corporations, government departments, and labor unions are not people; the relationships between them tend to be viewed increasingly as questions of cause and effect and of accountability and liability rather than praise and blame, reward and punishment.... [Thus] causalism comes to involve the application of the ethos of the law regulating bureaucracies to questions of individual morality and moral responsibility.[2]

Specific changes in the composition and duties of the Home Office bureaucracy promoted such a shift of mental frame. The period from the early 1890s to World War I saw a significant broadening of the scope of activities of the Home Office to areas of social regulation where the fixing of blame was less

---

[1] No Place of Grace (New York: Pantheon, 1981), p. 38.

[2] Christie Davies, "Crime, Bureaucracy, and Equality," *Policy Review*, 23 (Winter, 1983), 98, 99–100.

feasible. The period also witnessed the juncture of the retirement of the penal administrative generation of 1865 with the rise of the first generation of competitive examination entrants, admitted from 1880 on, to positions of influence in central government.[3] Whereas most of their predecessors had often entered government in their middle years from an already developed career such as the bar or from independent, usually landed, situations, these new younger men were professional civil servants, usually entering government administration directly from Oxbridge and intent on making it their career. They were less likely than their predecessors to be landed or to have practiced law, the profession in which voluntarist assumptions of personal responsibility were most deeply embedded.[4] They tended to be highly pragmatic, less moralistic or legalistic than their predecessors, and, while by no means ideologically collectivist, more attracted to the idea of scientific administration. They were convinced of their intellectual superiority and held a more expansive view of their job, ready to take on new tasks rather than complain of overwork or be afraid of infringing individual or local rights and responsibilities. Like their contemporaries in the ranks of politicians, men like Haldane, Herbert Gladstone, and Asquith, they looked askance at the rigid and "abstract" principles of the previous generation; instead, science – in the pragmatic rather than metaphysical sense – became their watchword.

It is instructive to look at the career of one of the most important of these new bureaucrats. Evelyn Ruggles-Brise (1857–1935) entered the Home Office in 1881, soon became Harcourt's private secretary, continued in that capacity under Matthews, was appointed to the Prison Commission in 1892 (replacing a retiring military man), and finally replaced the retiring Du Cane as chairman in 1895. Unlike Du Cane, Ruggles-Brise viewed penal policy "as a social sci-

---

[3] J. G. Legge, private secretary to the parliamentary under-secretary at the Home Office, Herbert Gladstone, eagerly looked forward in 1894 to the imminent retirement of a large number of prison governors and chaplains, all about to turn 65. Legge, whose father was an Oxford professor and who entered the civil service directly from Oxford in 1885, became chief inspector of reformatory and industrial schools the following year. [Viscount Gladstone Papers: B.L. Add. MSS 45,990/206, n.d.]

[4] "From 1908," Jill Pellew has observed, "when Troup became permanent under-secretary, the senior departmental adviser ceased to be [as he had been through the previous century] an experienced lawyer." Troup's elevation capped a major shift that had begun during the previous Liberal government. In 1894, the appointment of the first nonlawyer to the under-secretary level since before Gladstone's first government was proposed; opposed by Lushington on the principle that legal expertise was essential to the work of the Home Office, it was made in 1896, after Lushington's retirement. "By 1913," Pellew has remarked, "there would be only one legal expert among the [four] under-secretaries." [Pellew, "Law and Order: Expertise and the Victorian Home Office," in ed. Roy M. Macleod, *Government and Expertise: Specialists, Administrators, and Professionals, 1860–1919* (Cambridge: Cambridge University Press, 1988), pp. 70–1. See also Pellew, *The Home Office. 1848–1914* (London: Heinemann, 1982).]

ence."[5] By the turn of the century, he was deprecating what he called "artificial means of repressing crime," that is, "the elaboration of legal technicalities, so that by nice contrivances certain crimes may be followed by certain penalties, and be expiated according to certain fixed methods."[6] What he thus dismissed as "technicalities" had been the basic instruments of classical, or voluntarist, penology. Another of this generation, C. E. Troup (1857–1941) – who also saw his first service at the Home Office under Harcourt and was later to become permanent under-secretary – took on in 1893 the task of modernizing the annual returns of criminal statistics. The introduction to these returns, which he wrote in 1894, marked a change of tone; the earlier free use of moral and condemnatory language gave way to a more neutral, scientific discourse. At the same time, Troup urged that penal administrators be granted discretion to go beyond legal desert. "As there are some criminals who ought never to be sent to prison," he observed, "there are others who ought never to be released." He felt that the incurably criminal should "be treated in the same way as the incurably insane, and subjected, alike in their own interest and in that of the public, to some form of more or less permanent detention."[7]

The Liberal electoral victory of 1892 complemented, and stimulated, the changing of the guard in the civil service. This victory also abruptly moved to the fore new men less attached to Victorian concerns and principles and more interested in applying the methods and findings of science to government. The new Liberal government raised expectations of a fresh look at existing penal institutions, particularly since most conscience prisoners – antivaccinationist, Salvationist, Irish Nationalist, or otherwise dissident – tended to be part of the Liberal constituency. The change of government also specifically brought to the leadership of the Home Office two politicians of a new generation who shared the new outlook. H. H. Asquith and his parliamentary under-secretary, Herbert Gladstone, were more sensitive than their predecessors to the limitations of the image of the rational, responsible offender and, consequently, of the scope of the principle of deterrence. They were more sensitive to charges of inhumanity, more ready to extend administrative discretion to modify the judgment of the bench and to render penal administration more

---

[5] Pellew, "Law and Order," in Macleod, p. 70.
[6] *Report on the Proceedings of the Fifth and Sixth International Penitentiary Congresses,* 1901, p. xiii.
[7] *Report of the Departmental Committee on Identifying Habitual Criminals,* 1894, p. 224. (this committee was chaired and its report drafted by Troup). [P.P. 1893–94, v. 72.] As we have seen in Chapter 8, on the issue of creating less severe degrees of prison discipline for lesser offenders, Troup had already struck a different note from that of his chief, Lushington.

flexible. They also had more faith in science (both medical and sociological) as an aid and model for policymaking.[8] Asquith and Gladstone found the moralistic, antiinterventionist liberalism of their permanent under-secretary, Godfrey Lushington, who was nearing retirement, rather old fashioned and out of tune with their modern activism.[9]

With the Liberals in office, the penal system began to be criticized more energetically. The summer of 1893 saw parliamentary complaints that the local prisons in London were overcrowded and criticisms that the prison commissioners were out of touch with actual conditions. Then, in January 1894, the Radical *Daily Chronicle* published a series of articles denouncing the entire administration of the prisons; the controversy raged until Asquith appointed in May a departmental committee headed by Herbert Gladstone. It was not only the prisons that Asquith was interested in reexamining; a wide range of criminal policy soon came under fresh scrutiny, as he set up a series of inquiries into the treatment of habitual offenders, vagrants, and habitual inebriates in England and Scotland, and, subsequently, began investigations into the reformatory and industrial schools.

We can now see that the press attacks on the prison system and the official response represented the culmination of a long and gradual process of disenchantment with the Victorian principles of deterrent moralization as embodied in penal institutions characterized by uniform and severe discipline. By the early 1890s, a combination of developments within and without the criminal justice system had interacted to move public and official opinion, piecemeal and without great fanfare, toward receptivity to reform. As public security had risen and respectable behavior had ever more become the rule, a deterrent and sternly moralizing system seemed ever less necessary. And as images of lawbreakers, and, more generally, of human nature, had shifted with this alteration in public behavior and with wider currents of thought (from evocations of excess and insufficiently restrained power to those of weakness), such a system seemed less and less effective. Whether less necessary or less effective, the treatment of criminals in either case appeared ever less morally justifiable. What had at first entered penal thinking as exceptions to the inter-related rules of personal responsibility and disciplinary character development

---

[8] Herbert Gladstone applied the charge of his Departmental Committee on Prisons to consider the question of prison treatment scientifically. [Notes for Departmental Committee Report 1894-5, Viscount Gladstone Papers, B.L. Add. MSS 46,091/105.]

[9] See Viscount Gladstone Papers, B.L. Add. MSS 46, 117/118, 46,091/103–6. Asquith, while leaving most criminal matters to Gladstone, was eager to introduce compulsory commitment of drunkards to reformatory institutions. [HO 45/9729/A52921/37 (1893) and HO 45/9729/A5292 1E/14a (1894)].

had strained that paradigm to the breaking point. The outcome, not surprisingly, was to be an era of penal reform.

The nature of criminals

The problem of the habitual criminal

Recidivism – repeated offending – was the central issue around which criminal policy was reshaped in the 1890s. Once the scare of the 1860s had been met with the legislation of 1869 and 1871 and the threat of crime seemed to recede, this issue had faded from public consciousness. It returned, along with discontent with criminal policy, toward the end of the 1880s, albeit in a new form. The prison commissioners recognized recidivism as a distinct problem for the first time in 1890.[10] Thereafter, it drew increasing official attention, because while the total prison population was markedly falling, the proportion of repeaters in prison was rising. The proportion of offenders convicted on indictment and jailed who were known to have been previously convicted steadily rose throughout the later nineteenth century, from about 30 percent in the 1850s to 55 percent in the early 1890s and to between 60 and 75 percent by the Edwardian era.[11] This statistical fact was the product of a number of policy developments, including the end of transportation, the growing size and efficiency of the police, the greater accuracy of official record-keeping,[12] and the shrinking duration of sentences (which meant that a prisoner was quickly back on the streets, possibly to tangle with the law again). In this way the apparent rise of recidivism could be plausibly pointed to, as indeed it was by penal officials, as an index of progress in the war against crime. In addition to being a testament to improved identification, and thus to one sort of improved control, recidivism also bore witness to another form of success; if the prison population showed a growing proportion of repeat offenders, it was also by the

[10] *Report of the Prison Commissioners for 1889–90*, pp. 5–6.

[11] The annual returns of criminal statistics devote particular attention to recidivism after 1893. In particular, the (apparent) recidivism rate continued to rise seemingly inexorably while the first official committees on recidivism and on the prison system were being appointed, meeting, and reporting. In 1893, the proportion of repeaters among assize and quarter sessions convictions was 55 percent, of those sentenced to imprisonment 50.1 percent; in 1894, 56.6 percent and 54.5 percent; in 1895, 57.6 percent and 55.6 percent.

[12] Particularly from the end of the 1880s, the advent of Bertillon's body measurement system of identification and Galton's finger mark system gave authorities the first scientific tools for identifying criminals; after 1900, modern fingerprinting would arrive. Civil servants were well aware of this and sought to deflate some of the habitual criminal hysteria. See the remarks of Troup, who had supervised a departmental committee on the identification of habitual criminals, to the Gladstone Committee. [Q. 11,596.]

same token exhibiting a markedly diminishing proportion, and number, of first offenders, which had been an aim of policy at least since the 1879 Summary Jurisdiction Act. Both the general reduction in the statistics of serious crime and the growing rarity of first offenders in prison suggested to Du Cane that "the supply from which the habitual criminal is recruited is being cut off," and he found "no reason . . . why the prison system should not claim a share in the result."[13] Similarly, *The Times* saw the rise of the habitual criminal as a consequence of success: "The police are too strong and too active, the risks too great, for the amateur burglar to succeed."[14] Thus, the greater prominence of recidivists supported the argument that the Victorian war on crime was a success.

Nonetheless, recidivism became a widely accepted indictment of the prison system. It came to be interpreted (even by *The Times*) as evidence for the prison's inability either to deter or moralize criminals. Every repeat offender was taken as a testament to the failure of a system of uniform and strict penal sentences. Du Cane's system produced, in W. D. Morrison's phrase, "an increasing proportion of failures, a diminished percentage of success."[15] This reformist response by no means logically followed, even if one were disinclined to accept the claims of optimists. A concern over the continuing existence of crime also led to arguments that the problem lay in the *erosion* of the system's uniformity and severity. After all, for many years sentences had been getting shorter, the proportion of convicted offenders fined or probated instead of jailed had been growing, as had the number of exceptional cases considered unsuited for regular penal discipline, while even the harshness of that regular penal discipline itself had passed its peak and was now steadily relaxing. It was a common complaint by hard-liners that most judges were failing to use the extensive powers that were on the books against habitual criminals.[16] The new commissioner of the Metropolitan Police, E. R. C. Bradford, for example, in his first annual report in 1890 praised the "exemplary sentence" handed a group of housebreakers who had used firearms as teaching the criminal classes a clear lesson. He lamented the fact

---

[13] "The Prison Committee Report," *The Nineteenth Century 38* (July–Dec., 1895), 287.

[14] *The Times*, May 30, 1896, p. 11.

[15] "Are Our Prisons a Failure?," *Fortnightly Review N.S. 55* (Jan. – June, 1894), 463.

[16] Despite all the attention given habitual offenders in the early 1890s, this judicial reluctance only mounted. H. B. Simpson, head of the Home Office Criminal Department, referred in 1896 to "the growing disinclination to give long sentences of Penal Servitude for 'trifling' offences." [HO 45/10027/A56902C/2 (Feb. 22, 1896).] By 1902, Home Secretary Ritchie could refer in passing to the "well-known [fact of] a growing indisposition to send [the repeated petty offender] to the ordinary convict prison . . . the judge and the public alike feeling that for [such persons] the discipline of the convict prison is too severe." [PCOM 7/286/17201/5AT) (March, 1902).]

that "the belief now prevails [among habitual criminals] that short sentences are all that at present they have to fear."[17] This belief seems to have been justified. Though dissatisfaction mounted from both left and right with a regime of "short sharp shocks" and though plenty of room was available in the prisons, the appetite for inflicting longer sentences of the same sort, for other than heinous offenses, failed to expand beyond a small number of judges and their backbench Unionist supporters. As Morrison observed, the easy defeat in 1892 of a police bill for Scotland that would have established cumulative sentences bore witness to "a strong feeling with regard to long sentences."[18]

Another solution was tried in the Penal Servitude Act of 1891; to its humanitarian reduction in minimum length of sentence and easing of some prison rules was appended a disciplinarian expansion of the terms of the Prevention of Crime Act of 1871 to include lesser offenders, making them also liable to reimprisonment on suspicion. Yet this powerful new legal weapon was little used in practice, and complaints about the ineffectiveness of the penal system to touch recidivism continued.[19] In 1893 a committee headed by Troup was set up within the Home Office to explore improving the methods for identifying habitual criminals; its report urged the importance of a more thorough knowledge of the personal history of offenders than existed. The following year the terms of the landmark Departmental Committee on Prisons, originally restricted to internal questions of prison regime, were widened to include recidivism. The committee's report, the most influential since 1863, cited it as "the most important of all prison questions and the most complicated and difficult" since "the retention of a compact mass of habitual criminals in out midst is a growing stain on our civilisation."[20] The report pronounced the existing prison system quite inadequate to deal with this matter. While the Gladstone committee held hearings, the secretary of state for Scotland, Sir George Trevelyan, set up another departmental committee, chaired by the physician Sir Charles Cameron, specifically to investigate the apparent growth of habitual criminality along with vagrancy and drunkenness in Scotland. Cameron's committee also found a large problem in the increasing numbers of reconvictions, a matter with which the existing penal system was again failing to deal.[21]

[17] The exemplary sentence was penal servitude for life given to the Muswell Hill housebreakers who had created a public sensation by wounding the occupant of a house in the course of burglarizing it. [*Report of the Metropolitan Police Commissioner for 1889*, p. 4; *Report of the Metropolitan Police Commissioner for 1892*, p. 5.]

[18] *Report of the Departmental Committee on Treatment of Inebriates*, 1893, p. 60. [P.P. 1893–4 v. 17.]

[19] The chief effect of this provision seems to have been simply to increase further the recidivist proportion of the prison population.

[20] *Report from the Departmental Committee on Prisons 1895*, p. 5.

[21] *Report from the Departmental Committee on Habitual Offenders, Vagrants, Beggars, Inbriates and Juvenile Delinquents (Scotland), 1895*. [P.P. 1895, v. 37.]

Who were these habitual criminals? They had changed their appearance since the 1860s; while the legislation of 1869 and 1871 had been confined to those persons who had been sentenced to four months or longer, the new discussion of habitual criminality showed much more interest in the lesser offenders. As Troup observed in his introduction to the criminal statistics for 1893, "the persons who have a long list of previous convictions are not the worst criminals, but belong to the class who are constantly committing petty thefts."[22] Two different types of recidivists were usually distinguished: some were professional criminals, who had chosen a career of some form of theft, while others, the majority of repeat offenders, were social inadequates – drunkards, vagrants, and other sorts of social misfits[23] – a category soon to be described as the "unfit" or the "socially inadequate." The criminal was ceasing to frighten and consequently ceasing to draw fierce moral denunciation. At the same time, as we have seen, many nonhabitual criminals were also increasingly seen as not fully responsible for their acts, which were now described as accidental or the result of a moment's weakness. The social danger that criminals represented had by the turn of the century changed from that perceived by earlier generations. The danger was now a more subtle one stemming from the criminals' weakness, not strength; they represented a specter of social deterioration and degeneration, not explosion.

All agreed that criminals were now much easier to handle, whether on the streets or in the jails. The chaplain of Dartmoor told Edward Grubb, secretary of the Howard Association, in 1903 that "the system is much milder than formerly and characters less desperate." Both agreed that "men were not so bad as twenty years ago": hymn books, the chaplain noted, were now readily put out "for men to take into chapel service if they like" – in earlier years, such books would not have lasted long.[24] A prison doctor who became a prison governor, R. F. Quinton, reflecting in 1910 over his 34 years of service, noted the same change:

> Happily for us the type of violent and reckless prisoners who malinger themselves to death, or wilfully sacrifice an arm or a leg in order to evade labour, or make unprovoked ferocious attacks on warders is, if not extinct, at least much more uncommon now.... A prisoner of such a type was indeed of a hardened and dangerous character which it was well-nigh impossible to improve or reform. He was, however, to a large extent a product of his age, and of the time when compulsory education was unknown. Uneducated and undisciplined he had little self-control, and in prison his criminal passions ran riot.[25]

[22] *Criminal Statistics for 1893*, p. 83.
[23] *Report of the Prison Commissioners for 1889–90*, pp. 5–6.
[24] Notebooks of Edward Grubb, July 13, 1903 (Warwick University, Modern Records Centre, Howard League Archives 16A/7/6).
[25] *Crime and Criminals, 1876–1910* (London: Longmans, Green, 1910), p. 34.

A corroborative opinion comes from Thomas Holmes, Grubb's successor at the Howard Association. Reminiscing in 1908 over his years as a police court missionary of the Church of England Temperance Society, he noted the same development, though without Quinton's satisfaction:

> [P]risoners generally have changed: I am not sure that the change is for the better. Time was when prisoners had character, grit, pluck, and personality, but now these qualities are not often met with.... Prisoners have put on a kind of veneer, for both youthful offenders and offenders of older growth are better dressed. They are cleaner too, in person, for which I suppose one ought to be thankful.... [But] they are devoid of strong personality, and the mass of people in many respects resembles a flock of sheep. They have no desire to do wrong, but they constantly go wrong; they have no particular wish to do evil, but they have little inclination for good. In a word, weakness, not wickedness, is their great characteristic. But weakness is often more mischievous and disastrous in its consequences than wickedness.[26]

It was hard to see most offenders as having somehow made themselves; rather, the feeling was that they seemed to have been shaped, to a greater or lesser degree, by forces extrinsic to their will. Consequently, it was felt that penal policy needed to shift from a preoccupation with the criminal act to an uncovering of those prior and more fundamental causes – in short, as Herbert Gladstone had remarked to his secretary on the departmental committee, to give attention to the process of the "manufacture of criminals."[27] Like most of his young fellow Liberals and Radicals, Gladstone stressed the social over the biological determinants of deviance; he led witnesses before his committee toward discussion of the influence of social conditions and questioned assertions about criminal natures.[28] The committee's report (1895) joined the two categories of greatest concern by locating the "headsprings of recidivism" in social conditions, particularly those leading to the neglect of the proper upbringing of youth.[29] As John Burns was to complain during the debate on the prisons bill that stemmed from this committee's report, "I have seen in the exercise ground of the prison these professional enemies of society, as they have been called – these derelict human beings – and they have been there often because society has been cruel and unjust to them, first making them criminals, and then punishing them."[30] Others, usually more conservative, also spoke of

---

[26] *Known to the Police* (London: E. Arnold, 1908), pp. 10–11.

[27] J. G. Legge to Gladstone, Jan. 26, 1895, Viscount Gladstone Papers, B.L.Add. MSS 45,990/245.

[28] For example, see his exchanges with Reverend G. Merrick on juvenile criminality: *Report of the Departmental Committee on Prisons 1895*, Q. 1567, passim.

[29] *ibid.*, p. 11.

[30] 4 PD 56, 105–6 (April 4, 1898).

criminals as derelicts, but gave more attention to physiological in-fluences, and indeed the Edwardian era saw an efflorescence of eugenic think-ing. The lively controversy that developed by the turn of the century between nature and nurture in regard to the manufacture of human character drew heavily upon the example of criminals (as had, in its different way, early Victorian discourse on character).[31] Ruggles-Brise diplomatically took account of the arguments of proponents of both physical degeneration and bad social environment as causes of crime, seeing something in each, if not pushed too far.[32] The very terms of the current debate conceded the practical defeat of Victorian voluntarism; between the power of either nature or nurture, there was left precious little standing room for the self-determining individual.

At times between the early 1890s and 1914 the discussion of recidivism focused on professional criminals, at other times on the unfit, and at still other times the reference was left unfocused. Characteristically, witnesses to the Gladstone Committee were divided; some spoke of habitual offenders as rational and self-willed, others pictured them as incompetent. Proposals for their treatment varied with the diagnosis; those – most prison governors and some chaplains – who saw them as rational generally supported cumulative sentencing, while others – some chaplains and most medical officers – who saw them as incompetent tended to favor some sort of medical treatment of flexible duration, either curative or incapacitative. The committee's report itself was unclear, speaking sometimes in moralistic terms of "wilful persistence in the deliberately acquired habit of criminality" but at other times citing the need to understand "scientifically" the criminals' pathology. It suggested, albeit vaguely, a new form of sentence that was partly cumulative and partly indeterminate that would provide, in special new institutions, longer periods of less severe detention than existed in the present system. The Cameron Committee (1894), headed by a medical doctor, was more definite, seeing ha-bitual criminality as overwhelmingly a problem of social inadequacy. The committee viewed the typical habitual criminal as a drunken or vagrant petty offender, posing no great menace to society, but frustratingly resistant to either deterrence or reform. It indicted "the utter inefficacy of any of the systems adopted [in Scottish jails and prisons] to cope with the evil of the ha-bitual offender." The committee rejected the alternative of a general lengthen-ing of sentences, noting that "testimony from a large number of experienced witnesses [supported] the view that long sentences of imprisonment effect no good result." Instead, it proposed placing a ceiling of fourteen days on sentences for these petty offenses, while making recidivists – those committed

[31] See Mackenzie, *Statistics*, and Daniel Kevles, *In the Name of Eugenics: Genetics and the Uses of Human Heredity* (New York: Knopf, 1985).
[32] See, for example, his *Report on the Proceedings of the Fifth and Sixth International Penal Congresses (1895 and 1900)*, p. 103. [P.P. 1901, v. 33.]

to prison three times within one year – liable to commitment to a new institution, an adult reformatory, for a minimum period of a year.[33]

If conservative politicians rhetorically denounced highly skilled professional criminals, in practice few of these were to be found. Even the alarmist Sir Robert Anderson, former head of the Metropolitan Police's Criminal Investigation Department, urging immediate action against professional "outlaws" holding society at "siege," estimated their number at no more than 70 in the whole country.[34] Bureaucrats, while detaching themselves from reformers' sentimentalism, concurred with them in seeing the great majority of recidivists as not very competent, either mentally or physically. If prisoners were now being described as milder than their predecessors, they were also seen as weaker, because as the proportion of recidivists in prison rose, so did the proportion of prisoners judged unfit for hard labor.[35] The typical prisoner was being described by administrators as of poorer physique an lower mentality than ever before.[36] Ruggles-Brise observed to the Gladstone Committee that "the bulk of the recidivists" were suffering from "'moral imbecility'..... They are called 'half-sharps.'"[37] By 1899, there was consensus in the Home Office that, as one official put it, the habitual criminal should "be treated like a lunatic," and when public opinion permitted, confined for an indeterminate period.[38] The deputy commissioner in Lunacy for Scotland, Dr. J. F. Sutherland, noted in 1908 that two-thirds of petty-offender recidivists were "pathological" and required treatment "different from the present cast-iron system."[39] That year

---

[33] *op. cit.*, pp. 9–22. Sir Charles Cameron was the author of the Habitual Inebriates Act of 1879.

[34] "Our Absurd System of Punishing Crime," *The Nineteenth Century and After 49* (1901), 283. Anderson also recognized the separate problem of the inadequate habitual, the "poor wretch ... begotten and bred in crime." For them he proposed "asylum prisons" with a eugenic mission; there they would be unable to beget children.

[35] In 1881 75 percent of prisoners were classified fit for hard labor; by 1897–98, despite greatly increased efforts to prevent imprisonment of the unfit, this number had fallen to 56 percent. [*Report of the Prison Commissioners for 1897–8*, p. 27.]

[36] *ibid*, pp. 16–17.

[37] *op. cit.*, Q. 10,235.

[38] F. J. Dryhurst; also similar remarks by C. S. Murdoch and Ruggles-Brise. [HO 45/ 10,027/A56,902C (1899).] But see the doubts expressed by H. B. Simpson (the most Victorian of the senior officials) about the abilities of prison officials to determine when such a person could be released: he questioned the assumption "that it is tolerably easy in a few months to obtain such a knowledge of a man's character as will make it possible to predict what will be his behaviour under entirely changed circumstances." [*ibid.*]

[39] J. F. Sutherland, "Recidivism Regarded from the Environmental and Psycho-Pathological Standpoints, Part Two," *Journal of Mental Science 54* (1908), 91–2. He suggested the creation of a new kind of institution somewhere between an asylum and a prison, "such as has been foreshadowed in labor colonies, inebriate retreats, and reformatories such as are to be found at Borstal and Chatham."

a limited form of indeterminate sentence was enacted in the Prevention of Crime Act.[40]

Many of these pathological petty recidivists were in fact habitual drunkards, so policies toward the two categories began to intertwine. Through the criminal justice system, efforts were beginning to be made to distinguish systematically "alcoholic mania" from mere drunkenness.[41] In 1893, on the recommendation of his department committee, Asquith ended the government's aloofness from the issue, coming out strongly in favor of the compulsory medical treatment of both criminal and noncriminal habitual drunkards. In doing so, he officially recognized the close links between crime, inebriety, and insanity perceived by the BMA, the Howard Association, and others:

> The connexion between drunkenness and crime and between habitual drunkenness and habitual crime is too well established by experience to be any longer in doubt. . . . I do not think it is possible from a logical point of view, or from the point of view of policy, to treat habitual inebriety, or, to guard myself, I will say certain forms of habitual inebriety, as standing upon a different level from insanity itself.[42]

These words were tested the following year, when the National Society for the Prevention of Cruelty to Children (NSPCC) – hitherto relentless in pressing criminal prosecution against abusive parents, whether sober or drunk – now urged upon a reluctant Home Office an anticruelty bill clause that allowed courts to sentence drunken abusive parents to a year's detention in an inebri-

[40] A 1908 Home Office memorandum found legal precedents for indeterminate sentences for habitual criminals in lunacy law. [Viscount Gladstone Papers B.L.Add. MSS 46,094/126.] But public resistance prevented such treatment of petty recidivists, however pathological, and the provision in the 1908 act for preventive detention was explicitly described as aimed only at the professional criminal, and even for him very mild. The Home Office was disappointed but philosophical, one memorandum writer noting that "no doubt the petty thief must be dealt with; but we cannot do everything at once." Since the petty thief "is usually weak-minded . . . the Royal Commission on the Weak-Minded, which is soon to report, may be expected to make valuable suggestions" [B.L. Add. MSS 46,094/48,/49.]

[41] In 1892 Dr. Gover recommended that "the police should . . . make it a practice to call in their surgeon in every case in which the person in charge is increasingly excited, and who is so violent, after abstinence from alcohol for several hours, as to require severe handling and such manual restraint as possibly to occasion extensive bruises and other injuries. Such a person is probably in that state of disease known by medical men as alcoholic mania and is in urgent need of skilful medical treatment." [HO 144/484/X35276 (Feb. 9, 1892).]

[42] Report of a deputation, in *The Times*, Dec. 6, 1893, p. 3. Whatever the differences in actual states, he went on, inebriety "seems to produce the same condition of irresponsibility" as insanity. [HO 45/9729/A52921/37 (Dec. 5, 1893).]

ate retreat rather than send them to jail.[43] The clause became law, and the precedent for medical treatment of inebriate criminals was set.[44]

In 1895 the Gladstone Committee seconded the conclusions of the Departmental Committee on Inebriety, arguing that "the physical craving for drink is a disease which requires medical treatment not provided by the present prison system"; sufferers should be "dealt with as patients rather than criminals."[45] As usual, the bench was slower to change its ways, but even Lord Chancellor Halsbury acknowledged in 1898 that habitual drunkenness was "more or less a sort of disease."[46] Case law began to reflect this change of view; in 1900, Justices Kennedy and Darling ruled that a man suffering from delirium tremens, even though he had brought on that state by willful drinking, could not be prosecuted under the Vagrancy Acts as "idle and disorderly."[47] By the later 1890s, even with the return of a Unionist government, there was little objection to special treatment of habitual criminal drunkards;[48] and only the effort to extend compulsory commitment to noncriminal inebriates obstructed passage of reformist legislation. The act of 1898, which was confined to criminal inebriates, permitted such persons, if repeat offenders, to be separated from other offenders and given distinctive treatment in special therapeutic institutions. This new treatment was to be modeled, it was repeatedly suggested in parliamentary discussion, on the existing treat-

---

[43] Behlmer, *Child Abuse and Moral Reform* (Stanford: Stanford University Press, 1982), pp. 158–9. This change of front seemed to be linked to a broad change of attitude on the part of the society as to how much one could expect ordinary people, particularly women, to stand unaided against the power of drink; in the same years it was coming to support statutory restrictions on the sale of liquor. [Behlmer, p. 178.]

[44] However, as with some other such precedents of this era, use was only slowly made of this clause. As Behlmer noted: "Required to gain an alcoholic parent's consent to commital, and burdened with the full costs of institutionalization, the NSPCC was slow to exercise its new power. Between 1894 and 1898, during which time the society dealt with 2,084 cases involving habitual drunkenness, only a dozen adults entered retreats. With the advent of compulsory institutionalization under the 1898 Inebriates' Act, however, child-savers could be more systematic in this phase of their work. By late 1902 over a hundred parents per year were being placed in retreats." [p. 180.]

[45] *op. cit.*, pp. 31–2.

[46] 4 PD 64, c. 17 (Aug. 4. 1898).

[47] *St. Saviour's Union* v. *Burbridge* (1900), 19 Cox C.C. 573.

[48] Here also the changing of the guard in the civil service marked a shift in outlook. Where Du Cane had shown no interest in inebriate asylums, and Lushington had questioned whether habitual drunkards could be cured in asylums without stays so long as to cause excessive hardship to themselves and their families, Ruggles-Brise was a cheerleader for such institutions, pushing after 1898 for the state to establish them, rather than leaving the task to charitable organizations and local authorities. See *Report of Departmental Committee on Prisons 1895*, Q. 11,509–10, and Ruggles-Brise, *Report on the Fifth and Sixth International Penal Congresses, 1900*, p. 77.

ment of lunatics and juveniles.[49] The act's post-Victorian rationale was later recalled by the inspector of inebriate asylums:

> How necessary it was that some curative or restraining power should exist capable of direct application to drunkards themselves ... something applicable to inebriates more powerful than mere temperance teaching; something stronger and more physical, something that could make them reform, or, failing reform, could ensure their detention and care for the benefit of the community.[50]

At the same time that reformers, administrators, and political decision makers were now perceiving that habitual criminals suffered inordinately from inebriety, a growing proportion of habitual criminals, particularly petty ones, were also coming to be perceived as mentally weak or disabled. The police court missionary and Howard Association secretary, Thomas Holmes, concluded that

> the great amount of real crime comes from pathological causes.... I see, day after day, and take into my care, numbers of broken wretches, weak physically, weak mentally, weak in every direction, unable to cope with the difficulties of life, so weak that parasites prey upon them.

> I would prefer to have under my charge a hundred wicked, desperate men, rather than fifty of these poor weaklings. With God's good grace, I may exercise a good influence on the strong-minded man. The moment this is done, his environment begins to improve and my labour lightens. But it never lightens with the weakling; and though he may learn to love men, and I may feel that I have an influence with him, he knows, and I know, that as soon as I let him go, back to his misery and what we call his sin, he certainly goes. Pathological and social causes are too powerful.[51]

Holmes's pathological view of criminality fed his fears of national deterioration. In 1899, he drew attention to the way official statistics of insanity had been considerably outpacing population growth. Yet even this disturbing rise

---

[49] In this area, practice was to fall particularly far short of theory; Radzinowicz and Hood, pp. 307–15, describe "the fiasco of unenforceable legislation" as it was discovered that no one really knew how to cure habitual criminal drunkards.

[50] *Report of the Inspector under the Inebriate Acts, 1879–1900, for the Year 1908*, 4. [R. W. Branthwaite.] Such lack of faith in voluntarist remedies, not surprising in a medical doctor, had however become common coin; in greeting the report of the 1893 Departmental Committee on Inebriety, *The Times* (which had poured scorn on the first calls for inebriate asylums in 1870) observed: "This much at least is certain, that without restraint the condition of an habitual drunkard is not likely to undergo improvement." [*The Times*, May 12, 1893, p. 9.]

[51] Letter, quoted in William Tallack, *Howard Letters and Memories* (London: Methuen, 1905), p. 202.

"represents but a small portion of the insanity that exists. Outside our asylums are great numbers of people, male and female, who suffer from mental disease and who are not really responsible for their actions, and who present to those that know them a more woeful spectacle, than the altogether mad."[52]

It was not only reformers like Holmes who stressed the mental weakness of criminals. Prison officials themselves took a leading role in propagating such characterizations. Ironically, the charges thrown against the prison system in the 1880s and 1890s (particularly by Irish Nationalists) of being so harsh and inhuman as to drive prisoners insane had encouraged administrators to defend the system by stressing the preexisting tendencies to mental weakness and instability of their charges, especially those sentenced to longer terms. Imprisonment, even with the maximum of nine months' separation, did not cause insanity, insisted most prison governors and medical officers; indeed, imprisonment was defended as normally a healthful experience. As public attention was drawn to cases of breakdown, these officials complained that persons already mentally weak were being inappropriately sentenced to prison. The Gladstone Committee heard this argument from both the medical inspector of prisons, Dr. Gover, and its own medical member, Dr. J. H. Bridges. Gover acknowledged to the committee a rise in the number of insane and weak-minded prisoners but attributed it in large part to an increase in the *admission* of mentally ill persons. The prisons, he complained, and Bridges agreed, had become a dumping ground for persons unsuited to penal discipline. Magisterial missentencing was, however, not the whole story; Gover also traced part of the rise to closer medical supervision of the mental state of prisoners. In any event, significantly both Gover and Bridges also argued, one should expect a disproportionate number of mentally weak or insane persons among criminals, since insanity and crime were related.[53] As Gover had written earlier that year in his annual report on convict prisons:

> Many of the convicts are persons of low type who have never developed any degree of mental capacity. [Most] are of normal physical development and do not manifest any mental defect until they are subjected to discipline, or are put to some kind of work requiring an average amount of intelligence for its proper performance. A proportion of these semi-imbeciles tend to degenerate and to become wholly irresponsible so as to necessitate their removal to an asylum.[54]

Indeed, the very fact of a person's being sentenced to a long term of penal servitude, in the judgment of the medical officer of Parkhurst Prison (where

---

[52] Thomas Holmes, "Obscure Causes of Crime," *The Contemporary Review* 76 (July–Dec., 1899), 578.
[53] J. H. Bridges, "Memorandum on Insanity in Prisons," *Report of Departmental Committee on Prisons 1895*, pp. 48–9.
[54] *Report of the Directors of Convict Prisons for 1893–4*, Appendix no. 18, p. xxxvii.

weak-minded convicts were being concentrated), "points to an unstable mental equilibrium" and "latent mental illness."[55] As the new head of the Broadmoor Criminal Lunatic Asylum reflected in 1896, "the criminal mind is . . . predisposed to insanity."[56]

Whereas the Gladstone Committee rejected the wilder charges that prison discipline was systematically driving prisoners mad, and moreover concluded that only 2 or 3 percent of the prison population could be said to be *seriously* weak-minded, it nonetheless gave official recognition to mental weakness as a major problem among prisoners. Indeed, despite its Civil Service caution, the committee's work was cited by one Radical the following year as having proven that insanity in prison "is going up by leaps and bounds."[57] The report did urge a variety of changes to ensure that no mentally unsound prisoner was subjected to penal discipline.[58] "It is indeed a question," it noted, "whether the epileptic and obviously weak-minded class [of criminal offenders] should be sent to prison at all. They cannot be said to be fully responsible for their actions." It recommended establishing a special institution for them, along the lines of an asylum.[59] The association of mental inadequacy with the prison inmate, however, went deeper than this few percent; most of the evidence ot the Gladstone Committee, as well as to the Cameron Committee, suggested, as even W. D. Morrison, perhaps the leading public critic of the mind-destroying qualities of the prison system, acknowledged, that most prisoners were below average in intelligence and, most significantly, in mental balance and stability.[60]

After 1895, the Prison Commission under Ruggles-Brise not only followed many of the recommendations of the Gladstone Committee, but gave much greater attention to the mental state of inmates and to medical opinion. The reports of medical officers and the medical inspector began to be published in full; a medical man with experience in mental disease was appointed as a com-

---

[55] *Report of the Prison Commisssioners for 1896–97*, p. 22.

[56] Dr. Richard Brayn, November 9, 1896, PCOM 7/358.

[57] Bernard C. Molloy, "Insanity in Prisons," *Progressive Review 1* (Nov., 1896), 159.

[58] Dr. Gover, speaking for prison medical officers, objected to this aspersion; existing prison administration, he claimed, was quite successfully handling the weak-minded. Moreover, he warned that "weak-mindedness" was an "exceedingly vague term" that often was illegitimately extended to embrace "brutish and sensual" men who well deserved, and could stand, punishment. [Memorandum on the Recommendations of the Departmental Committee on Prisons, May 11, 1895, HO 45/10025/A56902/4.]

[59] *op. cit.*, p. 34. Simply to leave them outside the penal system altogether did not seem practical; as was noted in the Home Office when implementation of the committee's recommendations was being discussed, "they cannot be permanently detained in the workhouse or asylum, and when at large though they are too weakminded to resist their criminal propensities they have craft enough to thieve, to deceive, and to eake out a living by fraud." [HO 45/9750/A58650/1 (Feb. 19, 1897).]

[60] *op. cit.*, pp. 122, 126.

missioner; and Dr. Gover's successor as medical inspector, Dr. Herbert Smalley, adopted a more flexible line in defending existing practices. Though repeating in his first annual report Gover's explanations for mental disability among prisoners, Smalley abandoned the claims of his predecessors for the physical and mental benefits of prison regime. As he conceded: "I would not ... wish for a moment to deny that imprisonment is to many, indeed to all except the hardened criminal, perhaps, a certain mental and physical strain, which is a necessary corollary to any form of punishment."[61]

Thus, even as prison discipline was progressively relaxed, it was increasingly being acknowledged to be a strain, requiring a separation of the weak that could only be effective by "searching inquiry" into the mental condition of all inmates.[62] Such inquiry was no longer left to prison doctors; from 1897 all long-sentence prisoners were additionally and periodically examined by the medical inspector of prisons.[63] As weak-minded prisoners were being segregated and placed under special rules,[64] the government was beginning to push prison authorities to recognize more cases of weak-mindedness or insanity.[65]

Habitual criminality and mental disability were ever more associated with one another, and the average prisoner, ever more likely to be a recidivist, was ever more thoroughly assumed to be in some form or degree unfit. In the early years of the new century, as feeble-mindedness was for the first time acknowledged as a major social problem calling for state action, this problem was perceived to be particularly rampant among habitual criminals. The 1908 Royal Commission on the Feeble-Minded pointed to the connection between repeated crime and feeble-mindedness, calling attention to "a large number of offenders who are not insane, in the [legal] meaning attached to that word," but who were mentally defective and who without care would continue to offend.[66] The commission's recommendations were taken up with enthusiasm by Winston Churchill when he moved to the Home Office; he circulated to his cabinet colleagues a paper by Dr. A. F. Thredgold that argued for a close

[61] *Report of the Prison Commissioners for 1896–7*, p. 37.

[62] *Report of the Directors of Convict Prisons for 1896–7*, p. 39.

[63] HO 144/170/A43422 (1897).

[64] Special rules for the treatment of weak-minded convicts were promulgated in 1901 and made more detailed in 1905.

[65] Home Office files on individual difficult prisoners show an increasing readiness in the late 1890s to perceive mental illness or incapacity where previously only malingering was seen. For example, one man convicted of assault and of arson who was a discipline problem from his entry in 1886, was finally found insane in 1897; this case led to a new requirement, before any disciplinary punishment could be carried out, for medical officers to certify that "there is nothing in [the prisoner's] mental condition to justify a doubt as to his responsibility for the conduct with which he is charged." [HO 144/170/A43422.]

[66] *Report of the Royal Commission on the Care and Control of the Feeble-Minded*, 1908, 152.

blood relation between criminals and the feeble-minded, and, more widely, pointed to the "serious reality" of "national degeneracy."[67] Such concerns produced in 1913 the first general legislation on mental deficiency.

The problem of the habitual criminal was calling for more scientific treatment than had hitherto been available. In 1908 Dr. Sutherland set out a detailed scientific program for habitual criminality:

> first in importance, . . . a study of the post-natal environment in its numerous and far-reaching aspects from childhood to adolescence; second . . . a study of heredity, including ante-natal environment, which might reveal degeneracy, mental and physical defects of such a nature as to make the proper exercise of the will in conduct and duty a very doubtful one; and third, . . . criminal anthropometry, in order to view him in contrast with the entire population, and with the classes from which the different types of recidivists chiefly come.

In this prospectus Sutherland identified the two leading paths of Edwardian criminology, environmental and constitutional. Although the exponents of each were often locked in bitter conflict – a battle between nature and nurture, eugenics and social reform – their common ground, often obscured in the heat of struggle, was extensive. Both paths rejected the punitive approach of the past, stressed the powerful effect of external forces on an individual's will and character, and promoted increased state intervention to influence constructively the operation of those forces. "The knowledge of defective organisation in the case of many criminals," Sutherland reflected, "cannot but tend to justice and more tolerant views of . . . so many of the doubtful cases inhabiting the borderland between insanity and crime."[68]

The growing recognition of the power of environment encouraged the characterization of many, or even most, criminals as victims of oppressive social conditions and the act of crime itself as a natural product of social deficiencies and inequities.[69] In 1896, W. D. Morrison had argued that

> it is obvious that the connection between abnormal circumstances [of upbringing and economic state] of an adverse kind and an abnormal or criminal mode of life is not a mere accidental coincidence. It is in the main a relation of cause and effect. It is the abnormal circumstances which produce the abnormal conduct, and the abnormal conduct will

[67] CAB 37/108, no. 189: Dr. A. F. Thredgold, "The Feeble-Minded: A Social Danger" (written May 1909, circulated to the cabinet by Churchill in Dec., 1911).

[68] J. F. Sutherland, "Recidivism Regarded From the Environmental and Psycho-Pathological Standpoints, Part Two," *Journal of Mental Science 54* (1908), 79.

[69] See, for example, J. F. Sutherland, *Recidivism: Habitual Criminality, and Habitual Petty Delinquency* (Edinburgh: William Green, 1908), pp. 7–8, and Thomas Holmes, *London's Underworld* (London: J. M. Dent & Sons, 1912), p. 38 and passim.

> continue, and as a matter of fact does continue, till the abnormal circumstances are removed.[70]

By the era of the New Liberalism, the point was often made more directly. As James Devon, a prison medical officer of working-class origin, soon to be made a prison commissioner for Scotland, declared in 1912:

> Crime is largely a by-product of city life. It might be mitigated if we were more public-spirited; but it will always be an evil crying out against us, so long as we permit conditions to exist which shut men into dens under circumstances that make decent communion and fellowship between them difficult if not impossible, and compel them to remain there till they can pay a ransom to the man who holds up the land for his profit or his pleasure.

He denounced as both cruel and pointlesss the judging of a man without reference to the social conditions that he had to live in, and thinking about him solely in terms of abstractly determined concepts of vice and virtue. In the first place, Devon complained, the vices of the poor were much more likely than those of the rich to be interpreted by the law as crimes – street betting rather than private gaming, for instance. But even with the majority of crimes in which more than class prejudice was involved, the role of circumstances (as well as their variety) was by no means morally neutral. One could of course be poor and law abiding, but to be so was a far harder thing than for those who were not poor; "while a man may be poor and virtuous, his poverty will compel him to live under conditions in which any vices he has may easily develop into crimes or offences." Such compulsions of poverty, and of the social environment in general, Devon argued, needed to be paid much closer attention in the administration of criminal justice. Most generally, Devon criticized a system of criminal legislation and prosecution that took little account of the differential difficulties of life; "offences ... are manufactured without due regard to the injury that may be caused by their enforcement. It is an easy thing to place burdens on the backs of others, but in fairness to them it should first be ascertained whether they can bear them."[71] The influence of an offender's social environment, in Devon's judgment, needed to be assessed before determining his responsibility and fate. Indeed, in the same vein, Sutherland had a few years earlier called for the appointment of environmental observation officers to report alongside medical doctors in criminal cases.[72]

---

[70] W. D. Morrison, *Juvenile Offenders* (London: T. F. Unwin, 1896), p. 274.

[71] James Devon, *The Criminal and the Community* (London: J. Lane, Bodley Head, 1912), pp. 68, 90, 94.

[72] *Recidivism*, pp. 106–7.

Social criminology's relating of guilt and fate to circumstances was paralleled in Edwardian physiological criminology. If society bore down unevenly upon mankind, so did biology. The landmark work, *The English Convict* (1913) by Dr. Charles Goring, medical officer at Parkhurst and student of the biometrician, Karl Pearson, while on the one hand disproving notions of "the born criminal" and "the criminal type," on the other gave new scientific support to physiological criminology[73] and, more generally, the image of criminal offenders as weak and less capable than the average person of coping with the difficulties of life. As Ruggles-Brise noted in his introduction to the work, the "broad and general truth which appears from this mass of figures and calculations is that the 'criminal' man is, to a large extent, a 'defective' man, either physically or mentally."[74] Testing Lombrosian generalizations by the first large-scale and thorough physical and psychological examination of English convicts, Goring found that they did not form a clear and distinct category marked off physiologically from the noncriminal; in other words, "there is no such thing as a physical criminal type."[75] However, Goring did find statistically significant physiological differences; convicts, by his reckoning, tended to possess lower intelligence and poorer physiques than the norm.[76] Criminals were less "fit" than the average person, less able to cope with the demands of life; a purely moral judgment of crime was no more relevant in Goring's world than in Devon's. Goring's version of physiological criminology had rather different social implications than the original Lombrosian one he was dismissing. Rather than being an anomaly or an atavism, Goring's criminal was more representative of and less clearly marked off from the noncriminal population. Instead of contrasting the two types, he portrayed a continuum of strength of character; there is "a constitutional proclivity, either mental, moral or physical, present to a certain degree in all individuals, but so potent in some, as to determine for them, eventually, the fate of imprisonment."[77] In this scheme of things, both criminals and law-abiding citizens shared a common nature, but differed in their location on the

[73] This point is argued in Piers Beirne, "Heredity vs. Environment: A Reconsideration of Charles Goring's *The English Convict* (1913)," *British Journal of Criminology, 28* (1988), 315–39.

[74] Charles Goring, *The English Convict* (London: H.M.S.O., 1913), p. 8.

[75] *ibid.*, p. 173.

[76] This distinction could, of course, have been interpreted simply by the argument that the stronger of mind and body were less likely to be caught or, more complexly, as the result of social inequities (as has been done by modern criminologists). Goring, however, while accepting that his sample was biased by the fact of capture, nonetheless treated convicts as essentially representative of criminals. Similarly, while taking note of social influences on constitution, he gave them no place in his main arguments.

[77] *ibid.*, p. 26.

spectrum of susceptibility to crime. As Ruggles-Brise observed, "defectiveness is a relative term only."[78] If this analysis brought criminals back from beyond the Lombrosian pale, it did open dangerous cracks beneath the feet of law-abiding citizens, because no one could be sure of being free from criminal proclivities.[79] And because these proclivities were associated with an entrenched physical and mental weakness, this weakness infected the criminological vision of the normal population, itself now seen as increasingly in need of assistance and strengthening from professional authorities and the state.

The image of the youthful offender

At the same time that habitual criminals were being reconceived, attitudes toward offenders at the other end of the spectrum – juveniles – were shifting in a similar fashion. Like that of the recidivist, the growing visibility of the juvenile delinquent was not the result of any objective increase in criminal activity – despite some alarmist statements, such as during the hooligan panic of 1898 to 1900.[80] Indeed, insofar as it was related to patterns of traditional criminal behavior, such visibility was more the obverse of the growing rarity of older and more serious criminals. More fundamentally, however, the new prominence of the issue of juvenile delinquency seems to have emerged from the same sort of combination of a diminishing sense of the efficacy of deterrence and an expanding sense of the possibilities of more direct intervention, which was derived from the changing perceptions of human nature, that was bringing recidivism into the spotlight.

Indeed, these two poles of criminality were increasingly linked; as deterrent penalties were both becoming less acceptable and being seen as less efficacious against crime, more emphasis was placed on the role of preventive juvenile policies. "The difficulty of changing adult wild nature," *The Times* observed in 1893, "has been recognized as almost insuperable. It is a discovery of very recent date that the task of regenerating juvenile offenders is more pressing and far easier."[81] Offenders up to age 21 were described by the Gladstone

[78] *ibid.,* p. 8.

[79] The eugenicist Leonard Darwin drew out this implication of Goring in arguing soon after that "criminals are not a class apart, but merely ordinary individuals with certain innate qualities exceptionally well marked." ["The Habitual Criminal," *Eugenics Review* 6 (1914–15), 207.] See the discussion of this point in D. Garland, *Punishment and Welfare* (Aldershot: Gower, 1985), pp. 184–5.

[80] See Geoffrey Pearson, *Hooligan: A History of Respectable Fears* (London: Macmillan, 1983), pp. 74–116.

[81] Oct. 6, 1893, p. 7.

Committee as peculiarly "plastic," responsive to outside influences, an image reiterated by the prison commissioners thereafter under Ruggles-Brise.[82] Offenders and potential offenders in the age cohort of 16 to 21 were for the Gladstone Committee the second focus of attention after habitual offenders. This life period, the committee was "certain," was "when the majority of habitual criminals are made." Habitual criminals could "only be effectively put down in one way," it argued, "and that is by cutting off the supply" – preventing juveniles from becoming criminals.[83]

By the 1890s, a number of deep-rooted social trends were underway that tended to emphasize the distinctiveness of childhood – a falling economic need for child labor, alongside rising political opposition to it; growing need for an educated workforce; a rising standard of living; a falling birth rate. These developments also tended to extend childhood by definition upward to ages that had previously been reserved for adulthood.[84] In particular, adolescence was being "discovered" as an almost autonomous stage of life.[85] In this new age's classic text, U.S. psychologist G. Stanley Hall gave the years between 14 and 24 a unity and saw adolescence as shaped by its particular biological agenda revolving around puberty. For Hall, adolescence was a time dominated by the "storm and stress" associated with coping with puberty and its consequent emotional effects. Indeed, ratifying with the authority of science what others had already observed, Hall declared that because of this natural turbulence adolescence was "pre-eminently the criminal age."[86] Hall's work and its rapid transatlantic acceptance marked a new state of recognition of the problematic nature of both this age group and of puberty itself that had begun in the early Victorian period. Prior to the middle of the nineteenth century, John Springhall has noted, puberty was rarely seen primarily as a problem: "contemporaries associated puberty with rising power and energy rather than with the onset of an awkward and vulnerable stage of life."[87] Even the new Victorian concern had not changed this traditional image but only its valuation, injecting a strong note of fear of that "rising power and energy." It was left to the Edwardians to transform the dominant characteristic of this time of life from one of strength to, now, a kind of debility.

[82] *op. cit.*, p. 30.
[83] *ibid.*, p. 15.
[84] One official of the NSPCC remarked approvingly in 1898 on the "lengthening of childhood" in recent thinking. [See Behlmer, *Child Abuse*, p. 195.]
[85] See John Gillis, *Youth and History* (New York: Academic Press, 1974) and "The Evolution of Juvenile Delinquency in England 1890–1914," *Past and Present no. 67* (May 1975), 96–126, and John Springhall, *Coming of Age: Adolescence in Britain 1860–1960* (Dublin: Gill and Macmillan, 1986).
[86] *Adolescence: Its Psychology and Its Relations to Physiology, Anthropology, Sociology, Sex Crime, Religion and Education* (New York: D. Appleton & Co., 1904), Vol. 1, p. 325.
[87] Springhall, *Coming of Age*, p. 34.

The emerging concept of adolescence had immediate implications for criminal policy. In a sense, the new concept naturalized the imprecise category of juvenile delinquents, whose members – now extending in some senses up to age 21 – came to be seen as even more powerfully shaped than their elders by patterns of biological development and thus less responsible for their behavior. This perception could simultaneously point in several directions. As with inebriates, naturalization could lead *both* to greater tolerance and heightened interventionism. On the one hand, tolerance was encouraged by perceptions of juvenile criminality as a natural and, more important, a temporary stage, and indeed such deviance could be seen to possess positive characteristics. With the reign of respectability now well established, it became possible to appreciate the very aspects of youth – impulsiveness and energy – that had seemed threatening earlier. An established tolerance for childish misbehavior gradually made its way up the age scale. One worker for the National Society for the Prevention of Cruelty to Children criticized the "mistake of expecting too much of our children. The moral faculties evolve slowly, and overstimulation will have reaction. A boy of eight or ten years, who never transgresses . . . is lacking in physical or mental vitality."[88] Such sentiments began to be expressed about boys substantially older than age 10. Even C. E. Troup, in introducing the annual criminal statistics, soothingly observed in 1896 that youthful delinquency was in a sense only natural: "as youth is the time of activity and adventure, so it is necessarily the time when the tendency is strongest to run counter to law and custom and the precepts of morality." Many juvenile offenders, he went on, if not stigmatized by the law, could be expected in time to "settle down."[89]

The most successful of all youth movements, the Boy Scouts, was established in 1908 to meet the new felt need to assist this natural process of maturation in ways that would channel valuable juvenile energies into socially constructive tasks. Its founder, General Baden-Powell, made a point of praising such energies, even in lawbreakers. Conventional youth organizations, he told the National Defence Association in 1910,

> say to a boy, 'come and be good.' Well, the best class of boy – that is, the Hooligan – says, 'I'm blowed if I'm going to be good!' We say, 'Come and be a red Indian, and dress like a Scout', and he will come along like anything.[90]

[88] Quoted in Behlmer, *Child Abuse,* p. 195.

[89] *Criminal Statistics for 1894,* p. 21.

[90] Quoted in Pearson, *Hooligan,* pp. 51, 111. Upon General Baden-Powell's visit to Oxford in 1910, the mayor observed that people had been "accustomed to judge boys a little too harshly and to attribute mischief to them that ought to be put down to other causes." [Quoted in Gillis, "Evolution of Juvenile Delinquency," 126.]

The first English child psychologist of international repute, Cyril Burt, summed up the changing of opinion when he wrote after World War I that "most juvenile delinquency is, in the last resort, the effect, not of . . . sinning, but of misdirected energy, and is to be cured, not by an effort to stamp out that energy (a stark impossibility) but by directing it anew and guiding it aright."[91]

Burt, who was the first official educational psychologist in Britain, came to the study of delinquency from an interest in the general psychology of youth. Delinquency itself, he felt, was in a sense a natural aspect of growing up:

> There is . . . no sharp line of cleavage by which the delinquent may be marked off from the nondelinquent. Between them no deep gulf exists to separate the sinner from the saint, the white sheep from the black. It is all a problem of degree, of a brighter or a darker gray. [Similarly,] the insane, the neurotic, the mentally deficient are, none of them, to be thought of as types apart, anomalous specimens separated from the ordinary man by a profound and definite gap. . . . It is the same with the moral faults of children; they run in an uninterrupted series, from the most heartless and persistent crimes that could possibly be pictured, up to the mere occasional naughtiness to which the most virtuous will at times give way.

Burt put it more directly in the preface to his work: "Delinquency I regard as nothing but an outstanding sample – dangerous perhaps and extreme, but none the less typical – of common childish naughtiness."[92]

Yet the dominant picture of the juvenile delinquent as natural also had darker implications. For one thing, such normalization of delinquency also laid open to question the full range of normal behavior; in the words of one highly influential reforming magistrate, "There can be no such entity as the completely normal child."[93] For another, upon closer inspection the characteristics of the delinquent, from which the normal youth was no longer to be set apart, looked much like those of other types of the unfit. The newly appreciated vitality of youth could be, and often was, fatally weakened by unfavorable biological or environmental circumstances. While much childhood law-breaking might be a fundamentally beneficent expression of high spirits, its continuation suggested an inability to contend with the pressures of environment or constitution. At a time when an excess of social vigor was no longer feared, the growing concern after the Boer War over "national deterioration" had, as we have seen, stimulated a new concern with its opposite: an insufficiency of vigor.[94]

---

[91] Cyril Burt, *The Young Delinquent* (London: University of London Press, 1925), p. 474.
[92] Burt, pp. v, 13–15.
[93] William Clarke Hall, *Children's Courts* (London: G. Allen & Unwin, 1926), p. 31.
[94] See, for example, Reginald Bray, *The Town Child* (London: T. Fisher Unwin, 1907).

Already in the 1890s, the specter had been raised of a sizable population of debilitated youth. The reforming prison chaplain W. D. Morrison, in his influential 1896 book on juvenile offenders, portrayed them as pathetic physical and mental specimens who were unfit to cope on their own with life. With the juvenile prison population consisting of persons of below-average height and weight and suffering above-average mortality rates,

> the conclusion is . . . forced upon us that a high percentage of the youthful delinquent population is more feebly developed on the physical side, and more liable to succumb to the attacks of disease than juveniles of a similar age in the general community. In other words, the physical basis of mental life is in a worse condition amongst juvenile offenders as a body than amongst the ordinary population at the same stage of existence.

Morrison's impressions of the inferior condition of the juvenile prison population were confirmed by an 1898 study of youths discharged from Pentonville.[95] In each instance, the inferiority was explained scientifically as the result of delayed maturation. As the new science of child development extended the process of maturation in general, it connected delinquency with the special delays characteristic of youths growing up with unfavorable constitutional inheritances and in unfavorable social conditions. Morrison claimed that "bodily degeneration has a tendency to produce mental degeneration, and . . . there is often a concomitance between the two." Thus, "a large percentage of juvenile offenders are [sic] . . . in [a] condition of imperfect development and depressed vitality." Moreover, this was a condition they frequently shared with their parents, who demonstrated their unfitness by their inability to control or properly rear their offspring:

> the weakness of will in the parent reappears in the child in the form of an absence of power to resist criminal instincts and impulses. . . . According to the doctrine of mental inheritance, parents often hand down their moral defects in a more or less pronounced form to many of their children. We may therefore say on the grounds of heredity that a considerable proportion of juvenile offenders come into the world with defective moral instincts, and that their deficiencies in this respect, combined with external circumstances of a more or less unfavourable character, have the effect of making these juveniles what they are.[96]

Morrison's scientific view of juveniles was repeated by officials. Ruggles-Brise cited the agreement of scientific authorities on both the slowness of maturation, its susceptibility to surrounding conditions, and the linkage of physical with mental and moral development. "It is scientifically true," he noted,

---

[95] Cited in the *Report of the Prison Commissioners for 1908–9*, p. 15.
[96] Morrison, *Juvenile Offenders*, pp. 105–11.

that the body does not reach its full development until [age 21]; and with
regard to the mind, although cerebral development is not capable of
scientific demonstration, it is inferentially certain that the complexity of
the brain-structure . . . increases not only with the growth of the body
but also, in many individuals, long after coarse growth of the body.

Moreover, it was generally conceded that "the development of character is
closely allied to physical development." If so,

the character will not be developed in normal man before 21, and it has
been observed that the children of the poorer classes develop physically
much later than those of the more favoured classes, even as late as 25 or
26.[97]

Here was a rationale not only for decarceration, because prison discipline and
stigma only further weakened these not fully responsible young offenders, but
also for expanded intervention, because they clearly were in need of assistance
and direction. If the more disadvantaged youth could not be trusted to develop naturally through and out of criminality, external agencies might have to
intervene. The newly perceived plasticity of youth made it ever more incum-
bent on the state, as well as private reform societies, to bring the right sort of
influences to bear; in particular, to strengthen and revitalize modern youth.

There was much talk of raising the legal age of full criminal responsibility
from 16 to 17, in the view of the Gladstone Committee, and even to 21, in
Ruggles-Brise's opinion.[98] However, legal change was as usual slow, and in
the meantime practical policy moved on along two related paths – continuing
to reduce the numbers of juveniles subjected, even briefly, to penal discipline,[99] while creating new "penal reformatories" (that came to be known,
after the first, as "Borstals") for the more serious "juvenile-adult" offenders,
those between the ages of 16 and 23. These institutions were intended, in the
words of the Gladstone Committee, to serve as "a halfway house between

[97] "State Reformatories" in *Report of the Proceedings of the Fifth and Sixth International Penitentiary Congresses* (1901), p. 106, and *Report of the Prison Commissioners for 1908–9*, pp. 14–15.
[98] *Report of the Departmental Committee on Prisons*, 1895, p. 27; *Report of the Prison Commissioners for 1898–99*, p. 15; *Report of the Prison Commissioners for 1901–2*, p. 11.
[99] For example, the Children Act of 1908 required that a child (under 14) or young per-
son aged 14 to 16 should be given bail, except for certain specific circumstances; if
remanded in custody he had to be sent to a "place of detention" specially set up for that
purpose; if convicted a child was not to be sentenced to imprisonment or penal servitude
for any offense nor committed for failure to pay a fine, damages, or costs. A young person
was not to be sent to penal servitude and was only to be committed to prison if considered
to be of "so unruly" or "so depraved" a character that he was unfit to be detained in a
place of detention. As Radzinowicz and Hood note, "one thousand young people under 16
sent to prison in 1906 had, by 1910, dwindled to a mere 143." [p. 629.]

prison and reformatory";[100] they were established in 1900 (to quote Ruggles-Brise) "on the principle which has lately been sanctioned by Parliament for dealing with habitual inebriates, i.e. the principle of a long curative detention."[101] In order to achieve the declared aim of these new institutions, "to build up 'self respect,'" offenders would have to be held in the "care of the State" longer than previously allowed by law.[102]

By 1911, with revitalizing movements like the Boy Scouts well under way, Alexander Paterson, a young social worker crusading against repressive methods of dealing with slum youth (and who was to become the leading figure among the postwar prison commissioners), described most juvenile offenders as "drop-outs" from the "race of life." "Perhaps," Paterson wrote, "they had little stamina at the very start, or lacked the proper equipment for running in the heat of the day; possibly the rules were too hard."[103] By the aftermath of World War I, such sympathetic descriptions of juvenile offenders had moved yet further in the direction of pathos, paralleling the similar development in descriptions of habituals. Cyril Burt observed:

> Most repeated [juvenile] offenders are far from robust; they are frail, sickly and infirm. Indeed, so regularly is chronic moral disorder associated with chronic physical disorder, that many have contended that crime is a disease.... The frequency among juvenile delinquents of bodily weakness and ill health has been remarked by almost every recent writer.... When health deserts us courage is diminished; laziness increased; and the heated temper simmers over in perpetual peevishness or bursts out in some sharp blast of violence. The youth whose work needs energy and application, whose business entails long hours and irksome drudgery, finds it harder than ever, on these days of transient weakness, to rise promptly from bed in the morning, to toil punctiliously from eight till six, to withstand the onset of fatigue, and to do all that's incumbent to gain a hard-earned living in an honest way.... Parallel histories of ailments and of crimes will often make it clear that the child's offences were chiefly carried out when, owing to temporary ill health or transient weakness and fatigue, his moral control was at an ebb.[104]

Thus, the juvenile offender, as he had been a century earlier, had again become a social symbol, but now a symbol not of excessive and unrestrained

---

[100] *op. cit.*, p. 30.

[101] *Report on the Fifth and Sixth International Penal Congresses*, p. 104.

[102] *Prison Commissioners' Report for 1901–2*, pp. 11–12.

[103] *Across the Bridges, or Life by the South London River-side* (London: E. Arnold, 1911), p. 183. On Paterson and on juvenile delinquency policy from 1914, see Victor Bailey, *Delinquency and Citizenship: Reclaiming the Young Offender 1914–1948* (Oxford: Clarendon Press, 1987).

[104] *The Young Delinquent*, pp. 238–41.

vitality but of social enervation. For all their differences, and even oppositions, the most accepted images of the two most noted forms of criminality – the recidivist and the juvenile offender – bore witness to a broader uneasiness with an overcivilized and undervitalized social body. Both the criminals and the wider society would need different sorts of treatment than the Victorian era had developed.

Post-Victorian criminality

In the Edwardian years two reformist currents flowed together to constitute a new phase in the cultural history of criminal policy. The first stressed the ordinariness of most offenders, their difference only by degree from law-abiding citizens; the second, joined with the first, emphasized the weakness of most criminal offenders. The juncture both reflected and reinforced the weakening perception of the general population. By the First World War, the idea of a separate criminal class or subculture, which had flourished in the second half of the nineteenth century as a way of setting crime apart from society, had given way to a new readiness to see criminality as related to the normal life of society. In sum, whereas early Victorian policymakers had seen in crime a threat to swamping civilization by a flood of willfulness, their Edwardian successors found in criminality a social message of the weakness of the individual and the ineffectuality of his unaided will.

A new sort of program for criminal policy, corresponding to this new meaning of criminality, had emerged and begun to be acted upon. It was one that restricted nineteenth-century conceptions of universal free will and personal responsibility. While a consistent determinism was ruled out as compatible neither with liberty and the rule of law nor with generally accepted moral values, the notion of the autonomous individual was now labeled an illusion and an injustice. Rather than employing uniform deterrent and disciplinary action against all lawbreakers, in order to force individuals to take the responsibility for their actions that they were presumed capable of, policymakers increasingly sought ways to intervene more variously and positively to provide continuing assistance to a wide range of problem types in the population. The rationale had been set out by Dr. Sutherland in 1908. "The legal conception of free will," he concluded,

> is as ill-founded and as reprehensible as the unqualified Calvinist doctrine of predestination in which freedom of will has no part. Both are extremes, and the middle course of relativity [of will power] governed by environment and psychopathological conditions is one to meet with acceptance.[105]

[105] J. F. Sutherland, "Recidivism Part Two," 79.

Such new guiding principles of variable capacities and relative guilt entailed, as Sutherland noted, the kinds of institutions and modes of social intervention that the nineteenth century had not known.

New modes of dealing with criminals

> The vilest deeds like poison weeds,
> Bloom well in prison-air;
> It is only what is good in Man
> That wastes and withers there:
> Pale Anguish keeps the heavy gate,
> And the Warder is Despair.
>
> For they starve the little frightened child
> Till it weeps both night and day:
> And they scourge the weak, and flog the fool,
> And gibe the old and grey,
> And some grow mad, and all grow bad,
> And none a word may say.
>
> Oscar Wilde, *Ballad of Reading Gaol*, 1898[106]

Descriptions of criminals had altered; prescriptions for dealing with them had to change. In 1898, Asquith described in Parliament the prison population of the country:

> Some of them, not an inconsiderable number ... are what may be called trained and professional enemies of society. Some of them, again, no insignificant fraction[,] ... are people of a morbid, neurotic, and ill-balanced physical and nervous system, to whom it is very difficult to apply with anything like justice and humanity the ordinary canons of moral responsibility. Others again – and I believe these to be a very large class in our prisons – are men and women who, without any ingrained criminal instincts and habits, are paying the penalty of some sudden and perhaps unpremeditated act, an act committed in a gust of passion or during a bout of drink. Finally, there are among the inhabitants of our prisons what are called juvenile offenders; children, for the most part, of cruel or careless parents, who from their earliest years have spent their lives on the boundary line between poverty and professional crime.[107]

This description, increasingly accepted by public opinion, threw into question the overuse of the prison sanction. After World War I, Ruggles-Brise looked

---

[106] *The Poems of Oscar Wilde* (London: Methuen, 1908) [1969], p. 341.
[107] 4 PD 56, c. 73–4 (April 4, 1898).

back on the system he had taken over in 1895, as if from the far side of a great divide:

> It seemed to be assumed that the wit of man could devise no other method of punishment than by deprivation of liberty, by bolts and bars, and darkened cells, and all those devices of regulation and routine on which so much ingenuity was wasted since the day when Howard first called attention to the awful cruelty and barbarism of the prison methods of his day.[108]

The new attention to variation in clientele threw doubt not only on the previous overuse of the prison, but, within the prison, on its chief characteristics – disciplinarianism ("discipline," remarked *The Times* in 1897, was "the first and last consideration of an older generation"[109]) and uniformity ("the present system," Herbert Gladstone privately reflected in 1895, "[is] one of equality for all – does not this work out unequally?"[110]). The criminal law was now being described as an indiscriminate net that pulled in a wide range of social failure. In Asquith's phrase, the prison population was "a most heterogeneous body ... drawn from many different sources, and ... from the most diverse causes."[111] In such a situation, the hallowed nineteenth-century principle of uniform treatment made little sense. With its underlying assumptions no longer taken for granted, the Victorian prison system now appeared increasingly irrational in its very rationalism, in what the Webbs were later to call its "fetish of uniformity."[112] Ruggles-Brise later observed:

> The size and structure of the cell; the form of labour ... scale of dietary, so nicely adjusted according to the length of sentence, as if the weight of the body were a greater concern and business for the State than the saving of the soul; rules of discipline, by which every movement was regulated according to plan, and woe betide the wretch who deflected by an inch from the prescribed path of conduct ... a multitude of details which now seem to us foolish and unnecessary.[113]

No one regime could fit shrewd professional burglars, prostitutes, drunken brawlers, juvenile delinquents, weak-minded vagrants, respectable clerks who had succumbed to temptation and pilfered the cash register, misdemeanants

---

[108] Evelyn Ruggles-Brise, *Prison Reform at Home and Abroad* (London: Macmillan, 1925), p. 10.

[109] *The Times*, June 8, 1897.

[110] Viscount Gladstone Papers, B.L. Add. MSS 46,091/103.

[111] 4 PD 56, c. 73 (April 4, 1898).

[112] Sidney and Beatrice Webb, *English Prisons Under Local Government* (London: Longmans, Green, 1922), p. 204.

[113] Evelyn Ruggles-Brise, *Prison Reform*, p. 10.

who could not pay fines, and so on. Yet, of course, the previous generation had not been blind to these differences, as Edwardians often implied. Rather, beneath such differences early and mid-Victorian policymakers had seen a fundamental similarity, or at least the potentiality, of a freely willing subject who could learn, however painfully, to govern his impulses. By the end of the century, this vision – and the fear accompanying it of willful criminals who refused to restrain themselves – had faded, and with that fading, it was the variety rather than the unity of offenders that came to occupy center stage. Now, both sentencing and treatment were to be adapted to the varying nature of the offender.

Home secretaries on either side of the House endorsed flexibility and individualization. For Asquith, "the first principle of a wise system of prison administration is the recognition of the principle of discrimination;"[114] in a similar fashion, his Unionist successor, Sir Matthew Ridley, argued that his Prisons Bill of 1898 was aimed precisely at increasing the "elasticity" of the system.[115] *The Times* approved the new flexible prison rules proposed in 1898, arguing that with their adoption

> society will have satisfied its quickened sense of responsibility towards those whose crimes are accidents in their lives. There will be less lumping together the human wild beast and the helpless and unfortunate, the curable and the incurable, and a few months' imprisonment will not always leave an almost ineffaceable brand.[116]

Once the Prison Act passed and new rules that distinguished different classes of prisoner went into effect, the commissioners began to press the justices to take account of the new options. "The promiscuous consignment to the common form of imprisonment," they noted,

> – an attractive, because an easy remedy, in every case where the law has been broken – is, in our opinion, to be deprecated where the widely different circumstances in the character of different acts ought to, and under the Act of 1898 can, be recognized by a differentiation of penalty.[117]

Justices who lagged (as most did) in making use of the new flexibility were prodded and criticized even by many Conservatives, who were putting forth

---

[114] 4 PD 56, p. 74 (April 4, 1898).

[115] 4 PD 55, c. 836–7 (March 24, 1898).

[116] *The Times,* March 7, 1898, p. 11.

[117] *Report of the Prison Commissioners for 1901–2,* p. 8. "A consideration," as Ruggles-Brise later put it, "of the personality of the offender must enter into the legal conception of the degree of his guilt." [Speech to the 10th International Penitentiary Congress, London, 1925, in *Morning Post,* Aug. 5, 1935.] The personality not only of the offender but of those

further measures of scientific penology. Another Unionist home secretary, Aretas Akers-Douglas, in introducing a follow-up to the 1898 Prisons Act, the Penal Servitude Bill of 1904, claimed that it would make the punishment or treatment fit not only the crime but the criminal. Indeed, "it is more important to fit the criminal even than the crime."[118] Other Unionists shared the language of administrative flexibility with Liberals. The Tory magistrate (and eugenicist) Montague Crackenthorpe argued in 1901, seconding the views of Sir Robert Anderson, "that the uniform severity of penal servitude was a serious obstacle to the elimination of professional criminals, and that our existing methods of punishment were too monotonous and inelastic."[119]

Not only was the problem of crime taking on more varied shades, it was merging with the more general concern (sharply mounting after the Boer War) with popular incapacity and social inefficiency; as it did, the lines separating punishment and welfare blurred. J. A. Hobson characteristically joined the two realms in his influential argument for a New Liberalism:

> [T]he degradation of our Poor Law, the brutality of our casual ward, the damnable method with which our prison seeks to deal with the most delicate problems of human character must all give way to more humane and more intelligent modes of handling our battered types of humanity.[120]

Such arguments were readily echoed by younger civil servants. As Herbert Gladstone's private secretary remarked to him in 1911, after being named a prison commissioner on Gladstone's recommendation, prisons only constituted a small part of a proper criminal policy: "this prison business . . . cannot be isolated but is an integral part of the whole problem of the ineffective and anti-social and submerged. . . . The whole business of dealing with social

who deal with him was of new importance. Whereas the Victorian system had elevated impersonality, the natural accompaniment of uniformity, as a virtue, now the rejection of "machine-like" penality reversed that valuatin. "Yes," the penal reformer Arthur Paterson seconded Ruggles-Brise in 1909, "it's personality, – and, again, personality – everywhere that is needed. But you have done much in that way. The younger governors show this – and other officers. If once it becomes the tradition of the service, as it will, to choose men for high posts because of personality (combined with other necessary qualities) – but that *first* – all will come right." The following year he extolled Ruggles-Brise as "the supreme personality who has brought Personality and soul into what was almost dead." [Letters to Ruggles-Brise, Sept. 23, 1909, and June 28, 1910, Ruggles-Brise Papers, D/DRs addl. Essex Record Office.]

[118] 4 PD 135, c. 726 (June 3, 1904).
[119] "Mr Crackenthorpe on Crime and Punishment," *Journal of Mental Science 47* (July, 1901), 629; see Robert Anderson, *Criminals and Crimes: Some Facts and Suggestions* (London: J. Nisbet, 1907), pp. 71–5, and *The Lighter Side of My Official Life* (London: Hodder & Stoughton, 1910), pp. 266–9.
[120] J. A. Hobson, *The Crisis of Liberalism* (London: P.S. King, 1909), p. 174.

inefficiency has to be reformed."[121] Even *The Times* declared in 1914 that "a trial and sentence are not the chief concerns of the criminal law, but important mainly as reminders that the future of a human being has to be dealt with."[122]

Indeed, the penal system seemed now not only overused and misdirected, but cruelly counterproductive. Not only did it ignore, in its mechanical uniformity, the immense variety of individual conditions and categories of pathology, but its methods of stigmatization, separation, and severity, while doing little to deter crime,[123] in fact worsened the character of its inmates. The Gladstone Committee went out of its way to reject the old Evangelically rooted belief in self-reform through isolation and reflection, denying that separation "enables the prisoner to meditate on his misdeeds."[124] At the same time, the Cameron Committee described a pathetic stage army of social and biological inadequates trudging into, out of, and back into the jails. As the Edwardian reformer George Ives scornfully noted about the early Victorian moral advocacy of solitude: "The broken down, the cretinous, the neurotic, the unbalanced, once made to think, were somehow to solve all the terrrific problems of disease and environment, repent and so save themselves."[125] One middle-of-the-road member of the Gladstone Committee, while praising Du Cane's efficiency, observed that the prisons formed a "cast-iron system, crushing out to a great extent individual resource, and individual authority and responsibility."[126] Imprisonment, Reverend Morrison claimed in 1896, "aggravates the conditions which tend to make a man a criminal.... [I]t not only fails to reform offenders but in the case of less hardened criminals and especially of first offenders it produces a deteriorating effect."[127] By 1898, with Du Cane and most of his leading subordinates retired, *The Times* observed that "administrators, no less than irresponsible critics, own that every prison is more or less a failure."[128] As the prison commissioners put it the following

---

[121] B.L. Add. MSS 45,994/273, M. L. Waller to H. Gladstone, n.d.. "I don't mean to say that much can't be done inside," Waller went on. "But the greatest necessities are outside —*before* and *after*."

[122] *The Times*, July 8, 1914.

[123] As Herbert Gladstone, now home secretary, privately noted in 1908, "[that] severity of prison treatment does not deter . . . is admitted now as [an] axiom." [B.L. Add. MSS 46,094/125.]

[124] *op. cit.*, p. 20.

[125] *A History of Penal Methods* (London: S. Paul & Co., 1914), p. 176.

[126] Sir Algernon West, "English Prisons," *The Nineteenth Century 39* (1896), 151.

[127] *Juvenile Offenders*, p. 273.

[128] *The Times*, March 26, 1898. David Garland has observed, "if we sift through the official reports and documents of this period, we find the Prison Commissioners themselves doubting the efficacy of imprisonment as regards the professional or habitual criminal (Report on the Brussels [Penitentiary] Congress 1900: 107), the young prisoner under 21 years

year, for every type of criminal, "imprisonment should be the last and not the first resource."[129] If existing prisons were last resources only, what should be employed first? Two alternatives were found to the Victorian penal machine that crushed without deterring. The first was the path of decarceration, replacing sentences of imprisonment with supervision in the community and preventive social amelioration; the second was the path of therapeutic incarceration. In the following decades both would be taken.

As we have seen, decarceration in the form of shortening prison sentences had been under way since the 1870s. Penal servitude had been giving way to the shorter and less severe penalty of imprisonment for ever shorter terms. By 1896, only 2 percent of those convicted of indictable offenses were being given penal servitude, and only one-tenth of these for more than five years; similarly, the average length of simple imprisonment had fallen by the end of the century to less than one month. Moreover, as the scope of criminal sanctions enlarged through the Victorian era to embrace many lesser offenses, the proportion of convictions that led to prison sentences had steadily declined. Whereas in 1860 nine out of ten of those convicted of indictable offenses had been sent to prison, by 1896, that proportion had fallen to 54 percent. Now, in the 1890s, for the first time, the absolute number of such sentences began to markedly fall, from 158,000 in 1893–94 to 136,000 in 1913–14.[130] Once charges had been proved, the practice of release without conviction on recognizances or, especially, on probation was increasingly employed in place of imprisonment (especially for young persons and first offenders of any age).[131] Indeed, the greatest change in sentencing during the 1890s was the rise in the proportion released after charges had been proved without any sentence from 38.6 percent in 1893 to 55.7 percent in 1902.[132] In 1906, the criminal registrar called attention to the diminishing inclination to prosecute, attributing it to the "growing disbelief in the efficacy of punishment."[133]

After 1892, the Home Office became more active in seeking to reduce the

---

of age (Report of the Prison Commissioners 1906/7: 14), the short-sentence prisoner (Report on the Washington [Penitentiary] Congress 1911: 37), the vagrant (Report of the Prison Commissioners 1909/10: 8), the inebriate (Report of the Prison Commissioners 1908/9: 26), and finally, the feeble-minded offender (Report of the Prison Commissioners 1912/13: 31)." [*Punishment and Welfare*, p. 61.]

[129] *Report of the Prison Commissioners for 1898–9*, p. 16.

[130] *Report of the Prison Commissioners for 1893–4*, p. 7; *Report of the Directors of Convict Prisons for 1893–4*, p. vi.; *Report of the Prison Commissioners for 1913–14*, p. 9.

[131] See Radzinowicz and Hood, pp. 775–7, and *Criminal Statistics for 1896*, p. 25, and *Criminal Statistics for 1898*, p. 14.

[132] *Criminal Statistics for 1902*, p. 49.

[133] *Criminal Statistics for 1905*, p. 17. [John Macdonnell.]

prison population. Following the report of his committee on prisons, Asquith sought, in the brief time before he left office, to implement its recommendations on liberalizing convict remission and extending it to local prisoners (enacted in 1898).[134] The Home Office also stepped up its encouragement of prison doctors (begun under Harcourt) to send reports to courts regarding accused prisoners' mental condition, so as to prevent the sentencing of offenders of unsound mind; in 1899 this practice was made mandatory.[135] Between 1910 and 1911, Churchill carried decarceration much further, mitigating many more sentences than his predecessors (despite the recent creation of a Court of Criminal Appeal), urging abolition of imprisonment for debt, and drafting legislation (enacted in 1914) to require justices to allow time for payment of fines and to facilitate granting of bail.[136] The rationale of decarceration was straightforward; if imprisonment did little good, and moreover usually worsened its subjects, then it followed that it should be resorted to only when truly necessary for public safety and only after those charged had been given the fullest possible due process. Even as the number of prison committals fell, pressure continued for further reduction. "Prisoners," Thomas Lough complained in the debate over the false conviction of Adolph Beck, voicing an increasingly shared sentiment, "were far too lightly cast into prison."[137]

As the prison itself was viewed ever more negatively, concerns rose about unjust conviction and de facto imprisonment while awaiting trial.[138] Legislation between 1898 and 1907 greatly expanded the protection of defendants in criminal trials, allowing the accused to testify in his own defense, providing state-paid legal counsel for a much wider range of charges, and establishing a

---

[134] HO45/9958/V20544/30 (April 20, 1895). He found particularly "indefensible" the practice "under which prisoners forfeit marks which they might otherwise have gained, by mental or physical weakness, or by illness." Also from 1895, pregnancy was included among the grounds for medical release from local prison. [Prison commissioners' reports.]

[135] N. Walker, *Crime and Insanity in England, Vol. 1: The Historical Perspective* (Edinburgh: Edinburgh University Press, 1968), p. 231.

[136] See Radzinowicz and Hood, pp. 649–51, 770–5. "We must not forget," Churchill reminded the House of Commons, "that when every material improvement has been effected in prisons, when the temperature has been adjusted, when the proper food to maintain health and strength has been given, when the doctors, chaplains, and prison visitors have come and gone, the convict stands deprived of everything that a free man calls life. We must not forget that all these improvements, which are sometimes salves to our consciences, do not change that position." [July 20, 1910, quoted in Radzinowicz and Hood, p. 774.]

[137] 4 PD 143, c. 679 (March 21, 1905).

[138] In the first official published account, the criminal registrar noted with "surprise" that the period of pretrial detention had lengthened; he offered no explanation. [*Criminal Statistics for 1895*, p. 33.] Greater care for the rights of the accused may have been lengthening trials and thus increasing the waiting period after arrest.

Court of Criminal Appeal.[139] Meanwhile, the length of time spent awaiting trial became for the first time a major issue; with shorter prison sentences, the period of remand could often exceed the length of the sentence, if one followed at all. Asquith was the first home secretary to acknowledge pretrial detention as a serious problem,[140] and in 1898 magistrates were given the power to admit to bail without sureties.[141]

Reformers were less frightened by, and thus more tolerant of, working-class life, and consequently it now appeared less necessary to remove offenders in ordinary cases from their normal lives and put them into walled-off institutions in order to bring about criminal rehabilitation.[142] As a committee of the Howard Association put it in an influential report in 1898,

> It is under the conditions of life amongst the mingled good and evil of the community, rather than amidst the congregated and concentrated crime of Prison, that reform must be sought. Hence, in the future, it is to be hoped that Jails may be less and less resorted to, and that the more promising influences of strictly conditioned liberty, under authoritative Probation Officers, may become the chief instrumentality for dealing with both Juvenile and Adult offenders. Then the Prison would be almost exclusively used for the determined or violent criminal, or as the penalty and alternative for abusing the terms of 'Probation'.[143]

This committee also recommended restricting committal to reformatory schools to only the "more dangerous class of Juvenile Offender and their ringleaders" and not committing any juveniles amenable to admonition, a

[139] Criminal Evidence Act of 1898, Poor Prisoners Defence Act of 1903, and Court of Criminal Appeals Act of 1907.

[140] He ordered statistics be kept and published on the number and length of such detentions.

[141] Radzinowicz and Hood observe, however, that this new power (like others being granted them at this time as alternatives to imprisonment) was little used by the justices. Additional circulars and legislation thereafter sought to expand use of bail. [See Radzinowicz and Hood, p. 628n.]

[142] Or, for existing institutions, to isolate them so thoroughly from the former world of their inhabitants. Already in 1909, the inspector of Reformatory and Industrial Schools, T. D. Robertson, was sounding a new note of tolerance for working-class family life (a theme to be developed further by his successors): "The mother ... practically never loses her influence over the children ... one of the most promising signs is that the schools are gradually realising the advisability of making friends with the mothers. In this one must not be too puritanical, but must bear in mind that amongst those whom the world stigmatises as bad characters are to be found mothers capable of great sacrifices for the sake of their children." [*Report of the Inspector of Reformatory and Industrial Schools for 1908*, Part II, p. 28.]

[143] Howard Association, *Juvenile Offenders* (1898), pp. 15–16.

whipping, or conditional liberty.[144] The Cameron Committee had similarly warned that "reformatories, and especially male reformatories, are institutions where . . . young persons should not be lightly sent."[145] Even the less penal industrial schools were losing favor to noninstitutional practices, like boarding out, when dealing with destitute children.[146]

As society had become less turbulent, the desire among policymakers for the alternative controlled space of the prison – a place removed from society, intended to reform and moralize as well as deter – was diminishing. A new confidence appeared, particularly after 1906, in the ability to reconstruct successfully the character of deviants in the everyday life of society, with less use of penal institutions or even criminal sanctions. As Ruggles-Brise observed to his overseas colleagues in 1910, with imprisonment now reduced and reformed, the leading task for future penal reformers was "to limit by preventive measures the field of the operation of Criminal Law."[147]

At the same time, to achieve the kind of reform that now seemed necessary as the image of the deviant weakened, new sorts of nonincarcerative methods were called for. Although some accidental offenders might be safely released and never offend again, many offenders – unable on their own to cope successfully with life and in need of help from an increasingly knowledgeable and capable state – seemed to require more than simple lack of imprisonment. The Probation of Offenders Act of 1907 sought to introduce the positive alternative to imprisonment suggested by the Howard Association and other reformers, namely careful supervision and assistance in the community. Radzinowicz and Hood have called it "a charter for the establishment of social work within the system of criminal justice."[148] Henceforth, probation became, along with fines for nonindictable offenses, the chief alternative to jail.[149]

The social work of probation officers, however, seemed often too little too

---

[144] *ibid*, p. 20.

[145] *op. cit.*, p. 47.

[146] A sign of the times was the protest of the influential Unionist, Sir John Gorst, against the practice of sending to industrial schools children who he felt should be boarded out or helped to emigrate. [4 PD 135, 645–8 (June 2, 1904).]

[147] Ms of address to International Penitentiary Congress 1910, Ruggles-Brise Papers D/DRs addl. Essex Record Office. In 1921 he spelled out some of these measures: "Better housing and lighting, the control of the Liquor Traffic, Cheap Food, Fair Wages, insurance, even village Clubs and Boy Scouts" [Evelyn Ruggles-Brise, *The English Prison System* (London: Macmillan, 1921), p. xvi.]

[148] *History*, p. 643.

[149] Another side of probation from the purely benign picture painted by Radzinowicz and Hood has been pointed out by revisionist historians such as V. A. C. Gatrell and David Garland, who have shown how it fitted into a growing tendency to expand state intervention in the everyday lives of all sorts of people who were labeled as deviants.

late. If much crime, and particularly recidivism, had its headsprings in social and perhaps also biological influences, it followed that early intervention by experts, from both the state and voluntary societies, could do much to dry up the sources of criminality before they became unmanageable rapids. As the public health movement had been proclaiming, with increasing acceptance, prevention was often far more efficacious than attempts at cure. The generation's democratic politicians and meritocratic bureaucrats found common ground in expanding preventive intervention in society. Sweeping reforms of housing, health, and welfare, eugenic proposals to influence the production of the next generation, and more direct intervention in the most important nursery of character, the family, all entered the political agenda during the 1890s and 1900s, often justified by the promise of reducing crime.

Incarceration, however, was by no means discarded. One purpose, which came to be more prominently accepted as faith waned in the power of prison to either deter or reform, was simple incapacitation. Prisons could serve as places to hold hopeless criminals apart from society, just as lunatic asylums had in good measure come to do for incurable mental cases.[150] But such a negative role could not satisfy the growing self-confidence of policymakers. Even the strongest critics of the Victorian penal system nonetheless generally believed that new, scientific forms of incarceration could be constructive. This belief seemed clearest in regard to the most malleable offenders, juveniles and young adults. The line between juvenile offenders and merely potential offenders was blurring, and both sorts of youth were seen as being deprived, in need of assistance, and in fact responsive to such aid. Consequently, the reformatory schools – meant for offenders and increasingly in disfavor – and the industrial schools – meant for vagrant and uncared for children and less stigmatized by penal associations – drew closer together in the official mind.[151] Once imprisonment before admission to a reformatory was abolished in 1899, there was no longer any legal distinction between the two types of schools. The thrust of legislation thereafter was to remake the reformatories in

---

[150] The Howard Association secretary, Edward Grubb, noted in 1903 his conversation with the Chaplain of Dartmoor: "He is very hopeful about new departures with the Juvenile Offenders, but [the] ordinary convict seems fairly hopeless. Wishes professional criminals could be kept under lasting restraint.... But he thinks public opinion won't stand this yet." [Edward Grubb, notebook of visits to prisons, Warwick University Modern Records Centre, Howard League Papers 16A/7/6.]

[151] In 1908, the age limit for industrial schools was raised to 16, while it had been lowered to 18 for reformatories; meanwhile the state contribution to industrial schools was gradually rising toward the reformatory school level. As the once sharp line between prisons and reformatories were being blurred by Borstals, so too the line between reformatories and industrial schools was blurring; in their place was emerging a spectrum of penal-welfare institutions of varying emphases.

the image of industrial schools (themselves being reshaped in the image of the general state elementary schools). By 1906, their chief inspector referred within the Home Office to a reformatory as "[nothing] other than a senior Industrial School" and looked forward to their formal amalgamation.[152]

For older juveniles, repeaters in crime, or more serious offenders, a new sort of institution was created in 1900. The reformatory prisons for juvenile-adults that came to be known as Borstals were established in response to the newly felt need for a form of punishment that would give decidedly criminal but still impressionable youth "a place, not to end the character of the prisoner but to mend it."[153] Though they were a distinctive Edwardian innovation, Borstals themselves came to be seen by the following generation as still too Victorian. C. E. B. Russell, who after his 1913 appointment as chief inspector inaugurated a new era in reformatory and industrial schools, called in 1910 for Borstals to shed their penal character and develop "a scientific system of disciplinary therapeutics."[154] After the war this call became a guiding doctrine.

For many adults too, it seemed that imprisonment, if stripped of its severity and its unsympathetic moralism, could yet be made reformative. Indeed, therapeutic incarceration for both convicted criminals and merely potential offenders was seen as having a growing role to play in social improvement. "Our object," Herbert Gladstone had privately reflected while drafting his departmental committee report, was "a more scientific treatment of all classes of prisoners by [the] study of antecedents and by making the treatment penal, corrective, educational according to class *and* cases."[155] First, the penal elements of prison had to be reduced. One way was by exempting ever more types of prisoners from normal prison discipline – prisoners of conscience, fine defaulters, juveniles, nonserious first offenders, the physically weak, the weak-minded, the inebriate, even soldiers guilty of offenses against military discipline.[156] The other way was to ease the harshness of normal discipline by

---

[152] J. G. Legge, April 10, 1906, HO 45/10,340/139,444/1. Troup, about to become permanent under-secretary, agreed with Legge and another official, G. A. Aitken, that reformatories should indeed "be called Senior Industrial Schools." [HO 45/10361/154, 821/1 (July 17 1907).] By the time of the report of the 1913 Inter-Departmental Committee, Radzinowicz and Hood observe, "gone was all hint of the less-eligibility theory, all stress on punitive work, on restricting standards so as to deter parents from unburdening themselves of their children onto the schools. In theory, at least, the reformatories were to be residential educational and work training establishments for the children for whom the State had to stand *in loco parentis*." [p. 193.]

[153] C. G. Hay, 4 PD 109, c. 573 (June 12, 1902).

[154] C. E. B. Russell, *Young Gaol-Birds* (London: Macmillan, 1910), p. 226.

[155] B.L. Add. MSS 46,091/106.

[156] The prison commissioners in 1902 took note of recent public protests against the presence of this last group in civil prisons, under normal discipline, and agreed that they should be found other, less penal, accommodation. [*Report of the Prison Commissioners for 1901–2*, p. 16.]

reducing the period of separate confinement, doing away with penal labor, diminishing the number and severity of punishments for infractions of discipline, and relying more on positive rather than negative incentives to good behavior. The period of separate confinement was reduced in 1899 from nine months to six, in 1909 to three and in 1910 to one month for first offenders and three for recidivists, finally being altogether abolished in 1922. The use of treadwheel and crank was also steadily reduced and done away with in 1902. In the four years preceding the 1898 act, 301 men had been flogged in convict and local prisons; in the four years afterward, the total was only 92. By 1909 it had dropped to 10 cases only,[157] and from 1917 to 1919, no cases at all were recorded.[158] Overall, the number of prisoners punished for prison offenses, the number of instances of punishment, and the severity of these punishments steadily declined. These changes had portentous symbolic implications. "To abolish the tread-wheel and the crank," H. B. Simpson warned his Home Office colleagues in 1899,

> would remove the most characteristic symbols of the view with which society has hitherto regarded crime as distinguished from mere poverty, and without them it would not be easy to demonstrate the difference of treatment accorded to prisoners and to paupers who are made to work at oakum-picking and stone-breaking, are fed little or no better and are practically deprived of their liberty. The tread-wheel, it is said, is 'degrading' but is it not desirable that those who break the law should be treated in such a manner as to show that not only are they made to work – many honest men desire nothing better than to work – but must work in a humiliating way?[159]

The time for such symbols had passed. In place of reliance upon punishments came new "rewards and encouragement," as the prison commissioners put it;[160] for example, remission was made available to local as well as convict prisoners in 1898, and the conditions for obtaining remission and better living conditions were made steadily less stringent. It was a sign of

---

[157] Radzinowicz and Hood, p. 587.

[158] *Report of the Prison Commissioners for 1918–19*, p. 17.

[159] HO 45/10030/A57510/5 (July 22, 1899). Three years later, Simpson publicly pointed to a rise in the proportion of those fined who defaulted and were in consequence jailed, suggesting that this rise might be a sign of the diminishing fear engendered by the reformed prison. [*Criminals Statistics for 1901*, 16.] Although this proportion did continue to rise (as Simpson warned), it was taken solely as evidence of the need for allowing more time for payment. A revival of Victorian rigors was neither feasible nor imaginable; by 1912, the prison commissioners were scornfully referring to use in the recent past of "fantastic devices for causing pain." [*Report of the Prison Commissioners for 1911–12*, p. 27.]

[160] *Report of the Prison Commissioners for 1906–7*, p. 27. There was, of course, a self-serving quality to these accounts of advance. Nonetheless, they not only referred to a certain real change, they testify even more to a decisive shift in values.

the times that the Howard Association, upon the retirement in 1903 of its stern longtime secretary, William Tallack, chose to replace the hitherto ubiquitous term "prison discipline" in its annual reports with the phrase "prison administration."[161]

In place of inflexible and punitive modes of reform a succession of inquiries, form the Glastone and Cameron Committees on, proposed more scientific methods of treatment of those within prisons. These included greatly expanded classification of inmates and specialized treatment based on these classifications, and welfarist rather than disciplinary methods of treatment — education, vocational training, physical training, counseling, and reliance on rewards for good behavior rather than penalties for bad. The Gladstone Committee urged that, at a minimum, first offenders, juveniles, habitual criminals, habitual drunkards, the weak-minded, female prisoners with infants, and unconvicted prisoners be systematically separated and treated by means appropriate to their situations and natures. Beyond even this, the committee set out the goal of individualization, in which the prison administration would take account of the particular and variable conditions of each prisoner.[162] Ruggles-Brise made this official policy, describing in internal discussion the need to address the system's "want of elasticity" and lack of attention to the antecedents and nature of the individual prisoner.[163]

The prison commissioners took an accommodative stance toward proposals for positive rehabilitation, and for the first time in 1898 they described their goal as "the humanization of the individual."[164] By 1901 the editor of the *Journal of Mental Science* was noting "a wonderful change for the better" in the treatment of crime.

> Although we cannot yet say that rational and satisfactory methods prevail, we find that year by year more intelligence and more humanity is infused into prison administration. It is now recognised that primitive measures alone are not corrective, and the effective reformation of criminals can only be attained by making our prisons true schools and moral hospitals.... The Prison Commissioners now report in favour of modern ideas — they can, in fact, no longer remain impervious to the scientific knowledge of the age.

[161] See Howard Association, *Annual Reports*, beginning with 1903. At the same time, both escapes and assaults upon prison staff (reduced to rarities under Du Cane) seem to have been rising; a meeting of Birmingham magistrates at the beginning of 1903 noted with alarm that "in addition to violent assaults upon officers, other acts of gross insubordination by prisoners [have] been steadily on the increase." [Quoted in J. E. Thomas, *The English Prison Officer Since 1850* (London: Routledge, 1972), p. 134.]
[162] *Departmental Committee on Prisons 1895*, pp. 28–33.
[163] HO 45/9752/A59,678/2 (Nov. 28, 1896).
[164] *Report of the Prison Commissioners for 1897–98*, p. 7.

And, he continued enthusiastically, just as medicine now dealt with the individual patient in all his circumstances of heredity and environment, and not
merely with his disease, so was the judge now directed to study the criminal as
well as the crime.[165] Under the Liberal government after 1906, the principles
of positive penology came fully into their own. As home secretary, Herbert
Gladstone saw several of the as yet unacted on recommendations of his committee made into law – a probation act, a children act, and prevention of
crime act. Gladstone's penal creativity was overmatched by that of his successor. Soon after arriving at the Home Office in 1910, Winston Churchill,
eager to implement modern ideas, ordered his officials to draw up plans for
reorganizing the entire penal system into "a regular series of scientifically
graded institutions which would gradually and increasingly become adapted to
the treatment of every variety of human weakness."[166] Churchill left the
Home Office before these plans could be realized, but this vision of a scientific
and therapeutic penal system became the basis for the sweeping transformation carried out after World War I under the guidance of the former social
worker, Alexander Paterson. As a Fabian tract pronounced in 1912, "the old
idea of penal discipline was to crush and break, the modern idea is to fortify
and build up force of character."[167] Reflecting on Dr. Goring's study of
convicts, the prison commissioners concluded that its "principal lesson" was
"that crime can be combatted most effectively by segregation and supervision
of the obviously unfit, i.e., by removing them to a more restricted sphere,
where the stress and competitive conditions of modern existence are more
flexible and less severe; and that [the constitutional] tendency to crime can be
defeated by personal service."[168]

Thus, by the outbreak of a war that was to devastate most Victorian
assumptions and values, penal policy was already moving swiftly away from
nineteenth-century models. While practice lagged well behind principle, the
terms in which punishment was discussed, within government as well as for
public consumption, had substantially altered. Although the punitive impulse
had by no means evaporated, it was being ever more attenuated. The ratio-
nales of deterrence and disciplinary moralization were yielding to those of
welfarist administration. After the First World War, the seeds planted in the
late Victorian and Edwardian years came to fruition, and the criminal justice
system was thoroughly reorganized according to the new vision of criminality
and its solution. While law itself, held back by a judiciary ever more focused

---

[165] "The Treatment of Crime," *Journal of Mental Science 47* (1901), 354–5.
[166] HO 144/18869/196919 (July 8, 1910).
[167] H. Blagg and C. Wilson, "Women and Prisons," *Fabian Tract No. 163* (London:
Fabian Society, 1912), p. 5.
[168] *Report of the Prison Commissioners for 1913–14*, p. 24.

on precedent and ever more fearful of "making policy,"[169] was altered only slowly,[170] major changes took place in its administration. Long prison sentences were further shortened and, even more, very many short sentences were replaced by release with (or, sometimes, without) supervision and prolonged time to pay fines. By 1934, the annual prison intake had fallen by more than two-thirds since 1910, the number of prisons by more than half, and total prison population by almost half.[171] Similarly, for juveniles probation replaced incarceration. While convictions remained at the same level, commitments to reformatory and industrial schools fell in the 1920s by two-thirds, forcing between thirty and forty of them to close.[172]

With incarceration playing an ever less deterrent role, its new therapeutic rationale was being more fully defined. More and more negative facets of the penal regime were disavowed – in 1922, dress, grooming, and visitation rules were relaxed, separate confinement was for practical purposes abolished, and warders were renamed prison officers.[173] Incarceration – especially for young offenders, but for all as far as possible – was to become a positive experience, a system of individualized training not of generalized punishment. The Children and Young Persons Act of 1933 did away with the distinction between reformatory and industrial schools and established the principle that the chief if not exclusive consideration of juvenile courts should be the welfare of the child.[174] Even for adults, individualized training and rehabilitation became

[169] See Brian Abel-Smith and Robert Stevens, *Lawyers and the Courts: A Sociological Study* (Cambridge, Mass.: Harvard University Press, 1967), and Robert Stevens, *Law and Politics: The House of Lords as a Judicial Body, 1800–1976* (Chapel Hill: University of North Carolina Press, 1976), Parts 2 and 3.

[170] But nonetheless significantly, at least through Parliament; for example, in 1922 infanticide was recognized as a distinct and lesser crime than murder, in 1925 attempted suicide was decriminalized and a bill almost passed establishing degrees of responsibility for murder (this was finally enacted in 1957).

[171] Criminal statistics and *Prison Commissioners' Report for 1934*. The most dramatic change was a great reduction in short sentences, that is, in the deterrent use of imprisonment for relatively minor offenses like drunkenness, prostitution, vagrancy, and petty theft.

[172] See Bailey, *Delinquency*, pp. 52–3, 217–18, and Carlebach, *Caring for Children in Trouble* (London: Routledge, 1970), pp. 88–91.

[173] *Annual Reports of the Prison Commissioners*. As Ruggles-Brise's successor explained the change in terminology: "Safe custody is only one of the many duties of the Prison Officer at the present day. Reform, encouragement, and instruction, are instances of others whose importance increases." [HO 45/11,082/427,916, M. Waller to Home Office, Dec. 19, 1921.] As part of this program as it unfolded over the following decade, hard labor was to be transformed into vocational training and the mark system of earning privileges to be replaced by a more positive system of payment for work and conferring of privileges that could be lost by misconduct or idleness.

[174] See Bailey, *Delinquency*, p. 84. Indeed, once these institutions were clearly labeled therapeutic rather than deterrent or punitive, they began to enjoy a modest revival: in the 1930s committals rose, though their population never regained prewar levels.

the declared aims of the penal system. After 1922, in addition to the four-man Prison Commission being required to include a medical doctor with psychiatric experience, a second requirement was added for a person "with special experience of social work."[175] By the time these decarcerative and therapeutic impulses culminated in the Criminal Justice Bill of 1938, the symbolic role of the English penal system had undergone a metamorphosis.

As Whiggish historians have noted, this transformation exhibits a heightened reluctance to inflict suffering and a new sympathy for the social underdog. Also perceptible is the different sort of motive that revisionists have uncovered – a new sense of the possibilities of joining the developing human sciences with the instrumentalities of an expanding state to remake deviants according to the prescriptions of experts, while establishing social authority on a scientific basis. Yet, accompanying and flowing beneath these movements in policymaking mentality was a perhaps even more basic movement in perceptions of human nature and social action. Both the humanitarian and the social control tendencies of post-Victorian penal policy were crucially shaped by the replacement of a Victorian image of humanity by a less potentially dangerous but also less powerful image; the human material with which the makers of policy had to deal appeared both weaker and less autonomous. This shift in images linked criminal policy with general social policy, itself increasingly preoccupied with national inefficiency. And, less directly but as profoundly, this shift also developed from the personal sensibilities among the professional classes from which policymakers were drawn, sensibilities that were marked by growing discontent with the disciplines of respectability. The first image of humanity had presided over one era in criminal policy; the second presided over another, continuing into the 1960s. We now seem to be living at the close of this post-Victorian era of policy. Modern solutions to the problem of crime are now generally felt to have failed, just as modern reinterpretations of punishment have lost their persuasiveness. Philosophical argument about punishment has strikingly revived, along with practical conflicts over what to do with society's increasingly numerous lawbreakers. If the outcome is uncertain, this very uncertainty has at least reopened prematurely settled questions and made it easier for us to look more deeply into the origins of our own twentieth-century penal policies.

175 C. E. Troup, *The Home Office* (London: Whitehall Series, 1925), p. 117.

Index

secretary at the Home Office), 146n

Lingen, Ralph (permanent secretary to the Treasury), 290n

Livingstone, Edward, 95

Lombroso, Cesare, 234, 237, 254, 357–8

London, Jack, 244

Lough, Thomas, M.P., 372

Lowe, Robert (president of the Committee of Council on Education; chancellor of the Exchequer), 198, 199n

Lunacy Act (1867), 316–7

Lushington, Godfrey (permanent under-secretary at the Home Office): criticizes concept of "semi-insanity," 278; on liability for industrial accidents, 205; moralistic antiinterventionist liberalism of, 341; opposes appointment of nonlawyer, 339; opposes expansion of role of police, 305n; opposes proposed category of "conscience prisoner," 333

Macaulay, T. B., 37, 52, 60–2

MacFarlane, D. H., M.P., 281

MacKintosh, Sir James, 65–6

McConville, Sean, 105, 130n

McGowen, Randall, 65, 241n

McLennan, John, 34

McNaughten, Daniel, 86–7

McNaughten rules, 88–90, 269–76

Maconochie, Captain Alexander, 99–100, 114, 122

Magarey, Susan, 52

magistrates, 369, 373; missentencing of, 352; see also judges

Malthus, Thomas, 28–9, 40, 173

Manchester, A. H., 61, 67

manslaughter, 78–9, 82–3

Manslaughter Act (1822), 78–9

Manton, Jo, on Mary Carpenter, 140

Marris v. *Ingram* (1882), 69

Martineau, Harriet, 4, 62, 229

Matthews, Henry (home secretary): defends judicial autonomy, 302; lacks sympathy for issue of disability, 319; reluctantly establishes committee to examine prison rules, 330–1; resists penal reform, 292; Ruggles-Brise his private secretary, 339

Maudsley, Henry, 43, 168–9, 230, 232, 235, 267

Mayhew, Henry: on broadsheets, 15; contrasted with Charles Booth, 191, 230–1; criticizes silent system, 110; defines criminals as "those who will not work," 47; portrays criminals as akin to savages, 23–5, 31–3, 34n; supports Maconochie, 118

Mayo, Dr. Thomas, 44, 124

Meckier, Jerome, 249

Medico–Psychological Association, 231, 267, 276

Mental Deficiency Act (1913), 201

mental disability, 266–76, 313–21; see also criminals, mentally disabled

Mercier, Dr. Charles, 276

Mill, James, 39, 48–9, 55

Mill, John Stuart: critiqued by J. F. Stephen, 111; for increased criminal sanctions against drunken offenders, 80, 155; for increased criminal sanctions against receivers of stolen goods, 151; on law as preventive, 46; on necessary war with instinct, 38; on possibility of self-formation, 42–3; supports continuation of death penalty, 111n

Millbank prison: W. E. Gladstone's visits to, 145; medical officer of, 314

Milnes, Richard Monckton, M.P., 52, 134

Molesworth, Sir William, M.P., 98

Molesworth Committee (Select Committee on Transportation 1837–8): criticizes transportation, 98–100; decline of transportation and penal servitude since, 216n; evidence of Maconochie to, 114; see also transportation

moralism, 337–8

Moran, Richard, 85

Moretti, Franco, 223

Morning Chronicle, 134

Morning Post, 16, 95

Morrison, Arthur, 227–8, 240–4

Morrison, Reverend William Douglas: agrees most prisoners mentally subnormal, 353; agrees willful debtors should be treated as criminals, 209n; attacks penal system, 343–4, 370; on disappearance of idea of suicide as a sin, 267; on juvenile offenders as unfit, 362; on social and biological causes of crime, 236, 239–42, 355

Morselli, Enrico, 266

Morton, Peter, 171–2

murder, 15, 82–3, 86, 88–90, 272; efforts to reform law of, 273, 276–9; see also infanticide; killing; manslaughter; suicide

Murdoch, C. S. (Home Office clerk), 331n

National Association for the Promotion of Social Science (Social Science Association), 142–4, 152, 216, 271

naturalism, scientific, 159–184, 226

Newgate novel, 22

Nicholson, Dr. David (director of Broadmoor Criminal Lunatic Asylum), 129, 234

Nightingale, Florence, 111

Nihil, Daniel (chaplain-governor of Millbank prison), 110, 112

Northcote, Sir Stafford (chancellor of the Exchequer), 308

Norton, Lord; see Adderley, Charles B.

occupational injuries, liability for, 75–6, 206–8

O'Connor, Arthur, M.P., 330

Offenses Against the Person Act (1861), 64

"One Who Has Endured it," 311, 325

Orange, Dr. William (director of Broadmoor Criminal Lunatic Asylum), 231

Oxford, Edward, 86